CATAM...
CRUISE
TITICACA LAKE

- Full day or overnight on board cruises.
- Daily combinations between Bolivia and Peru.
- Unique itinerary providing the opportunity to interact
  with isolated indigenous communities of Titicaca islands.

INTI WATA
Titicaca Traditional Vessel
(Sun Island)

*Exclusive attraction only
for Catamaran clients.*

INTI WATA
Cultural Complex
(Sun Island)

*Exclusive attraction only
for Catamaran clients.*

TRANSTURIN
inbound
DESTINATION MANAGEMENT COMPANY

AMERICAN EXPRESS
Servicios
de Viaje

Courier Address: Calle Alfredo Ascarrunz Nº 2518
Mailing Address: P.O. Box 5311 La Paz - Bolivia
E-mail: info@transturin.com - Web: www.transturin.com
Phone: (591-2) 242-2222 · Fax: (591-2) 241-1922

The perferct combination between business and pleasure...

The perferct combination between business and pleasure...

This book is dedicated to my family who explored with me this wonderful, colorful and rich country.

AN INSIDER'S
GUIDE TO
BOLIVIA

QUIPUS
CULTURAL
FOUNDATION

FOREWORD

I t has been thirteen years since I published the first edition of "An Insider's Guide To Bolivia." With this edition, the fourth, we have completely updated the contemporary history of the country, added several new chapters, updated the information on cities and regions of Bolivia, and added a more complete table of contents. The toughest part has been keeping up with the new hotels, the opening and closing of many food establishments, and changing all the phone numbers in the book. In updating the guide book it became evident how much remains the same but at the same time the significant political, economic and social transformations that Bolivia has gone through in the last decade. New and comprehensive regional, town and city maps have also been added.

This fourth edition attempts to present a panorama of Bolivia's people, habitat, rich and varied cultural values, history and some of its problems, to visitors and English-speaking residents in Bolivia. By no means is it a complete picture, although with each subsequent edition we hope to add and revise chapters. In this edition we are adding dozens of new chapters including some on ecotourism, different ethnic groups, Butch Cassidy and Sundance Kid, "Ché" Guevara, Bolivian cinema, etc. We have also completely updated and revised the information on cities and departments. For this edition we welcome any suggestions, corrections and additions that will make the next guide more complete.

Since the first edition there have been quite a few changes in the political and social life of the country, with the rise and fall of populist parties, the privatization of nearly all state enterprises, the sharp reduction in illegal coca leaf cultivation, and new as well as traditional players in the country's political life.

Despite the problem that Bolivia has gone through, Bolivia is one of the most fascinating, colorful and varied nations in South America. In 424,165 square miles (1098.581 square km) of territory there are snow-covered peaks, lush valleys, spectacular salt flats, tropical rain forests and winding rivers that feed into the Amazon or Rio La Plata.

Contrary to the common perception, Bolivia has most of its territory in the tropical lowlands. With ethnic groups ranging from the Aymaras and Quechuas who inhabit the Bolivian highlands, to the Guaranies, Moxenos, Ayoreos, Chimanes and many other groups who live in the tropics, Bolivia's people are as varied as its territory. It is this cultural diversity and richness that makes Bolivia such a fascinating, enigmatic and diverse country.

In the last quarter century Bolivia has gone through a dramatic transformation, albeit maintaining much of its charm, mystery and cultural diversity. Santa Cruz, which in 1972 had a population of 40,000, is now a modem metropolis with a population of more than one million that has thrived on the region's natural gas and agricultural industries.

The country's economy has also shipped from a traditional mining country to an exporter of natural gas and soy beans. The discovery of large natural gas reserves has made Bolivia the country in South America with the second highest natural gas reserves.

There have also been significant changes in the economy with the closing of most tin mines, the rapid expansion of the country's natural gas industry with the discovery of important reserves in Santa Cruz, Cochabamba and Tarija, the construction of paved roads linking Bolivia with Chile and Peru, the migration of farmers to the cities, and a renewed dynamism of culture, including the naming of the Jesuit Missions, the Samaipata Fortress, Tiwanaku, Sucre and Potosi as UNESCO World Heritage Sites. New discoveries at Tiwanaku and in the Beni Amazon Basin are forcing a complete reexamination of their history and a keen appreciation for the highly developed forms of agriculture that developed in its environs.

On the political front there have been important developments, with former dictator General Hugo Banzer Suarez reaching the presidency through he ballot box but stepping down a year before the end of his term after he was diagnosed with cancer. The swearing in of the US-educated Jorge Quiroga symbolized the transfer of power from one generation to another. The 2002 elections marked an important shift in voter preferences, with the rise of the Movement Towards Socialism (MAS) party headed by coca leaf farmer Evo Morales, the death of the CONDEPA party and the election of the U.S.-educated mining executive Gonzalo Sanchez de Lozada to his second term as president. Morales' second place finish also changed the face of the Bolivian Congress with the election of many indigenous leaders.

The rise of indigenous political parties headed by Evo Morales and Felipe Quispe, the popular uprisings of October in El Alto, La Paz and other cities, the forced resignation of President Gonzalo Sanchez de Lozada in October, 2003 14 months after taking office, and the swearing in of Vice President Carlos Mesa Gisbert as Bolivia's 82nd President, had an important impact on Bolivia, its present and its future. Mesa, a highly-respected TV journalist and historian (his latest book is on Bolivian presidents) faces the daunting task of reviving the economy, satisfying the demands of an indigenous population that has been left out of the country's economic benefits, eliminating corruption and restoring credibility to the country's political class.

The conflicts also brought to the forefront the sharply divided social, ethnic and regional players and issues Bolivia faces. The protests were in part sparked by the possibility that Bolivia would export its vast natural gas reserves through a Chilean port to Mexico and the United States. The departments of Tarija and Santa Cruz, where many of the natural gas reserves are located, opposed the popular uprising lead by Morales and Quispe.

Some of the chapters are based on articles I wrote for the New York Times, Associated Press, Newsweek and the Bolivian Times, the newspaper I used to publish. People most familiar with each topic wrote other chapters on hand. The French photographer and good friend Frédéric Savariau was instrumental in organizing this information and in making sure all the corrections and updates were completed. A special thanks for his help. Without his commitment to the book I doubt it would have offered such a rich view of the country or even come out. Sarah Johnson, Diane Rothschild and Vanessa Arrington were also very helpful in editing the chapters and updating some of the information. Several journalists from the Bolivian Times contributed numerous articles to this book. I extend my sincere gratitude to all the people who made this edition possible.

I invite you to explore this wonderful country and its people.

Peter McFarren
La Paz, Bolivia
2003

AN INSIDER'S GUIDE TO BOLIVIA

PUBLISHER	Peter McFarren
EDITOR	Frédéric Savariau
EDITED AND COMPILED BY	Sarah Johnson, Diane Rothschild and Vanessa Arrington
CONTRIBUTING WRITERS	Fiona Adams
	Laurie Adelson
	Luis Antezana
	Vanessa Arrington
	José Antonio Aruquipa Z.
	Jorge Asin
	Ellis Auger
	Sarah Balmond
	David Boldt
	Yossi Brain
	Till Bruckner
	Daniel Buck
	Sarah Busdiecker
	Korey Capozza
	Erik Catari Gutiérrez
	Mike Ceaser
	Craig Cottrell
	Jonathan Derksen
	Marcelo de Urioste
	Ollie Englehart
	Clark L. Erickson
	Linda Farthing
	Eliana Flores Bedregal
	Peter Fraser
	Ben Garside
	Teresa Gisbert de Mesa
	Sergio Gomez
	Jamie Grant
	Paddy Grant
	Steve Hendrix
	Michael Herrera
	Sylvia Johnson
	Eimear Laffan
	Eric Latil
	Kip Lester
	Michael Levitin

Anna-Stina Lindahl
Erik Loza
Vicenta Mamani Bernabé
Charles C. Mann
John F. McCamant
Peter McFarren
Wendy McFarren
Jane McKeel
Anne Meadows
William Mullen
Katy Muncey
Bernardo Peredo Videa
Teresa Prada
Amy Oakland Rodman
Dino Scungio
Sita Shah
Stan Shepard
Anna Simon
Tamara Stenn
Matthias Strecker
Chris Sykes
Mark Taylor
Ryan Taylor
Cynthia Thompson
Alison Tilling
Patricia Tordoir
Adam Townsend
Arthur Tracht
Manuel Vargas
Kate Venner
Stacy Walker
Tom Walsh
Terry L. West
Tom Wilkinson
Tim Wilson
Jaime Rojas Zambrana

PHOTOGRAPHS Peter McFarren, BOLIVIAN PHOTO AGENCY
E-mail: photos@quipusbolivia.org

SPECIAL THANKS TO Sarah Johnson
Vivianne Cracknell
Moisés E. Pacheco Chambi
Diane Rothchild
Vanessa Arrington
The Bolivian Times Staff
Hno. Miguel Plaza Ramos
Julio Paco Coronel
Ernesto Rodrigo Lira
Bernardo Peredo

Caryn Hoff
Maribel Pelaez
Meagan Demitz
Dan Brinkmeier
Erin Raley
Doris Vera
Julio Alvaro Valenzuela
Beatriz E. García
Seth Nickinson
Bill Lofstrom
Alan Shave
Julio A. Rojas
Fredy Yapu Gutierrez
Primitivo Nina
David Edwards
Valeria McFarren
Verónica Martínez Caballero de Arduz
Avi Martins
María Fernanda Lujan
Domingo Izquierdo

PUBLICATION OF Quipus Cultural Foundation
Casilla 1696
Pasaje Jauregui 2248
Tel. 591-2-2444311
Fax. 591-2-2442848
La Paz, Bolivia
www.quipusbolivia.org
E-mail: insidersguide@quipusbolivia.org

COVER DESIGN Leonardo Cardenas

GRAPHIC DESIGNERS Leonardo Cardenas
Moisés E. Pacheco Chambi

MAPS Moisés E. Pacheco Chambi (black & white)
Instituto Geográfico Militar (color)
Sgto. Carlos Argoyo (Map design)
Cap. DIM. Marcos Zenteno
(Coordinator Dpt.)
Cnl. DAEN. Raul Virreyra Montero
(Manager)
Updated by Moisés E. Pacheco Chambi

PRINTER Editorial Bruño, La Paz - Bolivia
Julio Paco Coronel (Pre Press)

Deposito Legal: 4-1-14-03
I.S.B.N. 99905-0-277-3

TABLE OF CONTENTS

CHAPTER TWO — CITIES AND SURROUNDING AREAS

CHAPTER THREE – BOLIVIA'S CULTURAL PAST

CHAPTER FOUR – BOLIVIA'S TRADITIONAL PRESENT

CHAPTER FIVE – CONTEMPORARY ART AND CULTURE

CHAPTER SIX – THE MANY FACES OF BOLIVIA

CHAPTER SEVEN – EXPLORING BOLIVIA'S ENVIRONMENT

CHAPTER EIGHT – SPANISH, AYMARA, QUECHUA WORDS & PHRASES

MAPS

CHAPTER ONE

1

BOLIVIA
AN OVERVIEW

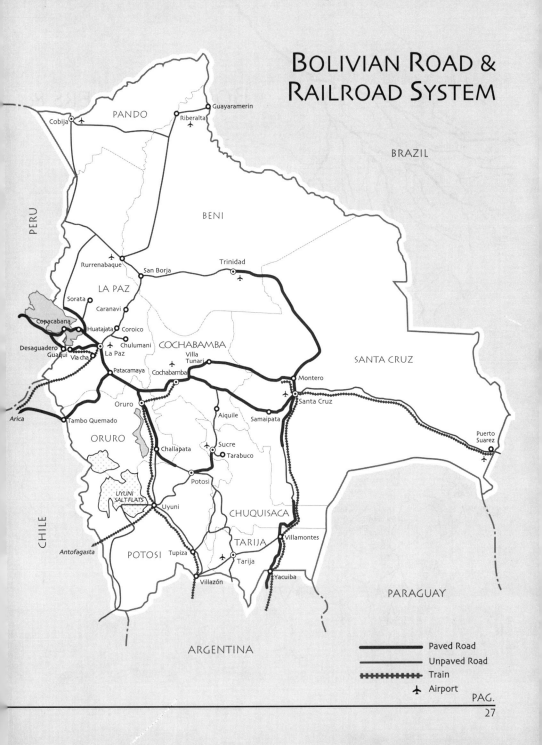

BOLIVIAN ROAD & RAILROAD SYSTEM

BRAZIL

PERU

PANDO

Cobija

Guayaramerin

Riberalta

BENI

Rurrenabaque

San Borja

Trinidad

LA PAZ

Sorata

Caranavi

Copacabana

Huatajata   Coroico

Desaguadero

Guaqui   Viacha   La Paz

Chulumani

COCHABAMBA

Villa
Tunari

SANTA CRUZ

Patacamaya

Cochabamba

Montero

Oruro

Aiquile

Samaipata

Santa Cruz

Arica

Tambo Quemado

Puerto
Suarez

ORURO

Challapata

Sucre

Tarabuco

CHILE

UYUNI
SALT FLATS

Potosi

Uyuni

CHUQUISACA

Antofagasta

POTOSI

Tupiza

TARIJA

Villamontes

Tarija

Villazón

Yacuiba

PARAGUAY

ARGENTINA

	Paved Road
	Unpaved Road
	Train
✈	Airport

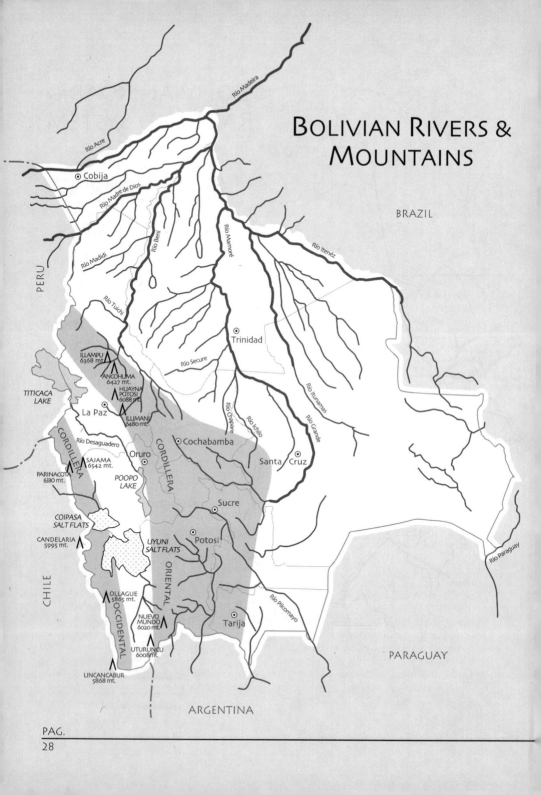

BOLIVIAN RIVERS & MOUNTAINS

BRAZIL

Río Madeira

Río Acre

⊙ Cobija

Río Madre de Dios

PERU

Río Madidi

Río Beni

Río Mamoré

Río Itenéz

Río Tuichi

⊙ Trinidad

Río Secure

TITICACA
LAKE

ILLAMPU
6368 mt.

ANCOHUMA
6427 mt.

HUAYNA
POTOSI
6088 mt.

La Paz

ILLIMANI
6480 mt.

Río Chapare

Río Ichilo

Río Itunamas

Río Grande

Río Desaguadero

CORDILLERA

Cochabamba

Oruro

SAJAMA
6542 mt.

CORDILLERA

Santa Cruz

PARINACOTA
6330 mt.

POOPO
LAKE

COIPASA
SALT FLATS

Sucre

CANDELARIA
5995 mt.

UYUNI
SALT FLATS

Potosi

CHILE

ORIENTAL

Río Paraguay

OLLAGUE
5865 mt.

OCCIDENTAL

NUEVO
MUNDO
6020 mt.

Tarija

Río Pilcomayo

UTURUNCU
6008 mt.

PARAGUAY

LINCANCABUR
5868 mt.

ARGENTINA

BOLIVIA, AN OVERVIEW

BY PETER MCFARREN

Bolivia is a country of superlatives. Landlocked in the western part of the continent, it sprawls over 424,165 square miles (1,098,580 square kilometers) and shares borders with Peru to the northwest, Brazil to the north and east, Paraguay to the southeast, Argentina to the south and both Peru and Chile to the west. It is a country which claims the highest navigable lake in the world, the highest commercial airport, the highest golf course, the highest ski run, the highest capital, one of the newest and wildest frontiers, one of the oldest ruins and what is said to be the highest concentration of cosmic rays on earth. Bolivia is also a nation of contrasts, which led Alcides d'Orbigny, a French explorer-scientist, to call it a "microcosm of our planet." It has every type of geologically classified land, flora, fauna, mineral and tropical product.

Bolivia lies wholly in the tropical zone, yet temperatures vary from the heat of its equatorial lowlands to the cold of the Andes. Therefore, to focus on Bolivia's diverse land, it is best to start with the inland sea of Lake Titicaca (12,600 ft or 3,780 m) and work east. The nation is developing economically and socially in that direction, much as the United States pushed its frontier westward.

Lake Titicaca is a major western boundary between Bolivia and Peru. Stretching some 3,500 square miles (9,065 square kilometers), this deep (700 feet, or 210m, in places), clear body of water is the highest navigable lake in the world. Notable along shallow parts of the shoreline is the totora reed that greatly influences life around the lake. The Aymara fashion the reeds together into exceptionally strong gondola-like boats. These thick reeds also become floating, inhabited islands. The pliable but durable material breaks loose from lakebeds and joins with other matter, forming islands. The reed is also used for building simple furniture, for making handicrafts, for feeding livestock and even for consumption as a special candy-like treat.

Lake Titicaca lies at the northern extremity of the Bolivian Altiplano (high plateau). The Altiplano is shaped by the Andes mountain range that hunches along the west coast of South America and slices southeastward through Bolivia. This two-pronged mountain range has formed between its peaks a rambling plain about 88 miles (142 km) wide and about 540 miles (870 km) long that cuts through southeast Peru and southwest Bolivia. About 40,000 square miles of this bleak, cold and windswept plateau lies in Bolivia. However hostile this 30 % of the nation's land is, it supports 52 % of the population. The otherwise impoverished Altiplano and its mountain rims are streaked with vast deposits of tin, copper, silver, lithium, gold, tungsten, lead, zinc and other minerals.

Centuries ago, the Aymara established elaborate systems of agriculture and irrigation that supported a large population. Today, archaeological digs are reviving these ancient forms of agriculture and trying to apply them—with much success—to improve the livelihood of present-day Aymara. Their diet consists mostly of a wide variety of potatoes, fava beans, grains and the nutritious quinoa cereal, (which is catching on in the United States and Europe as a delicious, high-protein grain). They also grow nutritious cereals and corn, which, when fermented, make an intoxicating brew called chicha, consumed mainly in the valleys.

The animal life on the Altiplano includes the wool-bearing sheep, llama, alpaca and vicuña, along with the fur-bearing chinchilla and red fox. The fabled vicuña, a rare and very delicate animal, still roams the high regions of the Altiplano, but articles made from its scarce fleece are hard to find because the government strictly prohibits its sale. You can, however, obtain rugs, ponchos and a number of other articles made from llama and alpaca wool. Designer-quality Bolivian alpaca products are being exported in large numbers to sophisticated foreign markets.

At the edge of the Altiplano, the city of La Paz (population 792,499), Bolivia's seat of government, is set in a large, spectacular canyon cut below the surface of the Altiplano at an altitude of about 11,900 feet (3,570m). The majestic beauty of the snow-capped mountains that encircle the city more than compensates for the discomfort of the thin air. Four of these peaks reach above 20,000 feet (over 6,000m).

The city of La Paz is the country's second largest, overtaken in the year 2000 by the City of Santa Cruz that has a population of 1,114,095. La Paz's sheltered location as inspired the spaniards to select it in 1548 the main silver route to the Pacific Coast. Colonial churches and architecture survive there. La Paz grew rapidly in the late 19th and early 20th centuries as the railway center and de facto capital of the country. The

industrial and lower-income areas of the city are located high up on the valley sides, the commercial district is at the upper level and the middle-class residential areas are at the lower levels. In the last two decades fancy neighborhoods have been built, now including modern supermarkets, fast-food stores and nightclubs.

The city center has changed dramatically in the last three decades. Dozens of skyscrapers now dominate downtown La Paz, and several five-star hotels accommodate a growing number of foreign tourists. Internet cafes have become common in La Paz and in other cities and towns.

On the outskirts of La Paz, the city of El Alto has grown dramatically in the last decade. Made up largely of Aymara immigrants from the Altiplano who continue to maintain ties with their traditional lands, El Alto is now considered the fourth largest city in Bolivia with a population of 694,749 and growing rapidly. Amidst the brick and adobe houses thrives a rich mixture of traditional Andean and western cultural traditions.

Further south is Potosí, which retains its colonial air and art treasures from an age when the nearby Cerro Rico (Rich Hill) mountain was one of the first great discoveries of the Spanish conquerors, and which pumped the equivalent of some 2 billion dollars into the Spanish treasury. Potosí (population 133,268) sits more than 13,000 feet above sea level (3,900m). Potosí continues to survive from mining and, increasingly, tourism.

From this high plain, the land spills off into lush, semi-tropical valleys to the north and east. These valleys, called the Yungas, are drained by the Beni River system, which then empties into the Amazon River. This land of beauty and future development begins about three hours out of La Paz. The mean annual temperature of this area is between 60 and 70°F (15 to 20°C), while the rainfall is between 27 and 31 inches yearly.

The soil of the Altiplano washes into the basin of the region, where many of the citrus fruits, coca, coffee, cacao, bananas, cattle and other products are grown, are exported to La Paz. Extensive road-building and river-clearing programs are linking this region with the rest of the nation. Altiplano Indians and others who formerly lived along the routes of these roads have, to some extent, already been resettled by colonization projects. A new route is beingf finished that will link the high plateau consumer areas and the productive plain of the Beni, ensuring the incorporation of the tropical lowlands into the economic life of the country. At the center of a colonization area, Caranavi, situated about 150 miles (250 km) north of La Paz, has grown from four huts to about 40,000 people.

From Caranavi, a new road connects with San Borja and Rurrenabaque, towns in the Beni Department, that are becoming important settlements in the tropical lowlands. The development of the tropical lowlands, however, is at the same time creating serious ecological damage and concern among environmentalists and government officials that, unless the migration is controlled, the area's fragile ecology will be endangered. Indian groups in the area are also being forced out of their lands by lumber companies that are cutting down mahogany and other fine woods without concern for the welfare of the Indians or for the area's fragile ecosystem.

In recent years Rurrenabaque has become an important tourist site and gateway to Madidi National Park. Since it was featured on the cover of National Geographic Magazine, the Park has gained international prominence and now offers first-rate accommodations.

Heading east and southeast from the Altiplano, the flatlands give way to hills and valleys that include the cities of Cochabamba, Sucre and Tarija (in the southeastern part of the country). These are the major population centers in the area, which includes fertile valleys as well as barren farmland that is barely able to sustain the economically poor but culturally rich Quechua-speaking population.

Cochabamba, Bolivia's third largest city, (population 778,422), has an average temperature of 65°F (about 18°C) and eternal sunshine, is situated at almost 8,500 feet (2,570m) and is described as the best living area in Bolivia. Sucre (population 194,888), still the nation's legal capital, has retained much of its colonial color and charm. Its elevation is about 9,150 feet (2,790m). The 135,651 inhabitants of Tarija are isolated, friendly, cultured and maintain traditions that have changed very little over time. These valleys spread out into the tropical lowlands that sweep from the Argentine and Paraguayan borders to Santa Cruz de la Sierra.

The Oriente is the largest and most sparsely populated region. Santa Cruz, the only major city, lies close to the Andean foothills but is very much a city of the plains. Since the mid-1950s it has been the fastest-growing center of agricultural colonization in Bolivia, and the center of oil and natural gas production and electrical generation. Thousands of highland residents have migrated to this region, as have groups of Mennonites and Japanese. Cambas, as the residents of this region are called, have converted the fertile Santa Cruz region (with the help of immigrants and migrants) into a production center of soybeans, cotton, sugar cane, sorghum, sunflower, poultry products and rice.

By the 1970s Santa Cruz had overtaken Cochabamba to become Bolivia's second largest city—a unique example of a long-isolated town in the Oriente overtaking a major Andean center. Today, the population of Santa Cruz has grown to 1,114,095, making it the largest city in Bolivia. Several five-star hotels have recently opened. A seventeen-year-old airport is considered one of the most modern on the continent and has become the country's main airport hub, serving nearly all neighboring countries and Miami. Golf courses, fashionable neighborhoods and some of the best restaurants in Bolivia are in Santa Cruz, a popular vacation spot for Bolivians and foreigners alike. The area's growth has also contributed to an important migration of residents from the highland, many of which have installed them in neighborhood lacking basic services.

Part of the growth of various cities and towns in Bolivia was attributable to cocaine. At least 45,000 farmers used to grow coca leaves in the Yungas, Chapare and Yapacaní regions located between La Paz and Santa Cruz. In the past, cocaine contributed to the growth of Santa Cruz and Cochabamba, as well as to a growing population of child addicts called pitilleros. Much of the wealth created by cocaine was invested in Cochabamba and Santa Cruz and oversees.

Illegal trade in cocaine has decreased considerably in recent years, and the Chapare, once the center of the country's illegal coca leaf and cocaine production, is now producing alternative crops such as a bananas, pineapples, spices, dairy products, etc. The former governments of General Hugo Banzer and Jorge Quiroga made the destruction of illegal coca plants one of their top priorities. These efforts have contributed to the economic slowdown of the region. Often violent conflicts, however, between coca leaf farmers and Bolivian police and soldiers have been one of the aftermaths of the coca eradication campaigns. An economic slowdown has also resulted because of the eradication of coca, destruction of many cocaine-processing labs and tighter custom controls.

The Quechua, Aymara and Guaraní Indian farmers and miners have chewed the leaves of the indigenous coca shrub for centuries as a relief against cold, fatigue and hunger. Small quantities of coca (from the Quechua kúka) have also been legally exported for many years for medicinal purposes.

The unprecedented expansion of coca cultivation in the Yungas, and especially in the Chapare region northeast of Cochabamba, began in the 1960s with the sudden growth in the illegal international market for cocaine. As demand soared in North America and Europe in the 1970s and 80s, Bolivian peasant farmers soon found that no other crop could compete with coca for profitability. It became the ideal cash crop—easy to grow, valuable, non-perishable and easy to transport, whether in dried leaf form or as cocaine. By the late 20th century, it was estimated that one-quarter of the world's coca was grown in Bolivia, with 80 % in the Chapare region alone.

Attempts by the government to introduce crop substitution or a voluntary reduction by the peasants of their coca acreage initially met with little success. Indeed, the area under coca cultivation continued to increase. In recent years, however, voluntary and forceful coca leaf eradication programs have sharply decreased the prevalence of coca leaf cultivation and cocaine production in the economy.

It is estimated that around $350 million worth of cocaine left Bolivia annually from centers around Cochabamba, Santa Cruz and from remote parts of the Oriente. Drug trafficking added to the country's gross national product and contributed to corruption among law enforcement and other government officials. Efforts by Bolivian and United States drug enforcement agents continue to make significant inroads against cocaine trafficking activities.

The political landscape in Bolivia changed after the 2002 presidential elections when coca leaf farmer Evo Morales became the second largest vote getter in Bolivia raising the possibility that Congress could have elected him president since neither he nor front-runner Gonzalo Sanchez de Lozada won a majority of votes. Morales' party, the Movimiento al Socialismo (Movement towards Socialism) is made up largely of leaders of the country's indigenous co::munities.

With much of its land, but few of the country's people, the lowlands are said to be Bolivia's future. Just as a comparison, the department of Santa Cruz is about the size of Bangladesh but a population of less than three million. Most of the area consists of dense tropical forests and pastures, swamps, dry tropical forests and scrub. Seasonal rainfall is high and the climate is usually hot, except when a cold, Antarctic-based wind from the south strikes in the tropical east around Santa Cruz. These fronts are called surazos, and they strike several times yearly for several days at a time. From Santa Cruz de la Sierra, rails and roads link the area with Brazil to the east and Argentina to the south. In the eastern section of Santa Cruz, a British government project has cataloged the tremendous mineral resources that exist in the area. Santa Cruz is also home to the Kaa-Iya National park in El Chaco, the country's largest, the Amboro National Park, the Noel Kempff National Park, the Ríos Blanco and Negro Wildlife Reserve, the Otuquis National Park and the San Matias Protected Natural Reserve, whose main gateway is the city of Puerto Suarez located on the far east on the border with Brazil.

The northern part of these tropical lowlands, from Santa Cruz to the Beni, was developed in the 16th and 17th centuries by Jesuit priests who established beautiful churches and communities rich in music, handicrafts and agriculture. The Beni area provided Europe with excellent tropical fruits, rubber, nuts and dried beef. This area fell into decay after the Jesuit priests were expelled, and channels to the outside world disappeared. Today, Indian communities are trying to survive despite the encroaching number of lumber companies and migrants from the highlands. The cultural heritage of the Jesuit Missions, however, continues to thrive as its Baroque music is recovered and played not only in the region but in Europe, the United States and other Latin American countries. The restoration of six Jesuit-period churches and its declaration as a UNESCO World Heritage Site has brought new life to the former Jesuit Missions.

Hunters, fishermen, birders and botanists come to the area and are accommodated in hotels in Trinidad (population 75,285), capital of the Beni and the only significant city in the tropical north. Riberalta, Guayaramerín, Rurrenabaque, San Ignacio de Moxos and Santa Ana de Yacuma are beautiful towns in the Beni that are rich in traditions and culture.

The northern department of Pando is breaking out of its historical isolation. A road now links the department with the rest of Bolivia during the dry season and a new airport now facilitates air travel. Once a rubber producing area, the production of Brazil (or Amazon) nuts has become the main economic resource in the region. The extraction of tropical wood products is also important to the Pando region, which borders and is heavily influenced by Brazil.

The People

Approximately 55% of the Bolivian people are descendants of the Aymara and Quechua pre-Columbian indigenous cultures. 20% of the population is mestizo and 25% is white. Socially, the population is in ferment. The once-stilted social structure of the nation was destroyed by the 1952 social revolution that took political control from a small, white oligarchy and passed it to the indigenous majority, under white and mestizo middle-class leadership. Aymara and Quechua city residents are commonly referred to as cholos. They are also referred to as campesinos (peasants) or mineros (miners).

This population pattern, like many other things in Bolivia, is changing. Anthropologists have noted that the unique Bolivian ethnic and social composition of Aymaras and Quechuas now discard some traditional ways and adopt western dress.

The mixture of rich native Indian cultures with the Mediterranean culture brought by the Spaniards is apparent everywhere in Bolivia. On religious feast days, for example, pre-Columbian rites that coincide with Roman Catholic celebrations are still practiced, and Aymara, Quechua and other ethnic groups express themselves through colorful dances and songs that blend the two cultures. In such festivities, some symbolic dress presents the Indian interpretation of European attitudes: the dance of the palla-palla or loco palla-palla caricatures the European invaders: the dance of the wakatokoris satirizes bullfights; and the morenada mocks white men, who are represented leading imported African slaves. The zampoña, quena and charango instruments are used to accompany these dances.

In the music itself, the mixture of cultures is also evident, since many of the tunes are based on Spanish dances. The more commonly-used instruments are the sicu or zampoña (panpipes) and the quena, tarka and pinkillo (vertical flutes). Percussion instruments of various sizes are used, including skin drums, bronze gongs and copper bells. Spain's influence is clearly seen in the charango, a stringed instrument peculiar to Bolivia. It has five double strings and is similar in shape to the guitar, although much smaller. Its sound box is made from the shell of an armadillo.

The costumes, highly embroidered and colorful, imitate the dress of the pre-Columbian Indian or the dress of 16th-century Spaniards. Elaborate plaster of Paris, cloth or tin masks and elaborate feather headdresses accompany many dancers.

There are at least 30 different ethnic communities in Bolivia. Even though the Quechuas, Aymaras and Guaraní are the best known, numerous other ethnic communities such as a Mojenos, Matacos, and Chiquitanos living in the tropical lowlands continue to maintain their rich cultural traditions.

A Short History

Historians usually raise the curtain on Bolivia's history at Tiwanaku about 600 A.D., although dissenting opinions date it as far back as 7,000 B.C. The Aymara Indians had developed a lesser civilization at this location between La Paz and the southern end of Lake Titicaca, but the second civilization was influenced by the Nazca and Chimú civilizations of Peru, and from these mixtures a truly great civilization emerged. This Tiwanaku civilization was characterized by immense buildings, massive monuments, ornate textiles, skillful pottery, attractive metalwork and sophisticated agricultural systems.

This flowering civilization began to wither for some unknown reason. When the Quechua-speaking soldiers of the great Inca Empire of Cuzco conquered the area about 1200 A.D., they found the Aymaras living about their decaying, but still impressive, ruins. The Incas controlled much of Bolivia until the arrival of the Spanish conquerors.

In 1535 A.D., Diego de Almagro, Francisco Pizarro's partner in conquest, founded a site near what is now Oruro. Five years later, Pedro Anzurez founded a site later named Charcas (Sucre), which became the Audiencia under the vice-royalty of Peru in 1559 A.D.

But Bolivia's destiny was shaped most by the discovery in 1545 of Potosí and its shadowing mountain of silver, Cerro Rico.

This find stirred great interest back in Spain and inspired a splendor at Potosí that rivaled the pretentious display at Lima. As the vast reserves of silver were shoveled out of the Cerro Rico Mountain, a crown mint established locally converted the metal into coins for shipment to Spain. For decades, a favorite Spanish description for untold wealth was "vale un Potosí" (worth a Potosí). The wealth of Potosí was taken by caravans of llamas and mules across the Altiplano to the Pacific Coast, a journey that is still carried on by herds of llamas carrying coca and corn from the lowlands to trade for dehydrated potatoes, fish and salt from the highlands.

The autocratic but well-organized social system of the Incas and their conquest of other indigenous sub-cultures was destroyed by Spanish colonization. The native population was pushed off fertile plains onto infertile mountainsides or incorporated into a peonage system. The Spanish colonial officials took over the vast lands and lived in relative luxury. Criollos, people of Spanish ancestry born in the Americas, also lived fairly well but resented their exclusion from high, appointed offices dispensed back in Spain.

The criollos and the mestizos were the first people in Latin America to sound the cry for liberty from Spanish rule. The first revolutionary movements developed in the department of Chuquisaca, La Paz and Cochabamba in the summer and fall of 1809. All were suppressed until 1825 when Bolívar pressed his liberation campaign from the north along the Andean region. Bolivia was named in honor of Simón Bolívar, the Liberator, in tribute to his leadership in the cause of South American independence. After General Antonio José de Sucre set up Bolivia as an independent nation and departed, his top general took over and proclaimed a Peruvian-Bolivian confederation in 1836. Dissident Peruvians defeated General Santa Cruz three years later and the confederation was dissolved.

Independence did little for the people of Bolivia. Political control of the nation switched from one greedy group to another. The new Criollo rulers lived lavishly from the profits of the vast, but ill-used, mineral wealth. Bolivia was a republic, but it was not a nation.

Since its independence, there have been 78 governments, half of them elected democratically and the rest imposed through coups. Weak governments made Bolivia vulnerable to the aggressive designs of neighbors. Several border disputes have dominated the nation's history, subtracted one-fourth of its territory and left it a land-locked country. Several incidents seemed to work along the same pattern—a neighbor would grab a piece of Bolivian territory, then build the loser a railroad. So, Bolivia ended up with several disjointed railroads and without its useful land.

When Chile defeated Bolivia and Peru in the War of the Pacific (1879-83), it took Bolivia's Pacific coast area and built a railroad from La Paz to Arica. When Argentina annexed some of the Chaco area, it too built a railroad connection between the two nations. When Brazil annexed the rich Acre area in 1903, it promised a railroad, which has yet to be completed. But in the Chaco War with Paraguay (1932-35), Bolivia surrendered a large area without the benefit of a railroad.

This war was to influence Bolivia's future greatly. Stunned by an embarrassing defeat, young officers and indignant intellectuals began examining the nation's conscience and prescribing solutions. The result was the formation of the National Revolutionary Movement (MNR) that gained power in 1952 and launched the first fundamental reforms in the nation's history. This party, headed by Victor Paz Estenssoro, Hernán Siles Zuazo, Walter Guevara Arce and Juan Lechín Oquendo, came to dominate Bolivia's political life for the next 35 years.

Social Revolution

Two events have symbolized this revolution and help explain the troubled nature of Bolivia's contemporary history. Returning from the Chaco War with an understanding of the world beyond their immediate misery, some Aymara and Quechua veterans began thinking about the lot of their people and ways to change it. Several veterans in the Cliza Valley, near Cochabamba, organized their neighbors into a union and began joint efforts to build a school. When union members tried to buy the land they had tilled for generations, the planters responded by flooding the valley and destroying their humble homes. Like-minded miners at Catavi on the Altiplano fared even worse. Hundreds were shot down by government troops in 1942 while striking for better wages and improved working conditions.

Cliza Valley and Catavi became symbols. The peasants and the miners emerged from the social revolution as the two strongest political forces, each armed and functioning as a militia because the traditional army had been destroyed by the 1952 revolution.

The farmers [151,434 family heads were given land titles under the revolution's agrarian reform program] have tended to support the moderate MNR majority. But the miners gave their support to the party's leftist sector. This sector has supported labor demands that have occasionally brought the nation's economy to a near standstill.

The 1952 revolution is perhaps Bolivia's most important political and social event this century, and one of the three most important revolutions in South America. It resulted in the nationalization of private mines, the enactment of universal suffrage and land reform legislation that significantly altered the political forces in the country. In the aftermath of the revolution, the COB (Bolivian Workers Central) under the leadership of Juan Lechín Oquendo became a major political force in the country. Mineral barons Simón Patiño, Hochschild and Aramayo lost the tremendous political and economic influence they once held, and a new leadership class developed.

Victor Paz Estenssoro, an economist and master politician, dominated Bolivia's political life as president from 1952 to 1956, 1960 to 1964 and 1985 to 1989. Also playing an important role was Hernán Siles Zuazo, a leader of the 1952 revolution who was vice president to Estenssoro between 1952 and 1956, and president of Bolivia between 1956 and 1960 and again between 1982 and 1985. During the early years, the MNR government exiled or sent to remote internment camps thousands of political opponents. Even when not in office, Paz Estenssoro was an important power player. For example, Estenssoro supported the 1971 military coup that brought General Hugo Banzer Suárez into office for a seven-year rule marked by severe human-rights abuses, as well as by economic growth and stability. Hundred of opposition political leaders, union officials and journalists were exiled during his regime. In the 1970s, the MIR (Revolutionary Movement of the Left) headed by former candidate to the priesthood and Marxist leader Jaime Paz Zamora, became, along with the COB, the main opposition to Banzer's rule. Paz Zamora was jailed and exiled by Banzer.

Popular opposition brought Banzer to call for elections in 1978, which were marked by violence and widespread fraud. Between 1978 and 1982, when democracy finally returned to Bolivia, there were 10 governments. After two military governments, Congress elected Walter Guevara Arce president in 1979. He stepped down in November after a failed coup and Congress elected the first woman president, Lydia Gueiler Tejada, who was scheduled to serve until elections slated for 1980, when 13 candidates, not including the incumbent, were in the presidential race. Siles Zuazo came in first with a relative majority, heading a coalition that included the Communist Party and the MIR headed by Paz Zamora. A bloody military coup interrupted the country's democratic evolution again in 1980 before Congress was able to elect a new president.

In the coup, one of the country's most brilliant authors and political leaders, Marcelo Quiroga Santa Cruz, was murdered. Murder, torture, exile, political persecution and widespread corruption by military officers headed by General Luis García Meza marked the period. For two years the country was run by right-wing officers who hired ex-Nazis, fascists and paramilitaries to attack opposition political and labor leaders. In this period, the involvement of military officers in cocaine-trafficking activities became widespread. Luis Arce Gómez, Minister of the Interior under García Meza, was indicted in Miami on cocaine trafficking charges and is now serving a 30-year-sentence. In December 1989, the government sent him to Miami to face the charges. Garcia Meza and many paramilitaries who supported his administration are now in a La Paz jail serving lengthy prison sentences.

Widespread opposition, domestic and international condemnation, and the deterioration of the economy led to the return to civilian rule in 1982. Congress elected Siles Zuazo president and Paz Zamora vice president. During his first year as president, Siles Zuazo took serious action toward placing Bolivia among the continent's few democracies. But differences within the ruling government coalition, the lack of congressional support, the heavy deficits of the state mining company COMIBOL and social unrest contributed to the collapse of the economy and a break-up of the ruling UDP (Popular Democratic Unity) coalition.

When Siles Zuazo stepped down in 1985, a year ahead of schedule, inflation had reached 24,000% and the economy was in a shambles, with banks virtually shut down, the Central Bank without any reserves, state mines suffering hundred-million dollar losses and the industrial sector on the verge of collapse. Siles Zuazo's main legacy, however, was to turn over the government to another democratically-elected president.

In the 1985 elections, Banzer's party, the ADN (Nationalist Democratic Action), came in first with 29 percent of the vote, followed by Paz Estenssoro's party, the MNR, with 26 percent and Paz Zamora's party, the MIR, third with 9 percent of the vote. The elections were peaceful.

Congress elected Paz Estenssoro president with the support of General Banzer. Soon after taking office, Paz Estenssoro said, "Bolivia is dying," and implemented drastic economic reforms to end hyperinflation, then the highest in the world. The peso was devalued by 95 %, gasoline prices increased ten-fold, wages were frozen and all price supports eliminated. The country's conservative government also shut down most of its tins mines and fired 21,500 miners—out of a work force of 27,000 — in response to the drop in international tin prices and large deficits by COMIBOL. To quell a general strike called by the COB and the mobilization of miners, the government declared two states of siege and sent hundreds of labor leaders to detention centers in the Bolivian tropics. Despite the tremendous social and economic upheaval caused by the economic reform programs, there was very little violence. To carry out the economic program, Paz Estenssoro formed an alliance with General Banzer's party (ADN). Paz Estenssoro dismantled the mining company that he helped set up after the 1952 revolution, and opened up the economy to foreign investors.

Paz Estenssoro ended his term in August 1989 as one of South America's most important statesman in this century.

Former dictator General Banzer emerged as an avowed democrat and major political player in the country and passed away in 2001.

In the May 1989 presidential elections, the main candidates were General Banzer, Paz Zamora and a newcomer to national politics, Gonzalo Sánchez de Lozada, a University of Chicago philosophy graduate, owner of the wealthy COMSUR mining company and the planning minister who helped carry out the economic reforms in 1985 under Paz Estenssoro. Sánchez de Lozada and the MNR came in first with 25 percent of the vote, followed by Banzer with 24 percent and Paz Zamora with 22 percent. With none of the candidates receiving an absolute majority, it was again up to Congress to choose Bolivia's next president. For the next three months, the economy came to a virtual standstill as the three leading candidates played political poker. To almost everyone's surprise, Paz Zamora, now a social democrat, negotiated the backing of General Banzer for a coalition government and was elected by Congress as Bolivia's 78th president. In most respects, Paz Zamora's policies were a continuation of his predecessor's (a distant relative), except for a new emphasis on national production of food and raw materials and negotiations with Brazil for the construction of a natural gas pipeline between the two neighbors. Under the threat of loss of U.S. aid, Paz Zamora continued to help fight the drug trade.

In the 1993 presidential elections, Sánchez de Lozada of the MNR party claimed victory. But since his party only won a relative majority, Congress again decided the election of the president, where Sánchez de Lozada formed an alliance with a newcomer to Bolivian politics, the Solidarity and Civic Union (UCS) party that was run by beer baron Max Fernández. Sánchez de Lozada was sworn in president on August 6 on a platform that included a complete revamping of the country's pension system and the capitalization of state companies. Sánchez de Lozada, who was widely known as "Goni," sold off half of the shares of the country's state-run electrical energy, transportation, communication, hydrocarbon and airline companies under a capitalization program. The 50% government stake in these companies was transferred to a new national pension fund system, while controlling interest in the new companies was turned over to the foreign partners.

Under this program, over two billion dollars in new investments started pouring into the economy. Sánchez de Lozada also finalized an agreement with Brazil for the construction of a $1.8 billion natural gas piping between Santa Cruz and Sao Paolo, Brazil that was completed in 2000. The prospects of selling natural gas to Brazil also sparked large investments by United States, Spanish, British, Argentine and Brazilian companies in the development of the country's natural gas reserves, which increased dramatically as a result of the investments sparked by capitalization.

Lozada's revamping of the pension fund system also revealed widespread corruption and inefficiency. Lozada ended his term in 1997 with a growing economy, increased foreign investment and with progress in reducing coca leaf cultivation and fighting the drug cartels.

Peaceful elections in 1997 gave Banzer only a relative majority with 23 percent of the vote. Congress once again had to elect Bolivia's new president. Banzer won the support of the UCS and a relative newcomer to Bolivian politics, the populist Conscience of Nationhood (CONDEPA) party run by the popular radio and television talk show host Carlos Palenque.

After taking office, Banzer inaugurated the Bolivia-Brazil natural gas pipeline and intensified the eradication of illegal coca plants and the war on drugs. He vowed to take Bolivia out of the cocaine trafficking circle before his five-year term ended in the year 2002. His US-educated vice president, Jorge Quiroga, played a major role in setting up anti-corruption programs, attracting foreign aid to Bolivia and addressing the dire social needs of Bolivians.

Banzer stepped down as president in August 2001 after doctors at Walter Reed Hospital in Washington D.C. diagnosed him with lung and liver cancer. The US-educated Jorge Quiroga, 41, was sworn in as president on August 6, and embarked on programs to eradicate corruption, rejuvenated the economy and spread the use of computers and the Internet throughout the country. His swearing-in marked a generational shift in Bolivia, and the hope that the traditional way of doing politics that included repaying political support with placing political supporters in key government posts, would come to an end. While Quiroga's reign brought a breath of fresh air to the country, he was unable to make significant inroads in eradicating corruption. He did support important institutional changes and promoted the introduction of Information Technologies into Bolivia. His American wife Ginger supported his efforts to combat poverty. Quiroga's term ended in August 2002, when Gonzalo Sanchez de Lozada, a U.S. educated philosophy mayor and millionaire was elected for a five year term. The 2002 presidential campaign was a turning point in Bolivia's political history. The leading candidates were the former Cochabamba mayor, Manfred Reyes Villa, the former president and mining executive Gonzalo Sanchez de Lozada, the former president Jamie Paz Zamora and the coca leaf farmer Evo Morales. Reyes Villa was considered the leader of the pack based on strong showings in political polls and growing interest by Bolivian in supporting new faces, Reyes Villa came in third in the country's elections, loosing the possibility of being elected president by Congress. Since none of the candidates received an absolute majority, the elections were decided by the newly elected congress. First-place winner Gonzalo Sanchez de Lozada managed a last-minute agreement with his erstwhile adversary Paz Zamora and was elected Bolivia's 77th president. His running mate, a highly respected journalist, historian and author, Carlos D. Meza, was elected vice president and took office vowing to lead a campaign to combat corruption in Bolivia. Evo Morales, the second-place winner, was unable to muster sufficient congressional votes to be elected president. Morales' surprising second place finish in the elections changed the country's political landscape through greater participation of indigenous leaders in congress. The elections also marked the death of CONDEPA, the near demise of the Nationalist Democratic Action Party (AND) founded by General Banzer and the fifth place finish of the Populist Party Civic and Solidarity Union (UCS) founded by former beer baron Max Fernandez and now led by his son, Johnny Fernandez.

Even though Sanchez de Lozada won only 23 percent of the popular vote, his alliance with Paz Zamora and support by AND and UCS assured him enough congressional votes to be elected government and have a relative majority in Congress.

Economy

Throughout the 1990s, inflation has remained under 10 %, and the economy had grown at an average of 4% until 1999 when a regional economic recession began affecting Bolivia. Economic growth came to a virtual standstill, the default rates at banks rose sharply, as did unemployment, and many companies collapsed throughout the country. The currency, however, has remained stable. The threat of military coups has evaporated and Bolivia's government is considered one of the most stable in South America. Stability in Bolivia, however, results in great social costs, with unemployment running at 15%, and affected by efforts to curtail contraband and the government's successful efforts to combat cocaine trafficking.

The minimum monthly wage is $60, while teachers earn an average of $75 a month. Economic stability has also brought a high cost of living. The price of dairy and poultry products is comparable to those in the U.S. and Europe, and malnutrition and infant mortality continue to be the highest in South America. The government says that its number one priority is to maintain economic stability and reactivate the economy, and it is counting on foreign aid and investment to do this. The government has also elicited the support of UNICEF, USAID, UNDP, the governments of Holland, Japan, Germany, the Nordic countries, the World Bank, the Andean Development Corporation, the Inter-American Development Bank and other aid institutions to improve the health and nutritional situation of Bolivians.

Bolivia now has duty-free access to Atlantic ports through the Brazilian border ports of Puerto Aguirre and Puerto Quijarro in eastern Bolivia. In the 1980s, Joaquin Aguirre, a Bolivian visionary and author, built Puerto Aguirre on the Canal Tamango that joins the Paraguay River a few miles downriver, with the support of USAID and the World Bank. Since then, the entire area, which includes Puerto Suárez, is booming. Five-star hotels, cement and soybean processing plants and an international airport have been built. Barges now regularly carry soybean and other crops on a two-week trip to Atlantic ports and return with food products, diesel and industrial goods.

In mid-1999, a 32-inch natural gas pipeline began pumping gas from Santa Cruz to Sao Paolo on a $2 billion pipeline that is a partnership between Enron, Petrobras and Shell. This pipeline is expected to bring badly needed revenues to the government and further fuel the economic growth of Santa Cruz and Tarija, where many of the newly discovered natural gas reserves are located.

Perhaps the most important economic shift in recent Bolivian history has been the discovery of vast natural gas reserves in Tarija and Santa Cruz that are considered the second largest in South America. Several projects to industrialize natural gas and export it to the United States as LNG are underway. Royalties and taxes derived from natural gas sales are expected to have a major impact on the Bolivian economy.

The capitalization and privatization of the economy has also led to important investments in other sectors. Entel, the former state telecommunication company that is now run by Italian investors, is modernizing the country's long-distance communications services and crisscrossing the country with fiber optic cable. Entel the Millicom-owned Telecel cellular phone company and Western Wireless through its VIVA partnership are also investing heavily in digital cellular phone networks. An opening of the telecommunications market in November 2001 has also brought in AES Communications and several other players to the telecommunications market.

The recent shifts in the economy has also resulted in important investments in the electricity and water service sectors, in air, rail and land transportation, and in large-scale soybean cultivation in the area around Santa Cruz.

Tourism is also playing an increasingly important role in the economy, bringing important foreign exchange earnings into the country. Important investments have been made in the cities of La Paz, Cochabamba, Santa Cruz and Sucre in hotel infrastructure. New hotels have also been built near the Lake Titicaca towns of

Copacabana, Huatajata, Isla del Sol, Puerto Pérez, the Jesuit Missions, Santa Cruz and other cities or regions. By the late 20th century, Bolivia had been added to an increasingly popular grand tour of South America— a package tour of continental highlights that attracts visitors from the United States, Europe and Japan and South America, who are attracted by the immense variety of natural and cultural resources, political stability and personal safety.

Bolivia's Rich Earth

From its earliest days, Bolivia's fortunes have risen or fallen with the riches extracted from its bountiful earth. Even before the arrival of the Spaniards, the Incas were mining the land's precious silver. It was this rich lode that quickly brought conquerors, colonists, adventurers and prospectors in search of fame and fortune to what became the greatest mining operation in the New World. Known then as Upper Peru, the area quickly prospered and then just as quickly declined as the mines were depleted of the valuable silver. But it was not long before those same rich hills in the Eastern Cordillera were found to contain tin, and the country's future course was shaped.

For a while, Bolivia's economy and the welfare of its people were largely dependent on the price of its principal product in the world markets. To a greater or lesser degree, the same is true today. But now the country is also mining bismuth, zinc, lead, antimony, wolfram and tungsten, as well as tin, gold and silver, and the prospect of rich natural gas and petroleum deposits is contributing substantially to the nation's economy and helping it achieve its goal of diversification.

The collapse of the world tin market and the drop in petroleum prices devastated Bolivia's export economy. Export earnings dropped from $1 billion dollars a year in 1980 to $500 million in 1985, but then increased to over $1 billion in 1991. This figure is expected to grow in 2003 when natural gas exports to Brazil increase. Non-traditional exports such as soy, sugar, wood, cattle and handicrafts have helped offset the drop in mineral exports. Foreign mining and petroleum companies are investing in Bolivia, and thousands of cooperatives are mining gold in the tropical lowlands.

Although mining has been and continues to be, along with natural gas, a chief contributor to the nation's economy, it accounts for less than 10% of the gross domestic product and represents less than 2% of the labor force. Nevertheless, minerals still account for close to a third of the country's total exports. Gas production has risen steadily and has become the country's principal export earner. Industrially, Bolivia is still running behind the economic goals it has set for itself. While manufacturing is changing slowly from handicrafts to industrial goods, the growth in these areas has been set back by contraband and lack of facilities and purchasing power. The country still depends in large measure on prices paid for a very limited number of mineral products overseas.

Lately, Bolivia has been cooperating much more effectively with its neighbors and integrating its economy with them through its membership in the Andean Common Market and ALADI (Asociación Latinoamericana de Integración), and through the development of natural gas projects with Brazil and for export to the US market

How to See Bolivia

A visit to Bolivia usually begins in **La Paz**. This city of over one million is the most important entry point to Bolivia. The city offers colorful Aymara Indian markets, Colonial churches, the highest professional golf course in the world, five star hotels, good restaurants and a variety of museums, including the Kusillo Children's museum.

From La Paz visitors head to Tiwanaku, one of the most important pre-Colombian sites in the continent and now home to a new museum, Lake Titicaca, the Andes and the Bolivian Highlands known as the Altiplano. After having seen the usual tourist sites around La Paz and the unusual tourist attractions farther south, the Bolivia of the past and future still lies ahead in all its charm and challenge.

Oruro is a mining center 130 miles southeast of La Paz. An important tourist attraction here is the colorful dances and ceremonies performed during Carnival, which starts on the Saturday before Ash Wednesday. This involves an elaborately costumed "bear" and "condor" clearing the way for a parade of similarly-costumed dancers led by alternate twosomes of Satan and Lucifer, and St. Michael the Archangel and China Supay, the devil's wife and sexual stimulant. After a leaping and shouting parade through the town, the participants crowd into the main plaza and perform dramatic rituals in which virtue prevails over sin. A mining theme is woven into the drama, in which the costumes represent a major portion of one's wealth.

Cochabamba is still a city of beauty, eternal spring and sunshine, but it has been caught in the crossfire of Bolivia's political turmoil and economic change. Once the prosperous center of a rich and vast area of plantation agriculture, the 1952 revolution's land reform program has sent many of the old planters into exile or to other livelihoods, divided up the big, absentee-owned plantations among peasants and diverted other peasants to colonization projects in eastern Bolivia and the Chapare, once an important source of coca leaves which were processed into cocaine.

The most important tourist attraction is the town house of tin baron Simón Patiño, which has been converted into a museum. The usual market here has the additional attraction of local Indian women with their unusual stovepipe hats. The newly discovered ruins of Incallajta, about 65 miles from Cochabamba, are accessible through special arrangements.

Potosí is 10 to 12 hours south by bus from La Paz over one of the world's highest roads, reaching an altitude of 15,809 feet (about 4,800m) at the junction of Condor. One of the first great cities of the Americas, with a population of about 160,000 early in the 17th century, Potosí has retained much of its colonial charm. Twisting, narrow streets pass aging mansions with colonial coats of arms, reminding one that this busy agricultural and mining center was once a majestic city. The city remains in the shadow of Cerro Rico that pumped silver into the Spanish treasury in the early colonial period. The Casa de la Moneda (Royal Mint), built in 1542 and rebuilt in 1759, still stands and has been converted into a museum. Some of the old homes and churches have oil paintings of considerable merit. Some 30 churches reflect good examples of Renaissance and Romanesque architecture.

Potosi and Oruro are important entry points to the Salar de Uyuni, Laguna Colorada and Laguna Verde region of southwest Bolivia. This region is now the second most important tourism destination in Bolivia, drawing at least 30,000 tourists captivated by the vast Uyuni Salt Flats, the red and green-colored lagoons, snow-covered volcanoes and the Andean flamingos, vicunas and Suri birds. The town of Uyuni is considered the main entry point because of its railroad link to Oruro. One of the continent's most important railroad graveyards is located in Uyuni.

From Potosí, buses head toward Sucre, which has an interesting display of buildings of both the Colonial and Republican eras. Many Latin American revolutionary leaders studied here at one of the oldest universities in Latin America. This city is still quite an oddity in Bolivia. Nearly 110 miles (183 km) northeast of Potosí, it is the legal capital of the nation, but the Supreme Court Building is the only vestige of what now unofficially belongs to La Paz, which became the de facto capital in the wake of the mining boom.

Well-paved roads join all these communities—La Paz, Oruro, Potosí and Sucre—. The only way to get to another important community, **Tarija**, to the southeast of these upland cities, is by a difficult road or by air. This settlement in the rich Guadalquivir River valley was founded in 1574 and has remained an isolated island apart from the rest of Bolivia. Thus cut off, the people have grown a variety of fine crops for their own consumption, produced a supply of skillful farm hands for Argentine agriculture and formed a pocket of advanced culture apart from the rest of the nation.

Returning to Cochabamba, one can continue eastward into the interior of the nation or take a river trip north to Trinidad. This latter trip involves traveling by road to Puerto Villarroel on the Ichilo River, which becomes, further north, the Mamoré. The boat trip up this river to Trinidad takes four days, from where the tourist might later fly back to La Paz. There are now two road links from Cochabamba to the city of Santa Cruz. The old, 315-miles (about 525 km) Cochabamba-Santa Cruz highway demonstrates what 20th century communication can do for a nation still existing in the 19th century. This highway, completed in 1954 after nine years of construction and a $50 million U.S. Export-Import Bank loan, actually united a nation that was falling apart and shaped an economy that was in serious trouble. There was a strong secession movement in Santa Cruz to join Brazil. Similar feelings were sweeping Tarija and several other communities. But this highway helped turn the nation's development inward instead of outward. Migrants from the highlands began settling in colonies and mixing with others along this road.

The old Cochabamba-Santa Cruz highway winds through the Cliza Valley, where the first important modern political movement among Bolivia's Indians began. Spurred by the 1952 social revolution, an indigenous peasant union in the valley community of Ucureña demanded that a planter return his land to peasants who had been evicted for union activity in the 1930s. When the planter stalled, these groups began a march on nearby towns and for a while the prospects of civil war between rural and urban groups hang over the nation.

Continuing east, the traveler can forget politics and take up geology. In the next 300 miles (about 500 km) he will travel through all four of the classified geological areas. First, he will experience the tundra area of the valleys, with its many flowers but no trees. Then comes the rain forest, with its mosses and ferns and damp, humid climate. Next, there is the desert, with pipe-organ cactus, much sand and little grass. Finally, near Santa Cruz, the tropical jungle breaks out in towering and verdant growth. Off this road are also the important pre-Colombian stone fortresses of Samaipata.

"This 331-miles (535 km) trip is like traveling from Ecuador to Alaska," one geologist remarked after traveling over the road and examining its specimens. Here one finds every temperature zone and practically every kind of vegetation.

A new road also links Cochabamba with Santa Cruz and is fast becoming the main route between the two cities. A paved road passes through the Quechua-speaking community of Sacaba before climbing to a lagoon that feeds water into hydroelectric generators that lie on the eastern slopes of the Andean foothills. From there the road winds down toward Paracti, a checkpoint where vehicles are examined for cocaine pre-constituents. In the rainy season landslides are common and the roads can be quite bumpy. After a two- to three-hour drive, the mountains disappear and the road flattens out.

The gateway to the Chapare is Villa Tunari, located 100 miles (162 km) from the city of Cochabamba. It has become an important transit point for travelers heading to Santa Cruz, as well as a base for development workers attempting to wean farmers away from coca leaf cultivation. Near Villa Tunari are some exceptional streams to bathe in and rivers to fish in, set amid spectacular scenery. The Carrasco National Park, with an incredible bird sanctuary, is reachable from Villa Tunari. Decent hotel accommodations are now available here. From Villa Tunari the main road passes Sinahota, Chimoré and Ivirgarzama before crossing the river at Puerto Villarroel. A new paved road now links Chimoré with Yapacaní, an agricultural region, en route to Montero and Santa Cruz. Roads from Villa Tunari and the Chapare highway head off into the tropical lowlands where hundreds of cocaine paste processing plants used to operate. Today, the former coca leaf fields now produce bananas and other products.

Arriving at the frontier community of **Santa Cruz**, an eastern, booming, tropical agriculture area, one can realize its importance as a commercial and industrial center. Its growing prosperity is seen in its oil fields, cotton plantations, sugar and lumber mills and modern airport, which links it with La Paz and other Bolivian cities, and which has become an important departure and arrival point for international flights. After visiting the city, one can decide whether to see more frontiers or return to La Paz. Near the city are areas undergoing rapid economic growth with the expansion of cattle and tropical farming and intense social change brought about by colonization projects. If a highway survey party cuts a small path through this jungle, colonists will line it

immediately and begin tilling its fertile soil. The center for this area's development is Santa Cruz.

There are still plenty of unexplored frontiers in Bolivia. A tourist can travel from Santa Cruz to Corumba, Brazil by railroad and experience the beauty of the tropics, the smell of the jungle and the bird life that at times seems to etch a rainbow in the sky. Over this 406-miles (655 km) railroad, one passes villages populated by Indians. Until several years ago, cousins of these residents occasionally attacked settlers encroaching on their lands. Now these people have disappeared further into the jungle brush to avert what they consider the annoyance of modern civilization, or to avoid being forced off their lands.

Midway through train ride from Santa Cruz to Corumba, an unusual type of topography stretches over about 10 miles (16.2 km). Beautiful mountains rise abruptly like polished stones from what is otherwise level jungle land. These small, stone-like mountains near San José have several colors, which, in the reflection of the noonday sun, provide an otherworldly atmosphere.

Upon reaching Corumba, on the Paraguay River, you can take a steamer down the river to Asunción, Paraguay, or Buenos Aires, Argentina. By entering Bolivia from Arica, Chile, the traveler could continue crossing the continent overland by following the route outlined above. It's rough, but rewarding.

Flora and Fauna

Bolivia's geographic range gives it a remarkable variety of flora and fauna. For example, more bird species have been found in Bolivia (over 1,250) than any other land-locked country.

In the Andes, llamas and alpacas are commonly seen; the rarer vicuña is restricted to special preserves. Armadillos and Andean condors, and the pink flamingos known as Pariguanas can also be found, but you will have to look in their own special habitats. In Comanche, southeast of La Paz, the Puya Raimundi plant grows. Taking 100 years to flower and reaching a height of 30 feet, it is the tallest succulent plant in the world. Lake Titicaca is home to salmon, trout, pejerrey, large frogs (with export-quality legs) and a wide variety of birds.

The Bolivian tropics, covering nearly two-thirds of the country, are incredibly rich in flora and fauna. While the area is developing rapidly, and thus losing habitats, the determined visitor can still find monkeys and macaws, peccaries and parrots, jaguars and jacamar, piranha and puff birds—along with several million head of cattle. Even travelers who never make it into the deep jungle can see parrots and three-toed sloths in the plazas of towns such as Santa Cruz and San Jose de Chiquitos.

Mahogany trees, though increasingly rare, spread skyward in the forest; in and under their canopy grows a botanist's dreamland of epiphytes, trees, shrubs, vines, ferns and grasses. One interesting tree in the area grows to some 100 feet and sprouts a bulb of cotton-like material used for making cloth.

The overwhelming biodiversity gives South America's heartland a beauty not to be missed. Numerous travel agencies now provide tours to experience Bolivia's great natural resources.

FACTS AT YOUR FINGERTIPS

WHEN TO GO

Due to its variety of altitudes and proximity to the equator, Bolivia has every climate and terrain imaginable. Temperature is largely determined by altitude; cities at lower altitudes are warm and tropical, cities at higher altitudes much cooler.

There is a rainy season that runs from October to March, with the dry season being from April to September. Rains can be heavy in the rainy season (which is actually summer), but generally last only an hour or two. During the rainy season, it is not advisable to travel by land to remote areas due to deteriorated road conditions. In the dry winter season, the skies over most of Bolivia are a pure, dark blue and sunny. *Carnaval* takes place in either February or March, when the heavy rains are nearly over.

In the mountainous regions of the country (particularly the La Paz, Potosí and Oruro Departments), temperatures reach 50 to 70°F (10C to 20C) in the sun but drop to freezing at night, and are also much cooler, even on sunny days, if you step into the shade.

The tropical Beni, Pando and Santa Cruz Departments are hot, often swelteringly so, year-round. Respite is offered, however, in the winter season when temperatures cool down a bit and with the arrival of the *surazos*, strong wind and rains coming in from other regions.

The most moderate, comfortable climates are found in the Sucre, Cochabamba and Tarija Departments, which have more sunny, warm days than anything else (think California). Here it rains during the rainy season, and gets cool during winter, but you will never be truly cold, or unbearably hot, in these places.

SPECIAL EVENTS

The **Oruro *Carnaval*,** scheduled for the Saturday before Ash Wednesday, and the **Pujllay Festival** in Tarabuco, scheduled for March, are important cultural festivals and very much worth visiting. Also recommended is the *Fiesta de la Cruz* (Feast of the Cross) that takes place the first weekend in May. In Achocalla, a village located one hour from La Paz, hundreds of area residents dance wearing elaborate costumes and the Aymara *Kusillo* mask. *La Fiesta de la Cruz*, one of the most important feast days, is also observed in Copacabana and other communities.

On **San Pedro**, which falls on June 28 and 29, many villages, among them Achacachi, Curva, Carabuco and Tiquiña, have festivals in honor of San Pedro. **The Feast of Santiago**, celebrated July 25, features native dances and processions. *La Entrada del Gran Poder*, celebrated in La Paz in early June, has thousands of dancers performing *La Diablada*, *Morenada* and a host of dances typical of the highlands. On **San Juan**, held on June 24, La Paz and other Andean cities are lit up by fires to fend off the cold winter. Several communities hold celebrations in honor of San Juan.

The Aymara New Year is celebrated on June 21st in the pre-Colombian town of Tiwanaku. Thousands of Aymaras are joined by tourists in a colorful and spiritual ceremony.

The **Alasitas Fair** of miniatures in honor of the *Ekeko*, the Aymaran Indian patron of abundance, takes place at the end of January in La Paz and other cities. Miniatures of handicrafts, household goods, houses, vehicles and figures are sold at the fair. For the opening, *paceños* stock up on miniature pesos and dollar bills, and have them blessed at the church with the hope that the year will be plentiful.

The cities of Sucre and Potosi organize yearly cultural festivals during the Bolivian Spring. Dozens of theater, dance and musical groups performs during this festival.

Every two years (2002 is the next scheduled festival) dozens of musical groups specializing in Bolivian Baroque Music from the Jesuit Missions come together in the Jesuit towns of Concepcion, San Javier, San Ramon, San Rafael and Santa Ana to perfom before backed crowds. A highlight of the festival that draws tens of thousands of fans are the performances by the Urububicha Children's Orchestra and Choir. Hundreds of Chiquitano Indian children and youths have mastered Baroque instruments and now perform them during the festival and on tours in Europe and other Latin American countries.

Check with the **Bolivian Tourist Agency** at Plaza del Estudiante or Av. Mcal. Santa Cruz, corner with Oruro, Edif. Palacio de Comunicaciones, 16th Floor, in La Paz for other festivals planned during your visit.

WHAT TO TAKE

For the highland regions (called the *Altiplano*), wool sweaters and a windbreaker are recommended. The sun in the Andes is very strong, so be sure to bring a good sunscreen and wear a hat. During the rainy season, an umbrella or raincoat is necessary. In the tropical regions, light clothing is worn year-round except during *surazo* fronts. (These can last up to three days and occur mainly in the winter). A good bug repellent is also recommended.

Jackets are expected at fancy restaurants, but informal clothing should do for most places. A good pair of hiking boots is a must, as well as sandals if headed for the tropical regions.

The bigger cities offer Western-style supermarkets with just about everything you can imagine from home. However, certain toiletry items, such as shampoos, contact lens' solution and sunscreen, are more expensive in Bolivia, and may be worth packing away before you board the plane.

TRAVEL DOCUMENTS AND CUSTOMS

U.S., U.K., Australian, Canadian and European visitors require passports. Visitors from other Latin American countries should check with their travel agency or Bolivian consulate to inquire about passport and visa requirements. Tourist visas are issued at airports or train stations upon arrival and are valid for 90 days. They can be extended at the immigration office located on Av. Camacho 1433, open Monday through Friday from 8:30. to 16:30. (not closed for lunch). If you stay longer than 90 days, you must stop by the nearest immigration office to get a visa extension. Customs are not very thorough about checking baggage.

Cigarettes and no more than two bottles of alcohol are allowed into the country. Cameras and computers can be brought in without much problem. Be especially careful about what you take out; many tourists who have tried to smuggle out a little bit of marijuana have ended up spending years in jail. There is a $25 dollar airport tax on international flights that can be paid in dollars or Bolivianos and a 15 Boliviano tax on domestic flights. Residents and Bolivians must also pay a 150 Boliviano departure tax. This is not applicable to tourists.

WHAT IT WILL COST

Bolivia has managed to control an inflation rate that reached 24,000% in 1985. As a result, prices have stabilized, though the dollar continues to gain purchasing power, and there are still many bargains to be found in Bolivia (particularly in handicrafts, silver and gold).

In the bigger cities, upscale travelers will have no trouble spending lots of money on fancy hotels and elegant restaurants. But in general, those who travel in Bolivia are amazed at how inexpensive it is. A comfortable, moderate hotel room for two with a private bath will usually cost about $25, and a good meal is easy to find for about $5, or 35 Bolivianos.

CURRENCY

The official and black market exchange rate is around 7.65 Bolivianos (sometimes referred to as "pesos") to the United States dollar as of June 2003. Since the government implemented an austerity program, the large disparity that existed between the official and black market rates has been eliminated. It is possible to legally change dollars in all Bolivian cities. In La Paz, people exchanging money have scattered all over downtown, particularly on the Prado (try Plaza del Estudiante) and on Calle Camacho. Money can also be changed at *Casas de Cambio* located throughout the main cities. **Prodem** offers also a good exchange rate at their offices all over the country. Your best bet for travelers checks is at a bank.

Bolivia probably has one of the most stable currencies in South America and dollars are considered legal tenders. ATM machines are located in all major cities and can handle dollars and bolivianos.

The official exchange rate is revised daily. Since 1990, only new bills are circulating. People still refer to *miles* or *millones de pesos*, but the new name of the Bolivian coin and the elimination of old peso bills should resolve any confusion. Dollars can be used for many transactions, and many hotels and stores now accept Visa, Master Card and American Express credit cards. If in a pinch, banks that handle credit cards can often provide cash advances. **Magri Tours** at Calle Capitán Ravelo 2101, can also cash checks and handle lost travelers checks for those who have American Express cards.

TIME ZONE

Bolivia is on Atlantic Standard Time, four hours behind Greenwich Mean Time. Bolivian time is constant throughout the year and throughout the country.

Bolivian time is Miami time, plus one hour from October to March, when Miami is on Eastern Standard Time (EST). From April until October, when the U.S. has Daylight Savings Time, Bolivia is the same as EST.

GETTING TO BOLIVIA

Lloyd Aéreo Boliviano (LAB) flies from Miami to Santa Cruz and La Paz with connecting flights to other cities. *American Airlines*, flies daily to La Paz and Santa Cruz. *Lufthansa* flies from Frankfurt to Caracas, Sao Paolo and Bogotá and connects with La Paz via LAB.

LAB airlines has service from Rio de Janeiro and Sao Paolo to Santa Cruz and La Paz; Buenos Aires to Santa Cruz; Santiago to Arica and La Paz; Panama to Santa Cruz and La Paz; Caracas to Santa Cruz; Asunción to Santa Cruz and La Paz; and Cusco and Lima to La Paz.

La Paz is also served by *Varig* from Sao Paolo and Rio de Janeiro, as well as, *Lan Chile* and *Líneas Aereas Paraguayas (Check if LAP still flies)*.

TACA, a Central American and

Peruvian owned airline now flies daily from La Paz to Lima with connecting flights to Central America, Mexico and Miami.

Check with your local travel agent for prices and schedules to and from La Paz and Santa Cruz.

GETTING AROUND BOLIVIA

By air: Lloyd Aéreo Boliviano, the national airline, and AeroSur serve most Bolivian cities. To reach some tropical cities and towns, Transporte Aéreo Militar (TAM) also provides regular passenger service. During the December to March rainy season, flights may be canceled or delayed due to bad weather.

By train: Bolivia has 2,624 miles (4,370 km) of railway. Trains link Potosí, Oruro and Santa Cruz, as well as linking Bolivia with Argentina and Brazil. Trains are infrequent and often delayed, especially during the rainy season. A great train trip is from Oruro to the Uyuni Salt Flats.

By bus: There is good bus service between major cities, with comfortable buses leaving regularly for very reasonable prices. Crowded buses often serve rural communities. Tickets must be purchased ahead of time for inter-city bus travel. Bus departures are usually on time. Be sure to bring food and a blanket for trips on the Bolivian Highlands.. The *main bus terminal* is at Av. Uruguay, Plaza Antofagasta (Tel. 2280551), and buses for the Yungas leave from Villa Fatima, and for Copacabana from the cemetery.

By boat: Boat service is available from Huatajata on the shores of Lake Titicaca to Copacabana and Puno, Peru. Crillón Tours, Transturin Ltd., Trimaran Service, Turismo Balsa (from Puerto Perez) and Atlas Tours offer boat service on the lake. Fremen tourist agency offers boat service on the eastern Bolivian rivers. Regular river boat services is available in the tropical lowland departments of Pando, Beni and Santa Cruz.

By car: Four-wheel-drive vehicles can be rented at a variety of agencies through-

out the country. Taxis can be hired by the hour and taken out to the surrounding countryside of almost every city.

BOLIVIAN HOLIDAYS

New Year's Day — January 1
Carnaval — Monday and Tuesday before Ash Wednesday
Good Friday — Friday before Easter
Labor Day — May 1
Corpus Christi — 60 days after Good Friday
Independence Day — August 6
All Saints' Day (*Todos Santos*) – November 2
Christmas Day — December 25

BUSINESS HOURS

Most shops open at 8:30 and 9:30, close at noon, re-open at 14:30, and close for the day around 19.00. Many shops are also open on Saturday morning.

Many government offices work straight through from 8:30 to 16:00.

Banks are generally open from 9:00. to 12:00. and 14:30 to 17:00 or 18:00. Some banks do not close for lunch. In some parts of Bolivia, post offices stay open all day, while others follow the *siesta* schedule. Most are open Saturday mornings.

HOTELS

Most Bolivian cities have good to excellent hotel accommodations. Always try to make reservations in advance for hotels, especially if you're planning on visiting Oruro, La Paz or Santa Cruz during Carnaval or the Jesuit Missions during Holy Week. Breakfast is sometimes, but not always, included in hotel rates.

Hotel rates are based on the official dollar exchange rate, which is practically the same as the black market rate, so it is usually the same to pay in Bolivianos or dollars. Before leaving the country it is also easy to sell Bolivianos for dollars. European currencies, however, are often difficult to change.

Credit card payments are based on the official exchange rate which is the same as the street exchange rate.

BOLIVIAN FOOD AND DRINK

One of Bolivia's little-known secrets is its great culinary tradition. Some day the cooking of the Andes may receive the credit it deserves. Corn, potatoes and quinoa, a high-protein grain, are native to the Bolivian Andes, and thousands of dishes are based on these and other products. The English-Spanish cookbook *Epicuro Andino* provides recipes for Bolivian and foreign dishes adapted for the altitude.

Unfortunately, few hotels will provide a good idea of the richness of Bolivian cuisine. Often the best way to be introduced to it is through Bolivian friends.

For a mid-morning snack, nothing beats a *salteña*, a hearty stew of beef, peas, potatoes, hard-boiled eggs, olives and a spicy sauce wrapped in a dough and baked. Served piping hot, it is popular at mid-morning celebrations. Some of the best salteñas are served in the City of Sucre.

Bolivian soups are second to none. Try a creamy peanut soup (*sopa de maní*) with chunks of corn, melted cheese and fava beans. Also worth trying are *chairo*, a hearty soup made with beef chunks and dehydrated potatoes, fava beans and potatoes; *sopa de papa lisa*, made from small, yellowish potatoes native to the highlands; and *sopa de quinua*, made from the quinoa grain, which can also be used in thousands of dishes including granola, bread, stews, casseroles and puddings.

La Paz and other cities also make an excellent French-style bread. In La Paz this typical bread is known as *marraqueta*. Baked early morning and afternoon, the *marraqueta* is one of the best options.

If passing through the Sucre airport, don't miss trying *chorizos*, pork sausages

flavored with green onions, fresh oregano, parsley, nutmeg and garlic. For lunch or dinner, be sure to try *ckocko*, a spicy chicken dish flavored with wine and a local corn brew. Also worth trying is *fritanga*, a pork dish flavored with fresh mint and ground, hot red-pepper sauce that is accompanied by hominy. For an appetizer, or even as a main dish, the *pastel de choclo* or *humintas*, made from ground corn, are delicious.

In La Paz, try *fricasé*, a spicy pork and hominy stew served at hotels and many restaurants (particularly on weekends). If interested in something mild, try the Lake Titicaca salmon trout, or excellent grass-fed filet mignon from the Beni or the highlands, accompanied by one of the 200-odd varieties of potatoes available in Bolivia.

In Santa Cruz or Trinidad, try a fresh heart of palm salad or a good juicy steak accompanied by rice with melted cheese and black beans. A delicious accompaniment is fried plantain or yucca. Perhaps the most delicious Bolivian pastry is the Cuñape, made from cheese and manioc floor and served fresh or dehydrated in the tropical Bolivian lowlands. Nothing beats the flavor of Cuñapes right out of the oven.

In terms of fruit, it is hard to equal the variety found in Bolivia. Because of the country's proximity to the equator, in Andean cities you will find a wide selection of valley and tropical fruits. Try *chirimoya*, a green and black-pocked fruit with a creamy white filling that makes great ice cream or mousse. Also worth trying are *tumbo* (a sweet-acid fruit), *maracuya* (passion fruit), *granadina*, *guayaba*, orange-colored bananas; most fruits common to the U.S. and Europe are also available in Bolivia.

Bolivia also has a thriving beer and wine industry. Beer made here by Germans and their descendants is superb, as attested to by many Europeans and Americans. Good and flavorful beer is sold throughout the country.

Bolivia's wine industry is based in Tarija, Camargo and other southern Bolivian regions. Best are *Concepcion, Campos de Solana, Kohlberg Fundador* and *San Pedro Cavergnet.* Bolivian wine is produced at altitudes of 1,000 to 1,500 meters and have recently gained international prominence.

Once you've adjusted to the altitude, be sure to try *singani,* a distilled spirit made from grapes. It is often served as a *pisco sour* or *chuflay,* which is a mixture of 7-Up, *singani* and lemon juice.

TIPPING

Many restaurants include a 16% value added tax, but not service, in the bill. Waiters expect a 10 to 15 % cash tip. Taxi drivers do not expect a tip, but for long distances or when hired for long periods in the city, a tip may be given according to the service received. At airports, plan on tipping baggage handlers one dollar for every piece of luggage.

COMMUNICATIONS

Local and long distance pay phones exist in all major cities and towns with populations of more than 1,000. Most require tokens or debit cards that can be purchased at nearby stores or food stands. It is usually more convenient to buy a telephone card from Entel and local cooperatives that provide long-distance telephone service. Central Entel offices, *Puntos Entel* as well as many hotels and airports, offer long-distance and fax service. Direct dial is available in all major towns and cities. Since the communications market opened in November, 2001, several companies, including AES Communications, provide long-distance and Internet service.

For information, dial 104. For domestic and international long-distance operators dial 101; you can also dial domestic long distance (city code+number) or international long distance (00+country code+city code+number) directly without operator assistance. One can also use your long-distance service providers by dialing the following access codes: SPRINT at 0800-3333; AT&T at 0800-101110; and MCI at 0800-2222.

Every major city and town offers Internet service usually through Internet cafés, the post office or Telecenters. An hour at a Café costs around one dollar. Several sites also provide Voice over IP services.

NEWSPAPERS

Bolivia has a weekly English-language newspaper called the *Llama Express.* Magazines such as *Newsweek, The Economist* and *Time* — are sold in many kiosks and at *Los Amigos del Libro* bookstore, which has branches in La Paz, Cochabamba and Santa Cruz, and offers a good selection of foreign-language books and magazines. There are also good bookstores in major cities-look for Lectura, among others.

La Paz has five dailies: *El Diario, La Razon, Jornada* and *La Prensa.* Three magazines, *Enfoques, Pulso* and *Cosas,* come out of La Paz. The weekly newspaper Nueva Economia is also widely read especially by business and political leaders. In Santa Cruz, you can purchase *El Mundo, El Deber, El Nuevo Día* and *La Estrella del Oriente;* in Cochabamba, *Opinion* and *Los Tiempos;* and in Sucre, *Correo del Sur.*

Bolivian dailies carry a good amount of foreign news. The U.S.-Bolivian Centers in La Paz, Cochabamba, Sucre, Tarija and Santa Cruz also have a good selection of English-language dailies and magazines. The British Council in La Paz also offers a library as well as English language training programs.

HEALTH AND SAFETY

Bolivia no longer deserves a reputation as an unstable, coup-prone country; it is one of the safest countries to visit in South America. There are periodic strikes and demonstrations, however, which occasionally make travel difficult. Foreign diplomats who have served at other Latin American posts say Bolivia is one of the safest and friendliest countries in the Third World. Muggings are very rare, but be careful of pickpockets, especially on crowded buses and at airports and railroad and bus stations. Be sure to carry your wallet in an inside pocket or body belt, and hold your belongings tightly. Be extremely careful with luggage and backpacks at bus stations and airports.

Water in most cities is treated, but to be on the safe side, drink only bottled water and avoid eating salads or raw vegetables in restaurants. Avoid the purchase of cooked food from street stands or in markets. Raw vegetables, fruits and salads should always be washed in water treated with a few drops of iodine. Cholera has become a serious problem in Bolivia, mainly in rural areas. If you take some basic precautions, such as not eating raw vegetables or fruit, you should have no problems.

In La Paz, Potosí and other places on the *Altiplano*, take it easy the first couple of days because of the altitude.

HIGH ALTITUDE HEALTH ADVICE

The sensations that you experience on arrival to the *Altiplano*, such as increased respiration, fast and pounding heart action, and some tiredness and lightheadedness, are all normal adaptive processes. Don't worry about them; the body will adjust. Apprehension, on the other hand, can increase the symptoms.

Much of what one feels the first days at altitude is an effect of dehydration. You need considerably more fluids (in the form of water, juices, broths and Gatorade-like drinks). Non-chocolate candies taken frequently on arrival to high-altitude places can prevent, or at least diminish, symptoms such as headaches if they develop. Also you need more carbohydrates; starches (pasta, potatoes, etc). should make up a large part of your diet. Frequent, small, light meals are best. *Mate de coca* (tea obtainable just about anywhere) is of benefit, especially with sugar added. Avoid alcohol and limit carbonated drinks or let them get a little flat.

Try to limit activity your first few days. You should avoid over-exertion, but the frequently-given advice to lie down during the initial hours in high altitudes can actually increase your headache if overdone. Children and young, athletic adults are more likely to develop serious complications, so guard them against overactivity until well-adapted.

Aspirin — two tablets every four hours, with a full glass of water— is the best medicine for a headache. Two tablets, taken preventatively on arrival, might be beneficial.

Avoid other medications claimed to be "*Soroche* (altitude sickness) Remedies" such as Coramine, Microren or various diuretics. They increase symptoms and can even be dangerous. One diuretic, acetazolamide ("Diamox"), might be beneficial for reasons other than its diuretic effect.

It is very unlikely that you will need oxygen. It can even delay the adaptive processes, and using it in the towns you'll be visiting is about as logical as using it while jogging.

Relax and enjoy the Andes. Extremely few major complications occur in healthy people at 12,000 feet.

SUGGESTED READING MATERIAL

Note: Many of these books are also available in Spanish.

We Eat the Mines and the Mines Eat Us: June Nash, New York, 1979.

Adventuring in the Andes: Charles Frazzier with Donald Secreast, Sierra Club books 1985.

Rebellion in the Veins: James Dunkerley, Verso Editions, London, 1984.

The Unfinished Revolution: James Malloy, Pittsburgh Press, 1970.

Let Me Speak: *An account of life in the mines*. Domitila Chungara.

The Ancient Civilizations of Peru: Alden J. Mason, Pelican, 1957.

The Great Tin Crash: John Crabtree, Latin America Bureau, London, 1986.

The Incas of Pedro de Cieza de León: Edited by Victor Wolfgang von Hagen, Univ. of Oklahoma Press, 1959.

Highway of the Sun: *A Search for the Royal Roads of the Incas*. Victor W. Von

Hagen, Plata Publishing, Switzerland, 1975.

Bolivian History: Charles Arnade, Ed. Los Amigos del Libro, La Paz, 1984.

Bolivian Indian Textiles: Tamara E. Wasserman and Jonathan Hill, Dover Publications, New York, 1981.

Aymara Weavings: *Ceremonial Textiles of Colonial and 19th Century Bolivia.* Laurie Adelson and Arthur Tracht, Smithsonian Institution Traveling Exhibition Service, 1983.

Hotel Bolivia: *The culture of memory in a refuge for nazism.* Leo Spitzer, Hill and Wang, a division of Farrar Straus and Giroux, New York.

BOLIVIA, Land of Struggle: Waltraud Queiser Morales, Ed. Westview Press, 1992.

A Brief History of Bolivia: Waltraud Queiser Morales, New York: Facts on Files Press, 2002.

Mission Culture on the Upper Amazon: *Native tradition, Jesuit enterprise, and secular policy in Moxos, 1660-1880.* David Block, Hardcover-February, 1994.

To Make the Earth Bear Fruit: *Essays on fertility, work and gender in highland Bolivia.* Olivia Harris, Paperback-April, 2000.

Snowfields: *The war on cocaine in the Andes:* Clare Hargreaves, Hardcover September, 1992.

Cocaine the Legend: Jorge Hurtado Gumucio, Accion Andina, Hisbol. La Paz.

The Aymara Language in its Social and Cultural Context: *A collection essays on aspects of Aymara language and culture.* Martha James Hardman-De-Bautista, M.J. Hardman.

Peasants, Entrepreneurs, and Social Change: *Frontier development in lowland Bolivia (Westview special studies on Latin American and the Caribbean).* Lesley Gill.

Inflation,Stabilization, and Debt: *Macroeconomic experiments in Peru and Bolivia (Westview special studies on Latin America and the Caribbean).* Manuel Pastor.

Raices de un Pueblo: *Afro-Bolivian history.* Juan Angola Maconde. Ed. CIMA, La Paz.

Palca and Pucara: *A study of the effects of the revolution on two Bolivian haciendas.* Roger A. Simmons.

Across South America: *An account of a journey from Buenos Aires to Lima by way of Potosi, with notes on Brazil, Argentina, Bolivia, Chili, and Peru.* Hiram Bingham.

The Fat Man From La Paz: *Contemporary fiction from Bolivia. A collection of 20 short stories by contemporary writer cover-ing a period of 50 years of Bolivian history.* Edited by Rosario Santos, Seven Stories Press.

Bolivia: A Climbing Guide: by Yossi Brain. Offers a selection of ascents on peaks in the four main Cordilleras: Apolobamba, Real, Quimsa Cruz and Occidental. Ed. The Mountaineers, Seattle 1999 (USA).

Trekking in Bolivia: *A compilation of about thirty treks across Bolivia, including photos and detailed maps.* Yossi Brain. The Mountaineers, Seattle 1999 (USA).

The ANDES of BOLIVIA, A Climbing Guide and Adventures : *The most com-plete climbing guide on the Bolivian Andes.* Alain Mesili, Ed. CIMA, La Paz 2003.

Back From Tuichi: *The harrowing life-and-death story of survival in the Amazon rain forest.* Yossi Ghinsberg. Random House, New York, 1993.

Digging up BUTCH & SUNDANCE: *The answer to a ninety-year-old mystery. First-class travel writing.* Anne Meadows. St Martin's Press, New York,1996.

Epicuro Andino: *Best bilingual cook book that includes Bolivian and international dishes adjusted for the altitude.*Compiled by Teresa de Prada, Peggy Palza, Wilma W. Velasco and Sus Gisbert. Ed. Quipus, La Paz, Bolivia, 1989.

Silver and Entrepreneurship in 17th Century Potosi: Peter Bakewell. University of New Mexico Press, Alburquerque, NM 1988.

Haciendas and Ayllus in Rural Societies in the Bolivian Andes in the 18th Centuries: Herbert Klein. Stanford University Press, Stanford, Cal. 1993.

Bolivia. The Evolution of a Multi-Ethnic Society: Herbert S. Klein. Oxford

University Press 1982.
Monumentos de Bolivia: José de Mesa & Teresa Gisbert. Edit. Gisbert La Paz - Bolivia 2002.

The Bolivian Times: A very funny true story of tear gas, heartbreak, bad Spanish, cocaine and deadlines by Tim Elliot. Ed. Random House Australia 2001.

Arte Textil de los Andes Bolivianos: Gisbert Arce y Cajias. Ed. Quipus, La Paz 2003.

Photo books:
Bolivia (1928): Roberto Gerstmann, Editorial Quipus, La Paz, 1996.

Bolivia Photos: Fred Kohler, Ed. Los Amigos del Libro, La Paz.

Vilacayma: Peter McFarren, Editorial Quipus, La Paz, 1992.

El Imperio del Sol: Photos and text by Hugo and Sonia Boero Rojo, Editorial Hispania, Spain, 1987.

Bolivia Desde El Aire: Willy Kenning.

La Paz, una Aventura Alucinante: Fernando Soria. A.

Bolivia, De la Raices al Futuro: Fernando Soria. A.

El Desfile Fantastico: Javier Palza Prudencio. Ed. Llave de letras. 2000.

Masks of the Bolivian Andes: Peter Mc Farren. Ed. Quipus, La Paz, 1993.

Temples of Bolivia: Peter Mc Farren. Ed. Quipus, La Paz, 1998.

La Fe Viva the Jesuit Missions in Bolivia: Peter Mc Farren. Ed. Quipus, La Paz, 1994.

Bolivia !magen y Palabra: Anouk Garrigues. Bustamante Editores, S.L. Bruch, 1994, Barcelona.

Potosi: Daniel Gluckmann.

I am rich Potosí: The Mountain that eats Men: Stephen Ferry, The Monacelli Press.

Bolivia Lo Autentico Aún Existe: Ed. San Marcos, Madrid. 2000.

Titikaka Lake: Peter McFarren. Ed. Quipus, La Paz, 2003.

Electric Current
La Paz runs on 220v and 110v current. The rest of Bolivia is 220v. The current is 50 cycle A.C.

Conversion Tables
To Metric
1 cup = 8 ounces = 227 grams
1/2 cup = 4 ounces = 113.5 grams
1/4 cup = 2 ounces = 56.75 grams
1 pound = 454 grams
1 arroba = 25 pounds = 11.35 kilos
1 quintal = 4 arrobas = 100 pounds
= 45.4 kilos
1 quart = 0.95 liter
1 gallon = 3.785 liters
1 inch = 2.54 centimeters
1 foot = 30.5 centimeters
= 0.305 meters
1 yard = 91.5 centimeters
= 0.915 meters
1 mile = 1.609 kilometers

From Metric
1 kilogram = 2.205 pounds
1 liter = 2.1 pints = 1.056 quarts
= 0.264 gallons
1 centimeter = 0.39 inches
1 meter = 1.095 yards
= 3.28 feet = 39.37 inches
1 kilometer = 0.621 mile

Celsius to Fahrenheit
(Celsius Temperature x 9 / 5) + 32
= Fahrenheit Temperature

Fahrenheit to Celsius
(Fahrenheit Temperature - 32) x 5 / 9
= Celcius Temperature

SAMPLE TEMPERATURES:
0°C = 32°F
5°C = 41°F
10°C = 50°F
15°C = 59°F
20°C = 68°F
25°C = 77°F
30°C = 86°F
35°C = 95°F
40°C = 104°F

OUCH! BOLIVIA HURTS

BY FIONA ADAMS

THE DEFINITIVE GUIDE TO NASTY THINGS THAT CAN HAPPEN TO YOU IN BOLIVIA AND HOW TO AVOID THEM.

Bolivia, unlike a pack of Marlboros, doesn't come with a government health warning. Just flying into La Paz is perilous enough. At 4,000 meters above sea level, the land rushes up to meet the plane. The pilot in turn speeds up because at this altitude the plane could stall in the thin air. At least your arrival will be exciting.

Welcome to Bolivia, a country of bugs, beetles and things that go bump in the night. The following guide should see you through your stay.

Withering Heights

Much has been written on the perils of living at high altitude. I won't bore you with repetition, but suffice it to say that at La Paz height — Potosí is even worse — most newcomers will get a nasty headache, blurred vision and breathing difficulties for the first day or so. If this doesn't put you off, then add thickened arteries, an annihilated mid-term memory and being winded to the list.

The Cure: coca tea, Alka Seltzer, lots of water and a day in bed. Actually, it's quite fun.

The World's Most Dangerous Roads

It is rumored that the road winding its way down from *El Cumbre* to the semi-tropical Yungas is the most dangerous road in the world. Some extremists claim that something topples off the edge every fortnight. The track only allows for passing vehicles in a few select spots — usually above a terrifying precipice. But, believe me, the views are worth it.

The Cure: Trucks have the worst track record; small minibuses the best. The decision is yours. Alternatively, you can opt for walking down on either the Choro or Takesi trails to arrive in the North or South Yungas, respectively. If you're still scared, wait a few years for the new road to be built.

Parasites and Other Animals

If you make it down the world's most dangerous road alive, you'll arrive in parasite territory. The following is not for the faint-hearted. Starting with one of the nastiest diseases, Leishmaniasis, otherwise known as white leprosy, is an especially awful affliction that eats your body away slowly and painfully. It's contracted through a type of sand fly. Another massive problem in Bolivia is Chagas Disease, transmitted by the Vinchuca beetle — 30 years after the bite, you drop dead.

Then there are all the other tropical but curable nasties such as ticks, malaria and the repugnant botfly. The latter lays a maggot under your skin. If left untreated, the maggot grows up to become a fly which eventually hatches out. Most hosts get rid of their revolting maggots by suffocating the buggers with nicotine or nail varnish then squeezing them out before they hatch.

Now for the real nasty: *El Candiru.*

This little creature lurks in the murky waters of the Amazon basin and is particularly fond of warm human orifices which it swims up and embeds itself with retractable spines inflicting horrific pain on its victim. It is only removable by surgical procedure.

The Cure: Don't swim in the nude, and use ample bug repellent, mosquito nets and anything else you can lay your hands on to avoid being bitten/invaded. For mosquito repellent, Off! is brilliant. Autan — orange with a red lid — is also good but does terrible things to your clothes. One friend swears by vitamin B complex, garlic and lemon juice.

Mountain Climbing

Hundreds of climbers attempt Bolivia's mountain peaks every year. Yet, astonishingly, Bolivia has no official mountain rescue service. On Illimani alone, there are four unretrieved bodies and a plane wreck. If this body count doesn't put you off, then stories of pulmonary endema — lungs filling up with water — and eye balls popping out of their sockets because of the pressure just might.

The Cure: Don't go solo, take a guide that knows the area well and acclimatize at La Paz height for at least a week before attempting any ascents.

If you're not put off by the above, Bolivia is one of the world's most exciting destinations for adventurous globetrotters. And parasites aside, it can proudly boast one of the lowest crime rates in Latin America. Just don't forget your Off!

2

CHAPTER TWO

CITIES AND
SURROUNDING AREAS

BOLIVIAN
DEPARTMENTS

PERU

BRAZIL

PANDO
Cobija

BENI

Trinidad

LA PAZ

La Paz

COCHABAMBA
Cochabamba

SANTA CRUZ

Santa Cruz

Oruro

ORURO

Sucre

Potosi

POTOSI

CHUQUISACA

CHILE

TARIJA
Tarija

PARAGUAY

ARGENTINA

EXPLORING THE CULTURAL
TREASURES OF LA PAZ

BY PETER MCFARREN

At dawn, mist and clouds can be seen rising from the lower valleys until the sun peers from above the Andes and bathes the surrounding hills with hues of red, ocher and blue. At dusk, as the sun settles on the *Altiplano* flat lands surrounding the valley of La Paz, a reddish glow envelops the city's greatest landmark, the snowy peaks of the 21,000-feet high (6,400 m) Illimani Mountain.

With the Andes and deep blue skies as a backdrop, Aymara Indian women, children in tow, sell their wares at roadside market stalls facing tin- and straw-covered adobe homes. Whether landing on the El Alto airstrip at 13,000 feet (3,962 m) or crossing Lake Titicaca by boat, the barren plateau known as the *Altiplano* is a visitor's first introduction to the city of La Paz.

The *Altiplano* hides the presence of a thriving metropolis of 900,000 inhabitants that opens up at its edge. Without warning, the plateau breaks and reveals below a deep, jagged valley covered with adobe and brick homes clinging to the hillside. Skyscrapers, rising to meet the jagged hills of the valley, cast shadows over cobblestone streets and tree-lined plazas that hide rich and colorful traditions growing out of centuries of Spanish conquest, revolution and Aymara folklore. And only three hours away by car, on the eastern slopes of the Andes, are banana and orange groves.

Before the sun is out, women, wearing bowler hats and multi-layered skirts known as *polleras*, men and children begin their daily trek by foot or bus to the center of La Paz. By the time the sun has risen, Aymara-speaking vendors are in place in the markets, ready to offer a wide variety of vegetables, fruits, clothing, household goods, steaming hot coffee and even whole pigs.

Aymaras live in the surrounding hills and market areas. Below are the homes and work places of a Creole class that has identified itself more with its European forebears than with the Indians who make up 70 percent of the country's population. The city then descends several thousand feet to the Zona Sur neighborhoods of Obrajes, Achumani, La Florida, Calacoto and Irpavi, where diplomats and wealthy Bolivians, including many in the military, live in sumptuous homes.

If you are arriving by plane, it is a good idea to take it easy the first day because of the rarefied air. Those who reach La Paz by crossing the lake from Puno, Peru, however, should be accustomed to the altitude. It is wise to drink and eat lightly at first, but drink plenty of *mate de coca*, a brew made from coca leaves, to help fend off the effects of the altitude.

To get your bearings and capture some of the color, bustle and contrasting life-styles found in La Paz, start your visit by taking a walking tour of downtown. With most good hotels located in the center, you'll only be a few blocks from the city's main boulevard, Avenida 16 de Julio, better known as El Prado, with its promenade of trees, flowers and monuments. In the evening it will be jammed with traffic and people returning from work. On Sundays, the Prado is filled with families out for a stroll. You will also see old homes with elaborate iron latticework and balustrades, which managed to survive the 1970s' building boom that transformed the skyline of La Paz.

Going upward, El Prado becomes Avenida Mariscal Santa Cruz, at the upper end of which, before it changes to Avenida Montes, is the San Francisco Church, built in 1549. Its carved stone portico is a fine example of the baroque Spanish architecture combined with native craftsmanship that flourished in Bolivia during the 16th, 17th and 18th centuries. The facade is decorated with carved images of birds of prey, masks, pine cones and parrots. The church offers one of the finest examples of religious colonial architecture to be seen in South America.

A visitor can spend several days exploring the roads and alleys that branch off from the San Francisco Church. Bordering it is Calle Sagárnaga, lined with shops offering leather goods, weavings, alpaca sweaters, silver and antiques. Vendors on the street sell old coins, irons that utilize charcoal, silver and pewter ware and small stone carvings made by the Aymara or Quechua people who inhabit the *Altiplano*. Sweaters range in price from $20 to $50, depending on the quality.

Adjacent to San Francisco, on the esplanade in front of it, is a handicraft gallery sponsored by the Catholic Church. You'll find weavings, sweaters and handcrafted Bolivian instruments such as the *quena, zampoña, tarka* and *charango*, a stringed instrument with a backing made from the carapace of an armadillo. At Rumillajta you can purchase these instruments of professional quality for $3 to $150. Be sure to ask the vendors, who are young, accomplished musicians, to try them out for you.

A block above San Francisco on Calle Linares to the right, and especially as you go along until you reach Calle Santa Cruz, you will find Aymara-speaking women, offering medicinal cures still used by the *Kallawayas*, the ancient medicine men who attended the Inca courts and used quinine to cure malaria long before it was adopted by Western medicine. Roadside stands offer herbs for curing rheumatism, stomach pains, etc. Also available are llama fetuses, incense, small bottles with sweet syrups, nuts, wool, copal and grease — items that are used for white magic ceremonies and to protect a dwelling from evil spirits. For about $2 you can purchase a bag of offerings to the goddess of the earth, the *Pachamama*, and be assured of a bountiful year.

Whenever construction on a home begins, these ingredients are burned and the ashes buried in the corner during a ceremony known as the *ch'alla*. The Tuesday after *Carnaval* most Bolivians *ch'allan*, or bless their belongings, by sprinkling alcohol and streams of colored paper on them.

Calle Sagárnaga continues up to market areas where shoeshine boys, vendors and peasants offer their wares. Tucked away in courtyards and alleys are *tambos*, where mountains of bananas, oranges and coca leaves are available. Coca leaves, from which cocaine paste is made, are widely used in restaurants as a mate, or chewed by peasants to help diminish the effects of hunger and fatigue. A former market area, Tambo Quirquincho located on Calle Evaristo Valle and Plaza Alonzo de Mendoza, is now a museum with a rotating exhibit of Bolivian masks and regional *sombreros*. The newly-restored building is impressive and dates to the Colonial period.

If walking the streets tires you, take a taxi for about fifty cents or a bus for even less up to Avenida Buenos Aires. It competes with the downtown business area as the most thriving commercial area of La Paz. The 30 blocks near Buenos Aires are filled with stalls offering contraband goods at low prices. Prices for televisions, radios and negative film are lower than those found in New York.

Above Buenos Aires are hundreds of workshops that make the elaborate costumes, masks and trinkets used for the **Entrada del Gran Poder** festival, the city's most important folkloric expression. In early June, thousands of dancers pay homage to the *Gran Poder*, the master of the Great Power. Three to four months before the *Gran Poder*, many of the participants invest their earnings in masks and costumes that may cost hundreds of dollars and weigh as much as 80 pounds. The procession begins near the Buenos Aires Avenue. First come the patrons of a particular group, carrying a banner and often a figure of the virgin. Then come vehicles laden with elegant embroideries, pewter and silverware, old coins and stuffed llamas next to blond, blue-eyed dolls. Dancers in the procession include *llameros*, llama drovers with their slings that recall the long caravans of llamas that continue to crisscross the Andes.

Near the end of the procession — which concludes around 10 or 11 o'clock at night at the Mercado Camacho — appear groups who arrived from the highlands surrounding the city. Perhaps the most colorful are the *Auki Aukis* who wear masks with long leather noses, wide-rimmed tin hats and twisted canes.

Ramona de Calle and her husband are two of the many artisans who make outfits for the *Gran Poder*. They and their assistants make elaborate costumes and banners for the *Moreno* dance. Their shop is located on the Calle Illampu 853. On Los

Andes street above Buenos Aires are several other embroidery shops.

At 1080 Calle Gallardo, one block above Buenos Aires, is a small workshop that belonged to the late Antonio Viscarra, a master mask maker who devoted 65 of his 74 years to making elaborate plaster and cloth masks representing the devil, his blue-eyed, blond mistress and a plethora of saints, African slaves and Incas that perform at the **Gran Poder** and other festivals that take place throughout Bolivia. Fortunately, his daughter Albertina and son-in-law, Carlos Fuentes, carry on this tradition. For about $50-$100 you can purchase an elaborate horned devil's mask that took a month to make or you can purchase beautiful miniature reproductions of larger masks.

After several hours of visiting this area you should be ready for a break. Many *paceños*, as residents of La Paz are called, take time off mid-morning to eat the *salteña*, a hearty beef, olive, hard boiled egg, potato and pea stew wrapped in a dough that is Bolivia's contribution to haute cuisine. They are sold throughout the city, but be careful where you get them if you want to avoid getting sick

An alternative mid-morning break is a visit to the popular Café La Paz, located on the corner of Ayacucho and Camacho. This quaint old café is a hangout for politicians, businessmen, tourists and labor leaders. It was also Nazi war criminal Klaus Barbie's favorite spot until he was expelled from Bolivia in 1983. They serve good expreso coffee, saltenas, lime juice among other foods.

Because of the altitude, it is wise to eat the main meal at lunch and have a light supper. A *siesta* after lunch is still a custom enjoyed by many.

Another alternative is to take an all-day tour offered by numerous travel agencies found in La Paz for about $18 (including lunch). Half-day tours will cost around $12. You can also hire a private taxi by the hour.

Heading downhill from El Prado you will pass the university and some high-rise apartments before reaching the neighborhood of San Jorge/Sopocachi and the presidential residence. The road bends and continues downward until it reaches the neighborhoods of Obrajes and Calacoto, which are several degrees warmer because of the drop in altitude. Since this route is downhill, it constitutes a pleasant walk.

Once at the Puente de Calacoto, the bridge which begins the main street of Calacoto, Avenida Ballivián, turn right and head to La Florida. Take the road bordering the river to Aranjuez, cross the La Paz River, and continue toward Mallasa and the Valley of the Moon, named for the rock and dirt formations that exist there. One of the areas's treasures is the ceramic workshop of Mario Saravia located on the left side of Calle 4 in Mallasa. He is one of the country's best ceramic artists. He has a charming exhibit and sales area at his workshop.

Just before reaching Mallasa is the **Valle de la Luna Park**. The area has some spectacular formations and a trail that takes about an hour to cover. The park also has a visitors center. One can see the La Paz Golf Club from the park. It is considered the highest course in the world.

Also worth visiting are the Animas, rock and soil formations beyond the neighborhood of Cota Cota. If you continue eastward on Avenida Ballivián, through the Cota Cota neighborhood and beyond, the road rises to La Palca and other fertile valleys where vegetables and fruits, including peaches, apricots and plums, are cultivated. Mount Illimani can be seen in all its splendor from this area.

On your way back, taking the detour to the Miraflores neighborhood, be sure to visit the square facing the city football stadium, Stadium Hernando Siles, where a replica of a Tiwanaku courtyard can be found containing authentic stone monoliths and figures that date from the 3rd to 12th centuries.

Miraflores is also home to the **Kusillo Museum** of Science and Play and the ArteFeria. The interactive children's museum offers exhibits on the environment, reproductive health, communications, nutrition, etc and serves infants to adults. On the lower part of the complex is probably the best intermitent craft fair in Bolivia that rotates its exhibits. The Kusillo Cultural Complex includes a funicular and the best lookout of the city.

From there you'll be five minutes away by car from Plaza Murillo, where the presidential palace and Congress are located. Before constitutional rule returned to Bolivia in October 1982, the palace was often guarded by tanks.

In front of the **Presidential Palace** is a statue of former President Gualberto Villarroel. In 1946 a mob attacked the presidential palace, dragged Villarroel to the square and hanged him from a lamppost; a nearby statue commemorates the event. The square is now filled with shoeshine boys, pensioners, city residents out for a stroll and children chasing after pigeons. Diagonally across from the presidential palace is the Congress building, which has a visitor's gallery from where you can see politicians at work.

Next to the Presidential Palace is the **Cathedral**, built in 1835. Facing it on the corner of Calle Socabaya and Comercio is the **National Art Museum**, which was built in 1775 for a Spanish nobleman and is the finest baroque building in La Paz. The exterior and the courtyard are ornamented with carved floral designs. In the center of the patio is an alabaster fountain surrounded by plants. The three floors of the museum contain some of the painting and sculptural treasures of Bolivia. The first floor is devoted to exhibits of contemporary Bolivian and foreign artists; the second to the colonial works of the grand master of Andean colonial painting, Melchór Pérez Holguín and his disciples. One room in the museum is devoted to Republican Bolivian painting. On the third floor there is an ample permanent collection of Bolivian artists. Some sculptures of Marina Nuñez del Prado, whose abstract stone representations of Aymara and Quechua Indians have earned her a worldwide reputation, are exhibited there. Art buffs can visit her former home, which now houses an exquisite collection of masks, colonial silverware and several hundred of her sculptures. The museum is located at Calle Ecuador 2034.

After leaving the museum take a stroll down Comercio street and take a right on Calle Yanacocha until you reach the corner of Ingavi. Around the corner, to the left, is the **Ethnographic and Folklore Museum**, a beautiful 18th century structure that is a repository of weavings, masks, feathers and other objects of Bolivia's great cultural traditions. The museum offers permanent exhibits on the Ayoreos, an Indian group from the Amazon area of the country, and on the Chipayas, who inhabit the most desolate area of the *Altiplano* and have maintained a distinct language and culture. Admission is free. It is open Monday through Friday from 8:30 to11:30 and 14:30 to17:45.

From the museum, go up one block on Calle Genaro Sanjines, take a left on Calle Indaburo and go two blocks until you reach Calle Jaén, a narrow, cobblestoned street that houses five museums. Admission tickets for the four museums can be purchased at the **Museo Costumbrista** for Bs. 4 (60 cents). Children are always admitted free. It is the best-preserved colonial street in La Paz and will give the visitor a glimpse into Bolivia's colorful, but often turbulent, past.

The **Casa de Murillo Museum** was once the home of the War of Independence hero Don Pedro Domingo Murillo, after whom the city square is named. In 1810 he was hanged by the Spanish for his anti-crown activities. The colonial-style building houses a handsome collection of Bolivian handicrafts, art and furniture. If you start to your right, you'll enter a room filled with over 40 masks, several of which are the work of Antonio Viscarra or his grandfather. Also shown are miniature representations of some of the traditional dances of the Bolivian highlands and several display cases showing diminutive hats, shoes, furniture, canned foods and street vendors. The objects are from **Alasitas**, a traditional fair that takes place for two weeks at the end of January. Bolivia's president and church officials make their yearly pilgrimage to bless over 20 blocks of stands offering candied fruits, sweets, handicrafts, plaster saints and animals, miniature pesos, marriage certificates, airline tickets, dollar bills and local dishes. The day the fair is inaugurated, city residents stock up on thousands of dollars of fake bills and miniatures, and pray that during the year their wishes will come true.

Across the same courtyard in the Murillo Museum is a room with a collection of silver masks, utensils, peacocks and saddles that belonged to Bolivia's aristocracy. From the courtyard a stairway leads up to several exhibit halls. In the first room, a collection of 16th, 17th and 18th century religious paintings and objects is displayed. In other halls are examples of colonial furniture and the rooms used by Pedro Domingo Murillo.

Farther up the street is the **Precious Metals Museum** that houses pre-Columbian gold and silver ornaments, Inca and pre-Inca ceramics and a description of Indian metallurgy.

Next to that Museum is the **Museo Litoral**, which houses documents, photographs and paintings relating to the 1879 War of the Pacific, when Bolivia lost its outlet to the sea. Bolivia is likely never to forget this loss, and stages marches, commemorative events and international appeals in an effort to recover access to the Pacific.

At the end of Calle Jaén is the **Museo Costumbrista**, an elegant colonial-style structure exhibiting ceramic figures representing historical events and local customs. In one case on the second floor are the remains of Indian guerrilla leader Tupac Katari, who was quartered by the Spanish in 1781 near La Paz. Other displays show the lynching of Murillo in 1810 and the traditional festivities of **San Juan**, when tens of thousands of fires and fireworks displays light up La Paz on what is said to be the coldest night of the year, June 24. Several cases show popular drinking places, markets, dances and outings dating to the time when La Paz was a provincial city of less than 50,000 inhabitants. You'll learn that the first auto made it across the Andes in 1913, and that by 1919 trolleys crisscrossed the city.

A visit to La Paz would not be complete without a visit to a *peña*. Worth visiting are: **Naira**, Calle Sagárnaga 161, Tel. 2350530; **Marka Tambo** on Calle Jaén 710. Tel. 2340416; **La Casa del Corregidor**, at Calle Murillo 1040, Tel. 2363633; and **Los Escudos**, Av. Mariscal Santa Cruz 1201, corner of Calle Ayacucho, Tels. 2322028, 2374485. Admission is about five dollars, and they all offer restaurant service. *Peñas* begin after 9:00 or 10:00 in the evening and last until past midnight. Be sure to bring a sweater along, since after the sun sets the night becomes brisk. Reservations are recommended.

On a clear night, as you walk back to your hotel or if you head to the Montículo Park in Sopocachi, you'll see the moon hovering over the eternal snows of Illimani. The entire canyon up to where it meets the *Altiplano* is ablaze with street lights, and the *Altiplano* above are brilliant stars that sparkle in the clear La Paz sky.

PRACTICAL INFORMATION FOR LA PAZ

La Paz Telephone Code: 2

• Useful Addresses and Numbers

Tourist Information Center, Av. Mcal. Santa Cruz, corner with Oruro, Edif. Palacio de Comunicaciones, 16th Floor. Tel. 2367463. Open from 8:00 to 16:00. Any cases of stolen valuables should be reported at this office. There is also another Tourist Center at Plaza del Estudiante, corner with Calle México, Tel. 2371044.

Police, 110.

Tourist Police, 2225016. Plaza del Estadio, Miraflores. Calle Sagarnaga corner with Murillo, Galeria Dorian Of. 6.

Emergency accident, 2371230.

Ambulances, 118.

Emergency Hospital Holandes, 2813919.

Emergency Hospital La Paz, 2454421.

Bus Station, Av. Uruguay, Plaza Antofagasta, Tels. 2280551, 2281055, 2281855.

Airport Information, Tels. 2810122, 2821010.

Train Station Information, Calle Interradial 11, Tel. 2467795.

Immigration Offices, Avenida Camacho 1468, open from 9:00 to 16:00. Tels. 2370475, 2203109.

Long distance Calls.

Entel,101.

AES, 0-11.

Cotas, 0-12.

Post Office, Av. Mariscal Santa Cruz, corner of Oruro, Tels. 2317028, 2333736.

Entel, the national telecommunications company, is located on Calle Ayacucho between Mercado and Camacho, and offers long-dis-

tance telephone, telegram and fax service.
Tel. 2313030. **Entel cellular**,
80010500.

For **Information**, dial 104. For the
local time, call 117.

**Visa, Master Card and American
Express** cards are accepted at many
hotels, restaurants and shops. Banks that
subscribe to Visa and Master Card can
also provide cash advances.

The American Express rep is Magri
Tours, Calle Capitán Ravelo 2101,
Tel. 2442727, Fax. 2443060.

• Consulates and Embassies

Argentina, Calle Aspiazu 497.
Tels. 2354404, 2434988, open from
9:00 to 13:30.

Australia, Av. Arce corner with
Montevideo, Edif. Montevideo. Tel. 2440459,
Fax. 2440801, open from 8:30 to 13:30.

Austria, Av. 16 de Julio 1616.
Tels. 2369863, 2326601, Fax. 2391073,
open from 14:30 to 16:00.

Brazil, Edificio Multicentro, Av. Arce
Tels. 2440202, 2443043, open from
9:00 to 13:00.

Britain, Av. Arce 2732. Tel. 2433424,
Fax. 2431073, open from 9:00 to 12:00.

Canada, Calle Victor Sangines
2678, Edif Barcelona, 2nd floor, Plaza
España, Sopocachi. Tel. 2415021.
Fax. 2414453, open from 9:00 to 12:00.

Chile, Calle 14, 8024, Calacoto.
Tels. 2797331, 2791203, open from
9:00 to 13:00.

Colombia, Calle 9, 7835, Calacoto.
Tel. 2786848, Fax. 2786841, open from
9:00 to 12:30.

Costa Rica, Calle 15, 100,
between Ballivián and Inofuentes,
Calacoto. Tel/Fax. 2793201, open from
9:30 to 13:00.

Denmark, Av. Arce 2799,
Edif. Fortaleza, 9th floor. Tel. 2432070,
Fax. 2433150, open from 8:30 to 16:30.

Ecuador, Edif. Herrmann, 14th
Floor. Tels. 2319739, 2331588,
Fax. 2391232, open from 9:00 to 13:00.

Finland, Av. Sanchez Lima 2560.
Tels. 2430500, 2430170, Fax. 8112221,
open from 8:30 to 12:00 and 14:00 to
18:30.

France, Calle 8, 5390 in Obrajes.
Tel. 2786114, Fax. 2786746, open from
8:30 to 12:30.

Germany, Av. Arce 2395. Tel. 2440066,
Fax. 2441441, open from 9:00 to 12:00.

Holland, Av. 6 de Agosto,
Edif. Hilda, Piso 7. Tel. 2444040,
Fax. 2444040, open from 8:30 to 17:00.

Israel, Av. Mariscal Santa Cruz 2150,
Edif. Esperanza. Tels. 2391112, 2358676,
open from 9:00 to 16:00.

Italy, Av. 6 de Agosto 2575.
Tels 2434955, 2434929, Fax. 2434975,
open from 10:30 to 12:30.

Japan, Calle Rosendo Gutiérrez 497.
Tel. 2373151, Fax. 2786517, open from
9:30 to 11:45.

Mexico, Calle Sánchez Bustamante
509, Calacoto. Tel. 2772133,
Fax. 2772212, open from 8:00 to 11:30.

Norway, Calle René Moreno 1096,
San Miguel. Tel/Fax. 2770009, open from
9:00 to 12:30 and 14:30 to 17:00.

Panama, Av. Ballivián 1110, corner
with Calle 17, Calacoto. Tel. 2792036,
Fax. 2797290, open from 9:00 to 12:00.

Peru, Av. 6 de Agosto/Calle
F. Guachalla, Edif. Alianza. Tels. 2444566,
2441240, Fax. 2441250, open from
9:00 to 13:00.

Russia, Av. Arequipa 8129 Calacoto.
Tel. 2786470, Fax. 2786531, open from
10:00 to 13:00.

Spain, Av. 6 de Agosto 2827,
Tel. 2431203, Fax. 2432386, open from
9:00 to 12:30.

Sweden, Av. 14 de Septiembre 5080,
Obrajes. Tel/Fax. 2787903, open from
9:00 to 12:00.

LA PAZ DEPT.

Switzerland, Calle 13 corner with Hernando Siles, Obrajes. Tel. 2423152, Fax. 2423221, open from 9:00 to 12:00.

U.S. located on Av. Arce 2780, Tel. 2430251, Fax. 2433854, open from 8:00 to 17:00. The U.S. **Consulate** at the same location is open mornings.

Venezuela, Av. Arce 2678, Edif. Illimani, 5th floor, Tels. 2431365, 2432023, Fax. 2432348, open from 8:30 to 12:30.

• Airline Offices in La Paz

Airport, Tels. 2810122, 2821010.

Aerolíneas Argentinas, Calle Reyes Ortiz, Edif. Gundlach, 2nd floor, Tels. 2351711, 2351624, 2391059.

Aeroflot, Av. Mcal. Santa Cruz 1322, Tels. 2358074, 2356552.

Air France, Edif. San Pablo, 3rd floor, Tels. 2390855, 2390856, 2390857.

Avianca, Av. Villazon 1940, Edif. Inchauste, 1st floor, Tel. 2375220.

TACA, Av. 16 de Julio, Edif. San Pablo, 4th floor, Tel. 2313132.

AeroSur, Av. 16 de Julio 616, Edif. Petrolero, Tels. 2313233, 2432432, 2430430.

Lan Chile, Av. 16 de Julio, Edif. 16 de Julio, Tels. 2315832, 2358377.

American Airlines, Plaza Venezuela 1440, Edif. Herrmann, ground floor, Tels. 2372011, 2355384. Galeria Telleria, Of. 203, Calacoto.

Iberia, British Airways (rep), Calle Ayacucho 378, Edif. Credinforma, Tels. 2203911, 2203885.

Japan Airlines, Calle Mercado, Edif. Mcal. Ballivián, 4th floor, Tels. 2201814, 2201871.

Amaszonas Av. Saavedra No 1649, Miraflores. Tel. 2220848, Tel/Fax. 2111104 E-mail: amascom@entelnet.bo

Transporte Aéreo Militar, Avenida Montes 738. Tels. 2121585, 2121582.

Lloyd Aéreo Boliviano (LAB), Av. Camacho 1460, Tels. 2353606, 2371020, 2367707.

Lufthansa, Av. 6 de Agosto 2510, Edif. Illimani, Tels. 2431717, 2810078.

Swissair, Edif. Gundlach Torre Oeste, 5th floor, Tels. 2355515, 2375057.

Varig Cruziero, Av. Mcal. Santa Cruz, Edif. Cámara de Comercio, Tels. 2314072, 2314040.

British Midland, Cathay Pacific, US Airways, Aero Mexico, Austrian Airlines (rep), Calle Capitan Ravelo 2101, Edif. Cap Ravelo, Tel. 2443306.

TamMercosur, Tel. 2443442.

• Getting Around Town

By bus: Large buses, called *micros*, serve most city neighborhoods (note the number of the micro, designating its route, on the windshield). Fares within the city center are Bs. 1.50 (25 cents). To outlying neighborhoods, fares are sometimes higher. Fares are paid as you board the bus. Watch out for pickpockets, who may slash purses.

By minibus: Small vans, called *minibus - es*, serve all of the city, along fixed routes. Touts incessantly shout out the many destinations of each minibus, and there are also signs on the windshield designating the route. Fares within the city are Bs. 2.50 (35 cents), slightly higher to outlying neighborhoods.

By taxi: Taxis in La Paz will pick up up to five passengers, following the route of the first passenger in the vehicle, and *trufis* (or shared taxis) follow fixed routes, i.e., down Avenida 6 de Agosto, up Avenida Arce, etc. Fares within the city center for both taxis and *trufis* are Bs. 3 (50 cents) per person. If traveling to Obrajes or Calacoto, check the taxi fare before boarding or take a *trufi*, which will charge a fixed Bs. 3 (50 cents) per person.

Radio-taxi: Service is efficient and comfortable: 6 to 12 Bolivianos ($1 to $2) total within the city and Zona Sur, no matter the number of passengers. Tourist taxis are also available in front of hotels. They charge an hourly rate of about $5 or according to distance traveled. Be careful you're not overcharged at the airport — an express trip to the city should cost no more than $8. If you share a taxi with four others, expect to pay about $1.70.

• Radio Taxis

Su Taxi, Tels. 2355555, 2366666.
Radio Movil del Sur, (for the Zona Sur), Calacoto Obrajes, Tels. 2792220, 2792222, 2795555. Aranjuez, Mallasa, Tels. 2792220, 2796544, 2799667, 2745050, 2799666.
Radio Taxi Service Sur, Tels. 2793333, 2799696.
Vip, Tel. 2721212.
Nano's, Tel. 2233322.
Pegasso, Tel. 2221616.
Gauchito, Tel. 2722323.

• Car Rental

International Rent a Car, Calle Federico Suazo 1942, Tels. 2441906, 2012951.
National Rent a Car, Plaza Sucre 1494, Tels. 2491945. 2376581.
Kolla Car, Av. Ecuador 2496, Tel. 2415088.
Oscar Crespo Rent a Car, Av. Simón Bolívar 1865, Tel. 2220989, Fax. 2242608.
Imbex Rent a Car, Av. Montes 522, Tel. 2455432.
American Rent a Car, Av. Camacho 1574, Av. Los Leones 11, Tels. 2202933, 2783230.
Localiza Rent a Car, Hotel Radisson, Av. Arce 2177, Tel. 2441011, Cel. 77635135.
Dollar Rent a Car, Tel. 800109010.

• Car Repair

Volk Auto, Av. Jaime Freire 2326, Tel. 2415264, specializes in European and Japanese vehicles.
Chino, Av. Saavedra 1249, Tel. 2222500.
Ovando S.A., Av. Estados Unidos

1118, Tels. 2227358, 2227361.
Taller IMCRUZ, Av. Saavedra 2407, Miraflores. Tel. 2226168.
Paravicini Motor Sport, Calle Posnanski 1044, Miraflores. Tel. 2220291. Calle 25, 129, Calacoto.
Toyo Service, Calle Guerrilleros Lanza 1347, Tel. 2221339.
Elite Motors, Av. Hernando Siles corner with Calle 8, Obrajes. Tels. 2786071, 2786074.
Moicar Motors, Calle Vicente Alvarez Plata 1126, Miraflores. Tel. 2224148.
Asisteca, Av. Alexander 220. Tel. 2799769.
Servitec, Av. Mario Mercado 401. Tel. 2784009, Fax. 2786822.
EASA, Calle Coroico 1453. Tel. 2203822.
Kairo Motors, Calle Gaspar Jurado 450, Irpavi. Tel. 2721947.

• Hotels

Note: Commercial or preferential rates can often be negotiated at nearly all Bolivian hotels, so check either with the hotel or travel agencies about improving on the hotel's published rates.

DELUXE
Hotel Europa, Calle Tiahuanaco 64, corner with Bravo, Tel. 2315656, Fax. 2113930. E-mail: reservas@hoteleuropa.com.bo Has 110 luxury rooms, a lovely sauna and exercise area, a cafeteria, a couple of restaurants and extensive meeting and banquet facilities. Rooms offer telephone and Internet service. Its lobby often presents exhibits of Bolivian artists. Single, $170; Double, $190; Single Suite, $230; Double Suite, $250.
Hotel Plaza, Av. 16 de Julio 1789, Tel. 2378311, Fax. 2378318. E-mail: plaza@plazabolivia.com.bo Hotel Plaza, located on El Prado, is elegant and

comfortable. 165 regulars rooms and 7 suites. Prices: Single, $130/$99 (foreigners/nationals); Double, $150/$119; Suite, $220; Additional bed, $30. Rooms offer private telephone, television and CNN, and the hotel has a sauna, swimming pool, rooms with a view of Mount Illimani and an elegant rooftop restaurant that serves excellent Lake Titicaca salmon trout and Bolivian dishes (try *fricasé* if interested in something spicy).

Hotel Presidente, Calle Potosí 920, Tels. 2406650, 2406666, Fax. 2407240. E-mail: hpresi@caoba.entelnet.bo Has 86 rooms, 18 suites. Offers private telephone, television and bathroom. Prices: Single, $125; Double, $155; Suite, $190; Presidential Suite, $235. This new hotel has a nightclub, sauna, swimming pool, and is located one block from Plaza San Francisco.

Radisson Plaza Hotel, Av. Arce 2177, Tel. 2441111, Fax. 2440402. E-mail:radisson@hn.radissonbolivia.com.bo Has 239 regular rooms and 7 suites. Prices: Single, $160; Double, $180; Triple, $210; Suite, $210-230; Additional bed, $30. Offers private telephone, television, bathroom and a panoramic view of the city and the surrounding Andes mountains. Good for large conventions or conferences. Has an indoor pool, sauna, exercise room, and a nice café in the lobby area that is great for business or social meetings. Ten minutes walking distance from El Prado. Several shops offer export-quality alpaca sweaters that cost three to four less than in New York. Be sure to check out the Millma shop. Tel. 2440737.

Casa Grande Apart Hotel, Av. Ballivian, corner with Calle 17, 1000, Calacoto. Tel. 2795511, Fax. 2771044. E-mail: info@casa-grande.com.bo This brand-new hotel has lovely rooms and is located in the lower section of the city with the side benefit of making it easier for those affected by the altitude. Single apart, $110; Studio apart, $110; Double apart, $140.

Camino Real Royal Suites Hotel, Calle Capitán Ravelo 2123, Tel. 2441515, Fax. 2440055. E-mail: caminoreal@ceibo.entelnet.bo Has 52 luxury-furnished, totally-equipped apartments. Offers breakfast, room service, laundry, parking and cable television. Prices: 1 bedroom, $88; 2 bedrooms, $98; Royal Suite, simple $98, double $118.

Ritz Apart Hotel, Plaza Isabel la Catolica 2478, Tel. 2433131, Fax. 2433080, E-mail:reservas@hotel-ritz-bolivia.com All suites: Suite Junior, $121; Suite Senior, $146; Suite Master, $177; Suite Ambassador, $299.

El Rey Palace Hotel, Av. 20 de Octubre 1947, Tel. 2418541, Fax. 2418521. E-mail: hotelrey@caoba.entelnet.bo Has 60 rooms and offers executive suites with whirlpool, single and double rooms with private bathrooms, heating and cable television. 24-hour room service. Conference room, sauna. Prices: Single, $70; Double, $80; Luxury suite, $105; Additional bed, $15.

Hacienda Villa Del Sol, Puente de Aranjuez, Zona Sur. Tel. 2740008, Fax. 2740193. E-mail: hacienda@villa-del-sol.com This hotel is located 5 minutes from the neighborhood of Calacoto and offers lovely rooms and suites surrounded by gardens. One bedroom Suite, $135, Deluxe, $155; Two bedrooms Suite, $185, Deluxe, $205; Three bedrooms Suite, $235, Presidential Suite, $395.

MODERATE

Hotel Libertador, Calle Obispo Cárdenas 1421, Tels. 2313434, 2310059, Fax. 2318924. E-mail: libertad@ceibo.entelnet.bo Has 53 rooms/51 regular rooms and 2 suites. Prices: Single, $40. Double, $52. Triple, $60. Suite, $70. Offers private bathroom and telephone. A five-minute walk from El Prado, on a side street.

Hotel Gloria, Calle Potosí 909, Tels. 2407070, Fax. 2406622. E-mail: gloriatr@ceibo.entelnet.bo Has 89 regular rooms and 3 suites. Prices: Single, $50; Double, $60; Triple, $75; Suite, $70. Offers continental breakfast and private television, telephone, bathroom. One block from Plaza San Francisco, this hotel offers comfortable rooms and a good restaurant with vegetarian buffet lunches.

Alcala Apart Hotel, Calle Victor Sanginés 2662, Plaza España, Sopocachi. Tels. 2412336, 2411113, Fax. 2411893. E-mail: alcalapt@zuper.net Single, $55; Double, $65; Triple, $75.

Hotel Oberland, 20 minutes from the city center, taxi fare 5 US $, between calle 2 and 3 in Mallasa. Also offers meeting facilities, an indoor pool and gardens. A great place to spend a day or weekend with kids. Tel. 2745040, Fax. 2745818. E-mail: wschmid@caoba.entelnet.bo Single, $30; Double, $38; Triple, $45; Suites, $60.

Hotel Copacabana, Av. 16 de Julio 1802, Tels. 2352241, 2352242, 2352244, Fax. 2312834. E-mail: hotelcop@ceibo.entelnet.bo Located on El Prado, this hotel is across from the Plaza Hotel and has 64 rooms. Prices: Single, $31; Double, $40; Triple, $46; Suite, $75; Additional bed, $12.

Hotel El Dorado, Av. Villazón, Tel. 2363355, Fax. 2391438. E-mail: eldorado@ceibo.entelnet.bo Has 73 rooms: 69 regular rooms and 4 suites. Prices: Single, $32; Double, $40; Suite, single $42, double $50; Additional bed, $8. Offers private telephone and bathroom and is located across from the University. Good service.

Sucre Palace Hotel, Av. 16 de Julio 1636, Tels. 2363366, 2363390, Fax. 2390251. E-mail: sph@kolla.net Located on the Prado. Has large rooms, a snack shop and a restaurant. Prices:

Single, $35; Double, $50; Suite $60.

Hotel Calacoto, Calle 13, 8009 (in Calacoto), Tels. 2799335, 2792524, Fax. 2799334. E-mail: hotelcalacoto@khainata.com Has 23 rooms with T.V. and heat. Single, $25; Double, $32; Triple, $40.

INEXPENSIVE

Apart Hotel Sopocachi, Calle Macario Pinilla 580, Sopocachi. Tel. 2410312, Fax. 2410512. E-mail: ahtsopo@caoba.entelnet.bo Rooms from $35, $5 for each aditional person. Centrally located it offers nice apartments.

Hotel Sagárnaga, Calle Sagárnaga 328, Tel. 2350252, Fax. 2360831. E-mail: hotsadt@ceibo.entelnet.bo Has 48 rooms. Prices for rooms with bathroom: Single, $20; Double, $25; Triple, $32; Above triple, $10 for each additional person. There are three rooms with communal bath, a double costs $12. Located near San Francisco Church, it is a few steps from Bolivian handicrafts shops and has *peñas* on its premises, Sunday and Wednesday from 8-10 p.m. Also contains Diego's Restaurant.

Hotel Alem, Calle Sagárnaga 334, Tel. 2367400, Fax. 2451785. Has 67 rooms. Prices: Single, $15 with private bathroom, $11 without; Double, $23 with private bathroom, $12 without. Prices include breakfast. It is next to Hotel Sagárnaga, very near *peñas*, handicraft shops and San Francisco Church. Also has travel agency.

Hotel España, Av. 6 de Agosto 2074, Tels. 2442643, 2441919, Fax. 2441329. E-mail: hespana@ceibo.entelnet.bo Has 22 rooms. Prices: Single, $22; Double, $32; Triple, $38. Prices include breakfast. A block down from the University and a couple of blocks from El Prado, this hotel has a great courtyard to write letters.

Residencial La Estancia, Calle México 1559, Tel. 2324308, Fax. 2369242. Has 14 rooms with T.V. and telephone.

Single, $15; Double, $25; Triple, $32.

Hotel Max Inn, Plaza Mariscal Sucre (Plaza San Pedro) 1494, Tel. 2491278. Offers 50 rooms with private bathroom, T.V. and fridge, and has a bar and a garage. Single, $35; Double, $47; Triple, $54; Suite, $70. Prices include continental breakfast.

Hotel Rosario, Calle Illampu 704, Tel. 2451658, Fax. 2451991. Has 43 rooms. Prices: Single, $28, Double, $37, Triple, $49. A charming colonial setting close to the outdoor market. Free internet. www.hotelrosario.com E-mail: reservas@hotelrosario.com

Residencial Copacabana, Calle Illampu 734, Tel. 2451626, Fax. 2451684. E-mail: combicop@ceibo.entelnet.bo Has 31 rooms.

Hotel Latino, Av. Perú 171, Tels. 2282828, 2280325, Fax. 2280340. Has 64 rooms, with T.V. and heat. Has a restaurant, meeting rooms and parking. Single, $21; double, $28; Triple, $36.

Hostal República, Calle Comercio 1455, Tel. 2202742, Fax. 2202782. E-mail: marynela@ceibo.entelnet.bo 25 rooms.

Hotel Continental, Av. Illampu 626 Tel./Fax. 2451176. E-mail: hotelcontinental@latinmail.com

• Restaurants

La Paz will not disappoint with its wide array of quality restaurants offering food from around the globe. Take advantage of being in the country's capital, and splurge on some exotic meals while in La Paz.

Rincon Español. Pasaje Hermanos Manchego 2550. Tel. 2435306. This small but charming restaurant offers some of the best food in town, including great fish and seafood dishes, including Paella. Reservations are recommened. Closed on Sunday.

Uma, Hotel Plaza, Av. 16 de Julio 1789, Tel. 2378311. Located on the main floor of the Hotel Plaza, this elegant restaurant offers a good selection of continental dishes and flamed desserts. Visa, MC, AmEx.

Utama, Hotel Plaza Skyroom, Tel. 2378311. Great salad bar and one of the few good restaurants that serves both continental and Bolivian cuisine. Prices are a bit higher here than in Uma, but the fabulous view of the city and lovely atmosphere make it worth it. Visa, MC, AmEx.

El Brasero, Calle Capitan Ravelo 2124 B, Tel. 2431034. Offers excellent Bolivian and International food.

La Suisse, Av. Muñoz Reyes 1710, Calacoto, Tels. 2793160, 2791387. Excellent beef and fondue as well as Swiss and European specialties. Offers raclet, fondue, good steaks, including llama cuts, and a Soufflé Glas au Grand Marnier. One of the best restaurants in town.

La Comedie, Pasaje Medinacelli 2234, Sopocachi. Tel. 2423561. Brand new french restaurant cafe in La Paz. Serves excellent french food in a very nice setting with live music and exhibitions of Bolivian artists. Open Monday to Friday from 11:30 to 2:00 and Saturday from 18:00 to 2:00.

Suma Uru Ansaya, Radisson Plaza Hotel on Av. Arce 2177, Tel. 2441111. Dinner specials change daily, including pasta, pizza and crepes.

Chez Lacoste, Calle Sanchez Bustamante corner with Calle 17, 1098. Tel. 2792616 . Run by a French and German-Bolivian couple, Lacoste offers great seafood and beef dishes and a good selection of Bolivian, Chilean, French and Argentine wines. Pricey, but a sure bet for an evening out or business lunch. Closed Sunday. Visa, MC, AmEx.

Blackie's House, Av. Ecuador 2442, Tel. 2415951. Offers continental food, specializing in trout. Closed Sunday evenings. Visa, MC, AmEx.

El Arriero, Calie 6 de Agosto 2536, Tel. 2441155, in the center, and also in Calacoto at Calle 17, 8185, Tel. 2771540.

Casa Argentina. Offers some of the best steak dishes in town with Argentine beef. Closed Sunday. Visa, MC, AmEx.

Restaurant Vienna, Calle Federico Zuazo 1905, Tel. 2441660. This Austrian restaurant offers private receptions, banquet, buffet and meeting rooms. Offers a wide and good variety of Bolivian, European and continental dishes in a very nice setting. Great desserts and expresso coffee. Closed Saturday and Sunday evenings. AmEx.

Giorgissimo, Av. Camacho 367, Tel. 2202919. Also located in Calacoto, Av. Ballivián. A favorite hangout for businessmen, diplomats and politicians, Giorgissimos offers good Bolivian, continental and seafood dishes. Get there early because it fills up fast.

Osteria del Pettirosso, Pasaje Gustavo Medinacelli 2282, Tel. 2310363. An Italian restaurant located in the Sopocachi neighborhood of La Paz, with classy decor and good food. A bit tricky to find.

Pronto, Calle Jáuregui 2248 (Jauregui is an alleyway in Sopocachi located between 6 de Agosto and 20 de Octubre, and Guachalla and Rosendo Gutiérrez), Tel. 2441369. This restaurant serves excellent Italian food and homemade pasta in an elegant and modern ambiance. Closed Sunday and noons. Visa, MC.

El Vagón, Calle Pedro Salazar 384, Tel. 2432477 in Sopocachi, and Calle 19 corner with Patiño, Tel. 2793700 in Calacoto. A sure bet if you are in the mood for trying local bolivian and creole dishes.

La Bodeguita Cubana, Calle Federico Suazo 1653. Tel. 2310064. La Paz's little piece of Havana. Excellent, reasonably-priced Cuban food and a lively atmosphere.

Highlanders, Calle Sánchez Lima 2667 (the end of the road), Tel. 2430023. A fun, comfortable Mexican restaurant with food as authentic as you'll find in Bolivia. Closed Sunday. Visa, MC, AmEx.

New Tokyo, Av. 6 de Agosto 2932, Tel. 2433654. Good selection of Japanese food, with excellent sushi. Closed Sunday evenings. Visa, MC, AmEx.

Wagamama, Pasaje Pinilla 2557, off of Av. Arce near the Ketal Supermarket, Tel.2434911. Offers sushi and other Japanese cuisine, all with unforgettably strong wasabi. A favorite hangout for diplomats and foreign residents, probably the best Japanese food in town. Closed Sundays and Mondays. Visa, MC, AmEx.

Furusato, Calle Batallón Colorado corner with Federico Zuazo, Edif. Sociedad Japonesa 2nd floor. Tel. 2442292.

Lu Qing, Av. 20 de Octubre corner with Aspiazu, Tel. 2424188. One of the best Chinese restaurant in La Paz in a very nice setting. It has a varied and complete Chinese menu at reasonable rates. VISA, MC, AmEx.

Chifa Emy, offers some of the best Chinese food in town in a handful of locations. Plaza Avaroa, calle 20 de Octubre. Tel. 2440551. In Los Pinos at Calle 7, 777, Tels. 2770909, 2795610. The latter is best for Peking Duck and Sunday brunch in outdoor gardens. Visa, MC.

Restaurant M'Dalali, Calle 1, #2, in Los Pinos, Tel. 2772873. Exotic Arabic cuisine. Only open for dinner during the week, weekends they open at noon. Visa, MC, AmEx.

Andromeda, Av. Arce 2116, Tels. 2440726, 2354723. French Mediterranean and vegetarian cuisine. Recommended for daily lunch special. Closed Sunday. Visa, MC, AmEx.

Mongo's Rock Bottom Cafe, Calle Hermanos Manchego 2444, Tel. 2440714. Without a doubt the most popular gringo hangout in La Paz, Mongo's offers delicious burgers, fish and chips and a guaranteed expat crowd. Great for lunch or dinner, although be prepared to wait. Visa, MC.

Restaurant Oberland, in Mallasa between Calles 2 and 3, half an hour from downtown La Paz, Tel. 2745040. Offers cabins, swimming pool and restaurant in a beautiful setting. Visa, MC, AmEx.

El Calicanto, Calle Jenaro Sanjinez 467,close to Plaza Murillo. Offers barbecue grill and Bolivian cuisine, monster steak and pretty cheap. Lovely setting in a restored Colonial building.

Café Montmartre, Calle Fernando Guachalla 399, Tel. 2440137, offering tasty food, an authentic French environment and live entertainment. Also has incredible set lunches during the week.

Café Bar Restaurant Dumas, Avenida Arce 2390, Tel. 2315089. Offers French, Spanish and Italian food.

La Quebequoise, Calle 20 de Octubre, Tel. 2371782. Offers Canadian and American style food.

Paladar, Calle Fernando Guachalla 359, Tel. 2441812. Offers good Brazilian style set dishes for a cheap price during the week. Open from Tuesday to Sunday at noon and Thursday to Saturday all days. Also in Miraflores at Calle Claudio Sanjines 1538, Tel. 2241520.

Restaurant Armonía, Calle Ecuador 2286, Tel. 2412858. Opens from Monday to Friday, offers a good choice of vegetarian food.

Maphrao On, the only Thai restaurant in town. Calle Claudio Aliaga 1182, San Miguel. Tels. 2793070, 1541720. Open Tuesday to Saturday from 19:00 to 24:00. Sunday from 12:00 to 16:00.

For quicker and cheaper meals, La Paz has plenty of cafés and fixed-menu lunch places. These range greatly in style — some have a strong local feel while others are modeled after American cafes, but all will satisfy your stomach.

Alexander Coffee Shops, Av. 16 de Julio (the Prado) 1832, Tel. 2312790. Calle Potosí, 1091. Plaza Avaroa and in the Zona Sur at Calle Montenegro "La Chiwiña," Tel. 2770465. Undoubtedly trendy and remarkably non-Bolivian, Alexander nonetheless offers some of the best sandwiches and beverages in town. The atmosphere is comfortable and relaxed, and definitely conducive to reading and journal writing.

For good expresso coffe try **Vizzlo** in the Shopping Norte.

La Terraza Café, Av. 20 de Octubre 2331, on El Prado, and in the Zona Sur. Similar to Alexander. Great for coffee, pastries and socializing or relaxing.

Café La Comedie, one of the best place in town to sip a cup of coffee a glass of wine or beer, whose French atmosphere makes it perfect for a date. Pasaje Medinacelli 2234, Sopocachi. Tel. 2423561.

Urbano Café & Grill, Av. Camacho between Loayza and Colón, Tel. 2316090, and Av. Arce 2142, Tel. 2443096. Not bad for deli sandwiches, crunchy french fries and satisfying desserts.

Café Banals, Calle Sagárnaga 147.

Café Ciudad, Plaza del Estudiante, corner with Batallón Colorados, Tel. 2441827. What this café might lack in ambiance, it makes up for in convenience. It is the only 24-hour café in La Paz, and is centrally located.

Café La Paz, Camacho, corner of Ayacucho, has good coffee as well as breakfast and tea pastries.

Café Club Lavazza, Hotel Plaza.

Euro Café Bistro, Hotel Europa.

Café Joyé Llas, Calle Loayza 273.

Café Berlin, Calle Mercado corner with Loayza.

Profumo di Caffé, Plaza San Francisco 502. Tel. 2313824.

Café de la Abuelita Aida, Calle 21 de Calacoto 8413, Tel. 2772348.

Café Mascaras, Plaza Murillo 542.

Café Pierrot, calle Potosi 909.

Café Royal, Av. Mariscal Santa Cruz corner with Almirante Grau.

If you are just looking for sandwiches go to **Hot Dogs** on Calle 20 de Octubre 2255 or **In "N" Out** on El Prado 1607.

For better or worse, La Paz offers

some unmistakably American food chains. Throughout downtown La Paz as well as the Zona Sur, you should have no problem finding the trademark signs of **Burger King** and **Domino's Pizza**, which will lead you, if you so desire, to a little piece of Americana.

If you prefer to dip into authentic fast-food cuisine from Bolivia, try **Eli's Pizza Express**, Av. 16 de Julio (the Prado) 1497, Tels. 2335566, 2319295, or 6 de Agosto 2548, Tel. 2434411, for a wide variety of pizza and sandwiches; the **Pizza Pub**, right next to Café Ciudad going down the hill on Batallón Colorados 2. For the best fried chicken in town, be sure to try **Pollo Copacabana**, Av. 16 de Julio 1866 near Alexander Coffee Shop, Calle Potosí corner with Socabaya and Calle Ballivian in Calacoto. Tel. 2371006. For *salteñas*, try **Salteñería El Horno** at 6 de Agosto 2235. There is also **Salteñas Potosinas**, on 20 de Octubre just up from Plaza Abaroa as well as on 6 de Agosto near Aspiazu. **Salteñas Paceña**, Calle 20 de Octubre 2379. **Salteñas Chuquisaqueñas**, 6 de Agosto 2187, **Salteñas Filipo**, **Romero** and **Salteñas Chic** on Plaza Avaroa. Also **Salteñas Potosinas** at Luigi's Pizzeria on 6 de Agosto 2048.

Don't miss dessert at **Kuchen Stube**, in Sopocachi at Calle Rosendo Gutiérrez 461, Tel. 2361689, and in San Miguel at Calle Montenegro 761, Tel. 2795407. Offers excellent Bolivian and German pastries, expresso coffee in authentic European cafe setting. Also has take-out service.

• Travel Agencies

BTI Travel Center Royal Tours, Avenida Hernando Siles 6106 corner with Calle 15, Obrajes. Tels. 2782380, Fax. 2782202. E-mail: btiroyal@acelerate.com Highly reliable for international booking and national tourism. www.enjoy-bolivia.com

Crillón Tours, Av. Camacho 1223, Tel. 2339047, Fax. 2116481, runs hydrofoil service on Lake Titicaca from Huatajata to Puno, and a hotel and a museum at Huatajata. E-mail: andes@ceibo.entelnet.bo

Balsa Tours, Av. 16 de Julio 1566, Tels. 2354049, 2356164. E-mail: Tbalsa@caoba.entelnet.bo offers Lake Titicaca and other regional tours.

Viajes Fremen, Av. Mariscal Santa Cruz, Galería Handal Center of. 13. Tels. 2407995, 2408200. Offers cruises on the Beni rivers that include fishing, swimming and visits to the Chapare and other regions of the country. E-mail: vtfremen@caoba.entelnet.bo www.andes-amazonia.com

Transturin, Calle Alfredo Ascarrunz 2518, (Sopocachi), Tel. 2422222, Fax. 22411922. Offers bus and catamaran boat service to Copacabana, the Island of the Sun and Puno with connections to Cuzco. E-mail: info@transturin.com www.transturin.com

Andes Expediciones, Avenida Camacho 1377, Tels. 2202983, 2319655, Fax. 2392344. Offers climbing and mountaineering. This agency is owned by Bernardo Guarachi, probably Bolivia's most experienced climber who is also the first Bolivian and the continent's first native American to have climbed the summit of Mount Everest. E-mail: andesexp@ceibo.entelnet.bo www.guarachibolivia.com

America Tours, Avenida on El Prado 1490, Tel. 2374204, Fax. 2310023. E-mail: jmiranda@ceibo.entelnet.bo Excellent for excusions all over the country. www.america-ecotours.com

Valmar Tours SRL. Calle Juan de la Riva 1406, Ed. Alborada, Of. 104. Tel. 2201470. Fax. 2201519. Expert in students and young tourists. E-mail: valmar@valmartour.com www.valmartour.com

Tawa Tours, Calle Sagárnaga 161, above Peña and Restaurant Naira, Tels. 2334290, 2334292, Fax. 2391175, offers adventure trekking tours in the Andes and tropics, where they have their own camps. E-mail: tawa@caoba.entelnet.bo

Gravity Assisted Mountain Biking, Av. 16 de Julio 1490. Tel. 2313849, Fax. 2310023. E-mail: gravity@unete.com www.gravitybolivia.com Probably the best experienced agency for mountain biking.

Paititi Tours, Av. 6 de Agosto, Edif. Santa Teresa, Tels. 2440061, 2440744, Fax. 2440999, offers excellent organized adventure traveling in the Andes, the *Altiplano*, the jungle and the valleys. Fully equipped trekking, mountain climbing, boat and jeep traveling.

Abotour, Calle Ayacucho 378, Tels. 2203916, 2203943, Fax. 2203878, specializes in nature, adventure and cultural tours. E-mail: abotour@kolla.net

Magri Tourismo Ltda, Calle Capitán Ravelo 2101, Tel. 2442727. Fax. 2443060. Offers tours to the most important sights in Bolivia. American Express representative. E-mail: info@magri-amexpress.com.bo

Eliana Tours S.R.L., Calle Sagarnaga 189, shopping Doryan 2nd floor, of 29. Tel/Fax. 2331090. Offers a whole range of tours all over the country.

Diana Tours, Calle Sagárnaga 326, Tels. 2350252, 2334152, Fax. 2351158, arranges city tours, trips to Tiwanaku, Lake Titicaca, Moon valley, Chacaltaya, Yungas, Zongo, Puno and Cuzco. E-mail: hotsadt@ceibo.entelnet.bo

Turisbus, Av. Illampu 704, Tel. 2451341. E-mail: turisbus@caoba.entelnet.bo

Turismo Balsa Ltda. Calle Capitán Ravelo 2104. Tel. 2440817. Fax. 2440310. E-mail: info@turismobalsa.com

Carlson Wagon-Lits Travel, Av. Mariscal Santa Cruz, corner with Colón, Edif. Litoral, Tels. 2358499, 2372822, Fax. 2373500. E-mail: carwagli@ceibo.entelnet.bo

Fortaleza Tours, Calle Sagarnaga 348. Tels/Fax. 2310866, 2415922. Offers excursions from high mountains to the jungle of Madidi Park. www.odissey-bolivia.com

E-mail: fortaleza_@hotmail.com

Peru-Bolivia Tours, Calle Loayza, Edif. Ayacucho, Of. 8, www.perubolivian.com Tels. 2338866, 2202956, Fax. 2200852. E-mail: info@perubolivian.com Offer culture and adventure tours.

Club Andino Boliviano, Calle México 1638, Casilla 1346, Tel. 2312875, offers trips to Chacaltaya ski slopes as well as trekking and mountaineering information. E-mail: clubandi@caoba.entelnet.bo

Andean Summits, Calle prolongación Armaza 710, Sopocachi. Tel/Fax. 2421106. Offers climbing and moutaineering all over the country. Run by Jose Camarlinghi. E-mail: info@andeansummits.com

Colibri S.R.L., Calle Sagarnaga 309. Tels. 2371936, 2378098, Fax. 2355043. Specializes also in climbing and moutaineering. E-mail: colibri@ceibo.entelnet.bo

Elma Tours, Calle Linares 888, Tel 2456823. Mountaineering, trekking and biking. www.excursions-bolivia.8m.com E-mail: illimani_yupanqui@hotmail.com

Toñito Tour, Calle Sagarnaga 189, Tel/Fax. 2336250. Organizes expeditions to Eduardo Avaroa Park and Salt Flats. E-mail: tonitotour@yahoo.com

Terra Andina, Calle F. Guachalla 662. Tel./Fax. 2422995. www.terra-andina.com E-mail: terra-andina@unete.com Offers adventure tourism.

Refugio Huayna Potosí, owners of the refugio in the Zongo base camp. Climbing, trekking, mountain biking. Of. Sagárnaga and Illampu. Tels. 2317324, 71581644. E-mail: berrios@megalink.com

• Museums, Art Galleries and Cultural Centers

The Kusillo Museum of Science and Play, an interactive museum for children with exhibits to get children and young people involved in learning about science and the world through fun and games. Calle Roosevelt

100, Tel/Fax. 2226187. Open Tues. through Sunday. 10:00 to18:00. Also has an outdoor play area and probably the best craft fair in Bolivia with rotating exhibits. A funicular reaching the childrens museum level is under construction. The museum offers a great view of the Illimani Mountain and the city of La Paz.

Museo Costumbrista, Plaza Riosiño at the end of Calle Jaén. Miniature scenes of old La Paz. Open Tues. through Fri. 9:00 to 12:30, 15:00 to 19:00; Sat. and Sun. 10:00 to 13:00.

Museo Pedro Domingo Murillo, Calle Jaén 790. Exhibits masks, weavings, miniature handicrafts, antique furniture and silverware. Open Tues. through Fri. 9:30 to noon, 15:00 to19:00; Sat. and Sun. 10:00 to 12:30.

Tambo Quirquincho, Calle Evaristo Valle. Has a mask exhibit and rotating shows on Bolivian popular art. Open 9:30 to 13:00; 15:00 to 19:00. Sat. and Sun. 10:00 to 13:00.

Museo del Oro, Calle Jaén 777. Exquisite collection of pre-Columbian gold, silver and ceramic artifacts. Open Tues. through Fri. 9:00 to12:00, 15:00 to 19:00. Sat and Sun. 10:00 to 13:00.

Museo Nacional de Arte, Plaza Murillo, across the street from the Cathedral. Fine collection of colonial paintings and contemporary art. Open Tues. through Fri. 9:30 to12:30, 16:00 to 19:00. Saturdays only in the morning.

Museo de la Catedral, Calle Socabaya 432, in the Cathedral building. Colonial art. Open Tues. through Thurs. 10:00 to noon and 14:30 to 18:00.

Museo de Etnografía y Folklore, Calle Ingavi 916. Permanent exhibit on Chipaya and Ayoreo cultures. A lovely textile exhibit area was recently opened. Open Mon. through Fri. 8:30 to 12:30, 14:30 to 18:00.

Museo Tiwanaku (Museo Nacional de Arqueología), Pasaje Tiwanaku 93 behind Hotel Plaza. This recently restored museum exhibits priceless pre-Columbian artifacts. Open Mon. through Fri. 9:00 to

noon and 15:00 to 19:00. Sat. and Sun. 10:00 to noon and 15:00 to 18:30.

Museo de la Coca, Calle Linares 906. Tel. 2311998. Open everyday from 10:00 to 18:00. Everything you've wanted to know about the coca leaf and never dared to ask.

Salón Municipal Cecilio Guzmán de Rojas, Located in the Casa de la Cultura, Av. Mcal. Santa Cruz, corner with Calle Potosí. Bolivian painting and sculpture exhibits. Open Mon. through Fri. 8:30 to noon, and 14:30 to 19:00.

Museo de Arte Contemporaneo Plaza El Prado 1698.

Taipinquiri Cultural Center, Av. Montenegro 1378, San Miguel. Tel. 2793716.

Alternativa Centro de Arte, Calle Gustavo Medinacelli 2268. Tel. 2423654

Goethe Institut, Av. 6 de Agosto 2118, Tel. 2442453. Cultural programs, lectures, concerts on Bolivian and German subjects. German Library.

Centro Boliviano Americano, Parque Zenón Iturralde, Av. Arce, Tels. 2431446, 2411156. U.S. and Bolivian cultural programs, films, art exhibits and concerts. Library with U.S. periodicals and books.

Alianza Francesa, Calle Fernando Guachalla 399, Tels. 2442075, 2441382. Bolivian and French cultural programs.

Teatro Municipal, the corner of Calle Genaro Sanjines and Indaburo. Concerts and theater.

Casa de la Cultura, Av. Mcal. Santa Cruz, corner with Calle Potosí, across from San Francisco Church. Art exhibits, cultural programs, cinema and concerts. Open Mon. through Fri. 8:30 to noon, and 14:30 to 19:00.

Spanish Language Institute, Calle 14 corner with Aviador 180 Achumani. Tel. 2796074.
E-mail: bolilang_in@bolivialanguageinst.com Specializes in spanish immersion programs, review courses. Bolivian and Latin America Culture.

• Bookstores

Lectura, Calle Loayza 271,
Tel. 2200865. Av. Montenegro 788, Galeria
Futuro, San Miguel, Tel. 2772631.

Los Amigos del Libro, Calle
Mercado 1315, Tel. 2204321.

Gisbert y Cia, Calle Comercio 1270,
Tels. 2202626, 2203680.

Juventud, Plaza Murillo 519,
Tel. 2406248.

Don Bosco, Av. 16 de Julio 1803,
Tel. 2441640.

Prurobin, Plaza del Estudiante 1923,
Tels. 2442202, 2430957.

Martínez-Acchini, Av. Arce 2132,
Edif. Illampu, Tel. 2441112.

Libreria Olimpia, Handel Center,
local 14. Tel. 2408022.

Librería Armonía, Av. Ecuador 2284,
Tels. 2412858, 2418454.

• Internet

You will have no problem finding
Internet cafes in La Paz. The areas most
densely populated with computers are
around Calle Sagárnaga/San Francisco
and all up and down the Prado. A bit
further south, in Sopocachi, is one of the
most comfortable, well-priced cafés:
Tenenet, Av. 6 de Agosto (just before
Aspiazu), Tels. 2338772, 2491442. But at
any hour of the day or night, you can log
on at **Café Ciudad,** on Plaza del
Estudiante, in their upstairs café.

• Shopping

For visitors interested in handicrafts, fine
alpaca ware, silver and gold jewelry,
La Paz is the place to shop. If you are looking
for the best crafts in La Paz visit the **Kusillo´s
Craft Fair** located in the central park area of
the city. Here you will always find both the
most innovative hand-made items and traditional crafts. You will also get the best city view on
the tram which takes you up to the Museum of
Science and Play. For more information,
Tel/Fax. 2226371. E-mail: wendy@kusillo.org

Galería Millma at Calle Sagárnaga
225, Tel. 2311338, offers beautiful Indian
weavings, wall hangings, natural dyed
alpaca and cotton sweaters, scarves and
ponchos. It is run by two Americans who are
authors of two books on Bolivian weavings.
They make most of their alpaca and cotton
goods at a workshop located two blocks
away from the hotel at Av. 20 de Octubre
1824. E-mail: millma@ceibo.entelnet.bo
www.millmaalpaca.com

Artesanías Titicaca, Av. Sánchez
Lima 2320, Tels. 2411102, 2418532, sells
good quality handicrafts and alpaca dresses.
Alpaka III, Av. 16 de Julio, offers Alpaca and
cotton products.

Galería Artesanal San Francisco
and **Mercado Artesanal San Francisco**,
both next to San Francisco Church on the
esplanade, offer a wide selection of
antiques, alpaca goods, weavings, old
coins and silver jewelry. Up from the
church along Calle Sagárnaga, you will
find **Galería Artesanal Chuquiago**,
Galería Artesanal Las Brujas, and small
shops and vendors selling leather alpaca
goods and handicrafts. Nearby at Calle
Linares 862, Tels. 2485159, 2393041,
Fax. 2485022, is **Artesanía Sorata**,
which offers jumpers, beautiful sweaters,
stuffed dolls and other gift items, also
located on Calle Sagárnaga 363. **Comart
Tukuypaj** on Calle Linares 958,
Tel. 2312686, **Lana Teñida,** Calle
Sagárnaga 177, Tel. 2314492. Has 100%
natural dyed products.

Designer **Liliana Castellanos** sells
unique creations of high-quality elegant
fashions made from delicate alpaca and
llama wools. Shopping Norte 3rd floor.
Tel/Fax. 2111453, and Av. Montenegro 770,
Galeria Lino, San Miguel. Tel/Fax. 2125770,
E-mail: milos@cotas.net Also worth visiting
for her high-quality design is **Beatriz**

Canedo Patiño just opposite Radisson Hotel.

For silver and pewter, try **Rafaella Pitti**, located in the Zona Sur, Tels. 2740292, 2797106, and at the El Alto International Airport, Tel. 2824805. For wonderful modern designs of very high-quality silver, **Joyeria Preziosi Milano**, Av 16 de Julio 1615, Tel. 2390540, and **Joyeria King's**, Calle Loayza 261. Tel. 2328178.

Chocoholics must try the Breick bittersweet or milk chocolate sold throughout the city — real chocolate that beats Hershey's. **Breick** has specialty stores on Calle Federico Suazo (just below the Mercado Camacho) and in San Miguel in Calacoto. Good chocolate can also be found at **Clavel's** on the Av. 16 de Julio (the Prado) 1566.

Casa Kavlin, Calle Potosí 1130 sells film and does color processing. **Casa Capri**, at the corner of Colón and Mariscal Santa Cruz, processes print film. **Kodak**, on El Prado Edif. Alameda sells and processes print and slide films. **Agfa** and **Fuji** have stores all over the city.

• Sports

There is a world-class **Golf Course** in Mallasilla. It is surrounded by mountains and hills and offers 18 holes, some of which are quite challenging. To reach Mallasilla, take the road to La Florida, Aranjuez, and head to the right after crossing the Aranjuez bridge.

There is also the **La Paz Tennis Club** on Av. Arequipa 8450 in La Florida, Tel. 2792440; the **Automobile Club** in Calacoto, Av. Ballivián 401 Tels. 2432136, 2792240; and **Los Sargentos Horse Riding Club** at Calle 10 in Obrajes, Tels. 2782522, 2784899.

A variety of hotels offer day passes to their spas, which generally include saunas, swimming pools, weight room, showers, etc. The best one is at Hotel Europa in downtown La Paz.

Bolivian **Soccer** is played at the Stadium Hernando Siles in Miraflores and Estadio Bolívar in Tembladerani. Check with the local papers for game schedules.

• Nightlife

If you're looking for family and/or cultural entertainment, your best bet is one of the many *peñas* — folkloric shows and dinner — that you will find in La Paz. The following *peñas* are reasonably priced and offer quality shows with good food.

Los Escudos, Av. Mariscal Santa Cruz 1201, corner of Calle Ayacucho, Tel. 2312133, Fax. 2312429.

Marka Tambo, Calle Jaén 710.

La Casa del Corregidor, Calle Murillo 1040, Tel. 2363633.

Naira, Calle Sagárnaga 161, Tel. 2350530. For drinks or to socialize, you will find a wide variety of bars and pubs throughout downtown La Paz and in the Zona Sur. If you want to bar hop, head to the environs of Plaza Avaroa in Sopocachi. From there you can head up 20 de Octubre where, within a block or two, you will come upon a string of options. Also recommended near the plaza is Calle Belisario Salinas, which has a few fun places to hang out (there are also many late-night meat eateries here where you can grab a sandwich before heading home). Listed are just a few of the best places.

Thelonious, Av. 20 de Octubre 2172, Tel. 2424405, is arguably La Paz's best jazz bar. The cover is high, but the music is worth it.

Cambrinus, Av. 20 de Octubre 2453 on Plaza Abaroa, Tel. 2430913, is an elegant bar with live music and sometimes theater performances on the weekends.

Matheus on Calle Guachalla near the corner of Av. 6 de Agosto, has jazz and a nice pub setting.

Beer's Pub, Calle Victor Sanjines

2866, Tel. 2411668, is a block and a half from Plaza España. So ridiculously American, it is worth visiting just to make fun of the name. (Also has good beer selection).

Talicho's, Capitán Ravelo 2465, Tel. 71570811, has a unique environment and lots of drink specials.

The Green Bar, a small and quiet bar that serves plentiful coctails and large measures and even a green beer for very decent prices. Just off Plaza Avaroa.

Somnus Pub, Calle Hermanos Manchego 2586.

Business, Av Arce 2164, in front of the Radisson Hotel, Tel. 2442218.

Fulvio Piano Bar, Calle 20 de Octubre 1947, Tel. 2393016.

La Obertura Café Rock, Av 6 de Agosto, Tel. 2443209.

Equinoccio, Calle Sanchez Lima 2191.

Reineke Fuchs, Pasage Jauregui 2241, Sopocachi,. Tel. 2442979, and Av. Montenegro corner with calle 18. Tel. 2772103.

Bizarro, Calle Fernando Guachalla opposite Cafe Monmartre.

Diesel Nacional, Av. 20 de Octubre 2271, Tel. 2423477.

Capotraste, Av. Montenego corner with calle 18, San Miguel, Tel. 2772856.

La Casa del Tapado, Calle Batallón Colorado 36. Cafe Bar with art exhibitions.

Dead Stroke, pub café, snooker club, Av. 6 de Agosto 2460, Tel. 2433472.

Occipucio, Av. 20 de Octubre on Plaza Avaroa, Tel. 77264078.

Malegria, Calle Goitia 155, Tel. 2440983.

If you're in the mood to dance, many places beckon in the country's capital:

Forum, Calle Victor Sanjines 2908, two blocks from Plaza España, Tels. 2414762, 2413669, is the most popular among La Paz's young, elite crowd.

Mongo's Rock Bottom Café, Calle Hermanos Manchego 2444,

Tel. 2440714, is the place where the expats go wild. Revisit your college years with some good old music and dancing on tables.

R S Club, in the plaza up the steps from Av. Arce before 6 de Agosto on Rosendo Gutiérrez.

Dragonfly, Calle Fernando Guachalla 319, Tel. 77622022.

Kokomo's, Plaza del Estadio 1354, Miraflores, Tel. 77555333.

Fantasy, Calle Agustin Saavedra 390.

• Movies

Cine Monje Campero, Av. 16 de Julio 1495, Tel. 2323333, is the most modern, comfortable movie theater in La Paz.

Cine 16 de Julio, Av. 16 de Julio, near Plaza del Estudiante, Tel. 2377099 comes in a close second to Monje Campero in comfort. Both offer the most up-to-date movie selections in La Paz (keep in mind that movies reach Bolivia a month or two after they feature in the United States and Europe).

Cine 6 de Agosto, Av. 6 de Agosto 2284, Tel. 2323829.

Cinemateca Boliviana, Calle Pichincha corner with Indaburo. Soon new direction at Calle Rosendo Gutierrez corner with Prolongación Federico Suazo, offers top-quality foreign and Bolivian films.

Cine Plaza. on the Plaza Murillo and **Cine Manfer** on Calle Comercio, corner with G. Sanjines offer second-run movies at bargain prices.

• Banks

Banco de Credito, Calle Colón 1308, corner of Mercado, Tel. 2330444.

Banco de Santa Cruz, Av. Camacho 1448, Tels. 2315800, 2351213.

Banco Nacional de Bolivia, Av. Camacho 1312, corner of Colón,

Tels. 2313232, 2354616.

Citibank, Av 16 de Julio,
Edif Hermann, Tel. 2369955.
Calle 15, Calacoto, Torre Ketal,
Tel. 2440099.

Banco Sol, Calle Evaristo Valle 136,
Tels. 2460044, 2457299.

Banco Mercantil, Calle Mercado
1190, Tels. 2315131. 2345000.

Bisa, Av. 16 de Julio 1628,
Tel. 2317272, Shopping Sur, Calacoto,
Av. Ballivian Calle 22, Calacoto.

Banco de la Union, Av. Camacho
corner with Loayza, Tel. 2333131.

• Money Exchange

Prodem, Plaza Avaroa, Calle Sanchez
Lima, Sopocachi. Illampu corner with Santa Cruz.

Cáceres Ltda., Calle Potosí 909,
in the Hotel Gloria, Tels. 2406761.

Cambios America, Av. Camacho
1233, Tel. 2340920.

Hermes LTDA, Av. Mcal Santa Cruz
1326, Tel. 2356126.

Sudamer Cambios Ltda.,
Av. Camacho and c. Colón 1311, Tel. 2203148.

Internacional Unitours, Calle Mercado
1328, Edif. Ballivián, Tels. 2201948.

Money Exchange, Calle Colon 330.

• Couriers

DHL, Av. 14 de Septiembre 5351
corner with Calle 7 in Obrajes,
Tels. 2785522, 2786909, is the central
office. But DHL also has a variety of locations throughout downtown La Paz (the
most centrally located one on Av.
Mariscal Santa Cruz 1297) and in El Alto
(including the airport).

Exprinter, first floor of the Herrmann
Building on the Prado, Tel. 2433802.

UPS, Calle Pedro Salazar 541,
Sopocachi, Tels. 2422110, 2422120,
2422132.

I.B.C., Av. Guerra del Pacifico 1194,

Miraflores, Tels. 2228558, 2224639, 2227975.

OCB, Pasaje Jauregui, Edif. Alamo,
Tel. 2443311.

SKY NET, Av. Arce 2031,
Edif. Victoria, Tels. 2440344, 2440029.

FedEx, Calle Rosendo Gutierrez 113,
Tels. 2443437, 2443403.

JET Courrier Express, Calle Pedro
Salazar 541, Tels. 2422110, 2422120.

• Laundries

Lavaya, Calle 20 de Octubre 2031,
Tels. 2325146, 2326833.

Zass, Calle Guachalla corner with
Sanchez Lima, Tel. 22423018.

Lava Centro, Calle Juan José Perez
268.

Profesional Pol Dry Cleaning, Calle
Belisario Salinas 350, and Av. Ecuador 2104.

Limpieza Ballivián, Calle Ballivián
1286, Tel. 2200792.

Express, Calle Santos Machicado
521, Tel. 2458571.

La Predilcta, Calle Villalobos 1675,
Miraflores, Tel. 2242531.

• Medical Services

Clínica Alemana, Av. 6 de Agosto
2821, Tels. 2432521, 2433023, 2433676,
2432155.

Clínica Cemes, Av. 6 de Agosto 2881,
corner with Clavijo, Tels. 2430350, 2430360.

Clínica del Sur, Av. Hernando Siles
3539, corner with Calle 7 in Obrajes,
Tels. (Central) 2784750, 2784755, 2784760.
Tels. (Emergency) 2784001, 2784002,
2784003.

Clínica Boston, Calle Ecuador 2475,
Sopocachi, Tel. 2422342.

Methodist Hospital, Av. 14 de
Septiembre 5809, corner with Calle 12 in
Obrajes, Tels. 2783509, 2783372, 2783510.

Dr. Esperanza Aid, English-speaking
dentist, Av. 6 de Agosto, Edif. Cordero,
Office 303, Tels. 2431081, 2441518.

Dr. Ciro Portugal, Av Arce, Edif. Escurial, Tel. 2434775. Highly recommended as a general practicioner.

Dr. Liang Wei Jun, Dra Yi Xian Wang de Liang, Edif. Estoril, 1st floor, between the bridge de las Americas and Plaza Isabel la Católica , Tel/Fax. 2442363. Chinese Traditional medicine, acupuncture and massage.

For **vaccinations**, Centro Piloto de Salud: Av Montes (End). Tels. 2458828, 2450026.

24 hour Drug Stores

Farmacias Bolivia, Av 16 de Julio 1473, Tel. 2331838.

Super Drugs, Calle Belisario Salinas 438 (Plaza Avaroa). Av. Julio Patiño 1188 corner with calle 18, Calacoto. Tels. 2771212, 2434444.

Gloria, Calle Garcia Lanza 330, corner with Calle 16, Achumani. Av. Arce corner with Golzalves, Sopocachi. Tels. 2434344, 2713030.

Super Farmacia, Parque Triangular, Miraflores.

EXCURSIONS FROM LA PAZ

Inca Trail

For the Takesi (Inca) road hike, take a bus at 8:30. From a street on the right below Plaza Belzu (which is below the Mercado Rodríguez) to Ventilla on Palca road (or take a taxi to the Ovejuyo vehicle checkpoint above Cota Cota, $6.50, then truck to Ventilla), then continue about six miles to the San Francisco mine. The Takesi trail goes over the pass at 15,250 feet (4,650 meters) and then follows the valley, which ends at Chojlla. Five kilometers farther is Yanacachi, where there is a very basic hotel, **Hotel Panoramic**. Some meals are available in private homes. The bus to La Paz leaves at 8:00. (If you miss that, it's a 45-minute walk to Santa Rosa, which is on the main road from La Paz to Chulumani). The Bradts' book, Backpacking in Peru and Bolivia, describes this

two-day walk, which shows exceptionally fine Inca paving in the first part. The tourist office in La Paz also publishes a leaflet with a sketch map. Please do not litter the route.

The highest point is 15,250 feet (4,650m) and the lowest is 3,500 feet (1,100m). The trail can also be used as a starting point for reaching Chulumani or Coroico. The scenery changes dramatically from the bitterly cold pass down to the Yungas. At Chojlla one can sleep at the school house for a fee.

Fundación Pueblo provides guides and information on this route.
Plaza Libertad, Yanacachi. Tel. 2413662.
E-mail: Pueblo@ceibo.entelnet.bo

Tiwanaku

Bolivia's most important archaeological site is located 50 miles (80 km) to the west of La Paz. It was once the center of one of the most ancient cultures in the Americas. Its monumental stone figures, stone courtyard and sun gate give a glimpse of a civilization that mysteriously surfaced around 600 B.C. and disappeared around 1200 A.D. Now located 20 miles (30 km) from Lake Titicaca, it is believed to have once been near the shores of the lake. A new museum was opened in June, 2002, in Tiwanaku that is now home to the Bennett monolith that was previously kept in the Stadium Plaza of La Paz. This beautiful museum offers a good overview of one of the most important cultures in the Americas. The Andean Rail Company is offering weekend train service from El Alto to Tiwanaku. Be sure to check with travel agencies or the Rail Company for service information.

Spanish-speaking guides are available at the site, although it is recommended to go with a travel agency that can provide English-speaking guides. A map and guide on Tiwanaku is available at bookstores.

The most imposing monument is the Gate of the Sun, which is thought to be a solar calendar. It is part of an elaborate observatory and courtyard that contain monoliths, the door of the Puma and a subterranean temple. It lacks the sheer splendor of Machu Picchu, but provides a glimpse into the ancestry of the Aymara people, many of whom still inhabit the area.

See "Secrets of Tiwanaku," in Chapter Three of this guide, for more background on Tiwanaku and recent investigations of the area.

La Cabaña del Puma restaurant, Tel/Fax. 2898541.

Hotel Restaurant Tiahuanacu, Av. Bolivar 903, Tiwanaku. Tels, 22137009, 2410322. E-mail: grcb5@hotmail.com

Lake Titicaca

If you did not arrive via Lake Titicaca, a trip there is a must. A paved road will take you to the lake past farming villages and farms where rows of potatoes, barley, fava beans and quinoa are grown. During the October through December planting season a visitor will see Indians using teams of oxen to plow the fields, much as their ancestors did.

An hour-and-a-half after leaving La Paz you will reach the waters of Lake Titicaca at an altitude of 13,000 feet (3,962m). Totora reed and wooden boats used for fishing or travel are visible from the shore. In Huatajata you can rent a boat and visit Suriki or other islands, Tel. 022135058. Four residents of Suriki built the *Ra Two* for the Norwegian explorer Thor Heyerdahl. Two of the builders have a small souvenir shop in Suriki, an island famous for its totora reed boats and furniture.

If you enjoy seafood you can eat some delicious salmon trout at the **Inti Raymi restaurant** or the **Inti Karka**, the **Sol Andes** and **Samawi** in Huatajata, also at the **Hotel Titicaca** which also offers comfortable accommodations and is located between the village of Huarina and Huatajata. Reservations for Hotel Titicaca can be made at the Hotel Libertador in La Paz, Tels. 2313434, 2203666.

At Huatajata there is the **Altiplano Museum** on *Kallawayas* and a health spa utilizing native herbs and products, providing an overview of cultures that inhabit the shores of Lake Titicaca. . They have also reproduced traditional Altiplano dwellings, burial grounds and a floating reed island. The museum is run by **Crillón Tours**, Tel. 2337533, which offers hydrofoil service on the lake and a hotel with private bathrooms and heating. **Balsa Tours** operates a hotel and conference center at Puerto Pérez on the shores of Lake Titicaca. **Hotel Las Balsas** offers comfortable rooms, restaurant service, jacuzzi, racket ball court, sauna and a covered pool. Reservations, Tel. 2440620, Fax. 2440310. In Puerto Pérez at 67 km from La Paz.
E-mail:hotel@turismobalsa.com
Prices, Single, $70; Double, $80, Triple, $99; Suite, $100 to $150.

Lake Titicaca sprawls for some 3,500 square miles (9,064 km2) and forms part of the boundary between Bolivia and Peru. The lake, fed by the melting snows of the Andes, is the lifeblood of the peasants who live in the area. The Islands of the Sun and Moon also hold an important place in the history of the Inca civilization. The Island of the Moon offers a look at the remains of the Temple of the Moon and a great view of the Andes.

Fremen offers ecotourism and cultural exchange from Tiwanaku to Machu Pichu around the Lake Titicaca, La Paz and Alto Peru. Tel. in La Paz, 2417062. Fax. 2417327.

Inca Utama Hotel & Spa, in Huatajata, reservation in La Paz at Crillon Tours; Tel./Fax. 2135050. E-mail:titicaca@caoba.entelnet.bo
The hotel co plex and port has a lovely museum, spa, observatory and a recreation of traditional village life on the Bolivian highlands Single, $81; Double, $100; Triple, $134.

Copacabana

If you continue past lake shore town of Huatajata, you will reach the Tiquina crossing. Cars, buses and trucks are loaded on wooden barges and ferried across the Titicaca waters en route to the religious sanctuary in honor of the Virgin of Copacabana, also known as the Black

Madonna. Legend has it that Copacabana was founded by the Inca Tupac Yupanqui as a resting place for pilgrims en route to visiting the Temple of the Sun located nearby. It is likely, however that the sites was already considered sacred during the Tiwanaku period. You can take a bus or minibus from the cemetery in La Paz, a bus from the main terminal in La Paz, hire a private taxi, or go on tours offered by several travel agencies.

During Holy Week, throngs of Bolivians spend several days walking to Copacabana to pay homage to the Virgin. On Sundays or holidays the main square is jammed with vehicles covered with flowers and colored strips of paper taken to be blessed by the Virgin. Priests and indigenous medicine men bless the vehicles and their occupants.

On the **Calvario**, a hill overlooking the village and the lake, visitors purchase miniature trucks or homes made from plaster and pray that the Virgin will provide them with a real truck or home during the year. Aymara medicine men also offer incense and their services to anybody needing spiritual or medical assistance. Not far from the church is the **Horca del Inca**, a pre-Incan astronomical observatory.

Copacabana has its share of good places to stay. Listed here are the best ones, in a variety of price ranges.

Hotel Rosario del Lago, Av. Costanera corner with Rigoberto Paredes Tel. 2-8622141 Fax. 2-8622140. Reservations in La Paz, Tel 2451341, Fax. 2451991. Single, $33; Double, $43.50; Triple, $58.30. A charming and comfortable hotel that offers 28 rooms with view on the lake, a game room, Internet and parking. E-mail: turisbus@caoba.entelnet.bo www.hotelrosario.com

Hotel Gloria Copacabana, Av. 16 de Julio, Tel. 8622094. Information and reservation in La Paz; Tels. 2407070. Fax. 2406622. E-mail: gloriatr@ceibo.entelnet.bo Located not far from the lake, this hotel offers great views from its dining area as well as from individual rooms. Single, $37; Double, $44;

Triple, $56. All rooms have private bath. Connected to the hotel is Café Sol y Luna, which offers snacks throughout the day as well as Internet service. Visa, MC.

Hostal La Cupula, Calle Michel Pérez, Tel. 8622029. Certainly the coolest place to stay in Copacabana, this hostel sits up on the hill with a commanding view of both the lake and the town. You can't miss it from town, you can see its bright white-domed roof. The grounds are beautifully designed, and the overall atmosphere is very peaceful. The hostel offers a vegetarian restaurant, an art center, an international library, tourist information, laundry services and free use of kitchen facilities. Rooms with private bath: Single, $11-22; Double, $17-28; Triple, $27. Rooms with shared bath: Single, $8; Double, $8-$15; Triple, $20.

Hotel Playa Azul, Av. 6 de Agosto. It is located not far from the church. Tel. 8622227, Fax. 2320068, offers meeting rooms and lovely gardens. Single, $14; Double, $20; Triple, $25; Quadruple, $30. All prices include breakfast. Visa, MC.

Hostal Colonial, on plaza Sucre.

Residencial Brisas del Titicaca, Av. 6 de Agosto, right on the waterfront. Tel. 8622178. Rooms with private bath, $7; rooms with shared bath, $5. Spartan, but a great location. You can change your money here as well.

Hotel Ambassador, Av. Jáuregui, Tel/Fax. 8622216.

Hotel 6 de Agosto, Av. 6 de Agosto, Tel.8622292.

Hotel Flores, Av. 6 de Agosto, Tel. 8622117.

Hostal La Luna, Calle José P. Mejia, Tel. 8622051, Fax. 8622160.

Residencial El Conquistador, Plaza 2 de Febrero 8, Tel. 8622093.

Residencial Aransaya, Av. 6 de Agosto 121, Tel/Fax. 8622229. Well located, only three blocks from the church.

Residencial Copacabana, Calle Oruro 555, Tel. 8622220.

You will have no problem finding a

restaurant with good Lake Titicaca trout. There are a handful of cafés around the main plaza and on the waterfront, all decent and very low-priced.

For a little something more, try one of the following:

La Orilla Restaurant, serves excellent international food from burgers to delicious Titicaca lake trouts and pejerrey in a very pleasant setting with a fireplace. Av. 6 de Agosto. Tel. 8622267.

Café Europa on the Calle 6 de Agosto offers good espresso coffee and German pastries.

Pacha Aransaya, on the corner of Plaza Sucre, on Av. 6 de Agosto. Definitely the place to go if you want great pizza, trout, espresso and a cozy atmosphere. They also have a book exchange.

Leyenda Restaurant Hostal, sitting right on the lake, this lovely restaurant offers a funky, rustic place to relax and enjoy great food. If it's sunny out (which it often is in Copacabana), make sure to grab a table outside. Menu includes breakfast, pizza, tacos, fish, vegetarian food, and lots of desserts. You'll know you're in the right place if you hear Bob Marley playing.

Sujna Wasi is a restaurant in a beautiful old building, great food and warm atmosphere, and a patio to enjoy the sunny days. Av. Jáuregui 127.

La Casa Colonial, near Plaza Sucre heading down to the lake. Offers Bolivian food, a great patio, and occasional peñas.

Buses leave from Plaza Sucre all throughout the day, heading for Peru (generally Puno and Cuzco) and La Paz.

Islas del Sol and La Luna

Getting to the islands is a must; they are one of the most magical places in all of South America and a great place for hiking, watching some spectacular views, eat great trout, visit pre-Colombian ruins and spend an unforgettable night. One can spend several days on the Islands, hiking, visiting the archaeological sites and enjoying the incredible views and sunsets.

The islands can be reached via boat from Copacabana or from Yampupata, a bay reached by land after a 45 minutes drive.

The entry point to the Island of the Sun is Yumani (see map). It is a lush, tree covered hill with terraces growing fava beans, corn and potatoes. A spring spurts from the middle of the hill and flows to the lake.

On the 8th of December the town of Challa has its feast day. Hundreds of Aymara residents pay homage to the Virgen of Concepcion by dancing the Quena Quena, Kusillo and Chunchos, some of the oldest and most beautiful dances in all of South America. The dances include the use of elaborate feather headdresses and shoulder pieces.

Hotel La Posada Del Inca is a lovely restored colonial hacienda situated on the top of the island with a great view of the Andes and the lake.   Reservations in La Paz at Crillon Tours. Tel. 2337533, Fax. 2391039. E-mail: titicaca@caoba.entelnet.bo Single, $81; Double, $100; Triple, $134.

Intiwata Cultural Complex, Andean museum run by Transturin, available only to catamaran cruise ship clients. Reservation in La Paz. Tel. 2310442, Fax. 2310647. E-mail: sales@turismo-bolivia.com

Ecolodge La Estancia, a new ecological hotel built and managed by Magri Toursmo. Reservations in La Paz at Magri Tourismo. Tel. 2442727, Fax. 2443060. E-mail: info@magri-amexpress.com.bo Single, $53; Double, $76. American breakfast included.

La Puerta del Sol, Clean and comfortable for 15 Bs. per person, have snacks, drinks and good family style dinner for 15 Bs.

The Island of the moon, located across from the Island of the Sun, has a very important pre-Colombian ceremonial site.

Numerous agencies offer tours to Isla del Sol. Boats usually leave Copacabana in the morning, around 8:30, and again in the afternoon, around 13:00. (For half-day tours), and take you on a tour of the lake or to visit the Inca shrines on the Isla del Sol.

The Zongo Valley

A delightful day trip from La Paz is to the Zongo Valley, where the hydroelectric plants of the Bolivian Power Company are located. A four-wheel-drive vehicle is advisable for the trip. Instead of taking the road to Chacaltaya, at the fork forty-five minutes from La Paz, continue to the Milluni Mine past lagoons that provide La Paz with its drinking water. Continue past the mine, and in fifteen minutes the road, bordered by snow peaks and crystal-clear lagoons, starts to wind toward the Zongo Valley. Within an hour you will reach mountain streams that offer good trout fishing. In another hour you will be in the tropics. The road drops from 15,170 feet (4,624 m) to 4,855 feet (1,480 m), during the course of twenty miles.

Devil's Tooth (*Muela del Diablo*)

A popular day hike from La Paz is a visit to Devil's Tooth. The start of this short but strenuous day hike, which offers a spectacular view of the city of La Paz and the surrounding mountains is only a five-minute drive from Calacoto. The path to Devil's Tooth is steep and can be strenuous, but is definitely worthwhile. Be sure to take along a light lunch, water, a hat, sun screen and a camera.

To get to the starting point of the hike, turn right off Avenida Ballivián on to Calle 21 in Calacoto (at the San Miguel Church). Go down Calle 21 almost its entire length, then turn left on Calle J. Aguirre Achá (the main road to Los Pinos). Take this street into Cota Cota for approximately one and a half miles (2.4 km). The other alternative is to take a **minibus number 288** or **207** with the sign Pedregal from Plaza del Estudiante and calle Mexico. The hike begins at a point where the road is directly next to the riverbed. Across the

riverbed is a dirt soccer field and a large sign that says, among other things, Calle 80. Park here and walk on the path across the riverbed. Stay to the left of the soccer field, and follow the path along the left of a wall. The trail continues into a canyon, and it is here that the hike really begins.

The trail will go up rapidly, intersecting with numerous other paths. Finding your way may be somewhat confusing, but if you continue to turn right and go up you are probably on the right path. The most important turn in this section of the hike comes as you approach a part of the hill covered with black, volcanic dirt. You must go left as you come to a fork in the trail, or risk a dangerous, rock-strewn climb up a narrow ridge.

After one and one-half hours of hiking up this part of the trail, you will reach a ridge. Go around a corner and you will come upon a beautiful, close-up view of Devil's Tooth. If you have had enough, you may stop here, eat lunch in a green field and hike back down. But the trail continues, running left through a tiny village, descending to a small creek-bed and then rapidly climbing to the Tooth itself. This will take an additional 30 to 45 minutes, but is well worth the trek for the magnificent view from the cavity between the two towers that make up Devil's Tooth. Climbing from the base to the cavity is treacherous, however, especially on the descent when it's necessary to be very cautious because of loose rocks.

The total time for the hike (including stops for lunch and water) is between four and five hours. Hiking boots are advisable, but the trek can be done in tennis shoes.

The Hot Springs of Urmiri

At Urmiri there are hot springs that feed into two swimming pools located next to a hotel. It makes a lovely day trip from La Paz. To reach Urmiri, which consists only of the hotel and springs surrounded by mountains, take the road to Oruro until you reach Villa Loza located 44 miles (70 km) from La Paz. Take a left on the road and head toward the mountains. The road is quite windy and narrow and it is advisable to take a four-wheel-drive vehicle. Fifteen miles (25 km) from Villa Loza there is a big sign indicating a crossing. The road to the left goes to Sapahaqui, a lovely valley where peaches, pears and corn irrigated by a clean river are produced. It also makes a lovely picnic and camping site.

To go to Urmiri, take a right and travel 1.5 miles (3 km) until you reach the hotel. The use of the pool costs $5. You may also have lunch or snacks at the hotel, which has small baths with water from the hot springs. The hotel is a bit run down, but the water in the pool is changed on a regular basis. You may also wander up the hill to where the boiling hot water comes out of the earth. Bring some eggs along and treat yourself to some fresh hard-boiled eggs. Reservations for **Hotel Gloria** in Urmiri can be made in La Paz at Tel. 2407070. Tel. 2407070, Fax. 2406622.

Chacaltaya

One hour from downtown La Paz is Chacaltaya. At 17,000 feet (5,180m) above sea level, it is the world's highest ski slope. On a clear day, Chacaltaya offers a breathtaking view of the *Altiplano*, neighboring peaks, and Lake Titicaca. To check on bus schedules to Chacaltaya, call the **Club Andino Boliviano** in La Paz at 2312875, Calle Mexico 1638, E-mail: clubandi@caoba.entelnet.bo or consult with travel agencies.

The ski lodge located halfway up the mountain provides a resting place and snacks for visitors. You will likely be out of breath or possibly feel a bit faint at this extreme altitude, but the fantastic view offsets any discomfort.

The ski season runs from November to April or May. The Club Andino provides bus transportation on Sundays and sometimes on Saturdays. Otherwise, hire a jeep or, if weather conditions permit, a taxi from in front of major hotels.

The Yungas
updated by Alan Shave

By traveling less than three hours from La Paz, you can cross a summit at 15,000 feet (4,572m) inhabited by llamas with occasional glimpses of condors, before descending to the tropical Yungas region where bananas, oranges, coca leaves, papaya, coffee and avocados are cultivated by Aymara, and Afro-Bolivian farmers. Just to experience the change in temperature and scenery is worth a visit to the Yungas. Minibuses (which are preferable to large buses, due to the road conditions), leave from the gasoline station on Tejada Sorzano Street, about 5 blocks from the market in Villa Fátima. Visitors can also hire private taxi or take a tour to the area. The first hour on the road to Unduavi, the crossroad to South and North Yungas, is paved. The new paved road from Unduavi to North Yungas is due to be finished by the year 2004 when a tunnel is completed .

Beyond Unduavi Nuevo, roads can be 'challenging' in Bolivia's Altiplano summer-the rainy season running from October to April when landslides can add to traveling difficulties. Best always to travel with an experienced driver familiar with the route.

Half an hour past Unduavi Nuevo, just after the traffic checkpoint with its colourful kiosks offering food for the journey, the road splits at a crossing called Chuspipata, signposted Nor and Sur Yungas. The paved route to the left goes to Coroico, Caranavi, and heads on to the gold mining regions of Tipuani and Guanay in Alto Beni. To the right, the dirt road descend immediately, winding down through the ghost town of Unduavi Viejo, abandoned when the road to Coroico was rebuilt some years ago, and toward Chulumani, a picturesque village famous as a vacation spot for city residents the road continues to **Irupana**, the Afro-Bolivian community of Chicaloma, to the Pasto Grande archaeological complex and eventually back to La Paz through Palca or Inquisivi.

On the way there are waterfalls, luscious forest covered hills, a rundown castle, views of the snow-covered Andes and a patchwork of miniscule agricultural fields clinging to the steep mountainside, many of them dedicated to coca leaf cultivation.

Along the way, on the side road to La Chojlla mine, is a detour to the right that reaches **Yanacachi**, a lovely village that is on the route of the **Taquesi pre-Colombian trail** that begins near Mina San Franscico just west of La Paz. The Taquesi offers a great view of the area, some old homes and many of the small communities along the Yungas roads nowadays offers a phone connection. **Fundacion Pueblo**, a German-supported foundation, is working with communities along the Taquesi trail, providing training and ecotourism promotional services. The foundation and community members have already finished a lodge that offers bathrooms, hot showers and basic accomodation. From the Taquesi at the old La Chojlla mine one can see of the start of the new Hidroelectrica Boliviana power plant, with its tubes and tunnels which cross the main road.

Fundación Pueblo, Plaza Libertad, Yanacachi. Tel. 2413662.
E-mail: pueblo@ceibo.entelnet.bo

Hotel Romulo & Remo, Sacahuaya, Yanacachi. Reservation in La Paz Tels. 2232621, 2229646.

Sixty miles (100 km) out of La Paz is the lovely **Santa Rosa camping** spot above a river with a swimming pool and cabins.

Hotel Tamanpaya is located just before the Puente Villa bridge. Signposted to the left just before entering Puente Villa village, crossing a narrow iron bridge on the spectacular road which eventually leads back to La Paz through Coripata, the Yungas coca growing capital, to Coroico: a road best avoided in the rains.

In Puente Villa village, immediately after crossing the main bridge, a road veers off to the right, following the cascading river. Ten minutes up the road is a camp site. From there a ten-minute walk will take a visitor to an old wood and stone bridge and heavily forested areas. Beyond it is Suichi village with the 17th century home of the Knaudt Family.

Hotel Tamampaya, Tel. 2796099. It offers comfortable cabins with private baths, a nice swimming pool, treks into the nearby woods and full restaurant facilities. This hotel is owned by a Bolivian-German couple, enthusiasts at protecting regional flora and fauna and promoting ecotourism.

The road continues on via Huancane, with its pretty main square, and a side road to the right to **Chirca** village, well worth a visit. **Chulumani** is situated on the side of a hill with a wonderful view of the entire area. Many of the surrounding farmers cultivate coca leaves, coffee and fruit. Be sure to try some of the local honey with a fragrance unlike anything you will buy commercially. Reservations to visit the **Hotel San Bartolome** can be made at the **Hotel Radisson** in La Paz. They provide a minibus that leaves Saturday mornings and returns Sunday.

Through Chulumani town, the road runs downhill and to the west is **Apa Apa Ecological Reserve**, run by Ramiro Portugal and his lovely American wife, Matilde. Their ecotourism complex is part of an hacienda that dates to the mid 16th century. The complex has great camping facilities, four rental rooms, great food, fresh milk and fruit-based shakes. The owners personnally attend visitors and take them on 2 to 4 hours tours of the nearby Apa Apa forest that is full of birds, animals and a diverse plant life. Reservations can be made in La Paz, Tel. 2790381, in Chulumani, Tel/Fax. 022136106.

E-mail: apapayungas@homail.com

Hotel San Bartolomé, Tel. 2441111, Fax. 2440261, In La Paz, Av. Arce 2177. Has 9 cabañas and 10 rooms, 2 swimming pools and a restaurant. This hotel was recently restored. Single, $20; Double, $30; Triple, $45; Cabaña, from $60 to $90. E-mail:sanbartolome@usa.net

Country House Hostal. This new lodge offers a lovely setting, a swimming pool, trails. Rates are $8 for a single, $12 for a double. This included breakfast.

Hotel San Antonio, Tel. 2341809.

Hotel Panoramica, Tel. 8116109.

Hotel El Monarca, Tel. 8116121.

Residencial Dion, Tel. 2361048.

Hotel Garcia, Plaza Libertad 20, Tel. 2224917.

Hotel Huayrani, Calle Junin, Tel. 8113117.

The road beyond Chulumani turns sharply to the left immediately after the petrol station and food stalls on entering the town limits. It continues to Irupana, with a side road to the right for Chicaloma, a traditional coca-leaf-producing region.

Irupana is a charming Yungas town, about the size of Chulumani and established some 250 years ago. Several new hotels have sprung up in the community, offering comfortable accommodations. Just outside Irupana is the Afro-Bolivian community of **Chicaloma**. The traditional Saya dance is performed during the Festival of the Gran Poder in May or June. Irupana also hosts colorful celebrations on July 24th and August 4th with dancing for days on end around the small main square. Rival bands compete for attention at each of the four corners, and there are fireworks and the lauching of colourful paper balloons with paraffin heaters to carry them aloft at dusk. The road from Irupana heads south, via Churiaca and up over the hills before descending again towards the Rio La Paz that originates in the city of La Paz. A bridge connects Sur Yungas with Providencia Loayza at the extended village of La Plazuela

and the towns of Inquisivi and Quime. Take the right hand fork on the road – ask direction in the village, the road is not obvious!. Before dropping to the bridge is a narrow road that heads west along the hills bordering the Rio La Paz. An hour after La Plazuela cross roads are the major pre-Colombian sites and the complex of **Pasto Grande** that includes terraced fields, sophisticated irrigation systems and extensive dwelling complexes buried under the forest canopy. A local guide can provide access to these sites. (The nearest accomodation is at Irupana- no lodgings at Pasto Grande. Fill up with petrol as well before leaving Irupana).

The road from Pasto Grande heads west towards Lambate, perched on a hilltop, and other small communities, such sd Palca, before eventually reaching La Paz. Allow four hours in a four-wheel vehicle to reach La Paz from Pasto Grande: longer if it is raining since there are several river points to be forded. The spectacular road passes between the Illimani and Mururata mountains, providing some of the best scenery and most diverse geography in Bolivia – a living geology lesson.

The road is stable but narrow so be on the lookout for oncoming vehicles, though the route back from Pasto Grande via Lambate has very limited traffic, particularly the rainy season. The area is also part of a pre-Colombian trail that begins near La Paz.

In Chicaloma in the Chulumani area, there is a large Black population who migrated to the region from mining centers in the highlands (see "Blacks of the Bolivian Yungas" and "Afro Bolivians reclaim their heritage" in Chapter Six of this Guide).

Irupana accomodation

Hotel Posada Buganvilla, Tels. 2136155. 8136155.

Hotel Posada Del Rey, Tel. 2136154.

Hotel Posada Soleda, (cabin in citrus landscape), Tel. 2136154.

If you had followed the paved road to the left at the Nor and Sur Yungas crossing after leaving Unduavi Nuevo, in a little over an hour, traveling over a windy road (said to be the world's most dangerous!) flanked by thousand-foot precipices on one side and waterfalls on the other, you would have reached **Coroico**.

(Several La Paz travel agencies offer moutain bike tours from the Yungas pass to Coroico-something really special for biking enthusiasts… and downhill most of the way. But don't go over the edge… parachutes are not provided).

Near this thriving old-established town, three hours'drive from La Paz and boasting luxury five star hotels, are several communities inhabited by Aymara-speaking, descendants of African slaves brought to work in Bolivia's mines, including one with its own crowned king. The hill overlooking Coroico is called Uchamachi, and is said to be the home of *Pachamama*, the Goddess of the Earth.

Parque Nacional A.N.M.I. Cotapata, Calle Sagarnaca, Coroico, Tel. 8136338. Tel. in La Paz 2434420.
E-mail: gabriel@latinwide.com

Five stars Hotels
El Viejo Molino, about one kilometer out of town, and also a lovely place to stay. Tel./Fax. 2895506. Rep. in La Paz, Valmar Tours, Edif. Alborada 1st floor, Of 104. Calle Juan de la Riva 1406. Casilla 4294, La Paz Bolivia. Tels. 2201499, 2201470, Fax. 2201519. Offer single to triple rooms and suites. price starts from $18.
E-mail: viejomolino@valmartour.com
www.valmartour.com

Hotel Rio Selva Resort, located a few km before Coroico. Offers cabins, swimming pools, sports, trekking, etc. Great for a family vacation. Tels. 2412281, 2411561, 2411818. Fax. 2411754.
E-mail: riosel@mail.entelnet.bo Single, $37; Double, $57; Triple, $65; Apartment,

$90; Cottage, $100.
Hotel Bella Vista, Tel. 1569237.
Hotel Cerro Verde, Calle Ayacucho 5037.

Four stars Hotels
Complejo Hotelero La Finca, San Pedro de La Loma, Tel. 2390061.
Hotel San Carlo, Tel. 2372380.

Three stars Hotels
Hotel Gloria, reached as you enter Coroico, a good place to eat and stay. Reservation in La Paz,Tel. 2136020, Fax.2406622. Single, $20; Double, $32; Triple, $40.
Hotel Esmeralda, Tel. 8116017, at the top of the hill of Coroico, with a swimming pool and fabulous view.
E-mail: esmeralda@latinwide.com
Hotel Don Quijote, Tel. 8116007.
E-mail: quijote@mpoint.com.bo
Single, $15; Double, $24; Triple, $30.
Hotel Lluvia de Oro, Tel. 8116005.
Single, $8; Double, $18; Triple, $20.

Residencials/Hostels
Hotel Sol y Luna, Tel. 1561626.
E-mail: sigfro@yahoo.com Single, $6; Double, $10; Triple, $15; Cabaña, $20/40.
Residencial Kory, Plaza Julio Cuenca 3501, Tel. 1564050, Fax. 2431234.
Hostal La Casa, Calle Antofagasta 964, Tel. 8116064.
E-mail: lacasa@ceibo.entelnet.bo
Hostal La Casa Colonial, Calle Gral. Pando, Tel. 2782707.
Hostal Dany, Tel. 1933979.
Hostal Claudia Paola Balnerio, Tel. 813264.

Delicious food options abound in Coroico, from **Back-Stube** one block from the main plaza, to **Hostal & Restaurant El Cafetal** Tel. 01933979, on the hill out of town, with more gorgeous views, and delicious cooking. For Italian try **Los Osos**, just off the main plaza, or **Las Hamacas** near the movie theater. Coroico is a wonderful place to spend a relaxing weekend walking, swimming, eating wonderful food and watching life goes by on the main plaza.

Pachama'Raft, only one hour from Coroico is Pachama'Raft offering cabañas for 20 Bs., a campsite for 10 Bs. where you can also rent camping gears, with kitchen, showers, bathrooms and swimming pool. There is also the possibility to go wild on various rafting excursion. Tels. 71500556 - 71255810. E-mail: southamericarafting@hotmail.com Or contact in La Paz **Terra Andina**. www.terra-andina.com

The road from Coroico continues to **Caranavi**, a growing commercial center for the Bolivian tropics. In Caranavi, the road

veers to the right to Alto Beni, San Borja, Rurrenabaque and Trinidad. To the left, the road heads to the gold mining villages of Guanay, Tipuani, and Mapiri. In the summer – the rainy season in Bolivia, it can be hot and humid, and Yungas roads may be blocked by landslides from time to time… So flexible travel plans are essential. The area is worth visiting if you are interested in seeing gold miners working in a Wild-West-type environment. Tipuani is an important gold mining center that dates to pre-Columbian times.

Rurrenabaque

(See Beni Chapter on this important tourist destination located in the Beni Department, across the river from San Buenaventura and the Department of La Paz).

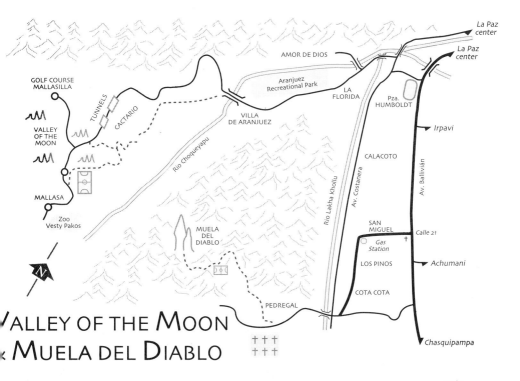

VALLEY OF THE MOON
& MUELA DEL DIABLO

La Paz

1 Tourist information
2 Police
3 Immigration
4 Entel
5 Post office
6 City hall
7 LAB
8 TAM
9 Aerosur
10 Amazonas

Markets
11 Bueno Aires
    Uyustus
    Graneros
12 Rodriguez
13 Sopocachi
14 Camacho

15 Bolivian Congress

Churches
16 San Francisco
17 Maria Auxiliadora
18 San Juan de Dios
19 San Sebastián
20 Santo Domingo
21 El Carmen
22 La Merced
23 San Pedro
24 La Recoleta
25 San Augustin

Museums
26 Kusillo
27 Costumbrista & Gold
28 Domingo Murillo
29 Quirquincho
30 National Art
31 Cathedral
32 Etnografia & Folklore
33 Tiwanaku
34 Contemporaneo
35 Coca

Cultural Centers
36 Goethe institute
37 Centro Boliviano
    Americano
38 Alianza Frances
39 Bristish Council
40 Teatro Municipal
41 Casa de la Cultu

--- Gran Poder Rou

LA PAZ
TITICACA LAKE

1

LOCATION	DISTANCE IN KMS		ALTITUDE
	PARTIAL	TOTAL	
La Paz	Kms	00	3577
El Alto	11	11	-
Rio Seco	5	16	-
Batallas	44	60	-
Huarina	14	74	3819
Achacachi	19	93	3823
Huarina	-	74	3819
Huatajata	13	87	3824
Tiquina	15	102	3414
Copacabana	56	158	3814
Rio Seco	-	16	-
Laja	20	36	3843
Tiwanacu	36	72	3943
Guaqui	19	91	3811
Desaguadero	23	114	3810
Achacachi	-	93	3823
Belen	3	96	-
Carabuco	58	154	3818
Pto. Acosta	39	193	3833

2

LOCATION	DISTANCE IN KMS		ALTITUDE
	PARTIAL	TOTAL	
La Paz	Kms	00	3577
La Cumbre	26	26	4643
Sacramento	43	69	-
Yolosa	22	91	1185
Caranavi	75	166	606
Santa Ana	76	242	372
Yolosa	-	91	1185
Coroico	7	98	1715
Coripata	34	132	1760
Caranavi	-	166	606
Teoponte	66	232	-
Guanay	-	-	-
Tipuani	-	-	-

3

LOCATION	DISTANCE IN KMS		ALTITUDE
	PARTIAL	TOTAL	
La Paz	Kms.	00	3577
El Alto	11	11	4082
Calamarca	16	58	3954
Ayo Ayo	24	82	3875
Patacamaya	20	102	3779
Sica Sica	21	123	3917
Panduro	19	142	4325
Caracollo	48	190	3772
Oruro	39	229	3709
Caracollo	-	190	3772
Vinto	22	375	2526
Quillacollo	4	379	2436
Cochabamba	14	393	5258

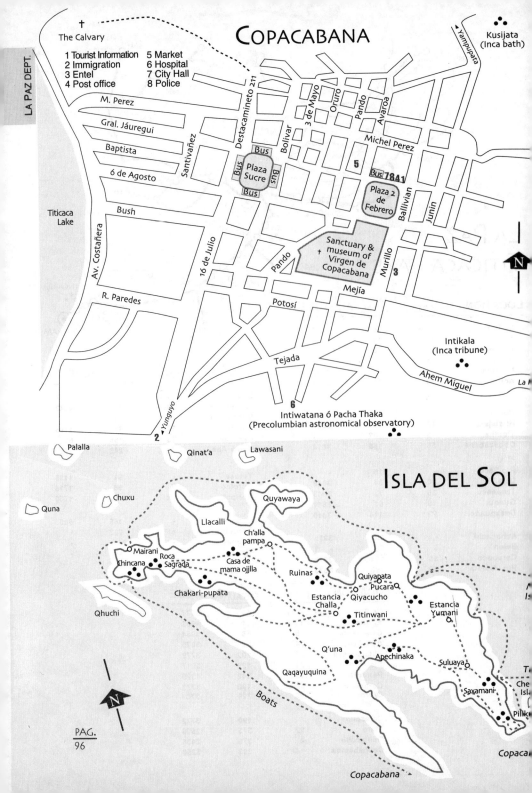

COPACABANA

The Calvary

1 Tourist Information 5 Market
2 Immigration 6 Hospital
3 Entel 7 City Hall
4 Post office 8 Police

LA PAZ DEPT.

M. Perez
Gral. Jáuregui
Baptista
6 de Agosto
Bush
R. Paredes

Destacamineto 211
Santivañez
16 de Julio
Pando
Yunguyo

Bolivar
3 de Mayo
Oruro
Pando
Avaroa
Michel Perez
Ballivian
Junin
Murillo

Titicaca Lake
Av. Costañera

Plaza Sucre
Bus

Plaza 2 de Febrero

5

Bus 7 8 4 1

Sanctuary & museum of Virgen de Copacabana

3

Mejía
Potosí
Tejada

6

Intiwatana ó Pacha Thaka
(Precolumbian astronomical observatory)

Intikala
(Inca tribune)

Ahem Miguel

Yampupata

Kusijata
(Inca bath)

N

2

ISLA DEL SOL

Palalla
Qinat'a
Lawasani

Quna
Chuxu

Llacalli
Quyawaya
Ch'alla pampa

Mairani
Roca Sagrada
Chincana
Casa de mama ojilla
Ruinas
Quiyapata
Pucara

Chakari-pupata

Qhuchi

Estancia Challa
Qiyacucho
Titinwani
Estancia Yumani

Q'una
Apechinaka
Suluaya

Qaqayuquina
Saxamani
Pilk

Boats

Copacabana

Copacabana

N

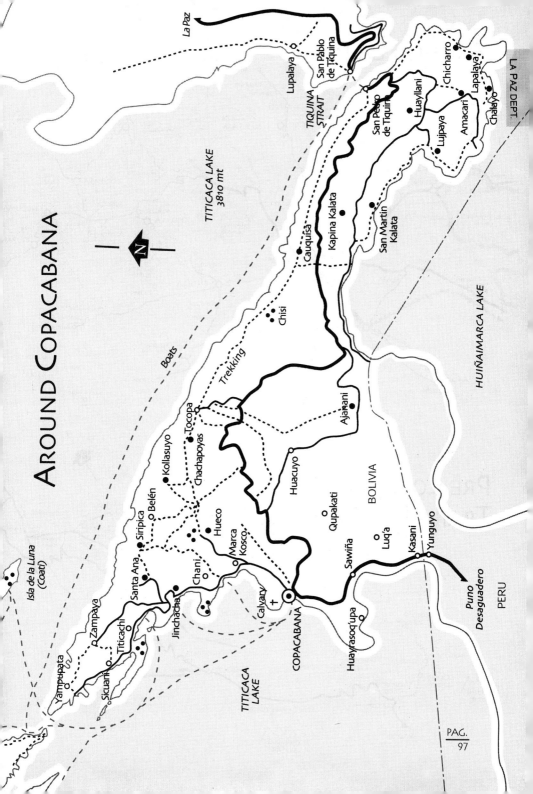

AROUND COPACABANA

N

La Paz

Lupalaya

San Pablo de Tiquina

San Pablo de Tiquina

TIQUINA STRAIT

Chicharro

Lapalaya

San Pedro de Tiquina

Huayllani

Lujipaya

Amacari

Challoyo

LA PAZ DEPT.

Cauquisa

Kapina Kalata

San Martin Kalata

TITICACA LAKE 3810 mt

HUIÑAIMARCA LAKE

Chisi

Boats

Trekking

Tocopa

Ajanani

Kollasuyo

Chachapoyas

Huacuyo

BOLIVIA

Belén

Qupakati

Siripica

Santa Ana

Hueco

Marca Kosco

Chani

Luq'a

Kasani

Yunguyo

Jindhacha

Calvary

COPACABANA

Sawiña

Puno Desaguadero

Titicachi

Zampaya

Isla de la Luna (Coati)

Yampupata

Sicuani

Huayrasoq'upa

PERU

TITICACA LAKE

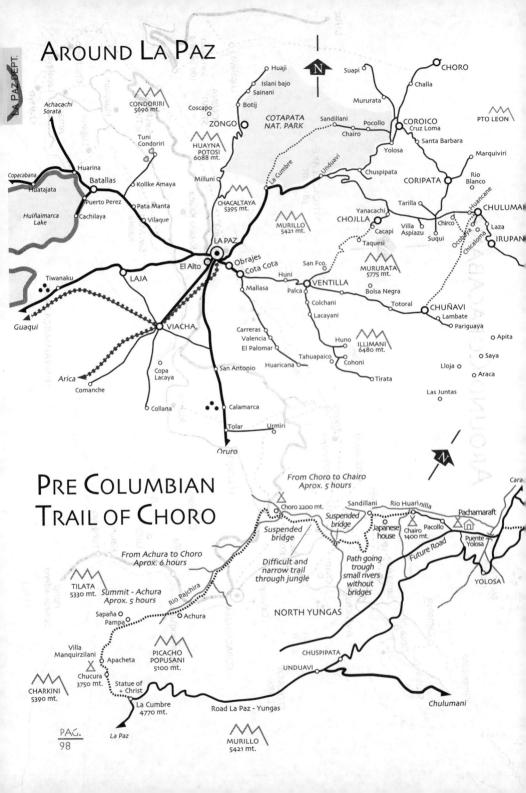

AROUND LA PAZ

Achacachi
Sorata

CONDORIRI
5696 mt.

Coscapo

Huaji

Islani bajo
Sainani

Botij

ZONGO

COTAPATA
NAT. PARK

Sandillani

Pocollo

Chairo

Suapi

Challa

Mururata

CHORO

PTO LEON

COROICO
Cruz Loma

Santa Barbara

Marquiviri

Tuni
Condoriri

HUAYNA
POTOSI
6088 mt.

Yolosa

Rio
Blanco

Copacabana

Huarina

Batallas

Kollke Amaya

Milluni

La Cumbre

Unduavi

Chuspipata

CORIPATA

Huatajata

Puerto Perez

Pata Manta

CHACALTAYA
5395 mt.

Tarilla

Huancane

CHULUMANI

Huiñaimarca
Lake

Cachilaya

Vilaque

MURILLO
5421 mt.

Yanacachi

CHOJLLA

Villa
Aspiazu

Chirco

Suqui

Ocobaya

Laza

Chicaloma

IRUPANA

Cacapi

Taquesi

Tiwanaku

LAJA

El Alto

Obrajes

Cota Cota

San Fco.

Huni

VENTILLA

MURURATA
5775 mt.

Guaqui

VIACHA

Mallasa

Palca

Bolsa Negra

Colchani

Totoral

CHUÑAVI

Lambate

Arica

Comanche

Copa
Lacaya

Carreras
Valencia
El Palomar

San Antonio

Lacayani

Huaricana

Tahuapaico

Huno

ILLIMANI
6480 mt.

Cohoni

Pariguaya

Apita

Saya

Lloja

Araca

Collana

Calamarca

Tirata

Las Juntas

Tolar

Urmiri

Oruro

PRE COLUMBIAN
TRAIL OF CHORO

From Choro to Chairo
Aprox. 5 hours

Choro 2200 mt.

Suspended
bridge

Suspended
bridge

Sandillani

Japanese
house

Rio Huari nilla

Chairo
1400 mt.

Pachamaraft

Pacollo

Puente
Yolosa

Cara

Difficult and
narrow trail
through jungle

Path going
trough
small rivers
without
bridges

Future Road

YOLOSA

From Achura to Choro
Aprox. 6 hours

TILATA
5330 mt.

Summit - Achura
Aprox. 5 hours

Rio Pajchira

Sapaña

Pampa

Achura

NORTH YUNGAS

CHUSPIPATA

Villa
Manquirzilani

Apacheta

PICACHO
POPUSANI
5100 mt.

UNDUAVI

CHARKINI
5390 mt.

Chucura
3750 mt.

Statue of
+ Christ

La Cumbre
4770 mt.

Road La Paz - Yungas

Chulumani

La Paz

MURILLO
5421 mt.

HIKES AROUND VENTILLA

1- Palca 4-5 hours

2- Taquesi trek 2 days

3- Yunga Cruz 3 days

Coripata 1734 mt.
CHULUMANI
Tajma
Loza
Ocobaya
Chirca
Chicaloma
Irupana
La Plazuela

La Paz — Florida — Sta. Rosa — Pte. Villa
Yanacachi

ACAMANI 4540 mt.

ASTILLERO

2

Chojlla 2280 mt.
Chajlla

YUNGA CRUZ 3920 mt.

MURILLO 5421 mt.

Laguna Wara Waran

Cacapi 3000 mt.

CUCHITUACA 3980 mt.

Taquesi 3800 mt.

KHALACIUDAD 4378 mt.

Apacheta

San. Francisco

Yungas

Tacapaya

3

Las mil gradas

Laguna Animas

VENTILLA

Palca

MURURATA 5775 mt.

Bolsa Negra

Chuñavi 3800 mt.

LA PAZ

Ovejuyo
Chasquipampa

Cañon de Palca

Colchani

Pacuani

Tres Rios

Totoral Pampa

Khanuma

Lambate

1

Copacabana

Aguila

Totoral

ILLIMANI 6480 mt.

Rio Coroico Santa Bárbara bridge
rata dge aña hrs

COROICO

Ayacucho

Caranavi ►

Iturralde

Coripata ►

Miraflores ►
Vagante
Cruz Loma

3 1

Julio Suazo Cuenca

2

+ 6

4

+ 7

Pool

Bus

R. Miranda

+ 8

Water falls 2:30 hrs

5

Pando

Antezana

Pacheco

UCHUMACHI 2548 mt. 1:30 hrs

Av. Monsignor Thomas Manning

Sagárnaga

R. Ortiz

Tomás Monje

Yolosita
Choro Inca Trail
Cotapata Nat. Park

9

Yolosa La Paz ▼

Carmen Pampa Universidad UAC ▼

1 Tourist Information	6 Church
2 Entel	7 Madres de
3 Post office	Clarisa convent
4 City Hall	8 Calvario church
5 Market	9 Hospital

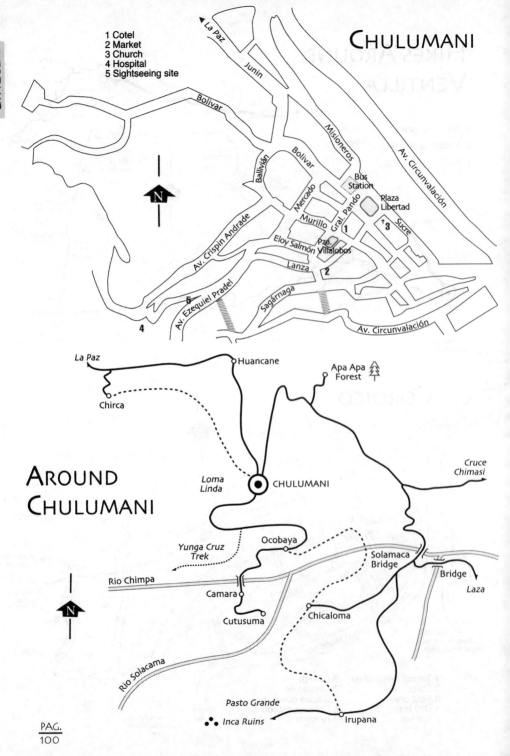

CHULUMANI

1 Cotel
2 Market
3 Church
4 Hospital
5 Sightseeing site

La Paz

Junin

Bolivar

Misioneros

Av. Circunvalación

Ballivián

Bolivar

Mercado

Bus Station

Plaza Libertad

Gral. Pando

Sucre

Av. Crispin Andrade

Murillo

1

† 3

Eloy Salmón

Pza. Villalobos

Lanza

2

Av. Ezequiel Pradel

5

Sagárnaga

4

Av. Circunvalación

AROUND CHULUMANI

La Paz

Huancane

Apa Apa Forest

Chirca

Cruce Chimasi

Loma Linda

CHULUMANI

Yunga Cruz Trek

Ocobaya

Solamaca Bridge

Rio Chimpa

Bridge

Camara

Laza

Cutusuma

Chicaloma

Rio Solacama

Pasto Grande

Inca Ruins

Irupana

KUSILLO:
MUSEUM OF SCIENCE AND PLAY

BY WENDY MCFARREN, PH.D.

Print, audio, video and computers are typical definitions of learning technologies. Interactive children's science museums extend this definition to include games, exhibits and other media that foment curiosity and learning in kids and adults. The Kusillo, in La Paz, Bolivia has further explored the notion of appropriate learning technologies and content for an urban population that is diverse culturally and socio-economically. Over the last four years the Kusillo has designed interactive educational programs on issues such as tuberculosis, measles, AIDS, ecosystem destruction and in this process faced two types of challenges: technology and content.

The technology challenge is to find the right combination of methods and to expand notions of interactivity so as to include: physical interaction (hands-on experiences), social interaction (communication exchange with others), and individual interaction (starting from personal experience). The content challenge is to develop socially relevant material and consider culture not only thematically but as a strategic resource.

Design of Educational Learning Technologies

Children who live in the city of La Paz/El Alto area internalize the contradictions and dynamic processes that Bolivia faces. Over 45% of the population still live in rural areas and speak native languages such as Aymara or Quechua. Although this rate is high for Latin America, urbanization is a reality and fuels the growth of cities such as El Alto, a twin city to La Paz. Children in La Paz and El Alto are diverse culturally and economically. Recent migrants still maintain language and traditions, but are rapidly absorbed into the world of pinball halls, television, Digimon and Pokemon. Other children may have great-grandparents who lived in rural areas yet no longer speak a native language, and reject an ethnic label. Families of other children are in the upper-middle classes, speak only Spanish, and have lived in urban areas for generations. These identity boundaries shift with education, with intermarriage and with the influence of media on knowledge and practices.

Economically, some children are very poor and suffer the ills associated with poverty: tuberculosis, diarrhea and respiratory infections. Others frequent McDonalds or Burger King and are beginning to suffer the ills of plenty, such as obesity. All Bolivians have some universal concerns, such as reproductive health, AIDS, and other infectious diseases including Chagas, a viral disease transmitted by a local insect. The kids from different socio-cultural groups interact with each other very little, although they share influences through the media and in cultural forms through dances and music. In La Paz and El Alto cultures are multiple, and constantly changing their boundaries of practices and forms of knowledge.

The Kusillo opened its doors in December of 1997 with the goal of creating a new educational experience for children that was interactive, fun and relevant. Its challenge was to create interactive educational technologies that respond to this diversity and to the social realities La Paz children face. How could it design educational materials that permitted multiple forms of expression, and that responded to the complex and dynamic cultural characteristics of the population, and to the social realities of a country with a high level of poverty indicators?

Within a perspective of the "democratization of science" (in Spanish the word is popularización), the Kusillo has two educational programs in health and the environment, in addition to exhibit areas on technology, pre-school development and body in movement. Each health program lasts three months and involves a semi-structured experience for school groups.

An Example: Learning Technologies About Tuberculosis

Tuberculosis is a serious health problem in Bolivia. Over 10,000 people are infected with tuberculosis every year. The Kusillo designers faced a social reality that children and adults needed to know the causes of this serious public health threat and how to prevent it. They wanted the public to understand the scientific nature of the problem, how the bacteria attacks and the role of antibiotics and good nutrition and hygiene in fighting the disease. Their intention was to make visitors curious about the subject, to find the materials relevant to their own experience and to feel like they were bearers of knowledge. The educational program designers knew that the public was diverse socio-economically, generationally, and ethnically. They set off to design "technologies" - instruments that would facilitate a learning process on this serious health problem.

The first "technology" was a puppet show called "Tb Tb," about a villain Don Tb who came to attack a community. He is a slimy elongated green character who emulates a nasty bacillo bacterium. The Kuzillo, the hero, comes to the rescue bearing his Andean clown face and vaquero hat, and to explain to the public about the different forms of bacteria and the importance of good nutrition and antibiotics. Before and after the puppet show, facilitators ask kids what they know about tuberculosis and if they know anyone with the disease. They open up a dialogue with the kids to get them to talk with each other about the problem and explore what they already know.

Kids then move to an area in the museum filled with interactive games and exhibits, the next form of technology utilized. Here they find a bingo game with body-sized playing boards (light boxes) constructed of wood and with graphic images of the Kuzillo and Don Tb figures. The bingo game invites the kids to play and touch which opens up their curiosity for learning about the dangers of and solutions to tuberculosis.

The kids then move on to an x-ray light box such as one finds in a doctor's office. Here they view large x-ray size transparencies of healthy and diseased lungs and images downloaded from the Internet on real tuberculosis bacteria. They can also see examples of antibiotics and different types of bacteria that they learned about in the puppet show. The Bingo game and x-ray station reinforces puppet show messages.

Kids can then pretend to be doctors in an examining room and play a Jeopardy game about the history of the vaccine. The next technology they interact with is a video about a man with tuberculosis, how he became infected and how he found treatment. Before they leave, kids who participate in the tuberculosis educational program receive a poster version of the Tb Bingo game for them to take home to play and thus remember key messages learned at the Kusillo. Those with access to the WWW can play a web version of the tuberculosis bingo game. Finally, the teachers receive a guide that allows them to follow up and reinforce key concepts.

This use of technologies successfully facilitates a learning process that takes two hours. When they leave the museum, children from various socio-economic classes and age groups are knowledgeable about the tuberculosis bacteria, how it causes disease and how they can protect themselves through antibiotics, good hygiene and nutrition. They come out feeling like they are knowers and can know even more. This feeling contrasts with low levels of self esteem that most students feel as a result of their experience in the formal educational system, which stresses that they know too little and need to be taught.

The Kusillo has used a similar methodology to turberculosis on issues such as measles, reproductive health, AIDS, ecosystems, biodiversity and urban contamination. In the following year it will develop interactive educational programs on nutrition, early childhood development, respiratory infections and Chagas.

THE TECHNOLOGY CHALLENGE

This narrative of the Kusillo's experience with tuberculosis points to a number of methodological lessons learned in the design of educational technologies.

Multiple Methods

The reaffirmation of messages through different media is important to foment curiosity, keep kids' attention, make learning fun and permit different points of entry. Technology as an educational tool should not be constrained by traditional definitions of print, video, audio or computer. In addition to the use of printed materials, videos, computer games and the Internet, the Kusillo defines technology more broadly to include instruments such as puppets, interactive games and exhibits. Some of the criteria for choosing the right media involve ease of interaction without guidance, graphic appeal, durability, safety, and effectiveness of the interaction of the child with the technology in stimulating learning.

Three Pronged Interactivity

These technological instruments must be interactive in three dimensions: they must be experiential, must foment communication with others, and must begin from one's own reality. Interactivity does not simply involve pressing a button on a computer keyboard.

THE CONTENT CHALLENGE

The second set of lessons the Kusillo has learned in the design of educational technologies on issues such as tuberculosis relates to content. Its concern was how to develop technologies that are socially relevant and culturally strategic (not just thematic).

Social Relevance

The Kusillo's challenge was to design technologies with content that made sense. Social relevance involves understanding the social problems and relationships of the diverse population the Museum served. In a country as poor as Bolivia, relevant content had to deal with problems in the environment and health, including tuberculosis, Chagas, diarrhea, other respiratory diseases and environmental destruction. However, in a highly stratified society, content developers could not assume that all the Bolivians faced the same set of problems. For instance, the nutrition program needs to consider the opposite extremes of malnutrition and over-abundance in its messages.

The content challenge also implied ensuring that even the poorest sectors of the population participated in the educational programs. This was accomplished with innovative ticketing, sponsorship and project counterpart policies.

An important content principle for the Kusillo is to center attention on health rather than on illness. Messages must be presented in a positive, solution-finding light, although they refer to serious problems. As citizens of a developing country, Bolivian children are accustomed to negative messages and generally have low levels of self-esteem about themselves and their country. Many educational programs offer a depressing and tragic image of illness. For the Kusillo, dwelling on poverty and illness does not stimulate a search for solutions, but, generates a passive and powerless attitude. The content challenge is to recognize that these issues are serious and often structural, yet it is important to stimulate a quest for knowledge and solutions where kids can be actors in change.

For instance, in the tuberculosis program, facilitators focused kids' attention on how to eat better to develop better immune systems, to recognize the importance of hygiene in the transmittal of the disease and to understand that vaccinations can protect newborns against the bacteria. Equally, the environmental program facilitates a process by which kids think of solutions to urban contamination and to ecosystem destruction, inciuiding positive actions that they can take.

Culture as a Methodological Issue

In the development of its educational programs, Kusillo designers consider cultur-

al issues as a strategic resource to better facilitate a learning process and not so much in thematic terms. In the tuberculosis case, for example, the figure of the Kuzillo is a known character in urban folkloric dances and kids easily identify with it across all social classes. They understand the Kuzillo as a hero and the good guy. He is the bearer of all the good news in regards to fighting tuberculosis. The selection of appropriate icons breaks down learning barriers and creates a personal identification with the learning process.

Another example of how the Kusillo uses culture as a strategic resource is in the pre-school area. Museum educators wanted to implement a space for pre-schoolers to explore pre-mathematics. They built a traditional street market where the kids weigh, classify, compare shapes and colors and count. They made an explicit decision not to build a supermarket as is common in other children's museums. They chose a local street market because kids from all social classes in Bolivia can relate to it as part of their daily experience. The street market is a strategic element to facilitate a pre-mathematics learning process.

Finally, culture is also strategic as far as language, vocabulary and selection of media are concerned. Children who come from bilingual families may not understand written forms of instruction and may relate better to oral communication. Children are the bearers of culture and the goal of learning technologies is to foment their self-expression rather than to teach them who they are.

Future Ideas: Putting Technology and Content Into Childrens Hands

Everyday brings a new experience for the Kusillo and its designers feel challenged to continue developing new educational instruments that facilitate a process of learning and communicating about issues that matter to kids and to society as a whole. The reward comes from thinking of new methods that go beyond traditional definitions of technology. The key question is what technology works best to facilitate a learning process that is relevant, fun, interactive and durable. A future challenge for the Kusillo will be to facilitate a process by which kids develop their own learning technologies and define their own content.

Wendy McFarren is Director of the **Kusillo Cultural Complex**, La Paz, Bolivia. She can be reached at wendy@kusillo.org. For more information on the Kusillo, visit http://www.kusillo.org.

IF YOU BELIEVE...:
LA PAZ'S WITCH MARKET

BY JOSÉ ANTONIO ARUQUIPA Z.

Just three blocks from the church of San Francisco, along Calle Linares, is one of the most mysterious places in La Paz: *El Mercado de las Brujas*. Almost unnoticed by tourists who are more interested in purchasing handicrafts, sellers of this market offer the most peculiar goods: countless types of herbs to cure illnesses, strange amulets to help "steal" the heart of the one of your dreams, offerings to be burned for *Pachamama* (the Mother Earth) and rare mixtures of ingredients to be used by sorcerers in their evil-doing.

A Family Legacy

Ninfa Aliaga, 78, has been in charge of the business of selling goods for witchcraft since her mother died. "My mother taught me all the secrets I know," said Aliaga, "and I am supposed to teach them to someone who will use the knowledge in a good way. As my grandmother instructed my mother: "What we know must be used to help people, not hurt them."

To find out the origin of a misfortune or foresee the future to avoid unwanted misfortunes, one must consult a *yatiri*, an Aymara fortune teller who can be found patiently sitting on the narrow street of the Witch Market, adding the final touch of strangeness to the place.

Julio Tudela, 45, a *yatiri* from Charazani, has many services to offer. "I can read your future for only 10 Bolivianos," he said. "No matter what, I discover the cause of your sorrow and help you fight against the sorcery that is making you unhappy."

"I'm not like the other fake *yatiris*, I'm strong. If you want to, I can prepare a good *milluchada* (a special offering for the goddess *Pachamama*). I guarantee positive results. The price? Only 350 Bolivianos."

Other *yatiris* at the *Mercado de las Brujas* charge more because, for them, it's merely business, said Tudela. But for Tudela, helping people is a sacred mission inherited from his ancestors.

Healing Ordinary Health Problems

Other than offering happiness and manipulating forces beyond human reach, herb sellers say they provide cures for ordinary health problems such as toothaches and headaches. They also sell medicinal plants that provide relief for serious diseases like heart attacks or rheumatism. There are herbs to cure just about everything.

"The herb I sell the most is *romero*," said Bertha de Zapana, 42. "It is good for headaches and taking baths with; it helps keep sorcerers away. Eucalyptus leaves are also a favorite of my customers and can be used for colds, coughs and sore throats."

However, little money is earned from the daily sale of these medicinal herbs; one woman said she only sells about 15-19 Bs-worth of products per day. But a wealth of secrets can be found.

"This is a place where you can find everything you need," said one vendor, "especially if you believe in witchcraft. But if you don't, I think it's better to stay away and not get involved."

For the true believers, taking the time to wander these streets might just be worth it.

BARGAIN HUNTING AT THE FERIA IN EL ALTO

BY TIM WILSON

For many *paceños,* there are only three reasons to go to El Alto. First, because you have to go through it if you want to catch a plane. Second, because you have to go through it if you want to drive to Lake Titicaca. The third reason actually involves spending some time in the much-maligned city itself — hunting for bargains at the *Mercado 16 de Julio* on a Sunday morning.

You name it, it'll be there somewhere in the shabby side streets off the town's main drag, Avenida 16 de Julio. From barbecues to shampoo, Amazonian herbs to truck tires, it is one vast outdoor department store.

But here there are no street signs, let alone floor plans telling you where to find the electrical goods, lingerie or lounge-room furniture departments. The best thing to do is just start at one end of the Avenida and wander up and down the seemingly-endless maze of back streets full of, well, stuff! After a while, you realize there are streets allocated to specific goods — one filled with stalls selling every imaginable part of a car, another clogged with dining and lounge suites, and so on.

Thousands of people from all over the province visit the market every Sunday. The air is filled with the smell and smoke from cauldrons of *chicharron,* except in the streets that double as open sewers. On a sunny morning, the atmosphere is carnival-like, a crazy muddle of vendors, buyers and suppliers, all set against the improbable pristine backdrop of the snow-capped *cordillera.*

But what attracts the most attention are the numerous streets filled with clothes stalls. Block after block is lined with small mountains of new and used clothes, and it is here that some real bargains can be found. If you're prepared to dig, the chances are you'll find something to your taste and size somewhere along the way. Size can be a problem though, especially for a lanky *extranjero;* most of the clothes are suited to the somewhat more vertically-challenged Andean.

Bartering is the order of the day, especially in the permanent shops behind the temporary street stalls. It's best to take a local friend with you and stay out of sight while they haggle if you want to avoid paying *gringo* prices. But for most of the goods on the street, the prices are so low it's hardly worth haggling.

I asked the vendor where on earth all this stuff came from. She said most of it was from the United States, imported in huge bales that she buys for between $100 and $120 each. While some of the clothes seem to be almost unused, there is also a lot of second-hand gear, so it's best to check for holes, stains, missing buttons, etc. The small mountains of socks are definitely second-hand; not too many for size 12 feet, but a real bargain at 2 to 3 Bolivianos a pair.

COCA MUSEUM EDUCATES AND INFORMS

BY ALISON TILLING

Tucked away in a courtyard off Calle *Linares,* it is easy to pass the Coca Museum without even noticing its existence. But visiting this informative and popular museum is well worth the Bs.7 entry fee.

Founded in 1997 by psychiatrist Jorge Hurtado, the museum's main aim is to inform people about coca, its usage and effects, and the difference between coca and cocaine. On entry, visitors are shown the order in which to view the exhibits — surprisingly many for such a small place — and are given a guidebook in their own language, or the nearest approximation to it. Guests can then proceed at their own pace, asking as many questions as they like of the person at the front desk.

Variety is the strength of this museum. Beginning with a factual time-line showing the first evidence of coca use through to today's cocaine developments, the visitor proceeds through exhibits on how to chew the leaves, how cocaine affects humans, and the manufacture of the drug. Most information is given through the guidebook and the huge collection of photographs, though there is also a growing collection of artifacts.

At first, emphasis is given to the long history of coca chewing in South America, and the beneficial effects it can have. Evidence of coca leaf usage has been found in pre-Columbian remains throughout the northern part of the continent. The con-

tinuing importance of coca in Andean culture is also discussed. Traditionally, the outside world has regarded coca as a retarding factor in Andean societies. The museum reassesses this view and demonstrates the ways in which coca is used in religious ceremonies and to read the future. The correct way to chew coca is also shown in some detail. After studying this you'll never get it wrong again!

The next part of the museum is the most interesting. Coca has nutritional value, long recognized by the Andean peoples, but only recently investigated by scientific bodies, such as the Altitude Biology Institute in Bolivia (IBBA). Their studies have shown that chewing coca provides the chewee with fiber, calcium and protein, as well as a greater tolerance of both hard work and altitude. The display of the findings immediately precedes the explaination of the use of coca in mining, and makes the miners' dependence on coca all the more understandable on a scientific as well as social level.

Another of the strengths of this tiny museum is its realism, and nowhere is this more evident than in its treatment of the development of cocaine.

Explaining that the aim is to inform and satisfy curiosity safely, the displays go on to discuss the way in which crude cocaine paste is extracted from coca leaves, the cost of this, and its impact on society.

Shocking pictures of cocaine addicts, their methods of consumption, and attempts to eradicate coca in Bolivia, are enough to put most people off even the thought of trying the drug. The attitude is one of detached information, and thus achieves its objective effectively. The role of the U.S. as the biggest consumer of cocaine, and as the force trying to eradicate coca in Bolivia (a policy that in itself is causing myriad problems) is emphasized and discussed, though the museum never becomes jingoistic: it does not have to. The facts themselves, shown as starkly and carefully as they are here, are enough for visitors to make their own judgments.

Finally, the displays treat the use of coca and cocaine in medicine, particularly as a local anesthetic, and in other products such as Coca-Cola. Some fairly gory pictures of early operations add an extra edge to this part of the museum, as does the realization of just how many modern, easily available medicines contain cocaine or its derivatives.

As museums go, this is one of the best I've seen anywhere. Space is well used, displays are varied, and the overall tone is one of dispassionate information rather than hysterical bias. Perhaps most telling of all is the Visitors' Book. A quick glance through shows that all nationalities and ages visit, and enjoy, this museum — and leave properly informed about one of the world's most infamous drugs.

Museo de la Coca: Calle Linares 906, Tel. 2311998.

For more information on Coca leave:
Cocaine The Legend by Jorge Hurtado Gumucio, Ed. Accion Andina , Hisbol; La Paz.

A Gringo's Guide to the La Paz Night Life

by Paddy Grant

From Cerveza to Ch'aqui in a City "Almost Crime Free".

Mongo's Rock Bottom Cafe on calle Hermanos Manchego is really the only English run bar suggested by the Lonely Planet, the travellers' useful guide book. However, it is not the only welcoming bar for us gringos in the city of La Paz. This week a team of volunteers set out on a bender, and for this reporter it was work!

The aims of this brief were really three fold: first, to investigate the bars who actively welcome gringos second to investigate safety for female visitors, and third, to keep going and avoid a hangover...

When entering a new city it is always a priority for those of us who are young at heart to investigate where to go and what to do. Sometimes it ends in disaster other times you find a gem. The conclusions are really entirely down to personal choice but its nice to think you are not going in blind.

So in a week that involved an interview with the general of the tourist police, immigration, five o clock bedtimes (a.m. of course) and really enough booze to float a small navy, hopefully there is enough to be going on.

Over the week seven bars in total were visited: the renowned Mongo's, Diesel, Dead Stroke, Waykis, Sol y Luna, La Luna and Malegria. It may have been fun to grade them, but that idea of that was discarded with the realization that as the week wore on the chances were that less

and less people would have the same appetite throughow the entire week.

There is, I am afraid, a rather sinister side to all this, many muggings, robberies and violent crimes occur in La Paz under the cover of dark.

Without trying to sound like a scare monger it is important to be objective with such things. Face facts-you could be drunk in the smallest of towns in England and encounter violence and theft. It's a risk here and it's a risk in China. The problem here is that drunken gringos could not be more obvious targets to criminals. How often does a Bolivian wail "I love you baby" on his way home in the early hours? On Tuesday, I popped in for a chat with the chief of the Tourism Police, Lt. Col. Juán Alanes Villarroel. We discussed the worrying numbers of muggings, not only in the street but also in the back of taxis and buses. Although a good number of tourist muggings occur at night, the tourist police do not have a clear statistic on these cases and they only work from 8 a.m. to 9 p.m. "La Paz Night life has become almost crime free," said Alanes.

When I asked the Colonel which bars to stay away from, he said: "La Luna is formerly a risk, but this year (by 15 January) there have only been 3 knife attacks."

So that's down to personal choice but really worth a visit for a pitcher of beer and a game of dice.

THE BARS...

Mongo's, on Hermanos Manchego 2444- Watch out for the slow service. The food took ages to arrive but to be fair it was worth waiting for. The menu is varied; you can have Bolivian or western. Good selection of drinks, although the European beers are served warm. And, the seats can be rather unaccomodating.

Malegria, on Goita 155-This is a nice bar; the most interesting thing is getting served. As a rule there are more people behind the bar than in the room, yet only 2 or 3 actually serve. What the others do is an enigma.

Again there is a good selection of the normal cocktails, beers and shots. It is very Bolivian but they make the effort to speak English, and as a gringo you generally do not have to queue. Taxis are constantly waiting outside in the early hours so getting back home safe and sound isn't a huge problem.

Waykis, near Plaza Uyuni- This is an amazing place. Den-like in ambiance, the fleece lined chairs and psychedelic murals create an atmosphere incredibly conducive to drinking. Here along with the usual suspects on the menu one can order a bucket filled with various intoxicants. At 35 Bolivianos they are a bargain. As the method of drinking is with a spoon and a straw, you have to see it to believe it. The staff is great. They do all they can to welcome you, even offering you a choice of music. They also provide complimentary coca leaves to chew on. nice...

Diesel, on Av. 20 Octubre- Very western, and slightly expensive, Diesel is one of those bars where you could be in any city in the world. They offer lots of western drinks including Gordon's gin, at a price you wouldn't argue about, in England. Overall though its atmosphere is good, the menus are in English, and they have an empty Bath tub outside for drunken reflection. Well worth a visit.

Sol y Luna, on Calle Cochabamba, one block up the Prado. We really enjoyed this bar. Not only is the service great but they welcome you with open arms. The cocktail list is expansive and they serve western lagers. Prices are very reasonable especially on the singani (Bolivia's most popular made out of grapes beverage). The bar itself is decorated by bizzarre pictures apparently by local artists. Downstairs is a television with comfy seats, a real group area.

Dead Stroke, on Av. 6 Agosto- pool and snooker bar with 6 tables, really very pleasant midweek for a game of pool and many glasses of lager. The bar staff is exceptionally friendly, the prices are great. Beers, shots and cocktails are all there. The menu is pretty expansive, buffalo chicken wings are a speciality. The music is great, everything from the Beatles to U-2. The decor is nice, many wonderful bar room signs including one comparing Pool and Sex, and claiming you can enjoy both without being particulary good at either activity. Go look, it tickles me every time.

La Luna, on the corner of Murillo and Oruro.On the upside there were no stabbings on our visit. I think its possibly a bit of a myth. The bar is nice, you can order coffe, tea, "mate de coca", and various proper alcoholic beverages. We visited it on a Tuesday and it was really pleasant.

Just the right atmosphere to chill out over a couple of paceñas and chat. The service was great, the staff friendly and the prices are reasonable. The positioning of the bar is not the very best, as they say in blighty, possibly not one for the lone females, but do visit.

HOW TO REMAIN A VEGETARIAN IN LA PAZ

BY ELLIS AUGER

VEGETARIANISM IS A RELATIVELY NEW TREND IN LA PAZ.

Whilst more and more people worldwide are committing to a vegetarian diet, it would appear, to the casual observer at least, that La Paz's restaurants fail to cater to this ever-growing and increasingly important niche in the food market. Whether this phenomenon is a large part in to the Bolivian culture which has yet to embrace vegetarianism is disputable and would need another article. It was against this background though, that I decided an article on the paucity of vegetarian restaurants in La Paz would be of some interest and use, both to the city's ever growing international community and to its native population.

As someone who has a number of vegetarian friends, my first outlet for finding out what La Paz has to offer was an obvious choice. The collective opinion was that the city presents two immediate alternatives in terms of restaurants or snack bars entirely devoted to vegetarian foods as well as a number of other options which proffer worthy vegetarian dishes in addition to meat cuisine.

The quaint **Laksmi Restaurant** is situated at 213 on the corner of Calle Sagárnaga and Calle Murillo. Essentially this is a Hindu Restaurant, with everything from the menus to the music reflecting this fact. For 4 Bs., I ate the recommendation of a Samosa de Vegeta, a pie stuffed full of exotic vegetables. Indeed, the most pricy option on the Menu was a dish of rice, fried potatoes, mixed salad and gluten, for the not so extortionate price of 15 Bs. There is a good selection of juices, though the dessert selection is limited, and the alcohol, for the more hardened (or should that be less), is non-existent (although to be fair this again reflects the Hindi culture). Open daily from 9:00 until 22:00, and on Saturdays 9:00 until 17:00 (closed Sundays), the lunch costs 10 Bs. and the Cena as little as 7 Bs.

Located in the heart of the tourist district, the English and Spanish Menu echoes this fact. As the friendly waitress tells you, this is Hindu Vegetarian, not Bolivian Vegetarian. My tip for this restaurant would be to stay clear of the bathroom facilities, which are best described as basic. In summary, I found the Laksmi to be cheap and cheerful, on account of the limited Menu and portions, perhaps more of a cafe than a restaurant but nonetheless well worth a visit. Their promotion is on Thursdays between 12:00 and 15:00, when 12 preparations of food can be bought for the bargain price of 18 Bs.

The more up market and predictably more expensive vegetarian option is the **Restaurant Vegetariano Armonía**, situated on Avenida Ecuador 2286, in the heart of the Sopocachi district. There is no set menu, but instead a buffet is run on weekdays only, between 12:00 and, they say, 15:00 (although the entrance door tells you otherwise, saying 12:00 till 14:00). The first discernible point to make is that the opening hours are obviously fairly limited so making a reservation is worthwhile (see contact details below), as it can get quite busy. The food is delicious, ranging from salad and sauces, to nuts and whole-wheat bread, from seasoned rice to tofu stir fry. This is an as much as you can eat buffet, not forgetting the soup starter, and the ever changing selection of gastronomic choices. The western music and daily papers all contribute to the thoroughly relaxing ambiance.

Besides these two vegetarian restaurants, what does La Paz have to offer in terms of meat restaurants with vegetarian options? I would strongly recommend **100 percent natural**, which is located slightly higher up Calle Sagarnaga from Laksmi. It prides itself on offering what the Bolivian Times has previously suggested is "The Best Breakfast in La Paz." Open between 8:30 and 21:30 every weekday and until 18:00 on Saturdays, 100 percent Natural offers a great soya burger, great value at 10 Bs., and true to name, a whole host of fresh and colorful juices and salads (I have come to not take green salads for granted so this was an added bonus). And the desserts here have to be seen to be believed. Again, in keeping with Laksmi, menus are in both Spanish and English. The service is prompt and, in fact, the only mute point to make about 100 percent Natural is its cheesy selection of music (fans of Michael Bolton and Peter Cetera will be in their element).

There is the excellent pasta house, **Pronto** (Pasaje Jauregui, Sopocachi), which offers any number of vegetarian variations on the meat alternatives and the service is friendly. For fish eaters, there is **Vienna**, just down from the Prado. Many of the embassies offer a wholesome selection of dishes, both vegetarian and meat, during much of the week. Chief among these is The **Italian Embassy**, situated on 6 de Agosto, which is an as much as you can eat for 50 Bs. on Sunday Lunch time. Finally, there is the ubiquitous **Mongo's Rock Bottom Cafe**. I'm sure this gringo's institution needs no introduction but I'll challenge anyone to find a better tuna melt in all La Paz (although the table service remains painfully slow- is this the price of a good reputation?).

What of the makeup of the clientele in the first two Vegetarian restaurants I reviewed? It can be no coincidence that these two restaurants' trade is almost solely reliant on the International community. In Laksmi´s case, this is no doubt because of its location in the heart of the tourist district and its more Indian theme, although it can compete with other local restaurants on price. However, it is the price of the food at the Restaurant Armonia which to a large extent undoubtedly dictates the nature of its clientele. It may seem harsh to criticize Armomia on the basis of the elitism it elicits, since it is situated in a well-off district and surrounded by international companies and embassies. 21 Bs. is also very reasonable by Western standards. However, in local terms, this is costly enough to deter the average Bolivian, at least on a regular basis. It could be argued that all concerned are content with the current situation in regards to the paucity of vegetarian restaurants in to La Paz. It seems some Bolivians are content because they are not worried about eating vegetarian food; and the International Community, whether that be tourists or ex-patriots, are content because their needs are just about catered for by the two most popular vegetarian restaurants, which are at opposite ends of the economic, religious and locational spectrums. And then there is the steadily growing number of places to eat out which make specific efforts to offer vegetarian alternatives. But I would argue otherwise.

In Bolivia, there seems to be a common conception that vegetarianism is an unhealthy option. However, according to the Vegetarian Society in the U.K., research has shown that this diet can reduce the risk of certain cancers by up to 40 percent, and decrease the possibility of heart disease by over 30 percent. At altitude, it takes four days to digest meat (at sea level this figure is two days).

But surely, and not just for reasons of health and satisfying the needs those of the small band of vegetarians in La Paz, eating out should not be so non-representative as to only cater for one sector of needs-those of meat eaters. If there are Chinese, Italian and Israeli restaurants, (and there are) and a lot of other countries' cuisine besides, it seems madness that what is a massive trend worldwide has yet to hit the streets of La Paz. But more than just a need for additional vegetarian restaurants, which would benefit the International Community (every vegetarian I know is crying out for more alternatives) , there is another clear reason why more vegetarian options are a must. By the same token that I came to La Paz to experience the local culture, including its cuisine, Bolivians should be given the opportunity to eat out, at reasonable local prices, and encounter other gastronomic cultures besides their own.

New comers on the list:
Manantial, Hotel Gloria, Calle Genaro Sanjinez 430 corner with Potosi.
"G" Bros, Av. 6 de Agosto 2335.

COPACABANA: WORTH ITS REPUTATION?

BY ELLIS AUGER

For the seasoned and uninitiated traveler alike, one piece of knowledge seems to hold true more than any other: when somewhere sounds too good to be true, it usually is. So after a brief trawl through the ubiquitous Lonely Planet, my next destination had been decided upon, and the immediate reaction upon and reading the section on Copacabana was: Would it live up to its billing as a must see?

Thus, last Friday saw eight friends and me board a bus to this small town, which sits on the western shores of Lake Titicaca. For the small price of 30 Bolivianos for a return ticket, we caught a large bus front the cemetery in La Paz and headed northwest up and across the Altiplano. Even for someone like myself, whose grasp of the Spanish language is somewhat less than perfect, buying the ticket proved no problem, with buses leaving on the hour, every hour, for much of the day.

The 158-kilometers journey, which included a ferry across a narrow strip of the Lake at San Pedro (the straights of Tiquina, took about four hours, and we pulled into Copacabana around 3pm. First impressions last as the saying goes; on arrival, mine was one of immediate relaxation. We headed straight to our hostel, Hostel La Luna, situated about two minutes from the Plaza San Pedro, where the buses pull in. For 15 Bs a night, we had a roof over our heads, breakfast in bed (small charge) and hot showers to boot. And given no less a respected traveler's assertion than Michael Palin, writer and comedian, that come night-time, temperatures drop to an unfeasibly cold level (due to the altitude of over 3800 m), there were blankets, lots of blankets (although next time I think it might be an idea to bring a sleeping bag as well). Another popular choice, for budget travelers especially, is the Hostel Ambassador, with a rooftop restaurant as one of the principal selling points. Understandably, these hotels dotted along the main street, La Calle 6 de Agosto, are slightly pricier.

The sedate atmosphere not withstanding, the first thing I noticed on arrival in Copacabana was the large number of fellow travelers. The town is, after all, firmly situated on the Beaten Track, which runs from La Paz to Puno, across the Peruvian border. But do not let this put you off; the town still retains much of its historical Aymara heritage, as typified by the manner in which vehicles from all over Bolivia come to receive the ritual blessings, made by Franciscan Priests, thus bestowing upon them luck and a warrant of safety.

As soon as we arrived and had unceremoniously dumped our bags at the Hostel, we headed back up La Calle 6 de Agosto to try our luck with the local cuisine.

I suppose there is no way I could write an article about Copacabana without mentioning the trout, which is fresh from the Lake, and for which I found the town to be justifiably renowned (although it would have been substantially cheaper if bought from the local market). But if trout is not your kettle of fish, you can be sure to find some gastronomic delight to suit all tastes and budgets.

And what of the local attractions? The grandiose Moorish-style Cathedral dominates the Main Square in the town and is considered to be one of the finest religious monuments in all Bolivia. Built in the 17th Century, it pays homage to the Virgen de Candelaria, also known as the Dark Virgin of the Lake. The Virgen de Candelaria is Bolivia's Patron Saint and during the Festival of the same name, held during the month of February, her statue leaves the Cathedral, to be processed around the town. The aforementioned market is also a must see, complete with everything from fortune-tellers to merchants.

The Cerro Calvario is the imposing hill, which sits like a shadow over the Northern edge of town. I can personally vouch for the fact that the effort required to climb to the top is at once exhausting and rewarding. Exhausting because the half-hour trudge is not for the faint hearted, rewarding because the steps, lined by the Stations of the Cross, lead to surely one of The more breathtaking views imaginable, both over Copacabana and the Lake. Come half an hour before sunset, you can be sure that you will not be the only person paying the small metaphorical price that the Cerro Calvario asks of you.

Following my exertions, where better to head than the local bars for a refreshing beer? The Sol y Luna, which adjoins the Hotel of the same name, offers a mean hot chocolate, a great selection of music and what is possibly the town's largest book

exchange (the beer was very good as well). Although I did not venture there, I hear that Tatu Carreta comes highly recommended and has the latest closing time in Copacabana of anything between 1.30 and 3.30 am. In general though, it is fair to apply the term "sleepy" to Copacabana's nocturnal interests, a surprise considering the number of "gringos" it attracts. One other minor point: Internet cafes are scarce here; so do not bank on checking your mail unless you are prepared to pay a much-inflated price.

About two hours by boat from Copacabana lies the Isla Del Sol and, so legend has it, the birthplace of the Incas. According to myth, it was here that Father Sun instigated the gathering of local communities to practice the arts of civilization and thus was born the Inca Empire.

I stayed here one night in a hostel, which rides an imaginary line over the top of Yumani, a small settlement in the south. Much like other hostels on the Island, facilities were quite basic although this was counterbalanced by its superb location. In terms of attractions on the Island, there are the pre-Columbian Stairs comprising about 1000 steps and the Fountain of Eternal Youth. For the more energetically inclined, hiking is a popular choice.

The Island itself is a maze of trails and the Northern and Eastern sides in particular offer the opportunity to truly take a step back in time as you witness the fashioning of the Tortora Boats, composed of long bundles of reeds.

Much like Copacabana, do not come here looking for a rousing time; La Isla Del Sol is a place for cogitation and reflection, a nice bottle of red whilst you watch the sun go down type of place. Put another way, it is a time capsule reminding us of a bygone era where time is dictated by the sun, and not by clocks.

How could I sum up my experiences

in Copacabana and the Isla del Sol? both have an appeal that sweeps across the board. For those on a tight budget, there are cheap though cheerful hostels and delicious though affordably priced foods.

For the more adventurous, there is a world of hiking options. For the visitor tending towards a more cultural experience, this is true Inca heartland, where tourism is a byproduct of their ancient traditions and not the other way round. The livelihood of a lot of attractions are won and lost on their reputation and I urge you not to be persuaded against visiting Copacabana on the strength of the tourists it draws, because it is one place that assuredly lives up to its lofty billing.

THE WORLD'S MOST DANGEROUS ROAD

BY DINO SCUNGIO

I braced myself as my trusty loaned mountain bike and I hurtled towards two water filled potholes (craters in any other country). A lethal concoction of inexperience, rain, testosterone, water logged brakes, poor visibility, and downright cockiness left us on an unavoidable collision course.

I went through the first pothole and emerged on the other side, still on my bike, but in a position not recommended in any biking textbook. I plunged into the second, wondering why the company hadn't issued us with a snorkel for such a hazard. It was there that my bike and I parted company. I vividly recall that frozen moment of freefall, other (equally bad) bike, horse and motorbike riders will tell you, you have time to dwell upon the thought, "I've fallen in trouble." This moment lasts a surreal amount of time; I was half expecting an in-flight movie and meal. Reality returned with a thud as body met bitumen, luckily my helmet, left cheek and right knee broke the fall. After a few bounces, the body stopped, providing another eerie, frozen, wonderful moment to take stock and conclude, "Hey not so bad... nothing feels broken."

Such ended my attempt to ride one of the world's longest and greatest ridable altitude descents. This takes place on Bolivia's notorious La Paz to Coroico (what for simplicity's sake, I shall now generously refer to as) road. The downhill section of this road is 64 km long and amazingly, drops 3600m

in altitude along the way. To put this in perspective, Australia's Eskyscraperi, Mount Kosciosko, from peak to sea level is just over 2000m.

In 1995, the Inter American Development Bank judged this road as the world's most dangerous, perhaps having something to do with the 26 vehicles which went 'over the edge' in 1994. A local tells me that the road's condition is now far worse, but there is more traffic, making racing far more difficult and thus it's a lot safer. The tell-tale stone and wooden crosses, which form (the only) grisly road barrier, are a lasting testimony to those who have 'met their maker' upon it. Rumor has it that a tourism group has had many crosses removed, apparently bad for business.

Reassuringly for the tourist, most of these incidents involve truck drivers, attempting to conquer the road late at night, fully loaded, often in more ways than one. Many of these fatal accidents occur during or after "Carnaval", or other similar "fiestas," when many Bolivians let down their long black hair, some neglecting to put it up again when life and its responsibilities continue. The annual death toll for the 96 km of winding spectacular road is decreasing. One accident in 1983 killed a staggering 100 people, thus making improvement easy. The death toll, the decrepit state of the road and the hardships it provide certainly earn it its dangerous reputation.

It's not surprising that there are numerous accidents, as the scenery to be enjoyed on this trip provides a fatal distraction on this demanding journey.

The journey starts at Bolivia's bustling capital of La Paz, under the shadow of the perennial snow-capped triple peaks of Mount Illimani, which at 6439m dominates the skyline. The journey then moves through a barren, sculptured, lunar landscape, peaking at the windswept, often snow covered, La Cumbre (4700m).

As your descent winds down through the Cordillera Real, the barren, brown landscape changes to green cloud forest, which makes way to thicker growth and finally, lush semi-tropical jungle. Be prepared to share the air with the majestic birds which dominate the sky, various members of the condor family and turkey vultures providing live entertainment. You'll also marvel at the delicate, startling array of vivid, colorful butterflies which grace the fresh air surrounding you. If the altitude hasn't already, its enough to leave you breathless.

Mountain biking is one wonderful way to take in all the joys that abound on this journey. Gravity Assisted Mountain Biking (GAMB) provides just that, having seized the opportunity to show the ever growing number of visitors, the beauty of Bolivia's Yungas, the Zongo Valley, Chacaltaya (the world's highest ski field at 5345m) and other remarkable areas around La Paz. GAMB's tours are professionally run, my incident being more indicative of yours truly rather than the company or the ride itself.

There are a variety of ways to travel from La Paz to Coroico. Most common (and advisable) are the mini-buses; these puncture prone vehicles offer the safest motorized option. For the brave, there are the local, full-sized buses; these larger buses known are as 'micros' (after being in Bolivia a while such logic does not surprise you). Hikers may prefer to follow in the footsteps

of the Inca's and tackle the Choro trail. This wonderful, downhill, three to four day trek begins at La Cumbre, travels across the Cordillera Real, finishing just before Coroico.

Those with rodeo experience and terrific life insurance may choose to travel on the back of the countless trucks which travel this route. More than likely (and appropriately), this option involves traveling atop a load of bananas or one of the variety of produce that the fertile Yungas sporns. These vehicles are mostly to blame for the monstrous pot holes and sorry state of the road. Previous to my biking attempt, I had completed the journey six times by mini-bus, such is the addictive nature of this wonderful journey and its quiet, jungle village destination, Coroico.

Simply to sit beside the driver and observe their mannerisms is a treat in itself. Being a busy narrow road, with two way traffic, there are inevitable confrontations as vehicles come head to head. Be prepared to share your personal space with fully laden trucks and buses as they gingerly squeeze past each other, on a road where one side offers a sheer cliff face up and the other a deadly drop down. In a startling piece of Bolivian logic, a driver going uphill has the right of way, meaning the driver going down must reverse until a wide enough section of road is found, allowing both vehicles to pass. When two drivers meet on a relatively flat piece of terrain, (often their bumpers within walnut cracking distance of each other) the drivers unleash their best "Clint Squint" (Eastwood) as they size each other up. All that's missing is the Spaghetti western soundtrack, this staring competition ends with the 'loser' reversing.

Look carefully and you'll notice your driver rapidly and continuously making the sign of the cross over himself. You then know its time to buckle up and perhaps rethink your religious responsibilities.

Another common practice is the sprinkling of alcohol on the tires as an offering to "Pachamama" (Mother Earth) in hope of a safe journey. Personally, I'd like to see them use tires with tread, just as an additional safety measure. Makes you wonder how they greet their families when they leave and return from work each day.

Besides the startling scenery which this trip provides, there is plenty of alternative entertainment to keep the passenger on their toes. When traveling, expect the odd flat tire, to become bogged in mud and perhaps even experience the odd landslide, but when you get them all in the one day, you've got your money's worth. These all too consistent landslides are a result of the terrific amount of rain the areas receives during the wet season, meaning you may have to wait while as a bulldozer creates a way ahead.

The wet season is the life source from which the tropical rain forest thrives, also providing countless spectacular waterfalls which you often have to drive through, thundering down onto the mini-bus roof. You may even have to play your part, pushing a bogged bus, or clearing the road of fallen rocks, always with one eye on the cliff face on the lookout for tumbling rocks. I'd also recommend taking a book; it gives you some thing to bite on while the driver negotiates the curves and hazards.

To further add novelty value to the journey, just out of La Paz, all vehicles are stopped and searched by the Bolivian military, searching for drug making materials, as they head towards the coca rich Yungas. Bolivia is the world's third largest producer of coca leaves, the raw ingredient of cocaine. To complicate the issue, coca is a traditional crop and has been used for centuries by native South Americans religious and cultural purposes, thus it' ,rown and used extensively.

In its natural state, chewed continuously, with a touch of carbonate as a cata-lyst, the coca leaf releases an alkaloid substance which sustains its user, relieving symptoms of thirst, hunger and providing stamina during period of extended work.

In a country whose history reveals countless years of slave labor and a shortage of food and necessities, the sense of well being which the substance provides has long been a necessity. Importantly, particularly for the traveling gringo, the coca leaf, when chewed or boiled and served as a tea, provides a natural relief from symptoms of altitude sickness. Vital in a country where approximately a third of its land is above 4000m and over 6000m peaks are common. To again give an indication as to the altitude at which many Bolivians live, the arduous climb to reach Mount Everest base camp ends at 5400m.

So once you have passed the guards, had your luggage searched, perhaps been frisked and been confirmed as a non-drug baron, the bitumen road continues for another 12 km before narrowing to a single lane dirt path, winding its way down the remaining 45km to Coroico. The drive itself takes a theoretical three hours, but I wouldn't make any appointments: three to five hours seems to be a fair estimate.

If the natural beauty isn't enough, the destination at the end of the road more than justifies the trip. Coroico is a beautiful Bolivian village, nestled in the lush Andes mountains. With snow capped peaks in the distance, it offers wonderful views of the valleys and the Amazon-feeding-Coroico River. Its narrow cobble stoned streets, bowler hatted women, smiling children and quaint central plaza, all provide a genuine experience of life in a Bolivian village. The semitropical climate allows you the option of living life by the pool, a real treat after the frigid nights on Bolivia's Altiplano.

As for my unsuccessful attempt to ride from La Paz to Coroico, well at least I got to know the staff at the Coroico Hospital quite well. They patched, stitched me and eventually sent me on my way. Mind you, there was a moment, just before the seventh (yes seventh) attempt to insert the unaesthetic needle in my knee (the first two with an item far more suited to be a fence post) when I cursed my infatuation with this road and town. This being my seventh trip on it, also leaving me to ponder whether to change my lucky number from seven (to perhaps one). But this was just a moment.

In summary, the journey from La Paz to Coroico is an experience which will live long in my (and other's) memories. The blend of natural beauty, adventure, landscapes, flora, fauna and culture make it a complete experience for the South American traveler. In two years (which in Bolivian time could be three to five.. ish) a new, safer road will be complete, allowing smooth passage for the week-end traveler from La Paz. This will no doubt leave many tourists much more at ease. Coroico and the path to it will not be the same. I'd get here quickly.

THE CHORO TRAIL

BY OLLIE ENGLEHART

I piled dizzily out of my "trufi" in Villa Fatima. It was seven o'clock in the morning on Thursday and I was feeling hideous. But I had an appointment with my friend and walking companion Robert which I could not miss. We were going to do the Choro trail, an old Incan route that passes from La Cumbre above La Paz down to the semi-Amazonian village of Chairo, deep in the Yungas. For a number of days I had yearned the countryside, the intoxicating fumes, barking dogs and hubbub of frenetic La Paz had finally got the better of me. I wanted open space, the musty smell of the Yungas and the opportunity to clear my head. I wanted to escape.

On Wednesday evening we met to discuss our plans. First, how long would it take us? The guide book said 3-4 days so we could do it in two, such was our arrogance and enthusiasm as we flexed our muscles and got ready to go. Second, what would we take with us? Well, a tent, obviously, and a pot for cooking with some noodles for supper, a couple of avocados, some tomatoes and minimal bread for lunch. A machete as well, not because we thought it was in any way practical, but because it would be fun and add to the general sense of adventure. We were sure that whatever we lacked could be picked up in one of the numerous *pueblitos* along the way. Little did I suspect that three days later I would wander out of the jungle in the dark, emaci-

ated, drenched and beaten and that after a further two days I would still be feeling the same way.

By ten o'clock on Thursday we were up at the 4600m of La Cumbre, strapped into our rucksacks and chomping at the bit. 'Choro Trail', a big blue sign said, and off we went, springing with each step and grinning through our coca-stuffed mouths at the adventure that was to come. "First left, second right" a muffled-up veteran of La Cumbre told us. We had read in the guidebook that there were signposts and splashings of paint at every turn indicating where trekkers should go, which stopped us from worrying that we might lose the way. Four hours later as we staggered down a decidedly Lord of The Rings-esque mountain to where we had started the walk, with our red faces having fallen victim to an especially vicious hailstorm at well over 5000m, it became apparent that we had gone wrong at the very first turn. I suppose that technically we were not lost because we always knew where we were but we had made that common mistake of thinking that it would be quicker to go over the mountain than around the mountain. Little did we realise that going over the mountain would entail a long walk uphill and then a 70m precipice on the other side. Our over-confidence had won it's first victory.

As we ambled down a well-trodden path after our first mishap, the tumbling hail turned into snow. The soft bed of snow creaked under foot as it melted with our descent and the lush vegetal valleys of the Yungas unfolded in the valley before us. Wet, but still grinning stupidly, we stopped at the remains of a *tambo* , or wayside inn, that dates back from Incan times to eat our first meal. It was all turning out to be very exciting. We marched on throughout the afternoon determined to make up some of the time we had lost on our earlier excursion. Walking through the rolling green valleys with streams of water that gush down from the mountain-tops, we came to our first village, called Samaña Pampa. There was only one man around, although evidence was present to suggest a couple more people lived there. We took the opportunity to sit down the goat-skin seats and purchased a refreshment from him. He told us about the Yungas' six-a-side soccer tournament which Samaña Pampa would be hosting on May 11th of this year. He even asked us to come back with some friends and enter the competition as one of the sixteen teams. First prize would be a bull, second a llama while third, fourth and fifth places would each take home a ram. Imagine winning a llama.

We reached a beautiful little location at about 3500m where we decided to spend the night. It was about three and a half hours after the first village. The going had been slow so far, but we attributed this to losing the morning up a mountain and remained confident that we could make up for it on Friday and enjoy a good couple of nights in Coroico. During the course of the day we had walked from snow-capped peaks into the dense, green, waterfall inhabited Yungas. Unfortunately, the tent, which we had failed to check, was in a rather depleted state. Indeed we spent a good 45 minutes deliberating over whether it was meant to be a dome-shaped tent or more of a sort of pyramid shape.

As darkness descended, a dramatic skyline moved over the valley. Soon the menacing clouds had hidden the sillouette of the hills and all we could see anywhere was an ominous blackness. Knowing that a storm was coming, building a fire and pitching the tent became a race against time. The sky had erupted on us in a matter of minutes, torrents of rain and thrashing lightening quashed our futile, inexperienced attempt at making a fire. Soaked to the bone and hungry we retreated miserably to the tent. The storm continued throughout the night, the sounds of the rain eventually lullabying us to sleep. We awoke late the next morning. The weather had cleared somewhat, although now that we were wet I knew it would stay that way until we reached our destination. We bathed in the icy river before starting the long day of walking that was ahead of us.

We went the morning starving and unfuelled, sure that when we reached the next village they could supply us with something to eat. The walking was difficult as we followed a makeshift path constructed in pre-Hispanic times. We kept slipping on the rocks as we ventured downhill, jarring our knees all the way. A girl in Cha'llapampa sold us some eggs at an extortionate price and we decided that if we could find nothing to eat before lunch we would have to build a fire and cook up the noodles from the night before and the eggs. Of course, within the next half hour all the eggs had broken. Following the river down the Yungas, our surroundings had become very Amazonian. Moisture dropped off the hanging vines and huge tropical plant-leaves. Our faces brushed against spider webs and swarms of black, yellow and multicoloured butterflies as big as the palm of one's hand frollicked about us. We realised how far we had come since yesterday morning as we looked back up the valley and saw the snowy mountain that we had scaled framed in a cloud halo.

While our legs kept walking, the conversation came to a standstill. We had found a rhythmn in our movement, trudging on, putting one foot steadily infront of the other.

Exhausted, we arrived at the Choro bridge for a late lunch. An old couple played host and plied us full of carbohydrates: A hot lunch of rice and potatoes for which we were most grateful. The limping old man, smiling maniacally chased and threw stones at his cats. I wondered about the lifestyle of these people, what they do and think about all day and what it must be like for them living their whole lives in the same place and then, since a few years ago, witnessing a sudden influx of tourists. Re-energized but with feet that felt like they were made of lead, the trek continued. Uphill and downhill we went, backwards and forwards across Indiana Jones style bridges. Our bravado concerning one of the most popular treks in Bolivia had worn off. We were very, very tired.

Our campsite for Friday night, despite the fact that we had expected to be in Coroico by then, was a great success. We had the tent set up in no time and were soon reclining beneath the stars gobbling up piping hot noodles with chopsticks. Our fire burnt for hours and we sat listening to the wild noises of the clear Yungeñan night. It must have rained after we fell asleep; all our things were utterly drenched again by the time we woke up on Saturday morning. Matters were not helped by the thick plant-life of the jungle, our tired legs had to fight to stagger on through the sodden creepers and long grass. Clouds rolled over our heads, through the valley beneath us and occassionally enveloped us completely, reducing the visibility to just a couple of metres. From time to time we would stop to watch a pair of humming birds or see a colourful parrot flap off into a neighbouring tree.

We were aiming to get to Sandillani for two o'clock and to find something to eat at the renouned 'casa del japones'. We had heard of the wise old man known only as 'el hombre japones' who had for many years been living on his own in the jungle and we were most excited by the prospect of meeting him. He alone made three days of hard walking worth it. As we arrived in Sandillani, passing an old lady chopping up root vegetables, 'el hombre japones' came scuttling crab-like out of his manicured Japanese garden. He looked like a mushroom with his arms held out on either side to balance him and a hunchback that showed his spine poking out at an angle through his tattered jumper. Surrounded by clucking chickens as we signed the guestbook of this querky figure, it felt like we had been launched into a García Márquez novel.

Mr Tamiji Hanamura de Furio told us how he had arrived in the Yungas. It was apparent that he was not altogether with it in his head, though he could not have been kinder or more hospitable. In 1955, he recalled, he had left his hometown in a mountain range of central Japan in search of new mountains. He travelled by boat to Bolivia stopping off in Cape Town, South Africa, on the way to see Table Mountain. He settled in the Yungas a few weeks later, building his Japanese house and garden facing the towering peaks of the Cordillera Occidental. At seventy years old, he has been there ever since. He showed us map after map of different mountain ranges and an intricate drawing of his route to Bolivia. When we told 'el hombre japones' that we were from England he quickly disappeared up his garden path only to pop up moments later with his collection of postcards from Great Britain. 'El hombre japones' collects postcards. He showed us postcards of The Royal Family, of The Tower of London and of the mountains in Scotland and Wales, which he was particularly keen on. When he showed us a picture of the Queen

Mother and we told him that she had recently died, he started scribbling away in his Japanese hieroglyphs on the back of the postcard. He does not recieve very much news, he said.

The walk to Chairo where the trail ends was only another seven kilometres, although we arrived in the dark due to an extended lunch break at the amazing 'casa del japones'. Very bedraggled and unable to speak from exhaustion, we scrambled into a *camioneta* which took us to Yolosa, just 7km from Coroico. Cold and wet we waited on the side of the muddy road for another *camioneta* to pass and take us up to our final destination. When we did get to Coroico, at about nine o'clock, we aimed straight for the French-run restaurant, el Cafetal, and like two cavemen devoured in silence the finest peppered steak that Bolivia has to offer.

For more information contact:
Bolivian Association for Conservation - TROPICO. Calle Campos 296 corner with 6 de Agosto
Edif. El Cipres, Of. 5B. Tel. 2435005, Fax. 2435027, Casilla 11250
La Paz - Bolivia.
E-mail: tropico@mail.megalink.com
Pachama'Raft
Only two hours from Chairo on the way to Coroico is Pachama'Raft offering cabañas for 20 Bs., a campsite for 10 Bs. where you can also rent camping gears, with kitchen, showers, bathrooms and swimming pool. There is also the possibility to go wild on various rafting excursion.
Tels. 71500556 - 71255810
E-mail: southamericarafting@hotmail.com
Or contact in La Paz **Terra Andina**.
www.terra-andina.com

AIN'T NO RIVER WIDE ENOUGH

BY TILL BRUCKNER

We were a couple hundred yards below the Abra Chucura pass, resting on the Incan paving that winds down into the valley below, when an old man and his son walked past. The man asked us where we were going. When we told him we wanted to do the Choro trek, he said that it was impossible. The bridge at the village of Challapampa had been washed away,' he told us, making the river impassable. We had been looking forward to this walk for weeks, and we'd finally gotten started, so our sense of reality gave way to wishful thinking. What is local knowledge against eight yards of rope in your rucksack and a survival handbook in your head? Even if the river really was insurmountable, the map indicated an alternative route from before the crossing—at the village of Chucura—to the Zongo valley.

In any case, nobody turns around voluntarily after having just walked steeply downhill for a long stretch. Rather, we continued down until we reached the point of reckoning, preferring to face the music if there truly was no way across. We met several other locals on that first day, all of whom told us the same story: there was no bridge, no way we could get to the town of Chairo at the trek's end. Disheartened, we entered Chucura, the first village on the route, where we registered with the park authority. The man in charge—a bouncy twenty-something we had met farther up, who was taking his

horse to pasturelands—echoed the locals' advice. With a big smile, he added that two other groups of hikers had passed along this road two days before and never returned. Apparently, he took this as an indication that they had successfully overcome the stream, but he admitted cheerfully that he didn't actually know. A little corner of my brain suggested dark scenarios of gringo corpses accumulating downstream. Walking on, we reached the river's banks and started to search for a nice camping spot as dusk began to settle. I toyed with the idea of hopping over some stones and pitching the tent on the opposite side, to camp where no man has camped before. But eventually my girlfriend dissuaded me, and we stayed between the trail and the river. After dark—just as we were cooking, of course—it started to rain and continued into the wee hours.

The following morning, the quiet stream we had seen only hours ago had turned into an awe-inspiring and deafening torrent of brown water. The rocks I had considered using as stepping-stones the previous evening were nearly totally submerged. As we were packing up to continue the trail, a villager walked past. He told us the water level should fall again by the next morning, causing my optimism to well up once again. Heading upwards towards Challapampa, we crossed several tributaries to the main river and made our acquaintance with Bolivian footbridges. There are two kinds:

miraculously stable Incan stone bridges; and the wobbly jerrybuilt contraptions of today. More and more water seemed to pour into the river from the surrounding hillsides at an alarming rate. Finally, the path turned steeply downwards, and from a distance we could spot a few huts right by the bank of the stream. The place where the bridge had been was immediately discernible. There were ramps on both sides, but nothing in between them save the raging waters. Heroically crossing this broad torrent with a rope I had never even tested seemed out of the question, and my heart sank as we drew closer. According to the Royal Geographic Society in London, I remembered, drowning is the most frequent cause of death during expeditions. I wished my brain would not randomly cough up such facts on inappropriate occasions.

Approaching the huts, we were greeted by a local family who seemed immensely amused by our predicament. Waving expansively at the stream, I asked how we could cross. One of the men said, "Swim." We looked at each other for a couple of seconds, until he couldn't keep a straight face anymore and burst out laughing, followed by the rest of his family. He then pointed to a man on the opposite bank that was just climbing into some kind of harness, holding a large Coke bottle in his hand. A few seconds later, he was gliding along a wire that I had failed to notice before, merrily waving his beverage to everyone. Once on our side, he passed around the bottle. Apparently, he was having an excellent time crossing to and fro, letting everyone have a sip. The first man grinned and said we could cross if we paid a fee of 10 Bs. each. Considering these people had an uncontested monopoly, and the only alternative was to lug our rucksacks from 3,000 m altitude to 4,800 m over the next two days, I didn't even attempt to haggle. Actually, I was relieved they didn't try to get even more out of us, considering our bargaining position.

We agreed I would go first, followed by our luggage, with my girlfriend last, so that our possessions would never be unattended. The two men strapped me into their mountaineer-type harness, which pointed me away from the river. There was a hook on wheels attached to the cable, and a rope would be used to pull me across from the other side. Altogether, it struck me as an ad hoc contraption rooted out from the dusty contents of an old shed. I could only ponder, if my harness falls off, I'll drown—game over. I was told to hold the strands of the harness just below the metal part to keep it from slipping. Having done as I was told, I looked at my helpers for further guidance, but they just displayed broad grins. "Do I jump now?" I asked. They nodded. "Backwards?" Another series of nods, even bigger grins, and I let myself drop backwards into nothing. Bungee jumpers must love that initial falling feeling, but then they don't use ropes from rural Bolivia. Once I was on the other side, happy the equipment had held up to my relatively large weight, I took a closer look at the setup while the rucksacks were ferried over. In reality, the construction was far more solid than it appeared at first. The metal cable was passed through a hole drilled straight through a big rock on either side, so it was firmly anchored. The whole thing was safe as long as the harness didn't slip off. What puzzled me was the contrast between such skillful engineering on the one hand and the use of a dangerous open hook, instead of a cheap and easily available carabineer, on the other—yet another Bolivian enigma. When the rucksacks had crossed and it was my girlfriend's turn, the man who had told me to swim yelled over the noise of the river. He motioned to me that he'd keep my girlfriend on that side and pretended to lead her to his hut. Laughingly, we exchanged threatening gestures from opposite banks, and he sent her over.

The moment we left Challapampa, it started to rain again and never stopped until sunset. Slipping and sliding down wet Incan stairs, with the occasional uphill climb in between, we wondered if the bridge at the village of Choro, indicated by the map, still existed. For some reason, now unfathomable to me, I believed there was a road from there to Coroico. Towards the evening, arriving at a cluster of huts precariously perched on a slope, we asked a small man how far it was to Choro. He replied with a cheery smile that this was it and asked if we wanted to pitch our tent. Evidently feeling a bit misinformed by me, my girlfriend gave me one of the filthiest looks our three-year relationship has ever seen. She asked our friendly host how we could cross the river, but we couldn't understand his reply, so we asked him to wake us up in the morning at half past six together with the other two groups of trekkers who were staying overnight. The next morning, we awoke and prepared to make our final crossing. Much to our dismay we were faced with a cable crossing rather than a bridge, much like the one we had encountered in Challapampa the day before, and we were only charged 5 Bs. The cable had to be negotiated with our own muscle power because there was no second rope to pull people across with. And far more worrying, there was no harness. Instead, an empty vegetable sack was used, which was somehow cut and knotted to form a kind of diaper. The highest knot was simply put over the hook. I just tried to get across at the highest speed possible, with as little thought as possible. Along the footpath between Choro and Chairo, running parallel to the Huarinilla River, there was only one bridge, which was intact. Personally, I would have preferred a hastily strung metal cable to this wobbly and creaky suspension bridge.

We camped overnight at Sandillani in the garden of the Japanese man who is a staple in every guidebook on Bolivia for offering free accommodation to trekkers. The next afternoon, we headed for the village of Pacollo, where we could flag down a truck to Coroico, everyone assured us. The only problem was that the heavy rains had damaged the road, so there was no traffic apart from bicycles. When we arrived, the owner of the local shop offered to drive us for 180 Bs., but we politely declined. Walking quickly, I thought, we should be able to reach the main La Paz-Coroico road by ten at night. Later, passing by two houses in the dark, a woman's voice called for us to stop. The lady, sitting smoking with a woman friend on her doorstep, advised us not to continue, because a big landslide had taken away a section of the road that morning "with a very loud noise." We were likely to fall down it if we continued, she said. We should wait until daylight, she said, when we would be able to see where we were going. I turned back to pitch the tent on a flat stretch of land by the road we had passed a minute earlier and nearly fell off the road into a mini-landslide that I'd forgotten about. I definitely wasn't going to continue that night. The next morning, we walked on, soon passing by a tractor that, incredibly, had started patching up the road already. Two hours later, we caught a bus at the ford in the river by the new Yungas highway construction project. And a few hours after that, we arrived safely in the Villa Fatima neighborhood of La Paz, though not before having witnessed a spectacular sunset at La Cumbre on the way.

CHULUMANI: A PERFECT DWELL FOR WEARY TRAVELLERS

BY SITA SHAH

On a glorious Friday afternoon, after just having heard the latest News that no further progress has been made between the government and campesinos, the earnest traveller can be left seething in despair. The prospect of foreseeable blockades for weeks to come and the thought of having to spend yet another weekend in La Paz is probably not most people's idea of a vacation. So if you don't fancy being stuck on a twelve hour bus journey heading South towards Sucre, and with the continuing inaccessibility of roads leading towards Sorata and Lake Titicaca, what are the likely alternatives?

One region that may spring to mind is the Yungas, perhaps better known for the tiny town of Coroico. However, another charming little town that is often overlooked by travelers is Chulumani. If you are truly in search of a weekend retreat and a place to escape the burdens of a bustling city then Chulumani is an ideal destination.

After having resigned ourselves to the fact that Sorata was no longer going to feature on our itinerary, we trudged up to Villa Fatima and embarked our journey to Chulumani. Even the fact that I felt like I was on a school trip, with a group of teenage girls giggling and screaming at the back, did not dampen my enthusiasm. The scenery was just spectacular, a close resemblance to a paradise on earth. Not to mention the idea of leaving behind the crowded, noisy streets of La Paz for just two days.

Situated in South Yungas, Chulumani lies at a height of only 1700m and has a sub tropically warm climate. It is also the center for growing coffee, bananas and Yungas coca. Having only been acquainted with the sights of La Paz for five weeks, arriving in Chulumani was like setting foot in a different country. Instead of being aligned by markets, the roads were simply littered with banana plantations of various heights and sizes. As soon as we got off the bus the change in climate was apparent. It was a welcome change to experience the warm air at eight in the evening and not feel the need to put on another Alpacas sweater. It was also a breath of fresh air to be able to walk up a moderately inclining hill without having to be rescued by an oxygen tank.

As we had arrived fairly late on Friday evening the only things that preoccupied our minds were food and bed. Although Chulumani is not as touristy as Coroico, there is no shortage of places to stay and it has its fair share of restaurants. However, if you want to be amidst the real country atmosphere and escape from the centre of town, I would recommend the Hostal Wiskeria Country House, which is about a fifteen minute walk from the Plaza. But, beware because there are no taxis in Chulumani. Do not pack to excess and bring along a torch.

Despite our weary legs the fifteen-minute walk to the hostel was certainly worth the effort. It is run by Javier Sarabia Sarbon and has a nice, cozy ambiance. As you will soon discover, Javier is the ever attentive host. On arrival we were presented with oranges, hand picked from his garden. He memorized our names within five seconds and only once during our stay did he make a blunder. The hostel only has a capacity of five rooms but they are equipped with twin beds, are spacious, immaculate and all come with their own bathroom. All the food is cooked by his wife, which does much to encourage a homely feeling. In addition there are an endless amount of activities. There is a bar, pool table, reading area, videos for rent and a swimming pool. As Javier will tell you, the water comes directly from the river and is free from all chemicals.

If all this is not enough to keep you entertained for the weekend then you can explore the surrounding areas. Hiking is a popular activity. Javier can suggest various routes or you can even ask for a guide to accompany you. There are plenty of options available. Alternatively, you can make your own way, as we did, to the lovely village of Ocabaya which claims to have the second oldest church in Bolivia. The actual route itself is breath-taking as you wonder through the forest. Never before have I seen so many banana plantations, orange and mango trees in such a confined space.

Another interesting day trip is the Apa Apa Ecological Forest, 8km from Chulumani. This cloud forest constitutes 800 hectares and is the last remnant of primary humid montane forest in the Yungas, abundant in tree, orchid and bird species. Just in the last five years this forest was declared as a protected area by the government. Recent research, in collaboration with a German scientist, has revealed the presence of 16 previously unknown plants. If the splendour of the forest is not enough to make this a worthwhile trip then the hospitality certainly will. Not only were we collected from our hostel by Señor Ramiro Portugal, but he was also our personal guide. A milkshake from his dairy farm was also included as part of the trip. In all my time in Bolivia so far, not even the juice stalls could compare with this strawberry milkshake.

Despite the relatively few visitors to Chulumani, it has so much to offer. It may not have scenic views of snow-capped mountains but scenic views it does have. As a weekend break I cannot think of a more idyllic location. Javier being a prime example, the locals are friendly and their hospitality is heart-warming. You can do as much or as little as you please and that is all part of Chulumani's rustic charm. The guide books simply do not do this town justice. Instead go and see for yourself just what ar exquisite place it truly is.

THE STRANGE PUYA RAIMONDII

BY CHRIS SYKES

If Rip Van Winkle had fallen asleep in Comanche a hundred years ago, he would have a woken to find that everything looked very much the same. On closer inspection, however, after a mighty 100 year yawn, he would have noticed that the mountain was a bit smaller, a neat little village had grown up around the base and the beginnings of an elegant farmhouse were now an abandoned, and decaying, yet still graceful ruin. Even the name of the town 'would have been subtly altered. Comanche is the anglicized version of *K'oma* and *Aycba,* two Aymara words meaning "clean or pure meat." Much of the mountain can now be found as the pavement on La Paz's streets, but the Puya Raimondii live on.

This prehistoric survivor is one of the more dramatic plants to be found in Bolivia. It survives in small pockets in Comanche, which has the largest and healthiest population, Peru and parts of the Cordillera de Vacas. The life cycle of the Puya Raimondii goes something like this:

A little seed is blown from the parent plant by the fierce winds that rip around the mountain. It lands in very rocky terrain, or in the cracks between rocks somewhere between 3,800m and 4,200m (nothing else will do, this is a very fussy plant) and takes root. Over the next 100 years it slowly matures into a robust but nondescript cactus bush with a root system covering an area with a radius of at least 16m. Then at some hidden and mysterious signal, the Puya blossoms. A huge spear of flowers is sent shooting into the air, reaching a height of 12m in only 30 days. The flowers bloom, little birds make their nests in between the flower stalks and the plant starts s secreting a highly flammable resin. Three or four months later, after the seeds have again been scattered, the plant ignites and bids farewell to this world in an incandescent blaze, leaving only a skirt of unburned leaves and perhaps a charred remnant of the once magnificent flower stalk as testimony to its passing.

It seems slightly unfair that the Puya only gets a couple of months of glory once in its life, and this after waiting a hundred years, but the sheer awe inspired by these plants more than make up for it. The shaft is made up of hundreds of pearl white and yellow flowers, which emit a surprisingly lovely smell. They tower above all the other plants in the area, reaching heights in excess of 12m. They were first documented by French botanist, Alcides D'Orbigny, when he traveled through the Cordillera de Vacas in October of 1830. According to Aymara legend, these plants have very powerful properties. You can be healed of your spiritual woes by merely spending some time near a flowering Puya Raimondii. They are also believed to be capable of a bit of matchmaking on the side. Any person who is worried about finding a suitable partner need only ask the plant and it will intercede with the gods on their behalf. Its a shame you can only do this every 100 years or so.

Sadly, the survival of the species is at risk. Because of the resin, they burn spectacularly and many people are tempted to give them a helping hand and light them before the flower has matured and been given a chance to scatter its seed. If this happens, the line of that plant is forever extinguished. Souvenir hunters have also been throwing rocks at the flower stems in order to knock a couple of blossoms off to take home. Many of they specimens in Comanche have large bare patches and rocks embedded in the inflorescence. The mining of granite blocks from the mountain still continues and this is eating into the habitat of the plant. All these factors contribute to the dangers of extinction that face the Puyas.

They are endemic to the Andean system and can be found nowhere else, in the world. Not enough studies have been completed on them to allow us any deeper insight into their role, but it is vital that efforts are made to save this stunning and spectacular plant from extinction. The Bolivian "Amigos de Naturelaza" recently took a tour group of interested people up to Comanche to learn more about the Puya. Mr Eduardo Machicado, whose family built and still owns the farmhouse that at the bottom of the rocky hill that is home to the Puyas, talked knowledgeably and enthusiastically about both the history of the area and the Puya Raimondii. If concerned groups like these persist in their efforts to save these plants, they may well be around for your grandchildren to witness the next flowering in 100 years' time.

SORATA, THE GARDEN OF EDEN

BY PETER McFARREN

egend has it that this charming valley town was the site of the biblical Garden of Eden. The perpetually snow-covered Illampu Mountain at 20,892 feet (6,368m) looms over Sorata and the surrounding corn, potato and wheat fields. The town, once a flourishing commercial center and the gateway to the gold mining regions of Tipuani and Mapiri, is laid out in the classic Spanish design, with two well-kept parks and a grid pattern of narrow, cobblestoned streets. Two streams carrying the melt-off from Illampu meet below the village. Sorata, located at 8,784 feet (2,678m) above sea level, is in the temperate zone and is an ideal place to visit for a weekend. During the December to March rainy season it may rain for an hour or two, but normally it's sunny. The remains of elegant estates that once housed rich landowners or gold miners still exist near Sorata, which is located five hours by bus from La Paz (or four hours by private vehicle).

Sorata is a village; therefore, the best way to get around is on foot. Almost everything you need (such as buses back to La Paz) can be found in the central plaza.

PRACTICAL INFORMATION FOR SORATA

Sorata Phone Code: 02

Asociacion de Guias Turisticas y Porteadores, Calle Sucre 302,

Tel. 81355044, Fax. 8115218. E-mail: guiasorata@hotmail.com Offers trekking in the Cordillera Real and the surrounding areas.

Tourist Office Illampu, Calle Murillo 212 at the Hostel Pnachita, Tels. 8135038, 8133700.

Trek Bolivia S.R.L. Calle Sagarnaga 392, Tel. 2317106, Fax. 2460566. E-mail: trekbo@ceibo.entelnet.bo

Bolivia Tours, Calle Sagárnaga in La Paz. E-mail: info@bolivia-tours.de Tel. 71255559. www.bolivia-tours.net

Club Sorata, located at the **Hotel Landhaus**, is the most reputable trekking agency in the area. They offer a variety of adventures, from nearby three-day treks to the seven-day Illampu circuit to the 24-day Knut-Berg-Hansen Trek, which starts in Carabuco on Lake Titicaca. Prices for these treks are usually $20 per day per person, which includes equipment, food, mules and guides.

• Hotels

Sorata has a wide selection of hotels for its size. Here are a few of the best:

Gran Hotel Sorata (ex-Prefectural), Avenida Samuel Tejerina, Tel. 2135201. Located at the entrance to Sorata above the *tranca*, this hotel offers guests beautiful views of Illampu and the valley, a swimming pool, garden, game room and dis-

LA PAZ DEPT.

cotheque on the weekends. Rooms with private bath cost $13, with shared bath, $12. For groups of 10 or more, each person pays about $8. All prices include breakfast, lunch and dinner. If you book through a travel agent, the prices will be much higher. Visa, MC, Am Ex.

Residencial Sorata (Casa Gunther), on Calle Villavicencio on the corner of the main plaza, Tel in La Paz, 2793459. Tel. 2-2136672. Fax. 2-2136680. E-mail: resorata@ceibo.entelnet.bo This is the former residence of a German merchant who became wealthy trading in gold and selling imported crystals, fabrics and household goods to the rich gold miners who passed through Sorata en route to La Paz. This hotel offers large bedrooms, clean bathrooms with hot showers and a lush, tranquil garden where one can eat breakfast, lunch or dinner amidst hummingbirds, bright flowers and palm trees. Rooms with private bath cost $7, a garden side room is $5 and the cheapest rooms on the second patio are $3. Prices do not include breakfast, which costs $2. The restaurant offers a fixed lunch and dinner for $2.50. The hotel also offers laundry service for $1.80 per kilo, book exchange, game room and videos. Visa, MC. E-mail: resorata@ceibo.entelnet.bo

Hotel Paraiso de Oro, Calle Villavicen- cio about a half block down from the main plaza, Tel. 2135043. This immaculate, modern hotel contains nine rooms with private baths, each costing $6. The rooftop terrace affords nice views of the valley, and guests can have their laundry done for $1.50 per kilo. The hotel serves breakfast, as well as a fixed lunch or dinner at about $2.75.

Hotel Landhaus, on the outskirts of town along Calle Marquilla, Tel/Fax. 2135042. E-mail: kramer@caoba.entelnet.bo This hotel offers comfortable and clean facilities at $6 per person on the ground

floor with private bath, $8 for rooms with a special view and $3.50 for rooms with a shared bath. Hearty, diverse breakfasts cost between $1-$5, lunch is approximately $5 and a set dinner costs $2.50. Guests can also change money or cash traveler's checks for a 2% commission. E-mail costs $10 an hour (much higher than in La Paz, due to long distance telephone costs). The owners have over 1,000 movie titles, and there always seems to be something playing in the lounge. A jacuzzi can be hired for $10 per half-hour, and a book exchange is also available. Club Sorata trekking agency is also located at this hotel. E-mail: clubsorata@mail.megalink.com

Hostal Panchita, Calle Enrique Peñaranda on the main plaza, Tels. In La Paz, 2329395, 2312939. Tel. 08115038. Offers 34 beds in 10 rooms, all with shared bath for an economical $2.50. This hostal also offers guests a T.V. salon and garden patio.

Hostal El Mirador, at the foot of Calle Muñeca, offers the "best view" to its guests. Dorm rooms go for $2 per person and regular rooms cost $3.50. All rooms have communal baths. The hostal serves a set breakfast at extra cost, but also allows guests to use the kitchen facilities. Also has free hot showers anytime.

Hostal Las Piedras, just outside the village on the way to the cave next to the soccer field.

Villa Sorata, Calle Fernando Guachalla 238. Tel. 2135241.

• Camping

Sorata offers two inexpensive camping options, each in a beautiful setting.

Altai Oasis Campground, an eco-friendly Shangri-La with Roxana or Johnny complete with lilies, waterfalls and sociable animals, offers camping, bathrooms, hot showers and fire pits for about $1.60 a night.

Café Illampu rests on a rise along the road to the San Pedro Caves and affords its campers an exquisite view of the mountains. For 80 cents you can pitch a tent and use the bathrooms and hot showers. Follow the signs out of town on Calle Marquilla. The owner Stefan will also provide all the necesary information about the caves.

For delicious pasta, pizza and other international dishes, try the German/Uruguayan-run restaurant **Kon-Tiki**. Restaurant has pizzas for $2 to $10, pastas for $2 to $5 (don't miss the gorgonzola pasta) and a famous crepe suzette. All art on the walls is Bolivian and is for sale.

• Restaurants

Due to the influx of tourists, Sorata has expanded in recent years, and has a handful of high-quality restaurants and cafes.

Diagonally across the plaza from the church is **Pete's Place**, it offers excellent European and vegetarian menu featuring dishes as varied as big breakfasts, hamburgers. Meals cost $ to $5. The restaurant is open Tuesday through Sunday from 8:30 a.m. to 12:00 p.m. Tel. 2895005. Also a useful tourist information.

For more national fare, try one of the two terraced restaurants on Calle Muñeca. **Restaurant El Ceibo**, on the left-hand side heading downhill, is open from 7:00 a.m. until 11:00 p.m., offering vegetarian fare, steaks, *pique macho*, sandwiches and other large-portioned meals in its expansive dining room. Prices range from $2.50 to $6. It also has an extensive bar, and is planning to add a *peña* stage and karaoke. On Sunday mornings, its specialty is *salteñas*.

Sorata also has one bar and one cafe, each with gorgeous views.

Hostal El Mirador (look for the sign), is open daily from 8:00 a.m. to noon, and 8:00 p.m. until whenever. Its comfy, sofa-chair atmosphere and patio garden make it a great place to meet people from all over the world. Breakfast costs between $1-2 while sandwiches run about $1.50.

Café Illampu, besides being an exquisite camping spot, is a relaxing place to sip tea, lie in a hammock and gaze at the magnificent view. In addition to tea, you may order coffee, juice or beer, then sit in the hand-carved wood pavilion while eating pastries or sandwiches that cost about $1.50. The cafe can be accessed by either a windy foot path (15 minutes from town) or longer road (1/2 hour). It is open every day except Tuesday from 9:00. to 19:00.

• Internet

The only Internet facilities in Sorata can be found on the main plaza for 5 Bs. per 15 mins. = 20 Bs./hr. (US $3). It just opened in August 2002, and has a very slow connection.

• Shopping

Residents of Sorata make some charming stuffed dolls, wall hangings and dresses from natural-dyed and hand-woven wool. These can be found on the main square at the **Artesanía Sorata**, which also sells beautiful postcards and has a book exchange. The Artesanía Sorata, owned by Diana Bellamy, is also located in La Paz on Calle Sarganaca.

• Laundries

Most hotels in Sorata offer laundry services, so your best bet is to check wherever you're staying.

• Medical Services

Renovated in 1995, the **Hospital Sorata** is modern and offers quality medical care. It is located straight up Calle Illampu from Obispo Bosque Plaza and is open every day until 10:00 p.m.

EXCURSIONS FROM SORATA

Sorata is the starting point for a number of climbs. For the daring, there is an Inca trail that begins near Sorata, crosses the Andes, and drops to the tropical gold mining region of Unutuluni and Tipuani. On this four-day trek you will travel from snow to jungle on a stone-paved **Inca highway** that crosses crystal-clear mountain streams and lagoons. This trail has been used since the time of the Incas to carry gold, coca leaves and other products to the highlands. On the trail you are likely to encounter herds of llamas or mules taking potatoes, corn and other goods to the tropics. For the trip, it is necessary to take a sleeping bag, tent and food supplies, including coca leaves to chew along the way.

Sorata is also the starting point for climbing the **Illampu Mountain**. For more information on climbing Illampu, as well as other treks in the Sorata area, be sure to read the book *Trekking in Bolivia* by Yossi Brain.

Those short on time can still enjoy day trips to the **San Pedro Caves**, the village of **Lakathiya** or **Laguna Chillata**. One of the most popular destinations around Sorata, the San Pedro caves offer views of bats, a subterranean lake and eerie, dripping rock formations. The winding road out of Sorata affords the hiker beautiful views of the surrounding valley and mountains en route to the caves (three to four hours each way). Information on these short trips is available at Club Sorata.

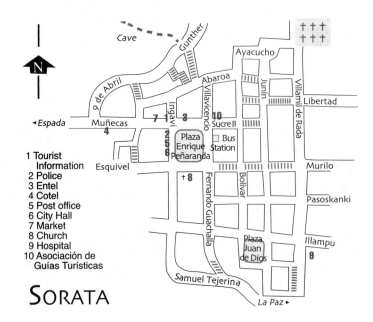

1 Tourist Information
2 Police
3 Entel
4 Cotel
5 Post office
6 City Hall
7 Market
8 Church
9 Hospital
10 Asociación de Guías Turísticas

SORATA

LA PAZ - SORATA - TITICACA LAKE

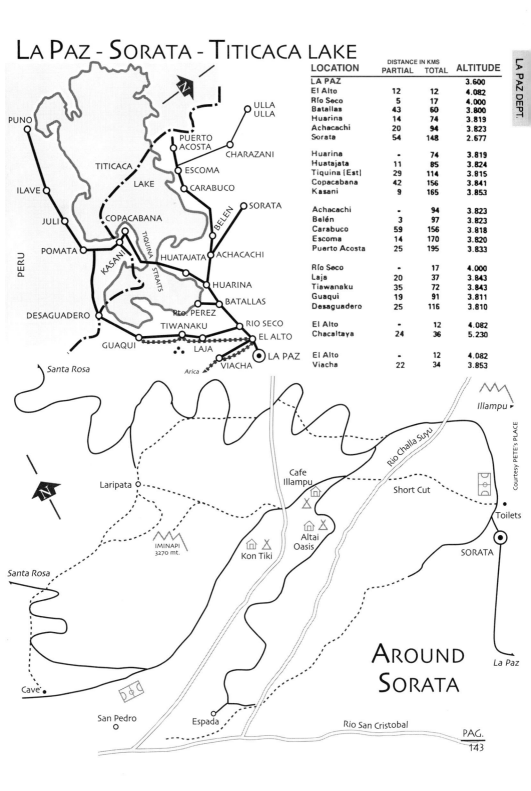

| LOCATION | DISTANCE IN KMS | | ALTITUDE |
	PARTIAL	TOTAL	
LA PAZ			3.600
El Alto	12	12	4.082
Río Seco	5	17	4.000
Batallas	43	60	3.800
Huarina	14	74	3.819
Achacachi	20	94	3.823
Sorata	54	148	2.677
Huarina	-	74	3.819
Huatajata	11	85	3.824
Tiquina (Est)	29	114	3.815
Copacabana	42	156	3.841
Kasani	9	165	3.853
Achacachi	-	94	3.823
Belén	3	97	3.823
Carabuco	59	156	3.818
Escoma	14	170	3.820
Puerto Acosta	25	195	3.833
Río Seco	-	17	4.000
Laja	20	37	3.843
Tiawanaku	35	72	3.843
Guaqui	19	91	3.811
Desaguadero	25	116	3.810
El Alto	-	12	4.082
Chacaltaya	24	36	5.230
El Alto	-	12	4.082
Viacha	22	34	3.853

AROUND SORATA

Courtesy PETE's PLACE

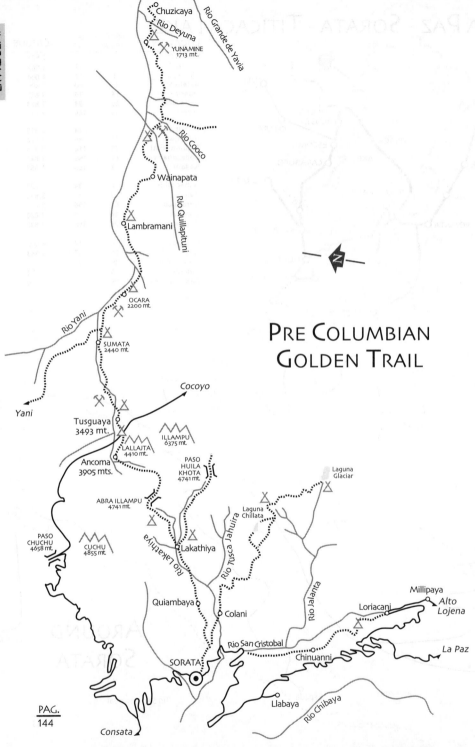

Chuzicaya

Rio Deyuna

YUNAMINE
1713 mt.

Rio Grande de Yavia

Rio Cooco

Wainapata

Rio Quillapituni

Lambramani

OCARA
2200 mt.

Rio Yani

SUMATA
2440 mt.

Cocoyo

Yani

Tusguaya
3493 mt.

ILLAMPU
6375 mt.

LALLAJTA
4410 mt.

Ancoma
3905 mts.

PASO
HUILA
KHOTA
4741 mt.

Laguna
Glaciar

ABRA ILLAMPU
4741 mt.

Laguna
Chillata

Rio Tusca Jahuira

PASO
CHUCHU
4658 mt.

CUCHU
4855 mt.

Rio Lakathiya

Lakathiya

Millipaya

Rio Jalanta

Loriacani

Alto
Lojena

Quiambaya

Colani

La Paz

Rio San Cristobal

Chinuanni

SORATA

Llabaya

Rio Chibaya

N

Pre Columbian
Golden Trail

Consata

A PARADISE LOST; SLEEPY SORATA

BY SARAH BALMOND

Imagine carpeted green hills, orange butterflies, sugar pink pastel blue homes, scattered palm trees - utter peace and quiet. A paradise lost? Not quite. Welcome to Sorata, a dozy, sleepy village nestled right in the heart of the Andes just four hours north of La Paz. It is a holiday choice for many Bolivians, and also a tourist destination for many gringos. Offering multiple treks for the active and a wonderful excuse to just sit and do nothing for the not so active, it is easy to see why Sorata has become so popular. A stressed out journalist made weary of all the hub bub of La Paz (if one more *truffi* honks I'll scream!) decided enough was enough and packed off her weary soul straight to Sorata in search of inspiration, good food and a bit of shut eye.

Sorata is easy to get to from La Paz. Just get to the cemetery and then from there find the Sorata Bus Depot only a short five minute walk from the cemetery center. The ticket to Sorata costs 11bs one way but it is important that you book at least a few hours in advance. The bus fills up very quickly and departure times, although supposed to be regular, are in fact very sporadic. The journey is pleasant enough, but beware - discomfort may be caused by all the standing passengers. These people hop off and on throughout the duration of the journey, and sometimes even sit in the aisle. You do feel like sardines, but it adds more to the sense of adventure. Just take note if you are claustrophobic.

The bus slowly climbs out of La Paz offering a spectacular aerial view of the city as you reach El Alto. The bus then continues in El Alto territory for a few hours, rocky lunar terrain giving way gradually to greener, more plush landscape. You skirt by Lake Titicaca seeing it from afar only as a dazzling blue smudge, and then pass by impressive mountains, snow capped but shrouded in low mist, so you can't distinguish between where the sky starts and where the mountains finish. If you're lucky the bus driver will tune the radio so that bright tones of folkloric music will fill the bus, making the journey seem all the more Bolivian. Then again, if you 're unlucky the bus driver will not bother tuning the radio, and all you will hear for four hours will be loud crackles and beeps. It's pot luck, but bring a walkman just in case.

Doze off for a while, wake up and you will be forgiven for thinking you have left Bolivia. As far as the eye can see everything is rolling green hills and tropical looking fauna. The browns and greys of La Paz are left behind and the lyrics of "Somewhere over the Rainbow" spring to mind. The climate of Sorata is eternally spring and forever warm because it is some thousand feets lower than La Paz. Bus passengers take off layers, open windows and begin to fan themselves.

The bus continues winding along skinny roads and then, suddenly Sorata comes in to view. Like a lazy cat it stretches itself across the valley, snuggled between mountains, basking in the sun.

The bus makes its way down into the valley and pulls into Sorata's main square, Plaza General Enrique Penaranda. As you get off children wave flyers at you, promoting different hotels and hostels. Its up to you where you stay and the good news is that pretty much all the places are within walking distance of the main square.

The square is undoubtedly the heart of Sorata. It is pretty landscaped with palm trees and plenty of benches. Lining the square are numerous restaurants and cafes. The hand painted signs advertising pizza and kitsch interior add charm to the eateries but also scream of gringos. To eat cheap, order the *almuerzo* or pizza personal. Tables are set outside, so you can peoplewatch and catch a tan. Ice cream vendors wander past tempting you with anonymous fluorescent goods, and children play in the street. If you're feeling in the mood, ask the owner of the restaurant for *"juegos"* (board games.) How lovely to pass an afternoon sipping a cool beer playing chess!

Wander off the square, and you will come across the various markets and stalls, selling everything from buttons to hair clips and Sangini. The main food market is held every Sunday, but avoid the meat market if you are squeamish. *Chola* women pluck and prune poultry whilst men line up pig's heads and intestines. You can walk the circumference of the city in about one hour (at a slow pace!) but is well worth doing, if only to fully see what is described by Lonely Planet as " medieval Sorata with steep stairways and a maze of narrow cobbled looking streets." The homes have simple facades but are decorated with baroque or renaissance touches like ornate window shutters or elaborate door frames. They are painted in a myriad of colors - azure blue, emerald green, hot pink, but paint is peeling

and flaking, giving Sorata the charm of a town that has seen its hey day in days gone by.

Indeed, Sorata used to be a very wealthy city. Alfredo Villamil De Rada, author of *La Lengua De Adan* (Adam's Tongue) says " In colonial days Sorata was a major trading center. Gold and rubber were produced here so all the merchants lived here." The rich from La Paz would come to Sorata to buy French champagne, imported silks and luxurious spices. Alfredo continues: "the farms were really well off as well. Everything could and was grown here because of the lovely climate. However, the 1925 revolution changed things. As land was divided amongst workers profits decreased. Now, nothing is farmed here. Everyone has gone off to work in the mines of Yahi, Conzata and Tipmani. The rubber trade quieted as well so for many years there was nothing here."

Sorata lay dormant, an impoverished city for many years, but it was Eduard Kramer, a German, who stumbled across the town whilst travelling, and who is now held responsible for injecting new life and tourism back into the area. A keen trekker himself, Kramer discovered the potential Sorata offered for hikers and ramblers. He says " Fourteen years ago when I first came here, there was nothing, Only three buses a week, two shops and one restaurant. The only tourists were hippies doped out on drugs. I came and just stayed. I fell in love with the region. who wouldn't? I developed the treks Sorata is now famous for, such as Gruta de San Pedro and Laguna Glacial. Now there are lots of European trekking agencies from Switzerland, Austria and Germany who have based themselves here." Restaurant owner of Pizzeria Napoles Mirtha de Quevedo confirms this: "Eduard has built this area up. Tourism has boomed the past years. Many Europeans come here to holiday, and many live here as well. There's quite a big ex-pat community." According to Eduard "high season is between May and October. Jesus, its so busy. English pubs and clubs open, and the town gets a real party vibe."

If, however, you go off season, expect very little to do at night. There are a few bars open and a peña where you can join in dancing, but apart from this, there isn't that much else to do. Still, all the more reason to just sit back and relax. Grab a cushion and curl up on the patio of your hotel with a good book. Listen to the crickets and the soft hum of the river, and fall blissfully asleep, dreaming of emerald green hills and a land once referred to as another Eden.

Trekking agencies to contact:
Trekking in Sorata, Guide Tourist Office "Illampu" Eco Tourism. Tel. 081315038.
Asociacíon de Guias Turisticas y Porteadores, Sorata, Tel. 08135044 and the highly recommended **Hotel Landhaus,** Ex-Copacabana and **Travel Agency Club Sorata,** Eduards agency. Hikes include "Knut Berg-Hansen trek" 24 days, "Laguna Glacier" 3 days, "Travers Trek" 4 days and " The Mamalaya Trail" 5 days. For additional information visit website www.khainata.com/sorata

Of interest to the region is the book *La Lengua de Adan* by Alfredo Villamil de Rada. The Bolivian writer Alfredo was so inspired by the greenery of Sorata and its crystal blue waters that he used it as an alternative setting for the Garden Of Eden. He postulated that Aymara was the natural language of Adam and that Cerro Illampu was the true Mount Olympus. The book is a poetic little gem and can be bought from Liberia Guisbert, on Calle Comercio Esquina Colon, La Paz.

Worth mentioning is Eduard's charming little **Hotel Club Sorata**, ex-Copacabana. The bedrooms are rustic and spacious, and cost anywhere between Bs.15 and Bs.25. The food is very good and service is attentive. The best thing though is the beautiful interior garden. Planted with tropical flowers and mini palm trees, the space is a wonderful Oasis, a place for quiet reflection guaranteed to de-stress.

CHAPTER 6

WITCH WAY PELECHUCO?

BY CRAIG COTTRELL

So here we were, a group of five hopeful hikers ready to take on the challenge of The Cordillera Apolobamba. Our starting point was Curva, an eerie fog-filled village straight out of a Boris Karloff movie. Luckily we'd chanced upon some simple accommodations though strange nocturnal noises and whooping children had us on edge. Curva is the capital for the Kallahuaya, the wandering magic men of Bolivia, so we were trying to do everything possible to invoke the favor of any local deities. "Don't punch that bag of bones!" Kat, one of my fellow walkers shouted. Then in a flash, shed covered the floor with our first meal, a pot of piping hot soup. "Pachamama" she lamented.

The rest of the night I spoke of spooks and ghoulish tales, not appreciated except by a Dennis Wheatley type homed skull, grimacing in the shadows of the room.

Nevertheless, sleep was demon free and we awoke to a wonderful sight of a gleaming mountain called Akamani, which spurred us into action. As we began the trail a corpulent toad flopped across our path. Another sign? "That reminds me", chimed in Kat, "there was a cauldron under our bed".

Skirting a knoll, according to our information, we dropped down to the stream we needed to cross and beared left. After a little way though it became apparent that we'd gone wrong. Turning back quizzically, we read and reread our directions, studied guidebook maps, and then lumbered up a grassy slope to find owselves in a valley. The guide said to cross a stream, then follow another. The problem was, which stream? We decided that the grassy plain was Jatunpampa and after more head scratching continued along side a stream, before heaving our way up what appeared to be the first pass.

By now it was late in the day and the mist was drifting up the next valley. Bemused by the map and unable to see a waterfall or a bridge, we took the most direct route down to the valley floor. In relation to my walks here, this has to be the most dangerous descent I've attempted, a steep, grassy incline, which had my heart fluttering as I stumbled laden down with a pack.

The three girls in our group were worryingly out of sight, not good in the ensuing gloom of twilight. But as they came into view above, a figure loomed below and thankfully offered the floor of his abode. He cleared a space and gave us a candle, lighting up our relieved faces and also directly dangling overhead, the woeful expression of a slime llama fetus. I think that was supposed to be auspicious.

The next morning was the kind that you dread. We discovered that Jatunpampa was in fact where we were now, not where we thought we were yesterday and the first pass was an extra we'd added in 'Blair

Witch' "forget the map!" barked my touchy Algerian friend. He was kind of right, though I wasn't about to throw it to the four winds. Thankfully there was no blue gunge on the tents or strange crosses in the trees (basically because there were no trees). "Be very careful", warned our host. "Two Dutch walkers went missing here in October and were never found". That was a great confidence booster. It was clear that we had to cross into the next valley. Bad weather didn't make this easy. It was a chilly ascent into mist once more with low morale. A ridge? There were bloody loads. And the only stream here was the stream of bad language I let flow as group mentality disintegrated. Basically we didn't know where we were and where we should be going. We dropped down once more and came to a full stop at the sight of a wall of rock around us. The circling condors provided a brief respite until we pondered as to why they were circling. It looked like game over and that we'd have to head back. However, after killing a few hours a man appeared in the distance tending some sheep. I went off to talk to him and gulped as he pointed up a huge edifice.

It was time for action. Huge lumps of thick stodgy porridge would be the key to success. The slow walk turned into a precarious clamber up an incline of unsteady stones and rocks, where adrenaline replaced tiredness. Two hours later we'd reached a plateau just in time for the clearing clouds to reveal a bewitching range of powdery white peaks on the horizon. This put a spring in our step even at 4900m. Just as well, as the supposed times between each places would have tested the lungs of Michael Johnson.

We sank into the next valley to arrive in a small gold mining village known as Sunchuli. The houses looked made for the likes of Sleepy, Grumpy and Dopey so we steered clear of rosy red apples and plumped for hot alpaca instead. Two men staggered in spellbound, and choked out that they'd been walking day and night in the heights for three days having also got lost in the fog - we'd got off lightly. A poster of the two 35-year-old Dutch couple fluttered sadly in the brisk air.

The next day was fortunately the domain of the fairy godmother. A cloudless sky provided heavenly vistas as we made it up to 5000 meters. Jumping onto a bank of snow, we spied a spot reachable above a snowy slope and a ledge. There, exaltation was found amid an amphitheater of summits, glaciers and icy ridges. The dark shadow of a condor passed ridiculously close and we could see viscachas bouncing in and amongst their rock pile colony.

For two hours we sat in bleary wonderment. After the doubts and the hardship this was a perfect reward, difficult to take in and harder to leave. But leave we had to. The guide said drop down steeply and connect with the path by the glacier lake. It might well have said, throw yourself off the cliff and hope you don't break too many body parts. After nearly coming to a messy end I decided there was no way down, so we chose the moss side, something I would avoid in England (our most notorious estate). We squelched through the boggy grass and followed a route into the village of Illo Illo.

The final day of the walk was upon us; traversing more picturesque plains before another a 1000 meters ascent, then testing the knees with a 400 meters descent to the charming community of Pelechuco. Far from being an anti-climax to the mountains, we were treated to lush expanses and the beautiful village itself a collection of stone houses with thatched roofs, cobbled streets and flower-rimmed lanes. Buckets of water for washing and a steamy brew of hot chocolate; luxury at last. All in all a magical experience.

For more information contact:
Area Natural De Manejo Integrado Apolobamba, Av. 20 de Octubre 2659, La Paz. Tel/Fax. 2434472.
E-mail: rmfuu@unete.com

Buses leave La Paz for Curva 3 times a week, Tuesday, Friday and Saturday, takes about 8 hours, return to La Paz on Wed, Sat. and Sun. Albergue is located outside of Curva, in Lagunillas. They have solar lighting and hot water for showers. Delicious meals available from the local community—only vegetarian food. Lodging costs Bs. 20, and dinners cost Bs. 20.

The other albergue is outside of Pelechuco, in Agua Blanca. Buses leave La Paz on Wednesday, return on Friday or Saturday, approximately 10 hours. Albergue has solar hot water and lighting. Lodging costs bs. 20, dinners cost bs 20, menu quite diverse, offering chicken curry, carne de llama, chocolate cake, guacamole, etc.

Each albergue has a fireplace, 2 dormitories with 6 beds in each room, 2 bathrooms. Quite luxurious.

THE SPRING VALLEY OF COCHABAMBA

BY PETER McFARREN

Cochabamba is the city of eternal spring. Nestled at the foot of Mount Tunari and other peaks, this valley city, at an altitude of 8,430 feet (2,529 meters), is an important agricultural center, as well as an alpaca handicraft center and a popular vacation spot. With a population of 778,422 Cochabamba is the third largest city in Bolivia.

Cochabamba, originally called Villa de Oropeza, was founded by Sebastián Barba de Padilla in 1574 in a valley known as Canata. The word "Cochabamba" comes from the Quechua words *Cocha* and *Pampa*, which mean lagoon and plain, respectively.

The flight from La Paz to Cochabamba in itself makes a trip to this charming city worthwhile. Leaving La Paz, the plane flies alongside the Mount Illimani and other snow-covered peaks. After 15 minutes of flight, you can see the tropical lowlands in the distance.

Once in town, to get a good view of Cochabamba, you have two excellent options. One is to get to **El Cristo**, the huge statue of Christ overlooking the city, by driving, biking or walking up the hill, or taking the recently-opened Teleferico that provides a spectacular view of the city. The other option is to go to the Coronilla on **San Sebastián Hill**. The entrance is on Av. Aroma. From this monument, which honors women and children who defended the city during the War of Independence, you will see Mount Tunari and the road to the Chapare, a lush, tropical region that has gained world fame as the country's principal coca-producing region.

The trip to **Villa Tunari** in the **Chapare** is very rewarding — the road snakes through the mountains and then drops to the tropics, offering stunning views. Villa Tunari borders a river that feeds the Amazon. It is dangerous to venture beyond the Chapare, unless you do it in organized boat tours that will take you up the Ichilo River to the Beni. Check with Fremen Tours, Tel. 4259392 in Cochabamba, Tels. 2414069, 2417062 in La Paz.
E-mail: vtfremen@caoba.entelnet.bo

Back in Cochabamba, **Plaza 14 de Septiembre** provides the exuberance of the valley's colorful trees and the 19th-century architecture of the buildings surrounding it, including the **cathedral**. **El Prado** offers a very pleasant atmosphere and many good stopping spots to relax and have a beer before lunch or dinner. Crossing the bridge over the Rocha River, at the northwestern end of the Prado, you will reach Av. Libertador Bolívar (also called Av. de Cala Cala Park), where before lunchtime one can find excellent *salteñas*. At the **Casa de la Cultura**, on the corner of Av. Heroínas and 25 de Mayo, there is a library that offers lectures, exhibitions and historical archives. The **Archaeological Museum** at the university has an impressive collection of pre-Columbian objects.

La Cancha, on Av. Aroma, is a lively, open-air market where one can find the exquisite products of the valley and see women wearing the characteristic dress of the area. In the section of La Cancha that is part of the railway station area, you can find all sorts of black market products including TV sets, video cameras, tape recorders, handicrafts, clothing and food.

Palacio Portales, on Av. Portales, is a grand mansion built by the tin baron Simón Patiño who was originally from the Cochabamba area. He amassed one of the world's largest private fortunes. The mansion was decorated by French designers who used the finest materials money could buy. It now houses a cultural center, very active all year round, which is funded by the Swiss Patiño Foundation. Patiño also built a sprawling estate in **Pairumani**, just above Vinto, a 30-minute drive out of Cochabamba on the road to Oruro. Check with the **Tourist Information Center** on General Achá 144, half a block from Plaza 14 de Septiembre, Tel. 4221793, to find out the hours when visits to Portales and Pairumani can be made.

The beautiful countryside surrounding Cochabamba is filled with dairy farms and villages with century-old homes. If you have a day to spare, hire a car and head out of town. Twenty minutes out of Cochabamba on the road to Santa Cruz, veer to the right by the Angostura Dam. In another 30 minutes, you'll reach **Tarata**, an old village with adobe homes and overhanging balconies that has changed very little in recent decades. In December, there is a colorful festival with dancers using the masks from the *Diablada*. Check with the Cochabamba Tourist Information Center for dates.

Instead of veering right at the dam, you can also head out to **Cliza**, **Punata** and **Arani**. These villages are also served by buses that leave from Av. San Martin. This area, the Valle Alto, is famous for its pottery and dairy products. Small white flags that hang in front of adobe homes indicate the sale of *chicha*, a fermented corn alcoholic brew.

Just below the **Taquiña Brewery**, 20 minutes from the city of Cochabamba toward the mountains, you will find the **Taquiña Restaurant**, great for its food, beer and the beautiful view of the Cochabamba valley it provides.

The road out of town toward the mountains leads those looking for a peaceful afternoon to the lovely village of **Tiquipaya**, a Quechua farming town where *campesinos* cultivate flowers, strawberries and vegetables.

For camping, hiking and fishing, a visit to **Mount Tunari** is recommended. It is 38 miles (62 km) from Cochabamba on the road to Morochata and Independencia. The climate is cold, but the scenery is spectacular.

Another farming village worth visiting is **Quillacollo**, located only eight miles from Cochabamba. The town's Sunday market is quite lively, offering something to do on a day when everything is pretty much shut down in Cochabamba's city center. In August, Quillacollo becomes overcrowded with thousands of pilgrims from La Paz, Santa Cruz and other cities who come to pay homage to the *Virgencita de Urkupiña*, a miraculous virgin of the area. Three days of offerings, feasting and dancing celebrate the generosity of this popular virgin. Hotels are packed during this observance.

PRACTICAL INFORMATION FOR COCHABAMBA

Phone Code for Cochabamba: 4

• Useful Addresses and Numbers

Tourist Information Center, Calle General Achá 144, half a block away from Plaza 14 de Septiembre. Tel. 4221793.

Police, Tel. 110.

Tourist Police, Tel. 120.

Ambulance, Tel. 181.

Post Office, Av. Heroínas, corner of Av. Ayacucho.Tels. 4230979, 4290983.

Entel, Av. Ayacucho, corner of General Achá, Tel. 4225210.

Immigration Offices, Calle Jordán 286, corner of Esteban Arce, Tel. 4225553.

Airport Information, Tels. 4220120, 4591820.

Bus Station, Av. Ayacucho corner with Aroma, Tels. 4223360, 155.

Long distance Calls.
Entel,101.
AES, 0-11.
Cotas, 0-12.
For **information**, dial 104.

• Consulates

Argentina, Calle Federico Blanco 929, Tels. 4255859, 4229347.

Brazil, Av. Oquendo, Edificio Los Tiempos, Tel. 4255860.

Chile, Av. Heroínas 620, Tel. 4253095.

Germany, Calle España 0149, Tel. 4254024, Fax. 4254023.

Holland, Av. Oquendo 654, Edif. Sofer, Tel/Fax. 4257362.

Italia, Calle Ayacucho, Tel/Fax. 4238650.

Norway, Av. Guillermo Urquidi E-2279, Tel. 4231951.

Paraguay, Av. 16 de Julio, Edif. El Solar, Tel/Fax. 4250183.

Peru, Av. Pando 1325, Tels. 4246210, 4240296.

Sweden, Calle Barquisimeto, Villa La Glorieta, Tel/Fax. 4245358.

Switzerland, Miguel de Aguirre 1140, Tel. 4242441.

United States, Av. Oquendo, Edif. Sofer, Tel/Fax. 4256714.

Venezuela, Av. Blanco Galindo Km 7.5, Tel. 4268311.

• How to Get There

A new airport (perhaps the most beautiful in Bolivia) has been built in Cochabamba, and it is quite modern, with operations running quite smoothly there. You can catch a flight to Coch (as it is called by locals) from any of the major airports in the country.

Cochabamba sits practically right in the center of Bolivia; thus, it is probably one of the easiest cities to reach by bus, whether coming from La Paz, Santa Cruz or Sucre.

• Airline Offices

Lloyd Aéreo Boliviano, Av. Heroínas, in the Edificio Arzobispado, close to the post office, Tels. 800103001, 800104321 (both toll free) and 4230325.

AeroSur, Av. Ayacucho s-0218, corner of Santiváñez, Tels. 800103030 (toll free) and 4323206.

Transporte Aéreo Militar, Calle Tumusla, corner of Heroínas.Tel. 4734510.

Aerolíneas Argentinas, Calle Ayacucho 0127, 2nd Floor, Office 4, Tels. 4526104.

American Airlines, Calle 25 de Mayo 262, Tels. 4226337, 4220996.

Air France, Calle 25 de Mayo 262, Tels. 4229323, 4255110.

Avianca, Av. Pando 1271, Hotel Portales, Tels. 4285444-51.

British Midland,Cathay Pacific, AeroMexico, AllNipponAirways, US Airways, Calle Antezana 826, Tel. 4523921.

Iberia, Calle Colombia E-0463, Tel. 4258099.

Korean Air, Calle 25 de Mayo 262, Tels. 4229323, 4255110.

Lan Chile, Lufthansa, Av. Heroinas O-130, Tels. 4253335, 4256443.

Varig, Av. Ayacucho 409, Tels. 4251738, 4222248.

• Buses

The bus station is on Av. Ayacucho,

on the corner of Calle Aroma, in the south part of town. It is right across from Cochabamba's huge, sprawling market. Tel. 4223360.

The bus companies listed below offer services to every main town in Bolivia:

Dorado, Tel. 4226387.

Copacabana, Tels. 4221648, 4222827.

Mopar, Tels. 4223349, 4251237.

Nobleza, Tel. 4222394.

• Getting Around Town

If you're staying in the center of town, Cochabamba is definitely navigable by foot. Downtown is lovely, so definitely take a walk, at least from the main plaza, Plaza 14 de Septiembre, down to Plaza Colón and El Prado.

If you're staying in the Recoleta, you might want to take a cab into the center. You definitely need to go on wheels to get to the airport or Tiquipaya. And the bus station is only within walking distance if you're staying at one of the hotels southwest of downtown.

• Radio Taxis

America, Tel. 4245678.

Aranjuez, Tel. 4241212.

Ciudad Jardín, Tel. 4241111.

Radio Taxi Bolivia, Tel. 4250437.

Radio Mobil America, Tel. 4241212.

CBA, Tel. 4228856.

Cristo de la Concordia, Tel. 4246546.

Ejecutivo, Tel. 4242692.

La Rosa, Tel. 4241190.

Portales, Tel. 4246100.

• Car Rental

Barron's Rent-a-Car, Calle Sucre 727, corner of Antezana, Tel. 4222774. Offers four-wheel-drive Toyotas and other vehicles.

International Rent-a-Car, Calle Colombia E-0361. Tel. 4226635.

Localiza rent a car, Av. Pando 1187, Tel. 4283132.

JR rent a car, Calle Ladislo Cabrera 232 Tiquipaya, Tel/Fax. 4288465.

• Car Repair

Don Pancho, Av. Melchor Pérez de Holguín, between Chaco and Olmos, Tel. 4284467.

Marañon, Calle Acre 1969, Tels. 4241162, 4283164.

• Hotels

DELUXE

Hotel Portales, Avenida Pando 1271, Tels. 4285444-51, Fax. 4242071, is a fancy, five-star hotel that offers two swimming pools, a sauna, raquetball, and elegant accommodations. It is conveniently located in the Recoleta residential neighborhood, 10 minutes from downtown or the airport. Single, $77; Double, $95; Suite, $155. All prices include breakfast and a welcome drink. Visa, MC, AmEx. E-mail: reservas@portaleshotel.com

Santa Rita Apart Hotel, Calle Buenos Aires 866, Tels. 4284827, 4280305, Fax. 4280512. Offers a classy, long-term place to stay. Apartments have up to three bedrooms, kitchen and bath, and the complex itself offers sauna, a pool, gardens and a garage. One bedroom, $75; Two bedroom, $110; Three bedroom, $160. Prices include breakfast. Visa, MC, AmEx. E-mail: jburgrit@santarita.entelnet.bo

Gran Hotel Cochabamba, Plaza Ubaldo Anze E-0415, La Recoleta, Tels. 4282553, Fax. 4119961. E-mail: cbbhotel@bo.net Is located five minutes from the Patiño mansion and 10 minutes by taxi from downtown and the airport. It offers a lovely garden, swimming pool, a garage and two tennis courts. Single, $66; Double, $85; Triple, $100; Suite, $110. Visa, MC, AmEx.

Hotel Diplomat, Av. Ballivián 0611, Tel. 4250687, Fax. 4250897. E-mail: info@hdiplomat.com Offers good views and rooms with private baths. Single, $63; Double, $73; Additional bed, $15. Prices include breakfast. Visa, MC, AmEx.

Hotel Aranjuez, Calle Buenos Aires E-0653, Tels. 4280076-79, Fax. 4240158. E-mail: reservas@aranjuezhotel.com Offers elegant and comfortable rooms in a beautiful, tranquil setting. Single, $59; Double, $69; Triple, $84; Suite, $105. Prices include breakfast. Visa, MC, AmEx.

Gran Hotel Ambassador, Calle España 0349, Tel. 4259001, Fax. 4257855, is a four-star hotel located downtown, just a couple of blocks from Plaza 14 de Septiembre. It has a garage and an international restaurant. Single, $40/$45 (executive); Double, $50/$55 (executive); Triple, $60; Quadruple, $70; Prices for suites: Single, $60, Double, $70. Visa, MC, AmEx. E-mail: ambassrv@comteco.entelnet.bo

Apart Hotel Queen Elizabeth, Parque. D. Canelas 1555, Tel. 4245770, Fax. 4248350.

Hotel Cesar's Plaza, Calle 25 de Mayo 210-223, Tel. 4254032, Fax. 4250324.

Hotel Jordán, Calle 25 de Mayo 651, Tel. 4225010, Fax. 4224821.

Residenciale Concordia, Av. Aroma 437, Tel. 4257131, Fax. 4225452.

Hotel El Carmen, Av. B. Galindo Km 5, Tel. 4242436, Fax. 4244765.

Hotel Hacienda De Kaluyo, 15 minutes away from the city in direction to Tarata, Tel. 4576676, Fax.4576593. E-mail: info@kaluyo.com

MODERATE

Apart Hotel Regina, Calle España 636, between Reza and El Prado, Tels. 4234216, Fax. 4117205, has both regular hotel rooms and apartments with kitchen, bath and television. The complex offers a restaurant and laundry and room service. Prices for regular hotel rooms: Single: $25; Double: $38. For apartments: One bedroom: $42; Two bedrooms: $58; Three bedrooms: $68. Visa, MC.

Hotel Boston, Calle 25 de Mayo 1167, Tel. 4228530, is two blocks from Plaza 14 de Septiembre and three blocks from El Prado. The hotel offers laundry services, and all rooms have private bath and television. Single: $22; Double: $32; Triple: $42. All prices include breakfast. Visa, MC.

Hotel Emperador, Calle Colombia E-860, Tel. 4229343, is centrally located a few blocks from Plaza 14 de Septiembre. Its rooms offer private baths and television. Single: $15; Double: $25; Triple: $30; Suite: $35. All prices include breakfast.

Americana Hotel, Calle Esteban Arce S-788. Tels. 4250553, 4250554, Fax. 4250484. Single: $25; Double, $35; Triple, $45.

Hotel Ideal, Calle España 329, Tel. 4257930, Fax. 4259430.

Hotel Las Vegas, Calle Esteban Arce 352, Tel. 4229217, Fax. 4229976.

Hotel Mary, Calle Nataniel Aguirre 601, Tel. 4252488, Fax. 4251746.

Hotel Ovando, Calle Ayacucho 106, Tel. 4222450, Fax. 4501212.

Hotel Planeta de Luz, Quillacollo, Tels. 4261234, 4264324, Fax. 4291031. E-mail: planeluz@albatros.cnb.net

Hotel Regina, Calle Reza 359, Tel. 4257382, Fax. 4117231.

Uni Hotel, Calle Baptista 111, Tel. 4235065, Fax. 4235066.

Hotel Tropical Palace, Calle Nataniel Aguirre 880, Tel. 4228256, Fax. 4222856.

Hotel Gala, Calle Esteban Arce 852, Tels. 4252054-6, Fax. 4226272.

Hotel El Salvador, Calle Montes 420, Tel. 4227307.

Residencial Jordan, Calle Antezana 671, Tel. 4229294, Fax. 4224821.

INEXPENSIVE

Hotel Capitol, Calle Colombia 415, Tel. 4224510, Fax. 4223422.

Hotel City, Calle Jordan 347, Tel. 4229137, Fax. 4254614.

Hotel El Rey, Calle Barrientos 1425, Tel. 4229598, Fax. 4220620.

Hotel Heroinas, Av. Heroinas 239, Tel. 4230670.

Hotel Claros, Av. Aroma 152, Tel. 4234366.

Hotel Central, Calle General Acha 235, Tel. 4223622, Fax. 4254405.

Hotel Colonial, Calle Junin 134, Tel. 4221791.

Hotel Elisa, Calle Agustin Lopez 834, Tel. 4254406, Fax. 4235102.

Hotel Jardin, Calle Hamiraya 248, Tel. 4247844.

Hotel Internacional Inn, Calle Junin 468, Tel. 4248304, Fax. 4254884.

Hotel Masegal, Calle Junin 671, Tel. 4259485.

Hotel Oruro, Calle Agustin Lopez 864, Tel. 4224345.

Residencial Brasilia, Calle Brasil 560, Tel. 4222107.

Residencial Buenos Aires, Calle 25 de Mayo 329, Tel. 4224005, Fax. 4254005.

• Restaurants

Those who want to make a spontaneous decision on where to eat dinner should head to the Paseo Boulevard, a popular walking strip just half a block from Plaza de la Recoleta filled with fun, affordable and tasty dining options. Most of the other best restaurants in Cochabamba are found in the city center, near Plaza Colón and El Prado.

Gran Ambrosia Restaurant, Paseo Boulevard 687, Tel. 4485005, is arguably Cochabamba's most classy, elegant dining option. Don't miss it.

Casa de Campo, Paseo Boulevard 618, Tel. 4243937, is renowned for its authentic Bolivian food and affordable steak dishes. Visa, MC, AmEx.

La Estancia, Paseo Boulevard 718, Tel. 4249262, also offers excellent meat dishes and a great atmosphere. Visa, MC, AmEx.

Chifa Lai Lai, Paseo Boulevard 129, Tel. 4240469, offers tasty Chinese food in a comfortable environment. Very affordable, but not cheap. Visa, MC, AmEx.

Hotel Cochabamba, Plaza Ubaldo Anza E0415, La Recoleta, Tels. 4282551-55, is one of the best restaurants in Cochabamba, with both international and national food. Expensive, at least by Bolivian standards. Visa, MC.

Restaurant Suiza, Av. Ballivián (El Prado) 0820, Tels. 4257102-03, offers a good selection of quite expensive continental dishes, including tasty seafood, and has an ambiance to match. Closed Sunday.

La Cantonata, Calle España 409, on the corner of Mayor Rocha, Tel. 4259222, offers some of the best Italian food in Bolivia. Definitely recommended for a romantic night out on the town. A bit expensive, but worth it. Visa, MC, AmEx.

Montecatini, Av. Villarroel, Tel. 4281507, is another good choice for excellent, and less expensive, Italian food. Open only for dinner. Visa, MC.

Buffalo Rodizio, 2nd floor of the Torres Sofer Mall, Tel. 4251597, is the ultimate dining experience for beef lovers. Go with a big appetite for the extensive salad bar and the all-you-can eat meat. Open every day for lunch and every night but Sunday for dinner. Visa, MC, AmEx.

Quinta Guadalquivir, El Temporal (Cala cala), Tel. 4243491.

Fratelos, Av. Pando 1143, Tel. 4402050, offers a wide variety of meat and fish dishes. Visa, MC.

Restaurant Chop Las Palmeras, Calle Lanza 248, Tel. 4228559, offers traditional Bolivian food.
B & J Victors Restaurant, Av. Libertador Bolívar 1580, Tel. 4248629, offers seafood and steak.
El Gran Asador, Calle Junin 842.
America, Calle Bolivar 971.
Comercio Bar Shop, Calle Jordan 360.
El Prado, Av. Ballivian 571.
El Recanto, Av. Santa Cruz 1209.
Grill, Av. Santa Cruz 1335.
La Casa de Gordo, Av. Zamudio 1847.
Magui, Av. Blanco Galindo 1173.
Palacio del Fricasé, Calle Calama 530.
Palacio del Silpancho, Calle Baptista corner with Mexico.
Quinta Miraflores, Calle Tarija 1314.
Savarin, Av. Ballivian, 626.
For typical dishes look for **Doña Leo** on Av. Simon Lopez or **Doña Pola** on Av. America. For vegetarian, there are **Gopal** on calle España 250 and **Govinda** on calle Baptista corner with Mexico.

Pizzerias

Eli's, Calle 25 de Mayo corner with Ecuador.
Cozzolisi, Av. Heroinas 621.
Don Corleone, Calle España.
Guilley´s, Plaza Recoleta.
Rondevu, Calle 25 de Mayo corner with Colombia.
Cozzolisi Pizza, Av. Pando.

Salteñerias

El Canguro, Av. Ballivian on Plaza Colon.
La Jaya Salteña, Plaza Recoleta.
Bacia, Plaza Cala Cala.
Los Castores, Av. Ballivian 420.
Heladeria Dumbo, a colorful ice cream and hamburger joint that is border-line tacky but hard to beat for its value and desserts. Dumbo has two locations, one on Avenida Heroínas 345, Tels. 4253748-9, the other on Av. Ballivián (El Prado), Tel. 4234223.
Bambi, Calle 25 de Mayo corner with Colombia.
Globos, Av. Santa Cruz.
Imperial, Calle Sucre 322.
Los Escudos, Av. Heroinas.
Unicornio, Av. Heroinas corner with Baptista.

Café Tea Shops

Di K'afe, Calle Pando.
Edén, Av. Salamanca 639.
El Pahuichi, Calle 25 de Mayo 127.
Oriental, Calle My. Rocha on Plaza Colon.
Zurich, Av. San Martin corner with Colombia.

• Travel Agencies

Fremen Tours, Calle Tumusla 245, Tel. 4259392, Fax 4117790. Undoubtedly the best agency doing tours into the jungle, including the nearby Chapare. Fremen can also offer guidance to those looking to further explore the department of Cochabamba. E-mail: fremencb@pino.cbb.entelnet.bo
Delicias Tours, Av. Heroinas 165, Tels. 4225059, 4226551, Fax. 4234985. E-mail: delicias@pino.cbb.entelnet.bo
Lauretana Ltda., Calle Bolívar 425, Tels. 4289938, 4224672. Offers tours to Valle Alto, Parumani, Quillacolla, Portales, Incachaca, Toro Toro and the Chapare.
Caxia Tour, Calle Esteban Arce 563. Tels. 4226148, 4250937. E-mail: caxiasrl@supernet.com.bo
Jamali, Av. Ayacucho 471.
Turismo Santa Rita, Calle Buenos Aires 866. Tels. 4281843, 4280305, Fax. 4280512. E-mail: jburgrit@santarita.entelnet.bo

Carve Tour, Av. Heroinas 637.
Aventur S.R.L., Av. Ayacucho 113,
Tels. 4582124, 4582125.
E-mail: mirtha@aventur.zzn.com
Cobotur, Av. Ballivian 888,
Edif. Concordia, Tels. 4254257-59.
Exprintbol S.R.L., Plaza 14 de
Septiembre 242, Tel. 4255834.
E-mail: exprint@albatros.cnb.net
Exprintur, Plaza 14 de Septiembre
252, Tels. 4257790-93.
Genesis Tours, Calle Ecuador
E-470, Tels. 452322, 4223115.
Fax. 4524077.
E-mail: genesis@supernet.com.bo
Glowilden Tours, Calle Uruguay 454,
Tels. 4241795, Fax. 4227784.
Kanatur, Av. Salamanca 595,
Tels. 4258360, Fax. 4258361.
Prisma S.R.L., Calle Gral. Achá 127,
Tels. 4582160-61, Fax. 4234181.
Turismo Balsa Ltda, Av. Heroinas
184, Tels. 4580485, 4254503, Fax. 4225795.
Unitours, Av. Heroinas corner with
Baptista, Edif. Arzobispado, Tels. 4227711,
Fax. 4222109.
E-mail: unitours@supernet.com.bo
Premiere Travel, Calle Jordan 201,
Edif. Alba, Tel. 4502111, 4502207,
Fax. 4113802.
E-mail: premier@supernet.com.bo
Emete Ltda, Av. Salamanca 555,
Tels. 4524143, 4524068.

• Museums, Churches and Cultural Centers

Centro Portales, Av. Potosí 1450/1480,
Tel. 4243137. Guided tours are offered
Monday – Friday, 17:00 in Spanish, 17:30
in English, and on Saturday, 11:00 in
Spanish, 11:30 in English.

This lovely palace was built between
1925 and 1927 by Tin Baron Simón Patiño,
even though he never lived there. Its architecture depicts a Renaissance French

style, and its rooms have Morrocan, Gothic
and Baroque influences, imitating those of
the Palace of Versailles. On the upper floor
are chambers with reproductions of the
Sistine Chapel.

The Patiño Palace contains a vast
botanical garden, finely crafted sculptures,
and great halls with Napoleonic and Louis
XV furniture. The gardens alone, complete
with fountains and terraces, occupy ten
hectares of the estate, and were designed
by Japanese experts.

Patiño brought in dozens of European
laborers and material to build this palace,
decorated throughout with Carrara marble
and paintings. It now serves as an important cultural center funded by the Patiño
Foundation.

Portales sponsors the Luzmila Patiño
musical festival and a wide variety of cultural programs, including outdoor musical
and theatrical presentations.

Also worth visiting is **Pairumani**, the
Patiño family farm located 20 kilometers from
Cochabamba. Contact the Tourist Information
Center for visiting hours and directions.

**Museo Universidad Mayor de San
Simón**, Calle Jordán and Calle N. Aguirre,
Tel. 4428090. Open Tuesday to Friday 8:30
to 18:30, and Saturdays and Sundays 9:00
to 13:00. Partly owned by the University of
San Simón, this museum consists of
20,000 pieces from cultures such as the
Sauce, Mojocoya, Nazcoide; Tiwanacotas,
Yampara, Kolla and Chullpas.

Cathedral, Plaza 14 de Septiembre.
This is the oldest church in Cochabamba.
It was built in the 16th century and rebuilt
in the 17th century. The front of the
Cathedral is done in a neoclassical style,
and the church holds an interesting collection of colonial paintings and furniture.

Temple of San Francisco, Calle 25
de Mayo, on the corner of Bolívar. This
monastery church was built in the 16th
century and has some elaborately-carved

wooden galleries and gold-leafed altars.

Temple of Santo Domingo, Santiváñez, corner of Ayacucho. Built in the early 17th century and rebuilt in 1778, the temple has a beautiful facade and side portal.

Temple of Santa Teresa, Baptista, corner of Ecuador. Built in the 17th century, this temple has a beautiful dome, wonderfully-carved altars and colonial paintings in its galleries. The convent adjacent to the church is under restoration and should open in the near future.

Museo Arqueologico, Calle Jordan corner with Nataniel Aguirre.

Museo Cristo de la Concordia, Cerro de San Pedro.

Museo Simon Patiño, Recoleta.

Casa de la Cultura, Av. Heroínas, corner of Calle 25 de Mayo.

Alianza Francesa, Santiváñez 187 Tel. 4252997.

Centro Boliviano Americano, Calle 25 de Mayo. Tel. 4251225.

Instituto Cultural Boliviano Alemán, Calle Sucre 693. Tel. 4228431.

• Bookstores

Lectura, Jorge Wilsterman Airport, 1st floor, Tel/Fax. 4590469.

Los Amigos del Libro, Av. Heroínas 138, Tel. 4254114. Offers magazines and books in Spanish, English, German and French.

La Juventud, Plaza 14 de Septiembre 290, Tel. 4250127.

• Internet

Internet Bolivia, España 280 near Ecuador, on the mezzanine level, has 50 computers, where one can hop on the Internet for less than a dollar an hour. Open every day from 8:00 to 22:00. Definitely the best spot in town, though there are countless other Internet cafes dotting the center of town.

• Shopping

If you feel like doing some first-world shopping, go to the **Torres Sofer Mall** on Calle Oquendo, which is filled with shops and items you would find back home. Another locale that seems a bit out of place is **I.C. Norte**, a full-fledged supermarket with everything from bagels to Lucky Charms.

For those who want to feel like they're in Bolivia when they shop, head to the town's authentic market, **La Cancha.** In addition, there are a handful of small galeries worth checking out: for artisan ware, try **Fotrama,** Calle Bolívar 439, or **Kay Huasy,** Esteban Arce 427; for leather goods, go to **Chenza,** Calle 25 de Mayo 394, or **Roger's,** Av. Ayacucho S-108. **El Atico,** Aniceto Padilla 775, Paseo peatonal (Recoleta). **ASARTI alpaca,** Calle Mexico corner with Av. Ballivian, Edif. Colon, local 5, Tel. 4246901. **Puerta de Sol,** Av. San Martin corner with Bolivar. **Coimsud,** Av. Ayacucho 741. **Vicuñita Handicrafts,** Av. Rafael Pabón 777, Tels. 4255615, 4229694.

• Sports

Club Tenis de Cochabamba, Av. Ramón Rivero, Tel. 4257079, also at Plaza Montenegro, Tel.4257080.

Estadium Felix Capriles, Av. L. Bolivar.

Gimnasio Curasau, Calle Ayacucho 435.

Raquet Sauna Curasau, Calle Ayacucho 435.

Raquet Sauna Club, Calle Reza 359.

• Nightlife

If you're in the mood to be social, just head down to **Calle España,** near Ecuador and Mayor Rocha, where you'll find a plethora of bars and cafés, all filled with music and people. Two recommended hotspots are **Café Tío Lucas**, whose owner is known for his eccentricity, and **Metrópolis**, which is smoky but has great pasta.

Another option, especially if you're in the mood to dance, is to go to the **Recoleta**, where you can also wander and choose from many lively places.

The Prado (Avenida Ballivian) also offers a variety of venues, including the underground discotheque **Cortingles**, the nightclub **Champagne**, which offers live comedy acts and dancing, and numerous karaoke bars.

Bars, Pubs
Angel Azul, Paseo Boulevar.
Bambu, Av. Ballivian 694.
Géminis, Calle Jordan, Edif. Albugoch.
Gipsy, Av. Ballivian.
Aladino, Calle España corner with Mexico.
Carajillo, Calle España corner with My. Rocha.
La Cahatarra, Av. Ballivian 675.
Business, Av. Uyuni.
News, Paseo Boulevar.

Night Club, Karaoke
Versus, Paseo Boulevard.
Automania, Av. Prado.
Alcatraz, La Recoleta.
D'Mons, Calle Tarija 1535.
Nostalgias, Plaza Quintanilla.
Amor, Prado.
D'Caruso, Calle 16 de Julio.
Seul, Av. Ballivian.
EX, Paseo Boulevard.
Comics, Av. America corner with Potosí.

• Movies
Cine Avaroa, Calle 25 de Mayo, just up from Plaza Colón, Tel. 4221285.
Cine Capitol, also on Calle 25 de Mayo.

Cine Astor, near Calle Esteban Arce, Tel. 4224045.

• Banks
Banco Mercantil, Calle Calama E-201, Tel. 4251865.
Banco Nacional, Calle Nataniel Aguirre S-198, Tel. 4251860.
Banco Santa Cruz, Av. Ramón Rivero 708. Tel. 4252658.
Banco de Crédito, Av. Ayacucho, corner of Santiváñez, Tels. 4252752-53.
City Bank, Calle Nataniel Aguirre 501, Tel. 4500150.

• Money Exchange
American Ltda, General Achá 162, Tel. 4222307.
Exprintbol, Plaza 24 de Septiembre 252, Tel. 4254413.

• Couriers
DHL, Av. Ramón Rivero 310, Tels. 4523628, 4523460, Fax. 4257254.
FedEx, Calle Paccieri 662, Tel. 4225900, Fax. 4225903.
CBK Courier, Edif. La Promotora, Of. 7, Tel. 4255094, Fax. 4223612.
IBC, Calle Bolivar 682, Tels. 4258112, 4256532.
Mega Express, Av. Ayacucho 378, Tel. 4222605.
New World Trade Courier, Calle Nataniel Aguirre 685, Tel. 4290605.
OCS, Av. Calancha 1265, Tels. 4240084, 4241773, Fax. 4115118.
Sky Net, Calle J. Cruz Torres 1466, Tel. 4253773.
UPS, Av. España 280, Edif. Bolivar 2nd floor, Tel. 4258948.

• Laundries
Super Clean, 16 de Julio 392, Tel. 4254225.
España, Av. Juan de la Rosa 765, Tel. 4325535.

• Medical Services

Centro Oncologico, Av. Linde, in Tiquipaya. A bit hidden and hard to find, but definitely the best medical facility in town.

Clínica Belga, Calle Antezana 455, corner of Paccieri, Tel 4231403.

Clínica La Paz, Plaza Barba de Barba de Padilla.

Clínica San Pedro, Calle Aurelio Melean 154.

Hospital Viedma, Av. Aniceto Arce.

Clínica San Vicente, Tel. 4254322.

Drug Stores

Droguería Boliviana, Plaza 14 de Septiembre, Tel. 4226749.

Farmacia Moderna, Calle Jordan between San Martin and 25 de Mayo, Tel. 4256509.

EXCURSIONS FROM COCHABAMBA

The department of Cochabamba is filled with places to visit, ranging from jungle towns to quaint villages. Those who are the most adventurous should rent a car; otherwise, just hop on a bus (try the main bus station, or ask the Tourist Information Center for directions to smaller bus centers around town) or join a tour group.

Wara Wara

A lake situated on the mountain range above Cochabamba at approximately 13,300 feet (about 4,000 m). Ideal for hiking and camping.

Angostura

This artificial lake, originally built for irrigation, is located 10 miles (16 km) from Cochabamba on the old road to Santa Cruz. Cabins and restaurants are located on its shores. A favorite spot for fishing and boating.

Corani

This hydroelectric dam feeds the Santa Elena and Santa Isabel electricity-generating plants located on the road to Chapare, 40 miles (64 km) from Cochabamba. Also a good fishing spot, with scenic views.

Incachaca

Only 90 minutes along the road from Cochabamba to Santa Cruz the dry valleys give way to the rich tropics of the Chapare. The road breaks off to the East and heads to Incachaca, a pre-Colombian site. A few minutes off the main road is the Conquistador trout farm and restaurant. The farms rents fishing reels to children who are charged 10 Bs and then 22 Bs per kilo of the fish they catch. The road continues to what is left of an old hydroelectric plant and father along a lagoon and pine forest. A new hydro plant is also under construction just beyond. This area is visited largely on weekends and vacations by dozens of largely Bolivian and some foreign tourists. Rolling hills covered in heather, deciduous forest with the sweet smell of pine and, of course, low clouds and drizzle.

Cerro del Tunari

This imposing mountain within view of the city of Cochabamba is located at 17,000 feet (5,200 meters) above sea level. It is inhabited by condors, llamas and vicuñas.

Two routes can be taken to reach it. One route follows the road to Morochata until the crossroad to Cocapata, which is in the middle of the mountain range, and from where one can see the peak. A four-hour walk will take you to the peak, which is often covered with snow. The second route goes past Pairumani up to Scaypata, and then by foot to the top of the mountain.

Quillacollo

This Quechua and Spanish-speaking community is located on the road to La Paz and Oruro and is fast becoming an extension of Cochabamba. An important province of the department of Cochabamba, located 8 miles (13 km) from the city, it is part of the central valley and was inhabited 3,000 years ago by the Aymaras.

Every year during the week of August 15, tens of thousands of the faithful descend on the Sanctuary of the *Virgen de Urkupiña*, located near Quillacollo. Dancers perform the *Diablada*, *Morenada* and other traditional dances during this festivity. During this time, hotels in Cochabamba are packed, so plan ahead.

Tarata

Capital of the province of Esteban Arce, this colonial town is located 20 miles (32 km) from the city of Cochabamba. Inside the Franciscan convent are the ashes of the martyr San Severino, patron saint of the town, also know as the "Saint of Rain." The town's main festival takes place the last Sunday of November, when thousands of area residents converge for a day of dancing, drinking and eating.

Huayculi

An alfalfa-growing region, located a few kilometers from Tarata. Also has a thriving ceramic industry.

Cliza

Located 26 miles (42 km) from the city of Cochabamba, this is an old agricultural center that specializes in road pigeon. Cliza has a colorful market on Sundays.

Punata

Located 29 miles (47 km) from the city of Cochabamba, Punata is an important agricultural center that is famous for its *chicha* production. A farmers' market brings together city and rural residents; on sale are agricultural products, cattle and handicrafts.

Also worth visiting are the villages of **Mizque** and **Aiquile**, beautiful small towns that preserve the traditions and customs of Cochabamba. Aiquile is famous for its production of fine *charangos*.

Arani

This provincial capital is located 33 miles (53 km) from the city. One of the most important religious festivals of the Valle Alto is celebrated in homage to the Virgin *La Bella* here. The Arani Temple is one of the greatest architectural legacies left from the colonial period.

Incarracay

Incarracay is located 20 miles (32 km) from Cochabamba on the road to Sipe Sipe. In the central Cochabamba valley, the Tawantinsuyu, or Inca, organized the extensive colonization of the highland Aymara and other ethnic groups in the area. The groups were assigned lands to produce corn on a large scale. It is very possible that Incarracay operated as an administrative center to control these and other state activities.

In 1937, the site, which offers stunning views, was declared a national monument. In 1956 and 1960, the German archaeologist H. Trimborn carried out extensive studies of its structures, identifying the Incan origin of the site.

Despite the fact that the site has been abandoned and vandalized, it is still remarkably well-preserved. The greatest danger, however, is the problem of erosion.

Incallajta

The fortress of Incallajta is the most important architectural expression of the Tawantinsuyu expansion to the Cochabamba valleys. Beginning in 1532, the Tawantinsuyu state expanded to several regions of the Cochabamba valley, primarily in an attempt to benefit from the tremendous agricultural potential of the area. For this purpose, the rulers implemented an extensive road system, market centers and forts.

Sarmiento de Gamboa, a sailor, adventurer, writer and faithful aide to the Viceroy of Toledo in the Andes, states in his narrative written in 1572 that Inca Topa Yupanqui ordered the construction of "the Pocona fort" (Incallajta is the modern name) between 1460 and 1470 to protect the advancing Tawantinsuyu from the fearsome advance of the Chiriguanos. The settlement was abandoned as a result of the profound internal crisis that the Inca state went through before its collapse in 1532.

Almost four centuries after these events, the Swedish explorer E. Nordenskjold visited and explored the site, confirming with his discoveries its Incan origins. It was declared a national monument in 1929.

The Incallajta fort is composed of a series of buildings on an area of approximately 12 hectares, following the form of a sloping alluvial platform, bordered at the east and west by deep and torrential streams. The Machajmarca river to the south and the precipitous hills to the north offer the fort an important strategic importance and difficult access.

The fort, which was originally surrounded by a solid wall, is built into terraced levels and walls, using stone held together by mud found in the area. The rectangular rooms are some two stories high.

A four-wheel-drive vehicle is needed to reach these ruins, which are located 75 miles (about 120 km) from Cochabamba on the road to Santa Cruz. Follow the road to Pocona for eight miles (13 km) until you reach Collpa, where you take a road to the right. After another 6 miles (10 km) you reach Incallajta, located above the Machajmarca river.

It is recommended that you take along a guide who knows the road. Two temples and several dwellings remain at Incallajta. Be sure to bring food and warm clothing.

The Chapare/Villa Tunari (Carrasco National Park)

Villa Tunari is located in the Chapare, about 95 miles (153 km) from Cochabamba on the main road linking Cochabamba with Santa Cruz. The trip from Cochabamba is quite spectacular, but be careful in the rainy season, when landslides may interrupt traffic for several hours.

Villa Tunari has an average temperature of 30°C, and is located between the rivers San Mateo and Espiritu Santo, 993 feet (298 meters) above sea level. It is beautiful, and an ideal place for fishing, hunting and canoeing. There are many natural springs amid the luscious vegetation of this tropical region.

This is the country's principal coca-leaf-producing region, and tensions between farmers and U.S.-backed military are high. It is not recommended to venture off the main road in the Chapare, since many cocaine-trafficking operations are based in the area.

Near Villa Tunari, however, are two wonderful places to stay: **El Puente**, operated by Fremen Tours, and **Los Tucanes**. Both offer comfortable cabins, beautiful grounds and restaurants serving excellent fish from nearby rivers. Los Tucanes has a large swimming pool, and El Puente is just a short walk from the river and some great swimming holes carved by the water that drops down from the mountains. Both resorts are located after crossing the bridge from Villa Tunari on the road to Chimoré, and are reasonably priced. It is recommended to book ahead with a travel agency in Cochabamba.

Carrasco National Park, in

Cochabamba: Calle Emiliano Luján 2882, Tel. 4421057, Fax. 4421057. E-mail: tipnis@pino.entelnet.bo Will give you all the informations about touring the Park and accomodations.

La Jungla, Recreational Ecotouristic Park, Chipiriri, Chapare. Offers tours from Cochabamba for one or two days with group of 25 people and more to the Chapare. Tel. 07743186, Marcia Nogales.

Hotel El Puente, Run by Fremen Tours, Tel. 4259322. Single, $27; Double, $38; Triple, $54. 2 Km from Villa Tunari at the entrance of Agrigentro.

Hotel Los Tuscanes, Tel/Fax. 4136506.

Hotel Araras, Tel/Fax. 4114116.

Hotel Las Palmas, Tel. 4135710, Fax. 4114103. Av. Integración 777.

Hotel Sumuqué, Tel. 4114110.

Hotel El Paraíso, Tel. 4114136.

Hotel Las Pozas, Tel. 77498828, at the entrance of Agrigentro.

Hotel San Martin, Tel. 4136512. Av. Integración 779.

Complejo Turistico Surubi, Tel. 4136563.

Chapare Tropical Resort, Tels. 4119923, 4292609. At the entrance of Agrigentro.

Hotel La Querencia, Tel. 4136548. Av. Beni 700.

Hotel Los Cocos, Tel. 4136578. Av. Benigno Paz 800.

Hotel San Antonio, Tel. 4136543. Plaza Colonizador Oeste.

Pilunchi, Av. Benigno Paz.

Restaurants
San Silvestre, Av. Integración 778.
Amazonas, Av. Integración 772.
Dumbo Guadalquivir, Av. Benigno Paz.
Don Corsino, Av. Integración.
El Jasmin, Av. Benigno Paz, with discotheque.
El Bosque, Calle Arroyo 40.
La Jatata, Puerto San Francisco.

Parque Machia

Parque Machia is one of the eco-tourism options in the Chapare. Run by the Comunidad Inti Wara Yassii under a contract with the Municipality, it is supported by anywhere from 10 to 30 volunteers from Australia, Israel, Europe, etc. Machia was officially declared a park by the Municipality of Villa Tunari in 1994 and is being administered by Inti Wara Yassi since 1996. The municipality of Villa Tunari officially gave Juan Carlos Antezana, head of the organization "Comunidad Inti Wara Yassi" the administration of the park in August of this year, for one year. The park has 3.2 km of improved trails in the 36 hectare park. The Community rescues injured or caged wildlife and rehabilitates them, when possible, to their return to their original habitat. There are around 200 monkeys, as well as pumas, ocelots , turtles, a harpy eagle, toucans, macaws, etc. The administrators charge a small entrance fee to visit the park and an additional fee for taking photographs.

Inti Wara Yassi, Casilla 9519 La Paz. E-mail: ciwy99@yahoo.com www.intiwarayassi.org

Cavernas Del Repechon

This premier ecotourism attraction is located 15 minutes by car from Villa Tunari and is situated on the northwestern edge of Carrasco National Park. The road is stable year-round, having recently being stone-paved with financing from USAID. To reach the caves a manually-operated suspended cable car system ferries tourists and park officials across the San Mateo River. This is in itself a tourism attraction. The caves are reached after 20 minute easy walk from the river. The caves are home to the rare and unique Guacharos, or oil birds, known for their nocturnal patterns. These bird only come out at night to feed on area fruits and nuts. They remain during the day in a 30-meter high and 70 meter deep cave that is their breeding ground.

Orquidario Villa Tunari

This very interesting orchid reserve is an important attraction for any eco-tourism circuit. Run by three German biologists, this park covering several hectares presents over 100 species of rare and endangered orchids, a nice trail, and a river lookout. The owners have also built what is probably the best restaurant in town as well as a small ethno-eco museum that displays a few examples of native customs, handicrafts, tools and area insects. It costs 5 bs to visit the site. Casilla 4825 , Cochabamba, Bolivia.

Puerto Villarroel

This river port is located 149 miles (about 240 km) from Cochabamba on the main road to Santa Cruz. The river here feeds into the Ichilo, Mamoré and Madre de Dios, all in the Amazon basin. Fresh *pacú* and *surubí* fish are available in the restaurants. There is regular boat traffic linking the port with Trinidad and other jungle towns to the north.

AROUND COCHABAMBA

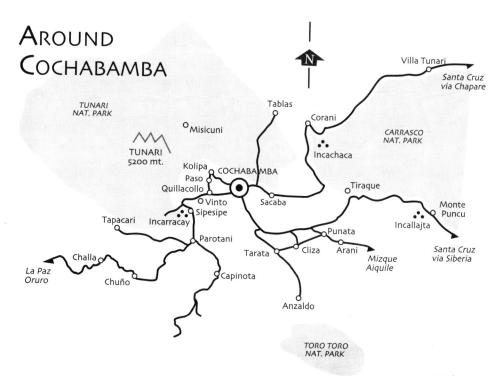

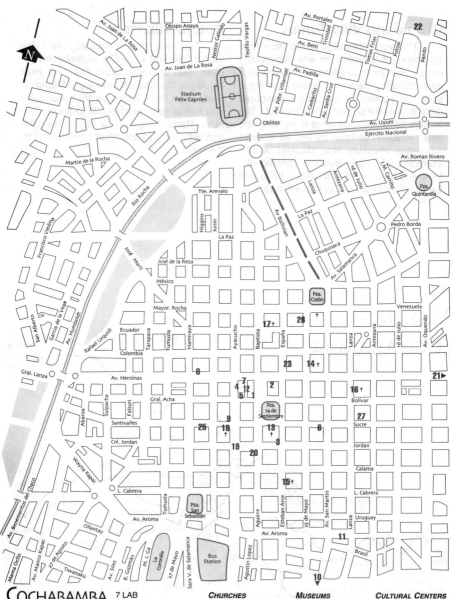

COCHABAMBA

1 Tourist information
2 Police
3 Immigration
4 Entel
5 Post office
6 City hall
7 LAB
8 TAM
9 Aerosur

MARKETS
10 Gran Mercado Ferial
11 Calatayud
12 Handicrafts

CHURCHES
13 Cathedral
14 Santa Clara
15 San Juan de Dios
16 San Francisco
17 Santa Teresa
18 Santo Domingo

MUSEUMS
19 San Simon
20 Arqueologico
21 Concordia
22 Centro Portales

CULTURAL CENTERS
23 Casa de la Cultura
24 Palacio Portales
25 Alianza Francesa
26 Centro Boliviano
   Americano
27 Centro Boliviano
   Aleman

LA PAZ - ORURO - COCHABAMBA

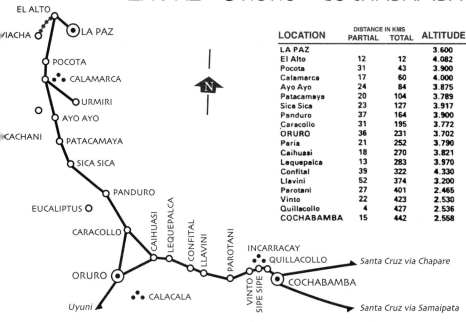

LOCATION	DISTANCE IN KMS PARTIAL	TOTAL	ALTITUDE
LA PAZ			3.600
El Alto	12	12	4.082
Pocota	31	43	3.900
Calamarca	17	60	4.000
Ayo Ayo	24	84	3.875
Patacamaya	20	104	3.789
Sica Sica	23	127	3.917
Panduro	37	164	3.900
Caracollo	31	195	3.772
ORURO	36	231	3.702
Paria	21	252	3.790
Caihuasi	18	270	3.821
Lequepalca	13	283	3.970
Confital	39	322	4.330
Llavini	52	374	3.200
Parotani	27	401	2.465
Vinto	22	423	2.530
Quillacollo	4	427	2.536
COCHABAMBA	15	442	2.558

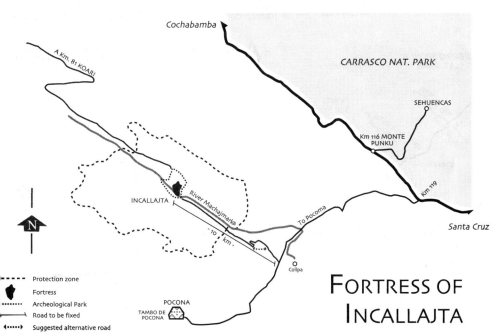

Protection zone
Fortress
Archeological Park
Road to be fixed
Suggested alternative road

FORTRESS OF INCALLAJTA

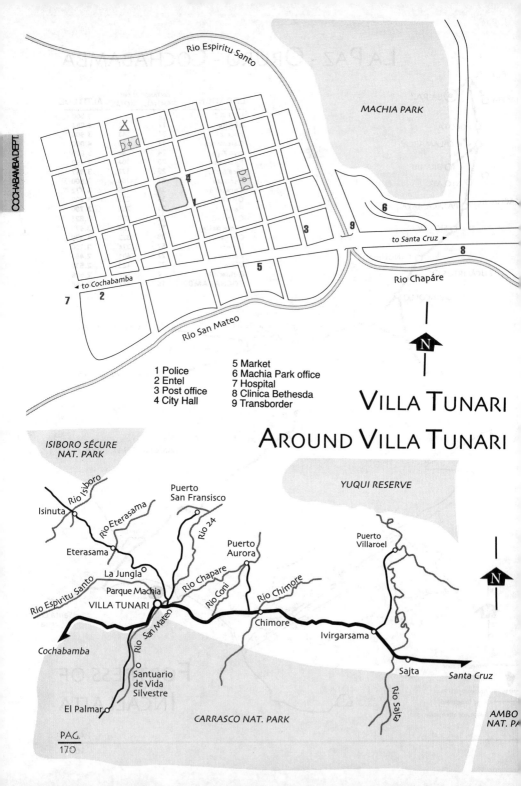

Rio Espiritu Santo

MACHIA PARK

to Santa Cruz ►

Rio Chapáre

to Cochabamba

7   2

Rio San Mateo

3   6
9   8

5

N

VILLA TUNARI

1 Police
2 Entel
3 Post office
4 City Hall

5 Market
6 Machia Park office
7 Hospital
8 Clinica Bethesda
9 Transborder

AROUND VILLA TUNARI

ISIBORO SÉCURE
NAT. PARK

YUQUI RESERVE

Rio Isiboro

Isinuta

Rio Eterasama

Puerto
San Fransisco

Rio 24

Eterasama

Puerto
Aurora

Puerto
Villaroel

La Jungla

Rio Chapare

Rio Espiritu Santo

Parque Machia

VILLA TUNARI

Rio Coni

Rio Chimore

Rio San Mateo

Chimore

Cochabamba

Ivirgarsama

Santuario
de Vida
Silvestre

Sajta   Santa Cruz

El Palmar

Rio Sajta

CARRASCO NAT. PARK

AMBO
NAT. PA

N

TOROTORO NATIONAL PARK

BY ERICK LOZA

Torotoro National Park wasn't supposed to exist. "The area doesn't have any biological value," argued critics in government. "Once the park is official you're going to lose your lands and livestock to the gringos," detractors murmured to a small population that rests within the reserve, located in the Department of Potosi, near the Cochabamba border. "But we've gotten past all of that," said the president of the Torotoro Conservationist Association (ACT), Dr. Rodolfo Becerra. Through informative seminars, ACT has gradually won over most of the Torotoro locals and the government eventually gave in. With the rocky road already traveled, he only has flush ideas ahead. ACT is devising a plan to make Torotoro—Bolivia's tiniest national park at 16,500 hectares—truly big, something that would make people refuse to believe that "Torotoro" is a word of Quechua origin meaning "mud plain."

"Torotoro National Park doesn't just exist as a legal resolution," said Becerra. Some of Bolivia's national parks are called "paper parks": they are acknowledged in the files of the Ministry of Sustainable Development and Planning, but the actual grounds of the reserve lack park guards, infrastructure, or proper administration. Before taking any steps to improve the park, ACT has contracted a French-Bolivian consortium to conduct a study of the park's protection, conservations and development lay-out. The study is being financed by the Inter-American Bank of Development and supported by the Ministry of Sustainable Development and Planning.

From the study report, ACT will be able to draw up a park management plan and a series of development project proposals. "We still have to make access roads, signposts, and divide the park into zones," said Becerra, who also wants to increase Torotoro's area to 45,000 hectares. He said he would approach international financial groups for project funding. ACT has already shown initiative by constructing a meteorological station in Torotoro and raising a new school that architecturally embodies the region's colonial legacy. By safeguarding the community's heritage, Becerra plans to transform the community into another of Torotoro's many tourist lures, thereby improving the residents' standard of living. "Our park project will provide job opportunities," he said, "because without a doubt this place will become a very popular tourist attraction." If there is enough visitor interest, guided tours, restaurants and handicraft sales are just some of the commercial ventures on which locals could embark.

Becerra is relying on a few baits and enticements to attract nature buffs. For one, the only place in Bolivia that the blind chaverti fish can only be found is in Torotoro. They ride the underground streams of its subterranean caverns—the most important in the country according to Becerra. "Because of these caverns, Bolivia was able to become a member of the Latin Federation of Spelunking." In August, 1998, Bolivia hosted the First Italian-Brazilian-Bolivian Spelunking Encounter in Torotoro. ACT, which began the Bolivian Spelunking Society in 1988, hopes that the park can lift the hobby/sport out of obscurity in this country, where many athlete-types prefer to hike up rather than down. Torotoro could cash in on residual Jurassic Park fervor, as well. Some of the park's rock formations bear the mark of dinosaur prints dating back to the Paleozoic and Mesozoic periods—somewhere between 130 to 350 million years ago. A team of Bolivian and foreign scientists discovered the markings back in the 1960s. Apparently, the impressions mark the end of a fossilized footprint trail that leads all the way to Brazil, according to the writings of paleontologist Rodolfo Faggione. "The whole national parks movement is recent," said Becerra, "maybe about ten years old or less." Many parks like Noel Kempff Mercado, Eduardo Avaroa, and Carrasco receive direct funding from the government, but not ACT. They've fought an uphill battle that seems to have finally leveled out.

For more information contact:

Parque Nacional Torotoro, Calle Emiliano Luján 2882, Cochabamba. Tels. 4421057, 4259173.

Fremen Tours, Casilla 1040, Calle Tumusla 245, Tels. 4259392; Fax: 4117790. E-mail: fremencb@pino.cbb.entelnet.bo

Famall Tours, Avenida Ayacucho S-0471, between Calles Jordan and Calama in Cochabamba. Torotoro National Park lies 198 km southeast of Cochabamba in the Potosi Department.

PEACEFUL POJO'S STREETS OF YORE

BY TAMARA STENN

The Cochabamba town of Pojo is a mini-Eden tucked into a small, steep valley extending from the old road to Cochabamba and winding down into the steamy tropics. Founded in 1615 by Pablo de Escalante, Pojo is surrounded by two rivers, the Grande and the Sunchalle, and is protected by the high peaks of Sipaskaya (4,100m) and Santa Barbara (3,800m). Pojo itself is situated in a pleasant tropical valley at about 2,000m.

Entering this town is like stepping back in time. There is no electricity and cars are scarce. Sleepy *burros* plod along the town's hand-laid cobblestone streets, and palm trees line the square. Quaint adobe buildings with low, shady front patios offer the best view of this perpetually green paradise.

Potatoes are harvested three times a year and rumor has it that the normally white *chirimoya* is pink here. Pojo also offers a plethora of fresh, succulent produce. The regular tomatoes and onions are complimented by wonderful papaya, oranges, pineapple and passion fruit, which arrive daily from the outlying lowlands.

The hot springs, which is so hot the villagers say you can cook an egg in them, are perfect for a relaxing soak after hiking Pojo's many footpaths to neighboring communities. More than 100 years ago, the springs were recognized for their healing properties and two pools were built, one for sick people and one for well people. Today, the springs have been returned to their natural state.

There are Incan ruins nearby in Koripalla, which is a short hike from the center of town. Here one can find remnants of circular houses and raised-bed agriculture. Pojo comprised the frontier between the territories of the tropical Samaipata tribes and the mountain-dwelling Inca. A nearby community, Chiriwano ("Killing Cold"), is said to have received its name from the war-time practice of suspending Samaipata and Incan prisoners in the cold river waters and leaving them to freeze.

Returning to the square at night, you'll find the street corners ablaze with lantern light and women barbecuing beef heart shish kabobs and selling sweet meringue-covered breads. Children dart in and out of the shadows shouting and playing. Older folk stroll the quiet streets. A steady wind blows down the mountain and if you listen carefully, you can hear the roar of the nearby rivers.

In one corner of the square, in front of the Jesuit Catholic Church, a bell hangs from an ancient princess tree. This is the original town bell, first erected in an adobe tower in 1895 and designed to be used to call town meetings. However, the tower fell down a few months after construction and the now-cracked bell has been securely suspended from the tree ever since.

COCHABAMBA DEPT.

There is daily public transportation to Pojo from the corner of 6 de Agosto and República in Cochabamba (next to the Mizque bus stop). When arriving in Pojo, visit Father Angel or Mayor Escóbar to arrange sleeping accommodations. There is no electricity, telephone or cellular service in Pojo. Remember to bring your own sleeping bag and flashlight, and get ready to sit back, relax and enjoy the peace of times long gone.

DON'T DO DRUGS – DO THE CHAPARE

BY JAMIE GRANT

The Chapare. Makes you think of drugs, thugs and American military "advisors" trying to blend into the foliage. Coca is what most people associate with the region, but even if you're not looking for any drugs, it's also an ideal weekend break out of Cochabamba. Coca is fast disappearing from the region, so tourism and alternative crops are the name of the game these days.

Only two hours along the road to Santa Cruz and you have dropped from the dry valleys outside Cochabamba into the rich tropics of the Chapare. If you have your own car, don't rush; we made the journey to Villa Tunari a slow amble, with plenty of breaks.

About an hour outside of Cochabamba, just the other side of the pass, we came across a wonderland for all cold-blooded Europeans. I never thought that I would find my Scottish homeland in Bolivia, but stop at the Hotel Apollo on the Corani reservoir and you'll find soft rolling hills covered in heather, deciduous forest with the sweet smell of pine and, of course, low clouds and drizzle. All that is missing are the midges (infamous biting insects).

The hotel itself is decked out as a bizarre hunting lodge with wildcat skins on the wall and a constant hum of Little Richie songs. We didn't eat there, but you must drink at least half a liter of their delicious home-made cherry brandy (*chicha de ginda*). For just $35 a night you can hire out your very own cabin for four. It comes complete with wood stove, rustic corrugated tin roof and breakfast in the morning. They have a range of sizes and prices for the cabins, but you can squeeze in twice as many people as they say using floor space.

Rolling on down the valley, the vista opens up to reveal a spectacular jungle that seems endless. Coming from La Paz, all that green is overwhelming; definitely stop to take photos of the beautiful vegetation.

A Face-Full of Fish

Everyone stops in Villa Tunari, from truckers and tourists to locals and the inevitable lanky, lost-looking NGO types. There is a string of restaurants and shops, and a little farther out, large hotels with swimming pools and saunas. We stopped at the restaurant San Silvestre, which is undoubtedly one of the best. For about $4 you can eat a slice of the local river fish, *surubí*, as big as your face. If the fish isn't enough, there is a selection of pickled snakes in the bar, with their mouths conveniently propped open with tooth picks.

And then on to the highlight of the whole trip. Only a ten-minute drive from Villa Tunari are the most stunning river pools in the world. Lost in trees, the idling eddies invite you to while away the afternoon, interrupted only by the sound of cicadas. The pools' true magic is their seclusion, so you'll have to find them yourself. You will need a jeep to reach them, and be prepared to spend ten minutes disentangling yourself from the suspension on arrival. It's best to avoid swimming in the main river; there are strong currents and sting rays with dangerous barbs on their tails.

Park Machia is the ideal place to finish your weekend odyssey into the Chapare. Forty minutes from Villa Tunari, Machia offers pristine tropical forests with three hours of safe walking on trails. At the entrance to the park is the Inti Wara Yassi headquarters, where you can play with monkeys that were saved from illegal captivity and are now slowly learning to cope again in the wild.

The Chapare was until a few years ago one of the biggest coca-producing regions in the world. Today it is an area of extraordinary natural beauty . . . and divine cherry brandy.

PLANETA DE LUZ HOTEL:
A PLACE OF PEACE, HEALTH AND HUGS

BY VANESSA ARRINGTON

Peacocks cooing in your ear as you sip on mountain-fresh water and indulge in a tasty, vegetarian meal. Funky, rotund architecture sending out waves of energy as you wander the lush green grounds shared by horses and llamas and birds of every sort. Refreshing air cleansing your lungs as you lay by the pool or relax in the solar sauna. It may feel like heaven, but it's really just time spent on another planet — Planeta de Luz.

Nestled away in the about a half hour from Cochabamba, *Planeta de Luz* (Planet of Light) is an alternative, ecological hotel where people from around the world come to relax and tend to their physical, emotional and spiritual health. Built in 1990, Planeta de Luz was designed by Luis Espinoza, a local artist who firmly believes in holistic health and ecological living, as a hotel and place to practice natural medicine.

One of the things that makes Planeta de Luz so unique is its physical appearance. The combination of blue-eyed llamas grazing next to Tiwanaku art symbols outside of curvy, Gaudi-esque buildings certainly makes for surreal and unforgettable imagery. But creating energy was what Espinoza had in mind when he designed Planeta de Luz. Every architectural line, every circle, every object has significance and "energy," which he believes contributes to the health of all those who grace the grounds.

In the center of Planeta de Luz rests the House of the Sun. A replica of Tiwanaku's *Puerta del Sol*, it guards the entrance of the building, reached by passing through a "tunnel" covered with aromatic jasmine flowers. Wind chimes blow at the entrance, which is decorated with engravings of the sun.

Shoes must be taken off before entering the building. Once inside the doors of this central meeting place, visitors shrink under the enormous domed ceiling and sparsely decorated hall. Though indigenous art from the Americas covers the walls, the rest of the design is minimalist. An "energetic column" that looks like a tree in the center of the room stretches from the ground up to the highest point of the ceiling. This, Espinoza said, is "the tree of life."

Sunlight peeks through four large windows shaped as stars, illuminating the altar to *Pachamama* as well as small tributes to the elements of fire, water and air. This serene, New Age environment is the setting for many of Planeta de Luz's activities, which range from yoga to music therapy to massage.

The vibrant skin, healthy bodies and happy, peaceful auras of those who frequent Planeta de Luz seem to attest to the physical and mental benefits of living an ecological life. Health is an overriding theme at Planeta de Luz, which does not tolerate smoking or drinking on the grounds.

The establishment's philosophy is not difficult to discern; mottos such as *"Te invito a ser libre"* (I invite you to be free), *"Urgente Amar"* (It's urgent to love) and *"Disfruto luego existo"* (I enjoy, therefore I am) decorate the walls of most of the buildings.

Each building on the grounds has a distinct purpose, and most have special names, such as *Rumihuasi*, Quechua for "House of Stone," or *Tikahuasi*, "House of Flowers." The House of Youth contains bunk beds where backpackers sleep for $25 a night (including all meals), while the funkiest building on the outskirts of the property houses couples for $55 a night (no meals, which cost $5 each). Those just wishing to have lunch and spend the afternoon at Planeta de Luz pay $12.

Espinoza chose the site — just outside of Quillacollo, the small city neighboring Cochabamba — because of its proximity to the neighboring mountains. The site is perfect, Espinoza said, because it is close enough to the city to be easily accessed, but isolated enough that guests can find some peace of mind.

And this they do. Even for those just passing through, Planeta de Luz makes a strong impression. Remarks in a book signed by visitors from all over the globe describe the place with glowing terms. "Life-changing," said one. "Planeta de Luz triggered a new love and appreciation for nature," said another. A third wrote that the place allowed him "to feel, to sing, to hug."

Correspondence can be sent to:
Planeta de Luz, Casilla 318, Cochabamba, Bolivia. Tels. 261234, 4292721, 4264324. Fax: 4291031. E-mail: pachaman@ngweb.com

THE BOOMING CITY OF SANTA CRUZ

BY PETER MCFARREN
UPDATED BY SETH NICKINSON

Less than forty years ago, oxen pulled carts through the streets of Santa Cruz de la Sierra. In the rainy season, city streets were covered with mud. Only the plaza was paved.

Today, Santa Cruz has boomed to become a thriving metropolis of nearly 1,2 million people and the vanguard of Bolivia's economic expansion. At an altitude of 1,460 feet (438 meters), this unique city contains modern office buildings that sit next to adobe homes with curved tile roofs. Santa Cruz has undergone a dramatic transformation in recent years, perhaps unlike any other Latin American city.

The Spaniard Ñuflo de Chávez founded Santa Cruz, the capital of the department of the same name, in 1561. Since the Department of Santa Cruz borders Brazil on the east, there is a strong Brazilian presence in the area, especially in February during *Carnaval*. Beautiful women wearing elaborate costumes, often similar to those seen in the Rio de Janeiro *Carnaval*, parade through the streets in an orgy of music, dancing and drinking. The weekend after *Carnaval*, local women, with their identities concealed behind masks, frequent the city's nightclubs, picking their dance partners. It is the day women get back at their unfaithful husbands. Santa Cruz and surrounding areas come to a standstill during Carnaval.

Cruceños, as residents of Santa Cruz are called, are easygoing and friendly. Due to the tropical climate, attire usually consists of short sleeves, miniskirts and sandals. But in the evenings or when cold fronts hit the area, a sweater might be necessary. Outdoor restaurants and nightclubs are popular, the nightlife is vibrant, and the city's restaurant and hotel accommodations are among the best in Bolivia.

The area around Santa Cruz is largely devoted to farming, cattle raising and tourism. Important crops are soy, sugar cane, rice, corn, cotton and tropical fruits. There are also several sugar, soybean and petroleum refineries in the area as well as several thermo-electric power plants. The boom in Santa Cruz is partly attributed to farming, natural gas and commerce with Brazil and Argentina, and partly to the trafficking of cocaine. The city itself is not a cocaine-producing region, but the profits from trafficking activities entered its economy until the Bolivian Government took Bolivia out of the cocaine trafficking circle.

Santa Cruz is also the gateway to the **Amboró Amboró National Park** located to the west of the city, the **Samaipata Fortress,** (a UNESCO World Heritage Site located in the outskirts of Samaipata and near AmboróAmboró), the **Noel Kempff National Park** that borders Brazil, and the **Jesuit Missions,** (also a World Heritage Site).

Worth visiting in the city is the **Basílica Menor de San Lorenzo** on the main plaza. It was built between 1845 and 1915 on the ruins of an old cathedral which was built in 1605. In the **Cathedral Museum**, within the basilica, there is an interesting exhibition of religious objects, sculptures, paintings and silverwork. Some of the objects are four centuries old. The museum is open Tuesday through Thursday from 9:00 to noon and from 15:00 to 18:00, and Sunday from 10:00 to noon, and 18:00 to 20:00.

On the main square next to City Hall is the **Casa de la Cultura Raúl Otero Reich**. It has regular cultural exhibits and and theatrical perfomances. If interested in art, be sure to ask for the works of the painter Kuramoto (one of the country's best) and the sculptor Marcelo Callaú. Around the corner and on the same block you will find **The Cultural History Museum**. To gain an understanding of the flora and fauna of the eastern Bolivian lowlands, a visit to **The Noel Kempff Mercado Natural History Museum**, run by the University in a space on Avenida Irala.

The murals by Lorgio Vaca, an outstanding and energetic artist, are on permanent outdoor exhibition at **El Arenal Park**, at the entrance to **Hotel Los Tajibos**, and at the zoo.

The **Santa Cruz Zoo** is the best Bolivia has to offer, though some may find the conditions quite woeful. But it does provide the chance to see many unusual animals from the tropical and highland regions of Bolivia. It is located on the third Ring, just west of the northern (airport) highway, and admission is US$1. The cabañas at the **River Piray** are an ideal spot for having afternoon tea with the various cheese and baked good specialties of Santa Cruz or a traditional lunch on the weekend in one of the many open-air restaurants. Located in the old botanical garden at the far western end of the Avenida Roca and Coronado, the site offers a rustic and interesting atmosphere, with bands and recorded music constantly playing in the background and cruceños of all types enjoying traditional foods and cold beverages. Best to visit on the weekend, when you can also rent time for horseback riding and Quadra track along the riverbank.

PRACTICAL INFORMATION FOR SANTA CRUZ

Santa Cruz Phone Code: 3

• Useful Addresses and Numbers

Tourist Information Center, Tel. 7131131.

Police, 110.

Tourist Police, 3225016.

Emergency Hospital,
Clinica Foianini Tel. 3436221;
Japanese Hospital, Tel. 3462031.

Bus and Train Station (Terminal Bimodal), (Extension of) Avenida Brasil and 2nd Ring, Tel. 3360320.

Airport Information, Tel. 181.

Immigration Offices, Tels. 3364435, 3332136.

Long Distance Call.

Entel, 0-10.

AES, 0-11.

Cotas, 0-12.

Boliviatel, 0-13.

Telecel, 0-17.

For telephone **information** call 104.

Post Office, Calle Junín, half a block from the Plaza 24 de Septiembre. Tel. 3364435.

Entel, central office on Calle Warnes 83, near the Plaza. Also one at airport, with telephone and Internet access. "Punto Entel" call centers scattered throughout the city. Help Line, 800-10-4040, Tel. 3350055.

• Consulates

All consulates below are open Monday to Friday, at the specific times listed.

Argentina, Calle Junín 22, on the 3rd floor, Tels. 3347133, 3324153. Open 8:00 to 13:00.

Austria, Calle Pilcomayo 242, Tels. 3525333, 3522780, Fax. 3525084. Open 14:30 to 17:30.

Brazil, Av. Busch 330, Tel. 3344400. Open 9:00 to 15:00.

Chile, Equipetrol C. 5 Oeste 224, Tels. 3434272, 3420051, Fax. 3434373. Open 8:00 to 12:45.

Denmark, Av. Landivar 401, Tel/Fax. 3525220. Open 8:30 to 12:30 and 14:30 to 18:30.

Finland, Calle René Moreno 258, Tel. 3371961, Fax. 3339871. Open 8:30 to 12:00 and 14:30 to 18:00.

France, 3rd Ring between Av. Alemana and Mutualista, Tel. 3433434. Open 16:30 to 18:00.

Germany, Calle Nuflo de Chavez 241, Tel/Fax. 3367585. Open 8:30 to 12:00.

Holland, Av. Roque Aguilera 300, Tels. 3581866, 3581805, Fax. 3581293. Open 9:00 to 12:30.

Italy, Av. El Trompillo, Edif. Honnen, Tel/Fax. 3531796. Open 8:30 to 12:30.

Israel, Calle Pailon Mercado 171, Tel. 3424777, Fax. 3424100. Open 10:00 to 12:00 and 16:00 to 18:30.

Japan, Calle Cochabamba 314, Tels. 3331929, 3351268. Open 8:15 to 11:30 and 15:00 to 17:30.

Paraguay, Manuel Ignacio Salvatierra, corner of Chuquisaca, Edif. Victoria, 1st floor, Tel. 3366113. Open 7:30 to 12:30.

Peru, Edif. Oriente, Tel. 3368979, Fax. 3368086. Open 8:30 to 13:30.

Russia, Calle 21 de Mayo 356. Tel. 3368778. Fax. 3336083. Open from 8:30 to 12:00 and 14:00 to 18:00.

Spain, Calle Mons. Santiesteban 237, Tel/Fax. 3328921. Open 9:00 to 12:00.

Switzerland, Av. Banzer 470, Tel. 3435540, Fax. 3423233. Open 8:30 to 12:00 and 14:30 to 19:00.

United States, Calle Juemes 6, in the Equipetrol neighborhood, Tel. 3330725. Fax. 3325544. Open 9:30 to 11:30.

Uruguay, Calle Moldes 436, Tel. 3329317. Open 7:30. to noon.

• How to Get There

A modern and spacious airport, inaugurated in 1985 and called Viru-Viru, now links Santa Cruz with the United States, neighboring countries and other Bolivian cities. Many flights coming in from overseas head first to Santa Cruz, and from there out to other domestic destinations. There are several flights a day connecting Santa Cruz with Cochabamba, Sucre, Trinidad and La Paz. The airport is about 30 minutes from the city center in a taxi or private car.

If already in Bolivia, you can also take a bus to get to Santa Cruz, but plan on a long, likely arduous journey; many travelers prefer overnight buses when arriving in Santa Cruz (16 hours from La Paz, 10 hours from Cochabamba, 18 hours from Sucre). There is also rail traffic linking Santa Cruz with Brazil to the east and Argentina to the south.

• Airline Offices

Lloyd Aéreo Boliviano, Calle Warnes, corner of Chuquisaca, Tels. 3344159, 3343998-9. The toll-free numbers for LAB are 800103001, 800104321.

AeroSur, Av. Irala 616, between Colón and Vallegrande, Tels. 3364446, 3367400. At the airport, Tel. 852181. The toll-free number for AeroSur is 800103030.

TAM (Transporte Aereo Militar), Tels. 3531993, 3333018, 3532639. Comercial service by the Bolivian military, to tropical destinations such as Trinidad, Guayaramerín, Riberalta, San Matías, Puerto Suárez, and Yacuiba.

Amaszonas, Aeropuerto El Trompillo Of. 10. Tel. 3578983, Tel/Fax. 3578988. E-mail: amas-srz@cotas.com.bo

TAM Mercosur, Calle 21 de Mayo, corner of Florida, Galería Florida, Office 101, Tel. 3371999.

Air France, Calle Independencia, Galeria Paititi, Tel. 3347661.

American Airlines, Calle Beni 167, Tels. 3341322, 3361414-15.

Iberia, Calle Casco Viejo Junin corner with 21 de Mayo, Tel. 3327448.

Lan Chile, Calle 24 de Septiembre corner with Florida, Galeria Martel, Tel. 3341010.

Lufthansa, Galeria Martel, Tel. 3372178.

Varig, Calle Celso Castedo 39, Edif. Nago, Tel. 3331105.

Aerolíneas Argentinas, Plaza 24 de Septiembre, Edificio Banco de la Nación Argentina, 2nd floor, Tels. 3339776-77.

• Buses

In 2001 the bus station moved from its previous location in a seedy market neighborhood to a spacious, modern building located on Avenida Brasil just past the second Ring. The new terminal is by far the cleanest and most organized in Bolivia, and has the added advantage that Santa Cruz train lines heading to Brasil and Argentina leave from the same station.

Santa Cruz is a hub, with buses going just about every place you'd need to go in Bolivia, including destinations all over the eastern lowlands. Here are just a few of the companies you'll find at the main bus terminal:

Jumbo Bus Bolívar, Tel. 3350762. Goes to Cochabamba, La Paz, Sucre, Oruro, Yacuiba, Trinidad and Vallegrande.

El Dorado, Tel. 3341197. Goes to Cochabamba, La Paz, Oruro and Potosí.

You can also find bus service to the Viru Viru airport from this main bus terminal. Buses leave approximately every 20 minutes

daily, from 5:30 until 20:30, from the corner of Av. Cañoto and La Riva, right next to the terminal. Tel. 3351137. (Service from the airport to the city is also provided).

Trans Illimani, Tel. 3377747, La Paz, Potosí, Sucre, Oruro, Villazon, Tupiza.

You can also find bus service to the Viru Viru airport from this main bus terminal. Buses leave approximately every 20 minutes daily, from 5:30 until 20:30. Tel. 3351137. (Service from the airport to the city is also provided).

• Getting Around Town

Santa Cruz is big, at least by Bolivian standards. It is also very flat, and appears to spread out for miles in every direction (it does).

The city is organized into a Ring system. The center of downtown is considered the first Ring, farther out you'll find the second Ring, etc, stretching to about nine publicly acknowledged Rings. Thus, if you see an address that is in the third Ring, you know it will be a bit of a drive to get there, especially if you're heading from downtown. But taxis are reasonably priced (ranging from $US1 to $US2 inside the city), and the drivers are friendly, so don't hesitate to hop in a cab and see some more of the city.

If you're staying in a hotel downtown, you'll be able to walk to many places of interest. Some of the best restaurants and nightspots, however, are those found in the Equipetrol neighborhood, which is also where many of the snazzier, luxury hotels are located. So if you're staying downtown, splurge one night and head to Equipetrol for dinner, drinks and dancing. (You should really take advantage of being in Santa Cruz, if for no other reason than you won't find nearly as many nightlife options in other Bolivian cities). Conversely, if you're staying in a hotel in Equipetrol, make sure to get downtown occasionally, to get some exposure to the city's older architecture and to see people from a wider variety of social classes.

• Radio Taxis

Radio Taxis are the most secure way to travel around Santa Cruz, and there are companies operating with bases all over the city. It may be convenient to find out which company operates in the neighborhood where you are staying. Nicer restaurants and all hotels will be happy to call you a radio taxi and / or recommend a service.

El Tucan, Tels. 3333222, 3333101.
Equipetrol, Tels. 3330660, 3321111.
La Cuba, Tel. 3340909.
Santa Cruz, Tel. 3322222.
Tropicana, Tel. 3520730.
Vallegrande, Tel. 3526162.
Viru Viru, Tel. 3520713.

• Car Rental

Across Rent a Car, Viru Viru Airport, Tel. 3852418. Also in the 4th Ring North and Radial 27 (400 meters from Av. Banzer Oeste), Tel. 3441717. Fax. 3441617.

Barron's Rent a Car, Av. Cristóbal de Mendoza 286, Zona El Cristo, 2nd Ring, Tels. 3333886, 3338823, Fax. 3360750.

International Rent a Car, Calle Pedro Antelo 5 (near Av. Uruguay), Tel. 3344425.

Localiza rent a Car, Km 3,5 on the North Road. Tel.3433939.

Dollar Rent a Car, Av. Uruguay 127, Tel. 3328490.

Abyss Rent a Car, 3rd Ring, Pasaje Muralto 1038, in front of the zoo, Tels. 3451560, 1332651.

Autocom, Av. Viedma corner with Brazil, Tels. 3321654, 3336306.

Save Rent a Car, Av. Suarez Arana 700, Tel. 3340828.

• Car Repair

Leo Arispe, Av. Busch 675, Tel. 3330560.

Enrique Sánchez, 3rd Ring, Tel. 3463863.

• Hotels

NOTE: While the listed rates are the officials posted by the hotel, good discounts can often be negotiated especially during low seasons.

Hotel Los Tajibos, Av. San Martín 455, Casilla 2966, Tel. 3421000, Fax. 3426994, not only is touted Santa Cruz's "best hotel" but is also considered to be either the first or second-best hotel in the country, depending on who you talk to (Los Parrales in Tarija is the other one vying for Bolivia's top honors). Los Tajibos sits on a huge piece of land a 10-minute ride from the city center. This luxurious, five-stars hotel offers a beautiful swimming pool, tropical gardens, large comfortable rooms, laundry services, a business center, a travel agency, a convention center, a cafe, a gourmet restaurant and a health club, which includes a workout room, saunas, racquetball, tennis, massage and a beauty parlor. Los Tajibos offers packages with special rates throughout the year, but the following are the average prices, for non-residents/residents of Bolivia: Single, $155/$106; Double, $175/$126; Suites, $165/$116. All prices include breakfast. Visa, MC, AmEx. E-mail: santacruz@lostajiboshotel.com

Hotel Buganvillas, Avenida Roca and Coronado 901, Tel/Fax. 3551212. E-mail: reservas@buganvillas.com.bo 1 Room, $60; 2 Rooms, $80; 3 Rooms, $90; 4 Rooms, $110. This new hotel offers lovely accommodations in rooms that are structured like apartments, a beautiful pool, first rate facilities including a full health club and soccer field, and a great way to get away with the family.

Hotel Camino Real, North Equipetrol on the 4th Ring, Tel. 3423535, Fax. 3431515. Though a bit out of town, this is definitely the place to go if you have children. Why? Because the pool at Camino Real in Santa Cruz sports the only known, full-fledged

waterslide in Bolivia. The hotel itself offers beautiful rooms, gourmet food, a conference center, a health club and a travel agency. Call and ask about any special prices. Visa, MC, AmEx.
E-mail: buganvillas@com.bo Single, $138; Double, $158; Suite, $188.

Casablanca Condominio Hotel, Av. Marcelo Terceros 205, 3rd ring between Av. San Martín and Canal Isuto, Equipetrol. Tel.3434444, Fax. 0911-5333.
E-mail: htelcasablanca@hotmail.com
www.hotelcasablancabolivia.com

Hotel House Inn, Calle Colón 643, Tels. 3362323, 800102323, Fax. 3371113. The most centrally located luxury hotel in Santa Cruz.
E-mail: ventas@houseinn.com.bo

Hotel Yotaú, Av. San Martin 7, Barrio Equipetrol. Tel. 3367799, Fax. 3363952.
E-mail: ventas@yotau.com.bo Single, $159; Double, $205; Suite, $300.

Hotel La Quinta, Calle Arumá, Casilla 1270, Tel. 3522244, Fax. 3522667, is located 10 minutes from downtown in the Urbarí neighborhood. It offers 73 apartments, equipped with kitchens, bathrooms and bedrooms. One-bedroom apartments cost $90 for one person, $100 for two; two-bedroom apartments are $110 for two people, and $10 each additional person. The La Quinta complex has three swimming pools, a restaurant and a sauna with a gym. Ideal for families wishing to spend a few relaxing days in Santa Cruz. Visa, MC, AmEx.
E-mail: laquinta@bibosi.scz.entelnet.bo

Hotel Cortez, Av. Cristóbal de Mendoza 280, Casilla 626, Tels. 3331234, 3351186, Fax. 3351186, offers friendly service, comfortable rooms, lovely gardens, a pool, a gym, a sauna, a convention center, a restaurant and a bar, and is conveniently located near a series of active cafes. Internet services are also available. This frequently recommended four-star hotel offers special family, weekend and honeymoon rates, but

the average prices are very reasonable: Single, $65; Double, $75; and Triple, $85. All prices include breakfast. Visa, MC, AmEx.
E-mail: hcortez@entelnet.bo

Hotel Arenal, Calle Beni 340, two blocks from the central Plaza, Tel. 3346910, Fax. 3335724, offers a swimming pool, sauna and cable in the rooms. Prices: Single, $65; Double, $75; Suite, $85. Visa, MC, AmEx.E-mail: reserva@hotelarenal.com

Hotel Continental, Av. Cañoto 238 corner with Junín. Tel. 3347272, Fax. 3324204.
E-mail: conmarketing@unete.com
www.hotelcontinentalpark.com

Hotel Las Palmas, moderate, is located at Av. Trompillo 604, corner with Chaco. It is a modern hotel with a swimming pool, Tels. 3520366, 3520975, 3526314.
E-mail: las-palmas@cotas.com.bo
Single, $65; Double, $75; Suite, $85.

Hotel Caparuch, Av. San Martin 1717, Sirari. Tel. 3423303, Fax. 3420144.
E-mail: caparuch@bibosi.scz.entelnet.bo
Single, $60; Double, $70; Suite, $80.

Hotel Canciller, Calle Ayacucho 220. Tels. 3372525, 3364847, Fax. 3361710.
E-mail: hotelcanciller@unete.com
Single, $59; Double, $69; Suite, $110.

Hotel Urbari, Calle Igmiri 506, Urbari. Tel. 3522288, Fax. 3332255. Casilla: 1020
Single, $59; Double, $69. www.urbari_resort.com
E-mail: urbacruz@bolivia.com

Hotel Lido, Calle 21 de Mayo 527. Tel. 3363555, Fax. 3363322.
E-mail: reservas@lido-hotel.com
Single, $55; Double, $65; Triple, $80; Suite, $90.

Hotel Enrico's, Calle Francisco Gutierrez 77, El Paraíso. Casilla 1952. Tels. 3364433, 3362801, Fax. 3362724.
Single, $50; Double, $60; Suite, $70.

Hotel Sirari, Calle Los Claveles 497, Sirari. Casilla Box 5240 Santa Cruz, Bolivia. Tels. 3451602, 3441300, Fax. 3420739.
E-mail: sirarisuites@mail.cotas.com.bo
Single, $48; Double, $60; Triple, $70.

Hotel Royal, Av. San Martin 200,

Equipetrol Norte. Tel. 3438000, Fax. 3438619.
E-mail: royalhotel@infonet.com.bo
Single, $55; Double, $65; Suite, $85.
Hotel Rio Selva Resort, Km 23
North road. Tel. 3231346, Fax. 3436342.
Cottage from $70 to $110.
Hotel Las Américas, moderate, Calle
21de Mayo 356,Tel. 3368778.Fax.3336083
Hostal Cañoto, moderate, is located
at Calle Florida 45, Tel. 3331052.
Hotel La Paz, inexpensive, Calle
La Paz 69, Tels. 3331728, 3334304.
Hotel Colonial, inexpensive.
A comfortable hotel in the downtown area.
Located at Calle Buenos Aires 57,
Tels. 3333156, 3323568.

• Restaurants

You can eat extremely well in Santa
Cruz, so be sure to put aside a bit of
money to try out some of these superb
restaurants. Definitely spend a night in
Equipetrol, where you will find many
restaurants offering fine dining.
El Candelabro Restaurant, Calle 6
Oeste (Tucuman) 11, Equipetrol,
Tels. 3337248, 3321085. A very classy
restaurant serving international food. It is
considered one of the best restaurants in
Bolivia. Closed Sunday. Visa, MC, AmEx.
Papagayo, located in Hotel Los Tajibos,
Equipetrol, Tel. 3421001. Offers dinner spe-
cials throughout the week, ranging from
Oriental food to paellas. Excellent cuisine.
Domenicos, Paseo Comercial
El Chuubi, Av. San Martin, Equipetrol,
Tel. 3349616. Expensive, one of the best
restaurant in town, has good variety.
La Maison, Calle Guemes Este 32,
Equipetrol, Tel. 3349616. Swiss, French
and Italian food. Open only for dinner,
Monday to Saturday. Visa, MC, AmEx.
Chalet La Suisse, Calle Los Gomeros
98, Equipetrol, Tel. 3436070. International
food in an elegant setting. One of the best
restaurants in Bolivia. Be sure to try their

llama steaks. Great seafood and fish dishes.
El Arriero, Calle Mendoza 929,
Tel. 3349315, also Av. Paraguay, 2nd Ring.
Offers great grilled Argentine beef, moderate.
La Herradura, Av. San Martín,
Equipetrol. Tel. 3331694.
Restaurant Yorimichi, Av. Busch
548, Tel. 3347717. Excellent Japanese
food, including fresh, tasty sushi, in a
comfortable, authentic environment.
Closed Sunday. Visa, MC.
Michelangelo, Calle Chuquisaca
502, Tel. 3348403. Easily Bolivia's best
Italian restaurant.
La Casa Típica del Camba,
Av. Cristóbal de Mendoza 539, 2nd Ring,
Tel. 3427864. Offers excellent Bolivian and
particularly "Camba" (lowland) food in a fun
atmosphere with music and dancing.
Las Castañuelas, Calle Velasco cor-
ner with Pari, Tel. 3364035. Upper-end
Spanish cuisine.
El Fogón, Av. Viedma 434,
Tel. 3329675. Probably the best Churrasco
place, pure meat. Go when you're hungry.
Don Miguel, Av. Viedma 586,
Tel. 3321823, moderate, offers excellent
beef dishes.
El Chico, Calle Libertad 350, 3
blocks from the central square. By general
consensus, the best Mexican restaurant in
Santa Cruz.
Texas Rodeo Grill, Av. 26 de
Febrero, 2nd Ring, next to Hotel La Quinta,
Tel. 3527214. Serves up Tex-Mex cuisine.
Visa, MC, AmEx.
Moosehead Canadian Grill and Bar,
3rd Ring Interno 1212, one block from
Av. Banzer, Tel.3434757. A bit hard to find, but
definitely worth the effort if you're feeling
homesick for that good ol' continent to the
north. This place brings together elegant dining with a raucous bar, in true North-American
style. The beef is excellent and the service
friendly, but don't bother ordering any of the
American or Canadian beers listed on the

SANTA CRUZ DEPT.

menu — they're out, indefinitely (this *is* Bolivia, after all). Closed Sunday. Visa, MC, AmEx.

La Tranquera, Hotel Camino Real, Equipetrol Norte, 4th Ring. Tel. 3423535. Grilled beef, pasta and international food.

Rodizio Brasargent, Av. Santa Cruz 1261, 2nd Ring, Tel. 3525354. Open for lunch and dinner Monday to Saturday, and just lunch on Sunday.

El Buen Gusto, Av. San Martin 50, Tel. 3338553. Offers Peruvian food, sandwiches and pastries.

Don Miguel, Av. Viedma 586, Tel. 3321823. More meat. Visa, MC, AmEx.

Nagasaki, Av. Uruguay 32, Japanese Social Center, Tel. 3322882. Moderate, offers good Japanese food.

Los Immortales, across from Los Tajibos. Tel. 3333455. Moderate, offers excellent pizzas.

El Boliche Creperie, Calle Beni 22. Tel. 3390553. Moderate, offers a variety of crepes, sandwiches and meals in an elegant setting.

Tapekua, restaurant peñas, Calle La Paz corner with Ballivian. Tel. 3343390.

El Lido, Calle 21 de Mayo 523 inside the Hotel Lido, Tel. 3326566. International and Chinese food. Visa, MC.

Mandarin, Alameda Potosi corner with Irala, Tel, 3348388. Chinese food in a lovely setting.

China House, Av. Banzer, near Km. 3.5 on the Montero highway, Tel. 3420926. Chinese food. Visa, MC, AmEx.

Restaurante Los Patos, Km. 8 on the highway to Cochabamba, Tel. 3524306. Offers only duck dishes.

La Sierra, Km. 23 on the highway to Cochabamba, Tel. 3840009. Only open on weekends and holidays for lunch, until 17:00. Also specializes in duck. Visa, MC, AmEx.

Y se llama... Peru Restaurante, Av. San Martin corner with Calle 9 Oeste, Equipetrol, Tels. 3360296, 0136486.

El Chile, on Libertad corner with Cristobal de Mendoza 112-B Tel. 3268629. Specializes in Mexican food.

Candilejas, Restaurant Bistrot; Av. Cristobal de Mendoza 1365, Tel. 3435086.

Don Caito, Calle 24 de Septiembre 166, Tel. 3366101.

If you're just looking for a quick snack, try one of these:

Roma, Calle 7 Oeste, Plaza Italia 46, Tel. 3433863. Pizza.

Ekipe, Av. San Martin, corner of Calle 7 Oeste. Offers a buffet of ice cream.

Saga, Av. Monseñor Rivero 359, Tel. 3326611.

Texas burgers, Av. Cristobal de Mendoza 2nd Ring 200.

Machi's pizza, Independencia, Tel. 3340082.

Cafes

Alexander, Av. Monseñor Rivero 400, Zona El Cristo, Tels. 3378653, 3378654.

Mr. Cafe, Av. Centenario corner with Ichilo, also at Av. Monseñor Rivero.

Petit Café, Av. Velarde, 1st Ring, Tel. 3325847.

Fridolin, Av. Canto corner with Florida, Tel. 3323768.

Kaffeehaus, Av. Velarde 145, Tel. 3377755. German pastries and cakes.

Café Girasol, Calle Independencia 683, Tel. 3372030.

Penalti, Calle 24 de Septiembre 651, Tel./Fax. 3362151.

Kfeina, Calle Velasco 75 between Ayacucho and Ingavi, Tel. 3332298.

• Travel Agencies

Contact any of these agencies to make travel arrangements or to book a tour in Santa Cruz or surrounding regions (including to the Jesuit missions).

Magri Turismo, Calle Warnes 238, corner of Potosí, Casilla 4438, Tels. 3344559, 3345663, Fax. 3343591. E-mail: magri-srz@cotas.com.bo AmEx.

Cambatour, Calle Sucre 8, Tel. 3349999.Fax. 3349998.

Tajibos Tours, located in the Los Tajibos hotel, Tels. 3429046, 3421000-4. E-mail: tajibostours@lostajiboshotel.com

Sudamero, Av. Busch 127, next to Plazuela del Estudiante, Tels. 3342909, 3363426, Fax. 3363806. E-mail: sudamero@mail.zuper.net

Fremen, Calle Beni 79, Tel. 3338535, Fax. 3360265. E-mail: fremen@cotas.com.bo The best agency to book exotic river trips.

ECO safari, Calle Mercado 457, Tel. 3368797. E-mail: ecosafari@mail.cotas.com.bo

Forest Topur Operator, Calle Cuéllar 22, Tel. 3372042, Fax. 3360037. E-mail: forest@mail.zuper.net

Gama Tours, Calle Arenales 566, Tels. 3340921, 3345266, Fax. 3363828. E-mail: gamatur@roble.scz.entelnet.bo

Balas Turismo, Calle Beni 218, Tel.3333933. E-mail: turbulas@roble.scz.entelnet.bo

Rosario Tours, Calle Arenales 193, Tel. 3369977 Fax. 3369656. E-mail: aventura@cotas.com.bo

Trotamundos, Prolongacion Beni 136, Tels. 3344146, 3322456. E-mail: trotamundo@scbbs-bo.com

Oriente Travel, Calle Bolivar 26, Tels. 3314142, 3348899, Fax. 3346702.

Chiriguano Tours, Calle Arenales 684, Tels. 3335850, 3344186, Fax. 3365180.

Uimpex Travel, Laguna Las Garzas, Zona Sur, Tel/Fax. 3336001. E-mail: uimpex@infonet.com.bo

Las Misiones, Calle Beni 340, Tels. 3346910, 3346933. E-mail: lasmisiones@hotelarenal.com

Elimar, Ñuflo de Chávez 13,

corner of René Moreno, Tel. 3332021. Fax. 3331719.E-mail: elimar@entelnet

Exprinter, Calle 21 de Mayo 327, between Buenos Aires and Seoane, Tels. 3335133, 3335134, Fax. 3324876. E-mail: xprintur@bibosi.scz.entelnet.com

Hurvatur, Calle Chuquisaca 561, Tel/Fax. 3364848. E-mail: hurvatur@yahoo.es

Bolivia Tur, Calle España 300, Tel. 3369393, Fax. 3340897. E-mail: bolivia.tur@hotmail.com

Orly Tours, Calle Libertad 268, Tel/Fax. 3349932. E-mail: orlytours@cotas.com.bo

Travel Tours, Calle 6 de Agosto 656, Tels. 3336196, 3346190, Fax. 3351685.

Tropical Tour, Calle Arenales 284, Tel. 3331888, Fax. 3361430.

Viru-Viru, Calle Ballivián, corner of Chuquisaca in the Edificio Oriente, Tel. 3364040, Fax. 3350023. E-mail: vvtravel@entelnet.bo

Amazonas, Centro Comercial Cañoto, Tels. 3338227, 3338350. E-mail: amazonas@roble.scz.entelnet.bo

Yanitur SRL, Calle Beni, Tel. 3363622, Fax. 3366988.

• Museums,. Churches and Cultural Centers

Casa de la Cultura Raúl Otero Reich, Plaza 24 de Septiembre on Calle Libertad 65, Tel. 3342377. Sponsors art shows, concerts and other cultural activities. Open Monday to Friday from 8:00 to noon and 15:00 to 21:00, and on Saturday and Sunday from 10:00 to noon and 16:00 to 21:00.

Museum of Cultural History, inside the Casa de la Cultura on the main square, Calle Junín, across from the post office. Open Monday to Friday, 8:00 to noon and 15:00 to 21:00.

Cathedral Museum, within the Basílica Menor de San Lorenzo. Open

Thursday, Friday and Saturday afternoons.

Museo de Arte, Calle Sucre, on the corner of Potosí. Open Monday to Friday, 9:00 to 12:30, and 15:00 to 19:00.

Museo de Arqueología, Calle Tiwanacu 93.

Museum of Natural History Noel Kempff Mercado, Av. Irala between Independencia and Rene Moreno. Run by the University, it displays exhibits about the geology, flora, and fauna of the region.

Agencia Española de Cooperación Internacional and Casa de España, Calle Arenales 583, Tel. 3351311.Often hosts concerts, including the excellent Bolivian guitarist Piraí Vaca, and art exhibits, and is known for its ever-popular admission-free Thursday-night film series.

Centro Cultural Franco Alemán, Av Velarde 200, Plaza Blacutt. Tel. 3329906. Offers language classes in French, German and Spanish for foreigners as well as other creative courses, such as photography. The center sponsors poetry contests, foreign films and speakers. It also has a library of books in French, German and Spanish open 9:00 to noon and 15:00 to 20:00 during the week.

Centro Boliviano Americano, Calle Cochabamba 66, Tel. 3350108. Offers English classes and a variety of cultural activities.

• Bookstores

Lectura, Viru Viru Airport, 1st floor, Tel/Fax. 3852387. Av. Monseñor Rivero 355, Tel/Fax. 3376782.

Los Amigos del Libro, Calle Ingavi 14, Tel. 3327937. This bookstore offers the best selection of foreign language and Bolivian books as well as foreign magazines.

ABC, Calle René Moreno 56, Tel. 3323277.

• Internet

There is no shortage of Internet access in Santa Cruz. Many hotels are equipped with computers, and just heading to the center of town you will pass many Internet cafes. Here are a few recommended sites:

Full Internet, Calle Ayacucho corner of 21 de Mayo, upstairs. Several years old, always reliable. Cost: $1/hour.

Softech Internet, tucked away in a little plaza on España, in between Junín and Florida. Cost: $1/hour.

Planeta Web, on Calle 21 de Mayo, in between Florida and Buenos Aires. Cost: $1.50/hour.

Music Computer Internet, yellow building right on the corner of Florida and Libertad. Cost: $1.50/hour. Continuing on Calle Florida, there is another Internet cafe between Calle España and Calle 21 de Mayo.

• Shopping

Arte Campo. A must in any visit to Santa Cruz. This lovely store offers the best handicrafts and folk art from Santa Cruz and the surrounding indigenous communities, including the Jesuit Missions. The non-for-profit CIDAC works to preserve the native arts and crafts of the area as well as serving as a showroom for local artisans. Calle Salvatierra corner with Vallegrande. Tel. 3341843.

Artesanías Inca Products, on the corner of Av. Cañoto and Landívar.

Inca Palace, Calle Sucre 25.

Camba, Calle Junín, in between España and Calle 21 de Mayo.

Near the pedestrian walkway, Paseo Peatonal Paititi, shoppers can find a cluster of stores with a wide variety of handicrafts, including jewelry. Start by heading to the corner of Independencia and Ingavi, and wander from there.

• Sports

Country Club, Av. Las Palmas, on the highway to Cochabamba, Km. 2.5, Tel. 3526566.

Club de Tennis Santa Cruz, Av. Tarumá and Av. Roca. (Villa San Luis), Tel. 3538080.

Urbari Racquet, Igmiri 590, Tel. 3525777. Non-members pay about $7 to play racquetball as a visitor.

• Nightlife

Your best bet for a festive night on the town is to go to **Equipetrol's Avenida San Martin** and just bar hop.

If you're on a date, head first to **Candelabro Piano-Sushi Bar,** Calle 7 Oeste 9, Equipetrol, Tels. 3377272, 3377271, where you can eat good sushi while listening to live music Monday to Saturday, from 20:00 to 3:00. Then just go to the main strip and dance, drink and people-watch to your heart's content.

If you're in more of a cultural mood, head to **Tapekua Restaurant**, on Calle La Paz and Ballivián, for a *peña* with assorted live music and excellent continental cuisine.

If your Spanish is good and you want to laugh, go to the **Chaplin Show**, a nightclub act on Sirai 202, Tels. 3420060, 3425473. The comedians make fun of everything to be made fun of in Santa Cruz, and in Bolivia in general. The entertainment also includes singing and dancing.

Live Music

Clapton, Calle Murillo 169 corner with Arenales, Tel. 3364757. Blues music on weekend nights with some of the better Santa Cruz bands, in a very small space.

El Muro, Calle Independencia 416. A candlelit bohemian bar with a large outdoor patio, live music on weekends.

Disco Beer, Av. Cristobal de Mendoza, 1205 2nd Ring.

El Trio de Oro, Av. San Martín corner with Calle 9 Este Equipetrol.

Kamikaze Bar, Calle Chuquisaca 113, Tel. 3354650.

Discotheques

My Club, Calle Ingavi corner with Vallegrande, frequently with live Brasilian music. Tel. 3372792.

El Loro en su Salsa, Calle Wames 280, Tel. 3372427.

Automania, Centro Comercial El Chubbi, Equipetrol neighborhood. One of the trendier spots for young people, along with **Friends** downstairs.

M@d, Av. San Martin, Equipetrol. A large, modern, dance club which is frequently host to concerts by better known groups from all over Latin America.

Classics, Av. Busch 682 between 1st and 2nd Ring, Tel. 3326021. Live music meant to get young people dancing, and a pool table.

Montecarlo, 3rd Ring, Calle Los Tucanes, Tel. 3421281.

Papilon, road to Cochabamba Km 4, Tel. 3435563.

Pubs

Irish Pub, two locations: upstairs in the Shopping Bolivar, east side of the main square and on the 3rd Ring, just west of Avenida Banzer and in front of the Zoo. Both locations are owned by a genuine Irishman, and attract and eclectic mix of expats, travelers, and Bolivians (many of whom speak English). The 3rd Ring location has live music on Wednesday nights, and is famous for it's St. Patrick's Day party when they close down an entire block. Good food as well, but unfortunately, no Guinness.

Tragomania, Equipetrol next to Picolo.

Rockal, Calle Ayacucho corner with Calle Sarah.

Insomnio, Calle Florida 517.
Lounge La Terraza, Hotel Los Tajibos, Tel. 3421000.
Los Violines Calle Mario Flores 98, Tel. 3524862.
Mauna Loa, 3rd Ring, Tel. 3462924.
Vertigo, Penthouse Torre Cainco, Tel. 3341111.
Friend's Pub, Paseo San Martín, Tel. 3329686.
Voodoo, next to Automania, Equipetrol.
Durango, in front of Voodoo.
Salamandra, Av San Martín 51.

Karaoke

Copa y Notas, Calle Tarija 447, Tel. 3364503.
Pentagrama, Pasilo 1, Av. Paragua, Tel. 3470620.
El Sotano, Calle Ingavi, Tel. 3331133.
Caribe, Av. Mutualista, Calle 9, 2030, Tel. 3489258.

• Movies

Cine Center, Av. El Trompillo, 2nd ring between René Moreno y Mons. Santiesteban. Tel. 3375456. Multiplex teather with 10 screens
Cine El Arenal, Calle Beni 555, Tel. 3350123.
Cine René Moreno, René Moreno 448, Tel. 3347448.
Cine Palace, Plaza 24 de Septiembre, Tel. 3322617.
Cine Bella Vista, Av. Ana Barba, in front of the stadium, Tel. 3533909.
Cine Santa Cruz, Calle 21 de Mayo 247.
Florida, Calle Cañoto 259, Tel. 3334638.

• Banks

Banco Mercantil, Calle René Moreno, corner of Suárez de Figueroa, Tel. 3345000.
Banco Unión, Calle Libertad 156,

Tel. 3366869.
Banco de Santa Cruz, Calle Junín 154, Tel. 3369911.
Citibank, Monseñor Rivero, corner of Calle Asunción, Tel. 3346333.
Banco Nacional, Calle René Moreno 258, Tel. 3364777.
Banco de Credito, Calle 14 de Septiembre 158, Tel. 3368300.
Banco Industrial S.A., Calle Ñuflo Chavez, Tel. 3346650.

• Money Exchange

Prodem, Arenales, 779.
Mendi Cambio, Plaza 24 de Septiembre 30, Tel. 3326509.
Casa de Cambio Romero, Libertad and Junín, Tel. 3349766.
Cambio Alemán Transatlantic, Shopping Bolívar, on Plaza 24 de Septiembre, Tel. 3324114.
Exprinter, Calle Libertad corner with Junin. Tel. 3349766.
Sudamer, Av. Busch 127. Tel. 3342909.

• Couriers

DHL Worldwide Express, Av. El Trompillo 531, Tel. 3538181. There are two other DHL offices in Santa Cruz as well.
Federal Express, Calle Santa Fe 52, Tel. 3377210.
Jet Express Courier/UPS, Calle Landívar 366, Tel. 3362233.
Sky Net, Calle Ballivián 767, Tel. 3377440.
O.C.S., Calle Andrés Ibañez 67, Tel. 3340302.
CBK, Av. Radial 19, Tel. 3522471.
Express Cargo Services SRL, Av. 26 de Febrero 23, Tel. 3531958.

• Laundries

LaveFast, Avenida Viedma corner Irala, 1st Ring (several other locations around town). Rapid, reliable service. Cost: $2 wash, $2 dry per basket.

Lavandería Buenos Aires, Buenos Aires, between Libertad and Calle 21 de Mayo, Tel. 3360964. (They also have other locations around town).

Lavandería España, Calle España 160, Tel. 3328283.

• Medical Services

Hospitals and Clinics

Clínica Angel Foianini, Av. Irala 468, Tel. 3436221.

Clínica Lourdes, Calle René Moreno 352, Tel. 3325518.

Hospital Japonés, Av. Japón, Tel. 3462037.

Clínica Santa Maria, Av. Viedma 754, Tel. 3352001.

General Practitioners

Dr. Julio Enrique Aburdene, Edificio Oriente, corner of Chuquisaca and Ballivián, Tel. 3324693.

Dr. Jorge Tellez Balderrama, Av. Escuadro Velasco 480, Tel. 3536991.

Pediatricians

Ernesto Nostas, Calle Pari 476, Tel. 3344194.

Jorge Flores, Av. Cañoto, Clínica Niño Jesus, Tel. 3361662.

Carlos Vidal, Calle Cuellas 309, corner of España, Tel. 3336969.

Dentists

Clínica Dental Roca, Av. Argamosa 96, Tel. 3328464.

Plastic Surgeons

Dr. Rodolfo Vargas Abularach, Calle España 520, Tel. 3335562.

Drug Stores

Gutierrez, Calle Cañoto corner with Landivar, Tel. 3316777.

Santa Maria, Calle 21 de Mayo corner with Junin, Tel. 3363233.

Telchi, Calle Libertad 164, Tel. 3365555.

• English-Language Churches

Trinity Union Church is an inter-denominational church with an English-speaking congregation that meets frequently in a building on the highway to Cochabamba, Km. 6.5. There are many activities on Sundays, ranging from services to Sunday school to potlucks, and mid-week Bible studies. Contact Jenny Dirkson, Tel. 3522347, for more information.

EXCURSIONS FROM SANTA CRUZ

Lomas de Arena

These sand dunes are located 8 miles (13 km) south of the city in the area known as El Palmar. They have a nice fresh-water lake and lots of sand and sun. You must take your own food and drinks, as little is available and there are no bathrooms. On nice weekends, the area attracts families from Santa Cruz, who come with their 4x4 and all-terrain vehicles, and during the week the area is generally pristinely silent.

The dunes are found off the road to the Palmasola prison; a four-wheel-drive vehicle is recommended, or you can take a taxi to within several kilometers of the dunes. Lomas de Arena can be reached from Santa Cruz in about half an hour.

Espejillos and Las Cuevas

Los Espejillos is a forested area 29 miles (47 km) west of the city along the Samaipata-Cochabamba highway where the river has formed a myriad of natural swimming pools and waterfalls. The falls are pools 18 kilometers off the highway, thus a four-wheel-drive vehicle is recommended. Drivers should plan on spending about an hour getting to Espejillos, which makes a lovely weekend day or overnight camping spot. As well, there is a hotel and resort located close to the pools.

Las Cuevas, located 62 miles (100 km) out on the same highway to Samaipata, offers a lovely series of three waterfalls and pools just a short hike away from the road.

Porongo

Porongo is one of the most traditional towns in the area and is located just 10 miles (16 km) outside the city just off the Cochabamba-Samaipata highway. It is famous for its wood carvers and for the Sunday celebrations of its townspeople.

From Santa Cruz, Porongo can be easily reached within a half hour in a bus or taxi from the city's main bus terminal

Cotoca

Cotoca is known for its Roman Catholic church, the shrine of the *Virgen de Cotoca*, who is the patron saint of Santa Cruz. It is located 13 miles (21 km) east of the city along the Cotoca highway (just a 20-minute bus ride from the main terminal in Santa Cruz). A large variety of orchids are cultivated in Cotoca.

On December 8, a festival is held in honor of the patron saint, and thousands of people participate in the traditional all-night walk from Santa Cruz to Cotoca to thank the *Virgencita* for granting their petitions. This is a colorful event and many locals set up booths to sell food and drinks. There is music and an early morning mass.

Former Jesuit Missions

These mission villages have been declared a World Heritage Site by UNESCO and are some of Bolivia's greatest treasures. Several of the former Jesuit Mission churches have been restored to their former splendor, in the towns of San Javier, Concepción, San Miguel, San Rafael, Santiago, Santa Ana and San Ignacio, with San José de Chiquitos awaiting work. The churches are some of the most beautiful architectural sites in Bolivia.

Every two years the Missions district and the City of Santa Cruz are hosts to an International Baroque Music Festival that draws thousands of local and foreign visitors to concerts by Bolivian and foreign artists. This festival has grown in quality and attendance and become a must for any music lover. (See boxed articled in this section, "Mission Music," for more information on the missions).

There is plane service to some of these towns, a paved road linking Santa Cruz with San Javier and unpaved highways to almost all of them. Many hotels and just about all travel agencies can organize tours to the missions. Most tours last four days. A great time to visit the Missions is during Holy Week when the towns come alive with processions and colorful celebrations. Nice hotels have opened in recent years to accommodate the growing crowds of visitors, particularly in Concepción and San Ignacio. (For more information on the Missions, see the book "La Fe Viva- las Misiones Jesuiticas en Bolivia" with texts by Mariano Baptista and photos by Peter McFarren).

Amboró National Park, An Ecological Masterpiece

(With over 700 birds, jungle cats and the rare spectacled bear)
by Jonathan Derksen

Dawn's arrival over this untainted wilderness is accompanied by sounds of the awakening jungle. High overhead in the tops, pairs of **toucans** greet the morning with shrill whistles. In the dense canopy of mara trees, **howlers** groan loudly at the birdish babble upstairs while hundreds of feet below on the forest floor can be heard the gentle rustlings of **peccaries** and **horned curassows** in search of breakfast. This is Amboró. For many the idea of exploring an untouched jungles cape is but a distant dream: however, a three hour drive west from Santa Cruz will take the adventurous tourist into one of the most pristine and, as of yet, unspoiled tropical habitats in the world.

Amboró National Park, covering and area of over 630,000 hectares, lies within three distinct ecosystems: the foothills of the Andes, the northern Chaco and the Amazon Basin. The park was originally established as the Reserva de Vida Silvestre German Busch in 1984 but, with the help of native biologist Noel Kempff, British zoologist Robin Clark and others, the park was expanded to its present size.

The park hosts an incredible variety of flora and fauna. Because of its unique geographical locations, both highland and lowland species are frequent visitors. One can find many trees valued for their fine wood such as the Mara (Swielenia), palms like the Chonta (Astrocaryum) a huge variety of bromeliads and orchids, and limited forests of giant fern and bamboo. Recent studies place the number of plant species at 638, though many species have, as of yet, not been clearly identified.

Because the park straddles different ecosystems, the animal population is also extremely diverse. Perhaps most impressive is the huge number of birds that inhabit the area including such rarities as **horned curassows, quetzals, cock-of-the-rocks** (found almost exclusively in Bolivia), and the more frequent **chestnut-fronted macaws** and **cuvier toucans**. According to park zoologist Robin Clark, the bird species count has already passed the 700 mark.

Most mammals native to Amazonia are also represented. They include **capybaras, peccaries, tapirs,** several species of monkey such as **howlers** and **capuchins,** jungle cats like the **jaguar, ocelot** and **margay,** and the increasingly rare, **spectacled bear,** the only species of bear found in South America.

"Amboró is an ecological masterpiece", says Clark. "712 species of birds have been discovered already and only 50 per cent of the park has been thoroughly explored." He also pointed out that while people eulogize a place like Costa Rica which contains a total of nine life zones, Bolivia has a total of 13.

"I've dedicated so much time to this place because I believe this is one of the richest places on earth," he stated matter-of-factly.

Bird Lovers, contact: **Armonia/BirdLife International,** Tel. 3371005, Casilla 3081, Santa Cruz de la Sierra, Bolivia. E-mail: armonia@scbbs-bo.com

A recommended book: *A Guide to the World's Best Bird-Watching Place: AMBORO PROTECTED AREA, BOLIVIA.* By Robin Clarke Gemuseus and Francois Sagot. Published by Armonia, Santa Cruz, Bolivia, 1996. Clarke and his wife also own comfortable cabins near Buena Vista , the **Hotel Flora y Fauna,** Tels. 3943706, 1943706, where rooms include breakfast and lunch and ornithologist Clarke's knowledge of the local species.

Parque Nacional Amboró, Calle Limos 300, Barrio Fleig, Santa Cruz, Tel. 3453040, Fax. 3452865. E-mail: Amboró@latinmail.com

Amboró from Buena Vista

Amboró Tours, Tels. 9322093, 71633990, Buena Vista. E-mail: amborotours@yahoo.com In Santa Cruz, Tel. 71633990. Calle Bolivar 16. Wilderness adventure, offers one, two or three day jungle tours and bird watching tours.

Amboró Adventures, Tel/Fax. 9322090, 716811355, Buena Vista. E-mail: Donald@zuper.net Offers guided tours of the park, transportation, and also camping gear for rent.

Located in the Amboró National Park,

in the town of Buena Vista, **Amboró Eco resort** is a great place for anyone wanting to tour the park without roughing it. The resort includes a huge pool, fields, gardens, restaurants, bars and a gym, and there are planned activities to get you out into the wild. It is located on Km. 103 of the highway to Cochabamba. Tel. in Buena Vista, 9322048. Tels. in Santa Cruz, 3422372, 3428954.
E-mail: gerencia@Amboró.com Single, $80; Double, $90; Triple, $100; Quadruple, $110.

La Junta, Tel. in Buena Vista, 9322019. In Santa Cruz, Calle 4, Casa 2, Villa Brígida, Tel. 3422473, Fax. 3429632.

El Cafetal, located in the middle of a coffee plantation. Tel. 71645541.
Tels. in Santa Cruz, 1645541, 7953007. In La Paz, 2215708, 2215707. Cafetal produces the excellent Buena Vista coffee that is now available in many supermarkets.

Cabañas J.F. Gualtu, Tels. 3472779, 1942529, 1611682, 3472779.

Residencial Portachuelo, Calle Warnes. Tel. 9242034.

Cabaña Pozasul, Tel. 9322070.

Cabaña Quimori, Tels. 9322081. In Santa Cruz, 3427747, 1645266, 16463329. E-mail: hamel@cotas.com.bo

Hotel Sumuqué, Av. José Steinbach 250. Tel. 9322080. In Santa Cruz, Av. 6 de Agosto 250. Tels. 3365051, 3346658. E-mail: sumuque@latinmail.com

Residencial Nadia,Calle Mariano Saucedo 86. Tel. 9322049.

Lomas de Mirador, Tel. 3231807.

Refugio Ocorotú, Tels. 3231807, 716-122112.

Pension La Casona, Calle Virgilio Serrate corner with 6 de Agosto.
Tel. 9322083.

Complejo Campestre Lomas del Mirador, road to Guaytú. Tel. 3334118.

Complejo Campestre Amboró, road to Santa Barbara. Tel. 716-02741.

Complejo Campestre El Paraíso

Perdido, road to Santa Barbara. Tel.710-47485.

Hacienda Santa Maria, road to Arboleda. Tel. 716-40188.
E-mail: cosuma@bibosi.scz.entelnet.bo

Hotel Pablo Matzuno, San Juan de Yapacani. Tel. 716-02741.

Cámara Hotelera de la Mancomunidad Sara e Ichilo, Tel 9322081. In Santa Cruz, Av. Beni Calle Tacuarembo 2085, Tel/Fax. 3427747, 3428001. E-mail: hamel@cotas.com.bo

La Chonta, eco touristic complex located at 35 km from Buena Vista offers housing, camping, showers and restaurants. Tel. in Buena Vista, 3231222. In Santa Cruz, Tel/Fax. 3426077. E-mail: unapega@mail.costas.com.bo

Los Franceses Restaurant, Tel. 77949675. This apparently misplaced and unquestionably delicious French restaurant is owned by a charming French couple. It serves great Surubi fish, beef and chicken dishes in an informal setting, and homemade everything, including bread, fried potatoes, paté, and an outstanding flan. A must for any visit to the area.

Samaipata and "El Fuerte" (The Fortress)

The pre-Inca ruins at Samaipata, 75 miles (121 km) west of the city along the Cochabamba-Samaipata highway, are some of the oldest and most interesting archaeological finds in Bolivia. They were recently declared a UNESCO World Heritage Site. Located at 6,560 feet (about 1,970m) above sea level, this stone fort — called "El Fuerte" — is covered in intricate, carved geometric and zoomorphic figures.

The town of Samaipata itself, which can be reached in about two hours from Santa Cruz, offers a mild climate, laid-back atmosphere and stunning views of the

Santa Cruz Department. (For more details on Samaipata, see the article "Rock Art in Archaeological Parks" in Chapter Three of this guide). A recommended place to stay is the German-owned **Cabañas Landhaus,** which offers lovely, furnished cabins complete with living and dining rooms, kitchens and bathrooms for very reasonable rates. Landhaus has regular, hotel-type rooms as well. In addition to a pool, sauna and artisan shop, Landhaus also offers a fabulous restaurant that has everything from goulash to cassler on its menu.

For tours to sites around Samaipata, such as **Parque Nacional Amboró, La Pajcha** (a 50-meter waterfall located in beautiful mountain scenery), **Mataral** (the site of 15,000-year-old cave paintings surrounded by a cactus desert), **El Fuerte** and **Las Cuevas,** contact **Michael Blendinger,** a tour guide who speaks excellent English, German and Spanish, Tel/Fax. 9446186 and E-mail: mblendinger@cotas.com.bo Blendinger provides excellent information about natural history and wildlife, and is willing to lead tourists on more off-the-beaten-path activities. He also rents cabins around town. www.discoveringbolivia.com

Another reliable and less upmarket option are the guides operating out of the **Hamburg Restaurant,** Olaf Liebhart and Frank, who speak English, German and Spanish. Formerly known as Roadrunners, they can be reached at Tel./Fax. 9446294.

Amboró Tours, with Erick and Jacky Tel. 9446293. E-mail: erickamboro@cotas.com.bo

Don Gilberto, Tel/Fax. 9446050. Guide tours to Amboró, Samaipata with own vehicle.

How to get there

Taxis to Samaipata from Santa Cruz: Avenida Omar Chavez corner with Soliz de Holguin, two blocks from the buses station, Tel. 3335067. Price, $5 each person, there are also buses. There are buses leaving at 16:00 everyday to Samaipata on Av. Grigota, 3rd ring.

On Av. Omar Chavez 111 there are minibuses leaving at 17:00 for $ 2.5. Tel. 3362312

Lodging

Cabañas de Traudi, Tel/Fax. 9446094. E-mail: traudiar@cotas.com.bo Cabaña price between $20 and $60 the night.

Landhaus, Tel/Fax. 9496033. E-mail: landhaus@cotas.com.bo

La Vispera, Tel/Fax. 9446082. E-mail: víspera@entelnet.bo Cabañas from $9 to $15. Camping site; $4 per person.

Campeche, Tel/Fax. 9446046. E-mail: campeche@scbbs.bo.com Double rooms between $15 and $35. Cabañas from $30 to $70.

Achira Resort, Tel/Fax. 3522288. E-mail: urbacruz@bolivia.com. 8 km from town, European-style camping with all sorts of entertainments. www.achiraresort.com

Baden, Tel/Fax. 09446071.

Campo Sol, Tel/Fax. 9446063, in Santa Cruz, 3420336. 2 cabins available at $25 each.

Fridolin, Tel/Fax. 3340274. E-mail: fridolin@unete.com

Quinta Piray, Tel. 9446033, Fax. 9446136. E-mail: quinta-pirai@cotas.com.bo Cabañas from $15 to $130.

Residencial Kim, Tel/Fax. 9446161. The best of the lower-end places.

Hostal Saldías, Tel/Fax. 9446023.

Residencial Chelo, Tel/Fax. 9446014.

Camping Achira, Tel/Fax. 3862101. E-mail: Bolivia.resort@scbbs-bo.com

Camping La Vispera, Tel/Fax. 9446082. E-mail: vispera@bibosi.scz.entelnet.bo

Restaurants and Coffee Shops

Baden Café, bar restaurant, Bolivian and German food, ice cream.

Cabañas Traudi, Bolivian and European food.

Café Hamburg, excellent international and vegetarian food, also has Internet.

Café Villa, only open on weekends, serves excellent American pastries with the coffee.

Campeche, international and vegetarian food.

Descanso en las Alturas, pizzas, pastas, churrascos and vegetarian food.

La Chakana, delicious café-bar, with breakfast, sandwiches and vegetarian food.

Landhaus Restaurant, Bolivian, international and vegetarian food. Discotheque on Saturday night.

Landhaus Café, German pastries, sandwiches and ice cream.

Media Vuelta, right on the plaza, the best typical Bolivian food in Samaipata.

Mosquito Bar, a music-themed bar (think Hard Rock Café Bolivia).

Snack Dany, typical dishes, pastries and ice cream.

Panaderia Gerlinde, French bread, cookies, jam, cheese, yogurt and muesli…

La Yunga

This community of 43 families located on the border of the Amboró Park, 30 km from Samaipata in a beautiful natural setting with a temperate climate, will offer you medicinal plants, natural food, handicrafts, restaurant and guide services. Some guide services lead tours here to see the worthwhile Giant Fern Forest.

From Samaipata you can hire a taxi for Bs.70 on Av. Barrientos in front of the gas station. Tel. 9446133. You can also horseback ride all the way down to the community with a guide. Reservation at least 24 hours before at Tel. 9446295. E-mail: plancom@fan-bo.org

For more information contact FAN:

Fundación Amigos de la Naturaleza; Km 7 Carretera to Samaipata, Santa Cruz. Tel. 3556800. Fax. 3547383. E-mail: fan@fan-bo.org

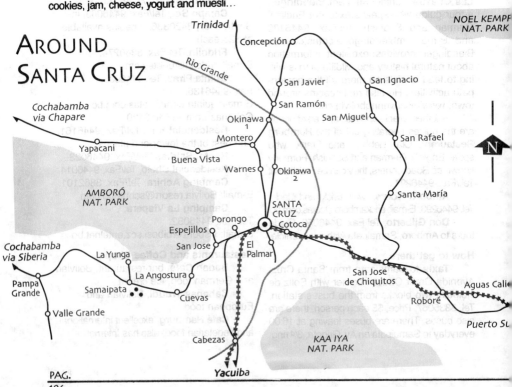

AROUND SANTA CRUZ

NOEL KEMPF NAT. PARK

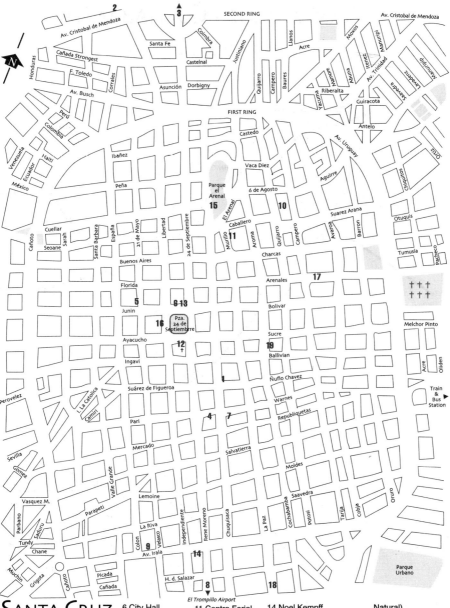

SANTA CRUZ

1 Tourist information
2 Police
3 Immigration
4 Entel
5 Post office

6 City Hall
7 LAB
8 TAM
9 Areosur

MARKETS
10 Los Pozos

11 Centro Ferial

CHURCHES
12 Cathedral

MUSEUMS
13 de Arte

14 Noel Kempff
15 Etno Folklorico

CULTURAL CENTERS
16 Casa de la Cultura
(Museo Arqueologico,
Antropologico, Historia

Natural)
17 Casa de España
18 Centro Franco
Aleman
19 Centro Boliviano
Americano

SANTA CRUZ - COCHABAMBA

ISIBORO SECURE NAT. PARK

TUNARI NAT. PARK

COCHABAMBA

SACABA

TOLATA

INCACHACA

VILLA TUNARI

CHIMORE

MONTE PUNCU

INCALLAJTA

CARRASCO NAT. PARK

EPIZANA

YAPACANI

SAN CARLOS

BUENA VISTA

CHANE INDEPENDENCI

MINEROS

TORO TORO NAT. PARK

AMBORO NAT. PARK

PORTACHUELO

SIBERIA

GUABIRA

MONTERO

OKINAWA 1

Sucre

1

SAMAIPATA

WARNES

Piray river

SANTA CRUZ

2

3

1

| LOCATION | DISTANCE IN KMS | | ALTITUDE |
	PARTIAL	TOTAL	
Santa Cruz	Kms	00	416
Samaipata	118	118	1639
Tolata	353	471	2780
Cochabamba	33	504	2558

2

| LOCATION | DISTANCE IN KMS | | ALTITUD |
	PARTIAL	TOTAL	
Santa Cruz	Kms	00	416
Warnes	33	33	332
Montero	20	53	293
Guabira	5	58	284
Portachuelo	14	72	289
San Carlos	32	115	328
Yapacani	13	128	282

3

Montero	-	58	284
Mineros	14	83	-
Chane Indep.	17	100	-

JESUIT MISSIONS CIRCUIT

Asención de Guarayos

Río Grande

San Javier   Concepción   Las Petas   San Matías

San Ramón

San Ignacio

Santa Rosa

San Julian

Montero   Los Troncos   Santa Ana

Puerto Pailas

Cotoca   Pailon   San Miguel

SANTA CRUZ   San Rafael

San Jose de Chiquitos

Roboré

Yacuiba

Puerto Suarez

N

to Cochabamba

to Santa Cruz

10

11   13

3

12

3

9   1

Bolivar

7   1

4

8 +

2   Campero

3   Pza. 15 de Diciembre   3

5   Sucre

6

N

Av. Roque Aguilera

SAMAIPATA

1 Tourist Information
2 Police
3 Entel/Cotas
4 Post office
5 City Hall
6 Market
7 Handicrafts

8 Church
9 Arqueological Museum
10 Hospital
11 Taxis
12 Sightseeing spot
13 Gas Station

MISSION MUSIC

BY PETER MCFARREN

Lisandro Anori, 14, a Guarayo Indian, divides his days between rehearsing on violin compositions by the Italian Baroque Composer Domenico Zipoli and looking after the family's cattle and small farm. Lisandro and five other brothers and sisters are part of a musical phenomena that has taken over a remote tropical region of Bolivia, where former Jesuit Missions are going through a musical and cultural renaissance, probably unique in the world.

The children of Urubicha and other Guarayo and Chiquitano Indian communities are at the center of this musical revival. "I'm so happy and honored to be part of the Urubicha Orchestra," says Hector Anori, 18, Lisandro's older brother, a violinist and now an instructor for other children from the community. "It is important for me that people in all the surrounding towns get involved with music."

Thirty children from Urubicha, a Guarayo Indian village located four hours from the former Jesuit Mission town of San Javier de Velasco, were taking part in the Third International American Baroque and Renaissance Music Festival that recently took place in six former Jesuit mission towns and churches and in the city of Santa Cruz.

Urubicha is a tropical village of 4,500 with wooden houses and palm-thatched roofs, where residents survive from tending their cattle, horses and small plots of land and handicraft shops. From this community,

350 children are being trained to read and perform baroque music from the former missions as well as other Bolivian and Latin American baroque composers.

Ruben Dario, a 28-year-old musician, is the conductor of the Urubicha Children's Choir and Orchestra. The local priest invited Dario in 1989 to play violin in the parish church so he could be a role model for other children in Urubicha. He became enchanted by the music and learned to play other instruments. His professional training came in 1994 in Venezuela under the tutelage of the well-known musician and conductor Jose Antonio Abreu.

Dario returned to Bolivia in 1996 and was invited by Marcelo Arauz to organize a children's choir and orchestra in Urubicha that would perform at a Baroque musical festival he was preparing in the Jesuit Missions, with the support of the French Baroque musicologist and organizer of the *Caminos del Barroco* French Festival, Alain Pacquier.

Dario started out by training 60 students. His former pupils are now teachers, working with over 1,000 students in several surrounding farming communities, including Santa Ana, whose children's orchestra and choir also participated in the festival.

"The musicians live in some of the poorest towns in Bolivia, but with some of the richest musical skills and traditions. Since the orchestra was organized, absenteeism has pretty much disappeared from local schools, as has alcoholism," said Arauz, a quiet but determined man who has greatly contributed to the revival of Mission music through the organization of the Urubicha Choir and the festivals.

"The discovery of a treasure-trove of manuscripts and their performance by the children of Urubicha has increased the self-esteem of local communities, and increased appreciation for the area's rich cultural traditions," Education and Culture Minister Tito Hóz de Vila said after a performance of the Children of Urubicha in the overflowing San Javier church.

Musical fever has caught on in one of the poorest regions of the continent, where the main concerns of the Chiquitano and Guarayo Indian farmers and artisans who inhabit the small towns and farms of the region, are to tend to their crops, livestock and handicraft shops. Artisan groups in Urubicha and other communities have begun recreating the elaborate, gold-leaf covered, wooden religious Baroque figures, and producing violins, violoncellos and wind instruments for area musicians.

Performances by the choirs and orchestras already brings income to the musicians and the community. The orchestra has already performed in 14 French cities and participated in the Sarrebourg Festival. It has also toured Venezuela and several Bolivian cities. Several more tours are in the works. They have also recorded several CDs.

Their performances at the three festivals that Arauz and his collaborators organized have received widespread acclaim. At the recent festival, 29 groups from Argentina, Brazil, Colombia, Chile, Spain, France, Italy, Mexico, Bolivia, Peru, Switzerland, Uruguay, Venezuela and the U.S. performed before an audience of 30,000 spectators from Bolivia and as far away as Japan.

Their repertoire includes music by the Italian Baroque composer Domenico Zipoli

and dozens of anonymous composers from the Jesuit Missions, including several Indians trained by the Jesuits. The joy the Guarayo Indian children felt in singing and playing the string instruments was evident.

"What is taking place in the Missions with indigenous communities, preserving and reviving musical traditions, is unique in the world," said Arauz. "We are so pleased that these communities are going through this musical revival in which parents and children are very proud to learn music."

This revival has coincided with and been sparked by the recent discovery by the Polish priest and musicologist Piotr Nawrot, of hundreds of compositions, including operas, masses and orchestra pieces. His incredible efforts to restore these musical treasures are providing Ruben Dario and his musicians, and artists from throughout the world, with a treasure gallery of Baroque music.

"Music reflects the grandeur of a people," said Piotr during an interview at the San Javier Church, where many of the 5,000 pages of manuscript are being preserved and recovered. "With this music the country revives a jewel hidden to the world. A jewel has fallen in my hands, and with this music we can search for the identity of the people and at the same time improve the living conditions of our communities."

"The seed planted four centuries ago is finally coming to bloom, not only in Santa Cruz but in Bolivia and abroad," said Cecilia Kenning, founding member of the Pro Art and Culture Association (A.P.A.C.), and with fellow organizer Alcides Pareja, a key to the festivals' successes. New hotels are being built to accommodate the growing number of tourists flocking to the missions that were declared a Patrimony of Humanity by UNESCO. The road from Santa Cruz to San Javier was recently paved.

A new museum was opened in Concepción in a Jesuit-period building donated by President Hugo Banzer, who was born and raised in the area. Banzer made two trips to the Missions in one month to participate in the festival. The new United States Ambassador Ramon Rocha visited the festival on his first trip outside La Paz.

The Jesuit Missions, considered one of Bolivia's and the world's greatest cultural treasures, are located in the Chiquitanía, a tropical region to the northeast of the city of Santa Cruz. The areas around the missions are inhabited by the Guarayo and Chiquitano Indians, who were colonized by the Spaniards and then organized into communities by Jesuit missionaries from Bavaria, Bohemia and Switzerland between 1720 and 1760. The Jesuits gathered Indian communities into settlements of 2,000 to 4,000 inhabitants and organized them into productive units. Architects, sculptors and musicians were brought in to build the churches that incorporated German baroque elements.

These churches survive in part thanks to the work of the late Swiss architect Hans Roth, who devoted 22 years to restoring the churches built by his fellow countryman and colleague over two centuries ago, Roman Catholic bishop Antonio Eduardo Bosl, who had mobilized the resources and his parishioners to restore the treasures.

The missions were kept in the hands of the Jesuits until they were expelled from the region by the Spanish crown in 1767. After the expulsion, many of these settlements fell apart and the Indians fell prey to colonizers, rubber merchants and loggers. Today, the church and other institutions are supporting greater Indian participation in local government affairs and in the cultural revival.

San Javier, located 231 km. from Santa Cruz, is surrounded by dairy farms, a cheese processing plant and cattle ranches. The town was founded in 1692 by Jesuit missionaries, who made San Javier the first Mission in the region. Father Schmid arrived in San Javier in 1730 and founded the first

music school in the region that trained musicians and established a choir. Schmid also established a workshop to produce organs, violin, harps and other instruments used in the missions. He designed and built the church between 1749 and 1752. The church began to be restored in1987, and some of the old wooden columns that support the slanted tile roof remain next to the new ones.

The paintings currently on the altar were made by local artisans out of wood and then painted, replacing paintings that had deteriorated over the years. The paintings represent biblical scenes as well as the missionary work carried out by the Jesuits until their expulsion. In the middle of the altar is a small image of a child. This child represents the highest authority in the village and leads the processions along with the indigenous *cabildos.* (community organizations) The entire church is covered with floral, animal and human designs using natural earth pigments.

In the rear of the church, the baptistery is located and contains the original ceramic angels covered with mica on their wings. One of the texts reads: Only one God, only one faith, only one baptism.

There is also a lovely garden and convent next to the church that contains a wooden bell tower. The walls of the patio are covered with lovely floral designs, protected from the tropical sun by tile-covered walkways. This church is one of the most beautiful in the region and the restoration has managed to preserve as much of the original designs and religious figures as was possible.

For more informations contact travel agencies in Santa Cruz.

Hotel Resort Cabañas Totaitu, Tel. in San Javier, 9635063. Tel. in Santa Cruz, 3326406, Fax. 3333672. E-mail: totaitu@em.daitec-bo.com

SANTA CRUZ DEPT.

NOEL KEMPFF MERCADO NATIONAL PARK: WORTH THE JOURNEY

BY TOM WALSH

The Huanchaca Plateau is part of the Brazilian Shield, the weathered remains of a mountain range that was old long before the Andes were born. Rising some 300 to 500 meters (about 1,000 to 1,600 feet) above the surrounding alluvial plain, the plateau is the dominant geographic feature of Noel Kempff Mercado National Park in eastern lowland Bolivia.

The physical isolation from people that has kept the area's environment relatively protected through the ages also makes it difficult to reach. The easiest way by far is by small plane. Flying the 350 kilometers from Santa Cruz de la Sierra, you will first pass over thousands of acres of cattle and crop land carved from the lowland tropical forests — evidence of the migration underway to these lowlands from the *Altiplano*. Eventually, forest cover dominates, broken only by a ribbon of unpaved road, a red clay seam cutting through the jungle.

Nearer to the park, the Huanchaca rises abruptly. Numerous waterfalls plunge off its sheer sides feeding the Río Iténez, and eventually, by way of the Río Madeira, the Amazon. British explorer Percy Fawcett wandered through the area in the early 1900s; some people believe his descriptions of the Huanchaca inspired Sir Arthur Conan Doyle's dinosaur novel, *The Lost World*. (Others believe the inspiration was the tepui formations of Venezuela.)

The 706,000-hectare park lies in one of the largest undisturbed and least explored areas of lowland tropical forest and wetlands in South America. Five major ecosystems — Amazonian rain forest, gallery forest, *cerrado*, flooded savanna and semi-deciduous tropical forest — provide habitats for an incredible diversity of wildlife.

Limited studies have found 530 bird species living in the park, including harpy eagles, macaws, toucans, hoatzins, Amazonian umbrella birds and helmeted manakins. Endangered and threatened mammals in the park include jaguars, giant armadillos, maned wolves, giant anteaters and pampas deer. Anacondas, piranha and black caiman share the rivers and lakes with giant otters and pink river dolphins. In the trees you will find spider monkeys at play.

White-lipped peccaries, which run in groups of 50 to 300 members, are also quite prevalent, as are brockett deer and tapirs. Tapirs, in the same zoological order as horses and rhinoceroses, are the largest land mammals in the South American rain forests. The chunky adults can weigh over 500 pounds and stand three-and-a-half-feet tall at the shoulder, making them a prize catch for hunters. Quiet and active mainly at night, tapirs leave large, three-toed tracks along the trail.

Also commonly found on the trail are leaf-cutter ants, looking like lines of miniature wind-surfers as they carry triangular pieces of fresh-cut leaves and flowers on their backs. The leaves are not eaten but brought home to underground gardens where they are chewed into a pulpy mass and disgorged. With this fodder, the ants grow a fungus, their sole source of food.

For a long time the region of Bolivia saw little human activity; the flora and fauna were protected by isolation. But with the opening up of the Brazilian states of Rondonia and Mato Grosso to the east, and Bolivian colonists following logging roads punched in from the south and west, the area faced increased intrusions.

The park was established in 1979 and originally named Huanchaca. But without adequate on-the-ground protection, illegal logging (mostly for mahogany), hunting and poaching for the world's pet-and-hide trade took place unchecked.

Unfortunately, isolation also attracted drug traffickers, who were to play a tragic part in the park's history. While on a reconnaissance mission in the park in 1986, Professor Noel Kempff Mercado and assistants landed at what appeared to be an abandoned air strip on the plateau. The area was being used as a cocaine-processing lab and Kempff and two others were murdered. The park was renamed in his honor in 1988.

After the death of Noel Kempff Mercado, in 1988 Hermes Justiniano organ- ized friends and conservationists who found- ed FAN (Fundación Amigos de la Naturaleza), a grassroots conservation organization. Two years later, with help from The Nature Conservancy and private donors, FAN purchased Flor de Oro, a 25-000-acre cattle ranch inside Noel Kempff Mercado Park. A ranger station, scientific base and tourist facility are now located at this site.

FAN: Casilla 2241, Santa Cruz, Bolivia. Attention: Tourism coordinator, Tels: (591-3) 3535426, 3524921, Fax: (591-3) 3533389. http://www.botanik.unibonn.de/system/fan.htm

Parque Nacional Noel Kempff Mercado, Calle Bumberque 1100, PB Colegio de Bioquimiqua y Farmacia, Tel. 3547383, Fax. 3556800. E-mail: gpena@farm_bo.org

AT PLAY IN BUENA VISTA

BY TAMARA STENN

Buena Vista, just 101 km outside of Santa Cruz, is home to posh resort hotels, a colonial town, native villages, and one of Bolivia's largest nature preserves: the 450,000 acre Amboró National Park. Founded in 1694 by Jesuit Priests of the Mojos Missionary fleeing from the inquisition, Buena Vista is full of surprise and intrigue. The reconstructed temple, with its original tower, is said to house secret escape tunnels to the wilds of Amboró or neighboring towns, and sacred documents are supposedly still hidden in its thick walls. The 26th of November is the festival of the town's patron saint: Santo Deposorio Jose y Maria. The town's 3,000 inhabitants are joined by thousands more as statues of the saints are marched around the village, dececimo music is played, and eating and dancing is enjoyed by all. Perhaps even more spectacular is the town's Easter Celebration during *Semana Santa*. The twelve stations of the cross are visited, the *matraca* (a traditional tonal instrument) is played, and groups circle the village, sweeping it with red flags. The town is later bathed in candlelight for the *Cavildo* procession that evening.

The Amboró National Park was a source of gold for pre-colonial communities. When the Spanish arrived, they developed a transportation system where native tribes would carry sacks of materials to the edge of their region; the next tribe would then do the same until the gold reached Santa Cruz. This way no one really knew how much gold was being taken from Amboró, nor its origin. Founded by naturalist Robin Clark, Amboró has been a national park since 1984. It is a vast, jungle wilderness, home to a few Yuracaré and Yuqui communities, 900 bird species and countless animals, rare trees, and fish. "I don't like to promise people they will see certain things," explained English travel guide and expert bird watcher Guy Cox. Others are not so reserved. "You can see capybaras, anacondas, caimans and many endangered birds," said one park ranger. The park does seem full of life. On a recent visit, there were Martin and Orku monkeys, parrots, butterflies, bats, hawks, mahogany trees, and hiergeron trees, whose sap is used to kill fish. The park, for all its wilderness, is surprisingly easy to visit and just a short hike from the town of Buena Vista. It is best to go from June to November, and one should enter with a guide.

There are many guide options. The Buena Vista Amboró National Park Guides can be found near the plaza principal of Buena Vista; just ask at the mayor's office (also on the plaza) or call Ricardo Romello in the Santa Cruz office Tel. 3330623. Prices range from US$15 to $120 per day depending on the number of persons (four is recommended). Guy Cox also offers spectacular one and two-night camping and bird watching tours deep in the jungle to La Chonta. He'll go food shopping with you, and then prepare your meals on the trail. Tours cost US$50 a day for two people. Contact him in Buena Vista at 932-2054 or E-mail: guy_cox@hotmail.com

Another well recommended tour operator is Walter Guzman of Forest Tour Operation in Santa Cruz. Contact him at 3548738 or E-mail: forest@mail . zuper . net

All tours start with at least one wade through a river. Bring a sleeping bag, mosquito net or tent, and bug spray. Currently there are no camping equipment rental places in Buena Vista. Another entrance to the park is in Yapacani, an hour and a half from Santa Cruz, in the Department of Cochabamba. There one will find the Hombre y Medio Ambiente Information Center and guided day tours for groups of up to 11 people. Prices range from US$18 to $22 per person and include transportation from Santa Cruz, a forty-minute guided hike through the jungle, and lunch. Call or fax 933-6138 for more information.

Many traditional cultures live on the outskirts of Amboro Park, within walking distance of the town of Buena Vista. As a new tourism initiative, several communities, with the help of NGOs such as CARE International, and Cedet, are offering ethnotourism activities. One can visit the Chiquitanos to watch them weave beautiful baskets and hats out of wild jipijapa plants and visit their rustic mud and stick houses. The eighteen families of the Aiquiles Sandoval community donated 350 acres of their land along the Surutü River to form a cooperative, UNAPEGA, and to build a Reception Center and two kilometer guided jungle nature trail. They also plan to construct camping sites, athletic fields, scenic lookouts and riverside cabins. Currently UNAPEGA hosts groups of up to thirty people for a day visit, which can include a tra-

ditional feast of *locro* (chicken with sauce and rice), *sonso* (yucca, cheese, butter, etc), or *masaco* (fried pork and plantains). To arrange a visit to the Aiquiles Sandoval community, contact the UNAPEGA office in Buena Vista 932-1222 or Santa Cruz 3426077. The Buena Vista office is half a block from the church on the plaza principal.

There are six hundred beds and a large variety of hotels and restaurants in Buena Vista with prices ranging from Bs.20 to US$65 a night. The more economic hotels such as the Gladly Bal Tel. 932- 2018. Las Palmeras, Posa Azul, La Casona, and Nadia often have small restaurants that serve inexpensive meals from Bs.6 to Bs.30. The more elaborate EcoResort with swimming pool, and air conditioning, can be contacted at 932-2048. The Cabanas Quimoré, Buena Vista's first hotel, offers private cabins, entrance to the park, horseback riding, and two to seven day adventure tourism with scientific experts. Contact them at 932-2081 in Buena Vista or 3427747 in Santa Cruz.

While in Buena Vista, beautiful items of hand woven fibers, ceramics and other natural materials can be purchased at the kiosk in the plaza principal or at the Arte Campo store a short walk from the plaza. Started fifteen years ago with CIDAC, Arte Campo is an association of twelve rural artisan groups representing seven hundred women and their families. Arte Campo's objective is to strengthen communities and stem urban migration by creating profitable industries within the villages. Most of the products for sale are made by Buena Vista, Valle Grande and other women in their houses. For jungle exploration, a relaxing weekend get-away, or a "dia del campo," Buena Vista—a Bs.20 taxi ride from Santa Cruz—seems to have something to offer to everyone.

For more information contact:
CARE Bolivia, pasaje Jauregui 2248, Sopocachi, Casilla 6034, La Paz.
Tel. 2443030, Fax. 2440008.
E-mail: jschollaert@carebolivia.org
Also see E-mail and phone numbers for specific hotels and tour agencies in the Amboro section of Santa Cruz.

SANTA CRUZ DEPT.

THE ONLY GRINGO MAYOR

BY MARK TAYLOR

IT IS APPARENT THAT MIKE BENNETT IS THE DRIVING FORCE BEHIND PORONGO'S DEVELOPMENT AND THAT WITHOUT HIM IT WOULD BE PUT ON THE MAP BUT IN THAT LOVEABLE BOLIVIAN WAY OF MAÑANA, MAÑANA.

There is something surreal about Porongo. It lies half-an-hours drive from the center of Santa Cruz, Bolivia's richest city, yet it shares none of this wealth with transport being by horse rather than a flash 4x4. Even more surreal is to find an English born mayor running the show for the municipalities 11,250 inhabitants. Mike Bennett came to Bolivia 17 years ago to work on a British government mapping project. Even though he now has Bolivian nationality at 6ft 4in and with blond hair he can't hide his English origin.

Mike Bennett has been mayor for almost two years and wants to "put Porongo on the map" according to a past interview in the Financial Times an English newspaper, a particularly astute observation as it was not on my map. Still through his endeavors that aim is coming closer and has been helped in recent years by the Foianini bridge over the river Pirai. The river had proved a natural barrier to development and traffic South West of Santa Cruz but now a housing project, a "garden city," has started over the bridge and trucks from Cochabamba come in to pick up fruit grown in the area.

Only 5km of the municipalities 250km road network is paved and during the rainy season even with a 4x4 access is difficult, sometimes impossible. The mayor wants to tarmac the road from Santa Cruz to Porongo which would help promote tourism for a town that has the only Jesuit church outside the Missions circuit and has lost none of its character unlike the vast urban sprawl that is Santa Cruz. Also the nearby Amboro National Park, on the fringes of the municipalities northern border, is the closest national park to an international airport and has the second most biodiverse environment in the world providing a perfect potential tourist attraction. It is for this reason that an ambitious scheme of road building has been suggested with Palestina, a village near the national park, planned to be linked to Porongo by road and a tourist base set up along the lines of the Madidi national park. At the forefront of the roads project is the lobbying of central government for the highway to Argentina to bypass the congestion of Santa Cruz and pass through Porongo. This would do two things: firstly it would help locals in Porongo to develop via increased trade and secondly it would cut 42km off this proposed 'export corridor' reducing the time it takes to get to Argentina.

Tourism and increased trade are needed to improve the lot of locals where there is still no transport to schools; the mayor is hoping to set up a charity called "Ninos de Porongo" to provide 40 horse drawn carts for this purpose. A result of the lack of money is that illegal logging in Porongo is a problem. Hopefully by developing this municipality the incentive to carry out that activity will be reduced, benefiting the local environment. The dilemma of "tradition v development" is one that the mayor is acutely aware of and has not been over-looked, after all if the environment is destroyed the livelyhood, and potential future, of the municipality is also destroyed. An environmental and engineering feasibili-ty study could cost in the region of $1-$4mil-lion and so far there has been support from the Canadian government. The tide is turn-ing; "people are starting to come to us" rather than the mayor constantly having to fight to get recognition for his region.

And so what of Mike Bennett, the man with the big plans for a Bolivian backwater? Married with 2 kids and a farm in the munic-ipality as well as mining interests in the area he modestly describes himself as a "gener-al manager." However spend any time with him and it is clear he is a born leader who sets goals and achieves them, proved by the fact that 90 percent of last years proj-ects were completed and in the first year a 1.4 million Bs. debt was got under control. Since coming to office there have been rough times, like the attempted coup a little while back where people besieged his office and the oppositions attempted to unseat him through the courts by contesting his validity to be mayor! He has an agreement to step down in a year to let one of his coali-tion partners take office and claims not to have thought about whether to run for the position again. Asked if he would return to the UK he replied "perhaps if I wanted a more sedate life but there is still so much to do here." It is apparent that Mike Bennett is the driving force behind Porongo's develop-ment and that without him it would be put on the map but in that loveable Bolivian way of mañana, mañana. Porongo should not have to wait for its development and if Mike Bennett has anything to do with it the wait-ing could soon be over.

DOES GUERRILLA TRAIL PROMISES GOOD FORTUNE FOR GUARANÍ?

BY KATY MUNCEY

The Guaraní are set to reap the rewards of a new tourism project set to be completed in September 2003. The trail once trodden by the revolutionary Che Guevera traverses the Santa Cruz department that they inhabit and is going to become part of a 'ethno eco-tourism' venture initiated by the Vice ministry of Indigenous Affairs. The project has been supported by the UK based charitable organization Care International, who have donated $250,000 to the cause after selecting it from 250 other similar projects. The Che Guevera Trail is one of several recent 'ethno eco-tourist' ventures in Bolivia, which aim to establish a more sustainable and locally beneficial type of tourism. The Chalalán Ecolodge in the Madidi National Park is one example, which houses guests visiting the jungle for four or five days, with all profits going straight to the local community. The Che Guevera Trail is hoping to achieve similar success once it is up and running.

The concept of 'ethno eco-tourism' was established in Bolivia by the Vice ministry of Indigenous Affairs, in an attempt to create a new form of ethnically and ecologically sound tourism. The indigenous population of Bolivia had started to show an interest in participating in the tourist industry, which up until that point had been dominated by the private sector. The aim was to set up community companies that would benefit both the rural and urban indigenous population, improving the quality of life without deteriorating the cultural identity of the community. This was to be sustainable tourism, an economic opportunity that would avoid the depreciation of local cultural and environmental resources. It would enable indigenous people to link their local and everyday experiences to the wider experiences of globalization. However, for this kind of tourism to work it requires careful management, intensive training processes, and strategic alliances and support from all interested and affected parties.

The proposed tour will follow in the footsteps of Che Guevera into the area surrounding Lagunillas in the South-Western tip of the Santa Cruz department. Che Guevera spent the last five months of his life in the region, before being captured in La Higuera in October 1967. From Lagunillas, tourists will spend three days (two nights) hiking through the area, visiting an interpretation center, and staying in an ecolodge where they will learn about medicinal plants, local crafts, and perhaps learn to speak some Guaraní. This itinerary is aimed at the 18-40 age group, and will involve mountain trekking and long walks through the Rió Nancawasu, whilst older visitors can choose a less strenuous tour that concentrates more on learning about the Guaraní way of life. In essence, the tour aims to combine the legend of the revolutionary guerrilla with guided learning about Guaraní culture.

However, the tour is not going to be ready until approximately September 2003, and first and foremost these itineraries need approval. In line with the ideals of Bolivian ethno eco-tourism this project has the support of a multitude of groups, but it requires the approval of all of them. As well as Care International and the Vice ministry of Indigenous Affairs, the project is being marketed and promoted by America Tours in La Paz and Tajibos Tours in Santa Cruz. The general manager of America Tours Jazmín Caballero García has designed the possible itineraries and is particularly active in the project as a whole. She explained that as tour operators they need to remain neutral and have therefore involved the Red Cross, members of the military who were involved in the counter-insurgency movement at the time, the Assemblea del Pueblo Guaraní and the Capitania del Lupaguasu, who represent the Guaraní people, and the various municipalities of the region.

Once the itinerary has been approved the main task for the project organizers is to train the Guaraní as guides, teaching them English amongst other things to assure that they provide a first class quality of service that stands this project out amongst other tours. They will also need to ensure quality cooking, running of the lodges and the interpretation centre that is due to be built. Transport will need to be improved, particularly to Vodo del Yaso where Che's remains were discovered. This place attracts many tourists a year, and is reached by truck from Santa Cruz. In order for Vodo del Yaso to be included in the Che Guevera trail tour, a bridge needs to be built across the Rió Grande, a building project planned for the up and coming months. This proposed tour would most likely take five days and fours nights, as the distance covered is much greater.

Che Guevera will help this project to succeed because tourists know his name and are already visiting the site where he died (244 so far in 2002). Visitors are also becoming interested in the kind of sustainable tourism that is controlled by the people, where the profits (minus a 15 or 20% agency fee) go directly to the communities involved. In this case there are approximately four or five communities who will co-own the project and who will provide a source of employees. The Che Guevera Trail is set to provide up to 3000 jobs in the area and 1000s more overall. This will mean an improvement in the quality of life of Guaraní without damaging their way of life. In fact, it is hoped that their way of life will be preserved.

At the same time it is important to think about what possible long term consequences this kind of venture has on Indigenous people and Bolivia in general. Yes, it helps people to value indigenous cultural practices and to preserve them, but it can also prevent change occurring when change is what is natural. The Guaraní, like the Karen in Thailand who continue the repressive practice of neck stretching purely for the benefit of tourists, may continue to practice customs that would naturally cease over time. It is also important to consider the consequences of changing the local economy from an agricultural base to a money economy. Finally, this kind of tourism is not completely unable to escape the hierarchical relationships involved in tourism. However, tourism in Bolivia is a reality and will help bolster the national economy, and ethno eco-tourism will help benefit the people who need it most rather than line the pockets of private companies. The ultimate question will be whether tourists will pay the estimated cost of $35-$80 per day for a more sustainable and egalitarian form of tourism.

THE MINING CITY POTOSÍ, A COLONIAL TREASURE

BY PETER McFARREN

In 1650, with a population of 160,000 Potosí was the largest city in the Americas and one of the most important urban centers in the world, renowned for its silver mines, magnificent colonial architecture, churches glistening with gold, and theaters that presented the best of European productions. It was also known for its extravagance and vice. In 1553, 67 years before the pilgrims landed at Plymouth Rock, Potosí was decreed an "Imperial City" by Charles V, King of Spain.

Today, the echoes of its fabulous colonial past can still be seen in the churches bearing elaborate baroque facades, the private homes with wooden balconies looking over the narrow, winding streets, and the host of fine museums, among them the *Casa de la Moneda*, which has served the Spanish Empire as a mint, fortress and prison since it was first built in 1572.

Potosí is a city of contrasts. Some of the residents, dressed in fine, handwoven wool garments, carry on the cultural traditions of their Quechua Indian ancestors. Others, wearing modern clothing, are the Creole descendants of the Spanish and Indians who were drawn to the city by the silver mines. They can be seen mingling in the markets, attending mass in the baroque churches, sitting in the city square, or walking the narrow streets of Potosí, bound by an understanding of the Quechua language but separated by class and cultural barriers.

Nestled at the foot of the *Cerro Rico* (Rich Mountain), Potosí sits on a plateau about 13,500 feet (4,100m) surrounded by mountains and valleys that are part of the Andes' eastern edge. Seeing Potosí is simply a must on your visit to Bolivia.

Because of the altitude, it is advisable to take it easy the first day before making a round of museums, churches, mines and outlying sights. A drive around Potosí by taxi is a good initial introduction, especially until one's system is better suited to the rarefied air. You will frequent cobblestoned roads that once carried Spanish royalty but now barely allow passage of four-wheeled vehicles. Starting at the plaza facing the cathedral you can head toward the mountain of Potosí, passing what is left of 90-odd churches built three or four centuries ago and, farther up, the scattered remains of colonial mining operations. The symmetrical lines of the *Cerro Rico*, crisscrossed by over 5,000 tunnels, disappear as one approaches the mountain, distorted by the mounds of rock and debris accumulated over centuries of mining.

To the left of the *Cerro Rico*, the road heads toward a chain of mountains containing seven lagoons that date to the 16th or 17th centuries. Water channeled down the mountain once powered the rustic silver processing plants built by the Spaniards and their Indian and Black slaves. Remains of these stone plants still dot the landscape.

The city of Potosí, with some 133,651 inhabitants, opens up below, bordered by a chain of ocher-colored mountains that contain a few thermal hot springs and legends of wealth, hardship and intrigue linked to the rise and fall of the city.

Despite the harsh climate, the residents are easygoing and very hospitable. Women wearing multi-layered skirts and pilgrim-type hats can be seen walking the streets or selling *tawa tawas*, *chambergos* or *sopaipillas*, all delicious sweet pastries typical of Potosí. During **Corpus Christi** the residents of the city, dressed in their best attire, take part in a religious procession. The city streets are lined with women vendors who sell these pastries. The treats are taken home and eaten in the evening with hot chocolate.

It is advisable to drink plenty of *mate de coca* (coca tea) throughout your stay to help fend off the effects of the altitude. It is from the coca leaf that cocaine is made, but the leaf itself is harmless and a staple at any hotel. After a relaxing first day and early retirement, the visitor should be in good shape to visit the **Casa de la Moneda** early the next morning. Just off Plaza 10 de Noviembre, a carved doorway big enough to have allowed horses, mules and llamas to enter opens onto a courtyard with a stone water fountain and a colorful laughing mask created by a Frenchman. Included in the price of admission are guides speaking Spanish, English or French who give two-hour tours of the *Casa de la Moneda*.

This museum, which takes up an entire city block, has walls that in some places are four-feet thick. First built in 1572 and then rebuilt between 1753 and 1773, the *Casa de la Moneda* was established to control the minting of the colonial wealth. The sturdy yet graceful structure is of stone, brick, wooden beams and domed, tiled roofs.

One room contains wooden gears and wheels once operated by Indian and Black slaves and used for pressing silver ingots in the process of minting coins. Adjacent to this room, thousands of coins that were produced there for the Spanish crown as well as for several Latin American nations are displayed. Some of the coins were custom minted by some of the wealthier residents and distributed as wedding souvenirs.

The *Casa de la Moneda* also contains more than 100 colonial paintings, including the works of the celebrated 20th-century Bolivian painter Cecilio Guzmán de Rojas. Also worth seeing are the archaeological and ethnographic collections, sculptures, exquisite furniture and historical artifacts.

A morning at the *Casa de la Moneda* should test anybody's stamina. A cup of coca tea followed by lunch is advisable. The best place to eat in Potosí is El Mesón, across from the Cathedral on the main plaza on the corner of Calle Tarija and Linares, which offers steaks, soups and tasty local dishes such as *fritanga* and *asado borracho*. If you plan on spending two or three days in Potosí, ask them to specially prepare a traditional and delicious peasant dish called *kala purka*, a hearty corn soup served in a ceramic bowl with a steaming-hot volcanic stone in the middle that cooks the soup. Also worth trying is the *ckocko*, a spicy chicken dish served with olives and a native corn on the cob. You can enjoy a delicious lunch in a quiet, colonial-style ambiance, while paying very low prices for most dishes.

A *siesta* is a custom still enjoyed by many. Since most stores and businesses remain closed from noon until 2:30 or 3:00 p.m., you won't miss much if you take a brief nap.

A well-spent afternoon in Potosí could include a trip to the **market on Calle Bolívar**, where you'll be surprised to see a wide variety of tropical fruits, which seem out of place at nearly 14,000 feet above sea level. There are regions in the Department of Potosí that produce grapes, peaches and apples. Oranges and bananas are brought by truck from La Paz or from the south of Sucre. Much of the produce sold at the market comes from the surrounding valleys inhabited by Quechua Indians.

Near the entrance to this market on Calle Oruro are several stands that sell elegant, local handcrafted silverware. For a very moderate price you can purchase a lovely sugar bowl or a set of serving utensils. If you're fortunate, you might find some coins minted in the *Casa de la Moneda* several centuries ago. Also of interest are the silver pins made from spoons called *topos*, which are still used to fasten the traditional handwoven shawls used by the Quechua-speaking women of the region. Silverware and pewter are also real bargains.

Silver was the *raison d'etre* for Potosí, and the residents did not hesitate to make good use of it. The sinks and pitchers in the bathrooms of some homes were made from sterling silver. One old-timer recalled attending elegant banquets where the food was served on sterling silver platters and imported ceramic trays three-feet-long. In keeping with this standard of living, some homes were furnished with Persian rugs and English and French pieces transported across the Andes from the coastal city of Arica by mule or llama. And when the silk or flannel clothing of the well-to-do was soiled, it was simply (or so it seemed) transported by mule or llama back across the Andes and the ocean to France where it was expertly dry-cleaned.

It is said that the silver mined here could have paved a road from Potosí to Spain. It is not known exactly how much silver was extracted from the *Cerro Rico*, but it was enough to fill the coffers of the Spanish crown and provide for the growth of painting, music, architecture and literature in Potosí, Sucre and the surrounding regions of South America. By the 19th century, however, Potosí was in decline as the silver veins became exhausted, leaving only museums and buildings as reminders of the past.

Behind the market is the church of **San Lorenzo**, which offers some of the finest examples of baroque carving in Potosí, if not in all of South America. Elaborate arrangements of flowers, garlands, and mythical and indigenous figures are represented on high-relief stone carvings made by Indian artisans. Even though the church is closed to the public except for special occasions, it is worth passing by just to see the church's exterior. You may be able to get into the courtyard, as sometimes the attendants let visitors in.

Four blocks from the imposing San Lorenzo church, on the corner of Calle Sucre and Modesto Omiste, you will find a collection of handmade weavings, belts, ponchos, silverware and antiques for sale. The quality ranges from not very good to first-rate, so you have to shop around to make sure you get what you want. For anywhere from $20 to $50 you can purchase lovely weavings that may each take as long as six months to make. The Department of Potosí produces some of the finest weavings in Bolivia and, according to weaving experts, in the world. Unfortunately, the finest examples have been exported abroad, and what is now available is not always good.

Definitely worth a wander is the narrow street **Quijarro**, lined with brightly-colored, colonial-style houses and filled with children playing kickball and old women watching from their doorsteps. This street and others nearby were designed with bends to break the impact of wind gusts. Don't miss the **Seven Turns Passage**, located off Calle Junín near Bolívar. On the quaint old street of Quijarro, there are several hatmakers who carry on a tradition that is slowly disappearing. During the day, it's a pleasant walk back to the plaza and then three blocks

POTOSI DEPT.

down to the **Santa Teresa Convent** on Calle Chichas. This convent contains one of the important museums in Potosí and takes about an hour to tour.

After entering the thick wooden doorway of the Santa Teresa Convent, the present will seem centuries away. The small museum within the convent belongs to an order of cloistered nuns and contains a fine collection of colonial painting, altars and furniture.

An old wooden turnshide near the entrance is still intact, used since the 17th century by nuns to keep their faces safely protected from male visitors. If a male had to enter for any reason, the nuns vanished to a second courtyard, out of sight of the intruders. One local resident recalled that, only three decades ago, an area that was stepped on by a male visitor was always swept (once the male was out of sight, of course). Even today, if you go there for a tour or to purchase the delicious milk, coconut and peanut candies for sale, you'll only get to hear these women's prayers and voices.

This museum offers an interesting, if somewhat morbid, view of a religious lifestyle that to some extent has adapted itself to the contemporary world. One room displays sharp, star-shaped iron instruments used to inflict pain on the penitent nuns. One blouse is embroidered with wire mesh with sharp prongs sticking out against the flesh. (They are no longer used, although one nun recalled using the artifacts in the 1980s). The same room has leather containers used for transporting sugar from the Santa Cruz region of Bolivia and for storing grains and dry goods.

Adjacent to this room is the dining room, with a main table containing a skeleton resting on a bowl of ashes, a reminder that "ashes to ashes, we will become." It does not make for the most appetizing of places to drop in for lunch.

In the choir room you'll find gold-and silver-embroidered garments used by the priests, and beneath its wooden floorboards dozens of nuns have been buried. Even in death they were kept isolated from men.

Other rooms contain a valuable collection of colonial paintings, particularly those by Melchor Pérez de Holguín, one of three major Latin American colonial painters, and gold-leafed altars donated by wealthy residents.

Once you've adjusted to the climate and altitude, you may want to visit the mines. You can arrange a half-day **mine tour** through any one of the travel agencies listed below. Tours are available every day, both in the morning and the afternoon, but be aware that on Sunday or holidays there will be less activity and fewer miners actually working inside.

After leaving the center of town, your transport will start climbing the *Cerro Rico*, passing caves and remnants of excavation that began in the 16th century and that are still sifted through by independent miners and women.

At the mountain, miners guide tourists through dark and humid tunnels and descend through hand-cranked elevators into mine shafts where miners work almost naked because of the intense heat. Tourists will encounter an area where miners pay homage to *Tío Supay*. Miners and many tourists will sprinkle coca leaves on *Tío* and chew a few leaves, no doubt to help deal with the rarefied air.

In the late 16th century, the great Inca chieftain, Huayna Capac, ruler of an empire that spread 2,000 miles (about 3,200 km) from Quito, Ecuador to Chile, visited the mountain of Potosí and ordered that silver found within be made into jewels for his court. But just as his workers were beginning to mine the valuable veins of silver, they heard a thunderous voice that said in Quechua "do not dig, it is not meant for you; God has saved it for others." And so it was that shortly thereafter the first contingent of

Spanish explorers arrived in this desolate and cold region of Bolivia and established the first Spanish settlement at the foot of *Cerro Rico* in Potosí. They set in motion a stampede of Spanish adventurers that forever altered the landscape of the region. The Quechua-speaking descendants of Huayna Capac were uprooted from their lands, enslaved and put to work mining the silver. The mountain, resembling a giant anthill, has served as a tomb for hundreds of thousands of miners.

In less than 20 minutes your transport will reach **Pailabiri**, the principal mining encampment on the mountain. There you will be given protective headwear, boots and lamps before entering the mine. You'll have a chance to walk through dark and humid tunnels and descend via elevators into mine shafts where the miners work almost naked because of the intense heat. Tin has become the principal mineral extracted from the mine.

The miners you encounter will be chewing the coca leaves to fend off hunger — superstition says it is illegal to eat inside the mine — and exhaustion. A few leaves are also deposited on altars in the name of the goddess of the earth, *Pachamama*, and the entity thought to truly rule this "underworld" — *Tío* or *Supay*, the devil worshipped with cigarettes and alcohol believed to be responsible for keeping the miners safe — or in peril. The famous *Carnaval* festival of Oruro that takes place in February or March of every year centers around the figure of the *Tío* or *Supay*, who is the basis for a rich and colorful folkloric tradition that is a mixture of Quechua and Christian religious beliefs.

A week before *Carnaval*, as well as in June and August, a centuries-old ritual is repeated in the mines when a llama is sacrificed and its blood sprinkled upon the entrance. This is supposed to evict evil spirits and assure that a rich silver vein will be found.

(Note: Tours of the mines are reasonably athletic and not recommended for anyone who is claustrophobic, pregnant or having major trouble with the altitude).

PRACTICAL INFORMATION FOR POTOSI

Potosí Phone Code: 2

• Useful Addresses and Numbers

The **Tourist Information Center** is in a small building on the Plaza Alonso de Ibañez, just a block up from the main plaza. The office is open Monday through Friday, 8:00 to noon and 2:00 to 18:00. Tel. 6223140.

Entel, Calle Cochabamba, in the Plaza Arce, Edif. Entel, Tel. 6222023, 800104040 Open Monday through Friday from 8:00 to noon and 14:00 to 18:30.

Long Distance Call
Entel, 101.
AES, 0-11.
Cotas, 0-12.
Bus Station, Av. Universitaria, Tel. 6227354.
Post Office, Calle Lanza 3, Tel. 22513. This charming building is open Monday through Friday 8:30. to noon and 14:30 to 18:30.
Police, 110.
Immigration Office, Calle Linares corner with Sucre.

• How to Get There

As of publication, Potosí had yet to reopen its old airport. However, TAM, the military service airline, in theory has one flight a week from La Paz to Potosí, and Potosí to La Paz. These are quite unreliable, however, so your best bet if you want to go by plane is to fly to Sucre from La Paz or Cochabamba on LAB or AeroSur

POTOSI DEPT.

and then take a mini-bus to Potosí. There are three ways to get to and from Sucre and Potosí, all of which take about three hours on a paved road. The most expensive is in express taxi, which transports up to four people for a total cost of about $20. From Potosí, call **Auto-Expreso Infinito** at Tel. 6243348 or **Cielito Lindo** at Tel. 6243381, and **Correcaminos**, Tel. 6243383. Mini-buses for Sucre leave regularly from Mercado Uyuni in Potosí, or there are usually three regular buses a day leaving from the Potosí terminal around 7:00, 13:00 and 17:00.

Bus lines also offer regular connections from La Paz to Potosí, providing a chance to see some of Bolivia's varied mountain scenery.

• Airline Offices

Lloyd Aéreo Boliviano (LAB), Calle Lanza 19, Tel. 6222361, Fax 6222517. Open Monday through Friday 9:00. to noon and 14:00 to 18:00., and Saturday 9:00. to noon. Visa, MC, AmEx.

AeroSur, Calle Cobija 25, Tel. 6228933, 6229988. Same hours as LAB. Visa, MC.

TAM, Tel. 6226618.

• Buses

The **Bus Station** is located out of the center of town on Av. Universitaria, Tel. 6243361. It is open every day from 5:30 until 21:00.

Transtin Dilrey, Tel. 6243367, has three buses a day to Sucre.

TransImperial, Tel. 6243378, goes to La Paz and Cochabamba every day.

Andes Bus, Tels. 6243371, goes to Sucre, Tarija and Camiri.

Trans Copacabana, Tels. 6244514, 6226346, goes to Oruro, La Paz, Cochabamba and Santa Cruz.

• Getting Around Town

The center of Potosí is easily navigated by foot. The bus terminal, however, is about a half-hour walk; taking a taxi, particularly for the uphill part from the terminal to town, is recommended. Cost is about $0.50.

• Radio Taxis

Radio Movil Trebol, Tel. 6227070.
Potosí, Tel. 6225257.
Ejecutivo, Tel. 6222211.
Bronco, Tel. 6225257.
Garfield, Tel. 6263333.

• Car Rental

As of publication, there were no car rental agencies in Potosí. Often you can "rent" a radio taxi for the day, and the driver will take you where you want to go.

• Car Repair

Mechanic shops are found on the outskirts of town, such as along Calle Chayanta, north of the center.

Most car repair shops are open from 8:00 to 12:30, and 14:00 to 19:00.

Taller Mecánico Toyonissan, Calle 12 de Octubre, corner with Hnos. Ortega, Tel. 6243189.

Taller de Radiadores Rasi, Calle Camargo, corner with Max Fernández, Tel. 6243269.

• Hotels

Hostal Colonial, Calle Hoyos 8 near the main square, Tels. 6224265, 6224809, Fax. 6227146. Lovely courtyard, offers rooms with private baths, cable, hot water and stocked refrigerators. Single: $33; Double: $43; Triple: $48; Suites: $60. Visa, MC.

Hotel Claudia, Av. El Maestro 322, Tels. 6222242, 6228444, Reservations: 800107001, Fax. 6225677. A bit further out of the center, but very clean and modern with many amenities: room service, heating, garage and conference rooms. All rooms have private bath and television. Single: $27; Double: $35; Triple: $45; Suites: $40. Prices include breakfast. Visa, MC, AmEx.

Hostal Libertador, Calle Millares 58, Tels. 6227877, 6223470/71, Fax. 6224629. Offers very comfortable, heated rooms with private bathrooms and television. Has a nice balcony to look out over the city. Single: $26; Double: $34; Triple: $42; Suite: $65. Visa, MC. E-mail: hostalib@cedro.pts.entelnet.bo

Hostel Cerro Rico Velasco, Calle Ramos 123, Tels. 6223539, 6227067, Fax. 6223539. E-mail: cerrorip@cedro.pts.entelnet.bo Four star hotel.

Hostal Bolivar, Calle Bolivar 772, Tel/Fax. 6222087.

Hotel Nuevo Milenio, Av. Universitaria 450, Tel. 6243865, Fax. 6242536.

Hotel IV Centenario, Plaza Bolivar, Tel. 6222751.

Tambo Hotel, Km 5 road to Oruro, Tel. 6225187, Fax. 6222985.

Jerusalem Hotel, Calle Oruro 143. Tels. 6224633, 6226095. Fax.. 6222600. E-mail: hoteljer@cedro.pts.entelnet.bo Single, $16; Double, $26; Triple, $36.

Gran Hotel, on Av. Universitaria across from the bus station, Tel. 6243483 (also fax). All rooms offer private baths, hot water and television. Also has a garage, conference rooms and room service. Single: $12; Double: $15; Triple: $20. Visa, MC, AmEx.

Hostal El Turista, Calle Lanza 19, Tel. 6222492, Fax. 6222517. Very basic but clean, bright and centrally located. Good if you're on a tight budget. Hot water all day, with bathrooms and a small black-and-white T.V. in every room. Single: $10; Double, $15; Triple: $20.

Hostal El Solar, Calle Wenceslao Alba 41, Tel/Fax. 6227951.

Hostal Santa María, Av. Serrudo 244, Tel. 6223255. Basic accommodations, with garage for small vehicles. All rooms have bathrooms. Single: $10; Double: $15; Triple: $20.

Hostal Carlos V, Calle Linares 42, Tel. 6225121.

Hostal Fellmar, Calle Junin 14, Tel/Fax. 6224357.

Residencial Sumaj, Calle E Gumiel 12. Tels. 6224633, 6222495. Fax. 6222600. E-mail: hoteljer@cdro.pts.entelnet.bo Single $5; Double, $8; Triple, $12.

• **Restaurants**

All restaurants in Potosí are all very reasonably priced.

Restaurant Museo del Ingenio San Marcos, at a colonial silver processing plant that has been restored by the Spanish government. It is a great setting for a dinner or lunch.

El Mesón, Plaza 10 de Noviembre, Calle Tarija, corner with Linares, Tel. 6223087. Offers good traditional cuisine as well as pasta and tasty appetizers. The best restaurant in town. Open every day, from 9:00 to 14:30 and 17:30 to 22:30.

Sky Room, on Calle Bolívar 701 in the Matilde Building, Tel. 6226345. Offers lovely views of the city's architecture — particularly that of the *Casa de la Moneda* and the *Cerro Rico*. Good traditional cuisine for very reasonable prices. Open all day Monday through Saturday, and Sunday until 15:00. Visa.

Restaurant Las Vegas, Calle Padilla 1, close to Linares, Tel. 6225387, has a menu of the day and offers good roast pork. Located on the second floor with a good view of the pedestrians walking by. Open every day.

Parrilla Aries, Calle M. Ascencio Torrico 222, corner of Litoral, Tels. 6223612, 6229275. A good steakhouse. Open every day.

POTOSI DEPT.

Le Boulevard, Calle Bolívar 853, Tels. 6223975, 6227044. Offers national and international food in an elegant setting. Also has two computers with Internet access. Open every day from 11:00 to 15:30 and 18:00 to 22:30.

Kaypichu, Calle Millares 24, 2nd floor, Tel. 6222467. Offers vegetarian food and breakfast in a peaceful atmosphere. Their set lunch costs less than $2, and is served Tuesday through Saturday. Closed Monday. (Kaypichu is also located in Sucre, and there are plans to open another one in La Paz).

Picantería El Dulce, Plaza 10 de Noviembre, offers traditional food.

La Manzana Mágica, Calle Oruro 239. Offers vegetarian breakfasts, lunches and dinners. A bit crowded when full, but excellent value. Closed Sunday.

Chaplin, Calle Bustillos 979, Tel. 6226794. Offers a variety of food in the mornings until noon and in the evenings after 17:00. Excellent burgers and fries, though the portions are a bit small.

Den-Danske Cafe, on the corner of Matos and Quijarro. Offers a variety of food in a nice cafe atmosphere, candlelit at night. Closed Sunday.

All around town, especially along the Padilla, you will find *confiterías* where you can stop for a quick snack or dessert. Recommended are **Cherry's**, Calle Padilla 8, Tels. 6225367, 6227805, and **Confitería Capricornio**, Calle Padilla 11, close to Hoyos.

• Travel Agencies

All of these agencies offer city tours of Potosí, mine tours, visits to the therapeutic hot springs of Tarapaya, camping and trekking in the Kari Kari mountain range, and one- to five-day expeditions to the Uyuni Salt Flats. All the agencies are open Monday through Friday between 8:00 and 9:00 in the morning, closed for lunch

from noonish to 14:30., and close shop between 18:30 and 20:00. (Some agencies are open Saturday morning as well, and those with home or cellular numbers listed can be contacted any time).

Potosí Tours, Calle Padilla 16 in the Alonso de Ibañez Square, Tel. 6225786.

Koala Tours, Calle Ayacucho 7, Tel. 6224708. Fax. 6222092. E-mail: k_tour_potosi@hotmail.com

Elite Tours, Calle Quijarro, Edif. Camara de Mineria, Tel. 6225275.

Altiplano, Calle Ayacucho 19, Tel/Fax. 6225353, 6227299.

Silver Tours, Calle Quijarro 12, Cámara de Minería Building, Tel/Fax.. 6223600, 6228202. Guide Freddy Mamani is recommended for the mine tour.

Andes Salt Expeditions, Calle Padilla 3 in the Alonso de Ibañez Square, Tel/Fax. 6225175, Tel. 6225304. Open every day. (You can also make arrangements with this agency through the Hostal Colonial). www.andes-salt-uyuni.com.bo

Cerro Rico Travel, Calle Quijarro, Edif. COTAP, Tel. 6225175.

Magic of Bolivia, Calle Ayacucho 9, Tel. 6223126.

Sin Fronteras, Calle Bustillos 1092, Tel/Fax. 6224058. E-mail: frontpoi@cedro.pts.entelnet.bo

South American, Calle Bustillos 120, Tel. 6228919.

Sumaj Tours, Calle Oruro 143, Tel. 6222600.

Transamazonas, Calle Quijarro 12, Tel. 6227175, Fax. 6224796.

Trans Andino Tours, Calle Butillos 1078, Tel/Fax. 6226787. E-mail: tatours@cedro.pts.entelnet.bo

Turismo Balsa, Plaza A. Ibañez 3, Tel/Fax. 6226270.

Victoria Tours, Calle Chuquisaca 146, Tel. 6222232.

Azimut Explore, Calle Junin 9, Tel.6225487, Fax..6225489.

Amauta Expediciones, Calle Matos 14 , Tel/Fax. 6225353.

Catering to a more up-scale clientele, **Hidalgo Tours**, Calle Bolívar 19, corner of Junín, Tel/Fax. 6225186, offers tours all over southwestern Bolivia, including Potosí, Sucre, Tupiza and Uyuni. Their guides speak English, Spanish, German and French. Visa, MC. E-mail: uyusalht@ceibo.entelnet.bo

• Museums, Churches and Cultural Centers

Casa de la Moneda, Calle Ayacucho, Casilla 39, Tel. 6222777. Open Tuesday to Friday, 9:00 until noon and 14:00 to 18:30, and Saturday and Sunday, 9:00 until 13:00. Closed Monday.

Building was begun at the *Casa de la Moneda*, or Potosí Mint, in 1753 under the direction of Don Salvador de Villa. It was completed in 1773. It has become one of the most important repositories of historical and visual material from the Colonial period. The building, considered one of the most important architectural works in South America of the Colonial period, is made from stone, brick, wood and iron.

In the first courtyard a visitor is greeted by a large mask with an ironic smile. It is believed that the mask was placed there at the outbreak of the War of Independence to represent the end of Spanish rule. Inside, there are exhibit halls showing colonial paintings, especially those by the master Melchor Pérez de Holguín. There are also collections of regional clothing, numismatics and anthropology.

An important part of the museum is the mint and the equipment used to press and form the coins for the Spanish Crown. There are three groups of wood gears brought from Spain, the huge cedar beams supporting the floors, the roofs, and the elliptical dome where the main silver smelting furnace sat. Admission: about $1 for nationals, $2 for foreigners, children under 6 years of age get in free. Must also pay for the right to film or take pictures. E-mail: moneda@cedro.pts.entelnet.bo

Often overlooked but of great value is the **Potosí Archive** with its collection of 80,000 unpublished documents on the life of Potosí. Admission to the Archive, which is located inside the *Casa de la Moneda*, is free.

Santa Teresa Museum, Calle Santa Teresa 15, end of Ayacucho, Tel. 6223847. Open every day from 9:00 to noon and 15:00 to 18:00. Admission: $2 for nationals, $3 for foreigners.

The **Convent** and the **Church of Santa Teresa** building were completed in 1691. They hold a beautiful collection of colonial paintings and religious objects. The cloistered nuns sell delicious sweets made from ground Brazil nuts.

San Francisco Church, Calle Tarija, corner of Nogales Street. Tel. 6222539. Open Monday-Friday, 9:00 to noon and 14:30 to 17:00, Saturday from 9:00 to noon. This was the first church built in Potosí during the Colonial period. Made from granite, the interior shows beautiful arches and a brick dome. On the main altar is the figure of "Lord of the Veracruz," the patron of Potosí who is worshipped by city residents. A huge painting by Melchor Pérez de Holguín hangs in the sacristy. Be sure to ask to visit the viewing platform, which provides a panoramic view of the city. Admission: $2. Must also pay for the right to film or take pictures.

San Lorenzo Church was built between 1728 and 1744 and is one of the finest colonial churches in the city.

Museo del Ingenio San Marcos is a restored old silver mill worth the visit, Calle Betazanos corner with La Paz, Tel. 6222781. Open from Monday-Saturday, 11:00 to 15:30 and 18:00 to 19:30.

POTOSI DEPT.

• Bookstores

There are numerous bookstores all along Calle Bolívar, some of which sell books in English.

• Internet

C-Camex, Galería Matilde on Bolívar, between Bustillos and Quijarro. Located in the same building as the Sky Room Restaurant, offers numerous computers. Open Monday through Saturday, 9:00 to 22:00. Cost: $1/hour.

Plus Ejecutivo, also in Galería Matilde on Bolívar, Tel. 6227687. Open Monday through Saturday, 8:00 to 22:00 and Sunday from 8:00 to 20:00. Cost: $1/hour.

Tinkusunchaj Cafe/Internet, Calle Sucre 45, Tel. 6225011. Light, charming atmosphere in which you can work on the computer or eat snacks or Creole food. Open Monday through Saturday from 9:00 to 22:00. Cost: $1/hour.

On Ayacucho, just off the main plaza, you will find a handful of places offering Internet services with one or two computers:

Altiplano, Calle Ayacucho 19, Tels. 6225353, 6227299. Open every day, 8:00 to noon and 14:00 to 20:00. Cost: $1.70/hour.

Candelaria Internet Cafe, Calle Ayacucho 5, Tels. 6228050, 6226467. Open every day from 8:00 to 21:00. Cost: $1.70/hour. Cafe also offers food all day in a funky building that contains an artisan shop and book exchange.

• Shopping

Mercado Artesanal offers a good selection of local handicrafts. Plaza Saavedra, corner of Sucre and Omiste.

Central Market, located between Oruro and Bustillos near Bolívar, this market offers a wide variety of local produce and canned goods as well as silver and other handicrafts.

• Sports

Club Tenis Bolívar, Calle Bolívar, Tel. 6223560.

Sauna La Florida, Calle América 104, Tel. 6243598.

• Nightlife

Camaleón, Calle Matos 90, Tel. 6243113. Offers dancing and karaoke every day but Tuesday from 19:00 on.

Potocchi, in the Plaza 16 de Julio at Millares 13, Tel. 6222759. Offers *peñas* Monday, Wednesday and Friday nights as well as Italian, French and Bolivian food. Open every day. Visa, MC.

• Movies

Cine Imperial, Calle Padilla 31, Tel. 6226133.

Cine Universitario, Calle Bolívar 893, Tel. 6223049.

• Banks

Banco de Crédito, Calle Sucre, corner of Bolívar, Tels. 6223521, 6223522. Does cash advances on Visa and changes dollars and traveler's checks.

Banco Nacional de Bolivia, Calle Junín 4, Tel. 6223501. Changes dollars and traveler's checks.

There is an **ATM** machine located on Calle Junín, right before Bolívar as you heading away from the central plaza.

• Money Exchange

Prodem, Calle Bolivar 10

• Couriers

DHL has an office on Calle Quijarro in the Copacabana Building half a block from the plaza, Tel/Fax. 6223395. Open Monday through Friday, 8:30 to 12:30 and 14:30 to 18:30. On Saturday from 8:30 to 12:30. Office also contains a Western Union.

E-mail: grupoipo@cedro.pts.entelnet.bo
CBK LTDA, Calle Matos 143,
Tel. 6226864.
IBC, Calle Bolivarcorner with Junin,
Tel. 6228293.
Jet, UPS, Plaza Alonso de Ibañez 3,
Tel. 6226270.

• Laundries

Laveloz Laverap offers same-day laundry service at two locations: one just a block from the main plaza at Quijarro 12, corner of Matos, called **Laveloz**, Tel. 6226814, the other a bit further from the center at Camacho, near Bolívar going towards Oruro, called **Laverap**. Both are open Monday through Saturday, 8:30 to 12:30 and 14:00 to 20:00. Cost is $1.40/kilo.

• Medical Services

Hostal Libertador works in conjunction with Dr. Uribe, who will come to the hotel to help guests (some of the staff at Libertador speak English).
Clinica Britanica, Calle Oruro 221, Tel. 6225888.

EXCURSIONS FROM POTOSI

The Mills of Potosí

Near Potosí are the remains of the mills used to process the silver mined from the mountain overlooking the city. These mills were powered by water from the lagoons surrounding the city, which also provided drinking water for city residents. Several of the remaining lagoons continue to provide drinking water. To visit the mills, take a tour provided by a local travel agency or ask the local tourist office for information.

The Hot Springs of Tarapaya

Located 16 miles (25 km) from Potosí on the road to La Paz, these hot springs are surrounded by rolling hills and make a nice camping spot or picnic place. The springs have volcanic origins and the lake's water is hot and can be treacherous, especially toward the middle of the small lagoon, so be very careful swimming here.

Kari Kari

Set in mountains 4,700 meters (nearly 15,500 feet) above sea level, the lagoons of Kari Kari make for a great visit, providing the opportunity to get in a few days of trekking as well as see some Andean animals. Most tours include food and camping gear.

Hacienda de Cayara

This farm has several rooms showing furniture and paintings from the Colonial period. Through Hidalgo Tours in Potosí, you can arrange to stay a night in this hacienda. The trip, which includes transportation, a guide, food, a night's lodging and a tour around the premises, costs $104 per person.

The farm also produces some great cheeses. It is located 90 minutes from Potosí. Take the road to La Paz, veer left at the La Palca smelter and bear left along the river. Cayara is at a much lower altitude than the city of Potosí and grows vegetables and fruits.

Uyuni Salt Flats (Salares)
by Peter Fraser

Once a major railway junction, Uyuni now thrives on tourism and any backpackers arriving at the bus station are likely to be accosted by hordes of tour operators touting for business. They may offer you a "free" taxi ride to your hotel but this is likely to involve a commitment to the tour itself ("included in the price.") The reason why most tourists come to the town is to travel across the magnificent salt plains situated but half an hour away. Before you pay money to spend three or four days in a 4x4 it's best to shop around.

Check what's included in the price (food, accommodation), the state of the vehicle and whether you will actually have an informative guide or simply a monosyllabic driver. Get a full itinerary and, if possible, ensure that one of your party speaks Spanish if the driver does not. In high season particularly, the tour companies racing across the vast white expanse can seem reminiscent of the old Monte Carlo Rally - whizzing across salt rather than snow - but if something goes wrong, you will be dependent upon your driver.

None of the tour companies are perfect: there is a book of complaints in the Clock Tower on Plaza Arce ("For Gods sake don't travel with...etc") and this writer had his own share of discomfort when his tour jeep went off to help another stuck in the mud, leaving five passengers stranded for three hours in the baking sun without water. Altruism is all very well but you need to be able to remind your driver where his first responsibilities lie.

There are three-day tours with the option to cross the border into Chile (you may want to get your exit stamp in Uyuni, giving you three days to get out) and four-day tours available which return you to Uyuni. It's best to change some Bolivianos for Chilean pesos before arriving in Uyuni (where it is difficult) and certainly before arriving in Chile because the exchange rates there for dollars, bolivianos and particularly for traveler's checks are simply exorbitant. Traveler's checks can be changed at most tour companies in Uyuni at a minimum of 3%.

After the Salar you will continue to the Laguna Colorada and the Laguna Verde (red and green lakes respectively) where flamingos strut across strange oases. If you're feeling weary after the bumps and jolts then you may wish to take a bath in the Termas de Polques (Thermal waters) although not in the Sol de Mañana, which are sulphurous jets of steam. Oh and if you want to photograph the flamingos then beware not to be lured into the mud as I was. The lake in question is nicknamed "the

stinking lake" and needless to say I had the front seat of the jeep for the rest of the day.

Uyuni itself is a small, fairly desolate town but has increasing facilities for travelers. There is Internet, Entel and reasonable food for the most part clustered around the Plaza Arce (Uyuni does not have a large Italian ex-pat community but the food is mostly pizza). Opposite the Plaza is the train station on the Avenida Ferroviaria and arriving by train from Oruro or Potosi is reasonably pleasant. Certainly preferable to taking the bus in the wet season when you may have to get out and push.

At time of writing buses from Potosi leave from the railway line that crosses the road just up from the terminal at around 12:30 pm (although if they are lacking passengers then you may be delayed for any length of time). Getting a train to Chile (Calama) is an option but an uncomfortable one. The journey can last over twenty-four hours because you have to get off at immigration and wait for a Chilean train to pick you up. The same is true of buses. Although for the train last minute tickets may be available for the cargo hold.

The main tourist attraction apart from the Salar is the Railway Cemetery to the South, worth a visit for buffs. It at least gives a sense of past in a town that can seem a far outpost as dislocated as the travelers that now flow through it, onward into a barren but beautiful wilderness.

In Jirija, look for Carlos and Luppe who offer hot showers and a place to stay overnight for 15 Bs. at the foot of the Tunupa **Train Station**, Tel. 02-6932153

Hotel Palacio de Sal, Salar de Uyuni, Tel/Fax. 6225186.
E-mail: uyusalht@ceibo.entelnet.bo
Web site: http//:www.salardeuyuni.com

Hotels In Uyuni

Jardines de Uyuni, Av. Potosi 113.
E-mail: jardinesdeuyuni@latinmail.com
Tel. 6932989.

La Magia de Uyuni, Calle Colon 432
Tel. 6932541. E-mail: magia_uyuni@yahoo.es

Joya Andina, Calle Cabrera. Tel/Fax. 6932076
Hotel Kory wasy, Av. Potosi 304.
Tel. 6932670. E-mail: kory_wasy@hotmail.com
Hotel Avenida, Av. Ferroviaria. Tel. 6932078
Hotel Toñito, Av. Ferroviaria.

Restaurants
La Loco, Pub Bar Restaurant. Av. Potosi. Fire places, games, french food and good music. Definitely the unbeatable place in town to relax and enjoy yourself. Open from Tuesday to Sunday from 15:00 to 2:00 in the morning. Tel. 6933105.
Jardines de Uyuni, Av. Potosi 113.
16 de Julio

Travel agencies
Sajama Expediciones,
Tel/Fax. 6933202, contact Abraham.
Kantuta Tours, Tel/Fax. 6933084, contact David.
Paula Tours, Tel/Fax. 6932678, contact Dionicia Flores de Ticona.
Turismo Amanecer, Tel/Fax. 6933093, contact Fidel and Sonia.
Toñito Tours, Av. Ferroviara 152, Tel. 6932819, Fax. 6932094. In La Paz, Calle Sagarnaga 189, Tel. 2336250.
E-mail: tonitours@yahoo.com
Andes Travel Office, Calle Ayacucho 222, Tel/Fax. 6932227.
E-mail: atouyuni@cedro.pts.entelnet.bo
iverstraete@hotmail.com
Colque Tours, Av. Potosí 54, Tel/Fax.6932199.
Terra Andina, www.terra-andina.com

Tupiza
by Ben Garside

This charming small city is on the eastern edge of the wild Sud Lipez region and a bumpy 8 hours bus ride away. Dramatic rocky landscapes, cliffs and canyons surround the city and closely resemble scenes from a Wild West film.

Tour agencies in town can give horse, bike or jeep trips out to explore this spectacular area. (See box article Cowboy Dreams in Tupiza).

How to Get There
There is no airport nearby, so the best way to get there is by train from Oruro (via Uyuni) which takes between 11 and 13 hours depending on which train you take, or just 3 hours from Villazon on the Argentine border.

Tupiza's small bus station serves some long distance routes. Although the roads are terribly bumpy, they afford fantastic views. There are daily services to Potosi (8 hours), Tarija (8 hours), Villazon (2 hours), La Paz (20 hours).
Information
There is no tourist office in Tupiza, but hotels and tour agencies should provide all the information you could want. **Tupiza Tours** and **Valle Hermoso Tours** are especially knowledgeable and helpful.

Places to Stay
Hotel Reina Mora, Alamos Palala, Casilla 137. Tel. (591) 6943028.
Email: valentinab@mixmail.com
Tupiza's only truly upmarket option lies in a quiet spot on the edge of town, with swimming pool and prices include breakfast. Single $13, double $20, rooms have private bath.

Mitru Hotels, a Tupiza institution. the Mitru family have been hoteliers in town for nearly 50 years. **Hotel Mitru** 187 Avenida Chichas, Casilla 067. Tel/Fax. (591) 2-6943001. www.tupizatours.20m.com
Email: tpztours@cedro.pts.entelnet.bo
Pleasant atmosphere, 1 block from main plaza. TV lounge, internet. Newly built pool in rear garden. Apartment $50 (up to 6 people), single suite $20, matrimonial suite $35. Single with private bath 65bs, double with private bath 100bs. Single with shared bath

35bs, double with shared bath 60bs. All rooms have cable TV.

Hotel Anexo Mitru, Calle Avaroa. Similar style, very close to train station. Also houses **Los Helechos restaurant**. Singles and doubles available at the same price as Hotel Mitru.

El Refugio, Avenida Chichas. Budget option on same site as Hotel Mitru. Singles with shared bath 30bs, doubles with shared bath 50bs.

Country House "El Recreo", Relaxed private atmosphere 2km from the city center. $100 (up to 5 people).

Hostal Valle Hermoso, 478 Avenida Pedro Arraya. Tels. (591) 6942370, (591) 6942592. Friendly family-run hotel providing a clean, comfortable budget option. Sells breakfast and snacks all day. Internet access. Room with shared bath $3 per person per night. Room with private bath $7 per person per night.

Several smaller places are in town offering very basic facilities for between $2 and $3 per night. Try along Calle Avaroa leading out of the train station.

Tour Agencies

Tupiza Tours, Well established agency in Hotel Mitru's building. Offers horse, bike and jeep tours to nearby beauty spots. Also arranges 2 day jeep tours to the sites of Butch Cassidy and The Sundance Kid and 4 or 5 day tours to the remote southwest region ending in Uyuni. Changes traveller's cheques and can reserve bus and train tickets. Tel/Fax. (591) 6943001. Email: tpztours@latinmail.com www.tupizatours.20m.com

Valle Hermoso Tours, Helpful and informative agency based in Hostal Valle Hermoso. Av. Pedro Arraya 478. Tel. 6942370, Fax. 6942592. E-mail: hostalvh@cedro.pts.entelnet.bo www.bolivia.freehosting.bo Offers many of the same services as Tupiza Tours.

Roca Colorado Tours, Avenida Chichas. New agency set up in competition to the established firms. Also has budget accommodation available.

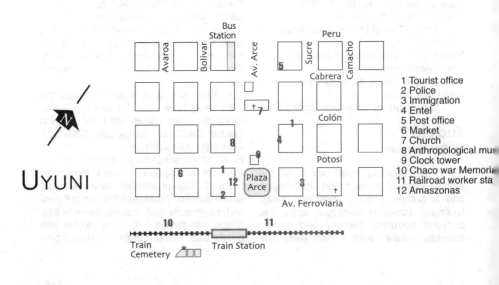

1 Tourist office
2 Police
3 Immigration
4 Entel
5 Post office
6 Market
7 Church
8 Anthropological mus
9 Clock tower
10 Chaco war Memoria
11 Railroad worker sta
12 Amazonas

Cerro Rico

Pari Orcko
Sight seeing

Bus
Station

POTOSI

Tourist information
Police
Immigration
Entel
Post office
City hall

MARKET

MUSEUMS
8 Casa de la Moneda
9 Santa Teresa
10 San Francisco
11 del Ingenio San Marcos

CHURCHES & POINTS OF INTEREST
12 De Jerusalem
13 San Bernado
14 Santa Monica
15 San Lorenzo
16 Pabellon de Oficiales Reales
17 San Augustin
18 Balcon de la Horca
19 Casa del Marquez de Otavi
20 Santa Teresa
21 Compania de Jesús
22 Cathedral
23 Belen Hospital
24 La Merced
25 San Martin
26 Tambo de la Cruz
27 Arco de la Cobija
28 Santo Domingo
29 Casa de Antonio Lopez de Quiroga
30 Cúpulas of the old Casa de la Moneda
31 Casa del Conde de la Carma
32 San Juan Bautista
33 Caja de Agua
34 Portada
35 Portada de los Leones
36 Portada del Sol 1
37 Portada del Sol 2
38 Ingenio Dolores
39 La Concepción
40 San Sebastián
41 de Copacabana
42 San Benito
43 San Pedro
44 San Cristóbal

POTOSI DEPT.

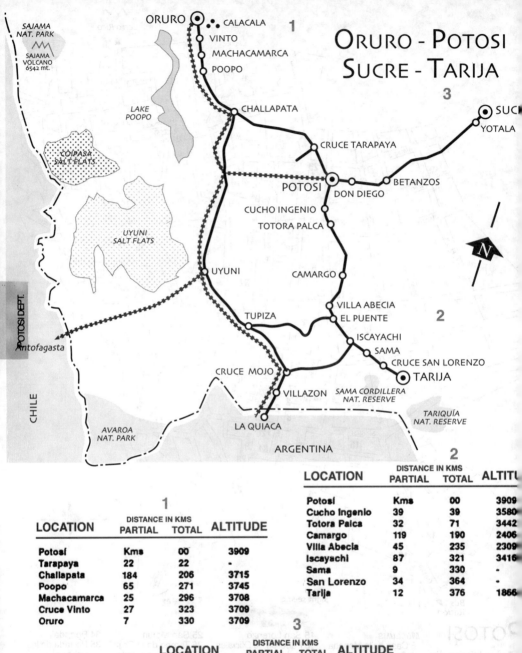

ORURO - POTOSI
SUCRE - TARIJA

1

2

3

SAJAMA NAT. PARK

SAJAMA VOLCANO 6542 mt.

ORURO
CALACALA
VINTO
MACHACAMARCA
POOPO

LAKE POOPO

COIPASA SALT FLATS

CHALLAPATA

CRUCE TARAPAYA

POTOSI
DON DIEGO
BETANZOS

SUC

YOTALA

UYUNI SALT FLATS

CUCHO INGENIO
TOTORA PALCA

UYUNI

CAMARGO

POTOSI DEPT.

Antofagasta

TUPIZA

VILLA ABECIA
EL PUENTE
ISCAYACHI
SAMA
CRUCE SAN LORENZO
TARIJA

CRUCE MOJO

VILLAZON

SAMA CORDILLERA NAT. RESERVE

CHILE

AVAROA NAT. PARK

LA QUIACA

ARGENTINA

TARIQUÍA NAT. RESERVE

N

2

LOCATION	DISTANCE IN KMS		ALTITU
	PARTIAL	TOTAL	
Potosí	Kms	00	3909
Cucho Ingenio	39	39	3580
Totora Palca	32	71	3442
Camargo	119	190	2406
Villa Abecia	45	235	2309
Iscayachi	87	321	3416
Sama	9	330	-
San Lorenzo	34	364	-
Tarija	12	376	1866

1

LOCATION	DISTANCE IN KMS		ALTITUDE
	PARTIAL	TOTAL	
Potosí	Kms	00	3909
Tarapaya	22	22	-
Challapata	184	206	3715
Poopo	65	271	3745
Machacamarca	25	296	3708
Cruce Vinto	27	323	3709
Oruro	7	330	3709

3

LOCATION	DISTANCE IN KMS		ALTITUDE
	PARTIAL	TOTAL	
Potosí	Kms	00	3909
Don Diego	20	20	3602
Betanzos	28	48	3316
Yotala	61	109	2503
Sucre	16	125	2790

AROUND UYUNI SALT FLATS

Oruro

Lago Poopó

Santa Ana de Chipaya

Huari

COIPASA SALT FLATS

Meteorite Crater

Tambo Tambillo

Rio Mulatos

Porco

NDELARIA 5995 mt.

Salinas de García Mendoza

Llica

Tahua

Jirija

TUNUPA VOLCANO 5432 mt.

ISLA DEL PESCADO

UYUNI SALT FLATS 3653 mt.

Pulacayo

UYUNI

S. Pedro de Quemez

Rio Grande

S. Juan

Atocha

Antofagasta

San Agustin

San Cristobal

Culpina k

San Vicente

Tupiza

OLLAGUE VOLCANO 5865 mt.

Villa Alota

CHILE

Laguna Cañapa

Laguna Hedionda

Laguna Ramadita

Laguna Colorada

San Antonio de Lipez

Soniquera

San Pablo de Lipez

Laguna Amarilla

San Antonio de Esmoruco

Quetena

Sol de Mañana

Salar de Chalviri

UTURUNCU VOLCANO 6008 mt.

AVAROA NAT. PARK

La Quiaca

Villazón

ARGENTINA

Laguna Verde

LINCANCABUR VOLCANO 5939 mt.

Valle Dali

ZAPALERI 5656 mt.

N

San Pedro de Atacama

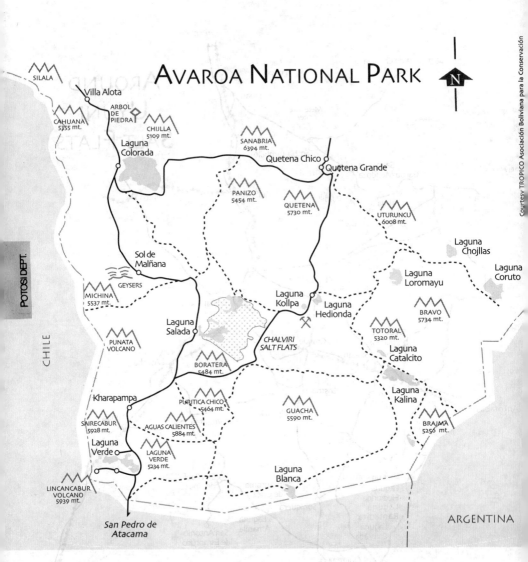

AVAROA NATIONAL PARK

SILALA

Villa Alota

ARBOL
DE
PIEDRA

CAHUANA
5355 mt.

CHIJLLA
5109 mt.

Laguna
Colorada

SANABRIA
6394 mt.

Quetena Chico

Quetena Grande

PANIZO
5454 mt.

QUETENA
5730 mt.

UTURUNCU
6008 mt.

Laguna
Chojllas

Laguna
Coruto

Sol de
Malñana

GEYSERS

MICHINA
5537 mt.

Laguna
Kollpa

Laguna
Hedionda

Laguna
Loromayu

BRAVO
5734 mt.

PUNATA
VOLCANO

Laguna
Salada

CHALVIRI
SALT FLATS

TOTORAL
5320 mt.

Laguna
Catalcito

BORATERA
5484 mt.

Kharapampa

PURITICA CHICO
5464 mt.

GUACHA
5590 mt.

Laguna
Kalina

SAIRECABUR
5928 mt.

AGUAS CALIENTES
5884 mt.

BRAJMA
5256 mt.

Laguna
Verde

LAGUNA
VERDE
5234 mt.

Laguna
Blanca

LINCANCABUR
VOLCANO
5939 mt.

San Pedro de
Atacama

ARGENTINA

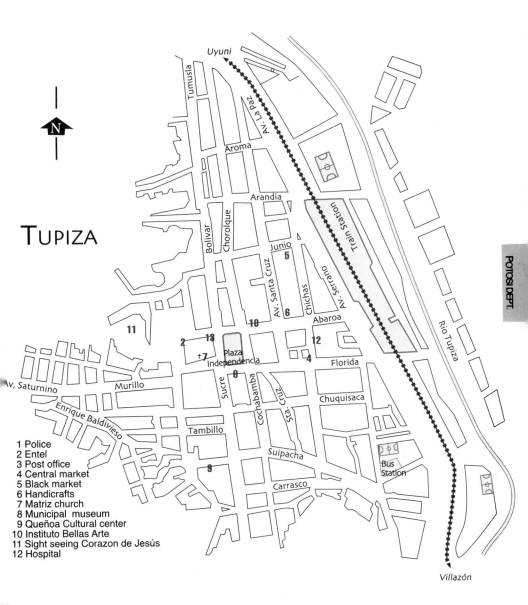

TUPIZA

1 Police
2 Entel
3 Post office
4 Central market
5 Black market
6 Handicrafts
7 Matriz church
8 Municipal museum
9 Queñoa Cultural center
10 Instituto Bellas Arte
11 Sight seeing Corazon de Jesús
12 Hospital

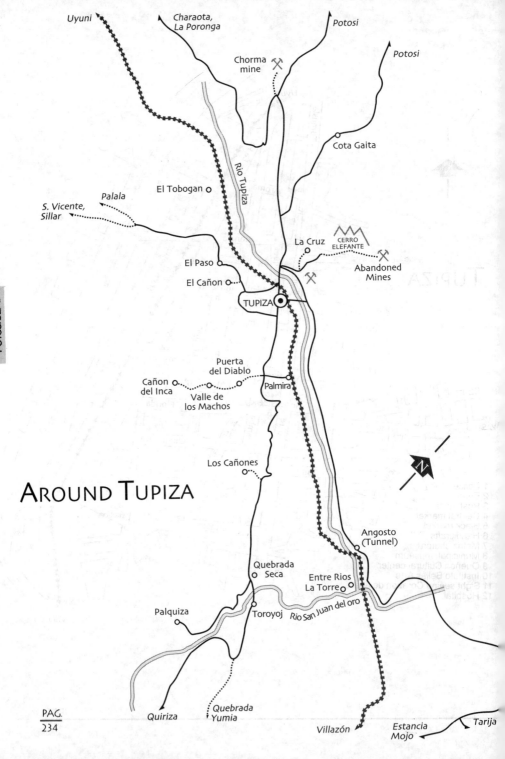

AROUND TUPIZA

Uyuni

Charaota, La Poronga

Potosi

Potosi

Chorma mine

Cota Gaita

Río Tupiza

Palala

S. Vicente, Sillar

El Tobogan

La Cruz

CERRO ELEFANTE

Abandoned Mines

El Paso

El Cañon

TUPIZA

Puerta del Diablo

Cañon del Inca

Valle de los Machos

Palmira

Los Cañones

Angosto (Tunnel)

Quebrada Seca

Entre Rios
La Torre

Palquiza

Toroyoj

Río San Juan del oro

Quiriza

Quebrada Yumia

Villazón

Estancia Mojo

Tarija

SALT HOTEL HAS A RULE: NO LICKING

BY PETER MCFARREN

On the bulletin board of the hotel rising out of a surreal moonscape high in the Andes, somebody posted a note: "Please don't lick the walls." The walls, you see, are made of salt. In fact, much of the hotel — the roof, some beds, chairs, tables and bar — are made of salt. Even the floor is covered with salt granules.

The hotel, recently renamed the Salt Palace and Spa, sits in the middle of the Uyuni Salt Flats — Salar de Uyuni — a prehistoric lake of salt near the Chilean border, covering 40 square miles at an altitude of 12,500 feet. The salt flat is bordered by a strange land of volcanoes and geysers, flamingoes and cacti, with a rich history and spectacular scenery that has become one of Bolivia's main tourist destinations. A railroad "graveyard" in the village of Uyuni southeast of the salt pan, was once an important railroad junction. It has vintage locomotives and boxcars that recall the days when Butch Cassidy and the Sundance Kid robbed trains and banks before being gunned down in 1908 not far from here.

Juan Quesada, an adventurous tourism operator, built the hotel with 14-by-14-inch hard blocks of salt cut with axes out of the salt flat. Twelve guest rooms with 24 beds and shared bathrooms surround a central courtyard. The intense sun heats the blocks of salt during the day and at night the bedrooms remain cozy while outside temperatures drop below freezing. I spent two nights at the hotel and found the rooms comfortable and dry with no salty smell. There are flush toilets, but no showers. One night we dined on barbecued llama meat. Quite tasty. The hotel, built four years ago, charges $50 for a single and $60 for a double. There is a separate building with cheaper rates for backpackers. As interesting as the hotel is, the scenery around it is breathtaking. During sunsets and sunrises, the sun casts shadows on the white expanse and geometric forms shaped by salt crystals. Star-watching is dazzling.

The nearest town to the hotel is Uyuni, once one of the country's premier railroad center, 220 miles south of La Paz. Minerals are still mined, but it's the tourist industry that is fast changing the region, bringing in money and creating jobs. An estimated 15,000 tourists last year visited the salt flats and Fisherman's Island that lies in the middle of the flats. On Fisherman's Island — Isla de Pescadores — there are thousands of cacti, some of them 30 feet high, and a stranded colony of vizcachas, long-tailed rodents related to the chinchilla. Around the flats, tourists encounter herds of graceful and shy vicunas (relatives of llamas) and dozens of pink flamingoes. Laguna Colorada in the highlands of this far southwest corner of Bolivia is a fiery-red lake. Birdwatchers are interested in the rare James' flamingoes that inhabit the lake.

Hundreds of Quechua Indians in surrounding villages make a living scraping layers of salt for processing into table salt, or by cutting blocks of salt. After a block the size of a shoe box is cut, brine that lies just below the surface rapidly fills the hole. After a few days, the surface becomes hard as rock. Today, the salt is carried on rusty trucks to nearby villages where residents make a living by drying, grinding, adding iodine and packaging the salt. Many quaint villages with beautiful churches that flourished around the salt flats for centuries are being revived thanks to tourism and aid-developed farming.

If you go. Reservations for the **Salt Palace and Spa** can be made through **Hidalgo Tours**, Tel/Fax. 591-6225186. The address is P.B. 314, Potosi, Bolivia. E-mail:uyusalht@ceibo.entelnet.bo www.salardeuyuni.com

Getting there: The Andina Train Company offers service to Uyuni on Mondays and Fridays. The **Copacabana** and **Nobleza** buses under contract to Andina leave La Paz at 6:00, connect with the train in Oruro and depart at 10:10. for Uyuni. Trains arrive at Uyuni at 16:25. For reservations contact **Andina** in La Paz at 591-2-2391770.

Tours: **Ecological Expeditions** offers a six-day, five-night tour to the Uyuni Salt Flats, Pescadores Island, Laguna Colorada and outlying communities. Reservations can be made at 591-2-2365047. E-mail: ecological@bo.net

BEAM ME OFF THE SALAR, SCOTTY

BY JAMIE GRANT

There are a few places on Earth that astronauts visit because they make such an impression on them from space. The *Salar de Uyuni* (Uyuni Salt Flats) is one of them. A glistening sea of white salt from above the *Salar* must look like another world amidst our own. The whole area is in fact straight out of a science fiction movie.

The *Altiplano* itself is weird enough. Traveling through its vast landscape, you are both entranced by the arid beauty and horrified by the endless monotony of it all. The South American Handbook was right when it described the *Altiplano* as a "luminous bowl of light;" there isn't much variety beyond the sun glare in your eyes. This must be the closest you can get to travel in outer space, but transport here is in bus or train rather than some fancy spacecraft that will hyper-warp you to your destination in a matter of seconds.

The small town of Uyuni is the gateway to the bizarre world of the *Salar*. The place has the feel of a frontier town— or perhaps the last space station before the final frontier. Old people crouch in market stalls clutching tin cups of tea with shivering, mittened hands. Kids hang out on street corners and in game halls, zapping asteroids and aliens in video games. When they are not writing in journals or hanging around the Entel Communication Center, tourists battle with tour companies for the cheapest

Salar expedition. The tour companies' Toyota Land Cruisers line up in varying states of decay outside their offices.

Uyuni is reminiscent of the town in Star Wars where Obi Wan Kenobi and Luke employ Han Solo's services on their mission to destroy the Death Star. Both are filled with the oddest bunch of travelers, hustlers and hostile locals in this "hive of scum and villainy."

Sitting at a bar packed with furry singing aliens in Uyuni, you can almost imagine Luke and Han haggling over the price for a *Salar* tour. "I have a state-of-the-art vehicle, on-board heating, trilingual guides and more food than you can shake a stick at," says Han. "It's a steal at $110." Luke talks him down to 65 bucks for three days all-inclusive — only to find that the Land Cruiser is a battered old pick-up, the food is an endless supply of *chuño* and rice, and the company answers are a miserable English couple who endlessly complain about their stomach bugs and the altitude.

Having committed your health, comfort and sanity for three days to one tour company or another, you finally approach the *Salar*, a mere half an hour from Uyuni. It's on the salt flats itself that reality truly clashes with science fiction. Walking across limitless white hexagrams you can't help but ask, "On which planet — or film set — am I?"

You almost expect Doctor Who to jump up with his long scarf and sexy assistant in tow. "This place is too weird for me," he'd say. "Lets get back in the TARDIS and transport ourselves to some disused quarry to fight polystyrene nematodes."

If not Doctor Who, that old dinosaur of the 70s, the *Salar* would make the ideal setting for Star Trek's *The New Generation*. Captain Picard is beamed down to earth, only to realize that all humans have vaporized each other and there isn't much left but a lot of salt. "Hmmm," he would comment, "if only the human race had respected each other and treated everyone as equals, they wouldn't have ended up as salt patties."

Of course there is much more to see beyond the outer limits of the *Salar* that most of the standard three-day tours cover. Bolivia's southern 'cosmos' also offers sulfur-spouting volcanoes, green and red lakes and deserts scattered with asteroids. But all these are for other film sets, sci-fi episodes and cliff-hangers with damsels in distress and overweight heroes poured into skintight jump suits.

A trip into the *Salar* is a trip into a fantasy world where only an over-active imagination can fill the hours of boredom, as you're thrown about on a dirt road in an overcrowded jeep with moaning Brits. So, if you do decide to go on this terrestrial space odyssey, fasten your seat belt and prepare to boldly go where no man or woman in their right mind has gone before. Oh, and remember that as much as you may like to, at no point during the trip can you flick open your communicator and give the order "Beam me up, Scotty."

POTOSÍ: A GOLD MINE FOR TOURISM

BY PETER MCFARREN

Miguel Angel Delgadillo helped a group of German tourists put on helmets, rubber boots and jackets and handed them a carbon lamp. As he chewed coca, Delgadillo led the group of tourists inside the *Grito de Piedra* mine shaft. After an hour of crouching, jumping over deep holes and avoiding protruding rocks, he led them to *Tío Supay*, the miners' devilish-looking protector, and told the visitors about the suffering, history and legends that surround this historical mountain.

Tourism in this colonial-period city of nearly133,651 has taken a new twist as miners and cooperatives linked to travel operators are cashing in on the growing number of visitors who are looking for something different and are interested in reliving one of the most tragic experiences in the Spanish conquest of the New World.

For decades, tourists visited Potosí to explore the beautiful churches with their gold-leafed altars and elaborate stone-carved facades and the Spanish Mint, all funded from the wealth generated by *Cerro Rico*. Today, the mines with their hundreds of kilometers of shafts and history of exploitation and suffering have become the main attraction for foreign tourists.

"Going into this mine is like going back centuries and seeing how the miners have worked under such difficult conditions," says Kurt Rabe, a German tourist who is visiting Potosí after several days of exploring the Uyuni Salt Flats, which are also located in the Department of Potosí.

Potosí is nestled at the foot of *Cerro Rico* on a plateau at 4,100m, surrounded by mountains and valleys that are part of the Andes eastern edge. The symmetrical lines of *Cerro Rico*, criss-crossed by more than 5,000 tunnels, disappear as one approaches the mine from the city's center. To the left of *Cerro Rico*, the road heads toward a chain of mountains containing seven lagoons that date to the 16th or 17th century. Water channeled down the mountain once powered silver processing plants built by the Spaniards and operated by indigenous and Afro-Bolivian slaves. Remains of these stone plants still dot the landscape. One of these, the former silver processing plant of San Marcos, has been converted into an elegant restaurant with the support of the Spanish Government, which is also financing the restoration of the most important colonial churches in Potosí.

At the mountain, miners guide tourists through dark and humid tunnels and descend through hand-cranked elevators into mine shafts where miners work almost naked because of the intense heat. Tourists will encounter an area where miners pay homage to *Tío Supay*. Miners and many tourists will sprinkle coca leaves on *Tío* and chew a few leaves, no doubt to help deal with the rarefied air.

"Millions died inside these mines," said Delgadillo. "Even today, this mountain, the source of so much wealth, continues to claim the lives of my fellow miners. But for us, until tourism brought in some additional income, mining is what sustained us," he said.

A museum under construction at the Cerro Rico will provide an introduction to the mountains' rich and tragic history.

SAN CRISTOBAL

BY MICHAEL HERRERA

If you happen to be mountain biking on the *Cerro Jayula*, just outside the town of San Cristobal, try to keep moving or, at the very least, look alive because those shadows looming from overhead are sure to be Andean Condors in search of a meal. In fact, the *Trinchera* ridge is a condor nesting ground and known to the locals who live in this remote area as "*casa de condor*". As for the mountain biking, it doesn't get much better than the rolling llama paths that zigzag through the boulder fields and bizarre geologic formations on these hillsides. If the majestic view over the Salar de Uyuni doesn't take your breath away, the 4500-meter summits will. All this can be found just two hours drive south and west from Uyuni, in a location that, until recently, was sparse vegetation and scattered rock. San Cristobal's history is, indeed, an interesting one.

The town itself was originally founded in the early seventeenth century by the Spanish to support the lucrative San Cristobal Mining District. Untold wealth was extracted and, sadly, exported from this bowl shaped mountain. Finally the supply became just a trickle and the mine abandoned. In a testament to the tenacity of these hearty people, the village lived on and, like their pre-Inca ancestry, they made good farming quinoa and raising llama their means for surviving. Then the big one hit. Modern mining technology discovered a sil-

ver reserve many times larger than what had been ever been imagined there and, as fate would have it, the reserve was too close to this old town. So the decision was made to move the town, it's people and it's history and by 1999 the population had it's new home some seven kilometers from the original location. Amazingly, the historically significant church and cemetery were moved stone for stone (or in the case of the cemetery, bone for bone) and rebuilt to their exact originals, thus preserving San Cristobal's heritage, something for which these townspeople are visibly proud.

Enter town these days (as a stop off on one of the many jeep trips that circuit the area, perhaps?) and one finds wide streets, traffic controls and obvious thought toward urban planning. It is clear that something is coming to San Cristobal and San Cristobal is ready. The center point of town is, of course, the church. The **church**, declared a National Monument in 1967, is a 17th century memorial to the history and traditions of the town and the region. See Alberto Colque at the **Hotel San Cristobal** (02-2138471) for a tour of this splendidly restored landmark. While you are at it, book a room at the hotel. It lays claim to the hottest showers in the region thanks to three large solar heaters on the roof making use of all that free southern Bolivian sun. Within the hotel lies the design brainchild of Bolivian artist Gaston Ugalde, "**The**

Mongo's Mad Max Café. Good food and drink in an atmosphere of *post-apocalypse meets Spanish iron-work* could only come from this mad, creative mind.

Aside from the *epoca de lluvia* (rainy season months of January through March) expect cloudless, panoramic skies and a fair dose of afternoon wind. This is a harsh climate, warm in the day, cold at night but well worth bundling up for.

So what about the aforementioned mountain biking? Well, if you are up to braving the elements by mountain bike, **Llama Mama Bicycle Tours** (www.llama-mama.com) offers full and half-day, predominately downhill trips with amazing views and kilometers of purpose-built singletrack. Just keep an eye out for the condors!

CULPINA K

BY MICHAEL HERRERA

The jeep trip from Uyuni to Laguna Colorada is a long one. The road (yes, there's a road out there somewhere) offers spectacular views of southern Bolivia's incredible geology and a lot of dust, but there's one more attraction that shouldn't be missed enroute: the small town of Culpina "K".

Culpina "K" (more on the "K" forthcoming) is a humble community one hundred kilometers south and west of Uyuni whose population of five-hundred continue longstanding traditions of farming quinoa and raising llama in a region that is as harsh as it is beautiful. Founded in the mid-fifties by the Copa, Calcina and Quispe families, not much has changed here over the years, but a new kind of tree is popping up around the plaza principal. Bolivian sculptor Gaston Ugalde (with support from the community, Minera San Cristóbal S.A. and Corporación Andina de Fomento) has undertaken a project to bring a modern flair to this area and his vision is quite eyecatching.

First are the arches as one enters town. These 15 meter-high adobe structures straddle the road at town's edge on both the north and south entrances and mark the start of Culpina's cobblestone streets.

Next one is struck by the architecture of the main plaza. Penned and constructed in 2002, the circular forms at the center of the plaza reflect a simple modernism and much use of the area's varied and colorful rock.

And finally, the trees. It is unusual to find trees in this region but the ones that run the perimeter of Culpina's plaza are worthy of a second glance. They are, in fact, steel and wood structures that form an odd forest of modern art. Ugalde's interest in the region, as well as his bizarre artistic vision, are readily appearant.

Curious about other attractions in the area of Culpina? A short distance from town lies Lago Vera, a small lake providing habitat for numerous bird and animal species including the pink flamingo. Nearby the lake are a large grouping of chulpas, Inca burial sites, making this an area of considerable archeological interest. For the adventure minded, Llama Mama Bike Tours (www.llama-mama.com) offers local mountain bike excursions both in Culpina and nearby San Cristobal. A small number of alojamientos (basic but comfortable lodging) are available, and each year brings a greater number of artisans to the area. Locally produced llama and alpaca wool products are top quality and thus in demand by travelers.

So what is the story behind the "K" in Culpina K? No mystery here. In the nineteen fifties, when Culpina made the big jump from a loosely scattered group of estancias to pueblo (with a school and church to make it all official) it was common

POTOSI DEPT.

practice to find more than a few towns all sharing the same family name. Enter the Bolivian army with a sound and suitable solution: a single letter designation to accompany the existing town name. So don't confuse Culpina "K" with Culpina "M" or "P" and do visit this model town.

For some interesting information on the various projects underway in Culpina, visit the town's website at www.culpinak.org.

COWBOY DREAMS IN TUPIZA

BY BEN GARSIDE

Overlooked by many visitors, Tupiza is a small city of distinct charm with a pleasant climate. But it is the spectacular Wild West landscape surrounding the town that really makes Tupiza "la joya bella" or beautiful jewel of Bolivia, leaving the lucky few who pass through with no regrets at having made the effort.

At a comfortable altitude of 2,950m, Tupiza is the capital of the Sud Chichas region of the Department of Potosi. Its small population of a little over 20,000 is one of Bolivia's youngest and most educated, many of whom are employed in agriculture and the mining of antimony, lead and other minerals. The city itself lies on the banks of the Tupiza River and is a stop on the railroad from Oruro (11 hours to the north) to Villazon on the Argentine border (3 hours to the south).

I arrived in Tupiza by train in the small hours of the morning and was relieved to have made prior reservations for a place to stay as I slipped uncertainly through the darkened chilly streets, yet upon knocking expectantly on the front door, I had an anxious wait until the night porter roused himself to let me in, his hair electrified with sleep. The following day a short stroll across town led me to the elegant plaza, dotted with palm trees, a colonial Catholic church and centered with a statue of Avelino Aramayo, founder of the Aramayo mining dynasty which was centered in Tupiza. I

continued walking up the gentle slope of the Cerro Corazon de Jesus, whose summit affords a good view of the city and surrounding area and ensured that I was already smitten with this agreeable little city.

Yet the highlight of any visit to Tupiza is the dramatic rock formations that surround the area. Best discovered by a trip on horseback to visit the numerous canyons, cliffs and cacti, some of which are only just outside the city. A small number of tour agencies run horseback trips ranging from a few hours to a few days in length, the longer trips really give an idea of the cowboy lifestyle and being out in the wilderness. Despite having never ridden a horse before, my initial fears soon departed as my small group did our best Wild Bunch impressions and headed out into the red hewn hills. Upon my return, the only thing smarting was my rear end but that could not stop my wide grin at having experienced an adventure to treasure for years to come. If you favor pedal power over horsepower, bicycles can be hired and tours taken, jeeps can be chartered for the less active or acutely saddle sore.

The rust-colored rock outcrops in Tupiza's outlying areas form an incredible and often crazy landscape straight out of a Wil-e-Coyote cartoon. El Sillar or "The Saddle" is a moonscape of craters and sky scraping formations lying about 15kms out of town. Closer by is the walkable

POTOSI DEPT.

Quebrada del Palala with its spectacular red fin shapes. Also nearby is the Quebrada Seca, a cathedral-like giant rock which often displays all the colors of the rainbow.

If Mother Nature has proven with these landscapes that she has fine artistic capabilities, in the Poronga rock she proves she has a sense of humor, with its amazing likeness to the male reproductive organ. Giggle-hunters will also be impressed with Valle de los Machos, also affectionately known as the Valley of the Penises.

The tour companies in town run jeep tours following in the footsteps of those lovable outlaws Butch Cassidy and the Sundance Kid who roamed these lands at the start of the last century. The shorter day out to Huaca Huanusca is a pleasant 4 hour jaunt to the site of their last crime, passing some beautiful country on the way before leaving the jeep for a 3km walk down to the picturesque and isolated spot where the outlaws held up the Aramayo payroll. The second day out to the site of their ultimate demise in San Vicente, taking a hefty 3 hours to get there by jeep through an increasingly wild and barren landscape is stricly for hardcore fans only. Upon reaching this cold and bleak mining town, population 50 and falling by the day, it may feel like reaching the end of the world. The glum adobe hut where the bandits were shot is a far cry from the picturesque square depicted in the film, and an inconclusive unmarked stone in the cemetery to mark their final resting place both make for a sorry and arduous day out.

A visit to San Vicente may only be worthwhile if it can be done as a stop en route to the Salar on the 4 and 5 day jeep tours which also run from Tupiza. Prices tend to be a bit more expensive than a similar trip from Uyuni but take in more lakes and can save on doubling back as it is possible to be dropped off in Uyuni at the end of the tour.

THE CARNIVAL AND MINING CITY OF ORURO

BY PETER MCFARREN

L ocated on the *Altiplano* on and beneath the slopes of a hill, earth-colored Oruro is one of Bolivia's major cities. Founded in 1601, it has since been a mining center of tin, silver and wolfram. Today it is an important transportation and communications center linking Bolivian cities by rail and road with points in Chile and Argentina. Oruro, with a population of 202,010, also has a university with a particularly strong engineering program.

The city of Oruro is visited by tens of thousands of Bolivians from other regions of the country and by foreigners from all over the world during the *Carnaval* celebration, which occurs at the end of February or beginning of March. It is definitely a must when you visit Bolivia: it is probably one of the most spectacular cultural events in Latin America. It is best if you make arrangements for travel and lodging with travel agencies in La Paz. The new **Museum of Archaeology**, located on the southern side of the city next to the botanical gardens, is also worth visiting. Especially notable are the stone llama heads from the Huancarani period and a first-rate collection of masks used in *Carnaval*. Maskmakers and embroiderers can be found on Calle La Paz. They make the elaborate plaster-of-paris and tin masks and the costumes used for the *Diablada*.

Also worth visiting is the **Virgin del Socavón Sanctuary**, located to the west of the city at the foothill of the mountain that overlooks the city. Here is where all *Carnaval* celebrations are focused, and also where the Virgin of Candelaria is worshipped. During *Carnaval*, dancers wearing devil masks and outfits end up at the church, where they pay homage to the Virgin. (For more detailed information on the *Carnaval* of Oruro, see "The *Carnaval* of Oruro," in Chapter Four of this guide).

Since it is part of the *Altiplano*, there are often strong winds that sweep through the city. Oruro is at an altitude of 12,143 feet (3,702m). Clothing for visiting Oruro would be the same as for La Paz.

PRACTICAL INFORMATION FOR ORURO

Oruro Phone Code: 2

• Useful Addresses and Numbers

Tourist Information Center, in the Prefectural Building on Plaza 10 de Febrero, Tel. 5250144, and Presidente Montes and Adolfo Mier, Tel. 5251764.

Post Office, President Montes 1456, Tel. 5251660.

Entel, offers fax, telex and long distance telephone service. Locations at Calle Bolívar/Soria Galvarro, Tels. 5250178, 5250301, and Presidente Montes/Adolfo Mier, Tel. 5250144.

Long Distance Call
Entel, 101.
AES, 0-11.

ORURO DEPT.

Cotas, 0-12.

Train Station, Calle Velasco Galvarro and Aldana. Tels. 5260605, 5260248.

Police Department, Tel. 110.

Bus Station, Calle Vakovic, between Av. Villaroel and Rodríguez, Tel. 5279535.

Immigration Office, Calle Montesinos corner with Pagador, 2nd floor.

• Consulates

Germany, Adolfo Mier 5999, Tels. 5255773. Open Monday through Friday from 9:00 to 12:00.

• How to Get There

You can easily reach Oruro by bus from either La Paz or Cochabamba. From other parts of the country, you will need to connect via one of these two cities to get to Oruro.

• Airline Offices

Lloyd Aéreo Boliviano, Calle La Plata 1544, corner with Junín. Tels. 5251620, 5251158.

• Buses

Copacabana, Tel. 5276263.
Oruro, Tel. 5275087.
Nobleza, Tel. 5274424.
Urus, Tel. 5277508.

• Getting Around Town

Oruro is a small town, and easily navigated by foot. Taxis are also readily available.

• Radio Taxis

Radio Taxi Oruro, at the bus terminal, Tels. 5273399, 5276222.

Tricolor, Tels. 5271441, 5272200.
Socavón, Tel. 5275456.
Sajama, Tel. 5272774.

• Car Rental

RENT-A-CAR, Calle Junín 621, Tels. 5256801, also 11-41183.

• Car Repair

Servicio Automotriz S.O.S., Calle Vasquez 210, Tels. 5241005, also 18-41889.

• Hotels

Note: Carnaval reservations must be made several months in advance and restaurant service is limited, so be sure to bring along extra food.

Three Stars Hotels

Hotel Terminal, Tels. 5253209, 5253797. Moderate, offers 108 rooms, parking and a restaurant. (It is one of the few places that serves food during *Carnaval*). Located at the main Oruro bus terminal.

Max Plaza Hotel, Plaza 10 de Febrero, Tel. 5252561. Fax. 5133003. E-mail: maxplazahotel@hotmail.com

International Park Hotel, Calle Rajka Vakovic, Tels. 5279209, 5276227. E-mail: lparkhot@nogal.oru.entelnet.bo

SM Palace Hotel, Calle Adolfo Mier 392, Tels. 5272121, 5255432, Fax. 5255132.

Hotel Monarca, Av. Del Ejercito 1145, Tels. 5254300, 5254222, Fax. 5279006. E-mail: h.momves@nogal.oru.entelnet.bo

Two Stars Hotels

Residencial Hostal Bolivia, Calle Rodríguez 131, Tels. 5241047 and 1841451.

Gran Sucre Hotel, Calle Sucre 510, Tels. 5272013, 5253838.

Hotel Lipton, Av. 6 de Agosto 625, Tel. 5241583.

Hotel America, Calle Bolivar 351, Tel. 5274707, Fax. 9526072.

ORURO DEPT.

Hotel Bernal, Av. Brazil 701, Tel. 5279468.
Hotel Gutierrez, Calle Rayka Backovick 580, Tel. 5256675, Fax. 5276515.
Repostero, Calle Sucre 370, corner with Potosí, Tels. 5250505, 5258001.

• Restaurants

Nayjama, Calle Pagador 1880, Tel. 5277699, serves national cuisine.
Pagador, Calle Pagador 1440, Tel. 5255387, open every day serving national and international cuisine.
Unicorno, Calle La Plata 5959, Tel. 5254002, serves national and international cuisine, and specializes in Argentinian beef.
Meat lovers should try **Complejo Sounder**, Calle Cochabamba 1126, Tel. 5255915 for grilled meats, or **Charcas**, Calle Camacho 1328, Tel. 5256919 for their specialty, *charkekan*. Also **Pompeya**, Calle Lira 685, Tel. 5241115, open every day. And on Saturdays and Sundays only, you can get good *fricasé*, *chicharron* and *wat'iya* at **Rosticería El Fogón**, at Av. Brasil 5021, opposite the bus terminal, Tel. 5279456.
Vegetariano Govinda, Calle 6 de Octubre 6071, Tel. 5255205 for a variety of vegetarian foods.
Gaviota, Calle Junin 676.
Pub the Alpaca, Calle La Paz 690.
For fast food, try roasted chicken at **Snack Cosmos**, Calle 6 de Octubre corner with Oblitas, Tel. 5246743, or for hamburgers and sandwiches, go to **El Hamburgon**, Calle 6 de Octubre 785, Tel. 5240175.
Salteñas Pizza Sum, Calle Bolívar 615, Tel. 5256312, open every day in the morning for *salteñas*.
Salteñeria Norita, Calle Cochabamba 664, Tel. 5251718, open every day in the morning only.

• Travel Agencies

Dalu S.R.L., Calle Potosí 6118, Tel/Fax. 5276805. E-mail: dalu@zuper.net
Jumbo Travel, Av. 6 de Octubre 6080, Tel. 5255203, Fax. 5255005.
Inti Tours, Calle Ayacucho 785, Tel. 5252515.
H.T. Viajeros del Tiempo, Calle Soria Galvarro 1220, Tel. 5271166, Fax. 5254491.
E-mail: viajerosdeltiempo@hotmail.com
Nature Tours, Calle La Plata 5868, Edif. Alvarez, Tel/Fax. 5252625.
E-mail: naturetours-bolivia@hotmail.com

• Museums and Cultural Centers

The **Museo Municipal** offers an excellent collection of old masks that were used in the *Carnaval* of Oruro. It also has one of the best archeological collections from Inca and pre-Inca cultures in Bolivia, including carved stone figures of llamas and other animals. This museum is very much worth a visit. Located in the Agua de Castilla suburb across from the Municipal Zoological Gardens. Best to take a taxi. Open from 8:30 to noon, and 14:30 to 18:00.

The **Casa de la Cultura** is a neo-classical building that once belonged to the billionaire tin baron Simón Patiño who made his fortune in the mines near Oruro. Here you will find a collection of colonial art and furnishings that belonged to Patiño. Calle Soria Galvarro and Ayacucho. Open Monday through Friday from 9:00 to 12:00, and 14:00 to 18:00.

Oruro is the mining center of Bolivia, and to understand its mining history, visit the **Museo Minerológico** located in the University. Tel. 5261250. Here you will find over 5,000 mineralogical samples, including precious stones and paleontological rocks. Open Monday through Friday from 9:00 to 12:00, and 14:00 to 18:00.

Lara Art Gallery and Workshop painting, ceramic and sculpture exhibit, Calle La Plata 6474. Tels. 5257737, 5254488.

Cardozo Velásquez Art Workshop, ceramic and sculpture exhibit, Calle Junin 738. Tel. 5275245.

• Bookstores

La Fuente del Saber, Calle Bolívar 570, Tel. 5252307.

Cultural Universitaria, Calle Caro 330, Tel. 5274468.

Pompeya, Av. 6 de Octubre 6056, Tel. 5270619.

• Shopping

Artesanías Oruro, Ayacucho 856, Tel. 5256331, also in the Mercado Fermín López.

Artesanías Kelkha, Calle Smith 428, Tel. 5228306.

Joyería Select, Calle Adolfo Mier 446, Tel. 5244525.

Joyería Asunción, Calle Adolfo Mier 456, Tel. 5277080.

Creaciones BYB Peltre Bolivia, Calle La Paz 4635, Tels. 5231488, 5271514.

Zona Franca (Duty Free), at Rodríguez 450, Tels. 5254855, 5276816, also at Km 10 of the Oruro-Manchacamarca Highway, Tel. 5278112 (also fax).

• Sports

Tiburones Swimming Club, Calle La Plata, corner with Ayacucho, Tels. 5250554, 5275473.

Raquet Club Sucre, Calle La Salle 321, Tel. 5260530.

• Nightlife

Bravo Bravo, Calle Montesinos between Pagador and V. Galvarro, Tels. 5277304, 5275506.

Harlem (Ex Nikei Plaza Hotel), Calle Adolfo Mier, Tel. 5272928.

VIP's, Calle 6 de Octubre 1408, Tel. 5277755.

• Movies

Gran Rex, Calle Adolfo Mier, between 6 de Octubre and Soria Galvarro, Tel. 5251720.

Imperio, Calle 6 de Octubre, corner with 1 de Noviembre, Tel. 5277661.

• Banks

Banco Mercantil, Plaza 10 de Febrero, Tels. 5253619, 5254079.

Banco de Santa Cruz, Calle Bolívar 460, Tels. 5254856, 5277710, Fax. 5252720.

Banco de Crédito, Calle Soria Galvarro 1291 and 5783, Tels. 5254852, 5251821, Fax. 5251820.

Banco Nacional de Bolivia, Calle La Plata 6160, Tels. 5255168, 5251380.

• Money Exchange

Prodem, Calle 6 de Octubre 643.

• Couriers

DHL, Calle Presidente Montes, corner with Sucre, Tels. 5272729, 5256729, Fax. 5256497.

UPS, Calle Soria Galvarro 599 (Parque Padilla), Tels. 5255773, 5250802.

International Bonded Courier, Calle Bolívar 359, Edif. Bolívar, Of. 205, Tel. 5255480.

CBK Ltda, Calle Bolivar 877, Tel. 5251045.

FEdEX, Calle Presidente Montes, Edif. Santa Teresa, Tel. 5250793, Fax. 5271369.

• Laundries

Dupall Limpieza de Ropa, Calle La Paz 5972, Tel. 5254433.

Andes Dry Cleaners, Calle Velasco Galvarro 757, Tel. 5276921.

• Medical Services

Clínica Urme, Calle Cochabamba 548, Tels. 5252580, 5252905, offers a wide range of medical services by numerous specialists.

Hospital San Juan de Dios, Calle San Felipe, corner with 6 de Octubre, Tels. 5275405, 5279830.

Policlínica Oruro, Calle Rodriguez, Tel. 5275082.

EXCURSIONS FROM ORURO

Mining Centers

An understanding of Bolivian society, politics and economics would not be complete without a visit to the mining centers located to the south and southeast of Oruro. Perhaps the most important is **Llallagua**, a three-hour ride from Oruro. It is in the Llallagua area that the Siglo 20 and Catavi mining complexes are located. At one point Siglo 20 was the largest mine in Bolivia, one of the most important tin mines in the world and the source of tin baron Simón Patiño's fortune. It boasts 500 miles (800 km) of tunnels which criss-cross the mountain. Most of the mines in the area were shut down in 1995 in response to a drop in world tin prices and large deficits by the state mining company COMIBOL. To try to arrange a visit inside the mines, check with the COMIBOL offices in Catavi. Visits have been restricted since the closing, even though private cooperatives made up of former COMIBOL miners continue to extract minerals. Because of the closings, Llallagua is slowly becoming a ghost town with many miners migrating to the cities and tropical zones. The Suggested Reading Material section in "Facts at Your Fingertips," in Chapter One of this guide, can provide a good introduction to the struggle of the miners and the tough living conditions in the mining towns.

Poopo

A one hour bus ride from Oruro to Poopo is an interesting excursion. From the town of Poopo, one may walk a few minutes to the former Patiño mines and watch people work slag tin.

Lake of the Uru Uru Miracle

Lake of the Milagro Uru Uru is eight kilometers from Oruro and may be reached by taxi. Formed by the Desaguadero River, it is the site of good fishing for *pejerrey* and other species. There is a restaurant, and row boats can be rented.

Birdlife on the lake includes flamingos, ducks and gulls. The lake contains several islands.

The Salt Flats of Uyuni

This is one of the spectacular sites in Bolivia and very much worth visiting. Using a private four-wheel drive vehicle, take the Oruro-Potosi road to Challapata, about three hours from Oruro. From Challapata head to Huari where there is, believe it or not, a beer factory. Bear right across the flat *pampa* on to the Santuario de Quillacas, which has an interesting church, then on to Salinas de Garci Mendoza, a colonial town. From there the salt flat (*salar*) is not more than 1-1/2 hours away, or 18 to 25 miles (30 to 40 km). Here, between Salinas de Garci Mendoza and Llica, is the safest place to cross the *salares*, or salt flats. Close to the edge of the flats the entrance and exit are well marked by tire tracks, as there is fairly heavy traffic across the route. The crossing, about 37 miles (60 km), takes about 45 minutes. It is advisable to take along somebody who knows the road, though. Warning: Never cross the salt flats at night. People have been lost and have died on the *salar*. Also only attempt the trip in the dry season (June to October).

The *salar* is impressive in its vastness and smooth white surface. If you plan on taking photographs, be sure to take into consideration the reflective glare of the salt and the ultra-violet light, which affect exposures.

For a guided tour of the *salar* and the impressive wildlife sanctuary at Laguna Colorada, contact Fremen Tours, TAWA Tours and Paititi Tours in La Paz. They provide vehicles, guides and the equipment necessary to visit the *salar*, Uyuni and the Laguna Colorada, famous for its pink flamingos.

Perhaps the best way to visit the Uyuni Salt Flats and the surrounding region is by taking the train from Oruro to Uyuni. For train schedules, contact the train station, Tels. 5260605, 5260248.

For more information on Uyuni and the salt Flats see chapter Excursions from Potosí.

The Chipayas

The Chipayas are an important community to the southwest of Oruro. Originally the Chipayas lived around lakes as did the Urus, but they were eventually pushed onto the desert salt fields of the southwestern *Altiplano*, while the Urus were pushed back to the swampy shores of Lake Titicaca. The Chipayas live in several scattered communities and survive on fishing, hunting and working in the Chilean copper mines. (See "Along the Inca and Silver Highway," in Chapter Four of this guide). The Spaniards tried to impose their religion on the Chipayas, but met with only limited success.

The architecture, clothing, religion, music and language of the Chipaya differ greatly from those of other Andean people of today. The most characteristic belief of the Chipayas is that they claim their origin from the Chullpas. These are mysterious tombs, square in shape, which are believed to be remnants of a people or culture which flourished between the decline of the Tiwanaku period and the birth of the Inca empire.

The Chipayas deify almost everything they know: little mounds of stone, mountains, dead animals, the river, the church tower. They build little altars in order to obtain magical protection. They also worship monuments that are conical in shape with a hole at the bottom carefully closed with a block of earth. The Chipayas make their offerings to the evil spirits of the region in the holes of these monuments. There are nine such monuments around the village within a radius of 3.5 to 9 miles (5 to 15 km).

The musical instruments of the Chipayas are of Aymara origin, with the exception of their drum, which is square. The Chipayas, particularly the women, vocalize in chorus, and it is said that they practice at midnight.

The Chipayas speak Aymara as well as their own language, Puquina. The women wear their hair in elaborate braids and wear coarse earth-colored garments.

To reach the Chipayas from Oruro, go to Sabaya. From Sabaya take a guide with you and proceed to the village, which is about 18 miles (30 km) away. The Chipaya communities can only be visited during the dry season since the rains flood the roads.

Cala Cala

21 Km. South East from Oruro is the **Cala Cala rock paintings archaeological park**.

For more information on Cala Cala see Rock Art in Archaeological Parks article in Chapter Three.

ORURO DEPT.

ORURO

Tourist information
Immigration
Entel
Post office

MARKET
5 Campero

CHURCH
6 Cathedral

MUSEUM
7 Municipal
8 Minerologico
9 Etnografico (Socavon
Sanctuary)

CULTURAL CENTER
10 Casa de la Cultura

POINTS OF INTEREST
11 Sight Seeing
Corazon de Jesús
12 San Jose Mine

--- Carnival Route

AROUND ORURO

La Paz
Caracollo
Obrajes
Capachos
Totora
Sepulturas
Curahuara de Carangas
Chiquichambi
ORURO
Cala Cala
Bolivar
SAJAMA NAT. PARK
SAJAMA VOLCANO 6549 mt.
Old Trains
Machacamarca
Toledo
Turco
Huanuni
Catavi
Corque
Lago Uru Uru
Poopó
Siglo XX
Llal
Panza
Uncia
Tambo Quemado
Macaya
Sacabaya
Huachacalla
Cutusuma
Challapata
Escara
San José
Potosí
Orinoco
Santiago de Huari
Sabaya
Santa Ana de Chipaya
Pampa Aullagas
Lago Poopó
Pisiga Bolivar
Coipasa
Challacota
Uyuni
COIPASA SALT FLATS
Meteorite Crater

ORURO DEPT.

SAJAMA NATIONAL PARK

CHILE
Larancagua
Tomarapi
Lago Huayña Kkota
POMERATA VOLCANO 6240 mt.
Sajama
SAJAMA VOLCANO 6549 mt.
PARANICOTA VOLCANO 6330 mt.
Lagunas

PÁG. 254 Tambo Quemado

Pataca La Paz

SAJAMA NATIONAL PARK: LUSCIOUS ANDEAN BIODIVERSITY

BY ELIANA FLORES BEDREGAL

The micro-habitats and micro-climates created by the Andean Cordillera make Sajama National Park Bolivia's most biodiverse protected area in Andean flora and fauna. Spectacular formations of volcanic lava and geothermal flows complete this unexpected panorama. In addition to the biodiversity, this region also has enormous scenic, historical and archaeological value, both colonial and pre-Columbian.

Sajama National Park, Bolivia's first protected area, was created in 1939 to preserve the Andean keñua woodlands. Located about 5 hours by road from La Paz, between 4,200 and 5,200 meters above sea level (between 13,800 and 17,000 feet), these woodlands constitute the highest altitude forest in the world and have become one of the principal attractions for visitors. Wood from here is still used as fuel and timber.

Standing proud in the center of the keñua woodlands is Mt. Sajama, Bolivia's highest mountain. Sajama, which reaches 6,542 meters (nearly 21,500 feet), offers a magnificent view of southwest Bolivia as well as great climbing and trekking opportunities.

Another reason to go to Sajama is to see the vicuñas, whose family groups consist of one male and two to five females and their young. Herds of bachelor males also graze on the plains. Other occasional visitors to the wetlands include flamingos, chinchilla rats that sit on the rocks and preen their coats and *suri*, a lesser rhea that runs from visitors. (Pumas, pampas cats and the Andean cats are more shy, and thus more difficult to spot.) Many species of plants, birds and butterflies also live in Sajama, as do many small *orestias* and *thichomycterus* fish.

The Sajama region has very important archeological treasures. The road is lined with *hullpas*, pre-Columbian grave towers that are a legacy of Aymaran culture. Brightly colored and well preserved, the most beautiful ones are found beside Macaya Lake. There are also ruins of a sanctuary at 4,850 meters (almost 16,000 feet) up Mt. Sajama, and a huge oval platform at the top of Winkuruta Hill, both of which are from the Inca culture. Pukara Huallila fortress and caves painted with llamas and deer are also worth seeing. Since this area was a historic route to the coast, today's visitor can find many traces of pre-Conquest inhabitants as well as vestiges of the Spanish colonial occupation, such as churches decorated with wonderful mural paintings.

Until 1990, when construction of the La Paz-Arica highway was completed using a loan from the Inter-American Development Bank, the park received little attention. Since then, the park has received funds from a roads program to create a master plan, provide training to guards and protect both the

ORURO DEPT.

biodiversity and colonial remnants of the region. Today, Sajama Park has a local administration, ten guards and extensive facilities to carry out its tasks.

Because of the area's unique natural features, it is necessary to combine conservation with human development. People have lived in Sajama since prehistoric times and the inhabitants have legal land tenure and historic rights to the lands. The management of renewable resources must be promoted in a way that meets the locals' needs and invites their participation in sustainable management of the area.

For more information contact:
Parque Nacional Sajama,
Tel. 8135260, Sajama.
E-mail: tblanco_mollo@hotmail.com
Albergue Ecoturístico Tomarapi,
run by the community Tomarapi, it offers accommodations and food services such as alpaca and llama meat. For reservations contact: **Millenarian** Tourism and travel in La Paz. Tel. 2414753.
E-mail: miletour@mixmail.com
www.BoliviaMilenaria.com

THE WHITEWASHED BEAUTY OF SUCRE

BY PETER MCFARREN
UPDATED BY BILL LOFSTROM

O n the cathedral towers in the city of Sucre, 16 life-size statues keep watch. Twelve of them are the Apostles, and the four figures closest to heaven are, of course, the saints of Sucre. So runs the story of the cathedral statues, as told by the residents of this colonial city of nearly 195,000 inhabitants located 672 kilometers (about 417 miles) from La Paz and 2,750 meters above sea level (9,020 feet). Sucrenses, as residents are called, have always held a special view of themselves, and the city's colorful history has tended to reinforce their vision.

Sucre's colonial architecture and museums are a reminder of the history, culture and traditions that have thrived in this city and have influenced a wide region of South America. Visitors can explore centuries-old churches and museums that exhibit priceless colonial paintings, furniture and religious figures adorned with gold and jeweled garments. And in March of every year, the traditional folklore of the surrounding Quechua inhabitants comes alive in Tarabuco, with one of the most important indigenous festivals in Latin America.

With daily, direct flights from La Paz on AeroSur or Lloyd Aereo Boliviano through Cochabamba, one can leave behind the rarefied air of the *Altiplano*, and arrive 45 minutes later in a city that embodies the perpetual spring of Bolivia's high valley region.

A 20-minutes drive from the airport serviced by modern jets will take you to the city's heart, the **Plaza 25 de Mayo**. There you will see veterans of the 1932 Chaco War with Paraguay spend their days seated on well-kept benches, watching the parade of students in white uniforms, Quechua peasants offering their wares to tourists, shoe-shiners, ice cream vendors blowing their horns, Sucre's many university students and children playing on the bronze lions surrounding the monument to the great Latin American "Libertador" Antonio José de Sucre.

Stately palm and ceibo trees, which in August and September bloom with red *galli - tos* (little roosters) shield the plaza from the blazing midday sun that beats down daily on Sucre, except for brief periods during the November to March rainy season. The sidewalks, bordered by well-groomed trees, are swept before dawn every day with palm branches by Quechua-speaking men and women.

Sucre, founded by the Spaniard Pedro de Anzures in 1540, is often called *La Ciudad Blanca* (The White City) for its cleanliness and for the houses and churches that, by government edict, are white-washed every year. Sucre is also referred to as the "City of Four Names" — Charcas, La Plata, Chuquisaca and Sucre.

The intellectual ferment that has characterized Sucre over the centuries comes alive every fall when tens of thousands of students return to study at a university founded in 1624, 24 years before Harvard. The **University of San Francisco Xavier** was behind many of the liberal ideas that gave birth to the first cry of independence on the continent.

After you check in to one of Sucre's comfortable colonial-style hostals or stylish hotels, head for the plaza, where converted right hand drive Japanese taxis, are available for a quick tour of the city. But because of Sucre's small size, most points of interest are within walking distance from the center.

Wherever you go, you will find that tradition is still an important part of life here. Near the Plaza, on calle Nicolás Ortíz , Jaime Soliz still cuts hair with hand clippers and shaves using blades sharpened on leather straps, much as his father, grandfather and great-grandfather did.

Before making the rounds of museums and Roman Catholic churches and monasteries, spend a few hours just walking around to savor a bit of Sucre's past and what remains of it. Imagine a time when gilded horsedrawn carriages trod through the city's cobblestoned streets carrying women dressed in the latest Parisian fashions, or a time when men in black velvet outfits tailored in Granada or Toledo, Spain walked the streets followed by their indentured Quechua peasants. Or picture the Plaza before the 1952 Revolution that abolished peonage and ended the rule of the tin barons, when life in the square reflected the social and professional divisions of the city.

Progressives and students gathered on the far side of the Cathedral, while doctors, lawyers and businessmen, shielded by palm trees, met opposite the **Casa de la Libertad** (House of Liberty), where Bolivia was founded and the constitution drawn up. The local blue bloods — descendants of the Spanish and Creole aristocracy enriched by the silver mines of Potosí and by government posts — sat and conversed on benches lined up adjacent to the Cathedral. Quechua-speaking peasants were relegated to the Plaza's inner circles unless they were servants attending the children of the well-to-do.

Two blocks from the square, on Calle Nicolás Ortíz, is the **San Felipe Neri Church** and convent from the late 17th century. Its size testifies to the power the Roman Catholic Church once held in Latin American society. The views from the domed roofs and towers, made of bricks bonded with a mixture that included silver from the mining city of Potosí, afford a marvelous panorama of countless churches, said to have numbered one per block during the colonial period. The extension of the graceful curves of ceramic roofs shields the tiny windows and balconies from the summer rains and piercing winter sun. Porticos, balconies and archways, visible in the corners of older buildings, are rich in symbolism depicting mythical gods and Christian effigies. Only the sounds of passing vehicles and a television tower on the Sica Sica mountain overlooking the city remind one of the present. Tours can be arranged to visit the roof and courtyards of San Felipe Neri Church.

Back in the Plaza, you will find yourself facing the portals of the baroque-style **Cathedral**, with neo-classic interior, famous for a virgin covered by a multi-million dollar garment of gold, diamonds, emeralds and pearls donated by wealthy residents during the colonial period of 1538 to 1825.

Adjacent to the cathedral is the **Cathedral Museum**, which displays colonial paintings, gold and silver ecclestical furnishings; volumes of parchment, and desks inlaid with mother-of-pearl. In the 18th and 19th centuries, musicians performed baroque works composed by Creole artists trained by Spanish clergy. These musical manuscripts, preserved at the **National Archives** on Calle España, have been commercially recorded and bring to life once again the great cultural activity that once took place in Sucre.

A walking tour of Sucre would not be complete without the traditional afternoon tea consisting of ice cream, fruit milk shakes and pastries. On the plaza and side streets are several *confiterías* open for this occasion. And be sure not to miss the delicious chocolate found in gourmet chocolate shops along Calle Arenales near the plaza.

If you are in the mood for something religiously sweet, head up Calle San Alberto until you reach Calle Camargo and the **Santa Teresa Convent**, whose nuns until recently spent their adult lives cloistered behind three-foot-thick adobe walls. Between 10 a.m. and noon, nuns and novices sell candied figs, oranges, apples and limes, reciting *Ave María Purísima*.

Two blocks from the plaza on Calle Calvo, just up from Calle Avaroa, you'll reach the small but precious **Santa Clara Museum**, adjacent to the convent of the same name founded in 1639. Ensconced within its thick adobe walls are valuable, anonymous paintings from the Colonial period, as well as exhibits of clerical silver-and gold- embroidered garments, statuary, furniture and other items. Of particular interest is the 18th century baroque organ now displayed at the rear of the church, which is played occasionaly in concerts of classical music. If you're an early riser, you might enjoy attending the 7:30 mass (8:00 on Sundays) that includes choral works sung by the Santa Clara nuns. Along the convent walls, lanterns light a narrow alley paved with stones, and indented knuckle bones in the shape of a cross that are a reminder of the inevitability of death.

As dusk approaches, walk up from the Convent Plaza toward the eucalyptus-covered Mount Churuquella until you reach the **Recoleta Monastery** founded in 1601 by the Franciscans. Paintings of religious figures line the hallways around the patios and lovely gardens with roses and geraniums in bloom. An adjoining restored chapel still contains intricately-carved choir seats that were once occupied by Franciscan monks. The only two monks who remain offer tours of the monastery.

Plaza Pedro Anzures, which has a stone fountain and sun clock, borders the monastery and offers a view of the city with its 15 colonial churches, white-washed homes, tiled roofs and parks surrounded by rolling farmlands and ragged mountain peaks that disappear into the horizon. At dusk, the horizon takes on hues of red, orange and gray that disappear with the advent of darkness, leaving the city lighted by a canopy of stars. Don't miss watching the sunset from the **Café Mirador** at the **Tanga Tanga Children's Museum**, located in this plaza, (see separate article on Tanga Tanga).

In the early morning you can enjoy a pleasant and lively trip to the **colonial-style market** located two-and-a-half blocks from Plaza 25 de Mayo. There, Quechua women are up before dawn arranging stalls of fresh vegetables, fruits and canned goods. They are protected from the morning chill by delicately-woven capes with abstract animal designs. Vendors at a row of stalls serve fresh vegetable and fruit juices and steaming hot *api*, a pungent brew of ground red corn, sugar, cinnamon and lemon which goes well with freshly fried cheese pastries called *empanadas*. Be careful when eating unwashed fruits and vegetables, but hot drinks like *api* should give you no problem. A command of Spanish words would help in bargaining with the vendors, but with prices so low, all you will miss out on without bargaining skills is some of the fun of shopping in a Latin American country.

Sucre is best known for its colonial past. There are so many monuments that remind some of its heritage that a selective list will have to suffice. A visit to the **Casa de la Libertad** on the Plaza is a must. This historical museum houses documents and artifacts related to Bolivia's struggle for independence. As you pass through heavy wooden doors and proceed along the hall to the left, you will reach a room dedicated to Bolivia's first president Antonio José de Sucre. Next is the former Senate chamber, which displays portraits of all Bolivia's presidents, including a huge carved wooden bust of Libertador Simón Bolivar. In another hall lined with carved pews, the Declaration of Independence was signed, and until1898 the House of Deputies met there. Depending on your time and interest, you could spend hours examining the many documents and relics of Bolivia's turbulent past.

La Casa Capellánica, on Calle San Alberto and Potosí, is a 17th-century building that, after having served many purposes, today houses the **Museo del Arte Indigena ASUR** — a textile museum most definitely worth visiting — handicraft shops, artistic workshops, *peñas* and a coffee shop. As the Center of Tourist Development, you will be able to find all the tourist information you need here.

The University Museum, at Calle Bolívar 698, exhibits fine weavings, archaeological artifacts and colonial paintings and furniture. Especially interesting are three mummified bodies that were once buried in a chamber attached to the Santo Domingo chapel. Within hours after they were discovered in the late 1940s, the city was rife with rumors of bodies buried alive during the Inquisition, and for days, thousands stood in line to view the well-preserved bodies of a couple and child. Local residents still talk of apocriphal torture chambers and of adulterous women forced to ride in the streets barechested on mules.

Sucre is becoming an important language training center. If interested in learning Spanish, contact the **Academia Latinoamericana de Español Sucre** at Calle Dalence 109 and

Nicolas Ortiz. Tel. 591-4-6460537. Their E-mail is: latin@sucre.bo.net They offer intensive private classes, living arrangements with Sucre families and organized activities such as cooking, dance and cultural classes. Students also have the opportunity to do volunteer work, including work at the Tanga Tanga Children's Museum.

PRACTICAL INFORMATION FOR SUCRE

Sucre Phone Code: 4

• Useful Addresses and Numbers

The main **Tourist Information Center** is at the Casa Capellánica, 413 Calle San Alberto. Tels. 6453841, 6462194. It is open Monday to Friday from 8:30 to 12:00 and from 14:30 to 18:00. Through the mayor's office, the city also offers **tourist information** at Calle Argentina 67, Tel. 6451083, open Monday to Friday from 8:30 to noon and 14:00 to 18:30.

Police, 110.

Airport Information, Tels. 6451445, 6461053.

Bus Station, Calle Alfredo Ostria Gutierrez, Tels. 6441292, 6452029.

Immigration Office, Calle Pastor Sainz 117. Tel. 64533647.

Post Office, on Calle Ayacucho, corner of Junín. Tel. 6454960. Open Monday through Friday, 8:30 to 19:30, and Saturday, 8:30 to 19:00.

Entel, the telecommunications office (long-distance telephone, fax and telegram service) is at Calle España 171, Tels. 6454141, 6453600. Entel is open every day from 7:30 to 22:00.

Long Distance Call
Entel, 0-10.
AES, 0-11.
Cotas, 0-12.

• Consulates

Brasil, Calle Arenales 212, Tel. 6452661.

France, Calle Bustillos 206, Tel. 6453018. By appointment, call first. E-mail: tere6@mara.scr.entelnet.bo

Germany, Calle Rosendo Villa 54, Tel. 6451369. Open Monday to Friday, 11:00 to noon.

Italy, Calle Manuel Martín Cruz 51. By appointment, call first at 6454172.

Panama, Calle Colón 338, Tel/Fax. 6455698. Call first.

Paraguay, Plaza 25 de Mayo 29, Tels. 6422999, 6453242. Open Monday to Friday, 10:00 to noon and 16:00 to 18:00.

Peru, Calle Avaroa 472, Tels. 6420356, 6455592. Open Monday to Friday, 9:30 to 14:30.

Spain, Pasaje Argandoña 25, Tel. 6451435. By appointment, call first.

Venezuela, Calle al Condominio Banacario, Tel. 6452462.

• How to Get There

AeroSur offers direct flights to Sucre every day from La Paz. **Lloyd Aéreo Boliviano (LAB)** flies every day from La Paz to Sucre as well, but via Santa Cruz or Cochabamba. Planes will not land or take off when there is heavy rain or cloud coverage, so be sure to keep this in mind when planning connecting flights.

Many bus companies offer service to Sucre, usually through Potosí if coming from the north. The road from La Paz to Potosí is about 80% paved, and the trip on the paved road from Potosí to Sucre takes about two and a half hours. Tarija to Sucre on a bus can take up to 20 hours; flying is recommended if coming from the south, but most flights now connect through Santa Cruz or Cochabamba.

• Airline Offices

Lloyd Aéreo Boliviano, Calle Bustillo 121, Tels. 6454994, 800103001. Open Monday to Friday, 8:30 to 12:30 and 14:30 to 18:30, and Saturday 9:00 to noon. Visa, MC.

AeroSur, Calle Arenales 31, Tels. 6462141, 6454895, 6423838 in office, 6451823 at airport. Open Monday to Friday, 8:30 to noon and 14:30 to 18:30, and Saturday, 9:00 to noon. Visa, MC.

Transporte Aéreo Militar, Calle Junín 742, Tels. 6460944, 6452213. Open Monday to Friday, 8:30 to noon and 14:30 to 18:00, and Saturday 9:00 to 11:00.

• Buses

The **Bus Station**, located on Calle Alfredo Ostria Gutiérrez, Tels. 6441292, 6452029, is open every day from 6:30 until 19:00. The following bus companies are recommended:

Copacabana 1, Tels. 6455409, 6454198. Goes to Cochabamba, La Paz and Santa Cruz.

Andes Bus, Tel. 6461549. Goes to Potosí, Tarija and Camiri. Calle Bustillos between Colón and La Paz.

Bolívar, Tel. 6453849. Goes to Santa Cruz, Trinidad, Yacuiba, Vallegrande, Cochabamba, Oruro and La Paz.

Transporte Emperador, Tel. 6440529. Goes to Potosí, Uyuni, Camargo, Oruro, Padilla, Monteagudo, Muyupampa and Camiri. Calle Junín 152.

Getting Around Town

As mentioned in the introduction, the major points of interest in Sucre are within walking distance of the main plaza. Given the mild, sunny climate and all the lovely architecture of Sucre, walking is definitely recommended. If you're short on time, however, but still wish to visit some of the areas on the outskirts of town — such as the cemetery, Plaza Pedro Anzures, or the

Parque Bolívar — just hop in a cab for 1 Bs. City buses go to the bus station, and radio taxis are recommended for getting to the airport (and are cheaper if you share with others; ask at your hotel).

• Radio Taxis

Chasqui, Tel. 6453535.
Super Movil, Tel. 6452222.
Diplomatico, Tel. 6451322.
Exclusivo, Tels. 6441414, 6451414.
Sur, Tels. 6451351, 6451321.
Sucre, Tels. 6451333, 6452204.
America, Tel. 6453030.
Bolivia, Tel. 6442222.
Charcas, Tel. 6460000.

• Car Rental

IMBEX Rent-a-Car, Calle Serrano 165, Tel. 6461222.
Chuquisaca, Av. J. Mendoza 1106, Tel. 6460984.
Shoping Car, Av. J. Mendoza, Tel. 6460908.

• Express Cars to Potosi

Exp. Colonial, Av. Ostria Gutierrez. Tel. 6445151.
Presidente, Av. Ostria Gutierrez. Tel. 6455638.
Cielito Lindo, Av. Ostria Gutierrez. Tel. 6441014.

• Hotels

Capital Plaza Hotel, Plaza 25 de Mayo 28/29, Tels. 6453242, 6422999, Fax. 6453588.
E-mail: cphotel@mara.scr.entelnet.bo
Conveniently located. Offers pool, sauna, conference rooms and Internet. Single: $45; Double: $55; Triple: $70; Suite: $80. All rooms have private bath and cable. Prices include breakfast. Visa, MC, AmEx.

Real Audiencia, Calle Potosí 142, Tel. 6451267, Fax. 6460823. Offers pool, sauna, restaurant and patios. Single: $40; Double: $50; Executive: $60; Presidential Suite: $80. All rooms are carpeted and have private bath and cable. Visa, MC, AmEx.
E-mail: realaudiencia2000@hotmail.com

El Hostal de Su Merced, Calle Azurduy 16, Tels. 6442706, 6445150, 6451355, Fax. 6412078. Inaugurated in April 1997 for the Andean Summit, this beautiful, charming hostel had as its first guests Andean diplomats and well-known politicians. Previously, five generations of the owner's family had lived in this 18th-century house, which was elegantly restored and furnished with antique objects. Su Merced has a lovely courtyard and the best rooftop balcony in town. Single: $30; Double: $45; Triple: $60; Junior Suite: $60 (for two people). All rooms have private bath and are fabulously decorated. Highly recommended. Visa, MC, AmEx.
E-mail: sumerced@mara.scr.entelnet.bo

Hotel Premier, Calle San Alberto 43, Tels. 6451644, 6452097, Fax. 6441232. Offers a restaurant and meeting rooms. Single: $25; Double: $40; Triple: $50; Suite: $60. All rooms have private bath and cable. Prices include breakfast. Visa, MC.

Hotel Independencia, Calle Calvo 31, Tel. 6442256, Fax. 6461369. This new and elegant hotel offers a restaurant, bar, garden and event rooms. Single: $25; Double: $36; Triple: $40; Suite: $45. All prices include breakfast. Visa, MC, AmEx.
E-mail: jacosta@mara.scr.entelnet.bo

Hostal Sucre, Calle Bustillos 113, Tel. 6451411, Fax. 6461928.
E-mail: hosucre@mara.scr.entelnet.bo
This Colonial-style hotel offers rooms with private baths. Breakfast is included. Single: $17; Double $ 24: Triple $30.

Hostal Colonial, Plaza 25 de Mayo 3, Tels. 6454709, 6455487, Fax. 6440311.

Has a garage. Single: $22; Double: $28; Triple: $31; Suite: $40. All rooms have private bath and cable. Prices include breakfast.

Hostal Recoleta Sur. Calle Ravelo 205, corner with Loa, Tels 6454789, Fax. 6446603.
E-mail: hostalrecoleta@hotmail.com
Offers comfortable rooms with private baths, Cable TV, Internet and Breakfast. Single: $17; Double $ 24: Triple $30.

Hostal Libertad, Calle Aniceto Arce 99, corner of San Alberto, Tel. 6453101, Fax. 6460128. Single: $18; Double: $25; Triple: $30; Extra mattress: $20. All rooms are carpeted and have private bath. Prices include breakfast. Visa, MC.

Hostal España, Calle España 138, Tels. 6460295, 6440850, Fax. 6453388. Offers "apartment" rooms, with kitchen and living room, for $30 per person. Also has regular rooms, all with private bath and cable. Single: $17; Double: $24; Triple: $32. Visa, MC.

Hotel Glorieta, Calle Bolivar corner with Urcullo, Tel/Fax. 6443777.
E-mail: mirusta@mara.scr.entelnet.bo

Complejo Hotelero Mendez Roca, Calle Argandona 24, Tel. 6452310, Fax.6454282 This hotel located just outside the Colonial section of the city offers comfortable rooms and lovely gardens.

Hostal Gobernador, Calle Gregorio Mendizabal 27, Tel. 6442338, Fax. 6461505.

Hostal Paola, Calle Colon 138, Tel. 6454978, Fax. 6912491.

Hostal Santa Cruz, Calle Lima Pampa 90, Tel/Fax. 6912498.

Hostal Los Pinos, Calle Colón 502, Tels. 6454403, 6455639, Fax. 6443343. Single: $16; Double: $23; Triple: $28. All rooms have private bath and television. Prices include breakfast. Visa, MC, AmEx.

Gran Hotel, Calle Aniceto Arce 61, Tel. 6452104, Fax. 6452461. Has a comfortable, quaint atmosphere; highly recommended. Single: $15; Double: $18; Triple: $27. Visa, MC, AmEx.

Hotel Los Solares, located at 20 minutes from the center of the city on the road to Potosí. Tels. 6440839, 6480300, Fax. 6446246.
E-mail: asolares@mara.scr.entelnet.bo

For **inexpensive lodging**, there are many clean, comfortable options.

Hostal Charcas, Calle Ravelo 62, Tel. 6453972, Fax. 6455764. Offers solar-powered showers, laundry services and buses to Tarabuco. Single: $10/$6 (with/without private bath); Double: $15/$10; Triple: $23/$15.Visa,MC.
E-mail: hostalcharcas@latinmail.com

Hostal Veracruz, Calle Ravelo 158, Tel. 6451560. Single: $12/$5 (with/without private bath and television); Double: $17/$8; Triple: $25/$12.50. Prices include breakfast.

Hostal Copacabana, Av. Hernando Siles, Tel. 6441790.

Hostel Del Rosario, Calle Azurduy 151, Tel. 6440464, Fax. 6460271.

Hostal El Conquistador, Calle Aniceto Arce, Tel. 6443498.

Hostal Recoleta Sur, Calle Ravelo 205 corner with Loa, Tel. 6454789, Fax. 6446603.
E-mail: hostalrecoleta@nhotmail.com

Hostal San Francisco, Av. Arce 191, Tel. 6452117.

• Restaurants

El Solar, Calle Bolívar 800, Tel. 6454341, is moderately priced and one of the best restaurants in town, although the service is slow. At this colonial restaurant you can dine on delicious, spicy Sucre dishes or on more traditional fare. Be sure to try *singani*, a fine grape-distilled liquor produced south of Sucre in Camargo and Tarija. Closed Sunday.

The newest entry in Sucre's culinary scene is **Joyride Café**, Calle Nicolás Ortiz

14, opposite the Cathedral, is owned by a Dutch expat and offers large portions, good service and a congenial atmosphere.

El Huerto, Calle Ladislao Cabrera 86, Tel. 6451538, with its lovely outdoor dining and superb local food, is pricey but definitely the best place to go on a sunny day. Open for lunch every day from 11:00 to 15:00, and for dinner at 18:30. Thursday to Sunday. Visa, MC.

The Plaza, Plaza 25 de Mayo 34, Tel. 6455843, overlooks the main square from its patio and offers continental and some local dishes. Open all day.

Arco de Iris, Calle Nicolás Ortíz 42, Tel. 6423985, offers fondue, international dishes and good pastries. Opens at 15:00, closed Tuesdays. (See Nightlife section). Visa, MC.

El Germen, Calle San Alberto 231, offers great vegetarian food and delicious German pastries in a very comfortable atmosphere. Also offers a book exchange. Closed Sunday.

Kaypichu, Calle San Alberto 168, Tel. 6443954, offers vegetarian food and cultural events. Closed Monday.

Kactus, Calle Espana 176, Tel. 6447376, offers a Café Bar, a variety of drinks, pizzas, pastas. Tel. 6447376.

Piso Cero, facing Parque Bolívar on Av. Venezuela 1241, Tels. 6452567, 6451206, offers a wide selection of continental and local dishes. Open every day for lunch and dinner.

La Esquinita, Av. Venezuela corner with Av. Del Maestro, Tel. 6427208. Fire roasted chickens.

El Refugio de Don Alfredo, Calle Aroma 90, Tel. 6455984.

Maxim, Calle Arenales 19, Tel. 6451798. Upscale , fairly sophisticated menu in elegant setting.

For Chinese food, try **Chifa Dragon Hong Kong III**, Plaza 25 de Mayo 46, Tel. 6443274. Open every day.

If you're in the mood for French food, go to **La Taverne** at the Alianza Francesa, Calle Aniceto Arce 35, Tel. 6453599. Open every day from 8:00 to 15:00 and 18:00 to 23:30, Saturday from 9:00 to noon.

La Vieja Bodega, Calle Nicolás Ortíz 38, Tel. 6424551, has a beautiful wood interior and warm decor. Offers a wide variety of fair food — from pizza to crepes to fondue — as well as live music on the weekends. Visa, MC.

For food from all over the world, as well as great coffee, don't miss **Café Kultur Berlín**, Calle Avaroa 326, Tel. 6452091 Open Monday to Saturday from 8:00 to midnight (See Nightlife section).

For great hot chocolate, coffee and snaks, try out the **Café Quito** at Calle Dalence 109. It is part of the Academia Latinoamericana de Espanol.

For the best view in town, go to the outdoor **Café Mirador** at the Tanga Tanga Children's Museum on Pasaje Iturricha 281, Tel. 6440299. Here you can snack on sandwiches, pizzas and hamburgers while taking in the sun and admiring Sucre. Open Tuesday to Sunday from 10:00 to 18:00.

Bibliocafé, Calle Nicolás Ortíz 50, a coffee shop where students and foreign visitors hang out, offers food, a bar and nighttime entertainment.

Salón de Té "Las Delicias", Calle Estudiantes 50, Tel. 6442502.

Café Al Tronco, Calle Topater 57, Tel. 01948182. Friendly ambiance with great variety of drinks and salads.

Café Confitería Pastelería Penco Penquitos, opens from 7:30 to 23:00, Calle Arenales 108, Tel.6443946, with branches on Calle Hernando Siles near Junin, and Calle Junin corner with Urcullu.

Café La Luna, Calle Argentina 65 (Casa de la Cultura).

Negro Café, Calle Dalence 95, Tel. 6452542.

Café Tertulias, Plaza 25 de Mayo 59, Tel. 6420390.

If pizza is what you're craving, there are a few places on and around the main plaza, such as **Pizzería Napolitana**, Plaza 25 de Mayo 30, Tel. 6451934 (closed Tuesday).

La Repizza, Calle Nicolás Ortíz 78 opens 24 hours a day. Tel.6451506.

Cozzolisi Pizza, Plaza 25 de Mayo 37. Visa, MC.

For *chorizos*, a spicy pork sausage not to be missed, try the **Airport restaurant** or **Siete Lunares**, in the Guereo neighborhood.

Las Bajos, Calle Loa 759, Tel. 6452531, open every day.

Doña Naty, Calle Olañeta 238, Tel. 6451172.

For *salteñas*, an indispensable pre-lunch element in the local cuisine, try **El Paso de los Abuelos**, Calle Bustillos 216, Tel. 6455173. Probably the best in Bolivia. Try their beef salteñas and Santa Clara chicken empanadas. Also try **Salteñería Lucy** at Calle Audiencia 21, Tel. 6423102, before lunch.

El Patio, Calle San Alberto 18, Tel. 6454917.

Confitería Fabiola, Plaza 25 de Mayo 58, Tel. 6451735, has good *empanadas* and pastries.

For the best ice cream in town, some of it made with the fruit of the season, try **Heladería Sandra** at the Parque Bolívar on Calle Pilinco. Be sure to ask for Tumbo or Chirimoya ice cream. Their specialty is the copa vienesa with vanilla ice cream, essence of coffee, and clotted cream.

• Travel Agencies

All travel agencies listed here offer city tours of Sucre as well as trips to Potosí and a variety of villages and natural wonders in the Sucre Department. They are all open Monday to Friday from 8:30 to noon or 12:30 and 14:30 to 18:30 or 19:00, and Saturday from 8:30 or 9:00 to noon or 12:30.

Abbey Path, Calle Arenales 215, Tel. 6451863, is a special-interest tour operator working primarily through e-mail. They offer one, two, three, five and seven-day trips throughout southern Bolivia, in which they guarantee that you stay and eat in the best facilities available. Tours range from visiting the dinosaur tracks at Cal Orck'o to retracing the routes of Che Guevara and Butch Cassidy and the Sundance Kid (For more details on the lives of Butch Cassidy and the Sundance Kid, see "Death in the Andes: Butch Cassidy & the Sundance Kid," in Chapter Six of this guide.)

Altamira Tours, Av. del Maestro 50, Tel/Fax. 6453525, specializes in rural tourism, offering tours to indigenous communities surrounding Sucre including textile producing communities, dinosaur tracks, Tarabuco, Monteagudo, Potosi, Salar de Uyuni and the Toro Toro National Park. Visa, MC. Email: altamirasucre@hotmail.com.

Solarsa Tours, Calle Arenales 212, Tel. 6460900, Fax. 6455386, offers tours to Uyuni and Tarija. Visa, MC. E-mail: asolars@mara.scr.entelnet.bo

Candelaria Tours, specializes in tours to the area's Quechua Indian communities and textile producers. It's owner, Elizabeth Rojas, is an expert on Bolivian Textiles and has one of the country's finest textile collections. Candelaria Tours also owns and operates a Colonial Hacienda in the Quechua town of Candelaria that is famous for its textile tradition. Calle Audiencia 1, Tel. 6461661, Fax. 6460289. Visa, MC. E-mail:catur@mara.scr.entelnet.bo www.candelariatours.com

Gumer Tours, Calle Junin 442, Tel. 6461575, Fax. 6441876.

Eclipse Travel, Calle Avaroa 310, Tel/Fax. 6443960. Offers three excursions every week in the surrounding countryside of Sucre from 8:00 to 18:00 for $18.

Isand Tours, Calle Calvon 161, Tel. 6455845.

CHUQUISACA DEPT.

Mall Tours, Av. Hernando Siles 813, Tel. 6461843, Fax. 6454627.
E-mail: malitour@mara.scr.entelnet.bo

Seaturs, Multicentro Cespedes 25, Tel. 6460353, Fax. 6462425.

Sur Andes, Calle Nicolas Ortiz 6, Tel. 6453212, Fax. 6452632.

Teresita's Tours, Calle Arenales 9, Tel. 6453206, Fax. 6460040, offers "adventure" tourism. Visa, MC, AmEx.

Turismo Balsa, Calle Argentina 49, Tel. 6451957, Fax. 69112484.

Turismo Sucre, Calle Bustillos 117, Tel. 6452936, Fax. 6460349. Visa, MC.
E-mail: tursucre@mara.scr.entelnet.bo

Tarco Tour, Plaza 25 de Mayo, Multicentro Céspedes, Mezzanine Oficina N°1, Tels. 6461688, 6461356, Fax. 6440938. Casilla 136. Offers tours in Sucre, to Uyuni, Cal Orck'o, Tarabuco, Potosí.
E-mail: tarco@mara.scr.entelnet.bo
www.statusprd.com/tarcotour

TrebolTours, Calle Dalence 140, Tel. 6462753, Fax. 6461893.
E-mail: trebol@mara.scr.entelnet.bo

Yeruti, Calle Calvo 21, Tel. 6442799, Fax. 6912480.

Joy Ride Bolivia (Moto Adventure Tours). Calle Nicolas Ortiz 14, offering tours on motorbikes and cuads to get to know the surrounding of Sucre. The standard tour of half a day costs $65 including protective gear and insurance.
Tel. 6425544, Cel. 719-73146.
E-mail: inf@joyridebol.com
www.joyridebol.com

• Museums, Churches and Cultural Centers

Casa de la Libertad, on Plaza 25 de Mayo 11, Tel. 6454200, is open Monday through Friday from 9:00 to 11:40 and 14:30 to 18:10, and Saturday from 9:30 to 11:40. Admission: $1 for nationals, $2 for foreigners.

Museos Colonial y Antropologico, Calle Bolívar 698, Tel. 6453285, contains a variety of interesting museums: the colonial museum, the anthropological museum, an ethnographic and folkloric exhibition room and a modern art gallery. The museums are open Monday to Friday , 8:30 to 12:00 and from 14:30 till 18:00. Saturday from 8:30 to 12:00. Admission: $1 for nationals, $2 for foreigners.

Museo del Arte Indigena "ASUR", Calle San Alberto 413, Tel. 6453841, E-mail: asur@mara.scr.entelnet.bo is a must-see museum in the Casa Capellánica featuring textile examples from regions all over Bolivia, with a focus on J'alqa and Tarabuco textiles. Local artisans are on site displaying how these textiles are made. Be sure to visit the new wings on Bolivian music and Tiwanaku that displays an incredible Tiwanaku textile. The museum also contains a store selling beautiful weavings; proceeds help the artists. Books, post-cards and ceramics are also available. Open Monday to Friday, 8:30 to noon and 14:30 to 18:00, and Saturday 9:30 to noon. Admission: $1 for nationals, $2 for foreigners.

Museo Gutiérrez Valenzuela, Plaza 25 de Mayo 23, Tel. 6453828, has a beautiful collection of 19th-century European decorative art, the legacy of Sucre's Late 19th Century silver boom. It includes sculptures, vases and furniture, open Monday through Friday from 8:00 till 12:00, and 14:30 to 18:00. On Saturday from 8:30 to noon.

The **Museum of Natural History**, in the same building, has paleontology, archaeology and herb exhibitions. Open Monday to Friday from 8:30 to 12:00, and Saturday from 8:30 to 12.00. Admission: $1.30.

Tanga Tanga Children's Museum, Pasaje Iturricha 281, Casilla 826, Tel/Fax. 6440299 , offers interactive and cul-

tural exhibitions for children, young people and adults as well as live music and theater. This hands on cultural complex has exhibits on renewable energy, science, Bolivian culture and a variety of art workshops. The complex also has an outdoor café with the best view of Sucre and the Ananay Handicraft Shop. It is open Monday to Friday from, 8:30 to 12:00, and 14:30 to 18:30.
E-mail: wawas@mara.scr.entelnet.bo

Museo Eclesiastico de Sucre, Calle Nicolás Ortíz 61, Tel. 6452257, is open Monday to Friday from 10:00 to noon and 15:00 to 17:00, and Saturday from 10:00 to noon. Included in museum entry is a tour of the beautiful 16th-century cathedral and the chapel housing the lovely Virgin of Guadelupe. Admission: $1.60.

The church itself is open to the public on Sunday for services at 9:00.

Museo de la Recoleta, Calle Polanco 162 in the Plaza Pedro Anzúrez de Campo Redondo, Tel. 6451987, is open Monday through Friday from 9:00 to 11:30 and 14:30 to 16:30, but recently foreign visitors have been frustrated by the museum's lax observance of the posted hours. Admission: $1 for nationals, $2 for foreigners.

The Recoleta church has services on Monday, Wednesday and Friday at 6:00 and on Sunday at 6:00, 8:00, 10:00 and 19:00.

Museo de Santa Clara, Calle Calvo 212, Tel. 6452295, is open Monday through Friday from 9:00 to noon and 15:00 to 17:00, and Saturday from 9:00 to noon. Admission: $1.

The convent is visited in the museum tour, but it is also open to the public during its daily service at 7:30 on weekdays and Saturdays, and at 8:00 on Sundays.

Universidad Mayor, Real y Pontificia de San Francisco Xavier de Chuquisaca is at the corner of Calle Junín and Estudiantes.

The National Library and Archives of Bolivia, Calle España 43, Tel. 6452886, is open Monday through Friday from 9:00 to noon and 14:30 to 18:30, and Saturday from 9:00 to noon.

General Cemetery, the end of Calle Linares, Tel. 6451075. Take some time out to wander through the peaceful, well-manicured grounds at what is said to be one of South America's most beautiful cemeteries. Filled with lovely fountains, exotic trees, stone angels and expansive mausoleums, the Sucre cemetery is worth a visit. Open daily from 8:00 to noon and 14:00 to 18:00. Entrance is free, though you can pay a small fee to get a tour from one of the many children out front offering to show you "buried presidents."

Consult with the Tourist Information Center for special events in the following **cultural centers**:

Casa Capellánica, at the corner of Calle San Alberto and Potosí, Tel. 6453841, offers *peñas*, theater and art exhibits. It also houses the lovely ASUR textile museum.

Alianza Francesa, Calle Aniceto Arce 35, Tel. 6453599, offers French, Spanish and Quechua classes, art exhibitions and video nights. Open Monday to Friday, 9:00 to noon and 15:30 to 19:30.

Instituto Cultural Boliviano Alemán, Calle Avaroa 326, Tel. 6452091, offers German, Spanish and Quechua classes as well as video nights and other cultural activities. Located next to Café Kultur Berlín. Open Monday to Friday, 9:30 to 12:30 and 15:00 to 21:00, and Saturday from 10:00 to 12:30.

Centro Boliviano Americano, Calle Calvo 301, Tel. 6441608, offers English classes.

• Bookstores

Lectura, Plaza 25 de Mayo 3, next to the mayor's office. Has English magazines and an excellent selection of books. Visa, MC. Tel/Fax. 6454619.

Juan Pablo II, Av. Aniceto Arce corner with Ravelo, Tel. 6462766.

Pompeya, Calle Calvo 38,
Tel. 6454088.

Tupac Katari, Calle Arenales 105,
Tel. 6461572.

Tauro, Calle Calvo 49, Tel. 6451964.

• Internet

Punto Entel, Plaza 25 de Mayo 7.

Cyber Cafe, Calle Arenales 11,
Tel. 6420617. Open 8:00 to midnight
every day. Cost: $1/hour.

Hyberlink, Calle Olañeta 125,
Tel. 6424965. Open 9:00 to 13:00 every
day. Cost: $1.30/hour.

Trebolnet, Plaza 25 de Mayo 4.

• Shopping

Probably the nicest craft shop in Sucre
recently opened at the **Ananay store** at the
Tanga Tanga children's museum just off the
Recoleta Plaza overlooking the city. It offers
handicrafts from Sucre, surrounding areas
and other parts of the country, including from
the Jesuit Missions in Santa Cruz.

If you want to purchase weavings and
handicrafts in general, you'll find a fine selec-
tion at the Sala Expo-Venta Artesanal of
ASUR in the **Caserón de la Capellanía**,
Calle San Alberto 413, and **Artesanía
Pujllay**, in the Mercado Baratillo at
Av. Hernando Siles 770, Tel. 6446297.
A new and good quality handicraft shop,
Ayllay Wasi, also offers a nice selection of
textiles from Macha, Pocoata, Jalq'a,
Tarabuco and Candelaria. It is located on
Calle Audiencia 17, next to Candelaria Tours.

For an excellent source of beautiful
weavings and information, go to Ulises
Murgia's shop, **Calcha Artesanía** on the
Plaza San Francisco; he can explain the origins and meanings of the textiles you find,
and if you're lucky, he might just show you
his collection of pre-Columbian textiles.

The best weavings originate in
Potolo, Macha, Ravelo, Calcha and

Candelaria. Several shops across from the
market offer weavings, as does an alley off
Calle Camargo near España.

Sucre is also famous for its miniature
dolls and fruit baskets made from dough.

• Nightlife

The hotspot on Calle Nicolas Ortiz is
Joy Ride Café. Kitchen doesn't close till
midnight (see restaurant section) and during
weekends the tables fly throught the air to
make space for those who want to dance.
Drinks are done right, funky music and good
atmosphere.

Café Tertulias, Plaza 25 de Mayo 59.
Tel. 6420390, opens from Thrusday to
Tuesday from 19:00 to 2:00.

Arco Iris, Calle Nicolás Ortíz 42,
Tel. 6423985, offers *peñas* every Saturday
night. With a day's advance notice, you can
arrange for a *peña* any other night, except
Tuesday. Just call Javier Ameller. Visa, MC.

Café Kultur Berlín, Calle Avaroa 326,
Tel. 6452091. A comfortable cafe that offers
films Thursday nights and cultural events —
plays, *peñas*, puppet shows — on Friday
and sometimes Saturday nights.

Klásicos Pub, Calle Dalence 39,
Tel. 6455706. Classy, mellow atmosphere
with live music on Thursday, Friday and
Saturday. Open on these days from
20:00 on.

Menfi's, Calle Bolívar 650. A lively bar
filled with smoke, dark wood tables and
funky art designs. Opens at 19:00, closed
Mondays. Live music on Thursday nights.

La Clave, Calle Hernando Siles 629,
Tel. 6446785. A long entranceway leads to
comfy couches and a small discotheque,
complete with karaoke. Open every day from
21:00. Visa, MC.

Mitsumania, Av. del Maestro, on the
corner of Venezuela, Tel. 6421616. A discotheque with a "car" theme, this is a good
place to dance if you don't mind the flashing

auto signals and numerous video games. Opens at 21:30, closed Sunday. Women get in free.

Micerino, Calle Bolívar 182, corner of Urcullo, Tel. 6443777. Discotheque, open Friday and Saturday from 22:00 on and Sunday at 16:00. Visa, MC.

There are also a handful of cafés around town, particularly on **Calle Nicolás Ortíz**, where you can snack, drink and hang out until at least midnight, oftentimes listening to live music or watching theater.

• Movies

Cine Libertad, in the Plazuela Monteagudo, Calle Calvo 120, Tel. 6451323.

• Banks

Banks are generally open Monday to Friday, 8:30 to 12:30 and 14:30 to 18:30, and on Saturday mornings.

Bisa, Calle España 2, Tel. 6443901.

Banco de Credito, Plaza 25 de Mayo 28, Tel. 6461858.

Banco de la Union, Calle Aniceto Arce 98, Tel. 6441780.

Banco Mercantil, Calle España 18, Tel. 6443952. Does cash advances and changes dollars.

Banco Santa Cruz, Calle San Alberto 102, corner of Calle España, Tel. 6455400. Does cash advances and changes dollars and traveler's checks.

There are numerous **ATMs** (cajeros automáticos) throughout the center of Sucre: on Calle Dalence, near the corner of Argentina; on the corner of Calles Argentina and Dalence at the tourist information booth; on Calle España, half a block from the main plaza.

• Money Exchange

Prodem, Calle San Alberto 70.

Ambar, Calle San Alberto 7,

Tel. 6461339, offers good rates.

El Arca, Calle España 134, Tel. 6460189.

• Couriers

DHL, Plaza 25 de Mayo 25 in the Cespedes Multicenter Building, Tel. 6441204. Open Monday to Friday 9:00 to 12:30 and 14:00 to 19:00, Saturday 9:00 to 12:30.

C&A Courier, Calle Dalence 170, Tels. 6424654, 6424698, 6445821.

IBC Courier, Plaza 25 de Mayo, Edif. Multicentro, Tel. 6461709.

UPS, JET Courier, Calle Argentina 49, Tel/Fax. 6451957.

SEC Courier, Calle Arenales 9, Tel. 6453206, Fax. 6460040.

• Laundries

Super Limp, Calle Estudiantes 26, Tel. 6460575. Same-day service if you bring your clothes in the morning. Cost: $1/kilo.

Laverap, Calle Bolívar 617, Tel. 6424501. Automatic machines, laundry done in just a couple hours.

• Medical Services

Clínica Sucre, Av. Venezuela, corner of Pilinco, Tel. 6451535. Dr. Aldolfo Menzoni, a general practitioner, is recommended.

Clínica Petrolera, Av. del Maestro, corner of Cobija, Tels. 6452105, 6454013.

Hospital Santa Bárbara, in Plaza Libertad, Calle Destacamento 111, Tels. 6451064, 6451900.

24 hours Drug Stores

Cruz Blanca, Calle Junín 558, Tel. 6444288.

San Augustín, Calle Arenales 214, Tel. 6441451.

Copacabana, Plaza 25 de Mayo 42, Tel. 6461141.

EXCURSIONS FROM SUCRE

A few of the many side trips from Sucre are especially interesting and recommended, especially if interested in Andean Culture, Rock Art, Textile Traditions and Ecotourism. All of those listed can be arranged through a travel agency in town.

Cal Orck'o Dinosaur Tracks

Sixty eight million years ago, dinosaurs tromped around what is now the Department of Chuquisaca. Just five kilometers (three miles) from Sucre, visitors can see the dinosaur tracks from this period. Discovered in the 1990s, these tracks have been luring paleontologists from around the globe who are coming to Cal Orck'o and proclaiming it one of the largest sites of its kind in the world. It contains more than 5,000 dinosaur tracks of 150 different animals, and is definitely worth a visit. Tours are often combined with a visit to the Museum of Natural Sciences and can be done in half a day. For excellent tours of the dinosaur tracks, contact Klaus Schuett of Abbey Path Tourism in Sucre, Tel. 6451863. The Dino-Truck leaves daily from the Cathredal at 9:30, 12:00 and 14:30. For reservations contact E-mail: kschuett@mara.scr.entelnet.bo

Dinosaur Tracks on the Wall

(Die Zeit, Sept. 1998).

The largest site with fossilized dinosaur tracks in the world, fascinates paleontologists and admirers of dinosaurs.

A few kilometers from Sucre, 3000 meters high in the central Andes, lies the quarry of the largest cement factory of this Andean country. The place is called Cal Orck'o in the local Quechua Indian language. Here, the history of dinosaurs is being re-written.

For some time, the workers of the factory where puzzled by the strange impressions on a wall, until in 1994 a local expert identified them as dinosaur tracks. Despite this, it was not possible to get foreign experts to visit the place, until a video made by the local Tourism Director reached Switzerland. The documentary made the investigators hearth of Christian Meyer beat faster, the specialist in dinosaur tracks traveled to Sucre and is still fascinated: "It was a vision that left you breathless". The scientist from Solothurn knows personally all the important sites in the world, from Canada, through the Seychelles all the way to Turkmenistan. A couple of weeks ago, the professor from the University of Basel has returned from his most exciting expedition.

Cal Orck'o is a stroke of luck for various reasons. To begin with, the magnitude of the wall is impressive: more than 25.000 square meters, the surface of several soccer fields, full of track impressions. Meyer deduces, that sixty eight Million years ago, the dinosaurs lived at the shores of a shallow, temperate, sweet water lake, which reached from the present Perú-Bolivian border all the way to northern Argentina.

That the dinosaur steps and the fossilized rests of turtles, crocodiles, fish and algae are from the late Cretacic period, is for the scientist something special; until now there was not much information about this epoch.

Nowadays a sheer wall of 70 degrees, with a height of up to 80 meters and more than one kilometer in length, testifies about the past of the history of earth.

To be able to make the measurements, a mountaineer's aptitude, hundreds of nails, hooks, rock perforating screws, one and a half kilometers of rope, climbing harnesses, a crane and infrared laser where necessary. The expedition was funded by the National Swiss Foundation and other private sponsors.

Not only the dimensions, but the characteristics fascinate the geologists. "Here we have examples of all kinds of dinosaurs, before they disappeared from the face of the earth. This shows us that the variety of creatures was much larger, than what we suspected until know. One of the most important discoveries, is that Anquilosaurius – a four-legged plant-eater – extended its habitat to South America. Previously its fossilized remains were unknown in the continent.

For Christian Meyer, these particular tracks document the most interesting aspects of the dynamic movement of the dinosaurs. While some Anquilosaurius moved rather slowly, others displaced their bodies with rapid movements and reached as much as eleven kilometers per hour. "This is very fast when you consider that these quadrupeds weighed between six and eight tons. We really need to revise our old image of these creatures as having been sluggish and slow" explains the forty-two year old expert. For many creators of expositions, this will mean reconstructing skeletons and models of the Anquilosaurius and re-writing the information that describes it. "The Anquilosaurius is often represented as having resembled an armadillo with widely separated feet, and a body that lies close to the ground. This however, is not correct, as we know that they were much leaner, and had a much more elegant construction."

The tracks of the Titanosaurius, according to Meyer, are the most spectacular of all. Reaching up to twenty-five meters in size, these were some of the real giants among the dinosaurs. These particular dinosaurs walked relatively slowly at around three kilometers per hour, while other species reached speeds of up to thirty kilometers per hour. In the case of one flesh-eating dinosaur, investigators were even able to determine that it had a limp. Cal Orck'o is a place of paleontological superlatives. Here we find one example of tracks that show a predator that walked for over 350 meters, which is the longest continuous record known to date. The sheer quantity of tracks is overwhelming: over 5,000 footprints-the majority of which are very well preserved- so many as in no other place in the world, are still waiting to be interpreted. Because many of the tracks are from young dinosaurs, it is possible to study the evolution of the species.

Meanwhile, this play area of the dinosaurs has given way to a growing community of dinosaur fans. "During our study, we usually had between seventy and eighty visitors per day", says Meyer.

In order to preserve this quarry for future generations, which is at the time being threatened by erosion, the scientist has spoken with government ministries and with the United Nations in hopes that Cal Orck'o will be put under the protection of UNESCO and declared a "World Heritage Site" before this Jurassic park of Latin America is invaded by hoards of uncontrollable tourists.

La Glorieta

A 10-minute ride toward the valley of La Florida on the road to Potosí will take you to La Glorieta, a grandiose monument to Sucre's past. At the end of the 19th century, the wealthy industrialist Don Francisco Argandoña built a miniature estate with Venetian-style canals, lovely gardens and fountains over which towered an exotic residential palace built in a mixture of Moorish, Gothic Spanish and French architectural styles. Doña María Clotilde Urioste de Argandoña, his wife became known as *La Princesa de la Glorieta*, a title bestowed by the pope in recognition of her work with abandoned and orphaned children. Today, the canals are gone and the gardens are in ruins but enough of the detailed ceilings and architectural forms remain to make this an attractive tourism destination. La Glorieta is being restored.

Yotala/Condor Khakha

Yotala, a small village 15 kilometers (9 miles) from Sucre on the highway to Potosí, offers a picturesque peek into its pre-hispanic and colonial past, with narrow cobblestone streets and unique charm. On August 30 Yotala celebratres the religious and folklore **Festival of the Virgen of Santa Rosa**. Weekend visitors to Yotala have two lunch options. On the main square, **El Molle Feliz** serves a limited menu of typical Bolivian dishes in the house's colonial patio on Sundays. Contact Janet Leyton V. de Ovando at 6480207. Overlooking Yotala's "riviera", where many of Sucre's more prominent families have summer homes, is **La Campana**, owned by Myriam Baptista Gumucio, a recent refugee from the hustle and stress of La Paz. On the covered gallery of her lovely home, on Saturday and Sunday, Myriam offers a delicious and sophisticated lunch buffet, for the equivalent of US$5, all included. For directions and hours call Myriam at 6480340.

You can combine a trip to Yotala with a visit to the protected Andean Wildlife Refuge of **Condor Khakha**, which lies just 35 kilometers (22miles) outside of Sucre and is replete with condors. Ask at a travel agency for more details.

Country Inns

Visitors to Sucre with more time to spend may want to consider one of several country inns at less than an hour's distance from the city. Any one of Sucre's travel agents can provide information about **Las Siete Cascadas** and **Hotel Los Solares**, both within a half hour's drive from the city. Sucre's premier country inn, however, is **El Bramadero,** an Andean lodge located 30 kilometers (about 18miles) from the city, on the road to Ravelo. El Bramadero consists of a main lodge and several stone cottages, attractively furnished and offering every comfort—except electricity! It is located in a large pine and eucalyptus forest on the slope of the Chataquila mountain range. El Bramadero's owner Raúl and Mabel Cagigao offer lodging, transport to and from Sucre and three gourmet meals, for US$29 per person. The area around the lodge offers opportunities for day excursions, hiking on pre-hispanic trails, rock climbing, visits to dinosaur tracks, and astronomic observations when the sky is clear using modern telescopes. Information at Calle Abaroa 472 in Sucre, Tel. 6455592, Fax. 6420356. Mabel will soon be opening her own restaurant at Calle Abaroa 510, in Sucre. **Salamandra** will feature delicious high teas, drinks, and gourmet dinners in a cozy atmosphere at reasonable prices, and will be open afternoons and evenings from Monday to Friday.

Chataquila- Incamachay Rock Art

Thirty kilometers from Sucre is located the Santuario de Chataquila at an altitude of 3650 meters. From here the road descends 8 km towards rock formations covered with Rock Art painted in red and white and showing abstract animal and human forms. Altamira Travel Agency provides tours to this site.

Resting Houses and Camping Samay Huasi, in Chaucana, Tels. 6452935, 6454129, 71161578. E-mail: 29avila@cotes.net.bo Offers transportation service from Sucre, rooms with private bath and hot water, and restaurant.

Patatoloyo

An archaeological site located 46 kilometers (about 28 miles) outside of Sucre, Patatoloyo contains pre-Incan cave paintings that are definitely worth visiting. You get to the cave by hiking through the beautiful Chataquila mountain range.

Tarabuco

The most colorful side trip from Sucre is to the town of Tarabuco at a distance of 60 kilometers (about 37 miles) in the Yamparáez province at an altitude of 3230 meters. Its Sunday market attracts peasants from the region who are famous for their conquistador-style leather helmets and multi-colored handwoven ponchos, *ch'us - pas* (bags for carrying coca leaves and money), *chumpis* (skirts) and musical instruments. The most popular of these is the *charango*, a stringed instrument whose back is formed by the carapace of the armadillo with hair that is said to grow even after the animal's death.

In March of every year, thousands of peasants from the area of Tarabuco join tourists and Sucre residents in the celebration of the **Pujllay Carnaval**, one of the best traditional festivals in Latin America. The event celebrates the Battle of Jumbate, in which the Indians of the area defeated the Spaniards on March 12, 1816. Area residents dance as music is played on the *charango, zampoña, tokoro,*

pinkillos and *bellspurs* and a lively mass is sung in Quechua. The lingering taste of spicy native dishes, washed down with the corn brew known as *chicha* also make a visit to the Pujllay a must.

Monteagudo

The road from Tarabuco winds southeast toward valleys and mountains that gradually take on shades of green and offer tropical air. Monteagudo, an eight-hour bus ride in good weather, is a region populated by the Chiriguanos, a sub-group of the Guaranís who inhabit southern Bolivia and Paraguay. Landslides and swollen rivers isolate the region from Sucre during the rainy season, but in the dry season the frontier town of Monteagudo is readily accessible. Also, a new airport now services the town and new hotels provide comfortable accommodations.

The area encompasses vast zones of semi-tropical virgin land that offer good fishing and adventure tourism. Years ago Che Guevara fought a losing guerrilla war not far from this town.

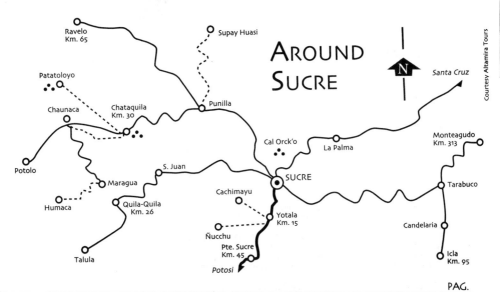

AROUND SUCRE

Ravelo Km. 65 · Supay Huasi · Patatoloyo · Chaunaca · Chataquila Km. 30 · Punilla · Potolo · Maragua · S. Juan · Cal Orck'o · La Palma · Monteagudo Km. 313 · SUCRE · Tarabuco · Humaca · Quila-Quila Km. 26 · Cachimayu · Yotala Km. 15 · Candelaria · Ñucchu · Pte. Sucre Km. 45 · Icla Km. 95 · Talula · Potosi

Courtesy Altamira Tours

CHUQUISACA DEPT.

SUCRE

1 Tourist office
2 Police
3 Immigration office
4 Entel
5 Post office
6 City Hall
7 LAB
8 TAM
9 Aerosur

MARKET
10 Central

MUSEUMS
11 Tanga tanga
12 Recoleta
13 Santa Clara
14 Universitario
15 Catedralico
16 Archivos Nacionales
17 Casa de la Libertad

48 Alianza Francesa
49 Instituto Boliviano Alemán
50 Centro Boliviano Americano

CHURCHES & POINTS of INTEREST
18 Arbol Milenario (Cedro)
19 Mirador de la Ciudad de Sucre
20 Capilla del Señor de Solano
21 San Lazaro (1st Sucre Cathedral)
22 Santa Teresa convent
23 Casa Capellanica

"La Madona"
Corporación Regional de
Desarrollo de Chuquisaca

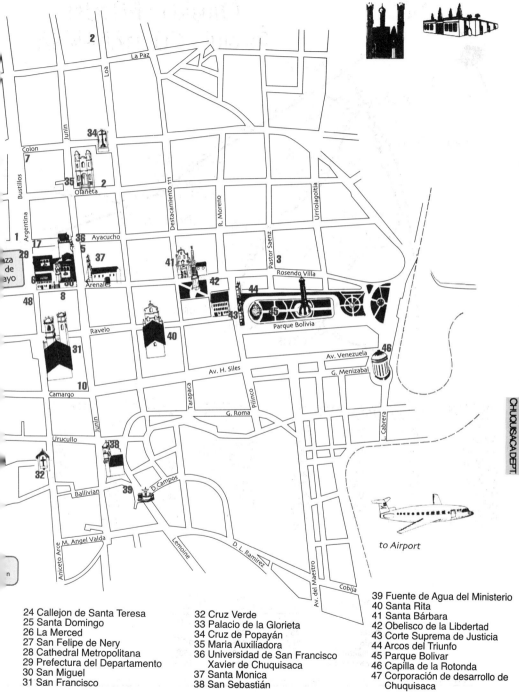

to Airport

24 Callejon de Santa Teresa
25 Santa Domingo
26 La Merced
27 San Felipe de Nery
28 Cathedral Metropolitana
29 Prefectura del Departamento
30 San Miguel
31 San Francisco

32 Cruz Verde
33 Palacio de la Glorieta
34 Cruz de Popayán
35 Maria Auxiliadora
36 Universidad de San Francisco
   Xavier de Chuquisaca
37 Santa Monica
38 San Sebastián

39 Fuente de Agua del Ministerio
40 Santa Rita
41 Santa Bárbara
42 Obelisco de la Libdertad
43 Corte Suprema de Justicia
44 Arcos del Triunfo
45 Parque Bolivar
46 Capilla de la Rotonda
47 Corporación de desarrollo de
   Chuquisaca

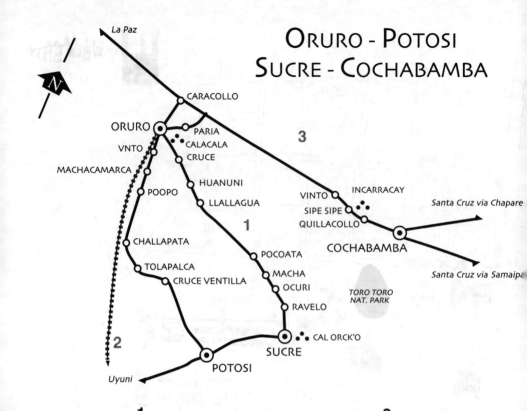

ORURO - POTOSI
SUCRE - COCHABAMBA

1

LOCATION	DISTANCE IN KMS PARTIAL	TOTAL	ALTITUDE
Oruro	Kms	00	3709
Cruce	28	28	3708
Huanuni	23	51	3962
Llallagua	47	98	3881
Uncia	8	106	3865
Pocoata	26	176	3376
Macha	21	197	3512
Ocuri	41	238	3990
Ravelo	64	302	3217
Sucre	62	364	2790

2

LOCATION	DISTANCE IN KMS PARTIAL	TOTAL	ALTITUDE
Oruro	Kms	00	3709
Cruce Vinto	7	7	3709
Machacamarca	27	34	3709
Poopo	25	59	3745
Challapata	65	124	3715
Tolapalca	67	191	-
Ventilla	28	219	-
Potosí	101	330	3909

3

LOCATION	DISTANCE IN KMS PARTIAL	TOTAL	ALTITUDE
Oruro	Kms	00	3709
Paria	23	23	-
Vinto	183	206	3526
Quillacollo	4	210	2536
Cochabamba	14	224	2558

TANGA TANGA CHILDREN'S MUSEUM: THE FUN IS SERIOUS

BY DAVID BOLDT

The name Tanga Tanga evokes an innocent and playful image, but there are a couple of ironic twists in both its origin, and its current application as the name of a children's. museum being created on a site high above the historic city of Sucre, Bolivia by the Quipus Cultural Foundation.

The legend of Tanga Tanga dates from the Spanish conquest and tells of how an Incan nobleman named Tanga Tanga was ordered by the Spaniards to present a huge treasure as ransom for the return of their captured Incan ruler. En route he learned that the ruler had been killed and decided to bury the treasure, along with himself and his soldiers. They were interred in a cave in the saddle between the two small mountains that tower above the valley in which Sucre lies — or more or less where the Tanga Tanga Children's Museum is located today. The cave was then sealed by a rock slide, and was never found by the Spaniards — or anybody else.

In a somewhat similar way, the light-hearted outward appearance of the scene at the museum, which includes a large children's playground, contrasts with its quite serious underlying purpose.

While close to being completed, the museum is very much a going concern at present. The sound of children's laughter echoes across the playground, with its intrepidly-constructed equipment made from old tires and huge wooden cable reels, along with a thatched-roof playhouse reached by a swinging bridge of chain-and-wood, or a notched climbing pole. On a white cylinder atop the building that houses the museum's offices and handicrafts shop is the smiling symbol of Tanga Tanga, a happy cross between a teddy bear and a flower.

Tourists and local residents often fill the tables at the cafe on the terrace above the playground, sitting in the shade of umbrellas, enjoying refreshments and light meals. The restaurant is a staircase level below the Mirador, a long building whose rounded arches offer a favorite vistas for taking in the city below, with its white buildings topped with tiled roofs of burnt umber, and the high, craggy mountains beyond. The visitors are drawn by the view and the Recoleta, a centuries-old monastery/museum across the square from the Mirador, which is renowned for its collection of religious art

But there is a serious side to the Tanga Tanga museum, exemplified at present by the library and classrooms adjoining the administrative building where on afternoons, school children can be seen reading, taking English lessons, making crafts, participating in dance workshops, learning clowning from a real clown, and other such playful, yet educational activities.

Across a narrow, cobbled alley is another component of the museum, not yet open to the public but nearing completion, consisting mainly of two large exhibit areas, as well as a theater, pediatric and dental clinics, and offices. The attractive modern buildings have been imaginatively re-created by architect Domingo Izquierdo, the museum's director, from what were once the 20th century concrete holding tanks for the city's water system.

One of the two exhibit areas contains "Balancing Acts," an exhibit on earth-friendly technology components of an energy exhibit that has been a star attraction on the circuit of children's science museums in the United States, and is being assembled largely by volunteers. One part of the exhibit uses ping pong balls and air currents to show how an airplane wing lifts a plane as air flows over it. Visitors can adjust the wing's angle and learn the effects. Other exhibits demonstrate the importance of conserving energy, and visitors also learn about Bolivia's rising role as a global supplier of natural gas and oil.

Plans are underway to create a dinosaur exhibit in a second area, which would tie in with Sucre's distinction as the dinosaur track capital of the world, thanks to the discovery of dinosaur tracks in a limestone quarry nearby. The tracks were made on rock sheets that had once been the bottom of a muddy lake on which dinosaurs made thousands of tracks preserved by a fortunate combination of geological factors. Dinosaur experts and tourists from around the world come to see them.

The exhibits will all make use of the "hands-on" approach to learning in which the children learn by manipulating the exhibits, an approach that has been shown to be effective in awakening children's imaginations at many other museums around the world, notably the Kindermuseum of Amsterdam, the Museo de la Ciencia in Barcelona, the Oregon Museum of Science and Industry in Portland, and the Please Touch Museum in Philadelphia. The key ingredient is the insight — long known but seldom effectively employed — that learning takes place when children are actively engaged in the process.

The same concept will be applied to museum's "youth gardens," laid out in the terraces adjoining and lying below the playground area. Eventually they will form four "microhabitats" each containing the cultures of Bolivia's diverse and rich ethnic communities and the plants that characterize one of Bolivia's four principal regions — the altiplano in the Andes to the west, the richly varied valleys of central Bolivia, the subtropical plains in the southeast, and the wet tropical forests of the Amazon Basin.

Besides demonstrating Bolivia's environmental diversity, the gardens will be constructed and maintained by the children at Tanga Tanga. The children will also perform science experiments there and hold discussions that deal with Bolivia's human diversity as well. Thus the gardens will function as both an outdoor laboratory and classroom.

The garden areas, one of the few environmental havens left in this city, also includes a 350-square meter greenhouse, an outdoor theatre that seats 250 people made from hand-carved stone and a botanical garden.

This kind of educational enhancement is particularly important in a place like Sucre, a city of 160,000, where many children often aren't exposed to the interchange of cultural and scientific ideas to enable them to understand how their lives are being influenced by increasing interdependence throughout the world. Ultimately, the experiences and knowledge they gain at Tanga Tanga should increase their own chances of success in life.

At the present time the opportunities of children in Bolivia, one of the poorest nations in Latin America, are sharply limited by circumstance. Bolivia has exceptionally high rates of infant and child mortality, as well as child malnutrition. There are insufficient funds for education. At some schools, even in the capital city of La Paz according to a recent newspaper story, children have to buy and bring their own chairs to school. Children in "el campo" — the countryside — often don't get beyond elementary school.

(The concept behind Tanga Tanga, it should be added, is congruent with the announced educational goals of the Bolivian government, and hundreds of teachers were consulted during the initial phases of the museum's development in the early 1990s).

The problems of deprivation are particularly acute in Sucre, where the survey of teachers commissioned by Quipus showed a major migration of families from rural areas and smaller cities into Sucre. It is estimated that about a third of the city's population consists of migrants, whose children often have very low levels of educational attainment.

Tanga Tanga will be a place where all of Sucre's children, and visitors as well, can have fun, while discovering along the way how they can contribute to both the Bolivian and global society. The museum demonstrated the power of its appeal when in 2000 it set up a pilot program under which entire classrooms could come to the museum for a visit — and almost 4,000 came. The museum could serve 30,000 schoolchildren a .year.

At present, dozens of children come to the museum on their own after school for supervised programs, or just to play. The desks in the library are often filled with children reading or doing projects. Model rockets made with paper and paste are tacked onto the representation of the solar system on one wall, indicating the number of books read by each of the participating children.

The remarkable thing about all this activity is that the museum hasn't been completed yet, much less officially opened, and the current efforts represent only a small portion of the institution's potential impact.

The Quipus Foundation has received important support for Tanga Tanga from the city of Sucre, which provided the water tanks and helped channel funds from the Governments of Spain and Holland. The 8,600 square meters of high-rent real estate the museum currently occupies was purchased with funds generated by a complicated debt swap supported by Plan International, USAID and a network of NGOs called PROCOSI. The complex construction and exhibits have been supported by the Spanish, Dutch and German governments, Transredes (ENRON-Shell), USIS, CESO, the Peace Corps, AFS, and the McFarren-Aviles and Marcos Iberkleid families.

However, more help is needed to complete the exhibit halls and youth gardens and additional space for library activities and workshops. More staff is also needed for programs and maintenance.

Wouldn't it be great if the kids, during construction of the gardens, should dig up the ancient treasure of Tanga Tanga? But whether they do or not, a treasure is already evident at Tanga Tanga in children's happy faces.

Tanga Tanga Children's Museum, which also has gardens maintained by local school children, a health clinic and library, is located near the Recoleta Church on Pasaje Iturricha 281, Tel. 6440299. The museum property contains a cafe as well as a gift shop with Bolivian art and cultural books.

CHUQUISACA DEPT.

ALL EYES ON SUCRE'S RECORD TRACK WAYS

BY ANNA SIMON

The excavation of the world's most important dinosaur footprint discovery drew to a close in Sucre. The site, on the property of the FANCESA cement factory, is a steep stone hillside one mile long and 200 ft. high. It is the largest and, being only sixty-eight million years old, youngest discovery of its kind. The site features over one hundred eighty-five dinosaur track ways, the greatest collection in a single site. Unearthed by factory workers fifteen years ago, the site was overlooked and mostly unnoticed for thirteen years until Swiss paleontologist, Christian Meyer, was notified. Since the beginning of July, Meyer, head paleontologist at the University of Easel in Switzerland, and FedericoAnaya, paleontologist from the Natural History Museum in La Paz, have led a team of Bolivian scientists in the site's excavation. "It's spectacular," said Martin Lockley, a geologist at the University of Colorado, Denver (U.S.), who is considered the world's foremost dinosaur track way expert. He reviewed the site at Meyer's request. "It's definitely a very big and important site," Lockley said. "How to preserve it and how it compares to other sites around the world are questions that we are just now beginning to answer."

Meyer and Anaya's work included mapping the site with infrared technology, stabilizing the wall with bolts for climbing and recasting the most important tracks.

Among the most significant of their finds were the tracks of six ankylosaurs, doubling the world finding of the armored dinosaurs to twelve. Also significant was the find of a 350-meter theropod track, the longest tracks discovered. Seventy-five percent of the tracks belonged to ankylosaurs, titauosaurs, theropods and ornithopods. "It's like the eighth wonder of the world," said Meyer. The tracks date from the Late Cretaceous period, the last appearance of the dinosaurs before their extinction sixty-five million years ago. The site is very important to dinosaur extinction theories, said Meyer. He speculates that an asteroid hitting TheYucatan Peninsula, creating a heavy cloud of dust that blocked the sun, prompted extinction. In a reverse greenhouse effect, the dinosaurs probably died out over five hundred thousand years as the climate became colder and their food chain deteriorated.

The Sucre site was at one time a large lake, said Meyer. A great diversity of beasts roamed its shores, including large, plant-eating dinosaurs that walked on four legs and smaller-sized dinosaurs that walked on two legs, as well as crocodiles and turtles. The muddy lakeshore eventually hardened and fossilized. When the Andes formed twenty-five to fifty million years ago, tectonics pushed the Earth's plates into vertical hills, resulting in the site's current state. Meyer said the area could be a source for more discoveries. He noted that although the FANCESA site is excellent for preserving footprints, the limestone, quartz and magnesium mixture is not ideal for preserving bones. Skeletal preservation is best along riverbeds where strong currents cover bones with sediment before they fossilize.

Meyer said he experienced a number of annoying and work delaying problems in Bolivia. "We had support from the regional officials, but the rest gave us some trouble," he said, referring to the local tourist office, who was eager to turn the site into a tourist location and some government officials, who were interested in promoting their image in connection to the site. Meyer implied that he had had to wade through some of Bolivia's infamous bureaucracy to complete his research. The crew was also the target of vandalism. Safety ropes were cut and climbing equipment was stolen, despite the posting of guards. This delayed excavations while the team waited for more equipment to be shipped from Europe.

The site's fate is uncertain but will likely be protected. President Hugo Banzer reportedly wanted to set up a foundation to preserve the site. Meyer was working with former Bolivian President and vice president of UNESCO, Jaime Paz Zamora, to declare the find a "World Heritage Site." The Swiss National Science Foundation funded the digging. Meyer will continue his work in Switzerland, where he will analyze the fossils and reconstruct the formation of the Andes to piece together more information on the site. Meyer says he may return for further excavations. He is also producing a book on the site with FANCESA.

For more information contact:
Tour agencies in Sucre for guided tours to the site. It is possible to get to the site by taking one of the Dino-Trucks that depart daily from the Cathedral on the Plaza. Expect the journey to take an hour and a half.

TARIJA, THE WINE CAPITAL

BY PETER MCFARREN

With about 135,651 inhabitants, an excellent valley climate and pleasant atmosphere, Tarija is the place to ease up the pace and enjoy life. It is best to reach the city by plane — you can fly there from La Paz, Sucre, Cochabamba or Santa Cruz. The roads that link Tarija with the rest of the country are extremely tortuous, and there is no direct train service. At an altitude of about 1,830 meters (about 6,000 feet), the city is located at the heart of a fertile valley of orchards and vineyards watered by the Río Guadalquivir.

Tarija was founded on July 4, 1574 by Captain Luis de Fuentes. The name originally given to the city was Villa San Bernardo de la Frontera de Tarija; it ended up retaining only the last part of its original name.

Tarija differs from other Bolivian cities in that it is situated far from the political center of activities, and it has always maintained a very peculiar personality. Its people declared independence from Spain in 1807 and founded their own little republic, producing a fierce struggle with colonial powers. But once the Spanish were defeated in the general insurrection, Tarija was absorbed into the new nation.

Tarija's geographic situation has led to a very close relationship with Argentina. Very early in the morning, when Bolivian radios have not yet gone on the air, peasants and people in the city and villages listen to Argentinian stations. The border is only a few hours away from the city and there are buses, planes (Bolivian and Argentinian) and trains crossing it constantly. The railroad reaches to Villamontes and Yacuiba in the Tarija Department and continues to the Argentinian border and its northern cities. But if your intentions are to continue to travel to Argentina, the best connection to take is not that of Villamontes or Yacuiba. Rather, because of road conditions, the best connection is at Villazón, a more accessible Potosí village bordering with the Department of Tarija and Argentina.

The best time to go to Tarija is from December to *Carnaval* time in February or March. Peasants are collecting all kinds of fruits and vegetables, the markets are full of produce, Tarija is crowded with visitors, and there is a very festive atmosphere. Nevertheless, Tarija has the advantage an excellent climate year-round, so if you go during early winter, you will catch the intense fishing and hunting season in the eastern part of the department. On August 16th, you will be able to see the **San Roque** religious festival, famous for its dances and rites. The procession and feast in honor of the **Virgin of Chaguaya** also take place during September.

Tarija is the grape-producing region of Bolivia, so you will be able to enjoy not only the excellent food, but also the different wines and distilled liquors (particularly *sin - gani*, a liquor derived from grapes). It is worth visiting the grape plantations in the beautiful valleys of **Concepción**, **Santa Ana** and **Chocloca**, which surround the city. Other valleys worth visiting for their beauty are the **Sella** and **San Lorenzo** valleys. The village of San Lorenzo, located in the valley of the same name, constitutes a necessary visit because of its historical importance; Moto Méndez, an Independence revolutionary hero, lived there and his house is now a historical museum. The valleys mentioned are irrigated by several rivers that contribute to their beauty and which provide excellent swimming areas. Ask at the tourist information center how to get to **Los Chorros de Jurina**, **La Angostura**, **Rincón de la Victoria**, **Tomatas**, **Coimata** and **San Jacinto**. Take your swimming suit and a picnic lunch. The **San Jacinto Dam**, located near the city, includes a large artificial lake with a shoreline where you can find lodging, food and boat rental.

In the city, **Plaza Luis de Fuentes**, the main square, is filled with exquisite roses and fragrant trees most of the year; young and old congregate there in the evenings. Also worth visiting is the **Cathedral**, a block from the plaza, on Calle Campero. The magnificent building of **La Casa Dorada**, once the house of a rich Tarijeño, is located at the corner of Calle Ingavi and General Trigo. It has been restored and can be toured. Another sumptuous house, interesting for its eclectic architecture, is **El Castillo de Beatriz** on Calle Bolívar.

The **Library of the Franciscan Convent**, one of the marvels of Tarija, holds an impressive collection of antique books and documents; a special petition has to be made to the Franciscans in order to visit it. The convent itself is also interesting for its collection of colonial and Republican paintings. Both are located at the corner of Calle La Madrid and Campos.

The **Archaeological Museum**, located at the corner of Calle Bernardo Trigo and Virginio Lema, exhibits, among other things, pre-historical Saurian remains found in the area. **The Loma de San Juan**, a park located ten blocks northwest of the plaza, offers an excellent view of the whole city.

The Department of Tarija now has the largest natural gas reserves in the country, discovered in recent years. The impact of this industry and the royalties it will produce is bound to change Tarija in the near future and result in mayor investments in road and other infrastructure projects.

Complete information about transportation and arrangements to visit all the places mentioned can be found at the **Tourist Information Center** at Calle Trigo 505, Tel. 6631000, and through the tour-operating agencies VTB and Vivo Tours (see below for contact information for these agencies).

PRACTICAL INFORMATION FOR TARIJA

Tarija Phone Code: 4

• Useful Addresses and Numbers

The Tourist Information Center is located on the main plaza on Calle General Trigo 505, Tel. 6631000. The office is part of the Prefectural building.

Police Department, Calle Colón and Cochabamba, Tel. 6642222.

Police Emergency, Tel. 110.

Bus Station, Tel. 6636508.

Airport Information, Tel. 6643135.

Immigation Office, Tel. 6643450.

Main Post Office, corner of Sucre and Virginio Lema, Tel. 6642586. Open Monday to Friday, 8:00 to 20:00; Saturday, 8:00 to 18:00; and Sunday 9:00 to noon.

Entel, Calle Virginio Lema 231, between Sucre and Daniel Campos,

Tel. 6642396. Offers long-distance telephone, fax and telegram service. Open all week from 8:00 to 22:00.

Long Distance Calls
Entel, 101.
AES, 0-11.
Cotas, 0-12.
Main Market is on Calle Sucre, in between Domingo Paz and Bolívar.

• Consulates

Argentina, Calle Ballivián 699, Tel. 44273. Open Monday to Friday, 8:30 to 12:30.

Germany, Calle Sucre 165, before Ingavi when heading from the plaza, Tel. 6642062. Open Monday to Friday, 8:30 to 12:30 and 14:30 to 18:30.

• How to Get There

It is recommended to fly into Tarija, rather than driving or taking a bus. AeroSur offers three direct flights a week to and from La Paz. LAB has daily flights to La Paz (though not direct), Santa Cruz and Cochabamba. TAM flies into Tarija once a week from La Paz, Cochabamba and Sucre on one flight, and Santa Cruz and Villamontes on another, and leaves Tarija once a week for Villamontes and Santa Cruz, and for Sucre, Cochabamba and La Paz.

• Airline Offices

Lloyd Aéreo Boliviano, Calle General Trigo 329, between Calle Virginio Lema and Av. del Carpio, Tels. 6632000, 6642195; at airport, 6642149. Open Monday to Friday, 8:00 to noon and 14:30 to 18:30. and Saturday from 9:00 to noon. Visa, MC.

AeroSur, Calle Ingavi, between Sucre and Daniel Campos, Tels. 6630894, 6630893 (also fax); at airport, 6634554. Open Monday to Friday, 8:30 to 12:30, and 14:30 to 18:30, and Saturday 8:30 to noon.

Transporte Aéreo Militar (TAM), Calle La Madrid 470, Tel/Fax. 6642734; at airport, 6645899. Open Monday to Friday, 8:00 to noon and 14:30 to 18:00, and Saturday from 7:00 to 8:30.

• Buses

The **bus terminal** is located on Avenida Las Americas and La Paz, Tel. 6636508. It is open every day from 6:00 to 21:00.

San Lorenzo, Tel. 6642653. Goes to La Paz, Oruro and Potosí every day, and frequently to Santa Cruz, Yacuiba and Bermejo.

Tarija, Tel. 6645557. Goes to Villamontes, Villazon, Yacuiba, Bermejo, Santa Cruz, La Paz, Oruro and Potosí.

Andes Bus, Tel. 6644125. Goes to Potosí, Sucre, Monteagudo and Camiri.

Flota El Chapaco, Tel. 6643137. Goes to Bermejo every day.

• Getting Around Town

Downtown Tarija is tiny, and easily navigable by foot. Given its natural and architectural beauty, Tarija is definitely a good place to wander.

• Radio Taxis

4 de Julio, Tel. 6642829.
Moto Méndez, Tel. 6644480.
Tarija, Tel. 6644378.

• Car Rental

BARRON's Rent A Car, Calle Ingavi E-339, between Mendez and Santa Cruz, Tel. 6636853. Visa, MC.

Localiza Rent a Car, Calle Comercio, corner with Juan XIII. Tels. 6627286.

• Hotels

Los Parrales, Urb. Carmen de Aranjuez, Km. 3.5, Tel. 6648444, Fax. 6648448, International Fax. 001-209-3157913. Los Parrales is hard to beat in

TARIJA DEPT.

Bolivia. Set atop a cliff overlooking the Guadalquivir River on a 7-hectare property, this five-star resort hotel is simply breathtaking. One can enjoy the magnificent views while drinking a glass of wine at one of the room balconies, eating delicious food at the gourmet restaurant, soaking up sun poolside or marveling at what's got to be the country's biggest hot tub surrounded by wall-to-wall windows. If you gawk at the prices, just think what you'd be paying anywhere else in the world, and go for it. Single, $80; Double, $95; Jr. Suite, $105; Presidential Suite, $145. Visa, MC, AmEx. E-mail: parraleshotel@mail.com

Plaza Hotel Victoria, in the Plaza de Armas on Calle La Madrid, corner of Sucre, Tels. 6642600, 6642700, Fax. 6642700. Offers 30 rooms, all with private bath, a small refrigerator and cable. Also has a restaurant. Single: $40; Double: $60; Triple: $80. Prices include breakfast. Visa, MC, AmEx.. E-mail: hot_vit@olivo.tja.entelnet.bo

Hotel Los Ceibos (ex-Hotel Prefectural), Av. Victor Paz, corner of La Madrid, Tel. 6634430, Fax. 6642461. Offers a restaurant and rooms with private baths and cable. Single, $34; Double, $50; Triple, $90; Suite, $90. Prices include breakfast. Visa, MC. E-mail: ceibohot@cosett.com.bo

Grand Hotel Tarija, Calle Sucre 770, Tels. 6642893, 6642684, Fax. 6644777. Offers sauna and carpeted rooms with private bath, refrigerator and cable. Single: $30; Double: $50; Triple: $65; Suite: $60. Prices include breakfast. Visa, MC.

Hostal La Costanera, Av. Las Americas 594, corner of Juan Misael Saracho, Tel. 6642851, Fax. 6632640. Offers comfortable accommodations in a family atmosphere, as well as a vegetarian lunch special. All rooms are carpeted and have private bath, refrigerator and cable. Single,$32; Double, $47; Triple, $59 (up to four people OK). Visa, MC. E-mail: costanera@olivo.tja.entelnet.bo

Viña del Sur Hotel, Zona Miraflores, Tels. 6632425, 6649041, Fax. 6112277. A bit out of the center, but within walking distance (or a three-minute taxi ride) from downtown. Very modern and elegantly decorated, brand-new, offers a swimming pool, gym and sauna, and rooms with private bath, refrigerator and cable. Upstairs rooms have balconies, some with views of the river. Single: $28; Double: $38 (separate beds), $43 (one bed); Suites: $64. Visa, MC. E-mail: vinasur@olivo.tja.entelnet.bo

Hotel Club Social Tarija, Plaza Luis de Fuentes and Vargas, Tels. 6642107, 6642108, Fax. 6814007. A very new hotel that offers conference rooms, a garage, a restaurant, room service and karaoke in the evenings. All rooms are carpeted and with private bath and T.V. Single: $22; Double: $30 (separate beds), $32 (one bed).

Gran Hotel Baldiviezo, near the main plaza on La Madrid 443, Tel. 6647686. This hotel has big balconies and lots of character. Offers Internet services to guests. All rooms have private bath and cable. Single: $15; Double: $30; Triple: $45. Prices include breakfast. Visa, MC, AmEx. E-mail:administracion@ghb.htmlplanet.com

Hotel Luz Palace, Calle sucre 921, Tel. 6635700, Fax. 6644646. E-mail: luzpalace@olivo.tja.entelnet.bo

Hostal Martinez Tarija, Av. La Paz 251, Tel. 6636518, Fax. 6640222.

Hostal Libertador, Calle Bolívar 649. Tel. 6644231, Fax. 6631016. All rooms have private bath. Single: $10; Double: $18; Triple: $21. Prices include breakfast.

Hostal Miraflores, Calle Sucre 920, Tels. 6643355, 6644976, Fax. 6633001. Offers a wide variety of rooms, with the range of prices depending on whether the rooms are carpeted and if they have a refrigerator or private bath. Single: $4 to $14; Double: $6 to $23; Triple: $10 to $18. Visa, MC.

Hostal mi Casa, Calle O'Connor 138. Tel. 6645267, Fax. 6114024. Single: $25; Double: $35; Triple: $45.

Hotel El Salvador, Calle Alenjandro Del Carpio, Tel. 6641920, Fax. 6645444. E-mail: savaldor@cosett.com.bo

Hotel Londres, Calle Campos 1072, Tel. 6641369.

Hostal Carmen, Calle Ingavi O-784, corner of Ramon Rojas, in the El Molino neighborhood, Tels. 6643372, 6644342, Fax. 611-3571. Offers free airport transfers, E-mail service, a garage and the tourism agency VTB. All rooms have private bath and cable and guests may rent VCRs. Single: $8; Double: $13; Triple: $17. Prices include breakfast. E-mail: vtb@olivo.tja.entelnet.bo

Hostal Bolivar, Calle Bolivar 256, Tel. 6642741.

Residencial Zeballos, Calle Sucre 966, Tel. 6642068.

• Restaurants

Mateos, Av. General Trigo 610, Tel. 6630797. Very elegant restaurant with artistic décor. Offers pasta and other international cuisine. Certainly one of Tarija's best places to dine. Lots of seating, but reservations recommended. Good selection of wines. Also has a bar that stays open late. Closed Saturday. Visa, MC.

Taberna Gattopardo, Madrid 318, in the main plaza, Tel. 6630656. Definitely worth having a meal here. With a warm, well-designed interior, this restaurant offers views of the plaza and roaming pedestrians. Extensive menu, including meats, pastas, pizzas and fondue. If it's hot out, don't miss having the lemonade. Open all day, every day. Visa, MC.

Cabañas are outdoor restaurants that serve traditional Bolivian food. The best are **Cabaña de Don Pedro** (accepts Visa and MC), on Av. Las Américas at the end of Parrilla, Tel. 6642681, and **Cabaña de Don Pepe**, Calle Daniel Campos 2681, between Av.

Las Americas and Abaroa, Tel. 6642426. Both are only open for lunch. Be sure to try *saice*.

Don Ñato, in the Villa Busch neighborhood on the San Jacinto highway, Tel. 6642894. Family atmosphere at moderate prices. Closed Monday.

El Amigo, Virginio Lema 685, Tel. 6646929. Offers excellent beef, a *must* for meat lovers. Traditional atmosphere, local dishes. Open every day from noon until 9:00 or 22:00, occasionally offers *peñas*.

Tommy's, Calle Madrid 178, between Colón and Suipacha, Tel. 6634409. This small restaurant offers good traditional food, especially *el pollo picante* and *chuño*. Closed Sunday.

Club Social, Calle Sucre, corner of 15 de Abril, Tel. 6642107. Offers regional food and a set lunch. Located inside hotel of same name. Visa.

El Solar Restaurant, Calle Virginio Lema, corner of Campero, Tel. 6638785, offers excellent vegetarian food in a cozy atmosphere. Closed Sunday.

Pizzería Europa, Calle General Trigo on the main plaza, Tel. 6647611, offers *salteñas* and the only pizza in town with a café-style ambiance. Also offers Internet services. Open 9:00 to 22:00.

For ice cream, try **La Fontana** on the corner of Calle Madrid and Daniel O'Campos.

In the morning, you can buy good *empanadas* at the **Main Market** on Calle Sucre, in between Domingo Paz and Bolívar. More to the south, you can buy freshly-squeezed orange, grapefruit or carrot juice. Fried *empanadas* known as *tucumanas* can be bought at the Parque Bolívar.

For those adventurous enough, try a meal at the Main Market. Recommended are the *saice* (a traditional meat dish in Tarija), *api* (a hot corn brew with a slight touch of cloves and lemon), *sopaipillas* (a fried bread that can be eaten for breakfast or tea) and *chicha*, a fermented corn brew. The market also offers a wide variety of fruits, cheeses and breads.

TARIJA DEPT.

While in Tarija, be sure to try the excellent wines and *singanis* produced in the region. The best-known brands are Kohlberg, Campos de Solana, Concepcíon, Aranjuez, Guadalquivir and Rujero. San Pedro wines and *singanis*, produced in Camargo to the north, can also be bought in Tarija. You will find a wine store, **La Vinoteca Tarijeña**, on the main plaza. They can also arrange tours to the wineries.

• Travel Agencies

The Department of Tarija is spectacularly diverse, offering everything from the jungle to the valleys to the desert. Two competing tour operators in Tarija specialize in adventure and eco-travel throughout the region. They both also offer city tours of Tarija and visits to nearby wineries. The tour operators are:

VTB, Calle Ingavi 784, in Hostal Carmen, Tels. 6643372, 6644341-42, Fax. 6113571.
E-mail: vtb@olivo.tja.entelnet.bo

Viva Tours, Calle Sucre 615, Tel/Fax. 6638325. Visa, MC, AmEx.
E-mail: vivatour@cosett.com.bo

Aldaluz Tours, Calle Sucre, Tels. 6635700-1, Fax. 6644646.

Andalucia Tours, Calle Ingavi corner with Sucre, Tels. 6630892-3.

Gaviota Travel, Calle 15 de Abril 190, Tels. 6647180-1, Fax. 6647181.
E-mail: gavioata_travel@hotmail.com

International Tarija, Calle Sucre 721, Tels. 6644446-7, Fax. 6645017.

Kenaya Tours, Calle Mendez 549, Tel. 6643075, Fax. 6112203.
E-mail: kenaya@cosett.com.bo

Mara Tours, Calle Gral Trigo 739, Tels. 6643490, 6643045, Fax. 6638874.
E-mail: marvin@olivo.tja.entelnet.bo

Paula Tours, Calle Sucre 532, Tel/Fax. 6640779.
E-mail: paulatours@cosett.com.bo

Tarija Tours, Calle Colon 585, Tel. 6640949, Fax. 6640948.
E-mail: tarija_tours@mixmail.com

The following three agencies do not offer tours, but they can book a flight for you or meet other transportation needs:

Guadalquivir Tours, Calle Sucre 405, kitty corner with post office, Tel. 6643914, Fax. 6634090. Visa, MC.

Danny Tours, Av. Belgrano corner with Raquel Darlach, Tel. 6633255, Fax. 6640606. E-mail: danny@olivo.tja.entelnet.bo Visa, MC, AmEx.

Aero Tours, Mendez 565, Tels. 6633004, 6633009, Fax. 6642299. Visa, MC.

• Museums and Cultural Centers

Archaeological and Paleontological Museum, Calle General Trigo, corner with Virginio Lema, Tel. 6636680, Fax. 6643403. Founded in 1945, this museum has a superb collection of fossils discovered in the Tarija Valley. Open Monday to Friday from 8:00 to noon and 15:00 to 18:00, and Saturday from 9:00 to noon and 15:00 to 18:00. Entrance is free, and you can take pictures as long as you don't use flash.

If you are interested in searching for fossils, you may visit **Las Quebradas**, to the north of the city near the airport and across the road bordering the gas pipeline. Here you can find fragments of mastodon bones that look like blue stones. Many of the fossils are quite fragile because they have not petrified.

La Casa Dorada Museum, Calle Ingavi 770, Tel. 6644606. Tour this lovely historic house, filled with antiques. Open Monday to Friday, 9:00 to noon and 15:00 to 18:00, and Saturday 9:00 to noon.

Centro Boliviano Americano, Suipacha 738, Tels. 6641727, 6648626.

Offers cultural activities such as plays and art exhibits, and English classes. Open Monday to Friday, 8:30 to noon, and 14:30 to 21:30.

• Bookstores

Cencotar, Av. Domingo Paz O-149, between Colón and Daniel Campos, Tel. 6643908. Offers books and magazines in English. Closed all day Sunday and Saturday afternoons.

• Internet

Café Internet, at the Pizzería Europa on General Trigo on the main plaza, Tel. 6647611. Open every day from 9:00 to 22:00. Cost: about $1.50/hour.

XLNET, Calle 15 de Abril on Plaza Sucre, right next to La Morocha discotheque. Open Monday to Saturday, 9:00 to 13:00 and 14:30 to 22:00, and Sunday 17:00 to 22:00. Cost: about $1.25/hour.

• Shopping

Artesanía 15 de Abril, 15 de Abril 161, Tel. 6640813. Offers wood and leather goods from Tarija. Closed Sunday.

Artesanía Sandy, Calle Madrid 163, Tel. 6635017. Closed Sunday.

Artesanía Vemar, Calle Bolívar 377, has some good postcards.You can also find a variety of jewelry and artisan ware on the pedestrian walkway next to the cathedral.

• Nightlife

There are a few cafes and bars scattered around the center of Tarija. Most people, however, gather in the Plaza Sucre and hang out there until going to the **La Morocha** discotheque, a lively place on the plaza on Calle 15 de Abril, which is open Friday, Saturday and Sunday from 22:30 to 4:00. Visa, MC.

• Movies

Cine Gran Rex, Calle Madrid, between Colón and Daniel Campos, Tel. 6643728.

Cine Eden, on Virginio Lema, between Sucre and Daniel Campos.

• Banks

Banco Bisa, in the main plaza on Calle Sucre 552, Tels. 6638101-2, Fax. 6638103. Changes U.S. dollars and traveler's checks, and does cash advances on credit cards. Open Monday to Friday, 8:30 to noon and 14:30 to 18.00, and Saturday 10:00 to 13.00.

There are a number of **Enlaces** (ATM) throughout town as well. Look for one on Calle Sucre, about 3/4 of a block up from the main plaza before you reach Ingavi; one on Calle Ingavi, in between Sucre and General Trigo; and one in Plaza Sucre on 15 de Abril.

Banco Nacional, Calle Sucre 735. Tel. 6642025.

Banco de Credito, Calle Ingavi corner with Sucre. Tel. 6642929.

Banco Mercantil, Calle 15 de Abril 283. Tel. 6642386.

• Money Exchange

You will find a plethora of money exchange houses on Calle Bolívar, in between Calles Sucre and Daniel O'Campos.

Prodem, Calle Ingavi 259.

• Couriers

DHL, Calle Sucre 419, Tel. 6646474, Fax.6640490. Office also contains Western Union.

CBK Ltda, Calle Colon 585, Tels. 6640348, 6640949.

IBC, Av. Belgrado, pasaje España, Tels. 6645037, 6634504.

UPS, JET Courier,Centauro, Calle Ingavi 449, Tel. 6636711, Fax. 9113526.

FedEx, Calle Suipacha, Tel/Fax. 6641919.

• Laundries

As of publication date, there were no public laundromats in Tarija. Many hotels, however, offer laundry services.

• Medical Services

Clinica Varas Castrillo, Corrado 176, between Colón and Daniel Campos, Tel. 6642051. Open 24 hours. Can handle emergencies and offers specialized medicine.

San Juan de Dios Hospital, Tel. 6645555.

EXCURSIONS FROM TARIJA

The road from Tarija to Potosí passes through some spectacular scenery and through the wine-producing towns of **Camargo** and **Villa Abecia**. As you leave Tarija, you can see the entire valley stretching behind you.

An outing to one of the many hamlets outside of Tarija is *de rigueur* for anyone wishing to get a good flavor for the unique culture of the valley. It is simple to get to most of the areas of interest since nearly all of them are close by and reachable by taxi or through some very pleasant hiking after short *trufi* or bus rides.

La Angostura

this is a dam that can be reached by taking the bus to **Padcaya** from the bus terminal and getting off at the road for the community of **La Angostura**. You will actually pass by La Angostura before you get off. From the turnoff, take the road toward the mountains, which are quite spectacular. Along the way, you will encounter a desert landscape with various cacti species and low-lying, tortured-looking bushes. When you come to a low ridge where you can see the river and some vineyards, veer left along the road, which ends at the river (**Río Tarija**). It is a little tricky if you want to get to the dam from there, so try to get one of the locals or a fisherman to show you the way. I'm told there is an equally beautiful angostura farther along the river toward the mountains.

Padcaya

An hour away in the same bus from Tarija is a lovely town that offers good hiking in the surrounding countryside. From approximately Aug. 15 to Sept. 15, the **Fiesta of the Virgin of Chaguaya** takes place in **Chaguaya** about 6 miles (10 km) away from Padcaya. During this period, Padcaya is the center for religious pilgrimages as people travel there by car and foot, sometimes walking as much as 60 miles (100 km) to be blessed by the Virgin.

San Jacinto

Take the *micro* or *trufi* for **San Jacinto** from the Palacio de Justicio, on Ingavi and Daniel Campos. San Jacinto is an artificial lake formed by a dam to produce hydroelectric power. There is a restaurant there that has good views of the lake and surrounding countryside, but the food and service are poor. There are also many small kiosks that sell fish on the other side of the dam. Also, below the restaurant, you can rent paddleboats, canoes and kayaks.

Tomatas

Rincón de la Victoria, **San Lorenzo** and **Erquis** can all be reached by the same *trufis*, which leave from just below the Loma de San Juan at the end of Calle Domingo Paz. After passing through about 3 miles (5 km) of monolithically-eroded landscape, one arrives at **Tomatas**, also known as **Tomatitas**, which becomes quite crowded during the weekends. Tomatas has a cou-

TARIJA DEPT.

ple of good restaurants, one being the **Cabaña** to the right just after you cross the bridge leading into the small town and another, a nameless place, about 300 meters further into town on the left-hand side, just past the turnoff for La Victoria and Coimata. It has a small store in the front and a patio to the left. Absolutely avoid the restaurant El Grillo. The best swimming is just below the footbridge and on the other side of the **Río Guadalquivir** behind the park.

Rincón de la Victoria

Coimata and **La Victoria** are reached by taking the turnoff mentioned in the above paragraph. The hike to **Rincón de la Victoria** is about two hours following this road southwest toward the mountains, keeping a knife-edged ridge to your left the whole way. Although far, the walk is well worth it, as there is a peaceful swimming hole in a lush, man-made forest. There should be rides back with taxis or trucks on the weekends.

Coimata

The swimming area in **Coimata** is a little more difficult to find. After about one-half hour's walk on the same road as above, one road will turn off to the right. Do not turn off, however, at the first right, as this road will take you to **Erquis**. Once you arrive at the football field of Coimata, turn to the left and follow that road toward the mountains. This road ends shortly before you reach a small kiosk; you will arrive then to the swimming hole after walking on a footpath for about 200 meters or so. In total, it takes about 1-1/2 hours of walking. This swimming hole is particularly nice in the summer, as it has a waterfall. If you are there at the right time in late November/December, you will see the ceibo trees in bloom, which provide a beautiful display of red flowers in the trees' large canopy. Also notice, just about anywhere, the ubiquitous *churqui* and *molle* trees, the former being spiny with tiny leaves and the latter having somewhat larger leaves and a peeled-bark trunk.

Erquis

To go to **Erquis**, take the same *trufi* to where a small stream crosses the main road and another turns off to the left. Follow this road uphill until it forks, taking the fork to the left downhill. Cross the riverbed and follow the road straight up that begins on the other side of the riverbed. Follow this road until it ends, then cross over to the other side of the river and follow this until it ends, too.

To get to the swimming hole, climb up to the irrigation ditch above and follow it until you arrive, about 20 minutes from there. The whole walk takes 2 to 2-1/2 hours. This swimming area, of all three I've mentioned, does not have the best swimming, but the canyon in which it is located is very picturesque.

It is also the best point from which you can climb **Cerro Morro Alto**, the tall and broad mountain observable from just about anywhere in the valley. I'm told by the locals that if you make an attempt on this summit, take some *singani*, coca leaves or cigarettes to offer to the *Coquena*, a coquettish and semi-friendly spirit who takes care of some of the animals on the mountain, among which are rabbits, deer and vicuña. The belief about the *Coquena* is that she will ask you for one of the above three pleasures and if you don't comply, she will make you disappear.

San Lorenzo

To get to **San Lorenzo**, take the *trufi* to the end of the line, the main plaza in the "land of Moto Méndez." Méndez's house is just north of the plaza, kitty corner to the park in a two-story building with a small balcony in front. It houses an interesting museum where, when you try to descend the precipitously steep steps adjoining the bedroom to the first floor, you realize how people actually did die falling down the stairs. There is a colorful *fiesta* for the town's patron saint the second week of August, in which the *chunchos* dance in the streets surrounding the plaza to *quenillas*, small flutes and *cañas* arranged in arcs over them.

San Roque Fiesta

The *chunchos*, in fact, are the most colorful part of the majority of the festivals in Tarija, especially the unforgettable **San Roque Fiesta** where nearly 500 of them dance to a variety of music, sometimes all playing at the same time, lending an almost chaotic atmosphere to the procession. (The celebration of the *fiesta* starts the first Sunday of September, but the actual day of San Roque, in which nearly every dog in the city receives a cloth flower collar, is August 16).

The *chunchos* are men and boys who have made promises to the Virgin to dance at *fiestas* for 10 to 15 years, although the promise can be more or less than this amount — some veterans having danced for upwards of 40 years. They wear brilliant costumes consisting of cylindrical feather headdresses decorated with trinkets, small mirrors, and pictures of the Virgin, veils, silk scarves and shirts, dresses, stuffed silk hearts slung over their shoulders with snail shells sewn into them, and stockings with frumpy shoes. All dancers carry a clicker adorned with feathers that is clicked during the dances. The whole spectacle is an unusual sight, indeed.

Beside its festive atmosphere, *Carnaval* is a good time to listen to the distinctive Tarijan folk music. One can also see folkloric performances during the **Fiesta de la Uva**, which lasts for three days in March. Two other folk festivals worth mentioning are the **Fiesta Santa Cecilia**, the

November 22, which has Argentine *Gaucho* music, music from the Chaco and typical Tarija valley music, and the **Fiesta del Palacho** in Bermejo, September 28-30, in honor of the Palacho tree. This *fiesta* features music from Tarija and other regions of Bolivia.

In sum, one is bound to run into a festival in Tarija; if not in the city, then somewhere in the country. As you meet the locals, you're likely to find the truth in the saying *en vino veritas* as you discuss anything from world events to local politics, to *chicha* to football.

Rodeo Chapaco

On April 28 is a traditional cowboy exhibit of *Gaucho* heritage.

Fiesta de Las Flores

On the second sunday of October the *Fiesta de las Flores* is dedicated to the *Virgen de Rosario*, which begins with the procession from the San Juan church in which faithful followers are showered with flowers petals. There is also a fair and a bazaar in which, there are local artesanal goods for sale.

Potosí, Villazón Tomatas, Coimata, Erquis

ARIJA

Tourist office
Immigration
Entel
Post office
LAB
TAM
Aerosur

MARKET
8 Central Market

CHURCHES
9 Cathedral
10 San Francisco
11 San Roque temple
12 San Juan temple

MUSEUMS & POINTS OF INTEREST
13 Paleontological
14 Casa Dorada
15 Loma de San Juan, Sight seeing site
16 Moto Mendez monument

17 Moises Navajas monument
18 La Tablada historical monument
19 Library of the Franciscan Covent

20 Hospital

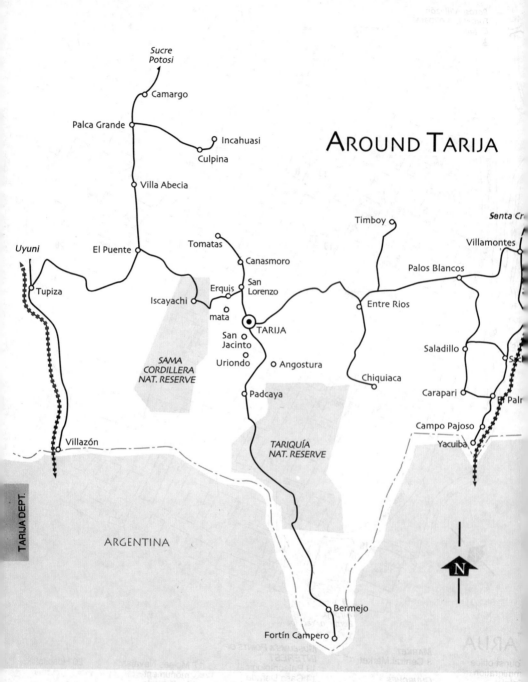

AROUND TARIJA

Sucre
Potosi

Camargo

Palca Grande

Incahuasi

Culpina

Villa Abecia

Timboy

Santa Cr

Villamontes

El Puente

Tomatas

Canasmoro

Palos Blancos

Uyuni

Erquis

San Lorenzo

Entre Rios

Tupiza

Iscayachi

mata

TARIJA

San Jacinto

Saladillo

Sa

Uriondo

Angostura

SAMA
CORDILLERA
NAT. RESERVE

Chiquiaca

Carapari

El Palr

Padcaya

Campo Pajoso

Yacuiba

Villazón

TARIQUÍA
NAT. RESERVE

N

ARGENTINA

Bermejo

Fortín Campero

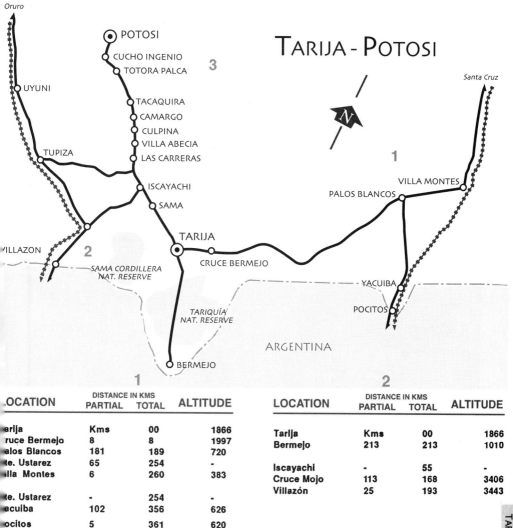

TARIJA - POTOSI

1

| LOCATION | DISTANCE IN KMS | | ALTITUDE |
	PARTIAL	TOTAL	
arija	Kms	00	1866
ruce Bermejo	8	8	1997
alos Blancos	181	189	720
te. Ustarez	65	254	-
illa Montes	6	260	383
te. Ustarez	-	254	-
acuiba	102	356	626
ocitos	5	361	620

2

| LOCATION | DISTANCE IN KMS | | ALTITUDE |
	PARTIAL	TOTAL	
Tarija	Kms	00	1866
Bermejo	213	213	1010
Iscayachi	-	55	-
Cruce Mojo	113	168	3406
Villazón	25	193	3443

3

| LOCATION | DISTANCE IN KMS | | ALTITUDE |
	PARTIAL	TOTAL	
Tarija	Kms	00	1866
Sama	46	46	-
Iscayachi	9	55	3416
Las Carreras	59	114	2328
Villa Abecia	27	141	2309
Cruce Culpina	34	175	-
Camargo	11	186	2406
Tacaquira	18	204	-
Totora Palca	56	305	3442
Cucho Ingenio	32	337	3580
Potosí	39	376	3909

TARIJA DEPT.

THE HIGHEST WINERIES IN THE WORLD

BY MIKE CEASER

From the start, Spanish colonists recognized that Tarija's Central Valley, even at 1,700 meters above sea level and higher, would be a good area for winemaking. In 1579 Tarija's founder, Don Luis de Fuentes, wrote a letter to the *Real Audencia* in Sucre describing how promising the land was for vineyards.

Winemaking had already started before then, however. The first Catholic order in the area, Santo Domingo, was founded in 1575 and must have certainly made wine for masses. The Dominicans were joined by the Augustinians in 1596, the Franciscans in 1606, San Juan de Dios in 1639 and finally, the Company of Jesus in 1690. But it was the Jesuits who got winemaking going in a big way to supply their missions in much of southern Bolivia and parts of northern Paraguay.

The Jesuits were expelled in 1767, leaving behind a now-crumbling mission in the Central Valley. The old mission property, still called *La Compañia*, now belongs partially to *La Concepción* and partially to a neighbor, on whose property the old winemaking equipment is located.

Other orders, however, continued the tradition. In the 293-year-old Franciscan monastery in Tarija, the monks, wearing their traditional long dark robes, still stamp grapes with their bare feet and squeeze them in hand-turned presses.

An Ulcer Launches an Industry

Winemaking never ceased around Tarija, but it took an ulcer to launch the valley's modern industry. Around 1958, auto parts store-owner Julio Kohlberg, ex-decathlon record holder of Bolivia, went to Buenos Aires for a medical check-up and learned he had a minor ulcer.

"The doctor told him that if he wanted to drink alcoholic drinks, it should be pure wine," said Julio's son Jaime Kohlberg, General Administrator of Kohlberg Wines. Julio Kohlberg began making wine at home, sold some to friends, and then bought land in the nearby Central Valley to expand production.

The doctor's advice was good, and Julio Kohlberg, now in his late 70s, is still healthy and works in the country. Meanwhile, Tarija's wine industry bloomed in the late 1960s and 70s and has matured and grown since. Kohlberg has been joined by three other major winemakers, *Casa Real*, *Concepción* and *Aranjuez*, as well as smaller jug wine makers and innumerable families who make wine at home.

The Advantage of Altitude

Planting vineyards at 1,700m above sea level would have seemed a heresy to the old French winemasters, whose crops grew between sea level and a few hundred meters elevation.

But Bolivia's nearness to the equator makes the elevation, that could be ski country in higher latitudes, apt for vineyards

TARIJA DEPT.

here. Seasons are well-marked, grapevines grow well in the alluvial soil, and the region has relatively dry micro-climates. Local winemakers say the elevation improves the grapes in several ways, giving them more cancer-fighting anti-oxidants and helping juices age faster into a sweeter, less-acidic wine.

In contrast to low-elevation grape-growing regions near the tropics, Tarija's elevation creates distinct seasons that allow the vine to rest in winter and flower naturally in summer. Grape-growers in places such as Venezuela must spray on hormones to cause the plants to pass through their life cycle. Tarija's Central Valley also receives lots of sun and afternoon winds that carry away the heat. It almost never freezes during the growing season, and the rains are usually well-timed for the crops, according to growers.

A Difficult Domestic Market

Bolivia may be wine country, but it's not wine-drinking country, complain winemakers. "Bolivians don't know how to drink wine," said Jaime Kohlberg. "They aren't educated about how to drink and how to recognize good varieties."

And the Bolivian market that does exist is inundated by foreign wines, particularly from Argentina and Chile. Bolivia's relatively small producers have difficulty competing with the foreigners' high-volume operations and established reputations. Not to mention the flood of illegal exports.

At the La Paz restaurant *Casa del Corregidor*, Bolivian wines sell well, but mostly to foreigners, said the administrator, Virginia de Guzmán. The restaurant also sells Chilean and Argentinean wines.

"We offer domestic and foreign wines, and they always prefer the Bolivian ones," she said. "They say they're very rich, well made and that the presentation is very good."

Even French tourists like the Bolivian wines, she said. Bolivian clients, in contrast, prefer beer.

MOSCATEL HERE TO STAY

BY MIKE CEASER

It was about 1763 when the Spanish Crown expelled the Jesuit order from Latin America, where it had created a huge network of farms and missions. But even today visitors to the site of the old Jesuit mission near Tarija will find one of their traditions, Moscatel making, still flourishing.

"I'm trying to follow [the Jesuits'] path," explained wine-works owner Carmen Blacud, whose father and grandfather restarted the tradition. "Distilling the ripe grape, paying attention to quality instead of quantity . . . all with the highest possible grade of sweetness."

After the Jesuits' forced departure, the family of the Marquis Campero, who had lent the land to the Jesuits, recovered it. Blacud's family later bought the section of land containing the wine works, and in the 1920s her father and grandfather re-initiated the Jesuit tradition.

Moscatel is the regional name for *sin - gani* wine. It is made from a type of grape named Moscatel of Alexandria. Moscatel makers use the green grape as their base.

The Jesuits produced Moscatel to supply wine for church masses in parts of present-day Bolivia and Paraguay. These days, said Blacud, the wine is either drunk pure, with ice, or mixed with Schweppes or lemon juice.

Blacud is one of many Moscatel makers in Tarija, she says she is the only one who uses the traditional methods. Though she does use electricity, she follows the Jesuit methods of using wood fires and storing the Moscatel in casks of baked clay. The process is delicate and time-consuming, she said.

While Blacud tries to stay loyal to traditional methods and standards, she will compromise for cleanliness' sake.

"One time I did stomp grapes (by foot)," she said, "but it's full of flies — very unhygienic."

TARIJA DEPT.

DISTANCE ONLY ADDS TO THE ALLURE OF LOS PARRALES

BY VANESSA ARRINGTON

Tarija is far. Los Parrales is even farther. But this isn't a setback, says Peter Bartmann, manager of Bolivia's new five-star resort hotel. Rather, it is a selling point.

"The principal reason we can be considered the best hotel in Bolivia is our location," says Bartmann.

Perched atop a cliff, overlooking the river and voluptuous hills of Tarija, this statement is hard to dispute. Los Tajibos in Santa Cruz, long the leader of Bolivia's top hotels, may offer a gorgeous swimming pool, tropical surroundings and a taste of Brazil, but your money buys something else at Los Parrales: serenity.

As you slowly wake up from the deep slumber guaranteed by what may be the world's most comfortable beds, you will hear the gentle sound of the river rolling by. As you wander Los Parrales' spacious grounds, you will be surrounded on all sides by natural beauty, and won't hear the sound of any cars racing by.

Combined with the earthiness is utter extravagance. Los Parrales is, after all, a five-star hotel, and the staff is trained to make sure you never forget that. So as you relax and reconnect with your inner being, you will also be pampered to the extreme.

Bartmann, a native of Germany who spent many years in Spain and Canada, has more than 30 years of experience in the hotel business, and it shows. From the gourmet food at the hotel's restaurant to the enormous hot tub situated next to floor-to-ceiling windows, it's clear that those who created Los Parrales knew what they were doing.

"People always pay for quality," says Bartmann.

So far, Los Parrales has had little trouble attracting people to do just that. From wedding groups to business conferences to Bolivians wanting a great place to party for *Carnaval*, the hotel has had a steady stream of guests since its opening. But for Bartmann, who believes Tarija is on the verge of being "discovered" by more mainstream tourists, the future holds much more.

"Tarija is very exotic," says Bartmann. "We must cultivate this market."

Tarija *is* far from Bolivia's gringo trail, he admits, but there's no reason for not expanding that trail. Not only does Tarija offer a taste of Argentina, it also has some of the best weather, tastiest food and friendliest people found in all of Bolivia.

Again, hard to dispute. And that's not even mentioning the wineries.

"There are resources here that no one has exploited," says Bartmann.

In an effort to change that, Bartmann is behind a movement of "cooperative tourism" in which other hotels, airlines, and tour operators in Tarija are plotting ways to attract more tourists to their fair city and offer them a memorable experience once they get there.

And if they come to Los Parrales, Bartmann promises, memorable is definitely what they'll get.

THE FRONTIER BENI REGION

BY PETER MCFARREN

Beni is one of the most fascinating, colorful, culturally and environmentally rich department of Bolivia, occupying 213,564 square km, or 22 percent of the country's territory. Within its tropical border a visitor will find pristine forests, incredibly diverse plant and animal life, traditional ranching communities and indigenous communities that have maintained century-old cultural expressions. Its capital, Trinidad, a city of about 75,285 founded by the Jesuits in the late 17th century, is what Santa Cruz was like 30 years ago. Most of the streets are still unpaved, and horses, motorcycles, four-wheel drive vehicles and carts are still favorite ways to travel.

Traditionally, Trinidad has been the center of Bolivia's cattle industry. Cattle were introduced by the Jesuits in 1675. Horses followed, and Benianos, as residents of the Beni are known, became expert horsemen. The Beni is largely made up of fertile grasslands that provide a natural breeding ground for cattle as well as tropical rains forests, savannas and lagoons. In recent years, farmers using the latest in agricultural technology diversified into rice farming. Until recently beef was flown from the Beni to La Paz and mining centers on World War II-vintage planes. Pilots who fly across the Andes, often without radar, are considered among the best — if not the craziest

— in the world. Today, most of the cattle are either taken by road to Santa Cruz, where modern meet processing plants have been built, to La Paz, or by river to Cochabamba.

In many regions of the Beni, indigenous native groups survive as farmers, ranch hands, Brazilian nut collectors and artisans. Yucca, rice, bananas, cotton and sweet potatoes are the most popular crops in the Beni. For nearly two decades the Beni became important cocaine producing centers and transient point for drugs. Towns such as Santa Ana flourished during from the early 1980s to late 1990's when the government succeeded in destroying much of the country's illegal coca leaf production.

Trinidad and the Beni are worth visiting if you are interested in adventure, a change of pace, the opportunity of seeing some rich cultural traditions that continue to thrive and to explore the area's rich and diverse fauna and flora. While Trinidad has excellent hotel accommodations, the rest of the Beni Department lacks modern-day comforts, with some exceptions. Rurrenabaque, for example, is a small village across the border of the Department of La Paz and located at the western end of the Beni Department. It is the gateway to the **Madidi National Park** and northern La Paz. It has become a popular tourist destination. Riveralta and Guayaramerin

BENI DEPT.

also provide decent hotel accommodations. These two towns are important river trading posts. Riveralta is an entry point to Brazil nut, wood and rubber producing areas. Guayaramerin borders Brazil and has become the most important commercial center in northern Bolivia.

The Beni elite used to send their children to study in Brazil and Europe. Area residents identified more with Brazil and Europe because the Andes separate the region from La Paz and the Bolivian highlands. Today, regular flights and a road usable only during the dry season are opening up the area to tens of thousands of highland settlers.

Traditional religious celebrations and folklore that date to the Jesuit period can be found in Trinidad and surrounding towns. These celebrations take place during religious feast days.

PRACTICAL INFORMATION FOR TRINIDAD

Trinidad Phone Code: 3

• Useful Addresses and Numbers

The **Tourist Information Center** is in the Prefectural Building on Plaza José Ballivián, Tel. 4621722.

Police, Tel. 110.

Bus Station, Calle Mendoza.

Entel, the telecommunications office (long-distance telephone, fax and telegram service) is at Calle Cipriano Barace 20, Tels. 4621400, 4620655.

Long Distance Call
Entel, 101.
AES, 0-11.
Cotas, 0-12.
Post Office, is at Calle Cipriano Barace 10, Tel. 4621266.

• Consulates

United States is at Panamericana (no number), Tel. 4626114. Open for consular services Monday through Friday, 9:00 to 12:00.

• How to Get There

You can reach Trinidad by plane with LAB or AeroSur, or by bus, from Bolivia's major cities. From Santa Cruz, buses leave at 18:30 and arrive in Trinidad the following morning.

• Airline Offices

Lloyd Aéreo Boliviano, Calle Santa Cruz 332, Tels. 4621855, 4622363, in office, 4621221 at airport.

AeroSur, Calle Cipriano Barace 51, Tels. 4621221, 4621277, in office, 4652120 at airport, Fax. 4652117.

TAM, Tels. 4620855, 4622363.

Save Regional, Tels. 4622806, 46250663.

Amaszonas, Calle 18 de Noviembre 267. Tel./Fax. 4622426. Aeropuerto, 4627575.

• Buses

Buses leave daily from Calle Mendoza to La Paz, Cochabamba and Santa Cruz during the dry season. There is also a service to Rurrenabaque, Riveralta and Guayaramerín.

• Getting Around

Trinidad is a small town, and best navigated by foot or by motorbike.

To reach many of the towns in the other parts of the Beni, often the only way is via plane.

Aero taxi Balcázar, Tels. 4622077, 4621340, rents single and twin-engine planes. Their pilots are experienced.

• Motorbike Rental

PAY, Av. Bolívar, corner with Cipriano Barace, Tel. 4625658.

La Veloz, Av. Bolívar 221, Tel. 4624942.
El Negrito, Av. Bolívar, corner with Nicolás Suárez.

Motorcycles can also be rented on the Plaza José Ballivián to visit the Mamoré River, to get around town or for trips to the airport.

• Car Repair

Chendo, Av. Ejército 354, Tel. 4621890.
Campesino Tatecam, Santa Cruz Highway, Km. 2-1/2, Tel. 4624046.
Taller General FM, Calle Martín Pascual, Tel. 4624271.

• Hotels

Flotel Reina de Enin, offers great ecological and cultural cruises on Beni Rivers on comfortable boats run by Fremen. Tel. in La Paz, 2414062, E-mail: vtfremen@caoba.entelnet.bo in Santa Cruz, Tel.3338535, in Trinidad, Av. Cipriano Barace 332, Tels. 4622276, 4621834. 4days/3nights: $349; 5days/4nights: $423; 6days/5nights: $497. E-mail: fremenfl@sauce.ben.entelnet.bo

Four Stars Hotels
Hotel La Hosteria, Av. Ganadera in front of Campo Ferial, Tel. 4622911, Fax. 4625622.
Hotel Mi Residencia, Calle Manuel Limpias 76, Tels. 4621535, Fax.4622464. E-mail: miresidencia@hotmail.com
Hotel Gran Moxos, Av. 6 de Agosto 146, Tels. 4622240, 4620002.
Aguahi Hotel, Av.Bolivar corner with Santa Cruz, Tels. 4625570, 4625569. E-mail: aguahi@sauce.ben.entelnet.bo

Three Stars Hotels
Hotel Bajío, Calle Nicolás Suárez 632, Tels. 4623400, 4622400. Offers rooms with telephone, T.V., air conditioning and room service. Pool, restaurant, bar and parking in hotel.

Hotel Beni, 6 de Agosto 68, Tels. 4622788, 4620522, Fax. 4620262. Offers rooms with telephone, T.V., air conditioning and bar. There is a pool, restaurant, cafeteria meetings rooms, beauty salon and parking in the hotel. E-mail: benihotel@latinmail.com
Hotel La Pascana, Av. 6 de Agosto 420, Tel. 4621583. Rooms have telephone, T.V. and air conditioning. Restaurant, tennis courts and parking in hotel.
Hotel Jacaranda, Calle Bolivar 229, Tels. 4621659, 4623990, Fax. 4652177.
Hotel Trini, Calle Sucre 353, Tel. 4622613.

One Star Hotels
Hotel Monte Verde, Av. 6 de Agosto 76, Tels. 4622750, 4622342, Fax. 4622044. This hotel, offers rooms with telephone, T.V. and air conditioning. Hotel offers laundry service and a boutique.
Hotel Copacabana, Calle Matias Carrasco 627, Tels. 4622811, 4620305. Fax. 4621978.
Hotel Yacuma, Calle Santa Cruz 303, Tel. 4622249.
Hotel Avenida, Av. 6 de Agosto 311, Tels. 4622044, 4623356.
Hotel Paulista, Av. 6 de Agosto, Tel. 4620018.
Residencial Brasilia, Av. 6 de Agosto 46, Tel. 4621685.
Residencial Castedo, Calle Luis Céspedes 42, Tel. 4620937.
Residencial Colonial Av. Antonio Vaca Diez 306, Tel. 4622864.
Residencial El Carmen, Av. Cipriano Barace 158, Tel. 4622688.
Residencial El Brete Calle 9 de Abril 38, Tel. 4620659.
Residencial Fatima, Calle Viador Pinto, Tel. 4622474.
Residencial Loreto, Calle La Paz 539, Tel. 4622999.
Residencial Oriental, Av. 18 de Noviembre 351, Tel. 4622534.

BENI DEPT.

Residencial Palermo, Av. 6 de Agosto 123, Tel. 4620472.

Residencial Santa Cruz, Calle Santa Cruz 537, Tel. 4620711.

Residencial Patuju, Calle Tomas Meliton 467, Tel. 4621963.
E-mail: anebeni@hotmail.com

• Restaurants

Restaurant Carlitos, Plaza Ballivián 38, Tel. 4622447, serves regional and international food in a nice ambiance.

For pizza try **Pizzeria Refugio**, Calle J. Chávez Bolívar, Tel. 4624800.

Excellent beef can be found at these two restaurants:

La Estancia, Calle Ibare 57, Tel. 4620022. Best restaurant in town. Accepts Visa, MC.

El Pacumutu, Calle Carmelo López, Tel. 4622751. Be sure to ask for fried yucca.

Be sure to try *pacú* or *surubí* fish when in Trinidad at one of the following:

Pescadería El Plátano, Av. Del Mar 365, Tel. 4620635, open every day.

Pescadería Moro, Calle Bolívar 707, Tel. 4620912, open every day.

Excellent fresh fish and rustic outdoor restaurants are along the Mamoré river banks, a few miles from the city on the road linking Trinidad with La Paz. Be sure to ask for fried *pacú* or *surubí*.

• Travel Agencies

Fremen, Av. Cipriano Barace 332, Tels. 4621834, 4622276. Fax. 4652251.
E-mail: fremenfl@sauce.ben.entelnet.bo

Fantasía Tours, Av. 6 de Agosto, Tels. 4621365, 4621087.

Tarope Tours, Av. 6 de Agosto 57, Tels. 4621468, Fax. 4652036.
E-mail: taroped@sauce.ben.entelnet.bo

Triniti Tours, Calle Cochabamba 100, Tels. 4622766, 4620172.

Turismo Moxos, Av. 6 de Agosto 114, Tels. 4621141, 17-80122, Fax. 4622189.
E-mail: turmoxos@sauce.ben.entelnet.bo

Paraíso Travel, Av. 6 de Agosto 138, Tels. 4625567, 4620946, Fax. 4620692.
E-mail: paraíso@sauce.ben.entelnet.bo

Vieira Tours, Av. Cipriano Barace 64, Tels. 4622547, 4621265, Fax. 4652178.
E-mail:rovieira@sauce.ben.entelnet.bo

Jarajorechi, Av. 6 de Agosto corner with 27 de Mayo, Tels. 4621409, 4621716.

• Museums, Churches and Cultural Centers

Parroqui de la Catedral, Plaza Principal, Tel. 4622928, lovely old Catholic church.

Casa de la Cultura, Av. Santa Cruz, Tel.4620796.

• Bookstores

Librería 2001, Calle Antonio Vaca Díez 24, Tel. 4621077.

• Shopping

Local handicrafts are sold at **Casa Bolívar** on Calle Cochabamba 609, Tel. 4620773, and at **Casa de la Cultura del Beni** on Calle Santa Cruz, Tel. 4620796. Native masks, hammocks and ceramics are sold across from the cemetery. **Boutique Moxos** on Calle La Paz 716, Tels. 4621252, 4621822, sells leather goods.

• Sports

Club Tenis Trinidad, Calle Nicolás Suárez 484, Tel. 4621020.

• Nightlife

Bongo, Av. José Chávez Suárez, Tel. 4620575.

Zeppelín, Av. 18 de Noviembre, Tel. 4621724.

BENI DEPT.

Oasis, Calle Julio Céspedes Añez 147, Tel. 4622141.

Discotheques
Discoteca Cachivateca, Av. 18 de Noviembre 670, Tel. 4624545.
Estación, Av. 18 de Noviembre 333, Tel. 4621917.
Discoteca Zodiak, Av. José Chávez Suárez.

Karaokes
Karaoke Meggers, Av. Santa Cruz, Tel. 4623330.

• **Movies**
Cine Trinidad, Calle Pedro de la Rocha 25, Tel. 4621850.

• **Banks**
Banco Mercantil, Calle Joaquín de Sierra 61, Tels. 4621950, 4620410, Fax. 4652051.
Banco Nacional de Bolivia, Plaza Mcal. Ballivián, Tels. 4621034, 4624180, Fax. 4624343.
Banco Ganadero, Plaza Mcal. Ballivián 30, Tel. 4623777, Fax. 4623888.
Banco Unión S.A., Calle Cipriano Barace 604, Tels. 4624500, 4621630, Fax. 4624501.

• **Money Exchange**
Prodem, Av. Antonio Vaca Díez.

• **Couriers**
Most courier offices are open from 8:00. to 12:00., and from 14:30. to 18:00.
Federal Express, Calle Antonio Vaca Díez 71, Tel/Fax.. 4626089.
SAS, Calle 6 de Agosto 84, Tel. 4626088.
CBK, Calle 6 de Agosto 140, Tel. 4622276.

IBC, Av. 6 de Agosto114, Tel. 4621141, Fax. 4622189.
UPS, JET Courier, Av. 6 de Agosto 57, Tel. 4621468.

• **Laundries**
Dry Clean, Calle Chaparral A-11, Tel. 4622505.

• **Medical Services**
Trinidad Hospital, Calle Bolívar 375, Tels. 4620776, 4621810.
Clínica Santísimas Trinidad, Calle Nicolás Suárez 56, Tel. 4621045.
Clínica Dental, Calle Carmelo López 27, Tel. 4623083.

EXCURSIONS FROM TRINIDAD

Puerto Almacén
Located 8 kilometers (about 5 miles) out of the city of Trinidad, it was originally established as a customs checkpoint and later became an important fishing and transit port. Taxis or motorcycles provide service to this port.

Puerto Varador
Located 13 kilometers (8 miles) out of the city of Trinidad on the shores of the Mamoré River on the main road linking the city with San Ignacio de Moxos, San Borja and La Paz. A floating hotel run by Fremen Tours docks at this port. Fish is often sold on the shores of the river. Vehicles travel east cross the river on barges and must often travel several kilometers upriver to rejoin the main road. Restaurants on the shore provide great fish and ice-cold beer.

San Ignacio de Moxos
This traditional ranching community has one of the richest cultures in Bolivia. The Jesuits established an important settlement in

BENI DEPT.

this town. In the dry season it is reachable by a three-to-four-hour trip on the main road going from Trinidad to La Paz. During the town festival the end of July and during Holy Week thousands of aread residents, many of them Moxenos, participate in festive and devotional celebrations that date to the Jesuit Missions period. Dancer suse colorful feather headdresses, old violins, wind instruments, drums and diverse masks.

Santa Ana del Yacuma

Another lovely Beni town that is a traditional cattle-producing center. Reachable by boat or by air from Trinidad. In the early 1980s and until a few years ago it become a haven for cocaine drug traffickers, and mansions to accommodate the cocaine kingpins were built t near the town. The indigenous Moxeno population has a rich culture that is expressed through dances with masks, feather headdresses and embroidered outfits.

Hotel Mamore, Av. Roberto Roca Suarez, Tel. 4842365, Fax. 4842090. Four stars hotel.

Hotel Tropical, Tel. 4842070.

Chuchini

This rural Beni center is an important archaeological site located 15 km north of the City of Trinidad on the shores of an artificial lagoon. Also know as the "Madriguera del Tigre" (the resting place of the tiger), is home to a small museum that was started in 1974 and rescues the rich culture of the Moxenos who inhabited the region long before the Spanish conquest. Over 1,000 ceramics and stone pieces that date back several thousands years have been collected by the owner, Efrem Hinojosa Hieber and his family.

Chuchini is also a wildlife refugee and home to dozens of species of birds and mammals. Located on a hill overlooking the lagoon, this site is a great place to spend a few days observing the wide variety of native wildlife.

For reservations contact in Trinidad the owner Efrem Hinojosa Hieber,

Tels. 4624744, 4625284, 71796198. E-mail: chuchini70@hotmail.com

Rurrenabaque, Madidi National Park Gateway
updated by Anna-Stina Lindahl

Rurrenabaque Phone Code: 3

One of the Beni's best-known treasures is this small farming, cattle-raising and fishing town on the shores of the River Beni at 230 meters (about 755 feet) above sea level. In recent years it has become one of the country's main tourism destination, especially for backpackers from Israel and Europe. It is bordered to the south by mountains that are part of the Andes Mountain chain, to the west by the Beni River that originates in the area around La Paz and to the north by the Beni grasslands. The wide Beni River is great for swimming, boating and fishing. At dawn you can buy freshly-caught *surubí* and *pacú* fish on the shores of the river. Be sure to rent a dugout canoe and travel upriver to a sandy beach. You can make a great fish barbecue accompanied by yucca and rice and swim in the river. Rurrenabaque has also become the entry point to the Madidi National Park that became world renown after it was featured on the cover of National Geographic. Visitors can either fly into the town or take a four-wheel drive vehicle, bus or truck from La Paz. The area's tourism boom has led to the opening of many restaurants, lodges and hotels. There is also a public swimming pool on Calle Santa Cruz between Bolivar and Busch that is very popular among visitors and offers a great relief from the humidity.

Madidi National Park, office and information, Av. Busch, Tel. 8922540. E-mail: info@madidi.com   www.madidi.com www.expedicionmadidi.com

Reserva de la Bioesfera y Territorio Indígena Pilon Lajas, Tel. 8922246, Fax. 8922445.

• How to Get There

TAM and **Amaszonas** in La Paz services Rurrenabaque. In the April to November dry season, the airport consists of a field just outside the town. Hence the flight cancellations when it is raining. It is possible to take a motorcycle taxi there for a couple of Bs. But it is then necessary to carry all your luggage on your back. For Bs. 5 there is a bus from the airline offices in the center of town, where you need to check in anyway. Sometimes planes will land in the neighboring town of Reyes, from which there is a bus service, although the buses are few and far between. Though it is possible for lone travelers to catch a ride with tour groups it is better to sort out transport before arriving.

Rurrenabaque can also be reached via a four-wheel-drive vehicle or public transportation. The road to Rurrenabaque runs past Coroico and Caranavi in the Yungas. At Caranavi follow the signs to Alto Beni until you reach Palos Blancos. There ask for directions to Rurrenabaque. The road splits towards the north and Rurrenabaque and to the east to the town of San Borja, an important cattle town in the Beni.

Amaszonas, Calle Santa Cruz. Tel./Fax. 8922472, Cel. 71149931.

TAM, Calle Santa Cruz. Tel. 8922398.

• Hotels

Plaza Tours, at the Hotel Plaza in La Paz, Tel. 2378322, offers weekend tours to Rurrenabaque and to the modern **Tacuara Inn** located near the shore of the Beni River.

Hotel Oriental, has a lovely garden with hammocks, There are a range of rooms with or without private bath from Bs. 10 to Bs. 30.

Hotel Carambola, offers private bathrooms and refreshing drinks made from the carambola fruit.

Hostal Berlín, offers economical lodging and also serves the catch of the day, Calle Comercio, Tels. 8922450, 8929999.

Hotel Las Garsas, Calle Eduardo Avaroa.

Hotel Rurrenabaque, Calle Vaca Diez, Tel. 8922481.

Hotel Safari, Calle Comercio Final, Tel/Fax. 8922410.

Hotel Santa Ana, Av. Avaroa, Tel. 8922399.

Hotel Tuichi, Calle Avaroa, Tel/Fax. 8922372.

Hotel Beni, Calle Comercio, Tel. 8922408, Fax. 8922407.

Jatauba Lodge in San Buenaventura, Tel. in La Paz, 2115283. www.jataubalodge.com

Jatatal Hotel, Av. Costanera 11, San Buenaventura. Tel. 38922054. Reservations Tel. 2414753, 71586818. E-mail: operations@boliviamilenaria.com www.boliviamilenaria.com

• Restaurants

For a nice but inexpensive dinner **La Perla de Rurre** on Calle Vaca Diez corner with Bolivar. It has excellent fish dishes and the house special is a must. For a light lunch, the **Taxuara restaurant** on Calle Santa Cruz makes wonderful sandwiches and fish dishes. Just opposite **Camila's** has a great ice cream bar as well as luxurious breakfast. **Café Motaco** on Calle Santa Cruz between Comercio and Abaroa is a cozy little café that offers some refreshments as well as handicrafts and a book exchange.

Rurrenabaque doesn't have much to offer in terms of a night life, but there is the **Moskkito bar** which offers expensive drinks to a mostly gringo crowd, happy hours between 19:00 and 21:00, when prices are half. Right next to it on Calle Comercio is the **Pizzeria Italia** with pool tables and is open late.

• Travel agencies

There are several travel agencies offering pampas tours and it is easy enough to find a group once you are there, it is also cheaper to book in Rurrenabaque.

Bala tours, Calle Santa Cruz,

BENI DEPT.

Tel/Fax. 8922527. www.mirurrenabaque.com
E-mail: reserva@balatours.com

Chalalan, Eco-Lodge, Calle Comercio Rurrenabaque. Tel. 8922419, Fax. 8922309. Offers a luxurious haven up in the Beni and once there at the Chalalan Lake experienced guides lead hikes into the jungle to look for animals.
E-mail: chalalan-eco@yahoo.com
In La Paz contact: Conservación Internacional, Calle Pinilla 291, Sopocachi.
E-mail: ci-bolivia@conseravtion.org

Ecological Trips, Tels. 8922571, 8922337, Rurrenabaque.
E-mail: donatours@hotmail.com

Flecha Tours, Calle Avaroa. Tels. 71143529, 71545450. In La Paz, Calle Illampu 747. Tel. 2461771.
E-mail: flechatours@hotmail.com

Fluvial Tours, Tel. 8922372.

Piraña Tours, Tel. 8922122.

Agencies in La Paz

Tawa, Tels. 2334290, 2350530.
E-mail: verney@ceibo.entelnet.bo

America Tours, Tel. 2374204.
E-mail: jmiranda@ceibo.entelnet.bo
www.america-ecotours.com

Bolivian Journeys, Tel. 2357848.
E-mail: boljour@ceibo.entelnet.bo
www.bolivianjourneys.org
If you are looking for a Guide **AndesMesili**, Tels. 71582376, 77500068.
E-mail: amesili@hotmail.com
www.andesmesili.com

• Shopping

Rurrenabaque does have a market in the center of town, but it consists largely of old clothes and other out of date materials. It is possible to find most things necessary to venture into the jungle, but other than practical matters, the market has little to offer. The only items that are of any consequence to buy there are hammocks, for which Rurrenabaque is also known for.

• Laundries

On Calle Vaca Diez there are several laundry places that offer one day services for weary travelers.

Isiboro-Secure National Park

This 1.2 million hectares national park is shared by the departments of Beni and Cochabamba. It includes heavily forested mountains, rivers, mountain streams and savannas. It is home to 714 species of wildlife, including 600 different birds, and a huge diversity of flora (3,000 species of larger plants), including an extraordinary abundance of flowers. The park is crossed and bordered by several rivers that are part of the Amazon River Basin. The park is also the northern frontier of Bolivian and within the area of the US government efforts to eradicate illegal coca leaf. Over the last decade thousands of highland Quechua farmers have migrated to the park area to cultivate coca. Some have begun leaving the area or are planting alternative crops. The presence of the colonizers has created conflicts with the traditional indigenous residents of the park who have eschewed coca leaf cultivation. The Moxeno Indian community of Espiritu Santos is located on the southern part of the park and can be reached by road from Villa Tunari. The Yuracare and T'simane indigenous communities also inhabit the park. The Moxenos are culturally and politically linked to the Beni and the area around its capital, Trinidad that can be reached after a weeklong river trip to the north. The Moxenos were part of the Jesuit Missions that were administered in the areas between the 17th and 18th centuries. The Missions established religious, handicraft and musical centers that continue to the present. Community members produce handicrafts, wooden masks, feather headdresses and colorful outfits.

Parque Nacional Territorio Indigena Isiboro Secure, Calle Julio Céspedes 139, Trinidad. Tel. 4620087, Fax. 4652166.
In Cochabamba, Tel. 4421056.

CIRCUNVALACION

Regimiento Ballivian

Roca

Simón Bolívar
Rafael Arteaga
Heroínas Caridad
Martiniano Fuentes
Rómulo Mendoza

Velasco Ávila
Julio Pinto
Viador Pinto
Beni
Vaca Diez
Itenez
Rómulo

Bus Station **12**

Davila
Antelo Aponte
Carranza

Reni Ibañez

Cortez Candia
Aponte

Ortiz Chavez
Claura

Velasco

Lopez

Moxos
1° de Mayo
Ibarre

9 de Abril **2**

11

Cochabamba

Barace
Carvalho
Luisa Viera
Coimbra
Sattori
N.Suarez
Pinto
Av. del Mar
Sucre
Limpias
Pza. Ballivian
Busch
La Paz
Mamore

5
9
3 **6** **1**
14 † **13**

18 de Noviembre
4
10
8
7
Sta. Cruz

Av. Circunvalación

Villavicencio
Meliton

Tarija

Av. 6 de Agosto

Av. del Ejercito

Pando
15

Av. 2 de Mayo

Airport

BENI DEPT.

TRINIDAD

1 Tourist office
2 Police
3 Immigration
4 Entel

5 Post office
6 City Hall
7 LAB
8 TAM
9 Aerosur
10 Amaszonas

MARKETS
11 Pompeya
12 Fatima
13 Municipal

MUSEUM & CHURCH
14 Cathedral
15 Casa de la Cultura

RURRENABAQUE

1 City Hall	6 TAM
2 Entel	7 Market
3 Post office	8 Campesino market
4 City Hall	9 Ferry to San Buenaventura
5 Amaszonas	10 Police 11 Immigration

AROUND TRINIDAD

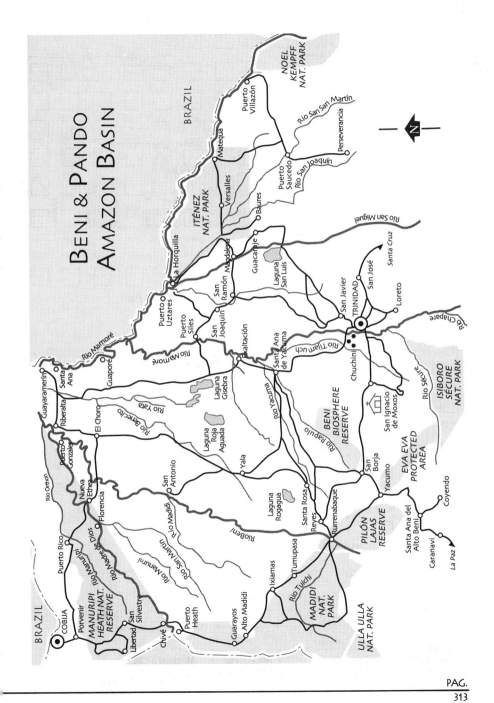

Beni & Pando
Amazon Basin

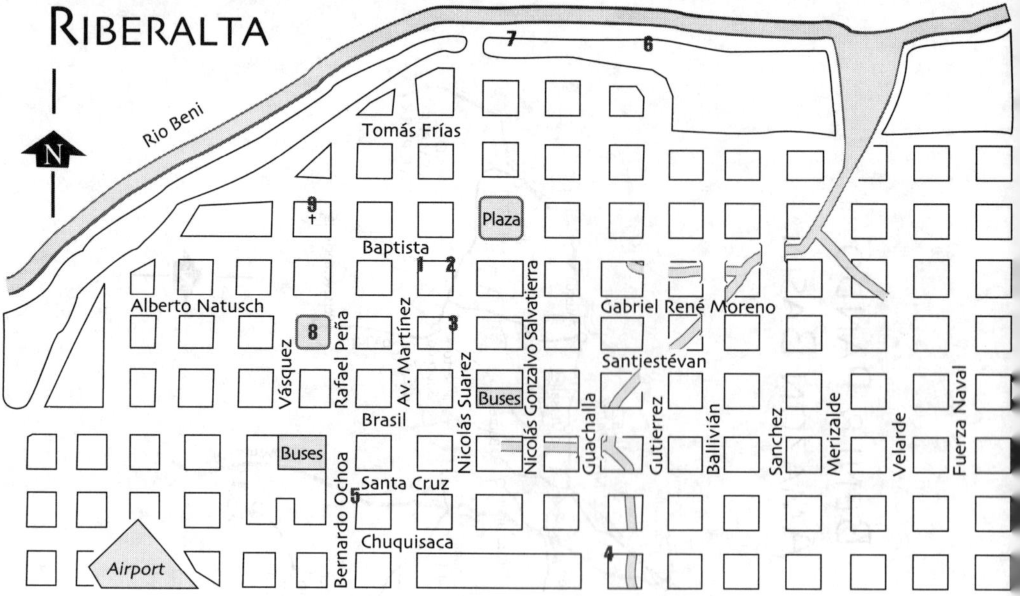

RIBERALTA

N

Rio Beni

Tomás Frías

Plaza

†

Baptista

Alberto Natusch

Vásquez

Rafael Peña

Av. Martínez

Nicolás Suarez

Buses

Nicolás Gonzalvo Salvatierra

Gabriel René Moreno

Santiestévan

Guachalla

Gutierrez

Ballivián

Sanchez

Merizalde

Velarde

Fuerza Naval

Brasil

Buses

Bernardo Ochoa

Santa Cruz

Chuquisaca

Airport

1 Entel	4 TAM	7 La Costañera Park
2 Post office	5 Amazonas	8 Market
3 LAB	6 Port	9 Church

GUAYARAMERÍN

11

N

Rio Mamoré

BRAZIL

Oruro

Plaza

Federico Roman

Beni

16 de Julio

Santa Cruz

Plaza

10 †

6 de Agosto

Mamoré

Costanera

Airport

1 Tourist Information	4 Post office	7 Amaszonas	*MUSEUM & CHURCH*
2 Immigration	5 LAB	8 Ferry to Brazil	10 Cathedral
3 Police	6 TAM	9 Port	11 Casa de la Cultura

BENI DEPT.

PRE-COLUMBIAN ROADS OF THE AMAZON

BY CLARK L. ERICKSON

Traditionally, archaeologists have studied "sites." Sites include monuments, settlements, cities, cemeteries, mounds, and other important places of the past. The cultural landscape of paths, roads, field walls, irrigation canals, terraces, and other features that fill the spaces between sites is often ignored. A relatively new subfield of anthropology, the archaeology of landscapes, treats the landscape as an artifact that can provide new, detailed insights about the everyday lives of peoples of the past. I will focus here on formal roads as an important element of the pre-Columbian landscape of the Bolivian Amazon.

All civilizations, past and present, require an efficient means of transportation and communication. Societies need to move goods, people, and information throughout the regions they control. Roads also have powerful social, political, and sacred functions. Formal roads are major transformations of the environment. Their patterns on the landscape provide information about the organization of settlements, social interaction, land tenure, ritual, standards of measurement, and the activities of everyday life (Trombold 1990).

The Aztecs, Maya, and Inka constructed impressive roads that linked the vast regions under their influence. Less known but equally impressive are the pre-Columbian roads in the tropical region of Bolivia, South America (Denevan1990). I

have been investigating the pre-columbian earthworks of the Bolivian Amazon since 1990 (Erickson 1995). The research team includes Wilma Winkler, a Bolivian archaeologist who is co-director of the project, and students from the University of Pennsylvania and the National University of Bolivia. In 1995, we were invited by the local government to begin a multi-year study of the archaeology of the Baures region. Baures is located along the upper headwaters of the Amazon drainage basin near the Brazilian border in northeast Bolivia (Fig. 1). The area can be reached by boat along a circuitous river route, by horseback, or by small aircraft. The complex landscape of gallery forests, crystal clear lakes, rivers, swamps, forest islands, and vast savanna is a spectacular sight from the air. During the rainy season, much of the flat savanna grassland is covered with shallow floodwater. As the rains end at the beginning of the dry season, the floods recede and the savanna slowly dries out. At this time, controlled fires rage across the savanna as ranchers and hunters burn the old grass to encourage growth of new grass for their cattle and game. Based on archaeological and historical documentation, I believe that this annual burning is an age-old practice that is necessary to maintain the open savanna. Gallery forests are found along the courses of rivers and streams, and forest islands are located on high ground surrounded by savanna. The native people

BENI DEPT.

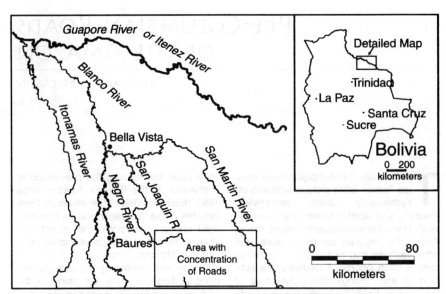

Fig. 1. Location map showing the area with concentration of roads and Baures, Bolivia.

practice slash-and-burn agriculture in the gallery forests and forest islands to raise maize, manioc, sweet potatoes, rice, and cacao for making chocolate, and wealthy ranchers raise cattle on the open savannas.

Early Spanish documents provide valuable information about the Baure, the native peoples of the region. The Jesuits wrote detailed eyewitness accounts about all aspects of Baure life in the early 1700s (Eder [1772] 1985). The Jesuits described them as "civilized peoples" who were "clean and tractable" in their fine cotton tunics (Fig. 2). Their chiefs had great powers to make war, mobilize soldiers, keep public order, and organize farming. Anthropologists of the 1950s considered the hereditary political organization of the Baure a classic example of "chiefdom." Their towns had large public plazas with a large men's house or temple in the center. Around the plaza were hundreds of houses arranged along streets and wide avenues. Deep defensive moats and tall palisade walls surrounded many settlements. In 1703, the Baure gave the Jesuits their first Bolivian martyr, Padre Cipriano Barace, who was killed for insulting a powerful Baure chief. In retaliation, the Spanish sent an army to punish them. In 1708, the remaining conquered Baure were gathered in new mission towns for indoctrination in Christianity and European culture. Crowded into mission towns, the Baure were nearly wiped out by European diseases to which they had little resistance. The population of the region today is probably smaller than in the past.

Reading the Landscape

While exploring for oil in the late IqsOs, a North American expatriate named Kenneth Lee discovered and reported the pre-Columbian roads and canals of the Baures region. Until he passed away in 1999, Lee was a determined promoter and interpreter of the archaeology, history, and culture of the region. To show off \ the huge network of pre-Columbian roads, Lee would fly visiting journalists and scholars over the region in a small plane. As a result, the national and international press rediscovered the "Lost Civilization of Baures" in regular ten-year cycles. Despite this sporadic attention, we were the first archaeologists to do a serious study of the region. The governor of the Department of the Beni loaned us his Cessna airplane for three hours of flight time. Like the previous visitors who flew over the region, we were immediately captivated by the extent, patterning, and size of the roads and other earthworks.

These pre-Columbian roads are raised causeways of earth. Abandoned roads are easily identified from the air as dark straight lines covered by small trees against the lighter-colored grasses of the savanna. The larger roads of Baures can even be seen from satellites orbiting 470 miles above earth. Most of the roads are perfectly straight for several miles and paired parallel roads are common (Fig. 3). Important questions immediately come to mind: (1) Who built these roads and when? (2) Why were they built? (3) What did they connect?, and (4) Why are there so many roads?

In 1995, my team and I landed on a tiny dirt airstrip in the town of Baures to begin an archaeological investigation to answer these questions. There are no modern towns or settlements in the area of the densest concentration of roads. The only people using the area are hunters who come each year in canoes to hunt the deer, peccaries, and tapirs that thrive in the savannas, wetlands, and forests. I hired three of the best hunters as my guides in 1996. We used mule, horse, canoe, and what the locals call the buey caballo-an ox saddled for a rider-for the three-day journey into the area. Most of the trip was on foot sloshing through the wet savanna.

Although abandoned and badly eroded, the roads are still prominent on the land-

Fig. 2. Drawings of native peoples of Baures from a 1772 Jesuit account. From Eder [1772] 1985: Figs. 6,8, 9, 10, and 11

Fig. 3. Aerial photograph of two palm-covered parallel roads crossing the savanna between two for-est islands in Baures. A smaller road can also be seen (center). Each road is approximately I mile long. Photo by Clark L. Erickson

scape. On the ground, we could see that the roads were constructed of earth removed from canals on one or both sides of the platform (Fig. 4). Raised road platforms IO to 15 feet wide and 2 to 3 feet high provided a dry walking surface. We assume that the roads were kept clear of vegetation, although shade trees may have lined the wider roads. Roads range in size and complexity from simple to truly monumental. Some raised roads in the savannas 100 miles southwest of Baures are 40 to 60 feet wide. In Baures, we have mapped several roads that are over 3 miles long. Most of the roads are straight from start to finish; thus, we assume that roads were carefully planned before construction. The impressive number of roads, their wide geographical distribution, and the effort put into their design and construction suggests that roads were important to the people who built them.

During eight field seasons in the Bolivian Amazon, our archaeological team perfected a strategy for recording and studying roads. They are mapped from the air with aerial photographs and satellite imagery and on the ground using surveying instruments. Long narrow trenches excavated through road platforms and canals provide clues about time of construction and abandonment, building technique, volume of earth moved, and function (see cover). In excavation trenches throughout the Bolivian Amazon, we recovered charcoal that could be radiocarbon dated, documenting that roads were built and used between 2000 and 400 years ago. A date from a causeway excavation in Baures showed that it was built before AD 1630. In the early 18th century, the Jesuits reported that old roads were still in use but not maintained. A T-mile pre-Columbian road was

BENI DEPT.

used between Baures and Guacaraje until the 1930s.

Multi-Functional earthworks

Roads served many overlapping functions. The tens of thousands of linear miles of roads provided a vast transportation network for foot traffic. The canals alongside them were probably just as important. These canals hold water much of the year; thus, heavy loaded dugout canoes could be poled, paddled, or pulled across the savannas. My workers continually complained about having to walk across the hot savanna carrying our heavy gear. They told me to return in the rainy season when they could pole a dugout canoe anywhere in the savanna. The native peoples of this region were a classic example of the "canoe cultures" of the Amazon. Using raised roads for pedestrians and canals for canoe traffic, the Baure had an efficient and sophisticated means of connecting settlements to navigable rivers, agricultural fields, and neighbors.

In other parts of the Bolivian Amazon, raised roads functioned as dikes for controlling flood-waters within raised fields. (In Expedition 30 [3] 1988, I described a similar raised field farming technique found in the Andes.) In Baures, the roads may have regulated floodwaters, extending the period when canoes could be used in the savannas (Fig. 5). They may also have maintained optimal water levels for the fish weirs built to control and trap fish migrating across the flooded savannas of Baures (Erickson 2000). Further, roads and canals may have been markers to define ownership of farmland and natural resources within and between communities.

In addition to transportation and water management, roads and canals probably had important political functions. Interactions between Amazonian communities are characterized in the historical and ethnographic literature as a complex and dynamic balance between alliance and warfare. Highly visible earthworks may have been used to establish and cement political alliances with neighboring communities. Most roads connect pre-Columbian settlements located on forest islands within the savannas and gallery forests on rivers. We can safely assume that

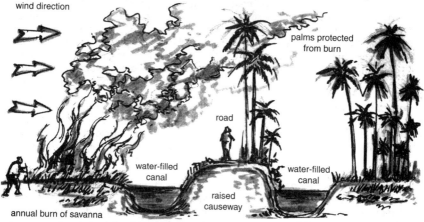

wind direction

palms protected from burn

road

water-filled canal

water-filled canal

raised causeway

annual burn of savanna

Fig. 4. Cross-section of a road platform and adjacent canals. Over time, the water-filled canals protect the palms that colonize the abandoned roads from the annual burning of the savanna. (Drawing by Dan Brinkmeier, Field Museum, Chicago).

BENI DEPT.

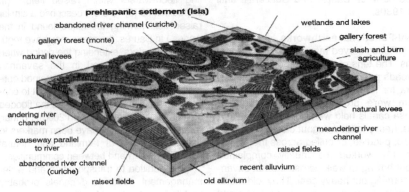

Prehispanic Hydraulic Systems in the Llanos de Moxos

prehispanic settlement (isla)

abandoned river channel (curiche)

gallery forest (monte)

natural levees

andering river channel

causeway parallel to river

abandoned river channel (curiche)

raised fields

old alluvium

recent alluvium

raised fields

meandering river channel

natural levees

slash and burn agriculture

gallery forest

wetlands and lakes

Fig. 5. An idealized landscape of roads, canals, raised fields, and settlements in the Bolivian Amazon. In addition to transportation, roads may have functioned as dikes to control water levels within raised fields and fish weirs in the rainy season.

settlements physically connected by artificial roads and canals were part of a larger political universe. We located several concentrations of roads associated with large settlements on forest islands. Between IO-SO roads and canoe paths converge on or radiate from each large island (Fig. 6). These roads can be followed to archaeological sites on smaller forest islands distributed over the landscape. Each of these interconnected concentrations of roads may represent an independent political, social, or ethnic group.

Symbols of Civic Pride or Ritual Raceways?

But why did the Baure build so many fine roads? My colleagues joke that every individual must have had his or her own road. The Baure had no draft animals or wheeled vehicles, thus they had little need for wide straight roads. Landscape archaeologists refer to roads that are much larger, straighter, or more numerous than what would have been necessary for basic transportation as "overconstructed," "overengi-neered," and "landscape oblivious." However, I believe these roads were conspicuous symbols of a community's political power, civic pride, and ability to mobilize labor. Rather than construct permanent public buildings, shrines, cities, or temples in stone, the pre-Columbian peoples of the Bolivian Amazon expressed monumentality in the form of prominent earthworks on the vast flat landscape. Guests attending feasts, pilgrimages, dances, and other events must have been suitably awed when approaching neighboring villages and towns on the wide avenues bordered by deep water-filled canals (Fig. 7). Competition between communities for the largest, widest, longest, straightest, and most impressive roads may help account for the emphasis on these earthworks. The social use of roads is specifically mentioned in the 1772 Jesuit account. Father Eder complained that the native peoples used roads for social visits with friends in neighboring villages, the sole purpose of which was to get drunk on the local beer brewed from maize and manioc!

In addition, the earthworks may have had specific sacred functions. As noted earlier, the roads are extraordinarily straight over long distances. As many as six canals and roads may run parallel to each other-a costly mismanagement of labor if the roads were constructed simply to get from Point A to Point B. Of course, we could argue that the roads were one-way streets, thus two were necessary for a round trip. Could the concern with precision and straightness be related to ritual processions, ceremonial races, or pilgrimage routes.? Could the roads be sacred or astronomical alignments? Some straight roads in Baures bypass forest islands and have no apparent destination. The similarity between the roads of Baures and the famous Nasca Lines etched on the coastal deserts of Peru comes to mind. Scholars have demonstrated that some Nasca Lines were used for ritual processions and determining astronomical events, and as indicators of sources of water and markers of social groups (Aveni 2000). We have begun to map and measure the orientations of the roads of the Bolivian Amazon to test the hypothesis that roads were constructed according to astronomical alignments or as a giant landscape calendar.

Roads may have converged on political centers or sacred sites. Early Spanish explorers reported entering towns on large formal roads. The larger towns of Baures had hundreds of houses organized around a large open plaza with public buildings and temples in the center. The indigenous peoples of central Brazil still live in similar, although much smaller, villages. Clean, wide straight roads cut through the forest and converge at the men's house in the center of the plaza. During important ceremonies, young men carrying heavy logs race each other along these ritual roads. Many important roads are deeply furrowed by years of use for ritual processions and racing.

How Were the Roads Built?

How difficult are roads to construct? The roads of the Bolivian Amazon are major, formally designed features of the built environment. Archaeologists often attribute the construction and use of formal roads to centralized state governments (Trombold 1990). This conclusion is based on the assumption that the labor organization and engineering for constructing roads were beyond the abilities of small-scale societies. The total labor involved in pre-Columbian earthmoving in the Bolivian Amazon is staggering, but our archaeological research shows that the work was spread out over many generations and could have been accomplished by small groups.

Although roads are often long and straight, the engineering and design of these earthworks are not complicated. The roads were built using simple tools of hardwood such as digging sticks, paddle-like shovels, and baskets documented in the historical literature. Similar tools are still used today for digging and moving earth, although the blades are now of metal. Our earlier experi-

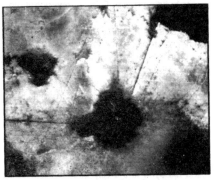

Fig. 6. Aerial photograph of a concentration of roads and canals crossing the savanna in Baures, Bolivia. The largest of several hundred roads are visible in the photograph as dark straight lines. Most of the roads radiate from San Martin Forest Island (dark area in center).

BENI DEPT.

Fig. 7. A landscape of roads and canals in the Bolivian Amazon. The raised road plataform was used by pedestrians, and the canals for dugout canoe traffic.
Drawing by Dan Brinkmeier, Field Museum, Chicago

ments building raised fields showed that digging canals and constructing platforms is relatively easy if done at the time when soils are neither too wet or too dry.

These issues of engineering and organization of labor became clear one day while doing fieldwork near a native village in Baures. I came across a "new" road 12 feet wide, 3 feet high, and over a half mile long. When I asked a local resident walking about it with me, he explained that he and a small group of neighbors built it in a week. I asked, "How did they make the road so straight ?" He rolled his eyes at the silly question and said, "We simply sighted along three wooden poles to lay out a direct route between the settlements. Anyone can do it." This modern example of the design and construction of roads by a community using hand tools demonstrates that many small groups working a few weeks a year could have easily constructed the entire road system given enough time.

I believe that roads and other earthworks were the Amazonian version of monumental, highly visible public construction. The monumentality of this engineered landscape at a regional scale rivals the works of better-known civilizations. Although most are abandoned, eroded, and neglected, the old roads, canals, and other earthworks continue to play a major role in shaping the landscape of the Bolivian Amazon. Pre-Columbian roads structure patterns of vegetation, soil fertility, water availability, and wild resources. Through their transformation of nature on a massive regional scale, the pre-Columbian inhabitants of the Bolivian Amazon left an indelible mark on the landscape.

Acknowledgments

The author thanks Wilma Winkler (co-investigator of the project), Kenneth Lee, Ricardo Bottega, Anita and Edwin Bruckner, Conrad Bruckner, Hans Schlink, Oswaldo) Rivera, and local government authorities who made this research possible. Wilma Winkler, Dr. Alexei Vranich, Dr. John Walker, Dr. Kay Candler, and Dante Angelo made up the archaeological team. Dr. Alexei Vranich, Freddy Bruckner, and Oscar Saavedra did the first archaeological research of the Baures roads in 1995. Grants from NSF, the Heinz Charitable Trust Foundation, the American Philosophical Society, Research Funds of the University of Pennsylvania Museum, and CORDEBENI supported field-work and analysis.

Bibliography

Aveni, Anthony F. 2000. *Between the Lines : The Mystey of the Giant Ground Drawings of Ancient Nasca*, Peru. Austin: University of Texas Press.

Denevan, William M. 1990. *"Prehistoric Roads and Causeways in Lowland Tropical America."* In Ancient Road Networks and Settlement Hierarchies in the New World, ed. Charles Trombold, pp. 230-42. Cambridge: Cambridge University Press.

Eder, Francisco Javier [1772] 1985. *Breve Descripción de las Reducciones de Mojos.* Cochabamba: Historia Boliviana.

Erickson, Clark L. 1988. *"Raised Field Agriculture in the Lake Titicaca Basin: Putting Ancient Andean Agriculture Back to Work."* Expedition 30 (3) : 8-16.

1995. *"Archaeological Perspectives on Ancient Landscapes of the Llanos de Mojos in the Bolivian Amazon."* In Archaeology in the American Tropics: Current Analitical Methods and Applications, ed. Peter Stahl, pp. 66-95. Cambridge: Cambridge University Press.

2000. *"An Artificial Landscape-Scale Fishery in the Bolivian Amazon."* Nature. 408:190—93.

Trombold, Charles, ed. 1990. *Ancient Road Networks and Settlement Hierarchies in the New World.* Cambridge. Cambridge University Press.

Clark L. Erickson is Associate Professor of Anthropology and Associate Curator of South American Archaeology in the American Section. He has over 25 years of archaeological fieldwork experience in Latin America. His research focuses on the pre-Columbian cultural or anthropogenic landscapes of the Amazon and Andes. Using landscape features as artifacts, Erickson is reconstructing social organiza-tion, land tenure, technology, and lifeways of past peoples. Information about past use of landscapes may provide models for contem-porary sustainable development. His team is helping the Bolivian government develop a plan for the conservation, management, and use of the landscapes of Baures.

Visit these websites for more information on the Archaeology of the Bolivian Amazon: Applied Archaeology in the Bolivian Amazon www.sas.upenn.edu/~cerickso/applied.html

We generously acknowledge EXPEDITION 43/2 magazine for granting rigths to repro - duce this article.

PRE-COLUMBIAN FISH FARMING OF THE AMAZON

BY CLARK L. ERICKSON

Popular images associated with the Amazon today include the towering continuous green forest canopy, Day-Glo poison dart frogs, and natives' faces painted red. These potent images have been used to raise funds for conservation, educate the public in "green" politics, and promote ecotourism. Two themes have long dominated the popular and scientific literature on the Amazon: 1) the Myth of the Pristine Environment and 2) the Myth of the Noble Savage. The Myth of the Pristine Environment is the belief that the landscapes of the Americas were largely undisturbed Nature until the arrival of Europeans, who have destroyed the environment with their agriculture, mining, urbanism, and industry. The Myth of the Noble Savage posits that indigenous peoples of the past and present exist as a harmonious part of an undisturbed Nature. We now know that much of what has been traditionally recognized as Wilderness in the Amazon is the indirect result of massive depopulation after the arrival of Europeans. The introduction of Old World diseases, slavery, missionization, resettlement, and warfare removed most of the native peoples from the land within 100 years. Many areas of Amazonia were not repopulated until this century and many still remain underpopulated.

My colleagues and I are documenting numerous cases of how native peoples of the Amazon (past and present) transformed,

shaped, and in come cases, constructed what is often misidentified as pristine "wilderness." We find that high biodiversity is clearly related to past human activities such as gap formation, burning, and gardening. Our approach, called historical ecology or the archaeology of landscapes, assumes that all landscapes have long complex histories. We find that high biodiversity is clearly related to past human activities such as opening up the forest, burning, and gardening. Since 1990, my research team has studied the vast networks of earthworks in the Bolivian Amazon built before the arrival of Europeans. These features include causeways of earth, artificial canals for canoe traffic, raised fields for growing crops in the savannas, and settlement mounds of urban scale.

In 1995, we were invited by the local governor to begin archaeological investigations in Baures, a remote region of seasonally flooded savannas, wetlands and forest islands in northeast Bolivia. He loaned us his Cessna and pilot for an initial aerial survey of the region. As the plane circled the landscape, we saw an amazing complex web of straight roads, canals, and moated earthwork enclosures below. During the dry season of 1996, I surveyed the area accompanied by a group of local hunters (Fig. 1).

One artificial feature, referred to as a zigzag earthwork, particularly intrigued me. Low earthen walls zigzag across the savan-

Fig. 1. Pre-Columbian fish weirs and ponds in the savannas of Baures, Bolivia. (painting by Dan Brinkmeier, Field Museum of Natural History).

nas between forest islands. Because of their changing orientations, they did not make sense as roads between settlements. As we mapped them with tape measure and compass, I noted that there were small funnel like opening where the earthworks changed direction. I immediately realized that these matched the description of fish weirs that are reported in the ethnographic and historical literature on Amazonian peoples. Fish weirs are fences made of wood, brush, basketry, or stones with small openings that extend across bodies of water. Baskets or nets are placed in the openings to trap migrating fish. While most fish weirs are simple ephemeral structures crossing a river or shallow lake, those of Baures are permanent earthen features covering more than 500 square kilometers. In addition, small artificial ponds are associated with the fish weirs (Fig. 2). Today these ponds are filled with fish as the floodwaters recede in the dry season. I believe that in the past these were used to store live fish until needed. Our studies show that the weirs were used before the arrival of Europeans to the region.

The scale of the fish weir complex is larger than any previously reported. The native peoples of Baures shaped the environment into a productive landscape capable of providing sufficient protein to sustain large populations. The people responsible for this impressive land management are long gone or have forgotten the technology. Archaeology provides the only means of documenting this important lost knowledge. As politicians, conservationists, and aid agencies seek sustainable solutions to both develop and conserve the Amazon, archaeologists can play a key role by providing time-tested models of land use.

Bibliography

2000. *"An Artificial Landscape-Scale Fishery In the Bolivian Amazon."* Nature. 408: 190-193.

200. *"The lake Titicaca Basin: A pre-Columbian Built Landscape."* In Imperfect Balance: Landscape Transformations in the Precolumbian Americas. Ed. David Lentz, Columbia University Press, New York, pp. 311-356.

For more information visit the websites Pre-Columbian Fish Weirs in the Bolivian Amazon: http://ccat.sas.uppen.edu/fishweir

We generously acknowledge EXPEDITION 43 (3): 7-8 (2001) magazine for granting rigths to reproduce this article.

Fig. 2. Remains of fish weir (lower to upper right) and fish ponds (circular features surrounded by palms) from the air.

CHALALAN:
A GRASSROOTS ECOTOURISM PROJECT

BY SYLVIA JOHNSON

In today's modern world of high-speed technology and rapid economic development, the terms "sustainable development" and "ecotourism" have become catch phrases. Have they lost meaning or do they still represent a feasible idea? When taken out of the context of written rhetoric and catchy tourism slogans and into the field, it turns out that preserving biodiversity is very closely tied to human sustainability.

During the month of October, I had the incredible opportunity to raft the Tuichi River in Madidi National Park and spend several days at Chalalan Ecolodge. Among the members of our group were two of the visionaries and founders of Chalalan, two of their naturalist guides, and a Madidi Park Ranger. It was an opportunity not only to journey through one of the most spectacular and untouched wild places on earth, but also to understand the source of a grassroots project that provides a way for a native Quechua-Tacana community to survive in this modern world while also protecting the environment that is their home.

Madidi National Park, located in the north eastern corner of Bolivia, spans numerous different ecosystems, from the heights of the Andes to lush lowland jungle. It is easily the most biodiverse park in Bolivia and one of the most biodiverse places on the planet. A thirty minute walk up into the jungle from the banks of the Tuichi River lies the village of San José de Uchupiamonas with some 500 inhabitants. The Quechua-Tacana's have lived in the region for over 300 years, subsisting first from traditional hunting, later from logging mahogany and panning for gold, then from agriculture, and, as modernization and development encroach on this forest community, they have turned to ecotourism in what is one of the most successful stories of its kind.

On one of our last days on the Tuichi, Zenon Limaco (one of the visionaries behind the ecotourism project), rowed the big oar boat rhythmically as he told me the story of Chalalan. In the community of San Jose of the early 90's, there was little economic income, and education didn't extend beyond primary school, which was forcing many of the community's youth to move to the frontier town of Rurrenabaque and beyond in search of employment. Problems with infant diarrhea and leishmaniasis (a disease transmitted by the bite of an Amazonian sand fly which can lead to death from gangrene if not treated) were widespread. In 1995, after receiving little response to their request for help from the Bolivian government, several of the community leaders sought out their Israeli friend, Yossi Ghinsberg, who they had saved from almost certain death in a disastrous venture down the Tuichi in 1982. They asked him to help them find support for an ecotourism project. Conservation International (CI), a prominent US based environmental NGO, was intrigued by an indigenous community initiating an ecotourism project in one of the world's "hotspots", as such biodiverse areas are often called by scientists. What evolved over the next six years is a unique and highly successful ecotourism project. Chalalan is a joint project between the community of San José, Conservation International, and the Inter American Development Bank (CI provided the development model, technical assistance, and funds, and the IDB contributed 1.5 million dollars originating from the Multilateral Investment Fund). Chalalan was just officially handed over in its entirety to the community of San José although it has been operating 80% autonomously for two years now.

The story that had come to me in bits and pieces during the course of our adventure down the Tuichi, solidified itself during the four days that we spent at Chalalan. Walking through the forest chatting easily with Ovidio Valdez as he pointed out wild boar trails, explained the various uses of different palm trees, and called back and forth to birds in the forest canopy, it was hard to imagine that this bright, incredibly helpful young guy who was so in tune with his forest surroundings had worked along with many of the other Josesanos as a mahogany logger several years earlier. Watching Alejandro Alvarez, a striking young Quechua-Tacana, lead a jungle tour in clear text-book English and recite the scientific names for the scarlet macaws, harpy eagles, hoatzins, and howler, spider, squirrel, and capuchin monkeys that he pointed out, I admired his passion and wondered at how this project had changed his life. Where before he probably would have been a mahogany logger, risking his life and raping the forest to make a living, he now converses comfortably in another language and dreams of going on to get a degree in

ornithology. It was during a formal interview we were doing for the camera, however, that I realized the full impact that this project has had on the community of San Jose, how it has transformed the way that they think about their environment and themselves. Alejandro Limaco´s contagious smile broke into an eloquent flow of thought as he spoke with pride about how Chalalan has given them recognition and a means of sustenance, but also of the struggles that still lie ahead.

This past year, the gross income for Chalalan was $30,000, not too shabby for a small forest community. Its profit is to be divided equally between maintaining the lodge, and building community infrastructure for the 70 plus San Jose families who own it. The year to come will be a real testing ground to see if the lodge is completely self-sufficient and there are still battles to fight. The people of San Jose do not yet hold the deed to the land on which Chalalan has been built, women need to be trained as guides so that they can be involved at a higher level, and the environment has to be monitored to see what long term effects the tourism will have.

Bordered by two Peruvian national parks, Ulla Ulla National Park in the high country, and Pilón Lajas Biosphere in the lowlands, Madidi forms part of one of the largest protected biological corridors in the world. However, these areas still face threats and the nearly 2 million hectare Madidi National Park has only 20 park rangers to protect the entire area. Sixto, our park ranger friend, gets paid approximately $110 a month with only a $10 bonus for any extras, and park resources are scarce.

Back at the Conservation International office in La Paz, the director, Juan Pablo Arce, referred to the Josesanos as "500 additional park rangers". The CI model used for Chalalan is an adaptable, grassroots model with a focus on enabling people to satisfy their basic needs while creating a vested interest in protecting the environment. It is an integrated model that includes ecotourism, craft sales, and agriculture in a business enterprise owned and controlled by the community. Arce remarked that although the process was long and at times difficult, "80% of the work was already done from the beginning because it was a project born from community initiative". It is a model adapted to suit a particular community and its needs, with the integral concept of creating a viable economic income makes possible the sustainability of the people while preserving a biodiverse environment.

An interesting book for animal lovers: ***Mammals of Madidi National Park***, by Teresa Tarifa, Enzo Aliaga R., Boris Ríos U. and Daniel Hagaman. Edited by Conservación Internacional and Chalalán Eco Lodge.

For more information contact:
Conservación Internacional, Calle M. Pinilla 291, Casilla 13593,
La Paz - Bolivia. Tels. 2434058, 2435225.
E-mail: ci-bolivia@conservation.org
Chalalán Ecolodge, Calle Comercio, Rurrenabaque, Bolivia. Tel. 8922419, Fax. 8922309.
E-mail: chalalan_eco@yahoo.com
Parque Nacional A.N.M.I. Madidi, Av. Busch, San Buenaventura.
Tel. 8922540. E-mail: info@madidi.com
www.expedicionmadidi.com
www.madidi.com

BENI DEPT.

ESCAPE FROM RIBERALTA

BY KATE VENNER

NOT THAT RIBERALTA IS UNATTRACTIVE OR UNPLEASANT, IT IS JUST SOMEWHAT BEWILDERING.

The road to Riberalta, though it may be new, is not smooth. The heat is stifling, the dust Incessant, and the juddering of the vehicle makes it impossible to do anything but contemplate your situation. For us, this was an onion truck, which, for the pricey sum of 25 Bs each, took us the rest of the way from Australia to Riberalta. Crammed with people from the surrounding villages, it did the job. There are buses that stop along the carretera highway but we were desperate and jumped on the first vehicle heading the right way. A bus should cost around $30 from La Paz (35-60 hours!) and $18 from Rurrenabaque (17-40 hours). The road is normally closed during the rainy season from November to March.

We arrived coated in dust, exhausted but deeply relieved to have made it to Riberalta. It is not the most inspirational town on first sight, and personally, I believe that in this case first impressions were accurate. Approaching the center through a sea of shanty huts and crumbling buildings we were impressed to see a few properly paved roads (our first in two weeks), shops actually selling food and drinks and streetlights. Hopping on a motor taxi for 2 Bs we headed for the most promising sounding hostel in the Lonely Planet. Hostel Katiti may not be the most salubrious or clean of pensions but it had showers, a bed and a fan. Although the showers were cold, in the blistering heat of Riberalta, anything warmer would be pointless. As for the fan, despite the fact that its sole function appeared to he stirring the air in our room, the psychological effects were significant.

Most touristy, if you can call them that, places are situated not far from the central plaza, which is a pleasant tree-lined place to sit and watch as the hordes of mopeds and motorbikes circle endlessly. It can be quite fun, particularly on a Sunday, to sit and watch the youth of the town in their motorized courtship. Girls ride around in gangs, sometimes squeezing four of them on one machine while boys follow them, shouting their names, making jokes and trying to impress them by steering with their eyes shut and fighting with their friends without breaking.

As for the sights, the pickings are pretty slim. In my guidebook a motorcycle monument is mentioned. To me, this sounded impressive and worth a visit, so I spent my five days there on the look-out for Riberalta's majestic landmark. It was only on the last day that we realized that the miniature arrangement of what appeared to be lead soldiers on a moped was this much-lauded sight. Be alert in Riberalta, it is very easy to miss anything of interest. There are a few nice buildings scattered about such as the Mogul palace and the old brewery, but this is not a tourist town.

One of the more attractive parts of the town is down by the river. There, on the banks of the Beni you can stand on what is known as the Parque Mirador la Costañera and survey the confluence of the rivers and the beached bulk of an African-style steamer, the Tahuamanu, as well as the enfolding jungle that surrounds Riberalta. However, as we had only just recently been looking at a great deal of both the Beni and the jungle, this vista was not as revelatory as it might otherwise have been.

Another proof that Riberalta is not out to trap the tourist market is the fact that you cannot change traveler's checks and visa is taken nowhere. No one speaks English and the hostels and restaurants are generally unsanitary, dusty and poorly organized. However, this is not entirely a bad thing. If you have been traveling for a while it can be a breath of fresh air to feel that finally you have stepped off the gringo trail. You are not fussed over and ripped off; often you are politely ignored or just treated as a benign but uninteresting presence.

After eight days of living on rice and yucca and the odd catfish, I had imagined a paradise of available food and ice cold drinks. This was not to be. There is a good pizzeria on the corner of the plaza and an ice cream parlor that makes its own ice cream. However, flavors are limited to chocolate, vanilla and cheese (a truly unique taste sensation). The rest of the restaurants and cafés offer pretty low quality fare with greasy meat, suspicious rice and mountains of rice pudding, although this is actually pretty good and a bargain when you only have 2 Bs left.

It was on Monday, when we, having believed ourselves to be reasonably prepared, discovered that the banks could give us no money in any form and the calculation of our entire funds resulted in a measly 40 Bs, we knew we had problems. I have learned my lesson now: never go anywhere without excessive amounts of US dollars. However, this left us with a distinct problem:

no way to get out of Riberalta. With this in mind, the town began to assume a distinctly malignant air, the heat increased significantly and the people appeared more threatening. Suddenly, all I wanted to do was escape as soon as possible.

This is where TAM comes in, and for their help I am eternally grateful. One phone call to our illustrious editor in La Paz and we had two tickets to Cochabamba the next day. I could have kissed the man in the office but settled for blowing our last 4 Bs on rice pudding.

The feeling of immense relief when the plane took off lasted all the way to Cochabamba. Not that Riberalta is unattractive or unpleasant; it is just somewhat bewildering.

Coming from a small-ish island, I was intrigued by the seam of life we found, isolated in deep Bolivian jungle. It is perhaps more Brazilian that Bolivian, considering its proximity to the border. If you are tempted to try a taste of the north and are prepared to rough it quite a bit, Riberalta leaves you feeling as though you really have done some serious traveling. A flight might be a less stressful way of getting there though, and while you're at the airport grab a couple of Brazil nuts on your way out.

TOURING THE JUNGLES OF RURRENABAQUE

BY STACY WALKER

As a frontier settlement located near the Beni River, Rurrenabaque is a superb starting point for trips to the rain forest or the pampas. The pampas have many lakes where one can fish for piranhas or swim with dolphins, or simply relax while enjoying a riverside view of animal wildlife on a boat tour. The jungle consists of the Bolivian rain forest that has many dense layers of trees, shrubs, and small streams that tour guides cut out paths for travelers while seeking tropical fruits or drinking water from trees branches. Locally known as "Rurre," this small town is surrounded by a variety of the natural wonders of the Bolivian lowlands, making it an excellent choice for the independent traveler. Rurre is growing in popularity among the full range of international tourists and it is not uncommon to find Norwegians, Israelis, Swedes, and tourists of many other nationalities roaming around the dirt roads. Since most of the roads are unpaved, most travelers prefer to explore this small settlement either on foot or with the local trufismotorcycle taxis that are quite inexpensive.

Despite being down in the lowlands, Rurre is easily accessible from the altiplano. One can opt for a twenty-two-hour bus ride from La Paz over the scenic Cordillera and through the tropical Yungas with one of the three bus companies that travel to Rurre daily. If time is of the essence, a one-hour flight on Transport Aeroe Militar (TAM) air-lines is available. For small groups, jeeps are available from Rurre to La Paz, which is a fourteen-hour trip. As for accommodations in Rurre, several hotels are easily accessible. Most hotels, including Hotel Rurrenabaque, Hotel Tuichi, and Hostel Beni, have rooms ranging from 15 Bs. per person for a double occupancy and access to a communal bathroom to 35 Bs. per person for a double occupancy with hot/cold showers in a private bathroom.

While Rurre is beautiful and accommodating, the main attraction is its location as a starting point for the many tours that head off into the unsettled regions along the Beni River. Although no two tours are alike, the prices for the tours are the same no matter which company one chooses. The most popular tour agencies are: Agency Fluvial, Aguila (Eagle) Tours, and Amazonia Tours— the newest of these three. With tours lasting two to six days, most jungle tour groups have between four to eight people per group, while groups to the pampas are usually larger. Tours to the jungle cost US$25 per person per day while tours to the pampas are a little higher at US$30; the pricing usually includes everything from transportation to food and lodging. On the jungle tours, transportation is simply cruising along the Beni river in a motor-powered canoe while accommodations vary from sleeping under a tarpaulin tent with mosquito nets to sleeping comfortably in a base camp with buildings and bedding that would satisfy even the most demanding tourist.

While the rain forest might bring to mind exotic wildlife, the jungle tour agencies advise travelers that it is only with luck that a tourist will see many wild animals in the forest. Tour guides— all are from the area— demonstrate their local knowledge about the flora and fauna with lectures on the forest's natural remedies for illnesses including stomachaches, colds, and fever. Another appeal of Rurre is its close location (about 1 km) to the famous Serpent Stone in the Beni River. This stone is known for its ancient rock art design of a serpent engraved with three sun images designed by Incas to warn boatmen against navigating the river. When the serpent was beneath the water level, this signaled that the river was too dangerous for travel.

During my trip to Rurre, we traveled by canoe to different regions of the forest with Nicolas, our tour guide, while his wife, Jackie, cooked delicious meals on either a small gas stove or a makeshift wood-burning one. After hours of trekking, hiking, and exploring the forest, it was nice to return, relax, dine and converse with the guide about his lifestyle, giving ecotourism a more personal appeal.

For more information contact:
In Rurrenabaque, **Parque Nacional A.N.M.I. Madidi**, Av. Busch, Tel. 8922540. E-mail: info@madidi.com   www.madidi.com www.expedicionmadidi.com

The Pampas of Santa Rosa

The pampas are located approximately 70 km. from Rurrenabaque, past the capital province town of Reyes. Santa Rosa del Yacuma is a very warm region located in the Department of the Beni. It has an average temperature of 32 degrees Celsius, an altitude of 155 meters and an approximate population of 7,000. It is a region rich in agriculture, livestock and vegetation. It has many neighboring communities and an air strip that operates throughout the year. The town was founded on August 30, 1907 by the General Jose Ballivian, a date that commemorates the patron feast in honor of the Virgin of Santa Rosa

In the navigable Yacuma river where the adventure tours take place, one can appreciate a variety of animals like: Pink dolphins, Tigers, Alligators, Capibaras, Monkeys, Anacondas, Turtles and many types of birds. The Pampas tour usually takes 3 days (most recommended). It has many Lagunas, the most important include, The Laguna de Bravo, Colorada, Rogagua and Mancornada, all of which are navigable and with plenty of fish. There are all the necessary means available to reach these places, first one arrives to the town of Santa Rosa del Yacuma, an attractive place with accomodations, restaurants and karaokes that provide great hospitality. With friendly locals and the support of the local Santa Rosa Tours Travel and Tourism Agency, one can easily get around the entire region of the pampas and lagunas, including the jungle of the Laguna Rogagua and other places.

For more information or to make a reservation contact:
Santa Rosa Tours Travel and Tourism Agency Tel. 71587755. E-mail: santarosatours@hotmail.com www.santarosatours.com La Paz: **Fortaleza Tours** Tel./Fax. 2310866 Tel. 71253615 E-mail: fortaleza_@hotmail.com

THE PANDO FRONTIER

BY PETER MCFARREN
UPDATED BY PETER FRASER, JULIO A. ROJAS

A city with much of the spirit of the frontier, Cobija, with a population of about 20,987, is the capital and largest settlement of the Department of Pando, named after General José Manuel Pando. It was formed after the Acre War, which resulted in the transfer of nearly 192,000 square kilometers of Bolivian land (73,750 square miles) to Brazil. Pando was considered a colony until 1938 when it was finally designated a department: the youngest in Bolivia.

That youth feels evident in Cobija. Founded in 1906 with the name of Bahía, it is a tranquil and pretty settlement located 252 meters above sea level and set among low hills with tall, stately royal palms lining the road to the river Acre. Students crowd the streets around the main plaza and their preferred transport is the motorbike (motor–taxis are the best way for the visitor to travel round the city).

Even the monuments you will see on entering Cobija by bus - or in the main plaza - are recently built and appear pristine. It creates an impression of a city looking to the future after a short but turbulent past – still maturing – and there seems to be a genuine optimism among its citizens.

Cobija has the caracteristic dual city of border towns. The town of Brasilea lies across the Acre in Brazil, and small boats cross back and forth in less than 10 minutes. There is active commerce between the two countries and therefore a strong Brazilian influence in Pando. Brazilian T.V. stations beam their signals across the border and Brazilian products are often more abundant than Bolivian ones (generally prices are slightly higher than elsewhere in Bolivia).

Cobija was named a tax-free zone in 1999, which is helping to expand commerce and trade with its Brazilian neighbors who cross the border to purchase tax-free goods. You can buy camcorders for about $600 and football trophies for considerably less. Travelers should be aware that while you can pay with VISA in most of these shops, flight agencies do not currently accept credit cards and there are no cash machines in Cobija.

In the 1940s, when Cobija belonged to the rubber-producing sector of Bolivia, the city was much larger. With the decline in the world market for natural rubber went the fate of the entire rubber-producing area, including Cobija. Today Pando depends on natural resources: lumber and Brazil nut production, most of which are exported to foreign markets. The area's main employer is the Tahuamanu Brazil Nut company. This modern complex located in the outskirts of Cobija provides work for many local residents.

From satellite, Pando is an island of green amidst the deforestation in the neighboring countries of Peru and Brazil. The Rainforest still covers 93% of the department and there are numerous schemes aimed at sustainable development in the area: fulfilling the potential of forest products and alleviating poverty without damaging the environment.

Ecotourism is one avenue being explored and a visit to Cobija is not complete without a riverboat excursion through the jungle; launches can be hired year-round. Be sure to take along mosquito repellent, rain gear, a hat and clothing appropriate for the tropics. **The Manuripi protected area** in the Amazon, only three hours by road from Cobija, is particularly worth a visit. The tourist office has identified four particular routes that take in the main sites of interest, including the black waters of **Lago Bay** and **Montevideo**, a town built over the river like a little Venice.

Here and elsewhere in the Pando, due to the relative isolation of the Department, the environment is extremely well-preserved and one can view rare and varied flora and fauna, including 21 species of birds found only in the Pando. Be warned that torrential rainstorms can arrive from an apparently clear sky, especially between November and March, but otherwise it is far more comfortable to travel by boat than by land, where the road network is poor.

PRACTICAL INFORMATION FOR COBIJA

Cobija Phone Code: 3

• Useful Addresses and Numbers

Airport Information, Av. 9 de Febrero, Tel. 8422260.

Long-Distance Operator-Assisted Calls, Calle Sucre, Tel. 100.

AES, 0-11.

Cotas, 0-12.

For **Radio Communications** with La Paz and areas nor serviced by Entel, contact Radio Serrano, Calle Sucre, Tel. 8422213.

Post Office, Calle Bruno Racua (on the Main Plaza), Tel. 8422598.

Entel, Calle Sucre, Tels. 8422290, 8422292, Fax. 8429712.

Police, Av. 9 de Febrero, Tel. 8422105.

Immigration, Calle Bruno Racua, Tel. 8422081.

Tourist Information, Calle 9 de Febrero (Prefectura) 8422235.

Telephone Information, Tel. 104.

Vida Silvestre Amazonica Manuripi National Reserve, Calle Bahia, Tel. 8422368, Fax. 8423399.
E-mail:pedromh@hotmail.com
E-mail: jenysruiz@hotmail.com

• Consulates

Brazil, Av. Fernández Molina, corner of Beni, Tel. 8422188.

• How to Get There

Flights: direct flights every week no matter which season.

• Airline Offices

Lloyd Aéreo Boliviano (LAB), Av. Fernandez Molina, Tels. 8422170, 8423272/3.

AeroSur, Av. Fernández Molina, Tel. 8423132. Fax. 8429710.

Transporte Aéreos Militares (TAM), Av. 9 de Febrero, Tels. 8422267, 8422692.

Save Regional, Av. Fernandez Molina, Tel. 8423090.

• Buses

Buses leave for Riberalta, Rurrenabaque and La Paz from Calle 2 de Febrero.

• Getting Around Town

You can easily navigate Cobija by foot, motor taxi or regular taxi. You can also takes boats to neighboring Brazilian villages.

• Radio Taxis

Radio Taxi Pando, Av. Fernández Molina, Tel. 8422969.

Radio Taxi Presidente, Av. 9 de Febrero, Tel. 8422101.
Radio Taxi Cobija, Av. 9 de Febrero, Tel. 8422828.

• Car Rental
Villavicencio, Av. Internacional, Tel. 8423228.

• Car Repair
Pipo, Av. 9 de Febrero 114, Tel. 8422863.
Auto Perno, Av. 9 de Febrero, in front of the Stadium, Tel. 8422009.

• Hotels
Hotel Avenida, Av. 9 de febrero Tel. 8422108.
Hostería Sucre, Calle Sucre, Tel. 8422797. Brand new hotel, offers six rooms, air conditioning, and gymnasium.
Hotel Asai, Km 3, Tel. 8422478. Three-stars hotel, offers telephone, T.V., air conditioning, bar and room service. The hotel has a pool, restaurant, bar, meeting rooms and parking.
Hotel Nanijo's, Av. 9 de Febrero, corner with Beni, Tel. 8422230, offers telephone and air conditioning in the rooms, with a gymnasium available for guests.
Hotel Diana, Av. 9 de Febrero, Tel. 8422073.
Hotel Villa Gloria, Barrio 11 de Octubre, Tel. 8422028.
Residencial Cobija, Calle Beni, Tel. 8422375.
Residencial Frontera, Calle Beni, Tel. 8422740.
Residencial Cocodrilo, Av. Fernández Molina, Tel. 8422215.

• Restaurants
Pacahuara, Calle Bruno Racua corner of La Paz, Tel. 8422080. Steak house.
La Palmas, Av. 16 de Julio across from the Plaza del Estudiante, Tel. 8422053. Serves steak, pasta and international food.

La Esquina de la Abuela, Av. Fernández Molina, Tel. 8422364. Serves traditional Bolivian food.
El Curichi de Cocodrilo, Av. 16 de Julio, Tel. 8422656. Serves traditional Bolivian food.
El Meson de la Pazcana, Calle Beni, Bolivian food.
El Negrito, Av. 16 de Julio, parrilladas.

• Travel Agencies
Promo Tours, Av. 6 de Agosto/Bruno Racua, Tel. 8423419.

• Cultural Centers
Casa de la Cultura, Av. 16 de Julio, Tel. 8422223.

• Internet
Universidad Amazonica de Pando, Av. Tcnl. Cornejo, Tel. 8422411.
Casa de la Cultura, Av. 16 de Julio, Tel. 8422223.

• Shopping
The **Main Market** is on Av. 9 de Febrero.

• Sports
Tenis Club Cobija, Barrio Miraflores, Tel. 8422241.
Balneario Los Cocos, Av. Internacional, Tel. 8423223, has a pool and football fields.
El Cartucho, 9 km. from Cobija, has barbecues, live music and pool.

• Banks
Banks are open from 8:30 to 12:30, and 14:30 to 18:00. U.S. Dollars can be changed, but not traveler's checks.

Banco Unión, Av. Tcnl. Cornejo, Tel. 8423268.

Cooperativa Jesús Nazareno, Plaza Germán Busch, Tel. 8422126, Fax. 8422591.

Mutual Pando A&P, Av. Fernandez Molina, Tel. 8422058.

Prodem (Fondo Financiero), Av. 9 de Febrero, Tel. 8422800. Also a good place to change money.

• Money Exchange

Horacio, Av. Internacional, Tel. 8422265. Do Not change traveler's checks. Does change to Brazilian Reales, which is advisable before visiting Brazilian towns from Cobija.

Cachito, Av. Tcnl. Cornejo corner with Av. 9 de Febrero

• Laundries

While there are no *lavenderias* as such in Cobija, most hotels offer laundry services, so your best bet is to check wherever you're staying.

• Medical Services

Hospital Dr. Roberto Galindo Teran, Barrio 11 de Octubre, Km. 2, Tel. 8422017.

Clínica Burgos, Av. 9 de Febrero, Tels. 8422013, 8422109.

Centro Odontologico de Cobija (Dentist), End of Av. Internacional, Tel. 8422893.

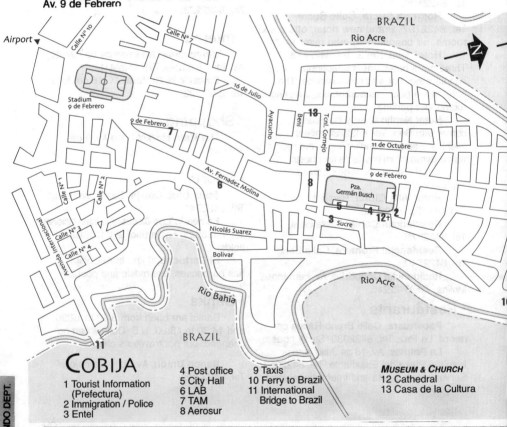

COBIJA

		MUSEUM & CHURCH
1 Tourist Information (Prefectura)	4 Post office	9 Taxis	12 Cathedral
2 Immigration / Police	5 City Hall	10 Ferry to Brazil	13 Casa de la Cultura
3 Entel	6 LAB	11 International Bridge to Brazil	
	7 TAM		
	8 Aerosur		

COBIJA, THE PEARL OF THE ACRE

BY JAIME ROJAS ZAMBRANA

As we took flight aboard an LAB one June winter morning from La Paz, the remnants of a heavy snowstorm still lay across the Andes, icing the mountains and broad plateau. As the plane flew to cruising altitude, we passed numerous snowcapped peaks and ridges, all humbled by the majestic Mount Illimani. On the horizon glistened Titicaca, the, sacred lake of the Incas, it's deep blue waters as blue as the surrounding sky of the clear day. The iridescent sun began to warm the barren slopes of the mountains and melt the snow on the highland plain.

In a short time we were above the clouds looking down on the immense Llanura Oriental, covered in cotton flake clouds all along its extension. The patchiness of the clouds allowed us the privilege of seeing the boundless emerald carpet of the Bolivian Amazon, with every conceivable shade of green on display, and countless rivers crossing its territory; the Beni, Madre de Dios, Manuripi, Tahuamanu, and lastly the River Acre.

Soon after, we could see the airport of Cobija. From the air, the streets and avenues of the city are surrounded by the Acre river with its waters meek and crystalline. As we exited the plane, we were blasted by a wave of warm air that immediately forced us to tear off the thick layers that are a necessity in wintertime La Paz. "A suraso (a bitter seasonal wind)

has just passed. You are lucky, and will have a good time," the locals told us.

As we strolled towards the center of Cobija, we already felt the gentle atmosphere of the town, with its clean, quiet streets, modern architecture, and beautiful town squares lined with mango trees and palms. Cobija deserves its reputation as the 'Pearl of the Acre' because of the hard work of its citizens and the support of the *Collas* who have collaborated efficiently in its urban and commercial progress. As the remarkable Alberto Lavadenz Rivera says in his book, *Pando Esta Avanzando,* Cobija is waking up to progress.

The Pando represents a landmark of sovereignty for Bolivia, with an impressive history of resisting foreign invasion. In particular Don Bruno Racua and the heroes of the Columna Porvenir, who defended the boundaries of Bolivia with great courage. Traveling inland to Nicolas Suarez country, the Manupiri, Madre de Dios, the Abuna and the Frederico Roman, the traveler receives an unforgettable experience amidst the beauty of the forests. There are abundante rubber and chestnut trees, plantations of rice, tobacco, peanuts and yucca, not to mention the kaleidoscopic array of native flowers. The paradise is completed by a rich variety of fauna including jaguars, periquitos, parabas, elks, monkeys, plus countless reptiles and types of fish. Pando is the future of Bolivia. It needs government support in order to reach its targets for development.

I interviewed some Pandinos. They are very gentle, kind, smiling people, as expressed through their melodies, songs and poems. The Amazonian Folkloric Ballet is an important and successful dance group from the region, directed and choreographed by Don Eduardo Velasco Zeballos. They took first place in the Sixth National Festival of Dances "Elay Pue", held in 1996 in Santa Cruz.

The Amazonian Folkloric Ballet was presented in a special show for an auditorium in a restaurant we visited. The beauty of the young women dancers was there for all to appreciate, and the talent and direction of the show was extremely professional. The folk dance of the Siringuero -Castanero, for example, expresses the process of collecting of rubber. The dancers wore skirts and chestnut blouses, taking a pail in their hands to extract and collect the milky liquid from the Siringa tree. The siringueros take a "Poronga" on their heads to light the path of the forest that is very closed, dark and dense until dawn brings natural light. The dancers carry a "Yamachi," a basket designed to hold coconuts and a shotgun in case of attack from wild animals. They also take a machete to make the cut in the tree from which the rubber bleeds. It is collected in a Tichelita, inserted into the gomero tree, and then transformed into the recognizable rubber compound in a Buyon oven. Afterwards the Siringueros remove the bolachas of rubber that weigh between 50 and 200 kilos, and the synchronized movements of the dancers represent the whole process.

The dance of the "pacahuaras"astonished the audience. The Pacahuara are a tribe of Indians who inhabited the banks of the Rio Negro in ancient times, a river that now marks the border with Brazil. The female dancers performed an interpretation of the life of the tribe. The dancers were wearingred and black knee-length skirts made with seeds of the Sirari. The male dancers wore skirts made of bark from different trees, beautiful feathered headdresses, and carried bows and arrows. Their delicate body movements complemented the beautiful slender figures of these warriors, together with expert choreography from Eduardo Velasco. The Taquirari Pandinista exalted the spirit of the dancers, and the audience accepted the show with great appreciation. The Third Interaction Folk Festival organized by the Centro Pedagogico Y Cultural Simon Patiño was held in Cochabamba later this year.

PANDO: AN UNTOUCHED PARADISE IN THE AMAZON

BY BERNARDO PEREDO VIDEA, MSC.

ocated at the North of the country, the Province of Pando is one of the last unspoiled areas in the Amazon. There are many undisturbed and pristine regions still in the department, especially in the northeastern provinces which has the highest rates of forestry, biodiversity and natural resources rates.

The Amazon basin and lowlands in Bolivia represents 66% of the total surface of the country. The entire Pando department, the North of La Paz (Iturralde Province), and North of Beni (Vaca Diez Province) composes the Bolivian Amazon River Basin. Furthermore, Pando is the only region that is 100% Amazonian.

Two National Reserves, Federico Roman and Madre de Dios, and one of the biggest protected Areas in Bolivia, the Vida Silvestre Amazonica Manuripi National Reserve, cover about 14% of the territory in Pando.

The Department borders with Brazil on the North and East, and Peru on the West. It is divided into five provinces: Manuripi, Madre de Dios, Abuna, Federico Roman and Nicolas Suarez. Because of Bolivia's decentralization reform process, there are 15 municipalities in this department.

Pando offers an unlimited number of opportunities and potentials based on the natural and ecological richness that exist in the different regions of this department. About 93% of the territory is covered by tropical forest, (one of the highest rates in the country and in the Amazon), offering plenty of opportunities related to biodiversity, non-timber products, medicinal plants, forestry under appropriate management, ecotourism, clean development mechanisms, Brazil nut production.

The region's economy depends on natural resources, rubber during the first part of the century and currently Brazil-nuts, which is the main economic activity in the region, producing the main income for rural communities and local families. In addition to Brazil nuts, there is subsistence hunting; fishing and agriculture developed by local communities. Rubber, once a pillar of the region's economy, is no longer a viable alternative for the population's income, due to the drop in international prices.

The main marketable natural product of the forest is the Brazil nut, which is gathered from the forest by local people during the months of November to March; Brazil nuts are taken to the gathering and buying centers known as Barracas through Pando river ways. It is the main economic activity for local people and doesn't affect the environment. In this sense, it is considered one of the most important allies for preserving the Amazon forest.

There are many communities in the rural area that have populations of less than 500 who maintain traditional ways of life, including different indigenous groups as the Takana, Esse-ejjas, Araonas, Cavineños, Yaminahua and Machineris. Pando has the lowest population density in the country with 0.6 people/sq.km.

The Department is very diverse biologically. It encompasses both black-water and white-water floodplain communities, characterized by a great abundance of Brazil-nut and Rubber trees. Many species in Pando are rare elsewhere in the Amazon and can be found nowhere else in Bolivia.

The primate fauna in the region is extremely rich, with fourteen species recorded, equaling the highest number reported in the Neotropics. This is the world's highest concentration of primates in a single area.

The composition of the flora indicates a rich soil, which is unusual for Amazonian upland forests, and a high productivity in the vegetation. These sandy-clay terraces are especially rich in tree species important to animals, and for extracting resources for local people.

However, rapidly expanding logging and ranching activities seriously threaten Pando's biological richness. Logging concessions now cover much of the Department, and cattle ranches, with their ecologically devastating practices, multiply as soon as areas have been logged for the most valuable timber. There is the need to provide alternatives for local development and income generation in order to avoid problems related to migration and degrading natural resources, thus conserving biodiversity.

Nevertheless, wild and undisturbed areas also offer incomparable beauty and biological richness that need to be protected

to avoid the depletion of natural resources, which are Pando's legacy and heritage.

By sailing the Manuripi River from San Silvestre, (the main camp of the Protected Area), for about 3 hours, you can reach the incomparable Lake Bay, with black waters that meet but do not mix with the brown waters of the Manuripi River. The Lake Bay, one of the most fascinating sites in Pando, is highlighted by unique beauty, scenery, exotic diversity of fauna and vegetation, which is one of the main attraction for ecotourists.

The proximity of natural sites and the Protected Area to Cobija, the capital of Pando, (which is accessible by road most of the year), offers tremendous potential both for careful development of ecotourism as well as for education and research activities. This provides alternatives that may reduce threats of different unprotected areas. Also, the countless navigable rivers offer one of the best options to discover this region through sailing.

There are numerous possibilities to explore, observe and learn about the Amazon richness in Pando, including biodiversity, wildlife, ecosystems and local communities. It is a place of magic and pristine areas with its people full of optimism and hope.

This region captivates visitors because of its unforgettable landscapes, majestic rivers and exuberant vegetation, where wildlife reigns and still roams in natural habitats. The Pando Amazon invites visitors to discover, enjoy and conserve this amazing untouched paradise.

For more information contact:
Oficina de Turismo de Prefectura de Pando, Calle 9 de febrero, Edificio de la Prefectura Ex- CORDEPANDO, Tel. 842 2235.
Centro de investigación y Preservación de la Amazonia, Universidad Amazónica de Pando, Tel. 842 2135.

LA PAZ, PLAZA SAN FRANCISCO

LA PAZ WITH ILLIMANI MOUNTAIN

LA PAZ, CALLE SAGARNAGA

Cordillera Apolobamba, La Paz dept.

La Paz market

Puya Raymundii, La Paz dept.

Copacabana, La Paz dept.

Titicaca lake, La Paz dept.

COCHABAMBA, THE PORTALES CENTER

COCA LEAVES DRYING ALONG THE COCHABAMBA - SANTA CRUZ HIGHWAY, CHAPARE

QUECHUA WOMAN FROM VILACAYMA, COCHABAMBA DEPT.   CARRASCO NAT. PARK, COCHABAMBA DEPT.

SANTA CRUZ, THE CATHEDRAL

Noel Kempff Nat. Park, Santa Cruz dept.

Amboro Nat. Park, Santa Cruz dept.

Noel Kempff Nat. Park, Santa Cruz dept.

Chiquitania Jesuit Mission, Santa Cruz dept.

Chiquitania Jesuit Mission, Santa Cruz dept.

ORURO CARNAVAL

PEACE IS NOT AN OBJECT FOUND BY CHANCE - IT IS THE RESULT OF EQUALITY BETWEEN MEN. ORURO

Sajama Mountain, Oruro dept.

Chullpa Aymara, burial site, Oruro dept.

Chipayas, Oruro dept.

Potosi

Potosi

Potosi, San Lorenzo Church

POTOSI, WOMEN WORKING MINE TAILINGS ON CERRO RICO

POTOSI, A MINER PAYING HOMMAGE TO THE TIO, THE PROTECTOR OF THE MINE

UYUNI SALT FLATS, POTOSI DEPT.

UYUNI TRAIN CEMETERY, POTOSI DEPT.

CARL ORCK'O DINOSAUR TRACKS, SUCRE DEPT.

SUCRE, SAN LORENZO AND LA MERCED CHURCHES

SUCRE, SANTA TERESA CHURCH

TARABUCO MARKET, SUCRE DEPT.

TARIJA, CASA DORADA

VINEYARD IN TARIJA DEPT.

RURRENABAQUE, SHORE OF THE BENI RIVER

MOJEÑO WOMEN IN ISIBORO SÉCURE NAT. PARK

MACHETERO IN ISIBORO SÉCURE NAT. PARK

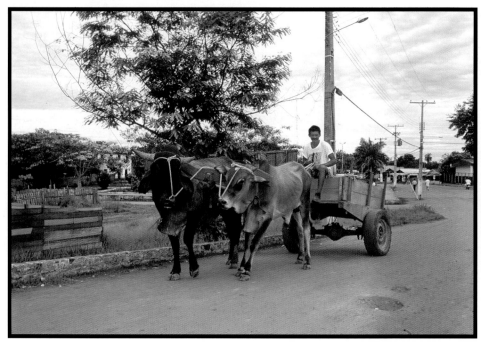

Around Cobija, Pando dept.

Cobija, Pando dept.

3

BOLIVIA'S
CULTURAL PAST

PRE-COLUMBIAN CULTURES OF BOLIVIA

BY AMY OAKLAND RODMAN

Bolivia's prehistoric civilizations are a product of the remarkable environment in which they evolved. The environment not only affected lifestyle at a fundamental level but also served as the source of religious beliefs. Three major natural features dominate the landscape: the Andes, the *Altiplano* and Lake Titicaca. In Bolivia, the Andes, rising to several majestic peaks of more than 6,000 meters, divide to form two separate ranges: the Cordillera Occidental, in the west, and the Cordillera Oriental, the wider eastern section. Between these barriers lies the *Altiplano* (or high plateau), an enormous flat expanse averaging more than 13,000 feet in altitude. The *Altiplano* is shaped like a huge oval, widest in the center, and is the largest plateau of its kind in the Andes. To the north of the *Altiplano* and lying at the base of the two Andean chains is Lake Titicaca, a body of water so large it creates the impression of an immense ocean in the sky. Coupled with snow-capped mountain peaks in the distance, the landscape has created a spiritual metaphor for human existence, one understood by native peoples to the present day.

Viscachani and Early Man Sites

The *Altiplano*, though a seemingly inhospitable environment, has been home to varied native cultures from early times. Beginning towards the end of the last glacial period around 7000-8000 B.C., human occupation has been detected through the non-perishable artifacts left behind. Worked stone tools, usually in the form of projectile points, have been discovered throughout the Bolivian *Altiplano*. Evidently, early man arrived to hunt the wild herds of camelids (llamas, alpacas, guanacos and vicuñas) which flourished in the area.

At one of Bolivia's early sites called Viscachani, an unusual quantity of early point types has been preserved close to the surface. In 1954, archaeologist Dick Edgar Ibarra Grasso discovered and recorded more than 12,000 individual examples. Similar lithic material has been reported in Bolivia near Oruro, Lipez, Potosí, Villa-Villa and Cliza in Cochabamba, and La Candelaria in Chuquisaca.

Because preservation of perishable artifacts is virtually impossible in the *Altiplano* (due to the severe climatic changes and soil conditions), we know very little of the material remains of these early people and even less about their spiritual life.

To attempt any cultural reconstruction, one must try to work from the non-perishable objects that remain, especially those objects which were essential to the lifestyle. The almost indestructible projectile points must have been lashed with fiber cords into wooden spear-throwers, arrow shafts or long wooden spears. Extra points were held ready for use in small bags from knotted fiber cordage or in looped nets. Hats and simple garments may have been formed from leather pelts or of knotted, interlinked or looped fiber textiles. Wherever preserved, the remarkable variety of early fabric structures shows a highly developed technology, one that played a large part in human environmental adaptation, and one that became the first major Andean art form. Simple, non-woven textile techniques perfected during these early periods continue to be used today in the form of basketry and netting. In some tropical areas east of the Andes, the identical structures are today shaped into bags, hats and carrying straps. The designs produced by the structures of these non-woven techniques were an important influence in the iconography of later loom-woven fabrics. Undoubtedly, the major fiber source in the *Altiplano* was the hair of the wild camelid herds.

In succeeding millennia, a process of collecting native grains and tubers was slowly developed in the *Altiplano* and within inter-mountain valleys. Early man followed a seasonal cycle of hunting and gathering around the lake borders, as well as traveling to the eastern valleys and the desert coast of southern Peru and northern Chile. Evidence dating to around 4000 B.C. attests to the collection of quinoa and perhaps the beginning of settled agricultural life coupled with pastoral activities. One of the most important aspects of early life in the *Altiplano* was the domestication of the llama and the alpaca. Early camelid pasturing centering around the Lake Titicaca basin, developed in conjunction with arable farming, proved to be the successful combination that gave rise to the great Andean civilizations.

To understand the importance of the llama to *Altiplano* people, one has only to view the hundreds of carved stone llama heads remaining from sites attributed to Wankarani villages. The mounds there

have been formed by continuous occupation of collapsed adobe constructions built within the confines of a large adobe wall. Circular Wankarani houses with thatched straw roofs were clustered inside the walled compound. As houses became obsolete, they simply tumbled to the earth and others were built on top. Some settlements were quite small, with about 15 house structures, while a few others contained over 780 units, suggesting a population of more than 3,000 inhabitants. Although none have been found in place, the form of the stone llama heads suggests that they were tenoned horizontally or vertically into walls. The large ears and squared eyes and mouth are prominent features. The llama provided protein to supplement a diet of grains and tubers and was valued for its wool and its capacity as a beast of burden. Llama dung was used as fertilizer in agricultural fields. It was perhaps also the valued fuel in kiln-fired ceramics, as it is used today for high altitude firing.

Wankarani ceramic llama heads

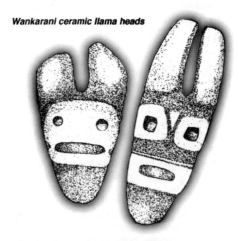

Reprinted from: Cuadernos de Investigación
UMSS Instituto de investigaciones Antropológicas
Cochabamba - Bolivia. Drawn by Ricardo Céspedes.

In addition to stone, ceramics are also major cultural markers used by archaeologists. Wankarani ceramics have simple shapes without design or applied colors. In clay, as in stone, the Wankarani people shaped heads of llamas. These are the only artistic products to survive the culture.

Perhaps the most important feature discovered in Wankarani sites is evidence of copper smelting in the earliest occupation levels around 1200 to 800 B.C. These dates are among the earliest in the Andes associated with metal working and are contemporaneous with other metal-using cultures of Chile and Peru.

Chiripa

At about the same time, around 1000 B.C., the cultural complex known as Chiripa developed around the southern shores of Lake Titicaca. Additional sites attributed to the Chiripa culture are found on the Copacabana peninsula, and as far south as the Moquegua Valley in southern Peru. The archaeological remains at Chiripa offer a fundamentally different view of early settled *Altiplano* life. The large mound visible today at Chiripa was formed artificially and faced with stone, perhaps an intentional imitation of the Andean mountain peaks visible in the landscape. In contrast to the scattered round houses of Wankarani, Chiripa houses were carefully arranged around a central courtyard. Their form was architecturally exact -- square, with double walls, perhaps used for storage -- and they were dug into the mound's surface forming subterranean structures. Sometime between 500-100 B.C., the central plaza was renovated. A subterranean temple became the new religious focus with a facing of elaborately-carved stone wall plaques. Stone stelae also carved with religious motifs of snakes and human or deity representations were erected in the central open space.

The classic Chiripa art style is evident in the iconography carved into one stone panel now housed in the *Museo Nacional de Arqueología* in La Paz, and a similar one found near Copacabana. In both, a central face is surrounded by scroll and arrow motifs facing the cardinal directions. Llama figures fill the central side space, and undulating snakes and cross designs fill the four corners. Each is carefully executed in shallow relief carving. The bilateral symmetry of the entire image and the two feet projecting above and below the central face are evidence of the duality understood in the social and religious life, the forces of male and female in the natural world, and perhaps even the divided leadership which would become common in the later Aymara populations. The entire mound was undoubtedly considered a sacred precinct and was reused later as a temple by the Tiwanaku culture and by the Incas. The execution of these monumental architectural embellishments is exquisite. It is probable that the stone carving tradition for which the Bolivian *Altiplano* is famous had its roots in the Chiripa and Wankarani cultures.

Exotic artifacts traded into the *Altiplano*, such as metals and semi-precious stones found at many Chiripa sites, suggest a connection with areas outside of the *Altiplano* such as the Cochabamba valley or the desert coast of Peru and Chile. Textiles, perhaps related to the Chiripa cultures, have been discovered near Arica, Chile. These fabrics, especially visible in the designs woven into interlocked tapestry blankets and tunic borders, are known in Chile as being part of Alto Ramirez, a culture with close ties to the *Altiplano*. Llamas are portrayed in profile with rayed deity faces and mountain images. Other important figures are designs of toads (perhaps water symbols) divided into four sections. The tunics were apparently worn with tall helmets of looped camelid fiber decorated with stepped mountain designs.

Clothing iconography in these remote periods has established a sound identity with a homeland high in the *Altiplano*. The beautiful red and blue dyes (relbunium, or cochineal, and indigo) used in all Alto Ramirez textiles attest to a strong and long-standing fabric tradition, and likely to an established trade or exchange in important dyestuffs.

The llamas carved into stone and woven into textiles must certainly have been a common sight, as organized llama caravans circulated within the different Andean zones. Local *Altiplano* products and status-validating goods such as brightly-dyed textiles, shells, metals, stones and feathers were exchanged for valley and coastal products. Life in the *Altiplano* was made easier from very early times through these continuous caravan connections.

This economic complementarity or verticality has been the subject of many recent studies. It remains impossible in most investigations to determine whether goods were exchanged through trade networks with local inhabitants, or were obtained through exploitation by colonies of *Altiplano* people placed specifically in a variety of productive ecological zones. Whether or not the Alto Ramirez people were in fact colonists of the Chiripa or another *Altiplano* culture remains uncertain, but their common ties are undeniable.

The Cochabamba valley was another area of constant *Altiplano* interaction, as well as one of the most important productive zones in Bolivia. Although little archaeological investigation has defined the early occupations of this region, it is apparent that settlements with early ceramic types were scattered throughout the area. Stylistic connections suggest *Altiplano* and coastal influences.

Cochabamba, Chullpa-Pampa and Chullpa-Pata

One site with very early ceramics discovered in Cochabamba is known as Chullpa-Pampa. Situated on the hills above the plain of Cochabamba (almost certainly in a depression formed by an ancient lake bottom), the area has yielded small globular ceramics with simple shapes and decorated with simple appliquéed human facial features, snakes or other animal forms. The ceramics are so similar to Wankarani *Altiplano* types and to others found in Arica, that early coastal/valley/*Altiplano* connections are obvious. No domestic architecture has yet been discovered, and only a few stone hoes suggest the presence of agriculture.

In 1982, other early ceramic sites were uncovered near Cochabamba. A site known as Chullpa-Pata was discovered near the community of Cliza, and another site was discovered in Sierra Mokko northeast of Quillacollo. Stratigrafic excavations yielding a variety of local ceramic types suggest an independent yet co-existing tradition in the valley. One large stone and adobe structure discovered in the lower levels of the excavation at Chullpa-Pata formed the base of a square or rectangular pyramid, another artificial mountain undoubtedly used for ceremonial functions. The most interesting art forms discovered in these early Cochabamba sites are the small, beautifully carved and often polished stone figures. Many decorated without obvious sexual symbolism apparently represented human fertility objects, while others suggest connection with natural phenomena such as water and rain.

Tiwanaku

No commentary on Bolivia's prehistoric cultures would be complete without a discussion of Tiwanaku. Most visitors are aware of the beautiful and mysterious *Altiplano* site located just south of Lake Titicaca, where stone sculptures and monumental stone architecture remain standing. But few understand the duration and extent of this important culture's influence throughout Bolivia, southern Peru, northern Chile and northwest Argentina, an area known as the South Central Andes.

About the same time that Chiripa was developing elsewhere, around 1000 B.C., a small village of the first Tiwanaku inhabitants was established in the area of the Kalasasaya at the site of Tiwanaku. The occupation is known by a particular ceramic type called Kalasasaya or Tiwanaku I. The first images of the puma or jaguar, an animal motif common to later Tiwanaku style, is evident in simple representations in the first Tiwanaku ceramic type. Birds, perhaps ducks, were modeled and painted, and human images were also formed.

Little is known of the layout or ornamentation of this early Tiwanaku settlement because the area was extensively renovated in subsequent centuries. Some investigators believe that at least some of the stone sculpture discovered in excavations at the site could belong to this early period. One candidate for an early date is the small monolith which was originally erected in the center of the subterranean temple in front of the Kalasasaya. The snake images on the monolith's sides recall Chiripa designs, and the duality expressed by the figures on the monolith's two faces could represent a sexual dyad similar to that suggested by the Chiripa image. To represent its sexual meaning, the Chave have termed this monolith style yaya-mama, which means "father-mother" in Aymara.

The appearance of a new painted style, designated Tiwanaku III or Early Tiwanaku, marks the first major architectural growth of Tiwanaku. Ceramics of this period were painted with designs loosely resembling pumas and birds. Some distinctive vessel shapes clearly influenced the more widely-known ceramics of the succeeding Classic period of Tiwanaku, or Tiwanaku IV, such as the open bowl with a scalloped rim, hollow base and appliquéed modeled feline heads. These particular vessels have been termed incensarios and have been discovered with obvious burned interiors giving evidence to their use.

Much of the architecture and monumental embellishment of Tiwanaku was probably carried out during this stage of Tiwanaku III, a period just prior to the Classic developments of Tiwanaku IV. Monoliths which have recently been uncovered, such as the curved lintel from Kantatayaita and the large anthropomorphic stele erected outside the walls of the Kalasasaya, reveal a style in contrast with the very standard iconography of the Classic period. It is possible to picture the site of Tiwanaku at the time as an extremely large ceremonial and urban center with palaces, temples and monumental stepped pyramids faced with megalithic pillars and cut stone blocks, further decorated with solid stone staircases and carved sculpture.

Tiwanaku III ceramics, architectural units and monoliths possibly dated to the same period have been discovered not only at the Tiwanaku site but in many sites surrounding the southern portion of Lake Titicaca, signifying a widespread cultural diffusion into this area. Tiwanaku *Altiplano* sites of lesser importance such as Lucurmata, Wankani, Mocachi and Qallamarka contain smaller-scale sculpture and architectural units which replicate those of the Tiwanaku site; still, no other center equals that of the Tiwanaku site in scale or degree of elaboration.

During the succeeding Tiwanaku IV or Classic period, the site of Tiwanaku and possibly the allied, smaller *Altiplano* sites as well underwent architectural expansion and a massive program of site beautification. Building projects complete with megalithic sculptural decorations were executed in all the major precincts. The Classic style and the following Tiwanaku V, or Expansive style, was spread throughout the South Central Andes in ceramics and portable art carved in wood and bone and woven into textiles. Classic style Tiwanaku pottery has been discovered widely dispersed around the entire Lake Titicaca basin and in the surrounding regions of the *Altiplano*, Cochabamba and the Mizque Valley, in Moquegua, Peru, and Arica and San Pedro de Atacama in northern Chile.

The iconography of the Classic Tiwanaku style, although highly stylized, reveals a great deal about the material culture. A central deity figure -- recognized with a rayed headdress and always portrayed frontally and holding staffs (perhaps spear throwers) -- was certainly the major Tiwanaku god.

Attendant figures are depicted in profile as human or animal headed images often holding staffs as well. In one image drawn in fine-line incision on the back of the Ponce monolith, attendants are depicted holding raised cups in some unidentifiable ceremony. Often staffs end in human heads, or heads are held by the hair in other clear images carved in portable Tiwanaku art. Headless bodies have been discovered in Tiwanaku burials. Burials of heads alone implies a certain cult of trophy head collecting or a value in the severed head. The tenoned stone heads of the semi-subterranean temple represent a monumental form of human sacrifice on permanent display.

Tiwanaku rulers may be represented in the monoliths carved in human form which were erected in the central plazas throughout the site. Recorded for later periods of Andean history, standing stones representing humans were important intercessors between the physical world and that inhabited by the gods. During the Inca period, the Inca ruler, himself considered a god, stood on a platform in the center of the plaza in the Inca capital at Cuzco. His func-

tion as intercessor with the natural world and with the other gods must have equaled the Tiwanaku stone figure's functions. It is possible that during an important rulers' reign (or to commemorate his death), Tiwanaku craftsmen shaped stones in recognition of his power.

Stone images wear clothing resembling garments have been discovered in Tiwanaku burials on the Chilean coast and desert highlands. Tiwanaku costumes were brilliantly-dyed and often highly-patterned. Furry hats formed of strips of dyed alpaca hair coiled or knotted over a straw foundation have been uncovered in burials of Tiwanaku affiliation in San Pedro de Atacama in the Chilean desert highlands. These hats closely resemble headwear worn by Tiwanaku people, shaped in Tiwanaku ceramics and carved in stone. Tapestry tunics also uncovered in the Chilean desert with Tiwanaku images show the high quality of weaving and dyeing produced, and which cover the monoliths carved in human form.

Other Tiwanaku textiles shaped into bags and narrow bands discovered in Bolivian dry caves and burials in the coastal desert. Once wrapped and protected objects of Tiwanaku's important cult of hallucinogenic snuff known as the complejo de rapé. Wooden and stone tablets, mortars, spoons and tubes often carved with Tiwanaku religious iconography have been discovered in sites located throughout the South Central Andes. The objects held in the hands of Tiwanaku monoliths could represent keros (cups) of chicha (maize beer) or drug tablets, all important ceremonial items.

During the Tiwanaku period, as before, large caravans of llamas (figures often carved on wooden snuff tablets) traveled throughout the South Central Andes carrying *Altiplano* agricultural produce, salt and manufactured items such as the textiles and cult objects connected with the rapé complex. As evidence of the importance given to ceremonial maize and drug plants, Tiwanaku llama images clearly carry maize on their backs and other vegetation symbols perhaps representing the hallucinogenic San Pedro cactus. The presence of these objects, decorated with Tiwanaku motifs, used with the snuff complex is the most often cited evidence for Tiwanaku influence in the South Central Andes. Instead of any major military conquest, it seems that Tiwanaku culture spread with the simultaneous exchange of economic produce and ideological doctrine. During the period of Tiwanaku IV and V (A.D. 500-1000), most formerly-independent cultures of Bolivia, southern Peru, northern Chile and northwest Argentina became part of the Tiwanaku empire.

**Mojocoya ceramics.
Source: Ibarra 1956.**

As Tiwanaku was consolidating its control of the Bolivian *Altiplano* around A.D. 200, other local cultures were developing outside of the Tiwanaku sphere of influence in the lowland valleys and along the broad river basins of Bolivia's eastern frontier with the region of tropical selva. In the Cochabamba valley, a ceramic style developed known as Tupuraya. A similar though distinct style and associated culture called Mojocoya have been found in the area near and to the south of the Mizque River. No archaeological investigations have yet identified house type or settlement patterns of either of these cultures. However, it is obvious from several ceramic vessel shapes, from the spears used in fishing and the textile techniques of simple looping, knotting and interlacing using plant fibers, that the cultures were influenced by their tropical environment and perhaps their tropical origins.

The Tupuraya ceramic style is painted with black and red ceramic slips on a white ground. Forms include tripod and tetrapod vessels and a wide flaring beaker similar to the Tiwanaku kero. Closely allied vessel shapes, the tripods and kero forms were used by the Mojocoya people who painted red and black colors on an orange slipped ground. Burial caves have been located with abundant Mojocoya pottery and textiles. White cotton bags and tunics were woven in simple warp-faced plain weave and were painted orange-red with iron oxide pigments. Tunics were often embellished around the sleeve and neck openings with embroidered geometric and zoomorphic figures. Warp stripes of brown- or blue-dyed cotton or more brightly-dyed alpaca were a common decorative feature in the many simple bags which have been preserved.

Mojocoya and Tiwanaku Influence

After about A.D. 500, Tiwanaku influence was felt in almost all parts of Bolivia, northern Chile and southern Peru. In addition to the local Mojocoya ceramic style and textile articles woven of cotton, the caves of Mojocoya were filled with ceramics of definite Tiwanaku origin and textiles which have been linked to the Tiwanaku culture through their particular structures and use of brightly-dyed alpaca yarns. Small bags, woven of interlocked tapestry around a circular warp, and narrow bands woven of a variety of complicated structures including supplementary warps, complementary warps, transposed warps and float weaves, have been discovered in portable articles of the Tiwanaku culture, especially those associated with Tiwanaku's drug cult of hallucinogenic snuff, snuff tablets, tubes and textiles. These remain the best documented markers of Tiwanaku presence in areas outside of the *Altiplano*.

After the fall of Tiwanaku around A.D. 1100, a proliferation of local groups, evidenced in a multitude of new ceramic types, evolved to control the vast territory formerly held under Tiwanaku influence. Undoubtedly, these late kingdoms and chiefdoms found in all parts of Bolivia were created from the local inhabitants established in earlier periods. The major characteristic of the regional development period is the political and social unrest evident in the establishment of fortified villages, or pucaras, high on hilltops. One ceramic type dated to the period of declining Tiwanaku influence is known as Yampara and has been discovered in a large variety of sites in the Departments of Cochabamba and Chuquisaca. Beautiful large pitchers and smaller cups with straight horizontal handles were decorated with a variety of complex designs suggesting geometric natural forms.

In another similar yet distinct ceramic type recently identified as Ciaco, the clay body is white kaolin and the decoration is painted in red, yellow and black. The Ciaco style represents the ceramic type made by the local inhabitants of the Cochabamba valley, perhaps the Chuis or Cotas described in colonial documents. Vessel forms and some decorative elements share characteristics with Inca ceramics which arrived in the valley during Inca military campaigns or with Inca colonists between 1450 and 1538. No large ceremonial precincts, decorated architecture or stone sculpture have been uncovered dating to this period. Instead of the standardized religious practices noted during Tiwanaku influence, it appears that a localized religion concerned with natural sacred places in the landscape was followed.

Altiplano and Aymara Kingdoms

With the fall of Tiwanaku, the Lake Titicaca basin -- which had been under central control for almost a millennium -- was severed into distinct political and possibly ethnic groups. These independent Aymara kingdoms shared a common language and many cultural patterns such as burial practices in stone or adobe towers known as chullpas. There is evidence, however, to suggest that domestic house structures varied between round and square preference within groups. Pottery was distinct and other practices may indicate ancient ethnic differences. Historical documents recorded at the time of the Spanish invasion reveal that the most powerful kingdoms were the Lupaca, with their capital at Chuquito located southwest of Lake Titicaca, and the Colla, located just to the north with their capital at Huatuncolla near present-day Puno. Apparently, territorial rivalry kept these two nations in constant warfare, and around 1430 the Lupaca succeeded in conquering the Colla and sacking the town of Huatuncolla.

Political control within the Aymara kingdoms was divided between two separate rulers, reflecting the dual division of Aymara territory into two groups called

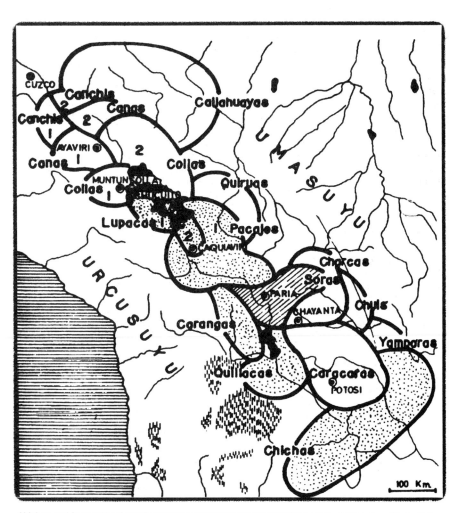

Altiplano and Aymara kingdoms. Source: Arte textil y Mundo Andino by Teresa Gisbert, Silvia Arce, Martha Cajías.

"moieties." One moiety division was known in Aymara as the Alasaa sector, and the other as the Maasaa sector. Within the Lupaca kingdom of the early 1400s, we know that the Alasaa ruler was Cari and the Maasaa ruler was named Cusi. Cari was given more deference and greater status and apparently controlled a larger territory than the Maasaa ruler Cusi. Each town was also divided into an Alasaa or Maasaa moiety with a separate lord governing each sector. This dual leadership was an important facet of Aymara political, social and religious life, and may have been a continuation of a similarly-divided system evident within the art of ancient Bolivian cultures.

Power resided in the lineages of kings and lords, and the architectural vestiges of the rule remains today in the standing burial towers, chullpas, the most obvious cultural marker of the period. Some were formed of blocks of highly polished stone decorated in shallow relief with shakes and other animal forms. Others were constructed of sections of thick adobe and straw, and some contained a mixture of the two materials. The chullpas were planned and built as a magnificent, prominent and obvious display of strength and grandeur. The grouping of several chullpas within a specific area suggests territorial markers, and may in fact represent cemeteries of specific lineages within the various kingdoms. In most, the dead were buried within a small chamber just above or below ground level.

There is evidence that the Aymara towns contained several standing stelae in human form. None have been excavated within any particular architectural precinct or obvious ceremonial sector; rather, it seems that monoliths during this period were worshipped in natural settings, particularly in locations on hilltops. Those carved stone statues that have been uncovered around the Lake Titicaca basin appear to have certain common resemblances to one another and to very early types discovered in the site of Tiwanaku, suggesting a long tradition of worship with similar form. It is possible that the statues themselves have survived intact from extremely early periods to be used even today in some Aymara villages.

Wealth of the Aymara kingdoms was measured in alpacas and llamas carefully bred for wool and used in great trading caravans. Like the Tiwanaku empire before them, and perhaps earlier Lake Titicaca groups, the Aymara exchanged potatoes, salt and high-altitude products for both necessary and desired valley and coastal goods. Trade or exchange was not the only method used by Aymara lords to ensure access to important complementary goods. Through historical documentation it is known that each lake basin kingdom held lands in the eastern valley and on the Pacific coast. These areas were managed by colonial occupations of *Altiplano* people who provided the corn, coca, dye plants and other products impossible to grow on the *Altiplano*.

Some authors have suggested that the large settlements on the eastern slopes of the Andes, identified as home to the Mollo culture, are actually colonial occupations of the lake-basin Lupaca nation. Although Mollo ceramics and the Lupaca ceramics known as allita Aymara do share a great deal of stylistic similarities, more probably the large, fortified and carefully-planned villages were constructed by separate political groups with close ties to the Aymara kingdoms.

Iskanwaya is one of the largest Mollo villages and may have served as the culture's center. Houses are constructed close together as U-shaped structures sharing

Mollo Ceramics
Source:
Ibarra 1965.

side walls. House groups are arranged on natural terraces, high on the slopes of hillsides. Through ceramic styles and radiocarbon dating it is apparent that the Mollo culture was established in valley sites around A.D. 1200, after the dissolution of the Tiwanaku empire. Ceramics of a style related to the Incas' ceramics have also been discovered at the site, testifying to a later Inca occupation.

While the Aymara kings were fighting among themselves to establish their territorial rights to lands around the Titicaca basin, the Incas of Cuzco prepared to invade the valuable region and incorporate the vast wealth into their own expanding realm. A first opportunity came during the reign of the emperor Viracocha when both Zapana, king of the Colla, and Cari, king of the Lupaca, asked for alliances with Cuzco. Apparently, when Zapana heard that the Inca Viracocha had decided to help the Lupaca Lord Cari, he invaded Lupaca territory. Zapana was killed, and sometime around 1430 Huatuncolla was sacked by the Lupaca.

One of the Inca origin myths describes the first Incas as rising out of Lake Titicaca. In this bit of propaganda the Incas were obviously attempting to associate themselves with one of the most important religious centers of the Andes. Temples were built on the Island of the Sun and Koati in Lake Titicaca, and at Incaracay and Incallacta in the Cochabamba valley. All the Aymara territories were incorporated into the Kingdom of Cuzco. Tawantinsuyo was a single suyo, one quarter of the Inca empire. Roads were refurbished and built to connect all parts of the empire and tambos, fortresses and temples were distributed throughout Bolivia.

Although the Incas left quantities of their material culture in architecture, ceramics and metal artifacts, and established their language, Quechua, in many locations throughout Bolivia, the duration of their occupation was no more than 70 or 80 years. In 1535, Diego de Almagro traveled across the Inca and pre-Inca roads through Bolivia to the Chilean coast with an army of Spanish and Indian forces. Hernando Pizarro, hearing of internal fighting among the Lupaca and the Colla, brought an army from Peru and finally subjugated the Aymaras. In 1542 the entire area was annexed as the Audiencia de Charcas of the Spanish Viceroyalty of Peru. The Spanish, European missionaries and travelers who arrived soon after began to record all elements of native life, and thus prehistory gave way to the historical record in the Andes.

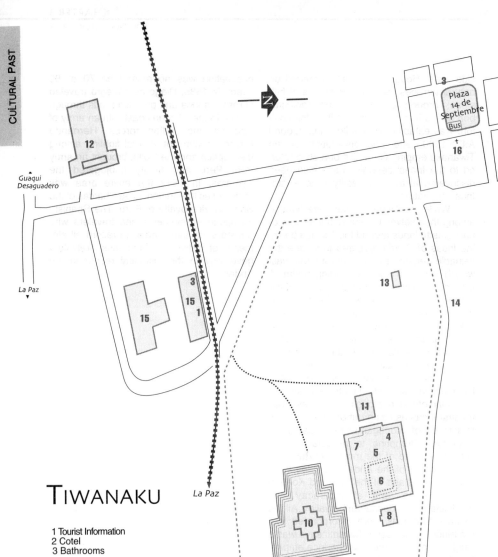

Guaqui
Desaguadero

La Paz

La Paz

TIWANAKU

1 Tourist Information
2 Cotel
3 Bathrooms

4 Puerta del Sol
5 Kalasaya
6 Ponce Monolith
7 Frail Monolith
8 Subterranean Temple
9 Kantatallita
10 Akapana Pyramid
11 Palace of the Sarcophajus
12 Pumapunku
13 Puerta de la Luna
14 Sukakollus
15 Museum
16 San Pedro Church

Plaza
14 de
Septiembre
Bus

SECRETS OF TIWANAKU

BY WILLIAM MULLEN

HOW INGENIOUS FARMERS BUILT AN EMPIRE THAT INSPIRED THE INCAS AND RIVALED ROME.

bout 400 years ago the first European, probably a Spanish conquistador or missionary priest, laid eyes on the Pampa Koani of Bolivia. History does not record whether that trailblazer lingered long in the cold, bleak, windswept valley on Lake Titicaca's southern edge, but it is not likely that many visitors since then have bothered to spend too much time there. Aside from a spectacular view of the eastern peaks of the Andean mountain chain, the Cordillera Real, at first glance there is not much about the place to recommend it.

The valley today is home to an impoverished farming community of 7,000. In the little villages that dot the pampa, or plain, you might occasionally see a few local oddities -- for example, the llama, alpaca and vicuña, the New World cousins of the camel that are native to the area. On the lake itself, you can watch the villagers fish from the graceful reed boats for which Lake Titicaca is noted. The few visitors who do come here, though, usually go to Tiwanaku, a small market town 10 miles west of Pampa Koani. It is the site of massive ruins of an ancient culture of the same name.

Discovery of a Grand Civilization

In the 1930s Wendell Bennett, an American archaeologist, came to Tiwanaku to examine its ruins. He also found some related ruins in the Pampa Koani, on a hill in a village called Luqurmata. Archeologists had long thought of Tiwanaku as a relatively unimportant era in the epic of Andean civilization. In most people's minds, it was a loose confederation of minor kingdoms that appeared and then disappeared some 400 years before the rise of the great Inca empire, which flourished in the area from

A drawig of the central deity figure on the Gateway of the Sun.

1438 to the mid-1500s. The ruins were thought to be not much more than ceremonial centers that were used only for occasional tribal ritual meetings. Bennett found nothing to challenge those assumptions.

But Bennett and the others who so dismissed the Tiwanaku era were premature in their judgment. In August 1986, Alan Kolata, a 37-year-old anthropologist from the University of Illinois at Chicago, led an archeological team to the hill in the village of Luqurmata. The team, a joint Bolivian-American effort, began to dig where Bennett had left off 50 years earlier, and started what they hoped would be a major five-year excavation.

In only three months' time, Kolata's expedition had come up with some extraordinary findings. Not the least among them is irrefutable evidence that the Pampa Koani, now barely able to sustain 7,000 impoverished souls, 1,500 years ago was a vast breadbasket area that grew enough to feed and support 125,000 people. The ancient Tiwanaku people must have known how to overcome the problems -- floods, droughts, frost, soil exhaustion and salinization from the slightly salty waters of Lake Titicaca -- that today bedevil the local farmers.

The Difficult Life of the Altiplano

The pampa here is a broad, flat, 40-square-mile basin that for 10 miles follows the Catari River in a southeasterly direction from the lakeshore. It is just one of many such basins surrounding the lake, which, at 13,500 feet above sea level, is the highest navigable body of water in the world. It is the central area of the great Andean Altiplano, the vast, rolling flatland nestled between the Cordillera Real and the Andean chain's western peaks, the Cordillera Occidental.

At this elevation, the extremely thin atmosphere makes life uncomfortable for all but the natives of the area, the Aymara, who are descendants of the Tiwanaku people.

They are squat and powerfully built, with massive chests and expansive lungs developed to cope with the rarefied air. Until Bolivia's agrarian revolution of 1952, the Aymara were virtual serfs to the few descendants of Spanish colonials who owned much of the valley and operated haciendas, large ranches and farms.

Now, thanks to the revolution, the Aymara campesinos, or peasants, own the land themselves, but they are extremely poor. Each family has a few cattle, pigs and sheep that graze on the undulating fields outside adobe-walled farms. Each farm consists of a few plots for growing potatoes and quinoa, a grain plant found only in the Altiplano. But the soil is so devoid of nutrients that after three or four years of cultivation, plots must lie fallow for 10 or 15 years before they can be planted again.

The result is a classic Third World subsistence-farming way of life. What each family grows it consumes; very little ever gets sold for extra income. When the family gets too large to live off the land, somebody invariably leaves home and moves to the shantytown sections near La Paz, a minimum of three hours by bus east of the valley, to search for work. Usually it is a fruitless search.

As the second poorest country in the Western Hemisphere after Haiti, Bolivia has few jobs for hungry campesinos forced to leave their farms.

Numerous international agencies have sent agricultural engineers to the Altiplano to see if anything can be done to improve conditions there. Most have gone away shaking their heads. At that altitude the climate seems too severe and the soil too poor to do much of anything that would make a difference.

The Agricultural Innovation of Tiwanaku

Kolata's expedition showed, however, that the Pampa Koani is just one Lake

Titicaca valley among many that every year for a thousand years produced stupendous harvests. He estimates that the harvests fed as many as six million people, just two million less than the entire population of Bolivia today, and allowed surpluses to be stored away for bad years.

The fields are proof of something Kolata has long suspected: that far from being a minor period in Andean civilization, Tiwanaku was one of the world's greatest and longest-reigning empires. And that the little market town of Tiwanaku was for a thousand years a fabulous imperial capital, the inspiration for the largest and better-known Andean empire of the Incas that came after it. Specifically, Kolata's expedition is uncovering an immense system of raised fields built and perfected by the Tiwanaku civilization more than 2,000 years ago.

The fields were so carefully engineered and constructed that many of them stand intact today. The undulating, precisely laid patterns of the raised fields still course across the Pampa Koani, creating a curious washboard pattern.

They are immense constructions, three to five feet high, their planting surfaces sometimes as large as 50 feet wide and 600 feet long. Each is a carefully layered structure, beginning with a thick cobblestone base which is covered with a layer of impermeable clay. Over the clay is a layer of large, coarse gravel and then another layer of finer gravel, and over it all sits the topsoil.

The raised fields lie parallel to one another separated by deep graceful curves. Forming precise geometric patterns, the fields and ditches cover some three-quarters of the 40-square-mile valley. To accomplish this, ancient engineers straightened the Catari River and moved it one mile to the east.

The design of the fields is both obviously simple and surprisingly complex. The irrigation ditches provided water in times of drought, and the elevated fields protected crops in times of flooding.

Among the more complex features is the impermeable layer of clay at the base of the fields. Its purpose seems to have been to keep the salty water of nearby Lake Titicaca from seeping up from below ground and into the topsoil. The precise positioning of the fields and ditches also seems to have a definite purpose: to take maximum advantage of the intense Andean sun. By efficiently exposing the ditches to the sun, the water in them gets enough heat by day to protect the fields from frost damage during the Altiplano's bitterly cold nights.

The heated water in the irrigation ditches also promoted the heavy growth of algae to nourish the fish. Furthermore, it attracted a resident population of ducks, which also entered the local diet both as meat and as eggs. Duck droppings, decayed algae and fish remains then formed a rich muck that was periodically scraped off the ditch bottoms to serve as an excellent fertilizer for the topsoil.

A colleague of Kolata, Clark Erickson of the University of Illinois at Champaign, had already spent three years cultivating raised-field test plots on the Peruvian side of Lake Titicaca with Peruvian agronomist Ignacio Garaycocha when Kolata began his work. Early results were more than encouraging. While local conventional farming methods yield two to three metric tons of potatoes per hectare (2.5 acres), their test plots of raised fields yielded 16 metric tons of potatoes per hectare.

These initial results are based on relatively small parcels of land, but the message is an alluring one. Bolivia once was a net exporter of food, but it now must import it, and malnutrition is a severe problem among its poor. Its treasury, however, cannot afford to buy the expensive western technology needed to upgrade its food production.

But if the ancient Tiwanaku could grow more than what they needed to eat, using these same fields and without the benefit of tractors, motorized water pumps and chemical fertilizers, why couldn't it be done again today? The idea sounds both absurd and appealing. A technology invented in antiquity and used profitably for hundreds of years was forgotten before its inventors could develop the written word and thus preserve it for posterity. Now, with the aid of 20th-century technology, the forgotten knowledge has been rediscovered, and across a gap of more than a thousand years is holding a bright promise for an impoverished land.

Alan Kolata certainly liked the idea. "It's called applied archaeology," he said. "It's discovering information that is not just fascinating in a scholarly way but has the possibility of being used for the good of people today. This is a case where you really can learn from the past."

The Tiwanaku Empire

The people modern scientists are learning from once had an empire that included nearly half of Bolivia, southern portions of Peru, the northwest section of Argentina and nearly half of Chile. It was an empire established on the abundant products of its agricultural systems. The surplus crops gave Tiwanaku the luxury of the time and the inclination to raise armies that began conquering the Andes before Jesus was born.

It was an empire that continued to grow until some time after 1000 A.D., establishing great agricultural colonies patterned after its own fields throughout the Andes. Its armies reigned supreme over people of many cultures and tongues. Its engineers built a vast system of paved highways over mountains and through deserts and jungles.

The highways enabled Tiwanaku to maintain a constant flow of goods throughout the empire. Royal bureaucrats traveled the highways along with the imperial armies and the endless chains of llama caravans. These bureaucrats kept tabs on far-flung imperial outposts, spreading Tiwanaku's considerable technology and an artistry that was unsurpassed by any other pre-Columbian Andean culture, even the Incas.

And as with ancient Rome, all the highways eventually led to one place -- to Tiwanaku, today a shabby little town but once the mighty imperial capital, lying in a valley a few miles south of Lake Titicaca.

Those visiting the capital city 1,500 years ago would have come to it by one of many paved highways over the mountains. Before descending into the Tiwanaku valley, they would have stopped to admire what lay before him, a city shimmering in the bright Andean sunlight, for much of it was covered with gold. The Tiwanaku skyline was dominated by imposing pyramids, temples and palaces.

The two largest structures, the Kalasasaya Temple and the Akapana Pyramid, ran some 600 feet on each side and rose to more than 50 feet in height. They were constructed of huge granite-like stones called andesite, some weighing more than 160 tons, that were ferried to the city on reed boats from quarries across the lake.

Much of the exterior of the city's grand stone buildings was covered with intricately carved friezes and bas-relief adornments. The finely carved surfaces, however, were not left bare but were covered with thin plates of gold that were formed to follow the contours of the carvings underneath. Portions of buildings not covered with gold were painted in hues of blue, red, gold and black. The effect was to give the imperial city a sheen of dazzling opulence.

Physical Appearance of the Tiwanaku

The most striking physical characteristic of the 50,000 Tiwanaku who inhabited the city was the shape of their heads. Both the elite and the commoners of Tiwanaku practiced a form of skull-shaping on their children that was popular in many Andean cultures. Shortly after the birth of a baby, its head was clamped between two boards to force the soft skull to assume a pointed shape. The boards remained on the child's head until about the age of five, by which time the pointed shape was permanent, leaving him with no brow and a forehead that sloped back dramatically from the eyebrows to a point at the back of the skull. This pointed head was regarded as a mark of cultural distinction.

On the city's broad avenues the people would have been dressed in the finest clothing and jewelry available in the realm, as anyone would in a thriving capital. "Costume and jewelry were immensely important in the culture," Kolata said. "We know they possessed combs, pins and mirrors made of polished metal, so we know appearance and beauty were important."

The men wore tunics over short pants cut just below the knee. Head coverings were indicators of position and status. The supreme rulers wore golden diadems that complemented chest pieces inlaid with turquoise. The more important people under the supreme rulers wore colorful, tightly woven, four-cornered caps; those next to them in status wore elaborate textile turbans.

Soldiers sported headdresses made of puma skin, the cat's head protruding from the front and the tail hanging from behind. As tokens of their ferocity and triumphs in war, the warriors collected the heads of the enemies they had killed in battle and wore them as trophies strung from belts around their waists.

For jewelry, the men had rings, bracelets, armbands, anklets and necklaces of copper, bronze, silver and gold. Those from the high ranks of Tiwanaku society set themselves off from the lower classes by wearing decorative plugs of turquoise, seashell, wood or gold set tightly in holes in their ears and lower lips. The women were less flamboyant, wearing simple wraparound tunics held together with decorative metal pins. Upper-class women also wore beaded cowl necklaces.

A Cultural Model for the Incas

The Tiwanaku way of life as practiced in the imperial city set the pattern of nearly every Andean culture that came after it until the coming of Europeans. "Tiwanaku was a seminal force in Andean culture," Kolata said. "Because they didn't have a written language to record it, we'll never know all the precise details of Tiwanaku life. But we know that the Incas modeled themselves specifically after Tiwanaku, and, luckily, we know a good deal about the Incas. Because of that, we can take what we know archaeologically from Tiwanaku and make some pretty good guesses about how they lived."

By extrapolating from what is known about the Incas, archaeologists have pieced together a fairly-detailed picture of life in the Tiwanaku empire. In the capital city 1,500 years ago, everything would have revolved around the comings and goings of the supreme emperor-priest of Tiwanaku. In the politics of the empire there was no separation of church and state. The emperor was both leader and god. He and members of his family, who were also revered as godlike mortals, conducted both the affairs of state and the culture's most sacred religious rituals.

The holiest precinct of the city was the Kalasasaya Temple, the burial place of Tiwanaku's ruling elite. Their palace Putani, stretching 300 feet on each side, lay directly behind Kalasasaya. The noblemen-priests inherited their positions and were raised from birth to lead their people in both spiritual and secular matters. As adults they took as wives the daughters of families of equally high status, perhaps even marrying their own sisters, as the Inca emperors later did.

The imperial city was filled with the most skilled artisans of the realm: sculptors, jewelers, weavers and potters. The elite patronized the artisans, lavishing their wealth on them and urging them to develop their skills further and produce the finest examples of their crafts.

Royal Life

Life for the lords of Tiwanaku was lived on a voluptuous scale. They were absolute powers over all they surveyed, with the power to possess anything or anybody they might desire in the kingdom. Royal retainers were sent out periodically throughout the realm to look for children of exceptional promise and beauty from the families of both minor elite and commoners alike. Those selected were taken from their homes and moved into the palaces of the rich to be sequestered and tutored in the finer facets of Tiwanaku life.

Some of the girls worked in the temples attending to the noble holy women. Some were assigned to entertain the men of the royal households as honored concubines. The most favored, as the evidence seems to suggest, remained virgins, guarded and schooled for their roles in the most important religious rites of the realm. In these rites, held only on special occasions such as times of bad harvest or war, these girls served as human sacrifices to propitiate or seek favors from the Tiwanaku deities. As for the boys, their destiny was to be castrated and trained to be palace servants and chamberlains watching over the household's royal women, priestesses and concubines.

Life in the royal household was sumptuous. Floors were covered with colored stone mosaics. Lamps burning oil from llama fat illuminated a central patio at night. Sculptures of pumas, condors and other important imperial symbols were arrayed along the patio's perimeter. On the walls were finely-woven tapestries.

Much of the royal household's time was taken up with the observance of religious ceremonies, in which extremely powerful hallucinogenic drugs seem to have played an integral part. The drugs were imported from the low-lying desert regions of the ocean coasts. Willka, a red hallucinogenic seed, was snorted as a powder from finely-carved snuff trays, and mescaline was used in mind-altering drinks. Even more powerful drugs, such as one extracted from the ayahuasca vine that produces violent behavior and visual hallucinations, were administered through syringes as an enema.

Sacred Life

All the great temples of the city were ornamented with an array of elaborately carved sacred monoliths that ranged in height from five to more than 20 feet, depicting idols in stylized human form. They were apparently positioned to remind the priests of the passage of important ritual days. One, the Bennett Stele (Wendell Bennett found it in the Kalasasaya temple area in the 1930s), bears complex markings that have been deciphered as a solar and lunar calendar more accurate than our own.

The calendar was extremely important as an agricultural guide, indicating when orders to plant the fields should go out through the realm. It also kept track of the religious rituals, including animal and human sacrifices, that had to be observed with the coming of the planting season.

On such occasions, members of the nobility would gather in the imperial city from all over the empire. It was a time of great celebration, the avenues leading to the temple and the lanes running through the adobe houses of the commoners awash with people getting drunk on corn beer. At the temple precincts, the crowd would gather as the young virgins, following the rites in which they had been so carefully trained, were offered as human sacrifices to Tiwanaku's gods.

The most important object in the Kalasasaya, however, was the Gateway of the Sun, a massive, carved portal hewn from a single block of stone 10 feet high, 11 feet wide and weighing 10 tons. The focal point of the gateway is a human figure wearing a tunic and holding two scepters topped with condor heads. The figure, found in every part of the Andes where the empire became dominant, is thought to represent the principal deity of Tiwanaku.

In front of the Kalasasaya is a large sunken courtyard that was filled with the sacred monolithic stone icons of the kingdoms Tiwanaku had conquered. They were put there for all to see that Tiwanaku's gods were more powerful than any others. Besides the captured icons, the royal families of the conquered kingdoms were also brought to Tiwanaku, held hostage there as insurance against rebellion.

Building an Empire

Conquest was in itself a form of insurance, giving Tiwanaku access to plentiful and regular supplies of those foods that could not be grown in the thin atmosphere of the Altiplano. It also assured them minerals, such as gold and silver, and medicinal and psychedelic drugs.

The job of conquest, of course, fell to the imperial army. The soldiers were armed with star-headed war clubs made of polished stone, bows and arrows, slingshots and spears. They armored themselves with thickly quilted tunics and carried circular and square shields constructed of wicker, leather and cotton batting.

"It is apparent from the evidence we have," Kolata said, "that the armies of Tiwanaku were pretty ferocious when they decided to do battle. They were organized, tough and certainly had no qualms about beheading anybody who opposed them. Ritual trophy head-taking is a very important component of Tiwanaku art."

The style of Tiwanaku conquest, Kolata said, was probably similar to that of the later Incas. A conquering army essentially was a siege army. Supplied from the home front by a secured route of llama caravans, it surrounded an enemy town, waited until the town began to starve, then moved in for the concluding battle.

Each time a kingdom or territory was conquered, masses of Tiwanakans, from 2,000 to 5,000 strong, were dispatched by the imperial city to establish administrative enclaves. At the extreme edges of the empire, traders and soldiers in groups of 50 established frontier posts to look after Tiwanaku interests and deal with primitive nomadic and semi-nomadic tribes.

Among the many administrative problems faced by the supreme emperor-priest was the maintenance and protection of the empire's far-flung outposts. Taxes had to be levied, armies maintained and communication kept open with distant administrators. Most importantly, Tiwanaku wanted access to the produce from the vast raised-field agricultural operations it established in its colonies.

Llama caravans provided transportation, and the government kept herds of up to 50,000 llamas in various locations around the Altiplano. A single caravan could include 500 or more animals. The highways were made secure by the military, and local communities along the route were under orders to maintain well-stocked posthouses to feed and provision the animals and traders.

For 1,000 years, llama caravans entered and left the imperial city in a continuous stream. Caravans from Chile and

Peru brought dried seafood, corn, hot peppers, coca, copper, tin, precious stones and gold ingots and dust. From the jungles of Bolivia came corn, coca, tropical fruits, wood and more exotic items such as wild monkeys, colorful bird feathers used in clothing design and the much-valued hallucinogens.

Outbound caravans carried local food products, particularly potatoes and quinoa, and such manufactured goods as pottery, textiles and jewelry. But the imperial city's most important export to the hinterlands, said Kolata, had to be its agricultural knowledge. All the other accomplishments of the Tiwanaku culture, he said, including its trade routes, architecture, artistry and even its city of gold, pale in comparison to its fields.

"These fields are the great monuments to their culture," Kolata said. "The hundreds of years of empirical science that went into perfecting them, the sheer amount of labor it took to move the stones, clay and earth to build them, the staggering amount of production that came out of them -- all was without parallel in antiquity."

Archeological Discovery and Investigation

The first raised fields were discovered in Bolivia in 1961 by William Denevan, a University of Wisconsin geologist, who found them in a tropical lowland area far east of Lake Titicaca. Since that first discovery, similar fields have been under archeological investigation in Mexico, Guatemala, Belize, Colombia, Venezuela and even as far north as Wisconsin and Michigan in North America.

In 1986, however, little archaeological investigation was done on the fields in Bolivia. For 50 years, the Bolivian government had banned foreign scientists from its archaeological ruins because early in the century archaeologists had stolen a number of irreplaceable cultural artifacts for American and European museums. The ban began to break down after Kolata, a native of Milwaukee, first came to Bolivia in 1978 after receiving his doctorate degree in anthropology at Harvard University. Intrigued by the raised fields in the Titicaca area, he was granted permission in 1979 to do some partial excavations on the fields in the Pampa Koani. Working with Oswaldo Rivera, a young archaeologist from Bolivia's National Institute of Archaeology, he set out to prove that the fields had been constructed by the Tiwanaku people.

The sheer immensity of the Pampa Koani field constructions piqued Kolata's interest in the Tiwanakans. Even by modern, industrialized standards, transporting the rocks, clay and topsoil for an area the size of the Pampa Koani would be a major undertaking. To have built the fields without benefit of wheeled vehicles or draft animals larger than the relatively delicate llama indicated an extraordinarily organized and highly developed culture.

Kolata then went to Chicago to work with the Field Museum of National History, but he continued to travel to Bolivia to investigate the raised-field systems. Until then he had only limited approval from the Bolivian government to do his work. But then two disasters hit the Altiplano and made Bolivian officials pay closer attention to Kolata's work.

The first was a two-year drought in 1982-83 that all but destroyed the Altiplano crops, except those in the Pampa Koani, where the ancient irrigation ditches continued to provide water. The second was a flood in 1985 when Lake Titicaca, rising to its highest recorded levels since the mid-1800s, inundated the surrounding farmland and ruined crops for two years -- except, again, in the Pampa Koani, where much of the planting surfaces of the ancient raised fields remained dry.

Support for Kolata's work began to grow rapidly both in Bolivia and in the United States. Shortly after Kolata accepted a teaching position at the University of Illinois at Chicago, the Bolivian government gave him a five-year license to conduct major excavations at Tiwanaku sites. He is the first foreigner to do unrestricted excavations in Bolivia since Bennett 50 years ago. In the U.S., Kolata received $330,000 in grants from the National Science Foundation and the National Endowment for the Humanities to underwrite the first three years of his Bolivian work.

"Though we may never succeed," Kolata said, "one of the first things we have tried to do is find out why the fields, after being cultivated for at least 1,000 years, were suddenly abandoned. If Lake Titicaca was smaller in those days, or if there was a sudden shift in climate in the area from a milder weather to the harsh conditions that prevail today, that would explain a lot. It would also make the attempt to restart the fields useless."

The best way, obviously, to see if the raised-field system can work again today is to begin planting those fields again. Kolata spent much of his time trying to convince local campesinos to lend him land for the experiment. The sight of the foreign scientists going around Luqurmata digging useless "holes" has given the natives cause for both amusement and suspicion.

That the mounds of now-barren earth in their pasturelands were built by their distant ancestors means nothing to them for the moment. But by showing them pictures of similar fields made verdant by Clark Erickson's work in Peru, Kolata has slowly begun to pique their interests.

Reconstructing the Origins of Tiwanaku

Virtually every discovery the team is making at the Luqurmata site is a new page in the history of the Tiwanaku. As a separate culture, Tiwanaku probably began as a village sometime before 1000 B.C. on the site, 10 miles west of Luqurmata. It was one of many cultures that emerged along the lake and around the Altiplano, a place well-suited as an incubator of civilization. The Andes have been described as a sort of "vertical archipelago." From Lake Titicaca, early men were only a day and a half by foot from radically different environments, including deserts, jungles, temperate plains and frozen glaciers.

As primitive Indians began to group together and settle down to a lifestyle of farming and animal husbandry in and around the Andes, they became increasingly adept at developing useful crops. In the Altiplano they developed quinoa and cañawa, grain plants unique to the region. They also developed hardy tubers well-adapted to the Andean cold: oca, olluco, mashwa and, above all, the potato, of which they grew more than 200 varieties, adapting them to the climatological conditions that changed with every 600 feet of elevation.

In the lower, warmer levels, other plants developed into important staple crops, particularly corn. Each climate had its unique staple products, and because of the close proximity of the various regions, inter-tribal trading began naturally. In the Altiplano the llama was domesticated into large herds and used for food, wool and as a pack animal, which probably encouraged trade even more.

As populations grew around the lake, agriculture also intensified. There is archaeological evidence that the first raised-field systems near the lake had begun by 1000 B.C. Nobody knows who originated the system, but Tiwanakans must have been foremost in perfecting it. By 100 B.C. Tiwanaku was emerging as the most important urban center on Lake Titicaca. The products from its raised fields fed the growing trade routes to neighboring kingdoms, and trade became the impetus for empire building.

"Most Andean cultures," Kolata said, "did not want to rely on simple trade to get the foods and goods they needed from other climatological zones. They wanted direct access to these things, so they colonized the areas that produced what they needed rather than rely on uncertain trade partners."

Tiwanaku simply followed that same colonizing pattern, but it was more successful in doing so than any civilization before it. By 100 A.D., it ruled all its neighboring kingdoms at the south end of the lake. By 400 A.D., it had defeated its main rivals, the Pukara people in Peru, and ruled the entire lake basin while continuing to push its boundaries west towards the Pacific and south toward Chile and Argentina.

The Site at Luqurmata

Luqurmata was probably one of the early conquests of Tiwanaku and one of the empire's first satellite cities and agricultural colonies. Today, Luqurmata is not so much a village as a group of scattered farms along the edge of Lake Titicaca. What distinguishes it from other villages in the Pampa Koani is a 100-foot-high hill sitting in its midst. The hill's slopes and crest rise in sharp, ruler-straight lines. The straight lines of the hill's slopes give it an appearance of being manmade. In fact, it is manmade. It was the temple hill of the Tiwanaku colonizers, constructed 2,000 years ago.

On the hill's slightly-flattened crest, the remains of two temple buildings poke through the tough, tundra-like grasses that cover the Luqurmata landscape. They were smaller replicas of the Kalasasaya temple in the imperial city and of the sunken temple that sits in front of the Kalasasaya. The two structures are positioned to face east precisely so that the rising sun falls through their doorways at dawn.

Kolata began his dig at Luqurmata in the summer of 1986 around the outer perimeters of Luqurmata's temple buildings on the hill. Three skeletons, two of them headless, the third with no head and torso but its legs and pelvis intact, were discovered buried at the base of a temple wall. The mutilated remains were testimony that even the priests in the minor temples of Tiwanaku's colonial areas had the authority to conduct human sacrifices.

The Luqurmata temples themselves are classic specimens of Tiwanaku's remarkably sophisticated architecture and construction techniques. Each block in the temple bears curious markings that hint at the complex organization of Tiwanaku's construction industry. On each block in the smaller, sunken temple is a symbol about eight inches across consisting of a single dot in the center and six dots forming a circle around it. Blocks in the larger temple have similar symbols, with eight dots instead of six encircling the central dot.

"These markings," Kolata said, "probably were made by architectural engineers constructing the temples, both of which seemed to have been erected at the same time. We believe the markings were made to show the workmen to which temple each block belonged, almost as though the blocks arrived at the site with a prefabricated design."

Each of the blocks was carved to exacting specifications, meticulously and precisely shaped to fit tightly together and form the temple walls. Corners are perfectly squared, indicating a knowledge of geometry, and the entire complex is undergirded with a network of drainage sewers that 2,000 years later continues to keep the temple floors dry.

But temples are not Kolata's central concern. His real quest at Luqurmata was an ordinary Tiwanakan house, so he dug in the slope behind the temples that tapers gently for several thousand yards toward Lake Titicaca.

Bermann, within days of beginning his dig, had found a floor and carbon ashes. He also found wall foundations, garbage heaps, burial vaults, bones and complete pottery pieces. Expanding his site, he found not just one floor but several, along with more burial vaults and more wall foundations separated by pathways. He had come upon not only the first Tiwanaku house to be unearthed in modern history, but a complete Tiwanaku workingman's neighborhood.

"Tiwanaku is no longer a cathedral in the sky," Kolata said after the discovery by Bermann and his team. Now he has proof that the temple sites were far from being largely uninhabited religious pilgrimage areas. "It was a real, live place, with people living in it. By the time we are finished, much of pre-Columbian history will have to be rewritten."

Each bit of bone, pottery, stone utensil and even some badly rotted bits of cloth recovered from the Luqurmata house sites and burial tombs will eventually add to the forgotten story of Tiwanaku. So will the ancient garbage heaps, archaeologically called "middens," found adjacent to the houses. Searching through a household midden, archaeologists can find evidence of what the occupants ate. Establishing what was in the daily diet of average citizens of a civilization can lead to much knowledge about the civilization itself.

The middens revealed llama bones, so llama meat was part of the diet, complementing such other local produce as potatoes, oca, olluco and mashwa, along with the quinoa and cañawa grains. This was no surprise.

But there were bones of ocean fishes in the Luqurmata middens. That would confirm the view that the Tiwanakans produced food in such abundance that they could trade the surpluses for desired foods from various and distant regions -- ocean fish as well as lowland corn, tropical fruits and hot peppers. The presence of remains of these foods in the middens of average Tiwanaku houses in Luqurmata can only mean that these foods came routinely and inexpensively over trade routes to all Tiwanaku citizens.

The pottery found in and around the houses bears the artistic markings of Classic Tiwanaku, a period roughly spanning 300 to 700 A.D., when the empire was at its artistic and technological zenith. By analyzing the pottery at a later time in the laboratory, the archeologists can fix the dates that people actually lived in Luqurmata.

That Classic Tiwanaku period coincides with the Roman Empire's final stages of collapse. At that time, much of Europe was still dominated by barbaric peoples barely past the stage of tribal, rock-throwing warfare. Luqurmata, on the other hand, had already enjoyed four centuries as a peaceful colonial outpost and was settled into the rhythms of planting and harvesting its fields, a rhythm that would continue for at least six more centuries.

The religious lords of Luqurmata, perhaps distant kin of the supreme emperor-priest in the capital city, inhabited the upper precincts of the temple hill in the town. The commoners living on the slopes below them paid obeisance to the lords and accepted the elitist state religion. But they were actually more prone to practicing animism, the worship of the spirits of hills, streams, trees and even household objects, much as the Aymaras of today continue to do while professing to be Roman Catholics.

Work and Artwork

To the elite, however, the animism of the commoners meant little so long as they paid their taxes, which were exacted in two ways. At harvest time, a certain percentage of the produce from the raised fields went to the state. Some of this was probably used for trade with communities elsewhere in the empire, and some was stored in state-owned warehouses for the common good, as a hedge against years of poor harvests. In addition to the harvest tax, commoners were also subject to a labor tax, whereby men and women were required to spend specific times during the year working directly for the state. The men labored on such public projects as building and maintaining raised fields, imperial roads and state-owned warehouses. Women probably were expected to weave for the state.

Weaving was a highly-developed art in Tiwanaku. Using the wool from the llama, alpaca and vicuña, artisans developed several highly specialized and sophisticated techniques that resulted in tapestries, batiks, tie-dyes and other styles of textiles. Using natural dyes, the women incorporated important religious and cultural symbols such as pumas, condors, snakes and llamas into their designs. Textiles were an important communication device in a culture without the written word, serving to record and transmit cultural information around the empire. Kolata believes, for example, that stonemasons designed elaborate building friezes and adornments in cloth first, and then used them as templates when they sculpted the designs into stone.

Indeed, while gold, silver and gemstones were valued commodities in Tiwanaku, real wealth was counted in textiles. No pre-Columbian Andean society, either before or after Tiwanaku, seems to have had any form of money for trade, but all of them valued fabrics to the extreme. Perhaps textiles were a major means of barter exchange.

Luqurmata was a regular stop for the llama caravans plying the trade routes of the empire. At Luqurmata the traders would pick up textiles and other objects fashioned by local artisans along with the produce from the fields. In turn, they would drop off the foods and goods from other colonial outposts, including great supplies of coca leaves.

The leaves were chewed universally as a mild stimulant in Tiwanaku times, by the commoners and elite alike. Not much more potent than a cup of coffee, it was used to counter the exhaustion easily brought on by the Altiplano's thin atmosphere. The practice continues today with the Aymara. Indeed, the local workmen hired by the archaeologists sometimes find themselves being mirrored by the faces of their ancestors depicted in pottery heads, the cheeks of both ancestors and workmen bulging with the ubiquitous leaf.

Social Stratification of Tiwanaku

If the 37 local workmen Kolata hired have any interest in the ancient houses they are uncovering, they hide it well. The only time they show much excitement is when the archeologists uncover tombs that were dug near the house sites. But the excitement is more a function of superstition than curiosity. Some workmen refuse to work when a tomb is opened. Those who do work often cover their mouths with their hands so as not to breathe in the spiritual essence of the tomb's occupant.

One day Bermann cut a finger while digging up bones from a tomb, and when his helpers saw blood on the bones as he handed them up it caused a complete work stoppage. Graffam fell ill with altitude sickness after opening another tomb. His helpers had not given an offering to Pachamama, Mother Earth, before disturbing the remains of the dead. They now insist that he pour liquor around a tomb before opening it.

Running Luqurmata was undoubtedly a difficult task. The lords of Luqurmata needed a lot of technical help to oversee the fields and administer the town. So they must have shared their enclave of better homes on the top of the hill with a second tier of elites who perhaps boasted some royal blood themselves.

Among this tier were architects, stone-masons, agricultural engineers, professional traders, soldiers and managerial overseers, including bookkeepers and historians. Despite the lack of the written word, a society as complex as Tiwanaku had to keep records of business transactions, both state and private. These records were kept by specialists who used knotted cords as memory aids and memorized past business transactions and the lore of the empire in order to preserve it all as oral history.

Farther down the hill, where Bermann uncovered the first Tiwanaku house, is an area that more than likely was reserved for artisans, specialists or personal servants to the nobility. Judging from the ruins Bermann has uncovered, their homes were not very large or particularly ornate and probably made of adobe brick and covered with thatched roofs. Agricultural workers and their overseers lived in numerous scattered sections away from the temple complex and close to the fields in which they toiled.

Death and Succession

Apart from times of war or the great disasters of failed crops, probably the most significant disruption of the routine of Luqurmata's daily life came upon the death of the supreme emperor-priest. On such an occasion, Luqurmata would be emptied of its highest-ranking citizens, who would get on their royal litters to be carried to the golden city and take part in the rites of succession.

In the case of an emperor's death, there would be several days of citywide mourning, while the royal kin gathered from far and wide for the state funeral. The mourning would be characterized by an almost-universal beer-drinking spree, the citizenry reeling and wailing through the avenues.

The dead emperor was buried in a tomb specially constructed for him in one of the temples, his body interred with an immense collection of his wealth, including golden objects, jewelry and textiles. If they were so inclined, the wives of the departed leader could have themselves put to death so they could accompany him into the tomb as well.

The empire's new leader would be selected from among his sons -- usually, but not always, the eldest of them. If other powerful lords felt that a younger son showed more forcefulness or capacity to lead, he would be installed after a period of court intrigue. At his installation, the city's broad avenues would again fill with reeling, drunken revelry. As soon as the new emperor was firmly in place, the various lords of the kingdom would disperse to their respective fiefdoms, taking up the business of the empire once again.

If life for the commoners and the colonial subjects of Tiwanaku was a good deal less sumptuous than that enjoyed by the elite, it was not without its benefits. First and foremost, the empire offered them security and freedom from hunger. With Tiwanaku's vast armies, there was constant protection from the hostile kingdoms and savage tribes that lurked on the empire's frontiers. That the empire existed for so many hundreds of years is testament to its success and the relative satisfaction with which its citizens regarded the government.

"Tiwanaku was the longest-lived empire of all the Andean civilizations," Kolata said. "There is no doubt about that. During the centuries of the imperium, there was probably a Pax Tiwanaku, a long, long period of almost universal peace, so it would not be surprising for people to trade their independence for the security of the empire."

Decline of Tiwanaku and Rise of the Incas

But sometime after 1000 A.D. it all ended. The empire collapsed, the raised fields were abandoned and Tiwanaku existed no more. No one has a very firm idea why.

"The only thing we are certain of is that in a 50-year period, Tiwanaku disappeared very rapidly and very completely," said Ponce, dean of Bolivia's archaeological investigators. "We don't know what the cause of the eclipse was. We can only disprove some of the early theories and speculate on some later ones."

One of the earliest theories was that Tiwanaku was wrecked by a cataclysmic earthquake. No archeological excavation, however, has produced any evidence of such a catastrophe, nor is there any geologic record of an event in the Andes powerful enough to have brought down an extensive empire.

Another of the theories was that the empire was invaded and routed by outside armies. Again, Ponce said, there is no archaeological evidence to bear out the theory. Except for the looting that occurred after Europeans arrived in the Americas, Tiwanaku's temples and religious icons have by and large remained as its people left them. Had Tiwanaku been conquered in ancient times, the temples and icons would have been smashed or carried away.

One untested theory holds that Tiwanaku was victimized by a prolonged drought. There is a very modern example of such a drought, the so-called "El Niño effect" of an upper atmospheric change that has denied adequate rains to equatorial regions in Africa, Asia and South America throughout the 1970s and 1980s.

"We can date the end of Tiwanaku as an organized state more or less between 1150 and 1200 A.D.," Ponce said. "In the United States a great drought ended the great pueblo civilization at the same time. A complex state like Tiwanaku, even with its vast storage facilities, would not likely be able to survive a prolonged drought and repeated crop failures for 10, 20 or more years."

Whatever caused the collapse of the empire, it was supplanted by smaller kingdoms made up of the former subjects of Tiwanaku. The smaller kingdoms were constantly at war with one another, retreating from the vast plains of the Altiplano to fortress towns on the mountainsides and adopting a form of terrace farming.

The former lands of the empire were torn by war for more than two centuries. Trade routes died, and technology and artistry regressed. The new mini-kingdoms that replaced Tiwanaku were still fighting among themselves for survival when the armies of the newly-emerged Inca empire marched down from Peru in the 1430s and conquered all of them.

Pachaquteq Inca Yupanqui founded the Inca empire in 1438, when the Tiwanaku empire had been dead for perhaps 300 years. Pachaquteq made the conquest of the former Tiwanaku lands his first order of business in establishing his empire. He personally visited the ruins of the Tiwanaku imperial city, and when he returned to Cuzco, he ordered that his own royal capital be remodeled along the lines of Tiwanaku.

The Incas were worthy inheritors of Tiwanaku. Within 90 years, the Incan empire far outstripped Tiwanaku's in size, subjugating lands from Colombia to Chile for 3,000 miles around. Trade routes, art and architecture began to flourish again in the Andes. Incan agriculturists, while not reviving the centuries-old raised fields of Tiwanaku, showed an amazing knowledge of irrigation and hydrology of their own, bringing mountainside terrace farms into bloom.

European Conquest

The Incas entrenched themselves so firmly that it appeared their reign over the Andes would match Tiwanaku's in longevity. But it was not to be. In 1492, when his three small ships landed on a small Caribbean island, Christopher Columbus in effect breached the watery barrier that had allowed the Americas to develop independently from the rest of mankind for tens of thousands of years of splendid isolation. The sudden appearance of Europeans proved to be every bit as incomprehensible, frightening and dangerous for indigenous American civilizations as if alien spaceships were to land among us today.

To be sure, the Europeans brought to the New World an overwhelming array of weaponry, technology and knowledge that the native Americans had never seen before: sailing ships, horses, guns, swords of tempered steel, wheeled carts and written language. But of all the things that the conquering Europeans introduced into the Americas, the most devastating were the diseases of the Old World, particularly smallpox, to which the long-isolated natives had no natural immunities. By the time the first Spaniards landed in Mexico in 1511, the aboriginal populations of the major Caribbean islands were already well on their way to total extinction. In 1528, news spread through the Incan empire that strange, alien men who traveled in large houses that moved through the ocean had been sighted along the Peruvian seacoast. By that time smallpox was killing hundreds of thousands of Aztecs in Mexico and had already moved through Central America into South America.

By the time Francisco Pizarro began marching on the Incan empire with his first full-scale invasion in December 1530, the deadly European diseases had done much of the conquering for him. Recent investigations indicate that Huayna Capac, the great Inca emperor of that period, and many of the most influential members of his court probably contracted smallpox and died around 1526. Their deaths set off a struggle of succession between two of the emperor's sons. The civil war that followed was still being waged by the time Pizarro arrived in Peru, and the combination of war and pestilence effectively destroyed much of the Inca's capacity to resist Pizarro's conquest.

So, like Tiwanaku, the Incan empire abruptly became history. Stunned and sickened, the Incan people looked on in horror as the Spanish invaders smashed their most sacred temples and idols, ripping them apart for gold and silver, which were melted down and sent back to Spain. The Spaniards went so far as to violate the tombs of the dead Incan emperors, ignoring, to the amazement of the Indians, what to them were the truly valuable caches of fine textiles, and grabbing only the gold and silver. To the Incas, it was clear that their conquerors were crude barbarians.

Barbarians or not, the Spaniards prevailed, and in prevailing they discarded the Incans' superior form of state management for their own. Wanting to control the countryside, the new rulers forced the Indians off their lands and into newly-created villages and into a form of tenant farming that drastically cut the amount of land under cultivation. The complex, finely engineered systems of Incan irrigation and crop management fell into disuse, and the soil became depleted.

Even the long-dead Tiwanaku culture along Lake Titicaca's shores was not spared from the destruction and greed that came with the Europeans. In the 1500s, the Spaniards learned of the existence of Tiwanaku and the fabulous ruins of its scattered outposts. The Spanish crown began to grant licenses to loot the ruins the same way it granted mining licenses. It did not take long before every known Tiwanaku temple site was hacked apart. Many of the exquisitely carved stoneworks in Tiwanaku's imperial city still lie on the ground, horribly gouged by Spanish looters when they stripped the ancient temples of their gold cladding.

In fact, until the middle of this century, vast quantities of the stoneworks of Tiwanaku's imperial city were used as building material for churches and houses. In the 1890s, a British construction company contracted by Bolivia to build a railroad from La Paz to Peru went so far as to dynamite temple stoneworks, including irreplaceable monolithic icons, in order to turn them into gravel for the train tracks.

Tiwanaku Today

Time is no respecter of tradition, including European tradition. Many of the grand churches built by the Spanish as they pushed into the Bolivian provinces are now crumbling ruins themselves. There are no priests to serve in them, and the colonial artwork and golden adornments inside them are often stolen by looters.

Bolivia's Aymara Indians, descendants of the ancient Tiwanakans, were introduced to Catholicism by the Spaniards, but to this day they are only grudging converts. They observe Christian rituals, but they also continue to pay homage to the ancient animist spirits and to celebrate the ritual days observed in Tiwanakan time. On those days they dress up in outlandish costumes that caricature the Spaniards as if to mock the people who erased their heritage. Bolivia now is much more aware of Tiwanaku's invaluable cultural legacy and, despite the country's poverty, is fiercely protective of it. Fortunately, the ancient Tiwanaku empire was so vast in size that many of its greatest works still survive in many sites.

Luqurmata is one of those sites, but Alan Kolata said it is only a starting point for preserving what is left of Tiwanaku. There are other satellite communities even larger and more important than Luqurmata that have never been closely examined by archaeologists. Kolata visited one -- Khonko Wankané, a day's walk from the imperial city of Tiwanaku -- and laid out plans to examine its raised-field system, which is even larger than that of Luqurmata.

The unexcavated temples and palaces of Khonko Wankané look like nothing more than mounds of scrubby pasturage. But underneath the mounds are temples and palaces Kolata believes were much larger and more significant than those in Luqurmata. The only visible evidence, however, are three great monoliths lying on the ground near the mounds. Lichen have already badly damaged the monoliths, much to Kolata's chagrin.

"This monolith is a cultural treasure, like the Taj Mahal," Kolata said as he strokes one of the fallen icons. "But because it's in Bolivia, nobody gives a damn. We've got to find somebody to fund the preservation of all this. There are a lot of secrets here. There's a dead city under our feet, just waiting to be uncovered."

THE TITICACA ROCK: SACRED WACA ON THE ISLAND OF THE SUN

BY ERIK CATARI GUTIÉRREZ

Lake Titicaca . . . one of nature's great wonders, a place of profound messages and enigmatic secrets, art and singular beauty. A sacred site in Andean mythology, where the god Viracocha created man, the sun, the moon and the stars.

Here arose the Tiwanaku civilization, the largest and one of the oldest in South America, a powerful influence on other Andean cultures. And it was from Titicaca Island (known today as the Island of the Sun), that the last great empire grew -- the Incas.

It is an island steeped in the folklore of Andean gods. When Mallku Willca (the Sun) realized that the island was too small to house his people and that the land did not produce enough to feed them, he sent his valiant son Mallku Khapaj and his sister/wife Mama Ocllo in search of more fertile lands for themselves and their descendants.

Ancient Gods

For the people of the pre-Colombian Andes, belief in supernatural beings was instinctive, and worshipping these gods was a form of appreciation for the benefits they offered.

The most sacred was Viracocha, who was said to have emerged from the lake in complete darkness to create the world. Then there was Willca or Inti (the Sun), whose light and warmth made the earth productive and supported life. Other important deities included Pachamama (Mother Earth), whose fertile womb protected the life of plants, animals and men; the vengeful Illapa (Lightning); Paxsi (the Moon); and Kota Mama (Mother Water), who ruled the rivers, lakes and seas.

The great peaks of the Andes (achachilas) were considered sacred ancestors, while unusual rock formations (apachitas) and some of the more ferocious and cunning animals were also worshipped.

The deities existed in a cosmic trilogy: Alaxa Pacha (the World Above), Aka Pacha (the World We Live In) and Manka Pacha (the World Below). The pre-Colombians also believed in a time-cycle doctrine, in which the world has a beginning, a middle and an end. According to legend, Viracocha created the sky, the earth and its inhabitants, and from Titicaca Rock he made the stars.

The Sacred Titicaca Rock

One of the most venerated wacas (sacred Inca sites) in the entire Andean region was the Titicaca Rock, also known as the Sacred Rock or the Rock of Origins. To many colonial historians, this rock was the most important Incan waca. Sarmiento de Gamboa wrote that, "the one they called Viracocha knew the world when it was dark, without sun, moon or stars. He decided to populate the world, and went to a large lake where there was an island they called

Titicaca. From a rock on this island he sent forth the sun, moon and the stars, giving light and warmth to the world."

In Inca times the adornments of the Titicaca Rock rivaled Cuzco, and thousands of worshippers visited from all over the Andes. The rock formed one corner of a triangular sanctuary, along with the Island of the Moon and Copacabana.

The chronicles of Bernabe Cobo relate that before their pilgrimage to the rock, worshippers would submit to confessional rites, and abstain from sexual relations and from eating salt, meat and chili peppers so as to arrive with great purity. On the island they passed three portals, where again they were subjected to purification rites. Not all would get to the Rock, as arrival there depended on the confessions given at each stage.

According to Ramos Gavilan, "the first portal was called Pumapuncu, the portal of the lion, guardian of the entrance. Before passing, pilgrims confessed their sins to a priest who lived there. "At the second portal, Kentipuncu, the pilgrims would make new confessions to a second priest, under a shade of tominejos feathers. The third portal was the Pillcopunco, the pillar of hope, adorned with the green feathers of the Pillco bird. At this gateway, the guardian priest subjected the pilgrims to a rigorous interrogation. They were not allowed to pass until he was satisfied."

The Northwest Face

The Titicaca Rock stands on a high ridge at the extreme northwest of the Island of the Sun, with views of the lake on both sides. In front of the Rock is a plain that, according to folklore, was artificially leveled by soil brought from the richest, most fertile regions.

The rugged features of the Rock include some intriguing natural formations that can be related to several mystical events in the folklore of the region. At the extreme right of the northwest face are two hollows where, legends say, the sun and the moon stayed before they rose up to the heavens to light the world. The story tells of two brothers that were sleeping in the hollows. When they awoke, the first one to get up would become the sun. This privilege was destined for the older brother, while the younger brother was supposed to be the moon. However, the younger brother woke first, threw ashes in his brother's eyes and rose up to become the sun.

From the altar on the western plain it's possible to see a large hollow known as the Sacred Cave. It was here that pilgrims left their offerings and poured chicha (corn beer) for Mallku Willca to drink. Locals say that above the Sacred Cave is the face of the cat Titi, a mysterious animal intimately related to the origins of the lake. According to legend, when the cat climbed onto the Rock, it was swallowed whole. Only the face of the cat remains, etched in stone.

To the left of the cat's face is the naturally-carved form of a bearded face between two grooves. This is considered by some to be the face of the god Viracocha. Finally, about 20 meters along the path from the rock are some large "footprints" that locals say were made by the sun as he leapt up to the heavens.

The Face of a God?

"It was evident, above and to the left of the Sacred Cave, there could be seen a face approximately six feet high, with an inverted trapezoidal beard similar to those of the ancient pharaohs," said U.S. anthropologist James Westerman, who discovered the bearded face in 1994. Westerman thought it logical that if Viracocha gave light to the world from this site, he would leave his image on the rock as a testimony of his presence there.

The penetrating stare of the bearded face can best be appreciated when the sun is exactly above the rock. Westerman's discovery is considered vital evidence that the rock was sacred, and his analysis fits well with the Andean mythologies.

In Inca times, Inti was more venerated than Viracocha, and it is possible that the rock was rededicated to this cult. This may explain why the colonial historians make no mention of the bearded face.

Westerman suggests another possible explanation. The local legends say that during religious ceremonies, only the Inca could look upon the sacred northwest face of the rock. Other worshippers were not permitted this privilege. Recent archaeological findings to the southeast of the rock support this suggestion. This site has been identified as the place where the worshippers stood, and from there they were unable to see the northwest face.

A Frayed and Weathered Mass

A 19th-century visitor named George Squier considered the Titicaca Rock to be the most sacred site in all of Peru. However, when he first saw it he said, "alas for gods dethroned! This rock today is nothing more than a frayed and weathered mass of red sandstone, part of a thick stratum that runs through the island, and which is here disrupted and standing with its associated shale and limestone layers. In the face there are many shelves and pockets, all apparently natural."

Squier found the rock much as it is today -- little more than a bare, rugged outcrop, with no obvious significance. A large part of the esteem in which it is held is obviously based on the legends relating to the site, but there had to be something more to cause this specific rock to be so venerated. If the bearded face is that of Viracocha, its presence would help to explain why the rock held such a revered place in Andean mythology.

EARTHMOVERS OF THE AMAZON

BY CHARLES C. MANN

ARE THE MOUNDS, CAUSEWAYS, AND CANALS IN BOLIVIA'S BENI REGION NATU-
RAL FORMATIONS OR THE RESULT OF 2000 YEARS' LABOR BY LOST SOCIETIES?
REPRINTED WITH PERMISSION FROM EARTHMOVERS OF THE AMAZON, SCIENCE, 4 FEBRUARY 2000
VOL287:786-789. COPYRIGHT 2000 AMERICAN ASSOCIATION FOR THE ADVANCEMENT OF SCIENCE.

TRINIDAD, BOLIVIA—In some ways, William Denevan says today, he didn't know what he was getting into when he decided to write his Ph.D. thesis about the Beni, a remote, nearly uninhabited, and almost roadless department in the Bolivian Amazon. Located between the Andes Mountains and the river Guaporé (a major Amazon tributary), the Beni spends half the year parched in near-desert conditions and the other half flooded by rain and snowmelt. But it wasn't until he made his first research trip there, in 1961, that Denevan realized the area was filled with earthworks that oil company geologists—the only scientists in the are—believed to be ruins of an unknown civilization.

Convincing a bush pilot to give him a flying tour, Denevan examined the earthworks from above. Much of the Beni is covered by a savanna known as the Llanos de Mojos (the Mojos Plains). But, to his amazement, Denevan saw what seemed to be the remains of transportation canals, pyramid-like mounds, elevated causeways, raised agricultural fields, and clusters of odd, zigzagging ridges scattered through the savanna. "I'm looking out of one of these DC-3 win-

dows, and I'm going berserk in this little airplane," recalls Denevan, who is now a professor emeritus of geography at the University of Wisconsin, Madison. "I knew these things were not natural. You just don't have that kind of straight line in nature."

Today, almost 4 decades later, a small but growing number of researchers believe that the Beni once housed what Clark L. Erickson of the University of Pennsylvania, Philadelphia, calls "some of the densest populations and the most elaborate cultures in the Amazon"—cultures fully as sophisticated as the better known, though radically different, cultures of the Aztecs, Incas, and Mayas. Although these still unnamed peoples abandoned their earthworks between 1400 and 1700 C.E., Erickson says, they permanently transformed regional ecosystems, creating "a richly patterned and humanized landscape" that is "one of the most remarkable human achievements on the continent." To this day,

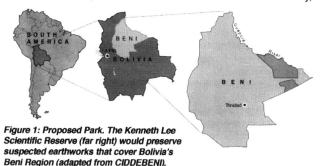

Figure 1: Proposed Park. The Kenneth Lee Scientific Reserve (far right) would preserve suspected earthworks that cover Bolivia's Beni Region (adapted from CIDDEBENI).

Lines in a landscape. Three pre-Columbian causeways run between raised mounds in Baures, Bolivia. Trees grow on the causeways and mounds, protected from the savanna's seasonal fires and floods (photography by C. Erickson).

according to William Balée, an anthropologist at Tulane University in New Orleans, the lush tropical forests interspersed with the savanna are in considerable measure anthropogenic, or created by human beings—a notion with dramatic implications for conservation.

These views have thrust the Beni into what Denevan calls "the Amazon archaeology wars." For more than 30 years, archaeologists have clashed, sometimes in bitingly personal terms, over whether the vast river basin could provide the resources for indigenous cultures to grow beyond small, autonomous villages. Until relatively recently, the naysayers had the upper hand. In the last decade, though, several archaeologists, including Anna C. Roosevelt of Chicago's Field Museum, have published evidence that such societies did exist throughout the várzea, as the Amazonian floodplain is known, and the bluffs above it (Science, 19 April 1996, pp. 346 and 373; 13 December 1996, p. 1821).

The dispute over the Beni is similar.

Using environmental arguments, skeptics contend that the Beni earthworks must be either natural formations or the remains of a short-lived colony from a richer part of South America—the Andes, most likely. "I haven't seen any basis for thinking there were large, permanent settlements there," says archaeologist Betty J. Meggers of the Smithsonian Institution in Washington, D.C. "But if they were there, where is the solid evidence?" In particular, critics like Meggers point out, there is no indication of hierarchical organization in the Beni. Without it, they say, the kind of sophisticated society envisioned by Denevan, Erickson, and Balée could not have existed.

Resolving the controversy may have important consequences for the region—and all of Amazonia. If the region is inherently too fragile to support intensive use, its most appropriate future may be as a biosphere reserve supervised by the United Nations Educational, Scientific, and Cultural Organization (UNESCO)—that is, as an almost uninhabited eco-park. But if human activity has played an essential role in the region's ecological processes for millennia, as Balée argues, then careful human exploitation of the land—such as allowing indigenous people to till land in areas used by ancients—is not only acceptable but essential to preserving its character. "Without a doubt the Llanos de Mojos represents one of the most extraordinary prehistoric landscapes anywhere on the face of the planet," says Robert Langstroth, a cultural geographer who did his 1996 PhD. dissertation at the University of Wisconsin under Denevan. "The question is, how much of it is archaeological, and how much did the archaeological parts affect the natural?"

Anthropological El Dorado

For centuries, the Llanos de Mojos guarded its story well. A shelf of alluvial deposits as much as 3000 meters deep, the savanna was once rumored to house the golden city of El Dorado. Protected by its clouds of insects, its climactic extremes, and its inhabitants' reputation for fierceness, it was among the last areas in South America reached by Europeans. In 1617, a ragtag band of explorers finally established that El Dorado did not, in fact, exist in the Llanos de Mojos. The Jesuits ruled the area from 1668 to 1767, while disease ravaged the indigenous people.

Even after the destruction wrought by the Spaniards, the Beni hosted a remarkable mosaic of indigenous societies until the mid-20th century. Its cultural diversity—and the relative lack of knowledge of the area— led the Smithsonian anthropologist Alfred Metraux to call eastern Bolivia "the El Dorado of anthropologists" in 1942. "Some of the Indians came in touch with the Spaniards during the First years of the conquest; [but] oth-

Life in the Llanos. An artist's conception of a settlement in the Llanos de Mojos, some 2 millennia ago. (painting by Dan Brinkmeier)

ers even maintain their independence today and are among the few natives of South America who still live as they did before the arrival of the whites."

Despite Metraux's enthusiasm—and the impetus provided by Denevan's later work on the earthworks—the Beni remained largely unexamined. U.S. researchers were put off by Bolivian political instability, by the difficult climate of the area, and by anti-American sentiments fueled by the heavyhanded presence of the U.S. Drug Enforcement Agency in the region. For their part, Bolivian archaeologists focused on the highland civilizations of the Andes, with their enormous, glamorous stone ruins. Only in the 1990s did a Bolivian-American team led by Erickson begin the first long-term archaeological research on the earthworks of the area.

Cultural mosaic

Climbing to the top of Ibibaté, a forested loma (mound) 18 meters higher than the surrounding savanna, Erickson comes to a bare patch of earth created by a fallen tree. Bending over the uncovered ground, he points out the dark, almost black soil, which is filled with fragments of pottery. Several pieces of pot rim are visible, along with the leg of a vessel shaped like a human foot. Both the richness of the soil and the abundance of the potsherds are typical, in Erickson's view. "Many of the lomas are almost nothing but enormous heaps of sherds," he says. "I've never seen anything like it—10, 20, 30 feet of sherds"

Ibibaté—"big mound" in the language of the local Sirionó Indians—is about 50 kilometers east of Trinidad, the provincial capital. The focus of ongoing study by Balée, Erickson, and a team of Bolivian scientists working with Erickson, Ibibaté is actually a pair of mounds connected by a short earthen wall. At the edge of the lower,

Re-Creating Prehistory: A patchwork of ancient raised fields. (Photo by C. Erickson)

Clark Erickson's team and local farmers studied how such fields work by erecting their own.
(Photo by C. Erickson)

southern mound is a Sirionó hunting camp; the higher mound is used for gathering fruit and nuts. Several earthen causeways radiate out like highways from the mound toward other mounds. Bordered by narrow canals, the causeways are about a meter tall, 3 to 5 meters wide, and straight as a rifle shot. Such features are rare in flood-plains, according to Denevan, which to him suggested an artificial origin. Indeed, in Balée's opinion, Ibibaté is "as close to a Mayan pyramid as you'll see in South America ... Beneath the forest cover is a 60-foot [18-meter], human-made artifact."

Although their research is incomplete and mostly still unpublished, Erickson and Balée have sketched out a rough outline of what they believe happened here. Ibibaté, like most of the hundreds of lomas in the Llanos de Mojos, was initially a much smaller mound, if it existed at all. It was built up, Erickson says, by the original inhabitants of the Beni, although how and why remain uncertain.

They could have begun by raising parcels of land to grow crops above the floodwater. Or, according to the late petroleum geologist and amateur archaeologist Kenneth Lee, they may have created the mounds when, for religious reasons, they buried their ancestors in ceramic urns and set up housekeeping on top of them. In either case, the people raised the lomas further by accumulating, garbage, the walls and roofs of collapsed wattle-and-daub houses, and, especially, smashed pottery. "The quantity and mass of material deposited indicates that a lot of people were responsible, creating the mounds over a period of at least 2000 years," Erickson says, "hazarding a guess" that Ibibaté typically housed 500 to 1000 inhabitants.

The villages, each on its own island of higher ground, were anything but isolated. By studying the geographic distribution and variety of the earthworks and their associated pottery, Erickson's team has tentatively concluded that the Llanos de Mojos was the home of not just one pre-Columbian people but a complex mosaic of societies linked by networks of communication, trade, alliance, and probably warfare. Beginning 3000 to 5000 years ago, Erickson has written, these cultures erected "thousands of linear kilometers of artificial earthen causeways and canals, ... large urban settlements, and intensive farming systems." For reasons that are still not completely understood, the whole social network unraveled about the time of Columbus or soon after. Smallpox may well have visited the area—many researchers think that an epidemic of the disease greatly weakened the nearby Incan empire in about 1525. In addition, Meggers believes that the Beni, like the rest of Amazonia, was subject to catastrophic droughts.

Erickson's team and local farmers erected their own raised fields to see how they might have worked. They concluded that the original inhabitants of the Beni probably employed traditional agriculture, growing beans, squash, sweet potatoes, and manioc on raised fields; agroforestry, planting groves of palm, nut, and fruit trees; and—perhaps surprisingly—aquaculture. Around the causeways in a northeastern region of the Beni known as Baures, Erickson says, run long, low, zigzag earthen walls that stretch for as much as 3 to 4 kilometers. The structures, he believes, were fish weirs, used when the rainy season covered the savanna with up to half a meter of standing water. Narrow channels up to 3 meters long open at angles in the zigzag. There, woven nets could be used to harvest fish and shellfish, Erickson says. The openings also funneled fish into artificial ponds as much as 30 meters across. In addition, the weirs are piled high with shells from apple snails (the edible gastropod genus Pomacea), possibly discarded after meals. The structures persist, although no one maintains them any longer; even today, the ponds pullulate with fish during the dry season. "They converted the savanna into huge fish farms," says Erickson. "When you see the weirs radiating out from the causeways, I don't think there's any doubt of the intentionality."

Archaeology wars

Others strongly disagree, in terms that mirror archaeology's long-standing disputes about Amazonia. In influential books and articles, Meggers and her husband, the late Clifford Evans, argued that despite its rich flora, the river basin's thin, acidic soils can't hold enough nutrients to permit sustained, intensive agriculture. And that means big, complex societies—which inevitably depend on agriculture—cannot long exist in Amazonia. Indeed, Meggers once proposed that Amazonian villages could contain no more than 1000 inhabitants before collapsing. "We call these cultures 'primitive,' " she says of contemporary indigenous groups, which are some of the least technologically advanced in the world. "But they are actually remarkable accommodations to severe environmental limits. They show us what's possible there."

When researchers claim that large, complex societies existed in Amazonia, she says, it shows only that "there's a lot of tricky environmental stuff that most archaeologists either ignore or don't know about." Because tropical lands are washed by frequent, heavy rains, she says, the traces of human occupation are flushed through the soil rather than being deposited in neat layers. Thus a place that was intermittently occupied by a few people can seem to have been settled permanently for long periods—the layers are smeared out. "The climate hides evidence of disoccupation," she says. "The charcoal samples get displaced. There's a whole list of pitfalls and problems."

In the early 1980s, Bernard Dougherty and Horacio Calandra, two Argentine archaeologists backed by the Smithsonian, excavated several Beni lomas similar to Ibibaté, though smaller. They concluded that the mounds were "not difficult to ascribe" to natural forces, especially "fluvial activity." In their view, the causeways and raised fields of the Llanos de Mojos were probably created by a higher culture, perhaps from the Andes, which set up short-lived colonies that winked out under ecological pressure. "It seems that here, as in other parts of the world, the environment had the winning ace from the beginning. Calandra and Dougherty wrote in 1984. In his dissertation, Langstroth argued, in parallel, that the isolated forests were not created by humans. "They were created by fragmentation and erosion of natural levees," he says. "It sounds nice to give people credit for doing wonderful things, but the evidence isn't there."

Erickson's critics have also pointed out that structures like lomas, causeways, and raised fields require sustained mass labor, which in turn requires the coercive, centralized authority and hierarchical division of labor characteristic of state-level societies. Yet in lowland Amazonia, as Erickson concedes, there is "no good historic or ethnographic evidence" for such vertically organized states.

Erickson has a different explanation: The earthworks, he suggests, were erected by "heterarchical" societies: groups of communities, loosely bound by shifting horizontal links through kinship, alliances, and informal associations. "There are some people working in South America who take a look at massive complexes of raised fields and say. This has to be organized by a complex polity,' " reports Peter Stahl, an anthropologist at the State University of New York, Binghamton. "Whereas Clark [Erickson] says, 'No, this is the accumulated landscape capital of generations of farmers who built it more or less on their own.' "

Like Erickson, Roosevelt believes that sophisticated pre-Hispanic cultures occupied the middle and lower Amazon areas she has

studied. With abundant fruit, nuts, edible palm, and fish, she says, river-basin peoples "had lots of options that people in [less naturally rich] places like central Mexico didn't have— they could always run away and do what they wanted." The result, in her view, was "much less coercive" societies—"more like epic chiefdoms, where the leaders sponsor buildings and ceremonies"—somewhat like the wealthy, relatively relaxed Indian cultures in the Pacific Northwest and California. "And we're still learning," she says, "about how they shaped this wonderful landscape they bequeathed us."

Researchers who deny the importance of the pre-Hispanic Beni cultures, Erickson explains, have been misled by "archaeology's traditional Fixation on individual sites." The traditional method of digging individual sites and measuring their contents is unlikely to produce clear data, Erickson says, for the very reasons Meggers cites: The area's heavy rainfall mixes up sedimentary layers, and the local practice of heaping up earth to create mounds and causeways farther jumbles the archaeological record. So, he argues, traditional site excavation must give way to a study of the landscape as a whole—"treating the landscape like an artifact, as if it were a piece of pottery." Such "landscape archaeology" uses nontraditional tools, including aerial photography, radar imagery, and multispectral satellite imagery, to prepare digital maps of large areas. "My main critique of the site concept is that it implicitly puts edges around each site. But here in the Beni, the 'sites' go on forever--the whole landscape has been organized and designed."

A flight in a small plane over the area makes Erickson's meaning clear. "This group of islands is connected with that one, but not those," he says, shouting over the noise of the propellers. "There's a relationship there. -. The raised fields are all aligned in a north-south direction. The landscape is telling us something."

Ecological adaptation

Erickson and others argue that the Beni mound builders began a process of ecological change in the region that continues to this day. Balée, for example, says the Beni, in his view, was "not favorable for well-drained tropical forests until after people—deliberately or not—made it favorable for them" by raising the mounds above the floodwaters and enriching the soils by burning, mulching, and depositing wastes. After the original inhabitants of the lomas disappeared 300 to 600 years ago, the mounds were presumably colonized by forest. When the Sirionó arrived on the scene—Balée believes, on linguistic evidence, that they emigrated to the Beni about 3 centuries ago, probably from the south—they altered the composition of these forests to suit themselves, creating what Balée calls "artifactual forests."

As evidence, Balée points to one of the most common tree genera on the loma: Sorocea, which is used by the Sirionó to make beer. In the Beni, Sorocea is found only on the mounds, not in the surrounding land with standing water, which to Balée is "strong evidence" that people brought it to the lomas. Similarly, the spiny palm (Astrocaryum murumuru), which has many indigenous uses, is much more common on the lomas than elsewhere—"there's 112 of these here," Balée says at Ibibaté, "as opposed to something like 15" in an equivalent nonmound area.

"There is more forest in the Llanos de Mojos because of people in pre-Hispanic times than in spite of them," Balée says. To him, this indicates "that there is no necessary incompatibility between human use and biodiversity in the tropics," and he hopes that conservationists, who sometimes view human actions as a priori destructive, will not seek to curtail the Indians' freedom.

Active efforts are being made to protect the Beni and its remaining indigenous peoples from over-development. After some hesitation, the Bolivian government has established more than a dozen reservation-like areas for Indian groups, although in some cases they provide little actual protection. Partially overlapping the indigenous areas for the Baures and Itonama peoples—the two easternmost reserves—is a proposed Kenneth Lee Scientific Reserve, named after the U.S. petroleum geologist whose vigorous advocacy of the Beni inspired many researchers, Erickson among them. (Lee died in 1997.) The Centro de Investigación y Documentación para el Desarrollo del Beni, a Trinidad-based nonprofit organization that seeks to develop the area in ways that would benefit indigenous groups, favors the plan. Meanwhile, some environmental groups would like UNESCO to create a World Heritage Site in the eastern Beni. There are already three such reserves in Bolivia, though none in the Llanos de Mojos. Presumably, the first priority in such a management scheme would be conservation—a stance that worries Denevan.

"The Indians created the environment we're trying to protect," he says. "They should get to stay there while we're learning what they did."

4 February 2000 Vol287:786-789 SCIENCE http://www.sciencemag.org/ © Charles C. Mann

Used by permission of the author, Charles C. Mann. Photographs by Clark L. Erickson. Painting by Dan Brinkmeier. Map by CIDDEBENI.

THE GOOD EARTH: DID PEOPLE IMPROVE THE AMAZON BASIN?

BY CHARLES C. MANN

REPRINTED WITH PERMISSION FROM EARTHMOVERS OF THE AMAZON, SCIENCE, 4 FEBRUARY 2000
VOL287:786-789. COPYRIGHT 2000 AMERICAN ASSOCIATION FOR THE ADVANCEMENT OF SCIENCE.

The debate over the existence of a major prehistoric society in the Beni area of Bolivia (see main text) is tied to a broader dispute over whether the Amazon Basin has ever been able to support big, complex cultures. That dispute centers largely on soil quality. Despite its rich flora, Amazonia has many thin, aluminum-rich soils that can't hold nutrients and are toxic to crucial soil bacteria. Societies that try long-term farming, say Smithsonian archaeologist Betty J. Meggers and others, will destroy the soil completely—and their resource base along with it. But evidence has gradually accumulated that the picture of the Amazon as a "counterfeit paradise," to use Meggers's phrase, may be overly simple.

Amazonia is usually divided into the várzea or floodplain, which occupies perhaps 2% of the basin's 7 million square kilometers, and the terra firme, the never-flooded uplands that comprise everything else. (Oddly, the Beni counts as uplands because 'it's flooded by rain, not river water.) According to Nigel J. H. Smith, a geographer at the University of Florida, Gainesville, "everyone agrees" that much of the várzea is fertile. What's in question is the fertility of the uplands. For more than 150 years, says Smith, individual researchers have reported that the terra firme contained pockets of good land—in particular the terra preta do indio (Indian black earth) often found beneath ancient indigenous settlements. In 1980, Smith summarized the evidence, including his own discoveries, for the prevalence of upland terra preta. "I got two reprint requests for that article," he says, laughing. "Nobody was ready to hear it."

One reason for the neglect, according to Emilio F. Moran, an anthropologist at the University of Indiana, Bloomington, is what he calls "the problem of scale." Three-quarters of the upland soils are indeed poor, he says. As a result, large-scale maps correctly show the basin as a wash of impoverished land. But on a smaller scale, Moran says, the land is dotted with patches of terra preta. "Even if it only covers 10% of the terra firme" he says. "the Amazon 's so big that 10% represents an enormous resource base. It's bigger than France."

The 10% figure, Moran says, is just a guess. Fewer than 1000 soil samples from the Amazon have ever been analyzed, according to William L. Woods, a geographer at Southern Illinois University in Edwardsville. Last year. Woods and Joseph 1. McCann of the New School University in New York City published their study of the soils along the Tapajós River, a major tributary of the middle Amazon. They found scores of black-earth sites ranging from 0.5 to 120 hectares, most of which were still in use by local farmers. Indeed, Woods and McCann believe that indigenous agriculture, far from destroying the soil, actually improved it.

In the past, archaeologists usually argued that terra preta represented ancient deposits of volcanic ash or former pond bottoms. Based on chemical analyses—and the constant presence of pottery—most researchers now believe that the black earth is created from old middens (deposits of waste). This explanation is incomplete, Woods and McCann say. They distinguish between terra preta proper, which they define as the soil directly around human settlements, and what they call "terra mulatta," slightly lighter soils that surround terra preta and often cover areas 10 times larger. The terra preta is the remains of ancient middens; the terra mulatta is soil used for agriculture—soil that has been deliberately altered by mixing with wood ash.

Farmers burned off the forest cover of their fields. Woods explains, then tilled in the cinders. The ash reduces the acidity of the soil, which in turn reduces the activity of the aluminum ions, fostering microbial growth. "In addition," he says, the ash "greatly increases the nutrient-retention capacity."

"I can't tell you how much of the Amazon Basin has been changed," Woods says, "but I can tell you that enormous areas have been modified, which implies a lot of people doing it." Woods would not be surprised, he says, if Amazonia turned out to have about the same percentage of excellent arable land as, say, the United States. Smith agrees: "The soils were a constraint, but people overcame them. Amazonia may have been a counterfeit paradise to start with, but it sure doesn't sound like it was one when they were finished with it."

GOLDEN RULERS OF AN ANCIENT EMPIRE

BY KIP LESTER AND JANE MCKEEL

The origin of the Inca civilization is "lost in the mists of time," although there are various legends and theories to explain it. According to Garcilaso de la Vega, a descendant of the Incas on his mother's side and Spanish on his father's side, the Sun sent Manco Capac and Mama Ocllo to gather the natives into communities and to teach them the arts of civilized life. This celestial pair, who were brother and sister and also husband and wife, advanced along the high plains of Lake Titicaca to the south. They had been instructed to live where the golden wedge sank into the ground without trouble. When they reached the Valley of Cuzco, the golden wedge sank into the ground and disappeared forever.

Another legend speaks of certain white and bearded men who advanced from the shores of Lake Titicaca and established power over the natives, bringing to them civilization.

It can be reasonably concluded that there existed a race advanced in civilization before the time of the Incas, and that this race derived from the neighborhood of Lake Titicaca. Who they were and where they came from is still unknown.

As far as dating the Incan civilization, the historian finds no firm footing on which to stand up to within a century of the Spanish conquest. The Incan dynasty is generally assigned 13 princes before the conquest, which would carry the foundation of the monarchy back to no more than 250 years before the Spanish conquest.

Cuzco was the holy city of the Incas, and the scepter passed from father to son, the eldest son of the lawful queen who was also sister of the Inca, thus maintaining the royal line free from any outside taint. The government was "a mild despotism." The ruler raised armies, usually commanded them, imposed taxes, made laws, provided for their execution and removed judges at his will.

Riches did not pass from father to son. The wealth of each ruler reflected what he had personally accumulated. When the Inca died, his palaces were abandoned, his treasures left and all but one of his mansions were closed forever.

Tahuantinsuyo was the name given to the empire. It was divided into four sections, each called a suyo: Chinchasuyo included northern Peru and Ecuador; the Atisuyo extended to the Cordillera; Contisuyo included the coastal lands; and the Collasuyo contained the rest of Peru, Chile, Bolivia and a strip of northern Argentina.

The agricultural products of the lands of the empire were divided into three parts: one for the sun, one for the Inca and one for the people. The part for the sun furnished the revenue to support temples and the priesthood; the part for the Inca supplied the royal state and government; and the part for the people was divided per capita. The tenant could not add to his possessions, and the lease was terminated at the end of a year. In this system there was no rich man, nor was there a poor man. The hardship was that a man could not better himself materially.

The Incas supervised the use of the wealth and resources of the empire. The sheep were sheared, the wool was put in magazines and used as needed. The same was true of products of the mines and crops. A register was kept of births and deaths, and surveys were made of the physical resources. The government then apportioned the labor to the provinces best equipped to accomplish it.

The remains of Incan temples, palaces, fortresses, terraced mountains, great military roads, aqueducts and other public works are proof of this civilization's industry. The two principal roads were the one that ran from Quito to Cuzco and the one that ran from Cuzco south toward Chile. The first one passed over the Altiplano, was 3,200 kilometers (2,000 miles) in length, over 6 meters (20 feet) in breadth and was made of freestone and bituminous cement. The second one ran between the Andes and the ocean.

About every 16 kilometers (10 miles) along the roads were accommodations for the Inca and his entourage. About every five miles, buildings were erected in which a number of runners (chasquis) were stationed to carry government dispatches. Dispatches were verbal or conveyed by a cord two feet long composed of different-colored threads twisted together from which a quantity of smaller threads were suspended in the manner of a fringe. This cord was called a quipus. Messages were carried 150 miles (240 kilometers) per day. The runners also carried fish, fruits and game to Cuzco.

The Inca was constantly at war, with religion as the pretext. He was wise and spared his enemies, and the gods of the enemy were tolerated as long as the sun was supreme. The Inca employed various measures to integrate the conquered into their society. The gods of the conquered people were moved with their rulers to Cuzco; the gods permanently and the rulers long enough to be inculcated with the general policies and the language. When they left the court, their eldest son remained. The Incas substituted Quechua for the great variety of dialects, thereby affording all their peoples with an important common denominator. The Inca had complete authority over the people and moved them from one place to another as he wished. He would move a group of unfaithful subjects into the midst of faithful ones. Thus, numerous independent tribes were melded into one by the influence of a common religion, common language and common government.

In effect, the government of the Incas was a theocracy. They believed in a supreme being whom they adored under the names of Pachacámac and Viracocha. Their special deity was the sun, and they also acknowledged other objects of worship such as the moon, stars and other objects in nature. The most ancient of the sun temples was the one on the Island of the Sun in Lake Titicaca. They believed in an afterlife, thus their attention to body preservation. The good were to pass on to a life of happiness, and the evil were to atone for their crimes by ages of labor. The belief in an evil principle of spirit was associated with these ideas and bore the name of Supay.

In the religious hierarchy, the high priest was second only to the Inca, and he was usually chosen from the Inca's brothers. His duties involved the ministration of his temples. The "virgins of the sun," or ñustas, cared for the sacred fire, wove the hangings for the temple and were often chosen as brides for the Inca. There were also wise men, or amautas, charged with the instruction of the youth.

The Incas had some acquaintance with geography, a moderate proficiency in astronomy and advanced skill in terracing and the use of guano as fertilizer. However, they used a clumsy substitute for a plow: a stake dragged along by six to eight men. There was no foreign commerce. They used maguey as a substitute for linen as well as cotton and llama fleece. Only the Inca himself used the wool from the vicuña. They cut emeralds and other stones, but were unacquainted with iron. Yet they added tin to copper, giving it a hardness nearly equal to steel. They gathered gold from the streams. Granite was used in construction, and although many constructions were accomplished without cement, they did use a mold mixed with lime or a fine, bituminous glue. They did not know how to mortise timbers, but they held beams together by tying them with maguey. Their buildings were suited to the climate and resisted the convulsion of volcanoes.

Little is known about the first six Inca rulers except for the accounts of Garcilaso de la Vega, which are not reliable. According to his accounts, the fourth Inca, Maita Capac, invaded the territory of the Collas and took the city of Tiwanaku "without resistance." He also won and settled lands around the Desaguadero River.

Viracocha, the eighth Inca (1400-1438), made a treaty of peace with Collasuyo, which was to allow the Incas to absorb them during the reign of the next Inca, Pachacuti. The investiture of Pachacuti in 1438 is the first verifiable date in Incan history, and it

marks the expansion of the Incan empire. Pachacuti, the Cataclysm, won his first great victory over the Collas, and the dominion of the Incas lasted until the conquest by the Spaniards. Atahuallpa, the Inca at the time the Spaniards arrived, was garroted despite the vast ransom paid by his subjects. Five Incas followed Atahuallpa, the last of whom was Tupac Amaru. The final demise of the Inca Empire came when Don Francisco de Toledo, the fifth viceroy of Lima, ordered the execution of Tupac Amaru, supposedly for the murder of a missionary, and thus exterminated of the Incan royal family.

ROCK ART IN ARCHAEOLOGICAL PARKS

BY MATTHIAS STRECKER

olivian rock art, largely unknown even to students of the prehistory of the country, comprises a wealth of petroglyphs (rock carvings and rock paintings in small caves and rock shelters, on vertical cliffs or on large boulders. More than 1,000 sites have so far been registered from all departments, though most are found in the Andean region and in the eastern lowlands. In the northern lowlands (the departments of Pando and Beni) a few sites are known that consist of engravings, mostly on rocks alongside or near rivers.

According to preliminary investigations carried out by members of Bolivia's Rock Art Research Society (SIARB - Sociedad de Investigación del Arte Rupestre de Bolivia, founded in 1987), these artistic manifestations span at least several millenia. The earliest rock art, which seems to date back to the Paleo-Indian period, may consist of painted hunting scenes with groups of camelids in vivid movement (possibly guanacos) and diminutive human figures, similar to representations found in Peru and Chile. In various sites ancient hand imprints also occur, but it is not known whether they have a similar antiquity as those of the caves of Patagonia (7,000 B.C.). In many parts of Bolivia, "cupules" or cup-marks (round artificial depressions) occur, some of which may belong to the earliest rock carvings.

Regional pre-Inca cultures produced a rich variety of rock art which, in the majority of cases, cannot yet be dated adequately. The exceptions are some representations in East Cochabamba and West Santa Cruz ("Estilo Tripartito") consisting of stylized animal figures with three-fingered hands, feet, and sometimes a tail. Identical figures occur on ceramics of the Yampará culture, which are estimated to have flourished at a time when Tiahuanaco influence declined (around 1100 A.D., cf. article by A. Oakland Rodman, Pre Columbian Cultures of Bolivia in Chapter Three.). Various sites of rock paintings include complex geometric designs, most likely representing textiles.

The relatively short period of Inca occupation of large parts of Bolivia produced peculiar rock carvings in the regions of Copacabana, La Paz, and the spectacular engraved rock of Samaipata, Santa Cruz. These historic sites are known to have had Inca settlements, and the style of these engravings show a close relationship to Inca rock art in Peru.

A unique feature of Bolivian rock art is that the artistic tradition continued in Colonial and Republican time. Post Hispanic manifestations can easily be identified by motifs such as Christian crosses, horse riders, and human figures with Colonial dresses and European utensils. At some sites, Christian crosses were painted or engraved over ancient figures in an attempt by

Spanish missionaries "to exercise whatever spiritual essence was believed to reside in the page sites" (R. Bednarik). However, the vast majority of post Hispanic rock art was produced by the Indians who incorporated elements of the European culture. Whereas most of the prehispanic art is geometric or highly stylized, later representations are mainly naturalistic. Among drawings in a rock shelter of Yaraque, Oruro, we see dramatic scenes in which a European ship appears, and a fight between two persons, one of whom fires a pistol. At one important site of rock paintings in the Dept. of La Paz, studied by Freddy Taboada of the National Museum of Ethnography and Folklore, numerous religious scenes are depicted, including pilgrims walking on pathways to churches and folkloric dances. Rock paintings in West Santa Cruz, investigated by Omar Claure and Roy Querejazu Lewis, include prehispanic, Colonial and Republican art all of which must be regarded as religious. The last representations, painted in the 19th and 20th centuries, represent saints and are still worshipped in annual feasts.

With possibly very few exceptions (battle scenes which may be historic, but could also have a ritual aspect) Bolivian rock art is clearly religious. Even in cases of prehispanic art, local Indians still regard these places as sacred and believe that they are inhabited by evil spirits. Superstitious beliefs are sometimes expressed by the names of the sites; for example "Diablopintapinta" in the Dept. of La Paz or "Supay Huasi" (Quechua: "House of the Devil) in the Dept. of Chuquisaca. Roy Querejazu Lewis (1987) proved the existence of modern rites in a cave with ancient paintings that are believed to have been made by the devil. A chewed coca ball was thrown or spat on the wall covering part of a painting. A stone was placed on top of another paintings, and a third one is partly covered by mud that was also placed "in a ritual offering".

The tourist will not be able to see much of the country's many-faceted rock art. Only three sites have so far been declared archaeological parks, protected by fences and controlled by guards. As vandalism has already affected part of the rock art, Bolivian archaeologists are not in favour of tourists visiting other sites.

A selection of photos of 10 Bolivian rock art sites are presented in a Web page: www.BradshawFoundation.com

Calacala, Dept. of Oruro

The best known Bolivian rock paintings are those of Calacala, about 16 miles (25 km) SE of the city of Oruro. The road passes half-way through Sepulturas (the name of this village denotes the existence of ancient burial burial towers) with a notable Colonial

LA PAZ

Copacabana

SANTA CRUZ

Calacala

Samaipata

ORURO

Localization of the three archaeological parks mentioned in the article.

Rock paintings of Calacala. (Photo by M. Strecker)

church and then reaches the village of Calacala ("place of many rocks") whose church and impressive "calvario" hill is visited on September 14th by numerous pilgrims. Large parts of the surrounding region are used as pasture for llamas.

The guardian of the archaeological park, Francisco León, lives in the village and must accompany tourists to open the gate of the small park, which is located off the road that leads from Calacala to the ruins of the former brewery (half an hour walk). At first sight an immense steep rock formation is visible at whose foot a small cave and a rock shelter are situated at a height of 4050 m.

Though a number of engravings exist (cup-like depressions and camelid figures), the majority of representations consist of paintings in red, white or black: camelids (most likely llamas), some felines, and a few very stylized human figures. Llamas connected by ropes to shepherds illustrate an important aspect of economic life of the artists. A large white llama (height: 60 cm), the favourite sacrificial animal in prehispanic times, dominates the panel of the rock shelter.

Ceramics found at the site date back to Wankarani culture and to the post-Tiwanaku period. Juan Faldín of the National Institute of Archaeology believes that the rock art has been exe-

cuted in the time of Wankarani as an expression of a religious cult of the llamas. However, the art apparently belongs to different periods, the last possibly just before the Spanish conquest. An archaeolical survey by Pilar Lima and three other archaeologists carried out in the valley of Calacala in September 2002 revealed a continuous occupation since preceramic times, including a notable presence of people during the Inca period all over the valley.

In 1999 SIARB began a long term interdisciplinary project in Calacala aimed at improving the archaeological park, supported by the Municipality of Oruro, the German and Dutch Embassies and Bradshaw Foundation. Part of this work has been a new recording of the rock art published in SIARB's Boletín 15 (2001). The most recent development is the construction of the visitors' platform which was concluded in October 2002. This wooden walkway in front of the cave and rock shelter enables visitors to view the rock art better than from the ground, prevents them from climbing the rock, and thus helps to preserve the art.

Calacala Archaeological Park. (Photo by M. Strecker)

Copacabana, carved rock at Intikala site. (Photo by M. Strecker)

Copacabana, Dept. of La Paz

In front of the village cemetery, to the east of the road leading to Tiquina-La Paz, two fenced-in areas contain a number of carved rocks, testimony to pre Hispanic activities. Unfortunately the site is now hidden behind a recently constructed petrol station. The larger precinct is called Intinkala (traditional Aymara name for "sun stone"). To its southwest, a second enclosure is found, known as Orkojawiora or Ticaticani. Both areas form an archaeological park that is open to visitors and whose attraction is the large rocks with carved steps which have been described as "rock architecture" and are popularly known as "Inca throne" or "Inca seats"- a very unlikely interpretation considering that several of these monuments exhibit low steps pointing in different directions. Investigators Teresa Gisbert and Roberto Mantilla assume that they were carved in the period of Emperor Pachacutec Inca Yupanqui (1438-1463). Similar carved stones exist in the Cuzco area (Kenko).

The traditional name "Intinkala" points to the use of the site for astronomical observations. In fact the German archaeologist Hermann Trimborn, who studied these rocks in 1960, believed that an Inca astronomer-priest stood on the steps of one of the largest monuments, looking east, watching the sun rise behind a mountain crest. Trimborn also observed another indication of ritual activities at the site: a serpent engraved on top of a large rock, its head represented by a deep basin and its writhing body by a groove leading down. Apparently liquid was shed into the basin and drained off the ground as an offering to the earth goddess.

Another monument popular known as "Horca del Inca" (Inca gallows), but definitely a place for astronomical observations, may be reached by climbing up the Kesanani (Seroqa) mountain, 600 meters south of Copacabana.

Samaipata, Dept. of Santa Cruz

A visit to the extensive rock carvings of Samaipata (which have been declared World Heritage Site by Unesco) may well be one of the highlights of a trip to Bolivia. The village of Samaipata lies 75 miles (120 km) to the west of Santa Cruz, on the road to Cochabamba. The archaeological site is reached in a walk of one hour starting from the road, about 3 miles (5 km) from the village (km384). The immense sculptured rock (longitude 250 m. or 820 feet, width 50 m. or 163 feet) lies 350 m. (1.150 feet) higher than the road, at an altitude of about 2,000 m. (6,500 feet).

All the sides of this crest are carved with terraces, niches, steps or seats; on the upper surface we find deep-cut basins, some of which are connected to channels and reliefs. Oswaldo Rivera Sundt (1979) distinguishes five sectors with carvings, beginning with the upper surface from west to east, and then describing the north and south sides:

Sector 1: Two reliefs representing felines are carved on circular pedestals at the western base of the monument.

Sector 2 (to the east): Two large rectangular basins are connected to channels flanked by three parallel rows of carved rhomboid lines extending in a W-E direction. This drainage system, popularly called "the back of the serpent", dominates the crest of the rock in a length of about 30 m.

Sector 3 (to the east): On the highest point of the rock there is a circular sculpture with eighteen rectangular or triangular seats that Leo Pucher, an investigator in the 1940s, named "priest choir". A subterranean channel unites this structure with a basin in the form of a T.

Sector 4 (north side): Five large niches in the form of trapezoids are found at the back of a recinct whose lateral sides are formed by two protruding portions of the rock. The German archaeologist Hermann Trimborn observed a long groove above the niches that may have been used to sustain a roof. Rivera Sundt assumes that these niches served for guarding certain religious objects, perhaps even Inca mummies.

Sector 5 (south side): Numerous niches, terraces, etc. At the foot of the mountain are the walls of several ancient buildings, possibly the dwelling palace of priests responsible for the maintenance of the sculptured rock and the performance of rites at the site. Finally, to the SE, 500 m. distant from the sculptured rock, a deep shaft exists ("chincana") whose purpose is unknown.

Scientific investigation of Samaipata already began in the 18th century. In 1795 Tadeo Haenke (a famous Bohemian schol-

ar) studied the rock carvings. In 1832 the French researcher Alcide d'Orbigny visited Samaipata and later published a plan of the sculptured rock. In 1909 the Swedish anthropologist Erland Nordenskiöld spent a week at the site measuring the most notable carvings. The next investigators were the local priest Adrián Melgar y Montaño and the Austrian Leo Pucher. In 1955 the German archaeologist Hermann Trimborn visited the sculptured rock and later published a detailed report.

A new phase of systematic studies of the regional archaeology began in 1974 when the first excavations were sponsored by the National Institute of Archaeology. From 1992 to 1996 large-scale excavations and a detailed topographic survey of the sculptured rock were carried out by a German-Bolivian team directed by Albert Meyers (University of Bonn).

Remnants of at least 53 buildings were found. Four phases can be distinguished: a pre-Inca settlement, two Inca phases (separated by an invasion of Chiriguano Indians), and a Colonial building. The largest Inca construction was a rectangular building (Kallanka) of 68 x 15 m which had a height of 12-14 m.

Different theories have been put forward for interpreting the sculptured rock. Some suggest that it was a fortress (the popular name of the monument is "El Fuerte") or a place where gold was washed out. Modern archaeologists agree that more

The Samaipata Fortress. © *P. I. A. S. (Samaipata Archaeological Project)*

CULTURAL PAST

probably it was a center of religious activities where the numerous basins and channels drained rain water and/or other liquids in fertility rites. There can be no doubt that at least part of the carvings go back to the Incas. Chronicles mention that the Incas had a stronghold in this region against the rebellious Chiriguano Indians. Among excavated objects on the mountain are small llama figures made of gold and silver and "Tupu" (pins decorating dresses).

Massive tourism to Samaipata has led to numerous acts of vandalism outside and even inside the fenced-in archaeological park. In order to protect the sculptured rock, which consists of fragile limestone, visitors are requested to restrict themselves to the area of a "lookout", a hill which allows a splendid view of the site and its scenery, and to a circuit around the sculptured rock and to some excavated ruins.

In the village of Samaipata there is a small archaeological museum.

Etiquette at rock art sites

Rock paintings and engravings are a very fragile cultural heritage whose survival is threatened by natural agents, but frequently much more by careless visitors. Here are some guidelines adapted from a leaflet by the Southern African Rock Art Research Association (SARARA) and from a publication by South African investigators David Lewis-Williams and Geoffrey Blundell (1998) which apply to South American rock art sites as well:

It is important that people realise that rock art is valuable and because of its antiquity it should be treated with respect. When entering a rock art gallery people should behave as they would in an art museum, that is moving slowly, standing quietly and admiring the work of the ancient artists.

Avoid touching the art. Never pour water or other liquids over the images. Avoid stirring up dust from a shelter floor

which would settle on the art. Never remove any stone tools or other archaeological artefacts from a site. Take only photographs; tracings or rubbings can and do damage the art unless you have undergone specialised training. If you see other people damaging the art, intervene. Follow the wilderness motto of 'Leave nothing but your footsteps behind' (but not on the rocks, do not intend to climb the carved or painted rocks)!

Bibliography

Boero Rojo, Hugo and Oswaldo Rivera Sundt, 1979. *El Fuerte Preincaico de Samaipata*. Cochabamba - La Paz: Los Amigos del Libro.

Meyers, Albert, 1993. *Trabajos arque - ológicos en Samaipata*, Depto. de Santa Cruz, Bolivia. Primera temporada 1992. Boletín 7: 48-58. La Paz. SIARB.

Meyers, Albert, 1998. *Las campañas arqueológicas en Samaipata*, 1994-1996. Segundo informe de trabajo. Boletín 12: 59-86. La Paz: SIARB.

Querejazu Lewis, Roy (ed.), 1992. *Arte rupestre colonial y republicano de Bolivia y países vecinos*. Contribuciones al Estudio del Arte Rupestre Sudamericano, N° 3. La Paz: SIARB.

Strecker, Matthias, 2001. *Rock art research in Bolivia*. International Newsletter On Rock Art (INORA) N° 30: 23-30. Foix, France.

Strecker, Matthias and Freddy Taboada, 1999. *Rock art protection in Bolivia*. Rock Art Research 16(1): 36-41. Melbourne.

Strecker, Matthias and Freddy Taboada, 2001. *Calacala, Monumento Nacional de Arte Rupestre*. Boletín 15: 40-62. SIARB, La Paz.

Trimborn, Hermann, 1994. *El cerro esculpido de Samaipata*. Investigaciones de arqueólogos alemanes en Bolivia: 97-136. Buenos Aires: Centro Argentino de Etnología Americana.

A HYBRID OF THE OLD AND NEW WORLDS

BY KIP LESTER AND JANE MCKEEL

COLONIAL ART AND ARCHITECTURE.

Much of what Bolivia offers the tourist is spectacularly evident: its breathtaking scenery, colorful markets and fine climate. One of its less conspicuous treasures is its wealth of Spanish colonial culture. To help the traveler appreciate the artistic riches scattered throughout the country, a brief description of colonial architecture, painting and sculpture follows.

The architecture of the colonial era in what is now Bolivia can be divided into three basic classes: Andean of renaissance, baroque and mestizo. Almost all the remaining examples of each type are churches.

The Renaissance churches, constructed between 1550 and 1630, were long and narrow. They generally had only one nave which was separated from the chancel by a great arch. The chancel, where the high altar stands, was often octagonal. Thick buttresses reinforced the adobe walls. The entryways were usually of brick covered with mortar with semi-circular archways above the doors, and flanked on each side with plasters and niches. The characteristic that distinguished these churches from their Spanish counterparts was what was constructed around them: an atrium and bell towers. These were essential to the task of converting the masses, which was often done outdoors.

The oldest examples of Andean Renaissance architecture are the churches of Caquiaviri (1560), Corque (1590) and Tiwanaku (1612). Also important in size and quality of construction are the following churches in Sucre which, incidentally, have Gothic vaults in the ceilings: the Cathedral (1561-1712), Santo Domingo (1583-1628) and San Agustín (1590-1632). The Moorish influence on the Andean Renaissance style may be observed in San Martín in Potosí (1592), San Francisco in Sucre (1581-1619), San Miguel in Sucre (1612) and Copacabana in Potosí (1685).

Baroque architecture began to appear about 1630. Churches from then on were in the form of a Latin cross with a dome over the intersection. The dome, a typical baroque element, was usually heavily decorated. The exterior entryway showed the rich ornamentation typical of the baroque style. The adobe walls were reinforced by great stone arches, or they were constructed entirely of stone and mortar. Among the Bolivian baroque churches are San Agustín in Potosí (1625), San Agustín of La Paz (1668) and, on the Altiplano, Jesús de Machaca. In Sucre there is Santa Bárbara (1663), and in Oruro the Compañía (1770). Baroque examples of non-church architecture are the Casa de la Vicaría in Potosí (1615) and the University of San Francisco Xavier in Sucre (1624).

After 1690 an architectural style appeared that is called either Andean baroque or mestizo. It reached its peak from

1690-1700, although after that it continued to exist in small towns with mainly indigenous populations. It could be described as applying a special decor to the European baroque forms or structures. This decoration varied, but generally the subject was either flora and fauna from the tropical lowlands, grotesque faces like satyrs or sirens, or pre-Colombian motifs like monkeys or pumas. In construction these 18th-century churches differed little from those of a century earlier. The most important examples of the mestizo style are San Lorenzo in Potosí (1728-1744) and San Francisco of La Paz (1744-1784).

Colonial painting, like the other arts, appeared in Bolivia in the 16th century as a European importation. The most influential painter in the Americas in the 1500s was Bernardo Bitti. Born in Italy in 1548, he entered the Society of Jesus and in 1571 was sent to Alto Peru (now Bolivia) to provide paintings and sculpture for the new churches. He worked in Lima, Cuzco, Juli, La Paz and Sucre, and many of his better works can be seen in Bolivia. He painted the high altar of the Compañía (now San Miguel) in Sucre, which was so splendid that the church authorities tried to buy it for the cathedral in 1600. Bitti's best paintings, including the Annunciation, the Adoration of the Shepherds and two fine paintings of St. John the Evangelist and St. James, can now be seen in the Cathedral Museum in Sucre. All this work was done between 1591 and 1600.

Following Bitti was Gregorio Gamarra, who worked in Cuzco and Potosí between 1601 and 1612. The influence of Bitti can be seen in Gamarra's best works: his Epiphany and Christ on the Cross in the National Museum of Art in La Paz and, in San Francisco in La Paz, his representation of the first convent of the Franciscan Order, The Vision of the Fiery Chariot and The Virgin of Guadalupe, signed in 1609. In

Peñas on the Altiplano, look for an example of the Bitti style in a painting of the Virgin of Peñas done by Matías Sanjinés in 1619.

In the 17th century, realism came to the New World painting scene via the Spanish influence and, particularly, via Surbarán. Unfortunately, most of his works today are in bad condition, for example, San Pedro Nolasco in La Merced in Sucre. However, in the latter third of the 17th century, native painting began to flourish in the Bolivian lake region. Many workshops with indigenous and mestizo artists sprang up, meeting the needs of the local churches as they were built. These workshops, generally with anonymous artists, were responsible for the great murals in the churches in Caquiaviri, Italaque, Guaqui and Jesús de Machaca. One of the best examples of this type of workshop art is a series of four large paintings in Carabuco representing death, justice, hell and glory, signed by José Lopez de los Ríos in 1699.

Another fine series of paintings is in the recently renovated church in Calamarca, on the La Paz-Oruro highway. The 20 or more pictures of military angels by the unidentified "Master of Calamarca" make the trip to this Altiplano village memorable.

The most important painter in the La Paz area in the late 1600s was Leonardo Flores. He was a prototype of the local master artist, and his work represents the highest in Andean mestizo art. He painted in 1683-84 in Puerto Acosta, where his work can be recognized by the small scenes that surround the central composition, and in Italaque, where his painting depicts colorful figures from the Old Testament in beautiful landscapes. In the church of San Francisco in La Paz, there are four Flores paintings depicting The Defense of the Immaculate by the Franciscan Order. In San Pedro in La Paz is his Feast of the Rich Epicurean.

The best-known painter in the Bolivian region in the 18th century was Melchor Pérez Holguín, who was born in Cochabamba c.1660 and died in Potosí c.1724. Holguín had a very accentuated style, detailing especially the head and hands of his subjects. His characteristic themes were ascetic saints and mystics, and as a painter of these subjects he is unrivaled. His second period was characterized by large murals. Many of his best works can be seen in La Paz in the National Museum of Art and in the Casa de la Moneda in Potosí.

Holguín was followed, chronologically and artistically, by Gaspar Miguel de Berrío (1706-1761) and Nicolás Cruz (1739-1761). Perhaps the best group of paintings by Berrío is in the National Museum of Art in La Paz: The Adoration of the Kings, The Adoration of the Shepherds and Adoration of the Angels. The painting of young St. John in the same museum by Cruz follows the general lines of a Holguín. Another imitator was Joaquín Carabal, and beyond these three masters Holguín's influence extended even into the 19th century in Sucre and Potosí.

Around 1760, the center of art activity shifted from Potosí to Sucre. The most important figure of this final colonial period was Manuel de Oquendo, whose signature appeared on a painting of Santa Teresa in the convent of the same name in Potosí. Also well-known in this epoch was Villarroel, whose painting of Jesús in the old church of the Mónicas in Sucre was signed in 1771. The last colonial period artist of note was Diego del Carpio, who was active in La Paz and Oruro from 1778 to 1812. Although he did some religious works, his most valuable efforts were portraits, and his influence was felt into the Republican years.

There were also two outstanding sculptors in Bolivia's colonial days: Francisco Tito Yupanqui, famous for his Virgin of Copacabana, and Gaspar de la Cueva. Yupanqui was an Indian born in Copacabana in the 1550s and fashioned the most venerated of all images in Bolivia. Gaspar de la Cueva was born in Seville in 1588 and came to the New World in 1623. His works reflected the realistic influence of Juan Martínez Montañes. Some of his best images are the effigy of Christ in San Agustín in Potosí, and Christ Bound to the Column in San Lorenzo of Potosí. The church of Sicasica (1725) contains a sculpture of St. Bartholomew, signed by Gaspar de la Cueva, which is one of the best of its era.

BOLIVIA'S
TRADITIONAL PRESENT

THE EXPLODING RAINBOW OF BOLIVIAN CULTURE

BY KIP LESTER AND JANE MCKEEL

The cultural heritage of Bolivia stems from various and diverse origins. This is a reflection of the population of the country, which can be basically divided into three distinct ethnic and cultural groups. These are the linguistically and culturally diverse Indians, or indigenous people, the descendants of the Spaniards who first arrived in the mid-16th century, and a large group of racially mixed people known today as cholos. Although it is extremely difficult to arrive at concrete statistics as to the sizes of these groups, it may be estimated that at least 55 percent of the total population are pure Indian, 20 percent make up the mestizo sector and the remaining 25 percent are of European heritage and background. Distinctions are more accurately made not on the basis of race or physical characteristics, but on lifestyle and language. However, there is often an overlapping and blending of group characteristics that blur sharp distinctions in many cases.

Both the Indians and those of European background have contributed in their distinctive and interesting ways to the evolution and development of Bolivian folk culture. This is observed, for example, in the music, some of which is purely Indian, some of which originated with the arrival of the Spaniards and some of which represents a blend of these two.

ETHNIC GROUPS

The Aymara and the Quechua

The two main Indian groups in Bolivia are the Aymara and the Quechua. In addition, there are many other smaller ethnic groups, such as the Uru and the Chipaya of the Altiplano, and those who inhabit the Amazonian jungle areas. The Aymara are a highland people, and the Quechua inhabit the high valleys and the Puna. They are either farmers or herders of sheep and llamas. At one time they were both dominated by the Incas, whose language was Quechua. However, the Aymara were allowed to retain their own language. As a rule, the Aymara and Quechua do not intermarry, keeping their languages and cultures distinct. The Aymara-speaking people of the northern Altiplano display strong cultural distinctiveness in their dress. Although variations are found, the basic dress for men consists of tight, ankle-length trousers slit at the lower end, a short, tight jacket, a poncho and a knitted wool cap with ear flaps worn under a home-made felt hat. The women wear either a large number of polleras (knee-length skirts) or one ankle-length skirt, an embroidered blouse, a manta (shawl) and a designed hat. The traditional dress is made exclusively of homespun textiles. In recent years, the Aymara have begun adopting the clothes of the cholo, machine-produced trousers and suit jackets for the men and felt derby hats for the women.

A piece of clothing worn by both the Aymara and Quechua is the awayo, a rectangular piece of wool or cotton, woven traditionally in the design specific to the region. The awayo is fastened across the shoulders to allow the wearer to carry upon her back a baby or an infinite variety of parcels; it may also be simply worn across the shoulders and tied or pinned in front as a wrap. Beautiful hand-woven woolen awayos are now giving way to brightly-striped cotton ones, often machine made. But in the more outlying areas, one sees handsome authentic awayos, sometimes for sale. They consist of two woven lengths stitched together to form a square piece or, in some cases, only one woven piece. Awayos can have fascinating patterns in both color combinations and design. The modern awayo, by contrast, has no merit as a handicraft, but it is colorful and lends a bright touch to city streets. (For more information on awayos and other clothing traditions, see "The Textile Traditions of Highland Bolivia" chapter in this section.)

The religion of the Aymara reflects a blend of pre-Conquest traditions and practices, such as reverence for various place spirits and the venerable Pachamama (Mother Earth), coupled with certain Christian beliefs, such as the Virgin and Catholic saints. Much of the social life which binds together Aymara communities revolves around the celebration of Christian fiestas. Most communities have specific patron saints, whose days are observed by masses, dancing, drinking and banqueting. The celebration calls forth the most strenuous and organized efforts of the residents. The sponsorship of these fiestas is closely bound with the structure of local leadership, for. Traditionally, prestige, respect and power have been given to those men who have more actively supported long and expensive festivities.

Dance is the focal point of Aymara ceremonial and recreational life, and every major festivity is celebrated by continuous dancing by individuals and groups. Although dance steps and costumes vary considerably among localities, many common themes are represented in dances throughout Aymara territory. The costumes, which are rich and often fantastic, made from brocade, silver thread and braiding, glass beads and mirrors, are purchased at great expense or rented from craftsmen who manufacture them in town workshops.

The economic self-sufficiency and the highly distinctive ceremonial life of the Aymara have produced a rich and varied pattern of handicraft, music and dance. The most utilitarian objects made by Aymara craftsman often display a high degree of technical competence and artistic beauty. Spinning and weaving of all available forms of wool (sheep, llama, alpaca and vicuña) are skills which were at one time known to almost all Aymara. The visitor to the Altiplano will inevitably see the pueblo women in doorways and walking down roads, spinning raw wool on small hand-held spindles. However, the introduction of industrially-produced clothing has caused a considerable decline in the weaving craft which now survives only in certain areas.

Although the great majority of Aymara adults are still reador and unable to speak Spanish, a significant percentage of their children are receiving at least a rudimentary education. Many aspects of traditional Aymara culture, more resistant to change, have been carried over into the newly emerging way of life. The fiestas, so important in defining local leadership, continue to be celebrated with enthusiasm. And traditional Aymara folk music has not been replaced by the more commercialized popular music, in spite of the increasing ownership of radios and cassette players by the indigenous peoples.

Quechua speakers in Bolivia include a variety of local groupings who consider themselves to be ethnically distinct from each other. The Quechua language was imposed by the Incas on several culturally and linguistically divergent people, and at the time of the conquest many of these groups still maintained separate social identities. This ethnic independence among the Quechua has, to a large extent, been maintained to the present, primarily due to their social isolation and relative immobility.

Their social identities are represented by the many distinct traditional costumes. Although the characteristic dress consists of garments patterned on old Spanish styles (as in the case of the Aymara), the headwear, color and poncho design vary greatly and often serve to distinguish Indians of neighboring communities. In addition, the Quechua language, much more than the Aymara, is divided by many variations in regional dialect. The areas occupied by the Quechua are more varied in altitude, climate and proximity to urban centers and markets than are those of the Aymara. There are Quechua speakers in the relatively low, fertile valleys of Cochabamba and on the high, bleak plateaus of Potosí, as well as in Chuquisaca, parts of Oruro and the mountainous western edge of Cochabamba. The social and economic environments in which they live are equally varied. The Indians living in settlements virtually uninhabited by mestizos or other Spanish speakers have largely been free of outside influence for centuries.

By contrast, the Quechua of the Cochabamba valley have long been in close contact with other diverse Bolivian groups, and with their intensive commercial activity, they form a somewhat special case. The relations between these Quechua and the cholos in the Cochabamba Valley have historically been smoother than in other areas, and the two groups have worked together for common causes. These same Indians have

always been bilingual to a greater degree than other Indian groups. They have also adapted much more readily to the cholo, or mestizo, way of life, and as a result their ethnic distinctiveness has been somewhat weakened.

They have abandoned their traditional dress over the years, with the Cochabamba Quechua men wearing manufactured cotton work clothes and the women wearing factory-made shawls and the high-crowned, white-enameled, starched hats of the Cochabamba cholas. The religious life of the Cochabamba Quechua includes many pre-Conquest survivals, such as homage to Pachamama. But in contrast to the Aymara, they lack specialized rituals and communal observances. The music and dance of the Cochabamba Indians are largely identical to those of the local cholo population. Only in the most outlying areas has there been any survival of either pre-Conquest instruments or melodies. Through widening educational opportunities, the Quechua youth of the Cochabamba Valley are becoming fluent and partially literate in Spanish.

The Chipaya, Uru and Lowlands Groups

On the northern and southern peripheries of the Aymara territory live the now-dwindled remnants of the two groups who managed to retain their ethnic identity through both the Incan and Spanish conquests. The Chipaya, llama and sheep herders of the inhospitable Carangas region of the western Oruro Department, speak Puquina and Aymara. This tribe has been driven from its lands, at various times, and has intermingled and intermarried to some extent with the surrounding Aymara. Today, the tribe is so small numerically that it is in danger of disappearing along with its language. According to estimates, there may now be no more than 600 Chipaya. The Uru, a fishing and herding people who inhabited the reed swamps of the Desaguadero River and nearby portions of Lake Titicaca, have suffered a similar fate.

The ethnic groups in the eastern lowlands include the Guaraní (numbering about 20,000), the Guarayo (about 15,000) and the Chiquitano (about 15,000). In addition, there are 25 other groups whose total population numbers approximately 15,000. Each group has its own language, many of which have never been classified.

In the lowlands, the tipoy, or low-waisted shift-like dress, is the most common clothing for women, who traditionally wear their hair in long braids. The men wear Western-style clothing. Although the Jesuits settled missions in some of these remote areas more than 300 years ago, these ethnic groups are only recently being assimilated into Bolivian culture. While the speed of acculturation has been accelerated, the difficulties of transportation to these areas still pose a challenge to the complete assimilation of these people into the language and customs of the country.

FOLK CUSTOMS

The Hair-Cutting Ritual

Some of the customs initiated by the Incas can still be found in modified form in present-day Bolivia. One of these is the hair-cutting ritual called ruthuchiku. The Incan custom was to hold a fiesta when a child reached the age of two years and was weaned from his mother's breast. This was often accompanied by the hair-cutting ceremony in which the child's head was completely shaved. The cutting of the hair followed a specified pattern: the first lock was cut by a padrino (godparent) chosen from all the relatives, and the remaining hair was then cut by other relatives in order according to age and rank. At the same time, each of these relatives gave the child a present. At the ruthuchiku, the child's name given him at birth was substituted by a new, permanent name. The occasion was celebrated with a banquet and singing and dancing for several days. For the Incan crown prince, the festivities lasted 20 days.

In present-day Bolivia, a small child's head is shaved and the accompanying celebration may last one day, with the child receiving gifts of money. One practical aspect of this custom is said to be a thicker growth of hair in later life.

Traditional Healers

For the Indians, there are three types of men who possess magic secrets: amauta (wise men), yatiri (fortune tellers) and collirii (said to possess both supernatural powers and practical knowledge). The yatiri practice fortune telling by reading coca leaves. The most common way of doing this is to place the leaves on a cloth after previously speaking to the spirits, and then to observe the design and direction among the leaves. Another method is to place the coca in the open hand, looking for interpretations in its shape. In this way the yatiri foretell the future and discover the location of the lost people or items.

Among the healers, the kallawaya deserve special mention. The kallawaya are the famous traveling healers and charm sellers of the Andes. With a bag of roots, herbs, ointments and amulets, the kallawaya travel the length of the Andes from Argentina to Ecuador, often spending their entire careers as traveling vendors and healers. The herbal remedies known to them number in the thousands and are prepared from plants of both the highlands and the eastern lowlands. Because of their reputed healings of both body and soul, the kallawaya enjoy prestige and far-flung fame. (For more information on the kallawaya tradition, see the "Traditional Medicine" chapter in this section.)

Compadrazgo

In Bolivia, as in other Latin American

countries, relationships are established with members outside of one's family through the institution of compadrazgo (godparent relationships). The visitor to Bolivia will find that great value is placed on interpersonal relationships, both within the family as well as outside it. Padrinos (godparents) are usually chosen in two ways: one is based on close ties of friendship generally among people of equal social status, and the other is when those in poorer and weaker positions seek to establish bonds of artificial kinship with the more affluent and socially prominent.

The visitor will find that in Bolivia the custom of asking for padrinos seems to be yet more ingrained than in other countries, and padrinos here are required for a larger variety of occasions than expected in other places. Thus Bolivians not only arrange godparents for the traditional baptisms, and civil and religious marriage ceremonies, but also for a specific part of the aforementioned ceremonies, such as buying the wedding cake, buying the bride's gloves, or joining with several other madrinas (godmothers) to buy the bride's veil. Men may be asked to sponsor the uniforms of a given sports club, to pay for the plaque at an inauguration site of a community development project (such as a new bridge), or to buy the trophy for a football championship. In all of these cases, the sponsoring man or woman receives the title of padrino or madrina.

In the case of baptism and marriage the godparent assumes a more lasting and binding relationship. If he is the godfather of a child, he will always be responsible as a padrino for the physical and spiritual well-being of this child and is expected to remember each birthday and other special events in this child's life, such as graduation, with gifts. He is also obliged to offer advice to the child when called upon. He enters into the compadre bond with the child's parents, through which they will be loyal to each other and help each other in times of need. The padrinos for a couple at marriage are expected to counsel the newlyweds later if marital problems arise and the couple seeks help. Traditionally, especially in rural areas, the large landowners, merchants and politicians assumed a large number of compadre relationships for purposes of cementing their authority over the population. Although this is slowly fading away, it is still common for poorer families to ask the more affluent to become their padrinos. The visitor and foreign resident in Bolivia should be careful in accepting, and feel free to reject becoming padrinos for specific events and ceremonies.

FOLK BELIEFS AND LEGENDES

Bolivian folklore, both Aymara and Quechua, is rich in legends and traditions. The natural world of mountains, animals and plants, and a supernatural world peopled with mythological beings, are the source of countless myths and beliefs. A small sampling of this indigenous folklore is offered here as an introduction for the visitor, but many more tales and traditions are chronicled in various Bolivian anthologies.

Pachamama

The strongest traditions surround Pachamama (Mother Earth), the most powerful being after the sun in Indian mythology. The Indian renders special homage to Earth, so that Pachamama, through centuries of strong beliefs, has become a true goddess. She is a goddess of good and evil, both adored and feared by the Aymara. Generous and loving, she protects people, animals and plants; but when angered, she is cruel and vengeful. To honor The Indians practice many rituals and sacrifices.

Pachamama presides over virtually all acts within the lives of Indians, both significant ones such as marriage and birth, and mundane ones like drinking and chewing the day's first coca. Pachamama has the first right to all things. Starting a trip, the Indian carefully places the first fistful of coca that he has chewed at a spot in the road as an offering to Pachamama, rather then throwing it away. She also receives tribute when the first furrows are plowed and before the harvest. At a gathering, each guest sprinkles the first drops of liquor upon the ground, another offering to the ever-present Mother Earth. In moments of highest joy or deepest bitterness, Pachamama is present as an intimate, indispensable symbol in the life of the Indian.

When a house is constructed, homage is rendered to Pachamama in a special ceremony called the ch'alla. Without the sacrifice to her, called cucho, the house could not be finished; or if finished, there would never be peace under its roof. When the foundations are laid, a small hole or niche is left at ground level. On the day of the cucho, which is always a Saturday, the owner and the people engaged in construction gather at the house. The cucho has been prepared, consisting of a wax figure of a man, a few grains of incense, some aromatic herbs, a few leaves of coca, cotton on a branch, and a few pieces of melted tin in the form of humans, animals and household objects. This collection of objects is placed together and wine or pisco sprinkled over it to begin the ceremony.

One of the workmen acts as a holy man and is left alone with the cucho. Placing the cucho over a pile of dried branches, he burns it in a fire, observing the direction of the smoke to determine if bad spirits will abandon the place. As he chews a handful of coca, he mumbles invocations to Pachamama and asks for her blessings. When the other participants return, the holy man places the coca he has chewed in the midst of the ashes and ties all of this into a sack which is placed in the prepared hole in the foundation. From that moment on, the cucho is the invisible guardian of the workmen and the inhabitants of the house. Now the festivities begin, but before drinking any liquor, each guest pours a few drops over the sealed niche that contains the cucho.

Creation Myths

Many and varied legends describe the creation of the Andean race. The most popular Incan account, which itself appears in various versions, is the myth of Tiwanaku, which says that Andean man came from the waters of Lake Titicaca. Another legend, and one with more historical backing, says that the founders of the race arrived by land or sea from a distant area.

By Aymara tradition, Huiracocha, the principal god, created the universe, brought light, and from stones made various human couples, each destined to form a community. Each place of origin was called an achachila, and each of the achachila contained an idol around which a cult developed. The major achachilas were Lake Titicaca, Illimani, the hills of Potosí, the Desaguadero River and certain rocks and caves. Often a small pile of stones is found along roads; these stones are offerings made by travelers to the nearest achachila.

Some Superstitions

The Indian reveres the world above his head, which he calls the alajpacha. This sphere includes celestial and spiritual phenomena, the heavenly bodies and the home of the souls. Akapacha (the earthly world) is also revered, and this includes the earth, wind and organic beings. The sun, Inti, is the father and protector, giver of light and life. The moon, Pajsi, indicates the time of sowing and of the harvest. The stars, Warawara, serve as guides to travelers, and rainbows, Curmi, are evil spirits. To stop the rainbow's bad influence, chewed coca is thrown at it. But one must not point at it nor view it from the front. Huairatata is fatherwind, husband of Pachamama. He frequently draws water from Lake Titicaca to the sky, from whence he causes it to fall upon the earth as rain.

Wind and Earth form an inseparable myth, and the idol with which they were traditionally represented was a two-sided statue encircled by snakes. This idol was considered more powerful than the sun. The underground divinity that produces seismic movements is a huge black boa with a flattened head and fiery eyes. He can reduce himself to the size of a worm and suck the blood of young people causing anemia and tuberculosis. The kindly deity of deserted places is Huasa Mallcu, who takes the shape of the magnificent and austere condor. When the wind stops, flowers perfume his way. His opposite is the devil, Supay, whose three servants cause great damage. The antidote against such evil is a certain plant and the image of Mama Sara, the deity of corn. Animals are also objects of superstition. Three totem animals that represent the vigor of the race are the condor, puma and vicuña. These traditionally favored animals constitute some of the principal decorative motifs in Tiwanaku art. Other animals with special powers include the armadillo, instrument of vengeance in witchcraft, the moth, which foretells death, and certain birds, whose singing is ominous. The lizard also has curative powers when held against the body, and the frog plays an important role in witchcraft.

A series of amulets, or protective charms, called huakankis, have developed from these beliefs in the supernatural powers of animals. These are small images made of stone, bone, wood or clay, and are used to attract the virtues or dispel the witchery of the various animals. There is a great variety. They appear as little hands, or simply as an image of the object desired: a good harvest, good oxen or cattle, or land. Some amulets are worn to attain the love of a woman and often take the shape of a rattlesnake. An amulet in the shape of a boar's tooth will bring the love of a man.

The Legend of Illimani

Many are the legends about Mount Illimani, the frozen, eternal guardian overlooking the city of La Paz. The following story tells how it came to pass that Illimani is the mountain with no rival in the La Paz basin, according to the best-known Aymara tradition. At the creation of the world, two gigantic mountains were formed over the basin in which La Paz now nestles. One of them, Illimani, was positioned so that the setting sun set it ablaze with colors. The mountain was especially lovely from this high canyon, but this same mountain viewed from its other side (the Yungas) appeared deformed. Farther north rose the second mountain, taller and thicker. Seen from the high canyon, its form was awkward and graceless and the sun's setting rays passed over it, leaving it colorless. But seen from the Yungas at the site today occupied by Coroico, it was distinguished and beautiful.

The god who created the two giants was greatly frustrated by his handiwork; he became an eternal pilgrim, traveling constantly back and forth from the high canyon to the Yungas, always asking himself, "Which mountain is the most magnificent?," from which side did he want to view his handsome son? Wearied of his journeying and indecision, he reposed one afternoon by the shore of the River Choqueyapu that runs even today through the canyon. His glaze rested upon Illimani, which that day appeared lovelier than ever. The other mountain, by contrast, was showing its ugly side. Suddenly he made his decision. Illimani was his favorite son, and the god would establish his permanent home in this basin by the river running with gold, so that he could daily feast upon the magnificence of Illimani's most beautiful side. Furthermore, he would destroy the second mountain. With a sling, he hurled a stone from the River Choqueyapu at the mountain, shouting, "Sajama" ("Go away")! The mountain split in two, and its head rolled far across the Altiplano to settle permanently among the Cordillera Occidental, and become known as Mount Sajama. The lower half of the mountain remained in its place, now flattened across the top. Since then, it has been called Mururata (beheaded). Thus, over the basin in which the city of La Paz was later founded, Illimani became the sole and undisputed sovereign.

The Legend of the Kantuta

Many legends explain the strong sentiment the Altiplano Indian has long felt for the graceful kantuta, now Bolivia's national flower. It is said that this affinity for the flower reaches back into the Incan period. Here is one of these legends, a poignant story of unfulfilled love.

Once upon a time, one of the cruelest Incas sat on the empire's throne. It happened that this tyrant had a daughter so beautiful that the fame of her loveliness had traveled to the end of the empire. The monarch, on a journey to the Island of the Sun, spent several days in the lakeside settlement of Copacabana. His beautiful, favorite daughter accompanied him, and during their stay in Copacabana she met a young man of the town. Kento was handsome but of lowly birth, the descendant of a people who years before had fallen under the Incan yoke and had been transferred to the shores of Lake Titicaca. The two young people fell in love with an ardent passion, but both realized the hopelessness of such love. The princess knew that, even if she confessed her love to her father, he would never permit marriage outside the customs and traditions of the royal house. Kento also recognized the undeniable barriers to their marriage, and the two young people faced the most serious dilemma of their lives.

Then the Inca announced that the following day his entourage would leave Copacabana for the return trip to Cuzco.

After a day busy with preparations for leaving, the princess secretly slipped out of her room by night. It was a dark and foreboding night with no moon or stars shining through the thick, ominous clouds. The princess, nevertheless, directed herself with resolution toward the house of her beloved, and had almost attained her destination, when she slipped and fell into a deep ravine in the depth of which grew a thicket. A sharp cry pierced the silence of the night. As the princess had plunged down into the ravine, drops of her blood had fallen on plants and thorns. And in the morning, these drops appeared like flower petals that had blossomed overnight. The body of the princess was discovered at the bottom of the ravine, and at that place a short time later a strange unknown bush began to grow. When this bush flowered, its delicate blossoms were in the shape of a chalice, and they were red, the color of the princess's blood. As this bush first appeared near Kento's house, the people called the flower kentuta pankara (flower of Kento's house).

Folk Dances

The music of Bolivia is perhaps the very heartbeat of the country. Each region of Bolivia has fostered music that reflects its distinctive lifestyle, the color, tempo and mood of the inhabitants, and their physical surroundings. Thus the music of the Altiplano is played in a minor key and tends to be sad and mournful. The music from the lowlands, on the other hand, is gayer and faster.

A recent and definite change has taken place in Bolivian music. With the advent of popular new musical groups, a trend has occurred whereby more importance is given to the vocal part of a group than to the instruments, which are used solely as accompaniment to the voice. This is in direct contrast to the origin of Altiplano music, where a voice was never heard among the musical groups, and the instruments were all-important. However, the voice has always played an important part in the music of the eastern lowlands, the region with more Spanish and Creole influence.

The traditions of the dance display a rich and ancient heritage that typifies much of the Bolivian spirit. A brief outline of some of the major dance types and forms is offered here as a mere introduction. To really know Bolivian dance, of course, you must witness the spectacle in person -- or actually join in the pulsating rhythms and movements yourself.

Comparsa Dances

The comparsas are organized groups of dancers who perform prescribed dances before spectators, following a set pattern of movements to a particular accompanying music whike wearing a specific costume or uniform. In almost every case the comparsa dances are very old, having originated among the people out of certain contexts and circumstances. (For a description of Bolivia's most famous comparsa, the Diablada (Devil Dancers) and several other principal dances, see "The Carnaval of Oruro" chapter in this section)

One such comparsa is the Auqui-Auqui, which is Aymara for "Old Man-Old Man." The dance is a satire of the solemnity and pomposity of Spanish gentlemen of the colonial period. Because of their dignified dress and quaint manners they seemed old, and a humped back is added to the dancers to emphasize age. The dance caricatures their solemn movements and dress. The costume is thus very exaggerated, featuring a tall hat and crooked walking canes of liana. The music is pretty, and the crooked cane is moved in time with the feet in quick, darting movements. Sometimes a woman appears during the dance, and the quaint little men take notice. The humped men of this comparsa create a humorous, appealing sight.

The Las lecheras dance recalls the time when lecheras (milkmaids) delivered milk to homes in metal milk cans. This vocation is now fading away. The dancers wear as many 15 or 20 polleras (wide skirts), a jubón (a richly-embroidered blouse), a manta (shawl) and bowler hat, and they carry miniature milk cans. The choreography is relatively simple.

Indigenous Dances

Many specific dances for couples and/or groups are danced spontaneously in fiestas in all parts of Bolivia. These include indigenous dances that have originated in and may remain typical of a particular region of Bolivia as well as bailes de salón (ballroom dances) that reflect a Spanish influence. The Bolivians are tireless dancers, and dancing is the most popular form of entertainment at parties.

Of the indigenous dances, one of the most popular is the huayño. It originated on the Altiplano, but is now embraced in most areas of Bolivia. As a dance of the Altiplano campesinos, the music had no words. Adopted later by the Creole, it was given words, and the dance itself developed more choreography and sophistication. Today at a fiesta, the huayño can become a frenzied sort of dance (locura, the Bolivians say), with everyone dancing and following as many different steps as they like. It concludes with a return to the main theme but faster and with more animation (zapateo). The dance may be accompanied by brass bands, zampoñas and all types of instrument groups.

Another interesting dance of the Altiplano is the kullahuada, in which men dancers hold a spindle in their hands and wear a distinctive costume. The carnavalito is another typical dance, used especially during Carnaval. It is popular in the lowlands, the valleys and the Altiplano region, but with definite mood differences among the three regions.

TRADITIONAL PRESENT

TRADITIONAL PRESENT

From the lowlands, especially Beni and Santa Cruz, comes the chovena. It is a dance that originated with certain tribal dances and has now evolved into a ballroom dance. A purely folkloric dance is the machetero, showing definite influence from the tribal areas of the lowlands. The dress includes a large corona of bright macaw tail-feathers, tipoy (a robe made of bark) and machetes of wood carried by the dancers. The traditional instruments used to accompany this unusual dance include a flute made of bird bones and a bombo (a very large drum).

The chapaqueada is a dance from Tarija, pertaining to religious festivals such as Christmas and Easter. The name comes from the word Chapaco, a person from Tarija. Typically Tarijan instruments accompany the chapaqueada: the erke, a wind instrument similar in form to the pututu; the cana, a very long flute that makes a very distinctive sound and is held over the shoulder; the caja, a type of drum; and the chapaco violín, a three-stringed violin.

Ballroom Dances

Of the ballroom dances, the cueca deserves special attention. Of direct Spanish influence, it is similar to the Spanish jota, a dance involving the use of castanets. In Bolivia the castanets are replaced by hand-kerchiefs held gracefully in the hands of both partners. As the cueca evolved in Latin America, it traveled from Peru to Chile to Argentina and, finally, to Bolivia where it ended its evolutionary circle. Today the cueca is very representative of Bolivia, being as typical of this country as the tango is of Argentina. The music has a measure of three beats, has a distinctly national flavor, and is more elaborate than primitive. The dance includes an introduction and three distinct parts. It is a dance performed by one couple; while a whole room of couples may be dancing the cueca at the same time, they never come together as a group.

During the introduction, the couple meets, actually standing and looking at one another in what may be a provocative manner. Then the word "adentro" is called out, which is the signal for the beginning of the dance. In the first part, the man tries to win the lady, who eludes him and escapes. In quimba (the second part), the step is softer and the music more lyrical; the idea is that an agreement between the two has been reached. The third part is signaled by the word "ahora." This part is called the zapateo, and is a repetition of the first part with more force. It is the climax of the dance, and the spectators applaud in rhythm with the beat. The entire cueca is always repeated once.

Oftentimes the second part of the cueca begins with the words "aro, aro, aro" shouted by the dancers. A tray is suddenly dropped upon the floor and all the music and dancing stop. The honored couple is then obliged to interlock arms, and each drinks a glass of liquor. After this dizzying ritual, the music and dancing resume to the finish.

The cueca is danced in the high valleys and in the Altiplano area. The rhythm and beat in both regions are the same, but there are distinct differences in spirit and mood. Among the cuecas danced in the high valleys, that of Tarija is particularly distinctive. The words of the cueca usually deal with love themes: asking for love, protesting a lack of love, etc. It is sometimes played solely as an instrumental.

The Bolivian composer Simeón Roncal wrote 20 cuecas in concert form for piano. These cuecas are slow and particularly beautiful, more suited for listening in concert than for dancing.

The harmonium, or red organ, and a battery of drums and cymbals have been the traditional accompanying instruments of the cuecas. This tradition is fading, however, and today all types of instrumental combinations are used: accordion, guitar, charango, piano and others. Complete bands are also used today.

The bailecito is similar to the cueca in several respects: it is danced in both the high valleys and in the Altiplano, though it has a different in mood in each area; it is an imitation of Spanish ballroom dances; it has an introduction and three parts, including the zapateo with spectators clapping. The partners carry handkerchiefs, and it can be played as an instrumental or sung, with a variety of instrumental groups as accompaniment. But there are also distinct differences between the cueca and the bailecito. The bailecito is finer and more delicate, and without the emphasis on provocative mannerisms. Shorter than the cueca, it is always played through three times. It reflects an influence from the minuet and other ballroom dances involving groups interacting in dance patterns. The bailecito is for four people, two couples, whose dance pattern is in the form of a square. The lyrics employ very evocative words with double meanings, many dealing with love themes. While the bailecito is still danced today, it is not nearly as common now as it was in the past.

Another interesting musical tradition is the copla, a contest between two people, each of whom has a guitar, who respond to one another through alternating verses of the song. The music is slow without much variation, but the words vary and are very important. The copla comes from Tarija.

A list of Bolivian dances showing Spanish influence should include the Villancicos (Christmas carols). The purpose of this music and dance is to adore the Christ Child, and it is performed in churches as well as on the street and in private homes. Traditional to Sucre and La Paz, this seasonal music is often gay.

The common custom is for costumed children carolers to visit various houses; they ask to enter the homes and then praise the image of the Christ Child through their music and dance, in return for sweets or coins. They approach the image of the Christ Child, marking the rhythm by hitting a castanet against their palm, and conclude their adoration by backing away from the nativity scene. The instruments used with the Villancicos are the chullu-chullo (which consists of flattened beer bottle caps strung on a circular wire), the harmonica, drum and pajarillo. The latter is a can filled with water that gives a birdlike sound when blown. In Sucre an unusual instrument known as the rekeke is used at Christmas to accompany these carols; wooden castanets are rubbed over tautly stretched cords strung between two wooden bars. The Municipality of La Paz traditionally awards a prize to the best caroler group.

TRADITIONAL PRESENT

THE CARNAVAL OF ORURO

BY MANUEL VARGAS

CARNAVAL IN ORURO IS A SERIOUS CELEBRATION STEEPED WITH DEEP RELIGIOUS MEANING. LIKE OTHER EXPRESSIONS OF BOLIVIAN CULTURE, IT IS A BLEND OF OLD AND NEW WORLD BELIEFS.

It is Carnaval Saturday in Oruro, Bolivia. Under the blue sky of the high plateau, surrounded by expanses of sand and low ridges, this mining town of 230,000 inhabitants will give itself over from eight in the morning until late at night to a celebration of music and dance that expresses the rich imagination of its people. Thousands of visitors from other parts of the country and around the world line streets, throng the squares and avenues, fill temporary bleachers, windows and balconies, festoon the tops of walls and roofs, and perch atop motor vehicles in order to watch the Entrada (entry march) of the Carnaval. The companies of celebrants, each with their own costumes, masks, distinctive music and dances, go hopping and dancing for 20 blocks to the church of the Virgen del Socavón (Virgin the Mine Shaft) on the Pie de Gallo (Rooster Foot) ridge.

If there are thousands of spectators, there are as many dancers from the town itself and elsewhere in the country, the most important of them being the Diablos (Devils) and Morenos (Blacks), who field eight of the 40 or 50 dancing companies. Considering that the smallest companies number 30 to 50 people and the largest 200 to 300, one can roughly estimate how many dancers there are, and thus visualize the magnitude of the spectacle.

In the Entrada, first come the cargamentos, a motorcade of vehicles laden with fine embroideries, jewels, gold and silverware, old coins and banknotes, which recall either the treasures once offered up in the worship of Inti (the sun) on the Incan Inti Raymi feast day, or the wealth of the Tío (Uncle) who dwells in the mine shafts.

Behind the motorcade comes the company of the Diablos, led by Lucifer and two Satans among a clattering din of reports from rockets and small cannon, and surrounded by five dancing she-devils. The masks of these Diablos, adorned with toads, snakes and lizards, sport plaster-of-paris horns, painted light bulbs for eyes, little mirrors for teeth and hair from the tails of oxen or horses. The group of dancers is followed by the angel guarding the Virgen del Socavón, who is carried by the standard bearer. A band brings up the rear of this section, and condors and bears (survivors from ancient totemic rites) walk in and out among the dancers.

Next comes the company of the Incas, representing historical personages from the time of the conquest: the Inca Huascar, the Spaniards Francisco Pizarro and Diego de Almagro, and the priest Vicente de Valcerde (who, failing to convert Atahualpa, the last of the Incas, to Christianity, allowed him to be sentenced to death). Just as the Diablos -- who on Socavón Square stage the relato (story) of the Seven Deadly Sins in which the Archangel Michael is victorious -- the Incas put on a fine theatrical piece. Theirs is called

La Conquista de los Españoles (The Conquest of the Spaniards) and is by an anonymous colonial author.

The Tobas, with large tropical feathers on their heads and lances in their hands, present war dances that remind spectators of the jungle tribes conquered by the Inca Yupanqui when he extended his empire eastward. The LLameros (llama drivers) call to mind with their slings the long llama caravans from the different lands of the Tawantinsuyo (the lands of the ports of Lima and Buenos Aires) for shipment to Europe. The kallawayas (witch doctors) dance with their bags of herbs and the other materials they use to fight diseases and preserve the heat of the body. There are also the kullawas, who spin and weave, as well as a host of other companies with intriguing names: the Chutas, Cambas, Antahuaras, Potolos, Tinkus, Corimaitas, Tollcas and Caporales.

The Morenada, led by the Rey Moreno (Black King) and the Caporal (Chief), advance slowly with their heavy costumes, whirling their rattles. According to tradition, for some they represent the black slaves brought over from Africa to stomp grapes for juice; for others, they are the blacks led off in chains to work the mines of Potosí in colonial times. Their richly-decorated costumes represent the wealth of the slave owners, the protruding eyes and tongues of their masks convey the black man's fatigue and the soroche (altitude sickness) from which he suffered.

The Entrada ends with the entry of all the masked companies into the church to hear mass in honor of the Virgen del Socavón.

Long preparation is needed for participation, beginning with the organization of companies of dancers in Oruro and their respective branches in other Bolivian towns. When Oruro's Carnaval was first held, only the miners danced; now they are joined by artisans, butchers, cattle brokers, workers in trade and industry, and professionals of all ages. Rehearsals go on for months, beginning on the first Sunday of November (the First Invitation) with a mass and vows to the Virgin, followed by a five-hour rehearsal every Sunday until the second or Last Invitation. The Entrada then takes place the following Saturday.

Carnaval, with all its music, dances, eating, drinking and ch'allas (offerings) to Pachamama (Mother Earth), continues for a week. At the despedida (farewell) on Temptation Sunday, ch'allas are held for the Condor, the Toad, the Viper and certain rock formations that are part of the town's myths. The celebration ends with an outing for participants and spectators to the country-side in the Agua de Castilla district, where the Carnaval is "buried" until next year.

The ch'alla consists of sprinkling drinks on all things, both fixed and movable, and in adorning them with confetti and streamers so that abundance will come, continue or increase. This is how the protection of the gods of increase and abundance is invoked, and how respect is shown to them.

A Unique Blend

Like other expressions of Bolivian culture, the Oruro Carnaval is a blend of aspects of indigenous culture and elements imposed by the Christianity of the Spanish conquistadors. On one hand, the Christian Carnaval underwent changes when it became part of the American tradition. In Andean Bolivia it not only changed, but also acquired a different meaning while retaining many Christian names and rites. On the other hand, the Andean myths and customs were adapted to the new situation of a conquered world. The result was to unleash a contest that, in the view of some, will end in mestizaje, or a blending of the two cultural forms. But in the view of others, it will have no end; rather it will go on indefinitely, ever latent. But all agree that Andean culture remains a window to the understanding of past and present, albeit one that is overlaid with Christian idioms and forms.

It is now believed that the Oruro Carnaval began in 1789 with the worship of the Virgen del Socavón. It is to that time that two similar traditions have been traced of an outlaw who lived in Oruro and who, being mortally wounded, was saved in his dying moments by an unknown woman of great beauty. She was the Virgen de la Candelaria, whom the outlaw had worshipped by lighting candles to her in the cave where he lived. Later, in 1881, the church of the Virgen del Socavón was built on that spot. This was how the Virgen de la Candelaria became the Mamita del Socavón (Beloved Mother of the Mineshaft), and her feast was changed to Carnaval because that was the day on which she had interceded for her votary.

The cult of this virgin is gradually merging with that of the devil or Supay Tío. It was around 1790 that a company of Diablos first came to the Carnaval. While it is known that the custom of dressing up as a devil is older, it was in those years that it became associated with the Carnaval and the worship of the virgin.

The music and the masks and costumes have also changed. The music used to be played by musicians with quenas, tarkas (two kinds of Andean flutes) and phutucas (native bass drums), rather than by a band. The masks were once of wood, with horns of ox or sheep that were not removable, but fixed, and less twisted. Also, the masks used to cover only the face, not the whole head.

In 1818 a Spanish priest introduced the relato depicting the struggle of the Seven Deadly Sins against Saint Michael. The intent, according to the author of the relato, was to counter the superstitions and myths that persisted in the mines, and to subdue the indigenous deities.

Sometimes declining, sometimes surging in popularity, the Carnaval has continued evolving down to the present in an endless contest --foreshadowed by the ancient myths of the locality and of the entire Andean region -- between tradition and novelty and sophistication, between the Catholic and indigenous religions. Always, Carnaval has reflected the changes that have taken place in Bolivian society.

Myths of Supay and Huari

As a mining town, Oruro pays homage to Supay Tío at Carnaval (as well as throughout the year). This worship is both background and complement to the Oruro Carnaval.

Supay, the malignant prowler in shadows and caves, inhabits ore-rich hills. The Andeans fear and respect him and must stay on his good side so that he will not become their enemy, for if he does, he will not give them wealth, but seek their ruin instead. Supay goes abroad at night, leading his trains of beasts bearing ores to be spread among the hills. Sometimes he allows men to hear him and even plays jokes on them. Whoever does not believe in Supay, or makes fun of him, can lose his mind or perish.

Local traditions hold that maleficent beings have existed since the world's earliest times. Some were created by Viracocha and Pachacámac (ancient Andean deities), others came even before these venerable gods. These formidable beings were gigantic, monstrous and eventually, under the rays of the sun, turned to stones and mountains. In other cases they sprang from beneficent sources, or appeared after an age of bonanza. An example is the myth of Supaya, as retold by an aged Aymara Indian of Puno, Peru.

"When the world began, the three were one: the Virgin Mary, her husband Jesus Christ and their son Supaya. . . Supaya had much wealth, far too much. His horses and mules wore magnificent shoes, but poor Jesus Christ had to walk in his bare feet. . ."

Two of the names are borrowed, but what is important are the parts played by the personages. The two generations of the family have opposite characteristics, one does good and the other evil, and a struggle arises between them. The myth ends as follows:

"In the end the father was vanquished. Today, say others, sometimes God wins and sometimes Supaya. . . Because of this, every man has something of God and something of Supaya in him; some more of God and others more of Supaya. When Supaya had finished persecuting his father, when he had vanquished him, all his friends came out and set to feasting, jumping about, drinking and shouting for joy. That's how the world is now."

This myth of the Aymara country on the Bolivian border of Peru is not an isolated case, but rather only one of many Andean myths that have features in common. Another example is the Huari myth, from which many elements of the Oruro Carnaval spring.

"Near where Oruro stands, there lived the Urus, who were chiefly fishermen and pastoralists. Huari, a giant, lived inside the Uru-Uru mountains. He fell in love with Inti Huara, the Dawn, who awakened him every morning. When he attempted to take her in his arms of fire and smoke, Inti buried him inside the hills. To revenge himself, Huari took human form and preached to the Urus against the rule of Inti and Pachacámac. He told them they would grow rich by seeking the metals concealed in the hills. He prompted them to steal the crops of the valley and made them drink chicha (a beer-like beverage made of corn in the Andean highlands, Mexico and Central America) until they became drunkards. The Urus turned to the practice of magic, using toads, vipers and lizards to bring illness and death to the followers of Inti, and they stopped worshipping, became apathetic and reclusive, and set to fighting among themselves."

"After a rainfall, a rainbow gave birth to a ñusta (Inca princess). She arrived accompanied by the chieftains and sages who had escaped the degeneration of the Urus. Huari would not give up though, and sent, one after another, a snake, a toad and a lizard, all of monstrous size, to wipe out the people and their crops, but the ñusta vanquished them by turning them into stone. The blood of the lizard became a lagoon, and from its mouth there streamed thousands of ants which the ñusta turned into mounds of sand."

Today the ñusta is the Virgen del Socavón in whose honor the Carnaval is danced. Huari is Lucifer, the chief of the dance of the Diablos, who in the early days of the Diablada was called Huaricato (representative of Huari). The plagues sent by Huari are depicted on the dancers' masks by vipers, toads and lizards. Other elements of the myth are found in local geography. The sands are there, as are the petrified remains of the lizard, toad and viper and the lagoon, called Cala-Cala.

According to the dancers and spectators of the Diablos, the dance is an act of adoration for the Virgin, but it can also be a celebration of the triumph of good over evil (and not just in the religious sense).

We see that the Oruro Carnaval is no isolated phenomenon, but rather a rich and most complex expression of myths and beliefs in which history and the present have blended to produce one of the most important social and religious events in Bolivia. At the end of the revels, the Carnaval is laid to rest, to re-emerge each year and give expression to a people and their culture.

ALL SAINTS DAY: UNITING THE LIVING AND THE DEAD

BY JOSÉ ANTONIO ARUQUIPA Z.

It's October 31, and the long-awaited Todos Santos, the eve of All Saints' Day, has finally arrived. One of the most mystic and important Aymara religious commemorations is about to take place.

In the Aymara belief system, Todos Santos is the day when all the animas (spirits of the dead), come from alajpacha (the hereafter) and stay here on akapacha (the earth) for two days.

Aymaras live in communion with their dead. The cooperative social rules that govern Aymara society have a strong influence on the relationship of the living with the spirits of those who have died. All the service-and-favor exchange patterns of the ayllu, or community, system are observed in dealings with the dead.

"We have to take care of them, so that they grant us their spiritual protection," said an Aymara yatiri (priest).

According to author Hans Van den Berg, the living ask for help from their ancestors, who have experienced the struggles and difficulties of life. "It is believed that the bones of the dead dry out at this time of the year, and Aymaras compare the situation to the dry season on the land," writes Van den Berg. The Aymaras believe both "the dead and the land are dehydrated and in need of fervent attention." Hence, by helping the dead satisfy their thirst and hunger, Aymaras receive favors from them. Their lands are fed with rains, presumably sent by the ancestors' spirits.

Other authors, like German philosopher Juliane Esch Jakob, define the relationship between the dead and the living as one in which "the souls of the dead punish the living if they don't behave well. These spirits keep watch and punish all human misbehavior. That's why Aymaras will avidly try to satisfy the spirits."

For most Aymaras, Todos Santos is simply an opportunity to be reunited, at least for a moment, with the dearly departed.

The Special Day

Perhaps what makes this celebration so interesting and fun is the preparation of bread figures to be placed at the "saint's table" on November 1. Tantawawas (bread babies), llamas, horses, ladders, sheep, birds and just about any figure imaginable take shape in the hands of parents and enthusiastic children working side by side on the eve of Todos Santos. Every figure has an ancestral meaning and specific role in this ritual. The bread horses, for instance, are thought to be helpful transportation for those nayra almanakas (elderly souls) coming from far away lands. The ladders are placed to help machaq almanakas (the souls of those who died less than three years ago) climb down to earth.

Todos Santos wouldn't be complete without a Mesa (Offering Table) for the visiting animas. "The table has three different levels," explains Esch Jakob. "The lowest is used to place two candles, a glass full of chicha morada, coca leaves, small pieces of sugar cane and a jar of water. The middle level is covered with a bottle of beer, bread and dishes of food. The top of the table is decorated with the bread figures. A crucifix and photos of the dead occupy the center-top space of the table." The Mesa must be set before noon so that all early animas can enjoy the food and drinks offered in the table.

In most Aymara communities, the arrival of the spirits is announced by the tolling of church bells. The ringing marks the exact moment to start praying for the animas, and all families get together and pray while calling and mentioning the names of those who died. A feast is served for lunch, and chicha is spilled onto the floor.

"On this occasion, you have to eat enough for two," says Freddy Ticona, an Aymara professor at the University of San Andrés in La Paz, "because what you eat goes to the stomach of the dead. And don't you dare kill the flies and bees that are attracted to the offering table; you may be killing an anima who decided to visit in insect form."

An Emotional Farewell

November 2 is a day of mixed emotions. It's sad because the animas of our beloved have to leave, and it's happy because the families have shared a good time with them. Another offering ceremony takes place to bid farewell to the dead.

This time the Mesas are set beside the graves in the cemetery. "All the spirits move to the cemetery before they leave the earth," Esch Jakob writes, so more food, drinks and special treats are placed on top of their tombs.

Beggars and volunteer resiris (suppli-cants) approach the tombs and pray for the dead, receiving bread, candies and drinks in exchange. Later, when all the bread and food have been consumed, the families head home while dancing to cheerful songs. "Todos Santos is over and our dearest souls have been appeased. In peace we may go," the Aymaras say as they sing and dance.

THE TEXTILE TRADITIONS OF HIGHLAND BOLIVIA

BY LAURIE ADELSON AND ARTHUR TRACHT

The textile tradition of highland Bolivia is a rich and highly developed art, with roots reaching back to pre-Colombian times. Yet this remarkable tradition has gone largely unrecognized outside of the Bolivian rural regions, where weaving is still the most important form of creative expression.

Originally, textile production arose out of the simple need for clothing. But gradually, complicated techniques and designs evolved, and cloth became a significant social element in the lives of the Andean peoples. Today in Bolivia, weaving is a well-respected, non-commercial art, and in most regions, cloth continues to play a major role in the lives of the Indians.

The simple indigenous loom and drop spindle are still used to produce a wide variety of weavings ranging from plain, utilitarian textiles for daily use, to highly sophisticated and refined pieces of extraordinary quality for use in ceremonies and festivals. When not tending animals, farming, or doing other daily chores, most people are engaged in weaving-related activities, and all members of the family are involved in textile production. Although in some respects costume has changed over the years, the complex weaving techniques of the past are very much alive.

Among the most beautifully woven and dyed textiles ever produced are the ceremonial weavings of the colonial and 19th-century Aymara Indians of Bolivia. These textiles are a reflection of an extraordinary textile tradition that has flourished in the Lake Titicaca basin plateau since ancient times. While other social and cultural traditions declined rapidly after the Spanish conquest (1532), Aymara weaving techniques, designs, colors and forms remained essentially intact in Bolivia until the end of the 19th century. This fact is not surprising when one considers that throughout pre-Columbian times, textiles were the most highly prized possession and the most sought-after trade commodity in the Andes.

Because of the physical nature of cloth, textiles were probably more important in spreading culture than any other art form. They were more durable than ceramics, which were susceptible to breakage, and had the advantage of mobility, which architectural stoneworks lacked. Moreover, as clothing, textiles were highly visible.

Although most Andean textiles were used as clothing, they were not merely utilitarian in purpose; they also, and in many cases more significantly, played major political, social and religious roles. In pre-Columbian times in the Andes, cloth was regarded as the most important gift. Used to establish and strengthen social and political relationships, it played an essential role in all important phases of the life cycle, as it still does in many parts of Bolivia today. Archaeological excavations of pre-

Colombian tombs in Peru and Chile give an indication of the tremendous importance placed on cloth during ancient times. Mummy bundles found in graves of the Paracas Necropolis (600-200 B.C.) on the southern Peruvian coast contained several hundred exquisitely made textiles.

During Inca times (1430-1532 A.D.), large quantities of the finest textiles were woven specifically to be burned as ritual offerings, a tradition that continued for centuries even after the arrival of the Spaniards. The Spanish conquistadors were astonished at the vast amounts of cloth they found in the warehouses that the Incas maintained in all parts of their realm. Some chroniclers reported that, upon retreating from battle, Inca soldiers sometimes left behind thousands of llamas and prisoners, and even gold and silver, but chose to burn entire warehouses filled with cloth rather than leave them for the Spaniards. In the quipus, the string knot recording system of the Incas, only people and camelids ranked above textiles, which came even before food and ceramics.

Even today, when acculturation has tremendously changed the Aymara lifestyle, the traditional Andean reverence for cloth remains. Ceremonial pieces are still handed down from one generation to the next and are brought out only for important rituals. Consequently, the finest textiles have survived until today, whereas ordinary garments were worn daily until they became merely patches to repair other pieces.

In one region of the southern Altiplano, local chieftains carry bundles called q'epis that are filled with old ceremonial weavings, including ccahuas (tunics), ponchitos, llacotas (mantles) and pillus (ancient headdresses). The q'epi is kept on an alter with burning candles and offerings of coca leaves, alcohol and pre-Columbian objects placed around it. The ccahuas are removed from the q'epi and worn by the chieftain a few

times during the year, serving as the symbol of his status as temporal head of his community, or ayllu. At the end of each year, the q'epi is relinquished to a successor during a special ceremony. A tax document found in one of the bundles and dated 1826 attests to the antiquity of the textiles. In a sense, the contents of the q'epi -- pre-Columbian artifacts, textiles and documents -- form a historical archive of each ayllu.

Most ceremonial weavings that have survived in Bolivia are matrimonial pieces of fine textiles used during rituals by chieftains or their wives. When these pieces are needed, they must be rented from someone else in the community if none are owned by the family. Textiles also play an integral role in the fertility ritual called k'illpa, in which the ears of young animals are marked.

The use of textiles in religious ceremonies has even carried over into Aymara Catholicism; on certain feast days the Indians carry images of patron saints from the church dressed in indigenous ceremonial garb.

Recent years have brought many changes to Bolivia and modernization has reached even remote highland areas. The influence of technology can already be seen as the rural people begin to wear machine-made, rather than hand-made, clothes. Many aspects of the ancient art are already lost. Little natural dyeing is done, and the skill of extremely fine spinning is preserved in only a few areas. Industrial wool and synthetics generally appear in modern textiles. Due to the breakdown of traditional values, the Indians themselves have forgotten much of the meaning that cloth once held.

The Development of Weaving and Dress

The heddle loom and other weaving implements used by present-day Bolivian weavers were developed by their ancestors over 3,000 years ago. Most of the weaving techniques which were eventually to be used all over Peru and Bolivia had already appeared by the first century A.D. The few pre-Columbian highland textiles that have survived indicate that a rich and impressive weaving tradition was already flourishing in the mountains well over a thousand years ago. By the time the Spaniards arrived in the 16th century, both coastal and highland weaving were at such a high point that the conquistadors were astounded by the richness and beauty of Incan clothing.

The influence of the Spaniards on weaving and costume soon began to show. Sheep, brought from Europe, provided wool as a new fiber, and the treadle loom was introduced. Certain aspects of Spanish dress, such as pants and European-style hats, were adopted by the Indians; the Spanish soon began to regulate native dress.

In 1780, the Aymara of Bolivia (then Alto Peru) and the Quechuas under Tupac Amaru, led a strong insurrection against the colonial government. The Indians were defeated but the government decided that in order to prevent further uprisings they must erase all signs of differentiation between the natives and the colonialists. The Indians were therefore prohibited from weaving their regional clothes and were ordered to adopt the costume of the Spanish peasant.

In the highlands and less accessible regions, the Indians were able to preserve their customs to a certain extent. The remoteness of many weaving communities has enabled Bolivians to maintain a tradition of high-quality, warp-patterned weaving. While Spanish elements still make up a major part of the Bolivian Indians' clothing, indigenous garments are worn along with them to form a costume that is distinctly Andean.

THE ELEMENTS OF WEAVING

Fibers

Before the arrival of the Spaniards, camelids (alpaca, llama and vicuña) were the primary sources for weaving materials in Bolivia. Alpaca was the preferred fiber and is still highly valued. When finely spun and woven, it yields a shiny, silky fabric. Llama hair is coarser and stronger than alpaca and is therefore generally chosen for utilitarian textiles such as costales (storage sacks). The rarest and most highly-prized fiber comes from the wild vicuña. In Incan times, only the Inca himself could bestow the right to wear vicuña. Since the Spanish conquest, indiscriminate killing of the animal has caused it to become an endangered species, so that vicuña hunting is now prohibited.

Sheep's wool, introduced by the Spaniards, is now the most available and commonly used material although it yields a rather rough fabric unless much care is taken in shearing and sorting the wool. By selecting fibers from different parts of the animal's body, various qualities of yarn may be spun.

Cotton is native to South America, but it is not often used in the highlands. It is rarely handspun, and its use is limited to certain regions and to particular types of weavings. In Tarabuco, for example, it is woven along with wool, but only in the patterned areas of the pieces. Obviously, in the cold climates of Bolivia, warmer materials are preferred.

Weavers have recently begun using machine-spun yarns, both natural and synthetic. These industrial yarns simplify the weaving process inasmuch as the initial spinning and dyeing are already done. Furthermore, there is a great deal of prestige in being able to purchase industrial products.

Spinning

Bolivian spinners have produced some of the most finely-spun sheep and camelid yarns in the world using only a simple drop spindle. The wool goes through three spinning processes. It is initially spun on a small spindle to obtain a single strand from the raw wool. Next, a larger spindle is used to make a two-ply yarn. After dyeing, the yarn is given a third spinning to produce a crepe twist, a spin so tight that the yarn, when not under tension, twists back on itself. This "over-spin" is an important feature of Bolivian yarns, giving it great strength, elasticity and a hard, smooth surface. These qualities aid the weaver, and the result is a fine, yet durable fabric.

Bolivians sometimes make deliberate use of 'S' and 'Z' twisted (clockwise and counterclockwise) yarns in their fabrics. Often, in a predominantly 'S' twisted fabric, one finds stripes or single warp threads of alternating 'S' and 'Z' twisted yarns. 'Z' twisted threads are called lloq'e, and are said to bring good luck and ward off evil. Not only do they add a lovely subtle effect to the weavings, but also, when near the edges of fabrics, they help prevent the corners from curling.

Color

One of the greatest achievements of the Aymara peoples was the development of a complex dye technology, the result of thousands of years of experimentation. The Aymara were skilled dyers who were able to produce an extraordinary array of colors, bright as well as subdued. The brilliant colors of most colonial and 19th century pieces found today have neither faded nor bled, a testimony to the exceptional abilities of Andean dyers. Unfortunately, the art of natural dyeing has been lost, and the few efforts that have been made to revive it in the Andes have not succeeded in discovering the secrets that produced such depth and evenness of color. In addition, there is a great lack of research in this area, resulting in scanty information about the dyes themselves.

Today natural-dye weavings are usually called makknu, a word that originally referred to the popular and widespread dye, cochineal. Cochineal, a parasite which lives on the cacti opuntia and nopalea, produces a vast range of reds and purples, depending on the mordant and the amount of dye used. Due to its great versatility and the depth of colors it produces, cochineal is one of the most commonly found dyes in the pre-Columbian, colonial and 19th century textiles of the Aymara. Two other sources of reds were chapichapi (R. microphyllum) and airampu (Opuntia soehrensii). Anil (indigo) was used for blues. A whole range of other colors were produced, although little is known of the dyestuffs employed. Bertonio, in his 17th-century dictionary of the Aymara language, gives the Aymara names for many dyes, including makknu, which he calls "a cake made of herbs which dyes wools red."

The great skill of the Aymara women at blending and composing colors is attested to in their weavings. Color was an essential element in the beauty of any textile, and this beauty depended on the individual weaver's ability to arrange the warp yarns pleasingly on her loom. Different color placement made a stripe or patterns vibrate or recede depending on the weaver's sensibility. The effect of certain juxtapositions created a bold cloth with much contrast or a subdued piece with gradual color variations. Occasionally, the dye process itself was utilized to create patterning, such as in the rare ikat banded ponchos.

Color, however, had symbolic as well as aesthetic significance. In many old pieces, particularly the llacotas (mantles), rectangular cloths, a yellow stripe appears near each weft selvedge. While the meaning of these yellow stripes is not yet known, they are too pervasive to be called random. Recent anthropological studies indicate that certain colors represent vertical land ownership and even the specific crops that grow at each altitude.

The Process

Most indigenous textiles are woven by women -- girls usually begin learning to weave before puberty -- on the traditional heddle loom. The loom is set up outside the house and may be positioned either horizontally, with the loom bars lashed to stakes in the ground, or obliquely (leaning against a wall) with the loom bars tied to two perpendicular poles. A backstrap loom is sometimes used.

Most weaving occurs during the winter season, after the harvest and before the next year's planting. The women spend many of their daylight hours at the loom, simultaneously attending to the children and other daily chores. A complex piece with a large patterned area may take several months to complete. Because of the time involved in weaving, these fabrics are made to last for many years.

An important feature of indigenous Bolivian textiles is that they have four selvedges. This is accomplished by using a continuous warp, which is woven entirely from one end to the other. Since these textiles are warp-patterned, the basic layout is determined during the warping process. In the areas where patterning is desired, two or more colors are warped together so that the weaver may "pick up" the color she needs to create the designs. The second color falls to the other side, resulting in a totally reversible cloth. The design motifs are identical on both sides; only the colors change. In a few regions, long supplementary warp floats are used, producing pieces which have designs only on one side.

Techniques and embellishments vary considerably according to the tradition of each region. Different structures are achieved, depending on how the loom is warped and the way in which the weft threads are inserted during weaving. A resist dye technique called watado (ikat) may also be used for patterning. The edges of fabrics are often protected with a woven tubing called ribete. Certain pieces are adorned with tassels or beading, depending on local custom.

Yardage, called bayeta, is woven in most regions on a European-style treadle loom. Usually woven by men, bayeta is then tailored into garments such as shirts, pants and dresses. In certain regions, men weave very bright plaids for their vests, jackets and sashes. A balanced plain weave is commonly used, but occasionally twills may be woven.

In the central highlands, men make belts for their wives or girlfriends on a lap loom called a cañar. A type of weft wrapping is employed with thick warp threads resulting in a stiff, but durable, belt.

Design

The Bolivian Indians' propensity for using stripes in textile design is not arbitrary, but rather based on two significant factors: weaving structure and ancient traditions. Because these textiles are warp-faced, the color composition of the cloth is determined by the layout of the warps when the loom is prepared for weaving. Generally speaking, stripes are inherent in the structure of warp-faced weaving. Unless a piece is completely patterned or completely plain, there will, of necessity, be stripes. Since the Bolivians were master dyers, most of their textiles incorporate many wide and narrow stripes and patterned bands of various colors. In pre-Colombian and colonial pieces, monochrome stripes predominated; later, patterned bands became more and more popular.

One concept of design composition, which is found in some pre-Colombian textiles and later became a classic layout for Bolivian Aymara weavings, is based on groupings of three. In ponchos, the most common setup is three groups of plain or patterned stripes on each side of the piece.

Awayos (mantles) usually have only three striped or patterned areas -- one in the middle and one at each outer weft selvedge. This awayo layout follows through on many ch'uspas (coca bags). Whether this composition is simply an adherence to tradition, a natural balanced result of the warp-faced structure, or a meaningful, symbolic representation is unknown, though it is obviously an important layout. A recent study of Bolivian textiles indicates that the disposition and number of stripes are symbolic representations of the Bolivian's social and physical world.

While design composition was ruled somewhat by technique and tradition, there was ample room for individual artistic expression. In the best striped pieces there is a profound sense of proportion in the placement, width and spacing of the bands. The possibilities of color choice and juxtaposition were vast, and there was a whole repertoire of local design motifs from which to select. However, since the symbols were obviously important and meaningful, they may have often been chosen more for their significance than for aesthetics. It is known that textiles have been used as visual communicators for spreading religion in the Andes for thousands of years. Images of deities appear on textiles as far back as 500 B.C.. This tradition carried through on colonial and 19th-century pieces, where masked dancers and mythological figures are sometimes represented. It is likely then, that religious ideas may also have been expressed through the abstract symbols so common in Bolivian textiles. Although most Bolivian motifs can be traced to pre-Colombian coastal cultures, many probably originated in the Andean highlands and were later used by coastal peoples. Eventually, Spanish designs also influenced Bolivian weaving.

Certain motifs, such as the horse, are clearly of European origin, while in other cases indigenous designs were simply altered stylistically, giving them a fancy, floral appearance. Unfortunately, little is known about the original names and meanings of the ancient symbols. Present-day informants often give conflicting information regarding them, perhaps because they are reluctant to reveal an important part of their culture to outsiders, or perhaps because the meanings have been changed over the centuries and now differ from region to region. In any case, the patterns on Bolivian textiles are not merely decorative, but represent religious, social and cultural ideas, symbolizing concepts relating to family lineages and/or land distribution.

WEAVING REGIONS

Bolivian weavings vary greatly from region to region in style, technique and use. The areas described here represent some of the important weaving centers of Bolivia. The names usually refer to small central villages, although most weaving occurs in the surrounding rural areas.

Calcha

Fine wool spinning is the mark of the textiles from the area around Calcha in southern Potosí. Calcheñas are still the best spinners in Bolivia and continue to produce weavings of high quality. Generally their weavings have little patterned area, but what design there is stands out strikingly due to the fine threads and forceful beating of the weft. For example, the aksus (overskirts) are entirely black except for two intricately-patterned bands, one near each weft selvedge. On these ends one finds the finest warp threads, sometimes over 170 per inch. Though camelid fibers are rarely used, the fabrics often have the shiny appearance of alpaca due to the dim, tightly over-spun threads.

Calcheño ponchos are especially handsome, and several of them can be found in every house. The panti is worn daily, its color varying from dark maroon to wine. It is patterned with stripes and tiny design bands of complementary warp weave. The luto, or mourning poncho, is always black with few decorative bands. Lastly, the boliviano is woven in very bright stripes and worn mostly for fiestas. Bands called watado (ikat) are frequently used on all three types of ponchos.

Women wear full almillas, dresses fashioned from homespun cloth, which are embroidered and sequined on the large open sleeves. Very fine, narrow belts up to five meters long encircle the waist many times, giving the appearance of a wide belt. The aksu is fastened at the shoulders by a topo, which is a pin of Bolivian spoons or coins. A lliclla (woven mantle) is worn around the shoulders, as well as an embroidered shawl, or waita.

Potolo

The textiles woven in the region generally referred to as Potolo are among the most graphically expressive weavings of Bolivia. Characterized by numerous birds and animals, these textiles reflect the lyrical nature of the Quechua-speaking people of Potolo. On the textiles one finds fantastic creatures such as winged, four-legged figures, headless or multi-headed animals, and even birds wearing human clothes. Many animals have comical or mischievous expressions on their faces. Frequently one figure is woven inside another as if it had been eaten, or as if the animal has a young in its belly. Scenes from nature may be portrayed, such as a bird catching a small animal. Humans sometimes appear, but it is interesting to note that plants, so prevalent in other regional textiles, are rarely depicted in Potolo. On the other hand, Inti, the sun, is a popular motif.

Unlike other areas where decorative designs are usually woven in bands, the figures on Potolo weavings may occur in seemingly random patterns, entirely covering a piece. Spatial relationships are free form. Figures can be arranged upside down or sideways and may vary in size from very large ones, which cover almost half the width of the piece, to tiny creatures the size of a thumbnail. The women's aksu usually contains the best array of figures.

When learning to weave, girls make little practice pieces called sakas on which they try weaving different motifs to learn how to form figures. When an experienced weaver actually makes a piece, there is no drawing to help her form the myriad of figures.

Potoleños wear clothes typical of the Quechuas, but some of their traditional pieces are unique to the area. The men, until recently, wore large festive ponchos called capotes (capes or mantles). Four detailed bands decorate these ponchos that are fringed with long yarns that swirl when the men dance. The costume is augmented by a tiny festival ch'uspa adorned with fancy tassels up to a half-meter long.

Tarabuco

Tarabucan costume reflects the strong influence of Spanish tradition on native Bolivian dress. Both men and women wear hard leather hats called monteras that are styled after the helmets of the conquistadors. The women sometimes wear a boat-shaped hat of European influence covered with ric-rac and sequins. The most widely used zoomorphic motif found on their textiles is the horse, an animal of European origin, although it is commonly found side by side with the indigenous llama.

Tarabucans also strongly adhere to the Catholic custom of wearing black clothes, called luto, for periods of mourning. This dress is identical in layout and motif to the everyday, red-colored garments, different only in that it is predominantly black.

The costume of the region is highly styled and recognizable as distinctly Tarabucan. Characteristic of men's dress is the tiny poncho called konga unku, which is worn around the shoulders over the main poncho, and the ahuasa uncu, a square cloth worn around the waist. For festivals, a pallai unku with elaborate designs is worn over the outer poncho. No man is found without his ch'uspa (coca bag), which either hangs from his wide leather belt or dangles from his shoulder. The white homespun corte pants are especially wide and fall just below the knee. Completing the costume is a blue and black embroidered shirt with a zigzag motif.

Tarabucan women wear a highly patterned overskirt called an axu, a simple striped lliclla (mantle) and an embroidered, homespun dress, called an almilla.

Sicasica

Of all the Aymara regions where natural-dye, 19th century and earlier textiles were found, the Sicasica area has the most prolific, abundant and varied textile material. They rank with the most beautifully woven and dyed textiles ever produced in Bolivia. Among the finest and oldest pieces are the one piece ponchitos. The central ground is usually brown or purple, but occasionally black or pink. A pink or red section with three contrasting stripes occurs near each weft selvedge.

Especially lovely are the large ponchos made from two rectangular pieces of cloth sewn together with a slot left for the neck. Often a separate woven strip was placed down the center of the poncho, and woven design border ornamented the perimeter of the piece. A woven multi-colored fringe was then sewn to that border. The traditional layout of six patterned bands with colored stripes

was maintained from pre-Colombian times. Small ponchitos made in two pieces reflect the construction of the larger ponchos. The most frequently occurring patterns in these garments are wavy, narrow bands that enclose the stripes in the design areas. These ponchos have either pink and red or black grounds with multi-colored stripes.

Unique to the woman's costume is the pleated or gathered full skirt called an urku. These pieces have wide stripes with only one patterned band. Red, white and purple predominate on a black ground. Completing the women's costume is the awayo. Sicasica mantles have extremely elaborate design bands, some containing up to 30 patterned stripes. The predominant motifs are birds and stylized medallions. The ground colors are usually purple, black or pink, and some even have two-color grounds. They are made from high-quality alpaca and are extremely finely woven.

Also exceptional in the region are ceremonial ground cloths called incuñas. Sicasica incuñas are characterized by various monochrome bands, sometimes interrupted by design bands. Accessory textiles such as wide belts and coca bags demonstrate the same expertise in spinning, weaving and dyeing.

Charazani

Textiles play significant social and cultural roles in the lives of the Charazani Indians. Consequently, symbolism and the use of color are important and meaningful factors in their weaving. The decorative motifs used in Charazani represent various aspects of the environment and the lives of the people. Zoomorphic figures are extremely diverse, and anthropomorphic images describe important social events. Occasionally, simple, decorative, geometric motifs have special correlations to nature. For example, a certain diamond motif depicts the ancient sun deity Inti.

The profuse symbolism that developed in Charazani was undoubtedly heavily influenced by the kallawayas, the famous medicine men of the area. The influence of the kallawayas is reflected in the scroll motif frequently employed by local weavers. Commonly regarded as a symbol of agricultural fertility, this design is a stylization of the churu, a type of land snail. The symbol, however, is also associated with the magic and power of the kallawayas. One of its forms, the wajra pallay, is worn only on the garments of the most experienced practitioners.

The way color is used in the weavings is significant. Llicllas are woven with design bands interspersed with monochrome stripes of plain weave. The colors of these stripes represent the levels of land of each community. For example, lower valleys where corn and wheat are found are represented by green stripes; red signifies the higher fields of potatoes and barley. The pastoral areas even higher are shown by maroon bands. Through these color bands and the predominant design motifs, the origin of a piece may be determined.

One unique aspect of the kallawalya man's costume is his multi-figured alforjas, or medicine bags. Characteristic of the woman's costume is the wincha, a head band woven in intricate designs and bordered with glass beads.

Pacajes

Although present-day Pacajes textiles are quite ordinary, 19th-century weaving of the area was of extraordinary quality. Special alpaca ponchos called challapatas were worn only by the chieftains. They have a silky sheen and drape elegantly over the shoulders. The black ground is interrupted by striped areas. Rarely are design motifs used. A striking effect on the poncho is achieved by the subtle use of natural dyes in the stripes. Cochineal was a favorite dye, producing colors ranging from pale pink to deep carmine.

The hilacata, (chieftain), wears an elaborate costume. Over his shoulders he wears a small ponchito, while a large challapata is folded lengthwise over one shoulder. The two ends of the challapata are pulled across the front and back of the body and tied on the side. A vicuña scarf encircles the neck and crosses in the back. Completing the costume is a highly decorative ch'uspa, a wood and silver baston de mando (staff of office) and a chicote (braided rope whip).

The women once dressed in equally fine garments. Their llicllas, also of alpaca, have a black or brown ground and narrow designs in the same natural dye colors as the ponchos. The urku (skirt) is quite full and made of shiny black alpaca. A wide, colorfully-patterned belt stands out against the darker clothes.

Calamarca

Because Calamarca is not far from La Paz, the contemporary daily dress of the region is modern. During many of the annual indigenous ceremonies, however, heirloom textiles handed down from past generations are still used. Most impressive are the wide belts of warp-patterned doublecloth figures of birds, cows, human forms and plants. Frequently, the Puerta del Sol (Gateway of the Sun) from the Tiwanaku ruins south of Lake Titicaca is depicted on the belts. Sometimes the figures are quite large and bold; at other times they are very tiny, appearing to float on the ample plain ground. Among the finest weaving done in the Calamarca region are narrow bands that display miniature versions of the figures on the belts. These bands, called tesnus, are attached to the end of the belts to hold them in place.

Symbolizing the stature of the Mallku (chieftain) is a natural-dye ponchito with bands of zoomorphic and ornithomorphic motifs, a vicuña scarf and wichiwichis, pompoms that hang from the waist and swing out from the body when the Mallku dances. A hat, felted from vicuña fibers, completes the costume.

The wife of the Mallku, the Talla Mama, is an equally impressive figure. Her urku, a very full pleated skirt, is patterned with a number of decorative bands running horizontally across a black ground. A wide belt, similar to that of the Mallku's, holds the urku securely in place as the woman dances. Over her shoulders she wears a number of awayos with the traditional designs of the area. One special piece is the iscayo, a wide, banded mantle in natural dyes. Lastly, the sleevelets of the Talla Mama are adorned with mangetas.

Northern Potosí

When referring to weavings, the jutting northern limb of the Department of Potosí is referred to as Northern Potosí. This rich textile region is typified by the weavings of Pocoata, Llallagua, Sacaca and Bolívar.

Traditional weaving is maintained in Northern Potosí more than in any other part of Bolivia. The textiles are so prolific and vital that they are the most widely sold in Bolivia. They are commonly found in markets throughout La Paz.

The woman's lliclla, which features a multitude of animal, floral and even modern day motifs (trucks, cars, trains) and is woven in pebble weave, is prevalent. At festivals, the women display their wealth by hanging many llicllas and silver pieces from their cloth. The patterned bands are usually set off on large fields of black or brown, but many other bright colors may also be used. The aksus are woven in the same colors and patterns, but in the typical aksu layout.

Even more numerous than the mantles are the finely woven double-cloth belts. During the tinkus, the ritual fights which take place several times a year, men wear as many as 10 belts criss-crossing their chests and wrapped around their fists. These belts display the entire range of zoomorphic, anthropomorphic and geometric motifs typical of this area. Men's ponchos are usually simple, striped garments with a dark ground color.

Bolívar

The people of the region of Bolívar have maintained a long and unbroken tradition of weaving excellence. Until recently, they strongly adhered to the Aymara customs of preserving and using old textiles. Consequently, a remarkable number of matrimonial and ceremonial pieces have survived from as far back as the early 19th century.

The oldest of these ceremonial pieces reveal the women's exceptional skill in natural dyeing. The large matrimonial aksus display impressive compositions of design bands interspersed with monochrome lines. Depicted on the aksu is usually the lymi linku or lymi tika, undulating floral or serpentine motifs. The bride wears her aksu hanging from a woven matrimonial belt and around her shoulders she fastens a matrimonial lliclla of the same style. On the shoulders of the groom rests a plain mottled rectangular cloth called a llacota. Ceremonial ponchitos and ch'uspas were also woven during this earlier period to be worn by local chieftains during councils. The ponchitos are small and decorative, usually with pink or indigo blue grounds.

A distinct change in weaving designs and technique occurred in the Bolívar region some time after the turn of the century. Instead of the narrow lines of traditional Aymara motifs, which characterized the previous period, bold representations of Intis (suns), condors and other animals were woven. These pieces, called kurti, were also woven for ceremonial use but contain bright aniline dyes. The patterned areas are woven in wide double-cloth bands.

Lique

The Lique region is virtually the last Aymara-speaking region in which traditional dress is still worn. The few remaining natural dye textiles, for the most part awayos, exhibit a multitude of typically Aymara figures woven in double-cloth bands. The iconography, mainly of zoomorphic or geometric medallions, is reminiscent of those seen on old textiles from Challa just south of Lique. Modern Lique weavings are characterized by impressive figurative motifs, although the cloth itself is relatively crude when compared with other Bolivian pieces. Most noteworthy of the present-day textiles are the wide belts, huakas, which show large, stylized mythological figures in bright colors of red, yellow and black. These same bold figures are repeated on fine, narrow tesnus (belt ties) and on the women's awayos.

Macha

One of the most distinctive weaving areas of the northern Potosí region is Macha. The Macha weaving style is based on the use of large and small geometric motifs, usually involving a network of diamond patterns. These diamond patterns can be found on all the textile forms except the man's poncho, which is usually striped. Some older pieces may feature rhomboid networks instead of diamonds. Macha textiles can be finely spun and woven even though they are made from sheep's wool. A few older pieces are made from alpaca. In the contemporary pieces, aniline dyes are used but in subdued, subtle shades of rust, amber, blue and purple on a black or brown ground.

Challa

Situated in the central Cordillera, on the road halfway between Oruro and Cochabamba, is the town of Challa. This weaving area shares many textile traditions with Bolívar and other areas of southern Cochabamba and northern Potosí. Especially noteworthy are the matrimonial aksus, llicllas and the large, matrimonial, blue-ground ponchos with pattern bands of birds motifs. Also outstanding are the wide condor belts, which may date to the turn of the century, and the extremely fine tesnus that are woven in myriad motifs in wool, cotton and synthetic yarns.

Some portions of this text were excerpted from the following books:

Aymara Weavings: Ceremonial Textiles of Colonial and 19th Century Bolivia. Laurie Adelson and Arthur Tracht, Smithsonian Institution Traveling Exhibition Service, Washington 1983.

Weaving Traditions of Highland Bolivia. Laurie Adelson and Bruce Takami, Craft & Folk Art Museum, Los Angeles, 1978.

Laurie Adelson and Arthur Tracht are owners of the **Millma** shops in La Paz. Radisson Plaza Hotel, Av. Arce 2177. Tel. 2440737, and Calle Sagárnaga 225, Tel. 2311338. E-mail: millma@ceibo.entelnet.bo www.millmaalpaca.com

TRADITIONAL PRESENT

ALONG THE INCA AND SILVER HIGHWAY

BY PETER McFARREN

A long the Inca road in pre-Colombian times, herds of llamas crossed the Andes from Bolivia to the Chilean coast carrying coca leaves, gold and food products. The Spaniards utilized the route to carry quantities of silver from the mines of Potosí to Arica en route to Spain.

Today, the route, which bypasses towns and villages virtually unchanged over the centuries, is used to transport contraband goods and bring in precursor chemicals used for processing cocaine, as well as the legitimate import and export of goods.

In the time of the Incas, who ruled a vast area of South America from northern Ecuador to Chile, a network of roads beginning in the Bolivian lowlands crossed the highlands and reached the coast of Chile near present-day Arica. Other roads linked Bolivia with the Peruvian cities of Cuzco and Lima.

Aymara-speaking herdsmen leading flocks of llamas began their journey in the tropical Yungas coca-leaf-producing region, located to the east of La Paz. Coca leaf, which continues to be chewed by farmers and miners, was carried on llamas to the seacoast and highland areas of the region. In the area near La Paz, the herdsmen traded for dehydrated llama meat and potatoes and continued their trek across the high flatlands known as the Altiplano.

This plateau, which includes lakes Titicaca and Poopo, is located 13,500 feet (4100m) above sea level and joins the two branches of the Andes that split in southern Peru and rejoin in northern Chile and Argentina.

Archaeologist Luis Briones, Director of the Archaeological museum of San Miguel de Azapa near Arica, said that coca leaves and other products brought from the highlands have been found in tombs along the coast of Chile.

In the 16th century the Inca rulers of the Tawantinsuyo empire were defeated by the Spaniards. In 1545, the Spanish conquerors discovered great silver deposits at the Potosí mountain. Between 1580 and 1620 Potosí produced a yearly average of 170,000 kilos of silver, said Clara Lopez Beltrán, historian and expert on Potosí.

By 1600 Potosí was the largest city in the Americas, with a population of 160,000, and was one of the most important urban centers in the world, renowned for its magnificent colonial architecture, churches glistening with gold and theaters that presented the best of European productions.

Today, Potosí, a city of 118,000 people located 14,200 feet (4100m) above sea level, continues to produce silver and tin, but retains only a shadow of its former grandeur. The echoes of its fabulous past can still be seen, however, in its churches and the mint, with its 3-foot-thick walls and arches that take up an entire city block. The mint still contains the equipment and smelters that produced coins for the Spanish empire.

Potosí, together with the Mexican mines of Zacatecas, became the most important silver producing center in the Spanish colonies, said Lopez Beltrán. UNESCO has now declared Potosí a Patrimony of Humanity.

A recent United Nations study indicates that the mountain of Potosí still has at least 4,160 metric tons of silver deposits in the residues from the mines -- twice as much silver as was taken out -- and could once again become a major world silver producer.

Caravans of llamas and the mules introduced by the Spanish carried the silver across the mountains of Potosí to the Altiplano past the city of Oruro toward Lima and Buenos Aires, or toward the Chilean coastal town of Arica.

On their return voyage to Potosí, the caravans carried French porcelain, Belgian lace, jewels and the materials used to process silver. In Oruro, founded in 1601 and part of the Inca and silver routes and today a mining city of 182,000 located 40 miles (225 km) from La Paz, U.S. drug enforcement and Bolivian police agents can be seen returning from raiding the Chilean border along the old Inca and silver routes.

The Inca and silver roads went past Corque, today a town of less than 1,000 residents who live in straw-thatched adobe houses located three hours by vehicle from Oruro. An enormous adobe and stone church built in the early 17th century evokes the wealth of the period. It has gold leafed altars, large printed canvases and frescoes. The adobe walls and saints are stained from the rains that pour in from the leaking tile roof.

Father Luciano Lachance, 55, a French Canadian priest who has spent 20 years in Corque, says that the church was built at the height of the silver rush in Potosí and was on the route to the coast. "It is sad to see this great church that has lasted since the early 17th century fall apart," he said.

"In my grandfather's time Corque was known as the city of silver," said Silverio Mamani, a school teacher, as he hung an archway decorated with silver dishes and vases during a ceremony in honor of the Patron Saint John the Baptist. Since there are no mines in the area, Corque was known as the city of silver because of the silver route. One of the routes from Potosí passed by the Chipayas, a sparsely-settled community of 2,000 residents reached after a 12-hour drive from La Paz. The Chipayas speak their own language, Puquina, and women wear elaborately-braided hair and coarse woolen garments.

Many of the Chipaya men must travel to Chile to find work in the copper mines as the fish, bird and sheep population, which provide them with their main source of livelihood, dwindle. The Indians live in beehive shaped adobe huts near the salt flats of Coipasa and hunt for birds using lead tipped slings, much as their ancestors did.

On their recent feast day, the village elders, or Jilacatas, sacrificed two llamas in honor of the goddess of the Earth, the Pachamama, and then entered a small church to pay respect to their patron, Saint Santiago.

Village residents then carried out an elaborate ceremony to obtain protection from the gods using coca leaves brought from the lowlands, alcohol and llama blood, before beginning hours of dance to the accompaniment of the zampoñas and quenas, native instruments made from bamboo.

From the villages on the plateau, the Inca and silver traders continued toward the borders of Chile and Bolivia. An important wind-swept crossroad was located at what today is called Tambo Quemado, 15,700 feet (4,800m) above sea level and near the 21,400 feet (6,520m) high Sajama, the highest mountain in the western Cordillera of Bolivia, and near several extinct volcanoes.

Just beyond, at Chungara, the Chilean border post located at the edge of a lake of the same name, 14 trucks carrying 26 tons each of soya were on route from the Bolivian tropical city of Santa Cruz to the city port of Arica. Bolivia is expected to export annually 50 million dollars worth of soya, and the road through Tambo Quemado and Chungara has become a major transit point from the Bolivian tropical lowlands to the Chilean coast.

Customs officials at Chungara said that they were on the lookout for electrical appliances, TV sets and other goods that were brought from the free ports of Arica and Iquique and smuggled across the border to Bolivian cities, where they are sold at prices comparable to those in New York City.

From Lake Chungara at the edge of the border crossing, the bumpy dirt road winds through Lauca National Park. Old Inca and pre-Inca trails that were used during the silver period are clearly visible from the road, as Briones, an expert on the old Inca and silver route, pointed out. On the route, near some rock overhangs, are several caves with blackened ceilings that, over the centuries, housed herdsmen. Today, llama herdsmen still find haven in the rocks, within sight of protected herds of the rare vicuña, a relative of the llama and alapaca.

Above the mining town of Putre is the 19,000 feet (5,815m) high Taapaca mountain where Johan Reinhard, an American anthropologist, in 1983 found an Inca figurine made with oyster shells brought from the Pacific coast. From Putre, the old Inca highway winds its way near the vehicle road that leads to Arica, past ruins of Inca fortresses and buildings used to house grains to feed the herdsmen who came from the highlands to the east.

The road past Putre rapidly descends towards the Lluta Valley, which cuts a green swath through the coastal desert of Northern Chile and reaches the Pacific coast, a few miles to the north of Arica.

Above the valley, which provided water and food for the caravans of llamas and mules that came from the highlands, are dozens of geoglyphs, some as large as 60 meters, depicting llamas, monkeys, wild cats and human figures. Briones says that these figures had a religious significance in pre-Colombian times and were also used as signposts for the herdsmen reaching the Pacific coast.

The llama and mule carriers crossed over to Arica from the Lluta valley and unloaded their cargoes in the protected harbor of Arica. Just below the Morro, a large rock and sand mound at the edge of the city, Inca rafts and later Spanish boats, loaded and unloaded goods.

At the Arica docks, several ships were unloading vehicles and containers that will be taken by truck or train toward landlocked Bolivia, continuing a trade that has gone unchanged for centuries. Some ships were waiting to carry the soya produced in the Bolivian lowlands. A journey that before took 25 days now takes 4 days.

HATS, THE CROWNING TOUCH

BY PETER MCFARREN

When Severino Vela got married in Jatamayu, Bolivia, he wore a mon-tera -- a black leather hat patterned after the 16th-century helmets of Spanish conquerors. The bride also wore a hat. It had a flat black cloth brim, two raised points on top, embroidery of green, red and black threads, and an assortment of silver beads and bangles.

Adult wedding guests appeared at the church in leather or felt headwear of different styles favored by the Quechua Indians who live around Jatamayu. Children under 18 wore knitted wool hats.

Hats are so common and varied in Bolivia that Vela, a middle-aged Quechua farmer, finds it good business to make them on the side. He often trades a new hat for a sheep.

"I learned from a master craftsman who died several years ago", Vela told a visitor as he fashioned his wedding hat from leather, which had been dyed with fermented corn juice and rusted iron.

Elsewhere in Bolivia, people cover their heads with tin, plaster, rabbit hair, feathers, straw, alpaca and totora reeds. South America's poorest country is rich in hat styles -- more than 100 for a population of about 8 million.

Bolivians have popularized a derby for women. They also make a Stetson known locally as a "J.R. Dallas" because it resembles the hat J.R. Ewing wore on the universally popular television series Dallas.

"I don't know of another region in the world that has such a variety of hats," said Gunnar Mendoza, director of the National Archives in Sucre, the colonial capital. "Aside from its use as part of an outfit, the hat serves as a way for people to identify themselves."

While urbanization and the covered automobile have put hats out of fashion in many other places, the demand for them in Bolivia remains steady. As a result, hat making is a thriving business, from Vela's busy shop at home to the industry-leading Charcas Glorieta factory in Sucre.

Born of Necessity and Style

One reason hats are so important in Bolivia is the high altitude of the Andes, where the sun's rays are more intense and few shade trees grow. Another is that the open-backed truck remains a popular means of transportation. A third factor is the survival of traditional costumes, hats and all, among Bolivia's Indian majority.

Former President Victor Paz Estenssoro, like other members of the country's European-descended elite, generally shuns hats. But during his election campaign in 1985, he wore a variety of colorful hats on trips to Indian farming villages and won most of the rural vote.

The feature of Aymara Indian women that most strikes visitors to La Paz is their derby. In English, the derby is referred to as a bowler, the name of the English manufacturer that introduced them to Argentina in the 19th century. But Bolivians call the hat a bombin. Aymara women, who dominate the city's retail trade, wear black, brown or gray bombines while selling fruits, vegetables, home computers and compact discs. In other countries the derby is a man's hat, but men here wear other styles.

According to one story, a shipment of felt bowlers arrived in Bolivia by mistake and an enterprising salesman convinced Aymara women that wearing them would guarantee fertility. As the idea caught on, a model made of rabbit hair by the Borsalino factory in Italy became a status symbol among wealthier Aymara women. One store, which has been importing Borsalino bombines for 30 years, now sells four to six a day for $75 each, according to Sonia Barriga, the store manager.

But the Borsalino factory, which manufactured hats exclusively for the Bolivian market, closed and much of the demand is now expected to be filled by Charcas Glorieta, a Bolivian hat-making company with a history as colorful as some of its hats.

The "Royal" factory

The Charcas Glorieta factory in Sucre was founded in 1929 by Princess Clotilde Urioste de Argandona, a Bolivian philanthropist who was given her title by Pope Leo XIII in the late 19th century when her husband was ambassador to the Vatican. With inherited wealth, she built a castle in Sucre, surrounded by Venetian-style canals, gardens and a small zoo. She also started the hat factory to provide jobs for the people.

Today the factory produces 400,000 hats or unfinished felt hat casings a year, supplying nearly half the Bolivian market. At least 2,000 hat makers in Bolivia, Peru and Chile buy the casings and mold them into finished bombines that sell for $10 to $20 apiece.

Most of the steam-powered machines at Charcas Glorieta date to its founding. Manned by 110 employees each shift, they turn Bolivian, Uruguayan and Argentine wool into 30 different hat forms, some based on U.S. and European designs.

Spare parts and molds must be made by hand because the factory that built the machinery no longer exists, said Mario Nosiglia Biella, who has managed the plant since emigrating from Italy in 1948. "In my hometown of Sagliano Micca there used to be nine hat factories," he said. "Now there is only one. Thirty years ago everybody in Europe wore a hat, but with the evolution of the automobile the use of hats has dropped considerably. Hat factories throughout the world are closing."

Yet Charcas Glorieta is unable to keep up with demand in Bolivia. So it purchased the Italian hat company Panizza's entire factory with a $2 million credit, $600,000 of it from the U.S. Agency for International Development. Nosiglia said the expansion will double the factory's output to one million felt hats per year while enabling it to make 60,000 rabbit-hair hats. He said that 20,000 rabbit-hair hats will be exported to Italy for Panizza's former clients. The enlarged factory will benefit farmers, who will supply the hair of at least 50,000 rabbits a year and wool from 10,000 sheep, according to company plans. "The economic impact will be extraordinary," Nosiglia said.

Charcas Glorieta already makes thousands of "J.R. Dallas" hats that sell here for $15 apiece, as well as traditional hats for nearly every region of Bolivia. For example, residents of Tarija, near the Argentine border, wear hats patterned after those worn by their colonial ancestors from Andalucia, Spain. People in Jatamayu, in the central highlands around Sucre, prefer helmet-like hats such as Vela's.

In Cochabamba, Quechua Indian women wear white hats made from felt and plaster of paris, decorated with black ribbon.

According to legend, a young, unmarried Quechua woman in Cochabamba was publicly reprimanded by a Roman Catholic priest for living with her boyfriend, a practice common among Indian couples intending to marry. For penance, she was made to wear a black ribbon around the base of her hat. The next day at Mass, much to the priest's chagrin, all the women present wore black ribbons, and the style stuck.

"The hat in Bolivia is not just to protect oneself from the sun," said Harold de Faria Castro, a Bolivian author on the subject. "It is the most important piece of an outfit. The hat accompanies an Indian while he sleeps and is always on his head, whether it rains or shines."

"The reason the hat is so important," he adds, "is because it is understood to be intimately tied to the head, and this is the most sacred part of the body and spirit."

TRADITIONAL PRESENT

ANDEAN FEATHER ART

BY TERESA GISBERT DE MESA

The art of feather work, along with that of textiles, is one of the few arts that has survived among the Andean peoples, though it has survived on a much smaller scale. Feather art was considered one of the most delicate arts. "The feather-work fabrics were of the greatest estimation and worth (greater than the cumbi (fine vicuña and alpaca textile) for the Incas, and the abascal (rough llama textile) for the people), and with much reason. They worked directly on the cumbi, but in such a way that the feathers showed on top of the wool, resembling velvet. The preparation for this type of material was great because of the innumerable multitude and variety of birds of such fine colors that this land breeds, which exceeds all praise," said Bernabé Cobo in 1620.

"They used only the smallest and most subtle feathers, which they attached to the weave with a thin wool strand and then placed to one side, making with them the same designs and figures which their most colorful cumbis had. The luster, brilliance and sheen of these feather fabrics were of such a rare beauty, that if they are not seen, they cannot be described."

Cobo also says that among "the other things that the Spaniards found when they came to this land, in the full coffers of the Inca, one of the principal things, was a great quantity of precious feathers for these weavings; almost all of them were iridescent with an admirable shimmer, which had the appearance of finest gold. . . There was another of a green gold iridescence, and there was an immense quantity of it; and there was an immense quantity of very tiny feathers which the small birds called tominejos (hummingbirds) grow on their chests."

Cobo's description is the most complete one we have of featherwork at the time, and his information gives a very exact idea of how this type of fabric was made before the Spanish Conquest. The feather fabrics of the Andes, like those of Mexico, had designs and figures of the same style as the cumbis.

Besides their use in textiles, feathers were also used to adorn headdresses. The Chinchasuyos and the Incas used them on their headgear. Ludovico Bertonio says that the plumage worn by both these groups -- which consisted of two plumes, like horns, placed in front of the llauto (headband) of the hat -- was called kausu. The Antisuyos wore a crown of feathers, which can be seen in a drawing by Guaman Poma. The Antisuyos also had a gala costume made completely with feathers.

The feathers of the flamingo and the parihuana (heron) are still used on headdresses, both of which breed in the cold lakes of the Altiplano . The Sicuris still use these feathers. Ostrich feather are also still used (called Nandu in the eastern lowlands and Suri by the Aymaras). These head-dresses are worn today in the dance of the Wila-Kawani.

A more significant feather design is the pectoral displayed by the Incas pictured in the series of the Procession of Cuzco (1680) that consists of a kind of bib with several rows of feathers of different colors. This piece, which was also used by the Aymaras, is called sipi of siphi according to Bertonio, who translates it as "plumage as diadem." He says of the Aymaras that "feathers of various colors were made as collars or ruffs which they wore around the neck, although the Chinchasuyos put them on their heads as diadems. . ." This collar dates back to the zenith of the of Pucara and Tiwanaku cultures. The most significant member of the Pucara culture, the Sacrifier (B.C. 400-100 A.D.) wore a siphi. A siphi was also worn by the Flute Player of that culture. The siphi was a symbol of authority and greatness.

However, most interesting is not the general use of feathers, which is a distinctive characteristic of all the indigenous cultures, but its use in tapestries or mosaics and its survival to the present day.

The Tiwanaku Expansion period, Huari I, had extraordinary examples of feathers worked in diadems as well as in uncus (shirts), though few articles are preserved; diadems and uncus of the Chimu or Chancay cultures are preserved in greater numbers. Monkeys, pumas and other symbolic animals are represented on the pieces. Cobo describes the method as attaching the feathers to the fabric, although sometimes they were glued on wood. The feathers used are those of the humming-bird, which is none other than the colibri, called qenti by the Aymaras, and valued for its iridescent and metallic feathers. Another valued bird was the guacamaya (macaw). Cobo says that these birds "are painted in red, blue, yellow and other colors, like parrots, and some are all blue. . . The feathers of these birds are greatly valued by the Indians to adorn themselves in dance and feasts." The tunqui (a bird with a very large crest of very small feathers) was also valued for his feathers, which according to the Cobo are red, though according to Bertonio they are yellow.

The feathers of the macaws had to be collected among the Antis, that is in the warm lowlands. They were a luxury that the Aymaras obtained through barter, likely through their settlements in the lowlands.

Featherwork was considered similar to working with flowers, possibly because (at least during the colonial period) flowers were considered to be "made" of feathers. Bertonio says that huayta means "feathers or flowers." This is still true today of the headdresses in various folklore dances. The artisans who use feathers are called huayta camana, and the those who provide feathers are called huaytancalla.

Documents on featherwork indicate that the four confederated nations -- Charcas, Caracaras, Chuis and Chichas -- worked in feathers for their use and adornment. The Charcas Memorial states that they were warriors, and that in the time of the Incas they were exempt from the mita (forced labor) as quarry workers in the city of Cuzco, and from "transferring a hill to another place by hand," which was the work of conquered peoples at the time of the Incas, as well as before them. For example, the Akapana in Tiwanaku "is a knoll made by hand," according to Cobo. In short, the featherworkers were free from what the Spaniards considered servile work.

The Memorial states that "the four nations made some featherworks, clothes and some weapons. . . for ourselves only." That featherwork was used for their own adornment is clear from the case of the Cacique from Moromoro, Pablo Humiro, friend to the Cacique Colque Guarache of the Quillacas, who presented Humiro as a witness for evidence at the succession of the cacicazgo (leadership). Humiro says that he was the servant of Huayna Capac, "who adorned him with the feathers that he wore." The Cacique Moromoro of the Caracaras nation was attached to the court with the honorary post of arranging the plumage that the Inca wore.

This post must have been similar to that of the "royal chamberlain" depicted by the painter Diego Velasquez in the Spanish court of Phillip IV. This post originally belonged to the servant who saw to the maintenance of the royal chamber, but in time became a position of confidence. In this position, Humiro forms part of the court of Huayna Capac. We can see from this the importance plumage as a royal symbol, as well as the participation of the caciques of the Collasuyo in the court of Cuzco.

Featherwork has died out with the exception of some rare examples that are found in Bolivia. Though feathers are used in headdress arrangements for dances, and are relatively abundant, elaborate compositions worked as mosaics, which are maintained in the so-called chacanas, have mostly died out.

The chacana is a band formed by several pieces of wood 20 cms high and 8 cms wide, joined by string. There are about 14 pieces that form this flexible band, which is adapted to the body. The colored feathers of the parrot, the macaw and the hummingbird are affixed to these bands, making a mosaic of different themes. The oldest chacanas show rampant lions facing each other, as in viceregal times. The more modern ones have lizards, pumas and anthropomorphic figures in addition to the lions. The background is usually yellow or red and, rarely, blue; the iridescent feathers of the hummingbird are used for the eyes, which are now made with silver paper. Some modern examples of these chacanas are made of cane instead of wood in certain areas. This featherwork is used also in hats and in rectangular pieces used as shields, where there is usually a mirror in the center surrounded by different motifs such as the national shield. Some examples use baroque themes such as sirens and monkeys.

The modern name chacana, occasionally called chakon, means ladder, and doubtlessly refers to the structure that holds the feathers, which is made of several pieces of wood in a ladder form. The chacana forms part of the wardrobe of the Quena-quena and is worn over the shoulder, covering part of the tiger pectoral of the dancers. The dance of the Quena-quena is a martial and war dance, explaining the tiger skin pectoral used in several regions, particularly among the Pacajes. The most significant chacanas come from the Quena-quenas of Patacamaya. This dance is danced as far away as the north of La Paz, in Mocomoco and Ayata.

Another remnant of pre-Conquest feather art is the cape of parrot feathers which is displayed by the dance group Green Parrot Quena-quena from the northern part of La Paz province. This weave reminds us, in a coarse way, of the fabrics adorned with velvet-like feathers, where each feather is attached to the weave with a ligature, not glued on as in the case of the chacana. Because the feathers are large, the cape cannot be pleated or tucked; it is instead held on the shoulders with a horizontal pole. Despite its rigidity, it is a garment of extraordinary beauty, reminiscent of the llacotas (very large rectangular pieces used as capes) worn by the Incas.

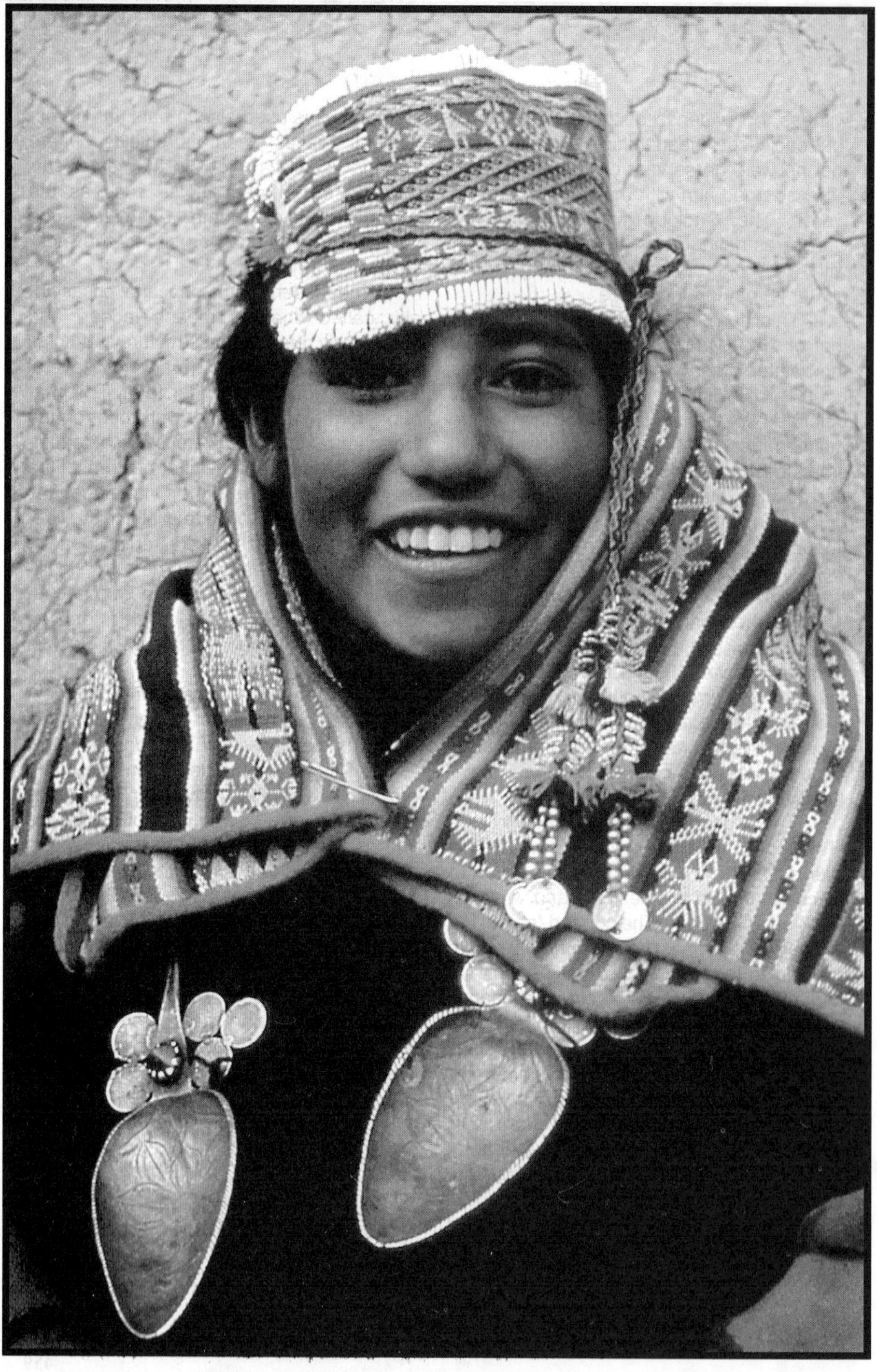

TRADITIONAL MEDICINE

BY LINDA FARTHING

In the land once known as Kollasuyo, the country of medicine, traditional practices still hold far greater sway than Western medicine. When confronted with a medical problem, 70% of Bolivians, particularly in the rural areas, first see the curandero (the local healer), and often utilize Western medicine only as a last resort. This reluctance stems from several factors. For one, Western medical care is expensive, as are its medicines. For another, doctors from cities usually can only communicate in Spanish, and often have little understanding or respect for indigenous culture.

In Bolivia, every village or community has its herbalist who knows which plants and herbs can be used for medicinal purposes. Traditional medicine is an integral part of the culture and responds to its values and beliefs. It takes into account the patient's own perception of his illness, and considers the emotional state of the patient important in selecting a remedy. Over the years, however, traditional medicine has begun to incorporate aspects of Western medicine. Increasingly, common Western medicines such as aspirin appear in the healer's bag.

Although Western medical practitioners are willing to acknowledge that 25 to 30% of the herbs used in traditional medicine are as effective as Western medicines, most cannot comprehend the use of ritual, magic and amulets in the healers' repertoire. The healers believe that illnesses in the body often have their origin in the soul, and in the ajayu (life force) leaving the body. The healer's job is to coax the ajayu back into the body and restore the body/mind equilibrium. Of equal importance is the equilibrium between the person and the natural and supernatural world.

According to Dr. Toribio Tapia, La Paz naturopath, "the medical philosophy of the Aymara is very different from the oriental or the occidental. Here we consider it vital to install confidence in the patient, to establish a deep dialogue, like confession in the Catholic religion, like softening psychological resistance and being purified."

"Man is a product of what he eats," says another traditional healer, Dr. Walter Alvarez. "If he knows what to eat he will not have parasites, he will not have diarrhea. We are lucky to have excellent plants that are food and medicine at the same time. Coca was the first anesthetic discovered, and soldiers of the Chaco war [the 1932-35 war between Bolivia and Paraguay] survived thanks to chewing coca leaves. Our plant Andrés Huaylla contains antibiotics and from fermented soil we get Terramycin. This is not witchcraft, it is knowledge from our ancestors."

Among Bolivia's traditional healers, the kallawayas -- legendary healers with considerable powers -- hold a special place. Why six small villages northeast of Lake

Titicaca became a center for wandering healers remains a mystery. Some theories hold that the kallawayas are descendants of Tiwanaku culture, others that they were sent as colonizers into this region by the Incas, and still others that they developed their knowledge in the past two or three centuries.

As many as 27% of the residents of these villages are considered kallawayas. Their travels throughout South America have given them access to and knowledge of an enormous number of herbs. It is estimated that each kallawaya has committed to memory information about 300 herbs and that the most capable knows the uses for 600 herbs. In all, they have accumulated knowledge of about 1,000 medicinal herbs.

The kallawayas recognize limits to their curative abilities; they don't try to cure serious hereditary diseases or diseases in very advanced stages. This is not so much fatalistic as realistic.

The kallawaya have their own language, linguistically derived from Quechua, which is slowly disappearing. Their knowledge is usually passed from father to son, or occasionally to apprentices.

Up until the 1950s, each student had to study eight to ten years and then prove his knowledge before a community council. They then traveled (and still do), gathering herbs and curing. They rarely worked as healers full-time; usually they worked the land at least part of the year. Although women were traditionally not allowed to become kallawayas, they played an essential role in medicine -- helping to gather herbs, as midwives and as healers of women's reproductive systems.

In the 1950s the kallawaya tradition started to disappear, but renewed interest in natural medicine has provided some support. Unfortunately, this support has also resulted in an increase of those who call themselves kallawayas in order to earn a living without the necessary training. To ensure both a thorough education and the continuation of the kallawaya tradition, schools have been established in the villages of Curva and Chajaya. However, the schools have only functioned intermittently, in large part because the kallawaya are not accustomed to this form of passing on their knowledge, and also because they still travel a great deal.

In recent years, even the World Health Organization has begun to encourage traditional medicine worldwide, in recognition of its importance in primary health care. The Bolivian College of Doctors in 1986 also urged the incorporation of traditional medicine into health projects. The integration of these two types of medicine, however, is far from easy. One European doctor who has been involved in such efforts believes that the greater degree of infrastructure required by Western medicine soon swallows the traditional medicine components. And a great number of doctors still associate traditional medicine with witchcraft, failing to recognize its contribution as a well-developed and researched herbal science.

Juan Villa, a kallawaya working in La Paz with 50 years of experience in collecting plants and healing, discounts the idea that traditional medicine is anything but a science. "We learn about herbs from the age of seven, about where they grow, how and when to collect them, how and where to store them, etc.," he said. "We know how to cure all the common diseases, like rheumatism, gall-bladder, colds, diarrhea, etc. And also the illnesses from wind or from lightning."

To Western medicine, which is often dehumanized, coldly scientific and analytical, traditional medicine has much to offer. Its emphasis on a psychic-biological-social equilibrium and the importance of the relationship between the patient and doctor/healer can add immeasurably to

developing a medicine that truly addresses
the needs and realities of Bolivian culture.

For a guide to medicinal plants utilized
by the kallawayas, see **Kallawaya,
Curanderos Itinerantes de los Andes**, by
Louis Girault, La Paz, 1987 (also available
in French).

A PANORAMA OF BOLIVIAN CUISINE

BY TERESA PRADA

To write about Bolivian cooking, one must write about three regions that have different foods and eating customs: the Altiplano, the valleys and the tropical region. Although each region has maintained a characteristic cuisine, over the years these different foods and eating customs have become, to a certain degree, integrated. This is especially true of the Altiplano and the valleys.

Recipes that came from Spain in colonial times -- and more recently, from other Latin American countries --have extended the Bolivian menu. However, all these recipes have become native by being adapted to local ingredients and methods of cooking.

The Altiplano

This very high plateau produces mostly grains and potatoes. A grain unique to this area is quinoa, which has an exceptionally high protein content and is the basis of the Altiplano diet. Cañawa is another native grain and is eaten as pito (roasted and made into a powder). Pito is said to relieve the symptoms of soroche, altitude sickness.

There are over 230 varieties of potatoes and dishes that utilize different types of potatoes. The following are some of the most commonly used potatoes. Papa runa has a high water content and is ideal for baking and for french fries. Papa imilla, especially the black skinned one, is the best for mashed potatoes. Papa pureja is one of the tastiest of potatoes; it is cooked and peeled and served with plato paceño, a meatless La Paz specialty, and in papas a la huancaina, a very popular piquant Peruvian dish made with a peanut sauce. Papa kati, which resembles long thin fingers, is also very tasty and used in these same dishes. Papa sani is boiled and peeled and served whole, as it holds its shape as it cooks. Papa lisa, a small yellowish potato is prepared as an ají, a piquant dish, and has a unique taste. These are the most commonly used potatoes. Oca is a very tasty tuber; if it is left to ripen in the sun after it is harvested, it becomes very sweet. It is very good baked and often accompanies roast meat dishes.

Potatoes are also dehydrated into dark chuño or white tunta. To make chuño, small potatoes are left outside in the wintertime for four nights. Water is poured on them each night. On the fifth day, the frozen potatoes are pressed to expel the water. They are then peeled and left out to dry. To make tunta, the chuño is put in sacks with straw, which are then put into running water for one month. When they are removed, the tunta is set out to dry. Tunta and chuño are cooked and served whole in many dishes. But the tastiest way to serve chuño is as chuño phuti. This is chopped, cooked chuño sautéed with eggs and condiments and then tossed with cheese. Chuño phuti can also be made with a peanut sauce.

TRADITIONAL PRESENT

Pasankalla is somewhat like popcorn, and is made from tonjo corn on the Altiplano. Just enough caramel is added to make it impossible to stop eating it. It is traditionally made in Copacabana on Lake Titicaca.

The Altiplano version of ice-cream is thaya, the Aymara and Quechua word for cold. Apple thaya is made by mixing apple purée with sugared water, cinnamon and cloves. It is formed into an adobe shape on a little board and left overnight on the rooftop. At 6 o'clock, sugar water, colored with airampu, a native herb, is sprinkled on it. It is usually eaten late in the morning or as dessert after lunch.

Thaya is also made with oca, pito (barley flour), milk thickened with bread crumbs or yams. Thayachas are frozen isaño ocas served with cane sugar syrup. Since the advent of freezers, this dessert is found only in the countryside.

La Paz Specialties

If you asked any Bolivian living in a foreign country which foods they longed for when thinking of home, the two things most likely mentioned would be salteñas and picantes. A paceño living far from home would also mention chairo and fricasé.

Salteñas are a meat or chicken turnover that are traditionally eaten sometime before lunch and accompanied by a cold drink (never coffee or tea). There are many heated discussions as to which salteñas are the best, but the Bar Social in Cochabamba, in Cala-Cala, behind St. Ann's church, always ranks high. The truth is that each restaurant and each region, mainly in the cities of the Altiplano and the valleys, has its own special way of preparing them.

A picante or ají is a meat cooked in ají sauce and served with boiled potato and chuño phuti. A raw sarsa -- sliced tomato and onion, parsley and sometimes a little thinly sliced locoto -- is served on top. Chicken picante or sajta de pollo is the most favored. The La Paz version of picante, the picante mixto, is by far the best and most complete: it contains sajta de pollo, charquecan (jerky), picante de lengua (tongue), picante de conejo (rabbit), saice (chopped beef) and ranga-ranga (tripe). This dish is also accompanied by tunta rellena (filled tunta, the best of the tunta recipes). Each region in the Bolivia's valleys and in the Altiplano has its picante specialty, usually a combination of chicken and tongue. Fricasé can be a respectable picante when the broth is very hot.

The picante sauce is made by cooking sliced onion and tomato in oil. When this is cooked, ají and water are added. The meat is then cooked in this sauce, which is seasoned with salt and cumin.

The most common piquant pod in Bolivia is the locoto. It is a small green, yellow or red pod. It appears every day at nearly every table in western Bolivia in llajua (an uncooked piquant sauce made with tomatoes, locoto and quirquiña, a local herb), which seasons every dish served. Llajua is as common as salt.

Ají is the name given to the long pods, which are either red or yellow. They are very different in taste and are very hot, but they can be less piquant if they are washed several times, and if the seeds and the fibers are removed. Ají is, by extension, also the name given to dishes prepared with ají powder. This long pod is seldom used fresh; usually it is dried and pounded into a powder.

There are other piquant plants such as the ulupica, which is a berry. It is so hot that it is best left to well-trained palates.

Chairo is a La Paz soup. It is made with beef, lamb and lamb jerky, chuño and pataska (ten condiments together).

Fricasé is another soup, made with pork and seasoned with yellow ají or hot pepper. The stock is slightly thickened with bread crumbs. It is served with boiled potato, chuño and pataska. It is usually served at lunchtime, but it is also a favorite in the wee hours of the morning after a late party.

Anticuchos are another favorite food eaten after late-night parties. Anticuchos are small slices of beef heart and a boiled potato on a skewer cooked over a grill and seasoned with yellow ají.

Thimpu is a popular lamb dish on native restaurant menus. After the soup is cooked, the solid ingredients are served on a plate and the broth is served separately.

Plato paceño, was mentioned earlier, is fried fresh cheese, served with boiled potato, mote de habas (cooked fresh broad beans), corn on the cob and llajua.

Oruro's Winners

Oruro is famous for one dish: rostro asado, baked lamb's head. This is a logical dish in sheep country. It is made with a sheep's head that has been cleaned thoroughly and baked for five hours, after cutting off the horns. It is served with yellow ají. Rostro asado takes a special talent to eat, but it's worth a try. It is served on weekend nights, after 11 p.m. on Av. 6 de Octubre.

El Intendente is a dish created by a government official from Sucre who was sent to Oruro in the early years of this century. He would go into a restaurant and tell the owner exactly what to cook for his dinner. The dish became so popular that it is still offered on the menu. It has one lamb's kidney, one piece of chicken, two pieces of calf's tripe, one pork sausage, one piece of beef sirloin and one pork chop. It is served with two peeled, boiled potatoes, rice, lettuce, locoto and onion.

Potosí's Pastries

Potosí, with the most opulent past of any city in Bolivia, is the city of the fritanga, confites and many varied pastries.

Fritanga is a fricasé without the broth and made with red ají. Confites are the most famous of the native candies. They are made from sugar syrup hardened around the center of a coconut, cookie, walnut, Brazil nut or despepitado (dried peach). There are three kinds of confites: first class, which are white and use the hearts mentioned; second class, which are violet or white and are hardened around aniseed or coriander seed; and third class which is not for eating. Rather confites of the third class are used as offerings at the ch'alla, a ceremony where coca leaves and liquor are offered to the Pachamama. These confites are made with a quinoa center or no center at all. They are colored with vegetable dye in red, green, blue or pink, but never in yellow or purple.

Not just anyone can make confites. There are traditional candy makers who come from the villages around the city, and who will not start working unless there has been a ch'alla. These candy makers have their secret methods, and will not let anyone look on while they work, for fear of the evil eye. They do not, however, own the candy industry; they work for the owners in the city.

Confites are a traditional candy. They are sold only at Carnaval time in every city and town on the Altiplano and in the valleys, or on special feasts such as Alasitas in La Paz, in January.

Potosí's famous pastries come from colonial times. The most famous are: tawatawas ("four-four" in Quechua), which are sweet pastries deep fried and served with chancaca, (cane) syrup (this recipe comes from colonial times and the name probably refers to "four for a penny"); chambergos, which are poached before they are deep fried and also served with the brown sugar syrup; and kispiñas, which are made with quinoa flour and steam cooked.

THE VALLEYS

The three valley Departments of Cochabamba, Chuquisaca and Tarija, are all characterized for excellent and lavish cuisine. These valleys are agricultural, and produce fruits, vegetables, grains, legumes and all domestic animals. However, their most important product is corn. When the Spaniards arrived in 1532 they found that corn was the most important food of the Indian population. Today it is still their basic food, and the people in the cities eat it almost daily.

There are several varieties of corn. Kulli is purple corn used to make api, a hot, thick drink, chicha, a corn liquor and tostada, a cold drink made by boiling toasted corn and barley with honey, cinnamon, cloves and fennel. Tostada is also made from the sweet ch'uspillo corn. In Tarija, tostada is called aloja. Willkaparu is also a very tasty corn.

There are many ways to prepare corn besides corn-on-the-cob. P'oshqo api is a thinned porridge made from purple or white corn that is an early breakfast drink served with llauchas (cheese turnovers) in market places. Mote de maíz is hominy. It is called pataska when it has lime peel. Mote accompanies many dishes such as chicharrón (pork cooked in its own fat), and it is an ingredient in other dishes such as the fricasé and chairo. It is served in Cochabamba with quesillo (fresh cheese).

Chicha is a traditional Andean drink of fermented corn whose origin is lost in pre-Columbian legend. In Cochabamba, chicha is sold in chicherías. Chicherías never have a restaurant sign, and rarely a name; instead you find a chichería by looking for a little white flag on a pole in front of a house or building. You go in through a zaguán (entryway) until you reach a patio, garden or orchard where tables and chairs will be set up. Chicha is also served at chicharronerías where you will eat chicharrón con mote with llajua and drink chicha or beer. In the chicharronerías, you can see the meat being cooked in big three-foot diameter copper vats set on adobe stoves or wood fires. On weekends the vats can be seen outside, in front of the restaurants.

Humintas, a dish now very popular in all three Bolivian regions, are tamales made with fresh corn pounded into a cream. The cream is seasoned with salt, sugar and ají and wrapped in corn husks, with a slice of cheese as a filling. Humintas are usually steamed, but they can also be baked, and they can be made sweet by adding more sugar and raisins instead of ají.

Tojori is a delicious dessert made by cooking pounded corn with sugar and spices. Pito is a flour eaten mostly by children, in which the corn is toasted and pounded with sugar and cinnamon. It is also made from other grains and legumes.

Not made from corn, but tasty nonetheless, orchata is a drink made from walnuts. Savor every sip, as orchata is difficult to make -- the walnuts are peeled by hand.

Cochabamba Segundos

There is no end to the variety of segundos, or second entrées, found in the valleys. Cochabamba, the dairy region of Bolivia, is no exception. A very typical dish there is the silpancho. It is a favorite with young and old (as well as with cooks because it is so easy to make). Silpancho is a steak pounded until it becomes very large and thin, and is served on a bed of rice with a fried egg on top. Potatoes are boiled, sliced thick and browned, and a sarsa cruda is served lavishly on top.

Cochabamba has many outdoor restaurants and sidewalk cafes on the Prado where you can find some of the city's best cuisine. Pique a lo macho, pieces of grilled steak mixed with sausages and fried potatoes, served on a bed of lettuce and tomato and lavishly garnished with chopped locoto, is a memorable specialty. Also worth trying is patitas en escabeche (picked trotters). The trotters should be accompanied by red wine.

Sucre Satisfies

In general, Sucre is perhaps the city that has remained closest to its traditions. This holds true for its food as well. Whenever salteñas are talked about, mention is always made of the justly famous salteñas served in Sucre. But "the best" depends more on the cook than on the place, so this title depends mainly on who happens to have a perfect recipe at the time. Nonetheless, Sucre has been noted for its salteñas for a many years.

Sucre is also famous for chorizos (sausages), especially los chorizos de Las Bajos, chorizos of the famous Bajos sisters, the pair who perfected the dish. Ckocko, pronounced "coco" at the back of your throat, is the most extraordinary of the many local dishes. It is chicken cooked in chicha, nuts and raisins and about nine condiments, including orange peel and is a "king" among Bolivian dishes.

Tarija is for Meat Lovers

Argentinian beef is one of the best in the world, and cooking the beef has become an art in which taste depends not so much on sauces but on the cooking itself. Tarija, which is on the Argentine border, has restaurants where you can eat meat such good meat, you'll think you're in Buenos Aires.

But of course there are many native Tarijan dishes that add still another facet to Bolivian cooking. Chancao is a chicken soup made with ají. Other picante specialties are ranga-ranga (tripe) and ají de patas (pigs' trotters). Saice is typical of Tarija, a picante made of beef and chickpeas. A popular place to eat traditional dishes is the Tarija market.

Tarija is also Bolivia's grape-producing valley, so make sure to accompany your meat dishes with some locally-produced wines and singanis (distilled grape liquor).

THE TROPICS

Pando, Beni and Santa Cruz Departments make up the tropical region of Bolivia. The foods they produce are yucca, rice, sugar, bananas, Brazil nuts, tropical fruits, soy and beef. Because of the heat, meat is often made into charque (jerky) and used in local dishes.

The favorite dish of people in the tropics is locro, a rice soup made with charque or with chicken. Fifteen minutes before serving, rice, cubed potatoes and green banana are added to the soup, and just before serving, eggs are broken into it. The condiments are chopped onion and green pepper, and yucca is served as a side dish.

Majadito is a jerky and rice dish served with an onion, tomato and green pepper sauce. Masaco is fried jerky and fried banana ground together with a little hot oil. It can also be made with banana and cheese or with yucca and jerky.

A typical method of preparing meat is as pacumutu. Beef is skewered on wooden poles and barbecued over hot coals, then served with boiled yucca. The most common accompaniments are jaku, broiled yucca or fried bananas. Rice is usually prepared with cheese. Chivé is fried grated yucca. Pasoka is chivé with jerky.

In the tropics, chicha is made from corn or peanuts, but it is not fermented. Sucumbé is made with milk, sugar, eggs, cinnamon and singani. Syrups are made from tropical fruits, such as tamarind, carambola, and guapurú, and are used to make cold drinks.

Pastries are also very different from those in the colder regions. Cuñape, a delicious tea-time pastry, is made with yucca flour and cheese. Corn is used to make bis-cocho de maíz, (corn biscuits), humintas and empanadas de maíz blanco (turnovers).

In such a humid climate as found in the tropics, the people have a very interesting method of preserving pastries. They leave them in the oven to dry until they become abizcochados, or hardtack.

Food Customs in Bolivia

Lunch is the main meal in Bolivia and offices and businesses are closed for two hours or more so that people can go home for lunch.

Lunch is never complete without soup. There are three kinds of soups: chupes, ch'aques and lawas. Chupe is a meat and vegetable soup with a clear broth. Ch'aque is a very thick soup that has a higher content of grain that has not been as finely ground. Lawa has broth thickened by a grain flour, such as corn or wheat.

Chupe is always served with a garnish, usually parsley or oregano. To make the soup tastier, the condiments -- onion, cumin, oregano, ají, pepper, parsley and tomato -- may be fried in oil before being added to the soup. It is common to find Bolivians adding some piquant flavor to this already spicy soup. Q'aspa is a locoto or a red or yellow ají which has been toasted and added to the soup five minutes before serving; this custom comes from Cochabamba. A locoto may be pounded to release all its flavor and then added to the soup. And there is always llajua to adjust the taste.

There are also special times of the day for some foods such as onces, literally "eleven o'clocks," where food, often salteñas or tucumanas, is served in the morning between breakfast and lunch. Picantes are usually served at 5 p.m. Barbecues are served at midday, but this constitutes a prolonged meal that may run into dinner time.

Weekend lunches also tend to go on and on. The sobremesa, the Latin after-luncheon conversation hour, is always pro-longed and the hostess is expected to serve tea before the guests get up from the table. But it does not end there. People continue the conversation in the living room into the cocktail hour. Sometimes a light dinner is served to the few diehards. This custom is always expected by hosts, and enjoyed by all the guests.

Just as lunch is the biggest meal of the day, holidays make for the biggest meals of the year. Bolivia has certain customs for hol-iday meals that are similar to the United States, such as eating turkey at Christmas. (In Bolivia, this is done at midnight on Christmas eve.) The New Year is celebrated with picana, a soup made with beef, chick-en, pork, lamb, ají and either wine or beer.

The Tuesday of Carnaval, the day before Ash Wednesday, is the day of the ch'alla, the offering to the native gods and the goddess Pachamama in which a special puchero (boiled dinner) is served with peaches and pears. On Good Friday bacalao a la viscaina, cod, is served in every Catholic home.

Suggested Reading Cooking Book:
Epicuro Andino by Teresa de Prada, Peggy Palza, Wilma W. Velasco and Sus Gisbert. Ed. Quipus, La Paz - Bolivia 1989.

QUINOA, THE MIRACLE GRAIN

BY JOHN F. MCCAMANT

In 1582 Spanish colonial administrators sent out a questionnaire asking, "What are the seeds, plants and green vegetables which serve or have served as food for the aborigines?" The answer that came back from the Andes: quinoa.

Garcilaso de la Vega, an Inca émigré to Spain, confirmed the prominence of quinoa in his Royal Commentaries of the Incas, writing, "the second most important of the crops which are grown above ground (after maize) is called quinoa or in Spanish 'millet' or 'little rice' which it rather resembles on the color and appearance of the grain." Note that de la Vega, who had left Peru when he was 20, reverses the ranking of maize and quinoa. In doing so, he may have expressed a bias of his new country for Spaniards took great interest in maize, which grew well at the altitudes where they preferred to live, but virtually ignored quinoa, which grew in the higher and cooler environments that supported the majority of the Inca population.

Four hundred and fifty years later, it seems strange indeed that the Spanish took such a dim interest in this exceptional food. Dazzlingly beautiful in the field, quinoa grows successfully in many environments that are inhospitable to other crops. Rich in flavor and supremely versatile in its uses, it is among the most nutritious of all grains. This unclaimed treasure of the Andes remains available thanks to generations of indigenous farmers working fields their North American counterparts would consider untillable. Even in the past 50 years, since its virtues were recognized by science, a series of political and agricultural obstacles have impeded quinoa from taking its natural place in the world's food basket.

The small grain of Chenopodium quinoa grows on a broad-leafed plant whose leaves take the shape of a goose foot. At maturity, atop stalks three to seven feet tall, its sorghum-like seed heads turn brilliant shades of white, yellow, red or black before they dry out and are ready for harvesting. The plant is closely related to spinach and beets and even more closely related to a common worldwide weed, popularly known as lamb's-quarter. A number of its wild relatives in the chenopod genus will cross quite readily with the cultivated plant.

Quinoa has been called a pseudo-cereal because it does not belong to the grass family, as wheat, oats and most other grains do. Those of us who work with quinoa prefer to class it as a leafy grain, along with amaranth and buckwheat, not only to avoid a negative nomenclature, but also to call attention to the fact that the leaves of these plants are valuable food sources. Quinoa contains a nearly perfect balance of essential amino acids, including lysine, which runs short in the grassy grains. Its protein level ranges as high as 22%, averaging about 16% as compared to wheat's 12%. Quinoa also supplies substantial amounts of iron, calcium and vitamin A, but the edible leaf has it in abundance. In short, the quinoa plant can satisfy all of our basic nutritional needs.

Quinoa has the telltale properties of a non-cultivated plant, including inability, under normal circumstances, to survive in the wild. Its seeds mature all at once and do not shatter, traits that make the grain easy to harvest and that native planters probably promoted by selection and preservation of the seed down through the centuries. The seed's thin coat and lack of dormancy also give it the quality of germinating very quickly when exposed to moisture, which is desirable as long as farmers husband the seed carefully. But this also means that quinoa, left to stand in the fields, will sprout in the fall (sometimes right on the stalk) and be killed by winter temperatures.

Quinoa's Origins

Archaeological evidence indicates that quinoa was cultivated as early as 5800 to 4500 B.C. in the Ayacucho basin of Peru, and was being traded by 1000 to 900 B.C. along the coast of what is now Chile. Archaeologist David Browman has found that quinoa comprises 70 to 90% of the seeds excavated from a site at Chiripa near Lake Titicaca, which dates from the period 1350 B.C. to 50 A.D. Evidently, quinoa was a staple in this high plateau, and Browman notes an increase in seed size at Chiripa after 1000 B.C., a clear sign of the crop's domestication and improvement. Interestingly, a closely-related chenopod still found in the wild has been discovered in several archeological excavations in the eastern United States and has now been established as one of the first agricultural crops grown within the borders of the present nation, dating from about 2,000 years ago and thus preceding maize by several hundred years.

Until recently, it has generally been accepted that quinoa originated in the Lake Titicaca region because that was the area of greatest diversity for the plant. Texas A&M botanist Hugh Wilson threw some doubt on that conclusion in 1979, when he found a wild North American species with a genetic structure similar to quinoa. Humberto Gandarillos, the grandfather of quinoa research in Bolivia, took up the challenge and sought possible wild precursors of quinoa in the La Paz region. Crossing several species of wild chenopods, he found one hybrid that produces fertile offspring with the characteristics of quinoa, including the shape of its seed head and the color and size of seed. He concluded that quinoa could have originated in any of the valleys of Peru and Bolivia, where both these apparent progenitors are found in the wild.

In any case, quinoa spread throughout South America to an area that closely coincided with the extent of the Inca Empire. Its northernmost reach was the Sabana of Bogotá in Colombia, and its southern limit was the Isla de Chiloé, two-thirds of the way down the coast of Chile.

Contemporary Peruvian agronomist Mario Tapia has identified four general types of quinoa. A great deal of variation exists within each of these broad types, but they provide a sense of the adaptability and prehistoric range of the plant. Valley quinoa grows in the valleys of Peru, Ecuador, eastern Bolivia and southern Colombia at elevations from 7,000 to 13,000 feet. These tall, slow-maturing varieties are usually planted in association with corn at the lower elevations, and with potatoes and barley at the higher elevations. Altiplano quinoa grows above 12,000 feet in the mountainous regions of Peru and Bolivia and also in parts of northern Argentina and Chile. It is a smaller plant than valley quinoa, quicker to mature and more often cultivated alone in small plots. The salt flats quinoa of southern

Bolivia grows at altitudes of 10,000 to 12,000 feet, has a medium maturing time and somewhat larger seeds than other types. Finally, sea-level quinoa is found along the coast of southern Chile. It has a medium maturing time and resembles the Altiplano varieties in size, but most of its varieties have a translucent starch not found in higher-elevation quinoa.

Its range and nutritive value made quinoa the basis for the great pre-Columbian civilizations of the Andes. The cultural center of Tiwanaku, which lasted from 600 to 1200 A.D., was particularly dependent on quinoa because maize would not grow at its 12,497-foot location (about 3,750m) on the shores of Lake Titicaca. The Inca Empire, which followed, was centered 1,300 feet lower at Cuzco and thus was able to make good use of both quinoa and maize. Before the Spanish conquest, two-thirds of Peru's population lived in the quinoa-growing areas of the sierra.

The ancient Andean people ate the grain boiled alone or with herbs, ground it into flour for cakes, cooked the green leaves as a potherb and drank the fermented grain in a kind of beer. They also used the plant for non-nutritive purposes: the seed's bitter coat of saponin for soap, ashes of the stalks to bring out the powers of coca, and the unwashed grain as a medicine. The Incas called it the "mother grain," and held it sacred. Each year the Inca ruler planted the first quinoa seed of the season with a golden foot plow, and priests offered it to the sun in vases of gold at the solstice.

Many theories can be suggested for the Spaniards' failure to adopt quinoa. They brought to the New World their own grains -- rye, barley, oats and wheat -- as well as sheep and cattle. Potatoes complemented these foods, but the well-balanced protein of quinoa lost its importance, given the abundance of meat produced by extensive ranching on lands that had swiftly become depopulated. Quinoa also lacked the gluten needed to make yeasted bread, the mainstay of the European diet; and if the quinoa samples tasted by the newcomers had not been thoroughly cleansed of their bitter coat of saponin, which it probably had not, the Spaniards could easily have failed to appreciate its flavor. Last but not least, the Spaniards may have directly suppressed the cultivation of quinoa because of its religious significance to the indigenous population.

In any case, what the Spaniards did not adopt they ruined. The sophisticated, highly-productive agricultural system of the Incas and their predecessors was allowed to fall to pieces. A complex social system of cooperation and labor exchanges that had been developed to maintain the agricultural infrastructure of roads, terraces and irrigation works could not be sustained by a population drastically reduced by epidemics, and with so much of its labor diverted to mining and other economic activities demanded by the Spanish. In the 1570s, resettlement of the indigenous population into reducciones (an early-day version of strategic hamlets) facilitated colonial control and labor recruitment and further hampered the collective work needed to preserve the farming infrastructure. Within a hundred years, the population of the sierra, although holding up better than that of the coastal regions, had dropped to one-sixth of the pre-Conquest level. Quinoa lapsed with the society and agricultural system that had sustained it. Remnants of the agricultural system remained in the indigenous villages, however, and there quinoa continued to be grown.

By the late 1970s, only a very limited area of the Andes was devoted to quinoa: 2,500 acres in Colombia, 3,750 in Ecuador, 62,500 in Peru and 30,000 in Bolivia, a total of just under 100,000 acres. (There is no data from Chile, but it is safe to say that production there would add little to this figure.) Even the Peruvian acreage devoted to quinoa amounted to no more than 1% of land under cultivation nationwide and represents a fall off of nearly 50% since 1951. Ironically, this modern phase of quinoa's decline is attributed in part to the U.S. Food Aid program, a misconceived undertaking that caused substitution of subsidized wheat and white bread for nutritious local foods throughout the Third World.

Revival of the Mother Grain

In the last 50 years, a small but burgeoning group of Andean researchers, seeking to hold on to and revive aspects of their pre-Columbian heritage, have investigated and promoted the use of quinoa. The U.N. Food and Agriculture Organization, Andean Pact and Oxfam contributed to this quinoa research in the 1950s and 1960s, as did bilateral assistance from the United States. After 1977, the most important support came from Canada's International Development Research Centre, through the Inter-American Institute of Agricultural Sciences, which has sponsored cooperation among the Andean countries on quinoa and seven other under-utilized Andean crops: kaniwa, tarwi, ulluco, oca, mashua, amaranth and bitter potato.

In order to stem the decline in quinoa production, agronomists collected specimens and built good seed banks in Ecuador, Peru and Bolivia; developed improved bread varieties; identified optimum levels of fertilizer application; found pesticides for various insects that infest quinoa; and devised improved harvesting techniques. Engineers assisted the endeavor by designing low-cost machinery for removing saponin and making this technology available to villages, while nutritionists analyzed the food value of quinoa and began actively promoting its use. The South American private sector also stepped in and started to market quinoa. The most notable firm in the field is Inca Sur, which merchandises a line of whole quinoa grain, flour and rolled flakes from its base in the ancient Inca capital at Cuzco, Peru.

Cash-poor South American governments, recognizing the importance of their indigenous food sources, have thrown support to the revival, including a law that required bread to contain a minimum of 5% quinoa flour. The area used for planting quinoa nearly doubled between 1970 and 1977, only to return to its former level two years later as bakers resisted, and the law went unenforced. Nevertheless, the government has continued to support efforts to revive quinoa within its extremely stringent budgetary limitations.

In the peripheral area of its production, quinoa still seems to be losing ground. Eduardo Peralta reported in 1985 that, in four southern provinces of Ecuador where quinoa was previously common, it is no longer found. Anthropologist Daniel Gade wrote in 1975 that, in the Vilacanota Valley of Peru, near Cuzco, "the seeds of quinoa, kaniwa and amaranth are less and less eaten." Likewise, botanist Hugh Wilson found in 1981 that "this plant is on the road to extinction in south-central Chile. Cultivation is declining, and in many instances, germplasm and information were available only from the most senior individuals of a given family unit."

Even where quinoa has received public support, it is the indigenous population that deserves most of the credit for maintaining production. For instance, in Nunoa, a mountain valley above Lake Titicaca, native farmers have continued to plant quinoa along with its close relative, the even more cold-hardy kaniwa. Anthropologist R. Brooke Thomas, who studied the area in the 1970s, observed that Old World grains grown there were "more susceptible than Andean grains to frost, hail and snow." He calculated that the Andean grains had far and away the highest energy efficiency of the food produced, much higher than livestock. Computing energy efficiency as a ratio of energy obtained to energy expended, Thomas found that quinoa yielded 50% more energy than potatoes per unit of land. Civilization could not survive in this harsh, cold climate without the Andean grains.

The peasant population of southern Bolivia's barren salt flats is even more dependent on quinoa than the people of Nunoa because there is not enough moisture to grow potatoes (except in very limited areas, and only if irrigated). Quinoa will not only grow with just five to ten inches of rainfall annually, but also tolerates salty, alkaline soils. Quinoa growers from this region are among the few who sell as much as half their production for cash. Their cooperative, Operation Tierra, holds an annual quinoa festival and is one of the most energetic promoters of quinoa in the world.

Today, the resilience of the peasant farmers and the five-decade campaign by Andean agricultural specialists appear to be bringing about the long-sought reversal in quinoa's fortunes. After an all-time production low in 1979, Bolivian land producing quinoa has increased by 34% annually, and similar, though less spectacular, increases are being seen in other countries.

One of the primary motivations for promoting quinoa and improving its cultivation in South America has been to improve the nutrition of the high-elevation population, most of which is indigenous. The 1948 U.N.-sponsored nutritional conference that first recommended investigation of quinoa suggested that the crop could "play a major role in feeding the Upland Indians, whose nutrition problems are among the most serious in the Americas." When the U.S. National Academy of Sciences added its voice to the encouragement of quinoa in a study of under-exploited plants in 1975, it

too sounded this theme, pointing out that "its grain, rich in protein and containing a good amino acids balance, may prove to be a better protein source than most of the true cereals. In the high Andes, quinoa is primarily a food of campesinos and poorer classes; increasing quinoa production and use could improve their inadequate diet."

Twenty-five years later, it seems clear that these well-meaning scholars misinterpreted the problem. The native populations certainly knew all about quinoa, and their organic farming techniques, passed down from pre-Columbian times, have proved to be among the best in the world. Chemical cultural techniques, which were being encouraged by the internationally supported research, would be appropriate for market production, but there would be little market unless the affluent whites and mestizos of low-lying areas started consuming quinoa. The Spanish-speaking middle classes of South America now largely reject quinoa, disdaining it as an Indian food, and do not need its protein since they consume large amounts of red meat, poultry and fish. Quinoa is rarely served at the restaurants of the two major cities in the center of quinoa production, Puno, Peru and La Paz, Bolivia; one has to go into the Indian markets to find it.

For quinoa to become more broadly accepted in South America, the negative attitude toward the grain must be overcome. Increased nationalist appreciation of the Indian heritage would certainly help, but recognition of quinoa's values by trendsetters in the industrial countries might help even more. As one Peruvian researcher suggested, the shortest marketing route for quinoa from Cuzco to Lima may be through the U.S. health food market.

A market for quinoa in the United States could develop entirely on the basis of imports from Latin America in the pattern of tea, coffee, cocoa and cocaine, but for three reasons, this pattern seems unlikely and undesirable. First, all the major foods consumed in the industrial world are also grown nationally; production in the northern hemisphere allows manufacturers to integrate foods into their product lines with confidence that the supply is secure.

Second, quinoa could provide a new means for economic development of some of the poorest counties in the United States, counties in the mountainous regions of southern Colorado and northern New Mexico. People in this area, whose economic struggles were accurately depicted by the novel and movie The Milagro Bean Field War, have little irrigation water and few crops aside from hay that grow well in their high-elevation fields.

Third, large-scale U.S. imports of South American quinoa would endanger the land and traditions of Andean indigenous communities, among the few places where Native Americans have been able to maintain their traditions. Andean communities have preserved their way of life in part because the agricultural products of their high-altitude plots have not yet found a strong commercial market. A high demand and price for quinoa exports would make their lands extremely attractive to entrepreneurs, who historically have always managed to usurp indigenous land once it proved its value for export crops. If quinoa became a bonanza in the Andes, indigenous communities would encounter pressures on their diet as well as on their land rights, as prices enticed them to sell large proportions of their quinoa crop and eat less of it themselves. North American production would moderate and stabilize the price of quinoa, preventing unintended harm to the very people who have preserved the grain while at the same time possibly giving them a chance to benefit from the expanding market.

The introduction of a new food to the mass market of the West is no small task, however. It was accomplished very successfully with soybeans in the 1930s, but this Asian crop had strong support from the U.S. Department of Agriculture, which spent thirty million 1930s' dollars to secure its present place in the affection of U.S. farmers. Amaranth has less government cooperation, but the Rodale Institute is giving it creative and energetic sponsorship. Quinoa has not yet found such well-endowed or well-placed supporters and has received almost no funding in the U.S. If it is to be successfully established in the United States, as it seems it will be, it will be due to the dedication of a loose network of people, all doing their bit with few resources and often without pay, in the belief that it is time to accept, even embrace, the gift of quinoa from the great civilization of South America.

Until recently, all attempts to transplant quinoa had failed. The first recorded trial, Inca Garcilaso de la Vega's 16th-century effort to grow quinoa in Spain, failed when his seeds did not germinate, probably because they had been obtained in the market and thus had been washed and dried to remove saporin, with a resulting loss of viability. Subsequent more scientific attempts did little better. When Elizabeth Eiselen surveyed the field in 1956, she found that "in spite of numerous attempts, quinoa has never been successfully introduced elsewhere. When it has been tried at high elevations in the United States, the plant has flourished during the long summer days, reaching heights of seven feet, but the seed does not mature before the plants are killed by winter cold."

Unfortunately, most attempts to introduce quinoa outside the Andes used seeds collected from Peru or northern Bolivia, where (we now know) quinoa varieties are sensitive to the day length and will not bloom until days and nights are equally

TRADITIONAL PRESENT

long. In the mountains of the northern hemisphere, these seasonal constraints do not leave sufficient time for grain to mature. Attempts to grow quinoa at lower elevations in Europe and the United States failed for another reason: the plants did not set seed, since heat kills quinoa pollen at temperatures above roughly 85°F.

Investors and established corporations are still leaving quinoa alone, but bit by bit the market and production are growing to the point where larger firms may become interested. It seems only a matter of time before food product giants, in order to gain an edge on the competition, will capitalize on quinoa's very positive image by adding it to their cereals, pastas, pancake mixes and soups. Indeed, John Marcille voiced concern at the inaugural N.A.Q.P.A. meeting that quinoa will soon become a fad in the United States and there will not be enough production in North and South America combined to fill the demand. Those of us who eat quinoa for breakfast, lunch and dinner see no reason why everyone else should not do likewise.

In these last years, I have learned to appreciate the words of an early quinoa advocate, who remarked that, "Quinoa has a life of its own." It seems to use people rather than the other way around; as some have become discouraged, it has found new people to take over. Spirits of the Andes may have placed all kinds of obstacles in the path of those trying to preserve and disseminate the "mother grain," but it seems destined, nonetheless, to take its rightful place among the crops of the world.

Cooking with Quinoa

Satisfying yet light, quinoa is so delicious that you may prepare the following simple recipes either for everyday fare or for entertaining. Prepare extra of the basic recipe; cooked quinoa lends itself to numerous dishes that will save you meal preparation time the next day. Quinoa may be cooked as is or toasted. Toasted quinoa is light with a full-bodied and rich flavor. Quinoa is not enhanced when pressure cooked or cooked starting with cold water.

Basic Quinoa Recipe
Makes 4 cups

1 cup quinoa
2 cups water
pinch sea salt

Rinse quinoa several times by running fresh water over it in a pot and pouring through a strainer. Place water and salt in a saucepan and bring to a rapid boil. Add quinoa, reduce heat, cover, and simmer until all of the water is absorbed (15-20 minutes).

Variations: For a rich, nutty flavor, toast quinoa (with or without oil) in a skillet, stirring constantly, before adding to the water.

Shrimp-Fried Quinoa
Serves 4

2 tablespoons unrefined oil
1 teaspoon grated fresh ginger
1 onion, minced
3 stalks celery and leaves, chopped
4 cups cooked quinoa
2 tablespoons shoyu
1 cup green peas
1 cup cooked shrimp, chopped
1 tablespoon sake or dry white wine (optional)

Heat a wok or large, heavy skillet. Add oil and ginger. Over medium high heat, sautée onion briefly and add celery, sautéeing until partially cooked. Add quinoa and shoyu, stir once, cover, and cool for 5 minutes. Add peas, shrimp and sake. Cook for 2 minutes, covered, or just until the peas are tender.

TRADITIONAL PRESENT

Quinoa, Leek and Tofu casserole
Serves 5

    1 1/2 cups tofu
    2 teaspoons sesame oil
    1 clove garlic, pressed
    1 leek, chopped
    2 cups cooked quinoa
    1 teaspoon sea salt, or 2
        teaspoons shoyu dash black
        pepper
    1 cup bread crumbs
    1 cup soy milk
    1/2 cup cheese, grated (optional)

Preheat oven to 350°F. Working with 1/2 tofu at a time, squeeze out water with hands. Set aside. Heat a large skillet or wok and add oil. Add garlic and then leek. Sautée until lightly browned. Add quinoa, then tofu, sautéeing for 2 minutes after each addition. Add seasonings.

Oil the casserole dish. Add 1/2 cup bread crumbs and rotate casserole to coat evenly. Gently add the quinoa mixture. Press a well in the center of the quinoa and pour in soy milk. Cover with remaining bread crumbs and cheese. Cover, and bake for 20 minutes. Remove cover and continue to bake until cheese is nicely browned.

Almond Quinoa Cookies
Makes 1 1/2 dozen

    1 cup almond butter (or tahini or peanut butter)
    1/2 cup maple syrup or honey
    1/4 cup unrefined sunflower or safflower oil
    1 tablespoon vanilla
    1/3 cup water
    1 cup whole wheat pastry flour
    1 cup quinoa flour
    1/2 cup toasted almonds,
        chopped
    9 whole almonds pinch of sea salt

Preheat oven to 375°F. In a mixing bowl, blend almond butter, sweetener, oil, vanilla and water. Sift together flours and salt, add chopped almonds and combine with wet mixture.

Using hands, form dough into small balls and place on an oiled cookie sheet. Press each cookie gently with the tines of a fork. Cut whole almonds in half and press one piece, cut side up, into each cookie. Bake for 12 to 15 minutes or just until golden.

Additional quinoa recipes by Rebecca Theurer Wood are available from the Quinoa Corporation.

Rita Del Solar has also published a Quinoa recipe book.

CLIMBING AND SKIING IN THE BOLIVIAN ANDES

BY STAN SHEPARD

When I search for ways to describe the mountains of Bolivia, "graceful, elegant, and peaceful," are the words that come. The quality of the light and clarity of the air here are astonishing. By day, these peaks and glaciers shine with a painful brightness, and at night they glow in the reflected starlight of the southern constellations. There can be few finer experiences than to walk up an Andean valley, your pack loaded with a week of supplies, your destination one of these splendid ice peaks.

With exceptions, the mountains are easy enough to approach, and many fine climbs do not exceed 1,000 meters in elevation gain from your base camp, a moderate day for a fit and acclimatized climber. The importance of training and acclimatization cannot be stressed enough, because while these are friendly mountains, blessed with exceptionally fine weather and stable snow and ice conditions during the climbing season, they still are big, serious mountains and there have been bad accidents here.

However, the alert and fit climber will find less danger and greater enjoyment in the Bolivian Cordilleras than in perhaps any other major range on Earth. The elegant ice wedge of Condoriri, the granite needles of the Quimsa Cruz, the dark fortress of Tiquimani, the giants Ancohuma and Illimani and Sajama - any one would

offer a worthy goal. Taken together, these peaks and the hundreds more like them can give you some of the best climbing you will find anywhere.

The Basic Geography

Most of the interesting peaks of the Bolivian Andes stand along the east rim of the Altiplano, on a roughly northwest southeast chain of three Cordilleras - the Apolobamba close to the Peruvian border, the Cordillera Real, Bolivia's principal mountain range, and the more compact Quimsa Cruz.

If you fly to La Paz from Lima, you will get a good view of the enormous Cordillera Real and can see something of the Apolobamba, with its many mid-size ice peaks, farther north.

At the northern end of the Cordillera Real stand Illampu (6,362m) and Ancohuma (6,427m). These major peaks, together with their many satellites and neighbors, including Aguja Yacuma (6,056m) and Casiri (5,828m), provide the greatest concentration of interesting climbing in Bolivia.

Three other major peaks, Calzada (5,871m), Chearoco (6,127m) and Chacacomani (6,094m), rise above extensive icefields and form the crown of the Central Cordillera Real. They are separated from the Ancohuma massif by the Casala pass (5,040m).

South of the icefields stands a line of sharp summits, including Wila Lloje (5,596m), Yanko Huyo (5,512m), Pacokeuta (5,589m), Jankho Laya (5,545m), Warawarani (5,542m), Kallhuani (5,492m), and the finest of all, Condoriri (5,648m). South of Condoriri the Cordillera flattens a bit until rising to a huge blunt pyramid north of La Paz, Huayna Potosi (6,088mm). East of Huayna Potosi stands Tiquimani (5,595m), notable for its large rock walls and aggressive form.

To the south of the capital you have a view of two major peaks, the oddly flat Mururata (5,868m) and Illimani (6,450m), an immense multi-summited mountain, which has become a symbol for the city.

South of Illimani, made insignificant by the distance, is the third of Bolivia's important ranges, the Quimsa Cruz, geolocally an extension of the Real, but separated from it by the stupendous Rio Abajo trench cut by the Rio Chuquiagu, a river fed by the glaciers of Chacaltaya, La Paz's local ski area. The Quimsa Cruz provides two distinct types of climbs - large snow and ice peaks such as Gigante Grande (5,750m) in the southern half, and small granite towers in the northern half. The dividing line is at Mina Viloco. The Araca group offers especially fine climbs on granite.

You also can see, to the west of the Altiplano and the salt flats, an enormous volcano rivaling the giants of Ecuador. This splendid mountain is Sajama (6,542m). Several other interesting volcanos, notably, Parinacota (6,330m), Pomerata (6,240m), and Acotango (6,050m), mark Bolivia's border with Chile.

Notes

Peak names: Tiquimani is incorrectly named Illampu on the "Instituto Geografico Militar" (IGM) topographic maps. These otherwise excellent maps contain numerous errors in the naming of peaks.

Altitudes: Agreement about the altitudes of Bolivian peaks is not complete. Sources used here are the "Instituto Geográfico Militar" (IGM), the American Alpine Journal and similar publications.

Pomarata: This peak is given as Pomarape on the IGM maps, apparently in error.

Maps: The IGM is located at the Cuartel Militar in Miraflores. The beautiful IGM maps do not cover the northern Cordillera Real or the Apolobamba, and some key sheets may be out of stock, so it is wise to scout the various alpine journals for maps before arriving in Bolivia.

THE CLIMBING

Some Generalities

On the whole, The Bolivian mountains are about the right size and shape - big, but not too big. During the cold and dry months, Bolivia provides snow and ice climbing outstanding for its quality and safety.

Superior rock - granite equal to the best of Yosemite or Chamonix - is found in several places in the Cordilleras Real and Quimsa Cruz, although much Bolivian rock tends to be an adequate, but uninspiring brown metamorphic. Pupusani and Kasiri, the sharp little peaks east of the Yungas Cumbre, provide high standard climbing on steeply tilted sedimentaries.

The northern Quimsa Cruz offers dozens of small granite towers above lakes and meadows. Sizeable granite walls will be found in the eastern cirques of Illampu and Ancohuma, which themselves offer mixed climbs - granite and ice - of a high standard. One such climb is the 1983 French route on the south buttress of Pico del Norte (6,085m). The first three pitches are vertical granite topped by a roof. The remaining 24 pitches provide free climbing on slabs and mixed terrain.

Some History

Today, hundreds of climbers are active each season in Bolivia, but as recently as the 1970's, climbing was relatively infrequent. With a few excep-tions, the leading climbers of the early days were Germans or Austrians resident in or visiting Bolivia.

Some of their climbs - the ascent of Illampu stands out - were outstanding achievements under difficult conditions. If these climbs seem moderate today, remember that those climbers did not own polypropylene underwear, their hardware was a joke and the approaches to their climbs took days.

In 1898, Sir Martin Conway and his two Swiss guides achieved the first ascent of Illimani, by a long route circling around from the south and east above Rio Abajo. In 1904, the first explorations of the Quimsa Cruz were carried out by the poet Henry Hoek. In 1911, Dr. Teodoro Herzog made several climbs in the group and published its first map. A German party led by Adolf Schulze repeated Conway's route on Illimani in 1915, and in 1921 and 1923, we find Schulze on Ancohuma, for its first and second ascents. The first ascent of Huayna Potosi took place in 1919.

In 1928, German and Austrian Climbers reached the summit of Illampu in a climb of advanced technical standard for the period. Sajama was climbed in 1939 by Pietro Ghiglione, and in 1940 Illimani was climbed by the "Nido de Condores" route, which since has become the "standard" line. Other important 1940 first ascents were Condoriri and Tiquimani.

Beginning in the middle 1960's, the major ridges and walls became the scenes of modern climbs, many of a high standard. Typical routes of the period can be found on the impressive and rather dangerous south face of Illimani, the beautiful west ridge of Huayna Potosi, the west face of Tiquimani, and the long lines on Illampu. Young Bolivian climbers have been infected with the chalk bag and sticky shoe ethic; the current standard is in roughly the 5.11 - 7a. range, which may not seem high by Smith Rock and Verdon standards, but remember that we are talking about 5000-plus meter altitudes and multi-pitch routes.

Weather

Bolivian mountain weather is incomparably superior to that of the Alps. Extended periods of good weather begin in April and hold through August. The climbing season traditionally covers June and July, when sub-freezing temperatures and cloudless skies make the Bolivian Andes about as safe for climbing as it is possible for large glacier-covered mountains to be. During the remainder of the year conditions tend to be warmer and wetter, with rain frequent in October and again from January to March. This neat scheme is upset now and then, when the Pacific ocean Humboldt Current is altered by "El Niño," a counter-current.

The "Club Andino Boliviano"

The "Club Andino Boliviano" (CAB) recently celebrated its sixtieth anniversary. The CAB increasingly is serving as central contact point for many hundreds of visiting climbers, and while it usually does not itself provide goods or services to visitors, it makes contacts for transportation, gives information about current conditions, bus schedules, etc. The Club is located on Calle Mexico 1638, corner of Otero de la Vega, behind the Hotel Sucre in down town La Paz, casilla 1346. The telephone number is 2312875. Hours usually are 5 pm to 7pm. E-mail: clubandi@caoba.entelnet.bo

Getting to the Mountains

The Cordilleras Real and Quimsa Cruz are well served by roads ranging from the modern La Paz - Yungas highway to terrifying Andean tracks on which a mistake would be your last. Several of the better roads have frequent bus service, and a number can be traveled by taxi. In some cases, the distance from the roadhead to the nearest glacier is less than a kilometer. However, some areas, including much of the Apolobamba and the central portion of the Real, require difficult jeep (4WD) travel and long walks. A few of the possible approaches suitable for taxis are described below. Precise directions should be obtained from the CAB, since finding the connections between the main highway and these approach roads can be frustrating.

The Cordillera Real: An important road is the link with the Zongo Valley which provides hydroelectric power for La Paz. This road gives access to Huayna Potosi and Tiquimani, and many small peaks such as Cunitincuta, and Charquini. Another important approach is the road into the Hichukhota Valley, starting point for Wila Iloje (5,596m), Pacokeuta (5,589m), Jankho Huyo (5,512m), Jankho Laya (5,545m) and dozens of other peaks offering hundreds of climbs.

Between these two important approach routes is the road to the Turn Condoriri valley, above which is found Condoriri, one of the more beautiful mountains on this planet. Again, dozens of other climbs can be made out of the Condoriri valley, a base camp location favored by many climbing parties. Another important approach route (4WD) is the road to Mina Palcoco, one valley north of Condoriri - more fine climbs.

Access to Illimani, Mururata and the Inca Trail is provided by the road leading south from La Paz via Calacoto, Cota Cota and Palca. At the northern end of the range, roads from the hilltown of Sorata provide access to Illampu and Ancohuma.

The Quimsa Cruz: Well maintained but unpaved roads snake along both the eastern and western flanks of the Quimsa Cruz, serving mining communities such as Viloco.

To reach these roads, take the La Paz - Oruro highway to the Viloco turnoff at the town of Conami. There is some bus service to Viloco, but hired vehicles provide a much faster, although expensive, alternative. Walking times from the Quimsa Cruz roads to the glaciers are as short as minutes at some locations.

The Apolobamba and Sajama: The CAB can provide information about access to these more isolated locations. To climb Sajama, proceed east to the town of the same name from Oruro and start walking. 4WD vehicles can be taken high into the Apolobamba.

Skiing and Chacaltaya: Raul Posnanski (1913-1943), with Alfred Hendel and other members of the newly - formed CAB, built Chacaltaya at the end of the 1930's. The first ski lift in South America pulled its first skier to Point 5,345 in 1940. The lift has been refurbished many times since then, but it retains the simple 1940 design - a steel cable, pulleys fashioned from automobile hubs, and an automobile engine for power. You attach yourself to the cable with a small hook, a rope and an uncomfortable little wooden bar, and you ski back down the mountain with this gear wrapped around you or stuffed into a pocket. The rig seems primitive and can be tricky to use, but it has proven fast and effective for half a century.

The lift spans about 1,000 meters, with a rise of about 340 meters from its base at roughly 5,000 meters. It gives access to two broad glaciers, with some first rate skiing, specially if you get good snow and are willing to explore a bit. The true summit of Cerro Chacaltaya is not the Point 5345 visible from the CAB cabin, but lies behind it, at an altitude of 5395 meters. The cabin itself is close to Benchmark 5238.

Skiing often can be found throughout the year, although from April to September - the winter months - the snow becomes rock hard, or even virtually unskiable blue ice. The real ski season is in the summer - January through March, when cover builds up and conditions range from glop to the finest powder.

On weekends ski buses provide transportation from the CAB headquarters. Reservations and payment should be made several days in advance, since seats can sell out. Prices vary depending upon exchange rates, etc, and are reasonable, although not necessarily low. (Remember that these fees are the only source of funds to keep the area operating.) Soups and sandwiches are available at the cabin, and the scene can be convivial.

Since most visitors go to Chacaltaya as an excursion and do not ski, the total number of skiers on a typical weekend averages perhaps two dozen - not a major crowd. A limited selection of equipment can be rented through the CAB or at the area.

Some Words of Caution

Do not leave your camp unguarded. If you do, it may be gone when you return. To a poor campesino or miner, an untended camp offers a painful temptation, and while theft is not endemic by any means, it does happen.

Do not have an accident. Although the "Federación Boliviana de Esqui y Andinismo," together with the CAB, has developed a respectable rescue capability, the size of the mountains and the time required to mount an effort ensure that rescue will be slow.

Do not leave trash - please. In recent years some climbers have left trash at their base camps. It is better to carry it out than to bury or burn it.

More advice: Obviously you will want to bring all of your climbing equipment with you. In general, the appropriate equipment for Bolivia is standard alpine climbing gear, with emphasis on warm boots and high tech clothing - the big 6,000 meter peaks can be quite cold.

It seems almost too obvious to mention, but don't bite off more than you can chew. It is not unusual for a group of technically skilled climbers to select a goal apparently within their ability, and then fail for reasons associated with lack of provision for a shake-down period. Take your time and get to know the environment.

The most successful climbing trips to Bolivia seem to follow a pattern: After a couple of days in La Paz, the party moves to one of the groups of mid - sized peaks, mountains in the 5,000 - 5,500 meters class, for their first week or so, and climbs the six thousanders only when well acclimatized and fit.

Hardware racks obviously should be appropriate to the types of climbing you have in mind, but remember that you will have to carry all of this stuff.

The winter days are short, so the best headlamp you can find is a necessary investment.

A wide variety of local and imported foods will be found in La Paz. Check with the CAB for sources for white gas and fuel cartridges, or for replacement equipment. **C.A.B.** Calle Mexico 1638, casilla 1346, Tel/Fax. 2312875. E-mail: clubandi@caoba.entelnet.bo

Guides

Several organizations and individuals in La Paz offer guide services. Making a name for himself is Jose Camarlinghi with **Andean Summits** offering mountaineering and climbing all over the country, Calle prolongación Armaza 710, Sopocachi. Tel/Fax. 2422106, Cel. 71944722. E-mail: info@andeansummits.com

Andes Expediciones, with Bernado Guarachi, who is highly respected for his vast experience. Avenida Camacho 1377, casilla 12287. Tels. 2202983, 2319655.

Fax. 2392344.

E-mail: andesexp@ceibo.entelnet.bo

Magri Tours, offers guided climbing tours. Calle Capitán Ravelo 2101, Tel. 2442727.

E-mail: magri_emet@megalink.com

Colibrí S.R.L. with Alain Mesili, Calle Sagarnaga 309, casilla 7456, Tel. 2371936. Fax. 2355043.

E-mail: acolibrie@ceibo.entelnet.bo

Quimsa with Gonzalo Jaimes, Calle Sagarnaga 189, local 101, Tel. 2317497.

A.G.T.M. Asociacion de Guias de Montañas en Bolivia. Tel. 2317497.

Refugio Huayna Potosí, owners of the refugio in the Zongo base camp. Climbing, trekking, mountain biking. Of. Sagárnaga and Illampu. Tels. 2317324, 71581644.

E-mail: berrios@megalink.com

Author Stan Shepard dramatically died on August 12th 1993 on a rescue mission in the Quimsa Cruz Cordillera.

Interesting books available in La Paz are ***La Cordillera Real de los Andes***, Editorial "Los Amigos del Libro" 1996, and ***The ANDES of BOLIVIA, A Climbing Guide and Adventures :*** Producción CIMA, 2003 by Alain Mesili. Mesili lived for years in Bolivia and is author of many fine routes. Another recommended book is ***Bolivia - A Climbing Guide*** by Yossi Brain, Ed. The Mountaineers, Seattle 1999.

A LIVING LEGEND

BY YOSSI BRAIN

UNRECORDED 1970 NEW ROUTE ON FITZ ROY DISCOVERED.

The French Alpinist and foremost pioneer of hard climbing in Bolivia is back in action. Alain Mesili, who wrote the only existing guidebook of any substance to climbing in the Cordillera Real, was released from imprisonment last year. Prior to this he had spent three and a half years in both American and Bolivian jails without any charge being brought against him.

Born a Parisian in 1949, Mesili was a political activist in France during the 1968 disturbance. Frustrated with the failings of the French Communist Party he left Europe in 1969 and went together with a number of other leaders of the failed uprising to Argentina. "We left to live other lives. At the time when I started to discover Argentina and Patagonia, virtually no one went there."

Mesili spent a year exploring Patagonia. He crossed the icecap and was probably the first person to trek around what has now become the Fitz Roy National Park. He also explored the Cordillera Darwin, crossing Chile at a time when Pinochet's Austral Highway did not exist.

Then came what appears to be a quite remarkable and, until the present, totally unknown event. In December 1970 Mesili, with the now unfortunately deceased Basque climber, Ricardo Arzela, crossed the Paso del Viento to reach the Patagonian Icecap. The pair attempted the West Face of Cerro Torre (only previously attempted by Bonatti) and climbed about 500 m before having to retreat due to excessive snow. They then turned their attentions to Fitz Roy. Due to the considerable publicity given in France to Lionel Terray's first ascent, they knew the line of the original 1952 French Route on the South East Ridge Face. However, they had no other information on the mountain. "There weren't any maps. You had to go there and see for yourself. We didn't have a good idea about what we wanted to do. We had a photo but there was no other information – it wasn't in fashion then. We went to see what there was. We just had the French Route as a reference. It was very difficult to find documentation in Buenos Aires. When we asked they didn't know anything."

Unbeknown to Mesili, by 1970 Fitz Roy had received only two more ascents. The Argentineans, Comesana and Fonrouge, had made the second ascent of the peak in 1965 with their historic climb of the Supercanaleta on the West Face and in 1968, Chouinard, Dorwort, Jones, Tejada-Flores and Tompkins had made the third via the South West Pillar. The fourth ascent has always been attributed to Dave Nicol's Anglo-American team, which made the first ascent of the South Pillar in 1972.

Arzela and Mesili started up the obvious line on the West Face-the Supercanaleta. Four days later they emerged on the summit. "We climbed the route free using pitons only for protection. There was a lot of wind. One night when we were sleeping on the ropes we were being blown about and we spent the whole night swinging wildly. It was impressive." The route they followed, shown on the accompanying photo, took a ramp line up the left wall of the couloir before breaking out left to reach the easier broken mixed ground of the upper North West Ridge.

Arzela and Mesili spent their fifth day on the mountain rappelling the 1952 French Route, finding big hand-made pitons. They then walked or rode horses to Calafate (in those days a small village of colonists) and subsequently travelled by vehicle a further 300 km to 'the big port on the Atlantic.' It took a total of two weeks to get out. "Very rarely were there any vehicles and we didn't have any money so we couldn't hire our own transport."

Their ascent of Fitz Roy, unrecorded in all the 'bibles' that have been written on the massif was, therefore, the fourth overall and by a new route. If Mesili's memory is correct in stating that the route was climbed without aid, then this would also prove to be the first free ascent of the peak as well as its first ever traverse.

Shortly after, Mesili arrived in Bolivia, where he began to climb extensively in the Cordillera Real, as well as exploring the less well-known range of the Apolobamba and Quimsa Cruz. "When I started climbing there, La Paz had three hotels plus a bar and it was three years since anyone had made an ascent of Huayna Potosi." Now this mountain just north of La Paz is probably the most popular 6000 m peak in South America.

Mesili climbed a multitude of new routes in the 70s, many of which were a generation ahead of anything-previous achieved in Bolivia. Mesili's main partner in the first years was the local climber, Ernesto Sanchez (tragically, Sanchez was killed on Illimani in 1975), although he also did plenty of new routes solo, or with visiting foreigners including a number of well-knownFrench climbers such as Anselme Baud and Georges Bettembourg.

Mesili's more notable first ascents include the Via del Triangulo on the 1000 m West face of Huayna Potosi (6088 m) and Via

de los Franceses on the same mountain, the latter the finest route on the East Face; Cabeza del Condor Directissima (5648 m) plus two fine solo ascents of steep 'goulottes' on Wyoming (5463 m) and Ala Derecha (5330 m), all in the Condoriri Group; several difficult mixed and rock routes on Illampu (6362 m). Pico del Norte (6050 m) Huayna Illampu (5956 m) and Pico Schulze (5943 m); a multitude of technically hard routes on lower peaks in the middle of the Real such as Jankho Layaka (5545 m); several long and committing new routes on both Mururata (5894 m) and Illimani (6439 m), including the only ascents to date on the remote and dangerous East Face of Illimani-two so far unrepeated routes.

A number of his new routes are now considered to warrant an alpine TD+ or EDI grade, though it is true that snow coverage was more extensive and climbing conditions distinctly better in Mesili's day. However, Mesili's routes pushed local climbers to new standards, as well as encouraging foreign Alpinists to visit and attempt hard new routes at high altitudes. His descents of Illampu and Illimani initiated extreme skiing to Bolivia, while his pioneering treks in the south west of the country are repeated today by an increasing number of adventure tourism companies.

Mesili worked with the Bolivian Alpine Club, instructing members in climbing techniques. He also had full access to archives, which held the most extensive record on what had been climbed in the country and by whom. Unfortunately, in 1974 the DIN (Direccion de Inteligencia Nacional), the intelligence force of the country's military ruler at the time, General Hugo Banzer, raided the Club's premises, confiscated all its archives and arrested Mesili. He was released after three days but the files, which the DIN suspected to be political in nature and written in some sort of code disguising their true content in amongst substantial information on Bolivian mountaineering, were never returned and have been lost forever.

Mesili continued to travel the country and collect what information he could, originally for his own interest but then later for work that was subsequently published in Liberation, the left of centre French newspaper. Mesili also translated into French the works of the revolutionary, Ché Guevara.

He continued hard climbing throughout the early 80s and in 1984 published what has now become the bible of climbing in the Real; La Cordillera Real de los Andes, Bolivia (for many years unobtainable but reprinted with a new soft back cover in 1996). He planned to write a guide to the Apolobamba but in 1990 a single incident changed his life.

Following terrorist attacks on the motorway that links the airport at El Alto with the capital and the murder of two Mormons, somebody bombed the US Marines building in La Paz. The marines were uninjured but a policeman was killed. The attacks were blamed on the Zarate Wilka terrorist group (named after a rebel leader from the colonial time), which had launched a campaign against the symbol of the US imperialism. Mesili was suspected of being involved with the bombing, and intelligence forces raided his flat. They took everything including all his notes and records, the most comprehensive information ever collected on climbing and exploration in Bolivia.

Mesili fled to the United States. "I went to Miami and had to learn English very quickly. I knew I was being hunted and that I was a suspect in the bombing. They called me The Jackal. They were mad." After four years on the run in America, Mesili was arrested and held in a series of jails before being transferred to Washington as a political prisoner. However, in 1995 the United States Government agreed to a swap with the Bolivian Government for a notable criminal. Mesili was brought back to Bolivia and held for two and a half years in the maximum-security prison of Chonchocoro near La Paz. No date was ever set for a trial. There was great pressure from France to obtain his release and during the latter part of this stay in jail he was persuaded by visiting climbers to write and article on Bolivia for the French magazine, Vertical. Then one day in 1997 his total innocence in the affair appears to have been accepted and he was suddenly released.

Mesili now seems relaxed about it all. Commenting on his time in jail he said:" It hasn't made me bitter. Someone once wrote that you need to have done three things in life; to have written a book, to have planted a tree and to know what it is like inside prison. I've done them all." He recently signed a one year contract with TAWA, running the mountaineering and trekking activities of this French adventure tourism agency that he previously helped set up in La Paz. Although much of last season was spent trekking with groups in the lowland area, he guided Illampu twice and Illimani four times. Recently he discovered a series of walls up to 500 m high in the Santa Cruz department and has plans to go back in the rainy season to attempt some climbing.

Author Yossi Brain, 32 years old, disappeared tragically on September 25th 1999 during an ascent of the Cerro Presidente in the Apolobamba Cordillera.

Bolivia: A Climbing Guide by Yossi Brain. Offers a selection of ascents on peaks in the four main Cordilleras: Apolobamba, Real, Quimsa Cruz and Occidental. Ed. The Mountaineers, Seattle 1999.

La Cordillera Real de los Andes by Alain Mesili, Editorial Los Amigos del Libro, La Paz, 1996.

The ANDES of BOLIVIA, A Climbing Guide and Adventures by Alain Mesili, Editorial CIMA, La Paz 2003.

LLAMA CARAVANS OF THE ANDES

BY TERRY L. WEST

FOR CENTURIES, LLAMA TRADE CARAVANS HAVE PROVIDED THE PRINCIPAL LINK BETWEEN PASTORALISTS OF THE ANDEAN HIGHLANDS AND AGRICULTURISTS WHO INHABIT THE VALLEYS.

From Lake Titicaca in Bolivia, the Desaguadero River meanders southward for 200 miles to Lake Poopó. Off the southern edge of this lake, at an altitude of some 12,000 feet, lies the canton of Pampa Auliagas. The 3.000 Aymara-speaking inhabitants of this cold and arid plateau region subsist on a combination of pastoralism and agriculture, raising sheep and llamas for meat and wool and cultivating potatoes and quinoa, a native cereal. Because frost and drought endanger even these high altitude crops, which are the dietary staples of the area, the people of Pampa Aullagas depend on exchange with people living at lower altitudes, where agriculture is less precarious. Like pastoralists throughout the Andean highlands, they not only have the motive to engage in trade but also possess the means-animals that can transport the products that come from the various levels of this "vertical environment." Llamas, in addition to serving as a source of animal products and as local beasts of burden, have for centuries been assembled into caravans for this long-distance trade. More sure-footed on the rugged terrain than the burros (and horses) imported by the Spaniards, the native llamas are also cheaper to maintain. They can forage along the route for their food, while burros, the usual beasts of burden in no pastoral areas, require fodder that has to be grown or purchased.

As accustomed as they may be to physical discomfort, the Aymara find journeying with llamas an extraordinary hardship. "To travel with llamas is to suffer," is the refrain of those familiar with the experience. In recent years, as the people of Pampa Aullagas have found alternative means of obtaining valley products, they have tended to abandon the arduous task of conducting llama caravans. Many drovers have so depleted their stock of male llamas by butchering them for market that they lack sufficient numbers to outfit future expeditions. When llama caravans were the rule rather than the exception, however, they helped occupy the dead time between the May harvest and the September planting. In years of poor harvest and famine, entire families embarked on such caravans in the search for food.

Because of a severe drought, the harvest of 1977 was a dismal one, giving me the opportunity to take part in a llama caravan that under other circumstances would probably not have been organized. The instigator was fifty-year-old Sergio, who was accompanied by his new son-in-law, Hilario, age twenty-seven. Hilario confided to me that at that time of the year he normally would be in the Department of Santa Cruz working as a migrant labourer, but he was going along out of obligation to his new father-in-law. The rather domineering Sergio had also succeeded in getting Hilario to convince his own father to join them. Four years older than Sergio, Gregorio had last gone on a caravan in 1974. Because of his age he had not anticipated going on any more, and he had gradually sold off the thirty mature pack llamas he had used on his last caravan, butchering them for the meat market.

Before we began to load for our departure, which took place May 17, there was a brief farewell ceremony. Sergio's aged mother provided a tin incense holder, and Hilario's older brother and wife supplied alcohol. Everyone present sat or squatted in a semicircle, exchanged coca leaves for ritual chewing, and drank sugar cane alcohol. By turns, the three drovers bared their heads and knelt in prayer. Holding the burning incense tray aloft, each beseeched the earth spirits for a safe and successful trip. Then we loaded our cargoes and set out on our journey.

Llama caravans from Pampa Aullagas may be termed salt caravans because salt is the bulk of the cargo the Aymara inhabitants take to trade. In the past, drovers made a one-week trek with their llamas to the salt flats of Uyuni, sixty miles to the south. There they purchased salt from the local residents, pausing a week before making the return trip. Now, most acquire the salt from truckers who transport it to Pampa Aullagas for sale. Then, following the harvest, troops of cargo-laden llamas and their drovers depart Pampa Aullagas on a three-month trade circuit to valleys in the east, where the salt is exchanged for the products of the local Quechua-speaking agriculturists. These include wood, medicinal herbs, and above all, foodstuffs, among which maize ranks first, both for domestic and ceremonial consumption. Until the last few years, no major ritual ceremony in Pampa Aullagas was complete without the serving of corn dishes and maize beer, and even

now, guests who enter the houses of local authorities on special occasions are expected to genuflect before a wall altar containing ears of corn. Drovers on caravans will kiss the first few ears of maize they receive en route in exchange for a handful of salt. They also recite prayers to the tunari, or "valley," where maize is grown.

On the basis of precedent, drovers from Pampa Aullagas visit specific valley destinations so that both men and cargo are dispersed equitably throughout trade areas. This enables drovers to estimate the quantity of salt they need to take and the amount of maize they will receive. It also assures long-term relations with specific caseros, or "trade partners." Since the Aymara drovers and their Quechua clients share neither ethnic, kinship, nor communal ties, the establishment of binding casero agreements represents the main link between two otherwise distrustful populations. The potential theft of cargo or animals worries drovers, whereas valley residents are concerned about crop damage from strayed llamas. If drovers have been known to cheat on measurements, valley people have been known to receive cargoes on trust and disappear without reciprocating. Establishment of casero ties-and concomitant personal ones-mitigates this mutual distrust. To further cement their bond, easeros exchange gifts and services and, in some cases, sanctify their ties through the institution of compadrazgo, the relationship of co-parenthood that is established between parents and godparents.

Drovers learn routes and acquire caseros by accompanying their fathers, uncles, older brothers, or other men as helpers. As one drover explained, "When one serves as a helper, you are introduced to people. The next year, when you return to the area, you have your clients. When you travel with your father, you make caseros with the sons of his caseros.

Most of the veteran drovers that I met began their apprenticeship as helpers to their fathers at age six to eight. A helper is usually a man's son or nephew but can be a daughter or niece if a male helper is not available. Also, young men whose own fathers lack llamas may volunteer to assist drovers to whom they are unrelated. In this way, they obtain maize for their parents, plus experience for their own eventual caravans. The standard compensation for such helpers in Pampa Aullagas in the 1970s was the free use of five of the employer's llamas for the transport of the helper's own trade goods.

Helpers are expected to perform irksome, low-prestige chores, such as fetching water and gathering dung for fuel. On our 1977 expedition, Hilario served as helper mainly to his father, while I acted as Sergio's helper. The caravan contained a total of fifty-five llamas, of which twenty-eight belonged to Gregorio and his family and twenty-seven to Sergio. There were also three burros to carry utensils and provisions and to serve as pack animals once we reached our destination. Each drover was responsible for looking after his own animals and for conducting his own trading, although on the march the animals intermingled freely, with one man walking behind them and one on each side of the caravan.

Only male llamas are used as pack animals, and they are usually castrated because the drovers believe that this makes them more resistant to fatigue. Caravan llamas range in age from three to seven, with ages four to six regarded as the best. Whenever possible, caravan veterans are selected as lead animals. The average mature male llama can carry a load of about seventy-five pounds, with some capable of sustaining a hundred pounds over short distances. To avoid unduly fatiguing their llamas, most drovers limit their cargo weight to between fifty and sixty pounds.

The salt we transported came in both solid blocks and in granulated chunks. The latter are carried in llama-hair bags, which weigh about fifty pounds when half full. The bag is draped across the back of the llama, with the salt separated into two equal compartments and tied on with an eight-foot length of thick, braided llama-hair rope. Salt blocks, purchased in pairs, are wrapped in coarse straw (to protect the llama's back) and are linked together with strands of llama-hair rope. Draped over the llama and tied on by ropes, two blocks are designated "one cargo" of salt, equivalent to a bag. We took fewer cargoes than animals to allow younger, weaker llamas a respite. Each morning we took care to leave unloaded the half dozen llamas that had been particularly fatigued the previous day, rotating their loads to stronger animals.

A typical day's travel for us averaged six hours, beginning at about 9:30 A.M. and ending at 3:30 P.M., in time for the llamas to graze. Once on the move, we seldom stopped to rest until camp was made. Veteran drovers attempt to pace their daily march so as to reach familiar campsites each afternoon. In addition to pasture, access to water holes and firewood were important considerations. Only occasionally are there stone corrals in which to herd the animals at night. The lack of corrals complicated our daily chore of loading and unloading the cargoes.

Although a relative of the camel, the shorter llama is always loaded when standing. Only semi-domesticated, llamas are not reared from birth to be pack animals. Our llamas were not trained to harness and only partially trained to voice commands, and we had to start, stop, and guide them by flailing a short length of rope, whistling, and making body blocks. The first few days of the journey were a constant battle to prevent the escape of llamas to their home territory, and throughout the trek we were kept constantly busy herding grazing strays back into the main mass of the caravan. Novice pack animals had to be load broken by tying light bundles, such as ponchos or blankets, on their backs.

Our principal morning chore, right after breakfast, was to load the animals for the day, through a hectic but well-established routine. First, we herded the animals into a compact mass close to the stacked cargoes. A number of pack ropes were then tied together to form one long rope, which was laid on the ground in the form of a large U. Once the animals were herded into this U, the ends of the rope were quickly raised off the ground, pulled together, and tied. This formed a corral around the midsections of the bunched llamas; a second rope was then wrapped around the herd at the knee level. While one of us remained on the outside, circling the corral to prevent escapes, the others climbed inside the ropes and, using shorter pack ropes, linked small groups of adjoining animals by binding their necks together. When all the llamas were bound into clusters of four to six, we could remove the outside restraint ropes and begin the loading. Scurrying back and forth between the stacked cargo and the waiting llamas, each drover tied his loads onto the backs of the pack animals with a slipknot. When a cluster had been loaded, the rope binding their necks was released and they were allowed to graze. Lastly, the camp utensils were loaded on the burros, the llamas united, and the caravan set off for the day. The whole procedure usually took us one hour.

Unloading was done in the same manner until the llamas became habituated. Then it could be accomplished without ropes, simply by forming the animals into a mass and darting in and jerking the slipknots loose with one hand while lifting the cargoes off with the other. This technique enabled us to unload in less than twenty minutes. Once unloaded, the scattered packs and tie ropes had to be gathered and arranged. Each drover on a caravan not only recognizes his own animals but can also identify his own cargo bags and ropes. Each man usually tends to his own tasks before helping a fellow drover with his.

Before being stacked, bags were inspected for holes, tears were sewn, the straw that protected the blocks was redistributed, and frayed ropes were replaced. We then stacked the cargo in piles to form a windbreak, and laid out bedding on the sheltered side. This done, one person was sent for water, while another prepared a crude fireplace. Only then would we take a rest break, eating a snack of flour mixed with water and sugar. Immediately afterward, everyone spread out to gather sagebrush or dried dung for the fire.

Once the sun went down, the winter chill came rapidly upon us. Huddled around the cook's fire, we would eagerly await our first meal since breakfast. For both meals we had lahua, a stew made of flour, lard, water, salt, fresh and freeze-dried potatoes, and an occasional slice of carrot or onion. A piece of dried meat bone would be added to the pot for Stock. Gregorio and Sergio took turns cooking. The diet was monotonous, but hunger made us lap up the last drop. Supper over, the 'voluble Sergio would discourse in Aymara until chill or fatigue drove everyone to bed. Once we had left the plateau and entered the eastern Andean mountains through a series of passes, the extreme cold prevented a sound sleep. Intermittently dozing and conversing, we would pass the night. Everyone slept fully clothed, wearing two pairs of pants and a jacket.

On our route we sometimes followed roads passable by truck and bordered by homesteads and fields. At other times we took shortcuts over wind-swept knolls along trails made by years of human and animal passage. Yet even in the coldest, most barren regions, there were signs of human habitation. We observed circular huts of straw or rock used by isolated herders, tiny potato patches tended by aged men, and women carrying infants on their backs in a blanket tied over the shoulder.

As we wound through trails cut through rock crevices so narrow that the packs would scrape on either side, we noticed droplets of blood spattered on the rocks. The blood was from llamas whose feet had been cut on the jagged surfaces. At night we would tackle the animals with the worst wounds and treat them. With me holding the animal on its side, Hilario would urinate into a can and pour the urine into the cuts as disinfectant. Gregorio would then use a knife to pry out chunks of gravel from the moistened wound. Once they were cleaned out, he would squeeze daubs of llama lard into the open cuts. Both men would then work together to slip each claw of the cloven hoof through slits in a four-inch square of llama hide. Thongs were then run through holes punched on each corner and the "sandal" was bound to the animal's foot.

On May 31 we began to enter the valley that was our destination, although the transition was not a clear one. Instead, there was a series of canyons that we had to drop into and then climb out of. Morning might find us in a warm, narrow river canyon where peach trees grew, while in the afternoon, we would be a thousand feet above it on a grassy, wind-swept knoll where only flocks of sheep and llamas grazed. Both men and animals being weary, it was with great relief that we reached the temperate valley floor on June 5. Now it was fleas, not the cold, which plagued us at night.

We camped on the banks of the Moscari River, which we followed downstream toward our destination. On June 7 we travelled up a small feeder streambed and took a narrow, uphill path that led to the hamlet where we would stray and trade. In single file the caravan wound its way up the steep path while we scrambled alongside to fight jams caused by irritated llamas. One would try to crowd ahead of the rest. "bile another, equally aggressive beast would take offence and begin to spit in the eyes and nip at the neck and ears of the offended llama. Until we parted them, the whole trail would be blocked by the combatants. Once, when out of frustration I used blows to separate a group, Sergio chastised me by casually remarking, "Gringo, one must have the patience of Jesus Christ to travel with llamas." Gradually the trail levelled on, and we made camp at dusk, exhausted. The next morning at dawn Sergio discovered that in the darkness he had spread his blankets over an ants' nest. This hillside was to be our final camp, where the llamas would remain pastured. From then on, one man would stay to guard the camp while the others would visit clients and arrange trades. The burros would be used to transport cargo to and from the houses of the local residents. June 8 was the festival of Corpus Christi, and my companions spent the morning in celebration of our safe arrival.

Sergio and Hilario arose before dawn and went uphill to a rock formation to await the morning sun. There, facing east, they made offerings to the mountain spirits in the morning solitude by burning llama lard, incense, herbs and coca leaves. On their return they continued their ritual libation of alcohol to the such an extent that Hilario was sent to buy another bottle. In our journey we had covered some 180 miles in twenty-two days, including seven rest days along the way.

Scattered throughout the canyon we had reached were tiny hamlets interspersed with farmland and isolated houses wherever the terrain was flat. Thorn bush and cactus grew in the dry grasslands that formed the mountainsides, but where there were clearings and water, the soil was rich in vegetation. People were at work in the fields trimming ears of corn off dried stalks or cutting other stalks to dry. Cattle used for ploughing were tethered in fields of stubble. Near people's homes were large trees on whose lower forks stalks of maize were stored for fodder. Next to the plots of maize were smaller ones of broad beans, peas, and squash.

Before the development of motor roads, llama caravans were the only outlet for surplus maize. Valley residents require salt for themselves, their draft animals, and goats. According to the drovers, the valley people are also anxious to trade their yearly surplus because insect larvae infest stored maize and render it fit only to feed to chickens and pigs. In contrast, on the arid plateau, maize, freeze-dried potatoes, and quinoa can be stored for years.

When a caravan arrives, valley people are generally busy with the harvest, they expect the drovers to shell their own maize. After the trade has been agreed on, a drover enters his client's patio and is presented with mounds of dried ears to shell. He spreads the ears over a blanket and, with bare feet, treads them vigorously to snap off the dried kernels. If the maize is still wet, then the kernels must be rubbed off by spindling the ears between the palms of the hand. The friction that results causes sores and even bleeding. This and the shrinkage that occurs as the maize dries explain why drovers will delay their departure from the valley until the end of June rather than accept water-soaked maize in trade. While it might seem burdensome for drovers to shell their own maize, they have the advantage of choosing the quality of ears to shell.

Those who still travel with llamas are mainly pastoralists who lack money for truck fare or market purchase. The beneficial exchange rate they enjoy also motivates them: "With llamas there is no transportation charge, only physical suffering-work. In the market, when you buy maize you get an exact weight. When we trade, it is done by estimate, and we always get an extra amount."

In remote areas frequented by llama caravans, traditional forms of measurement by volume are still used. At present, salt is traded on a volume-for-volume basis. If the harvest is good, the valley people will be especially generous with their surplus to compensate for the bad years, when they cannot reciprocate adequately for the cargoes of salt. When the maize is plentiful, the llamas return burdened to capacity, and sometimes fatigued llamas weaken and die.

Nineteen seventy-seven, however, was one of the poorer years, and when Sergio, Gregorio, and Hilario set off on July 12 for the return trip to Pampa Aullagas, they were not enthusiastic about the results of their venture. Although they returned with other foodstuffs as well, they were particularly dissatisfied with the amount of corn they had acquired: Sergio had fourteen cargoes of corn (700 pounds) and Gregorio only ten. Hilario declared his intention to work in Santa Cruz the next year and purchase maize in the valley with part of his earnings. None of them planned to travel with llamas any more.

Archaeological evidence indicates that llama caravans existed in the Andes almost 4,000 years ago, but the system of interdependence that has for so long operated between highland drovers and their valley trade partners is breaking down under the impact of commercialism. Markets have eroded the barter system that prevailed for centuries, and middlemen, travelling in trucks and buying maize with cash, have forced down the exchange rates, which once were more favorable to drovers.

Traditionally, the primary goal of all

drovers was the provisioning of their households, not monetary gain; they were concerned with the quantities of products traded, rather than their monetary values. This ideal is reflected in the traders' custom of not mentioning the cash value of exchange items during their transactions. Lately, however, migrant labor opportunities created by an agricultural boom in the Department of Santa Cruz have induced the new generation to take a more calculating look at the economics of llama caravans. The young men of Pampa Aullagas do not consider the profits sufficient compensation for the effort that must be expended. They can earn enough as wage laborers in the same amount of time to buy the maize they need and still have money to spare.

While recent increases in the price of oil in some Andean regions appear to have given llama transport a new lease on life, there are other considerations that spell a permanent decline in the caravans of Pampa Aullagas. Following the introduction of tractors in 1972, agricultural production rose as lands formerly used for grazing were opened up to cultivation. This both reduced the need for llama ownership and constricted the amount of pastureland. At about the same time, some local residents purchased large trucks, which are a more convenient form of transportation to the valleys, as well as to the nearby weekly market where maize and other valley products can be purchased. Finally, the construction of a secondary school has helped to deprive drovers of their apprentice helpers. Exposed to the opportunities and values of modern society, the youth of Pampa Aullagas have become both independent and disdainful of their parents' occupations. Many hope to be teachers or truck drivers or at least migrant workers, to earn money and emulate urban ways. To them, travelling with or herd llamas is old-fashioned and even degrading.

TINKU, MORE THAN A STREET BRAWL

BY EIMEAR LAFFAN

THE ANNUAL "TINKU" RITUAL IS MORE THAN MEETS THE EYE. THE VIOLENCE AT THE CENTER OF THE FESTIVAL IS A MEDIUM THROUGH WHICH SOCIAL HARMONY IS PRESERVED AND FUTURE PROSPERITY GUARANTEED.

At first glance the hills that descend over the small village of Macha provide the perfect backdrop for an annual festival. On seeing the natives who descend from these hills fight indiscriminately, one wonders how such beauty can breathe such violence. But all is not as it seems, and hidden beneath the brutality lies a rich Andean tradition that predates even the conquistadors.

Literally meaning 'to meet' in Quechua, "Tinku" is a gathering of the surrounding communities of Macha, in the department of Potosi. They come to give thanks for their crops, offer sacrifices to "Pachamama" and to fight. This year's festival took place from 3-5 May.

This is certainly a festival of contrasts. Dancing and drinking, families and fighting, worship and sacrifice all play a significant role. The first of the 62 surrounding communities descend on the small plaza in Macha on Friday night shortly after midnight. Each group, which represents a single community, arrives at a different time. Those communities that are bigger or come from farther away arrives later, even into the following day. Some dance and drink for up to 50 km to get there.

Dancing takes center stage on arrival amid a backdrop of charangoes and zamponas and the strange cacophonous singing of the women. The songs are about folklore and history, varying slightly from community to community. They play their instruments while forming a circle, the women occupying an inner circle. One member cracks a whip urging either faster movement or a change in direction. This builds up to a stomping dance unlike any you are likely to have witnessed before.

Most striking is the dress. Luminous socks of triangular patterns and multicolored hats abounding with tassels hanging from arms, legs and heads alike. "Bonito, no?" one of the locals inquired. "Si, muy bonito", I replied without hesitation. It wasn't an untruth.

Dating back to Inca times, the natives beliefs in the benevolence of spirits is still very much alive, along with their belief in the therapeutic effects of alcohol. The Queen of these celebrations is undoubtedly mother earth herself, "Pachamama," whilst there is some dispute about who is King; "chichi" and "puro," both alcoholic drinks, vie for the title.

Prior to drinking, some of the liquor is poured on the ground as an offering to "Pachamama." She is believed to help bring forth crops. The locals believe that in taking from the earth, they too must give something back, whether in the form of alcohol, animal sacrifices or even their own blood.

And here comes the seemingly strange conviction, that while fighting, the spillage of blood is something to appreciate and be grateful for. This ritual of fighting is one that marks the beginning of the harvest. The blood acts as fertilizer and in this way promotes the harvest. Fighting tended to be controlled at times, with the police cracking their whips to keep the crowd back, and uncontrolled at others, with the throwing of rocks at one particularly edgy moment. Rounds of gas were fired by the police at these times, but only served to disperse the crowds temporarily. Although the "Tinku" was previously a fight to the death, killings have largely stopped because of police control. Still, it is best to watch from afar at these moments.

While it is interesting to see the locals try to entice the foreigners to participate in the dancing and fighting, (whether because they believe they will win or because they believe the offer will be politely refused) it's probably best to avoid confrontation.

Indeed, if you found yourself unexpectedly in Macha (though unlikely considering its location) you would be taken aback by the random men lying along the pavements with blood flowing from their noses and faces, and perhaps even more surprised that everybody largely ignores them and carries on with their business. The only exception was the occasional irritated wife. Given the positive nature of the spillage of blood, I saw one farmer crying and had to wonder if it was because he had escaped unharmed.

The area that surrounds Macha has always been famous for its warriors. Similarly, the exchange of socioeconomic goods is an old practice predating even Columbus. To weaken and conquer the people, the Spanish created a division between the communities of the Altiplano and those of the lowlands that led to greater poverty and consequent tensions. Today, the communities still come together to exchange goods. Yet, while they may have grievances over prices, quantities and so on, confrontations are avoided by knowledge that the "Tinku" ritual will offer an opportunity to settle any issues or disputes.

One of the primary events of this festival is the Blessing of the Crosses, a tradition completely separate from the fighting. Each community, even those of less than 20 families, brings their crosses to be blessed in Macha. Prior to the arrival of the Conquistadors, some interpretation of the cross did exist and this continues to be a symbol of the community in addition to its now religious and Christian significance. But why Macha? Macha was where the tower was built as a focal point for the worship of the surrounding communities. Furthermore the area itself already had significance as a worship area. They throw puro on the tower as an offering and a symbol of their respect.

Something new this year was an actual meeting about the "Tinku." The movement towards the preservation of this native Andean tradition has to be welcomed. "Tinku" is more about giving thanks and offering sacrifices than about brutality. It is about tradition and pride and should not be reduced to a less significance.

CHANGING CHARM OF CHOLITA

BY SARAH BALMOND

"END OF CHOLITA? ARE YOU CRAZY? THAT MEANS END OF BOLIVIA."
QUOTE FROM A SHOP OWNER.

The cholita is quintessentially Bolivian and a defining feature of South America. Watch her walk heavy with a baby on her back, talk to her on the roads edge as she sells salteñas and see her selling fruit or homemade goods in a market. Bright skirts, beautifully embroided shawls and bolero hats add a touch of magic and surrealism to the Bolivian landscape. But what are the secrets behind this traditional costume? Why does the cholita dress this way, how has her fashion changed, and what does her future hold?

The word cholita refers to Bolivian women of Quechuan or Aymaran descent who have moved from the country to the city, but continue to dress in a traditional way. There is much debate concerning the origin of the word chola, but most seem to think it grew from either the Aymaran word "chulu" which means mestizo in Castillian Spanish or the word "chulo" used to describe people from lower class Spain.

Clothes are signs of specific cultures and can therefore be considered as forms of political expression. Traditional attire like that of the cholitas reflects national Bolivian identity representing a resistance to outside Western influences. Sociologist Charles Sacks says "cholitas are urban women who cling to tradition." The cholita outfit was first introduced into Bolivia by the Spanish King in the nineteenth century. He dictated that women wear a *pollera* (skirt) or *vestido* (dress), a *blousa paseña* (blouse), a *manta* (shawl), a *sombrero* (hat), *zapatos* (shoes) and some sort of jewelry. This fashion was very popular in Toleda, Spain at the time and was considered a respectable alternative to the women's indigenous clothes. There is a certain degree of homogeneity to the fashion of the cholita although there are minor variations between regions.

The pollera is perhaps the most distinctive part of the cholitas' costume. It is made up of four petticoats, "enaguas" including twelve meters of material, and fans out into a magnificent bell shape, giving the impression of a larger bottom half. The cholitas consider this to be both beautiful and feminine. The skirt has four to five horizontal pleats "alforzas" and is tied with a string "hilera." Some women complain of the sheer weight of the skirt but nowadays petticoats are made from lace, making it lighter and easier to wear. The petticoats were traditionally made from white linen or lambs wool.

The *pollera* is traditionally handmade and until 1920 would have been sewn from taffeta and brocade. Today, however, many cholitas, purchase factory made skirts for economic reasons. These cost around 150 Bolivians, are usually made of cotton, and come in a whole array of colors. For parties the cholita will wear a special pollera - something brighter, more ornate, and probably made from silk. These skirts are mini pieces of art work and reflect the craftsmanship of the cholitas. In some cases they become family heirlooms and are passed down from mother to daughter. Over the years details of the pollera have changed. Function now wins out over fashion. For example, at the beginning of the twentieth century all skirts would have featured a hemline "enagua" ten centimeters long. This has now been abandoned in favour of a more simple design which requires less handiwork.

The *blousa* is sometimes referred to as a *chaquetilla* and is the item which has changed most over the years. Traditionally made from silk or lace, but it is now more common to see a cholita wearing a machine-made *blousa* that is more loose-fitting and basic. The long fringed manta is still folded in a rectangle pattern similar to how the nunstas women (princess' of the Inca Empire) used to do. Traditionally the shawl would have been handmade or woven from llama's wool. These days, however, it seems that anything goes - the cholita will wear everything, from extravagantly decorated silk, to a simple acrylic cloth. The manta is pinned at the front with a large broach referred to as a tupa. This is typically disc shaped with a simple decorative head and set with jewels. The women also would have worn *faluchos*, earings of pure gold and cultured pearls. Today though cholitas wear all types of inexpensive fashion jewelry. Sometimes the cholita will simply fasten her manta with a safety pin whilst working.

Up until the 1930s cholitas would have worn high heels or midcalf boots. These would have been tied at the front and made from champagne colored leather or silk. These shoes however were thought to be specifically American (and impractical) and so were swapped for a flatter style, known as *plantillas*. Cholitas do not carry handbags, but rather *ahuyayos*, large

pieces of multicolored cloth which act as a carry all. This cloth is typical to a region and is made from a weaving technique that has been used in Bolivia for over three thousand years. Unfortunately as more and more cholitas purchase ready made cloth, this skill seems to be dying out.

Cholitas part their hair in the middle, braid it into two plaits, and join it with *tullma*, a long piece of black wool which gives the impression of added length. The longer the hair, the more beautiful the woman is considered. Single women at parties sometimes attach colored baubles to the cord in order to attract attention.

On top of their heads cholitas wear the *bolero* - this is considered the most important item of clothing and you will not see a cholita without one. The shape of the hat varies throughout Bolivia; in La Paz the hat is small and short, in Cochabamba the rim is broader. There is much debate over the origin of the hat, but local legend has it that a German factory man in 1925 imported derby hats, didn't know what to do with them, and so fobbed them off to the women. Fashion spread, and the hat stuck. Now an Italian company, Borsalino, mass produces them and ships up to twenty thousand hats to Bolivia each year.

As Bolivia accelerates in its race for modernization some worry that the cholita will be left behind. A shop owner who sells *polleras* says "We only sell to the older women. I can't remember the last time I sold something to the next generation." It seems younger women no longer want to dress and mothers tend not to encourage the cholita style, fearing it may hinder their daughters progress. Some even look upon the cholita as an embarrassing anomaly. A twenty five year old female dressed in Nike trainers, jeans and a t-shirt says "Why would we dress like that? We have nothing in common with those people." However, the end of the cholita is by no means near and most argue that the worry is all for nothing. One woman shop owner says "End of cholita? Are you crazy? That means end of Bolivia." It seems that the cholita is here to stay.

THE SACRED AND SEXY SPUD

BY PETER MCFARREN

BIOTECHNOLOGY AND GENETIC ENGINEERING USED TO HELP BOLIVIAN FARMERS.

TRADITIONAL PRESENT

Perhaps Bolivia's greatest and least credited gift to the world is the potato. It's a crop considered by the nearly half the world as its own. For McDonalds the home of the potato is Idaho, for the Irish it's as synonymous with life as Guinness. People fry them, boil them, bake them, roast or mash them —everybody seems to have their favorite technique. They have been described as great aphrodisiacs and pilloried as the food of the devil. Their adoption aided and abetted the growth of England through the industrial revolution and their failure wiped out almost half the Irish nation. While the potato has been spreading accross the world Quechua and Aymara farmers have been growing almost 800 different types of potato, oblivious to its gradual domination of a large part of the world's diet. Now scientists in Bolivia are trying to help the original cultivators of this crop to fight disease, drought and frost,while maybe learning a few tricks themselves from Bolivia's indigenous peoples.

The potato has completed an incredible journey since its origin on the shores of Lake Titicaca. Eight thousand years ago nomadic Indians began collecting wild potatoes from the altiplano. As the people turned to more sedentary farming lives, the potato became a cultivated crop and a staple for the Aymara and other Indian farmers that inhabited the region between the Peruvian city of Cuzco and the southern shores of Lake Titicaca. When the Spanish —-under

the command of conquistador Francisco Pizarro — conquered the region, they were unaware of the treasure that lay below their feet. They had eyes only for the gold of the Inca Atahuallpa. Yet this muddied lump was also to later make the crossing to Europe and become one of the world's four most important foodstuffs. Five centuries later it continues to reign throughout the world. "Compared to the vast benefits this versatile plant has bestowed on humankind, all the gold of Peru becomes small potatoes," said anthropologist Robed E Rhoades in a 1982 issue of the National Geographic.

The potato is produced in 130 countries and one year's crop is worth a billion dollars, more than the value of all the gold and silver the Spanish took out of the New World. The average annual worldwide crop could cover a four-lane superhighway circling the world six times.

The journey has now, however, come full circle with the latest in genetic engineering being used to assist the people that first gave the potato to the world.

The Potato Goes Hi-Tech

Ana Gloria Badani, a Bolivian lab specialist, carefully selects tissues from lab-produced potato seedlings and discards those that are damaged by viruses. She and another 45 employees of the Potato Research Project, working high in the Andes, are using state-of-the-art biotechnology to yield new potato seeds from native varieties that will be resistant to worms, drought, frost and parasites.

Their work is likely to have a major impact on improving yields for the more than 800,000 Bolivians who depend on potato farming for their livelihood. This work, carried out under the umbrella of the Peru-based International Potato Center (CIP) and supported by the Bolivian Government, the World Bank and the Swiss Government, is likely to have an impact far beyond Bolivia's borders.

Not far from the center, Elsa Lopez, 24, a Quechua Indian farmer and mother of three, uses a hoe to harvest one of the 800 varieties of Bolivian potatoes, much as her ancestors did thousands of years ago. Drought and frost have reduced her harvest by half, but for her this is nothing new.

"By increasing potato yields and lowering potato prices we should make a major impact on a large segment of the population," says Dr Campos of the Government's Bolivian Institute of Agricultural Technology (IBTA).

Potato weevils, late blight and bad weather destroy as much as 50 percent of potato crops in Bolivia, according to Dr. Andre Devaux, a potato scientist who is co-director of the Potato Research Center.

In the lab, Badani points out 1/8 inch potato seeds that have been produced in test tubes by combining commercially available potato seeds with wild native varieties still found in the high Andes. Through this process, scientists at the center are producing a new generation of potato seeds that offer resistance to destructive pests. Devaux, who has worked at the center in Cochabamba department since 1989 when the project began, says, "Since potatoes are originally from here we have all of the genetic elements and conditions on hand to carry out tests to control plagues and the effects of frost while taking advantage of modern techniques from the US and Europe."

Not far from the lab, computers regulate the climate of greenhouses, subjecting the seeds and young plants to below-freezing temperatures in an attempt to determine which hybrids best resist frost. Those chosen are taken to the fields where Quechua Indian farmers test them. A two to three degree resistance to frost should increase potato yields by up to one-third, says agronomist Willman Garcia. After developing 100,000 hybrids the center has identified five that are worth developing because of their resistance to pests, especially the potato late blight that was responsible for the Irish famine that killed a million people in the mid-19th century.

Through genetic engineering scientists are hoping to control late blight and are especially concerned with new resistant strains that have developed in recent years and could wreak havoc on worldwide potato crops. Another dire threat to the potato is the weevil. In many areas of Bolivia 80 percent of the harvest is attacked by this bug that lays its eggs while the potatoes are in the fields and can wipe out nearly a whole crop in little over a month. Scientists at the center have also developed and are selling bio-pesticides to control moths that destroy potato seeds in the Bolivian highlands. The current practice — clearly less than ideal — is for farmers to spray their potato seeds, which are often kept in their living quarters, with toxic chemicals such as DDT.

One of the most important activities carried out at the center is the development of a germplasm bank that currently houses 800 varieties of potato ranging in color from purple, to deep red to yellow. The different strains — like the Parko, Lunku Ayanhuir, Kaysalla and Janko Choquepito — are being analyzed for use in hybrids in the hope of developing a group of super potatoes to take the vegetable into the next millennium.

A Potted History

Archaeological remains of potatoes along with maize, peppers and other tuber crops have been found dating from Nazca and other ancient cultures.

By the time of the rise of the Incas potatoes were a major South American food crop and had also become a ritual offering to Pachamama., the Mother Earth, who gave them up as bounty. The half-Indian/half-Spanish author Guaman Poma de Ayalat provides probably the earliest illustrations of these ritual practices and the agricultural techniques used by the Incas in the 15th and 16th centuries. By the time of the Spanish Conquest, their use had spread to the northern extremities of the Andes in what is now Venezuela and Colombia.

The potato presence in Europe was first recorded in 1567 in Antwerp. The 16th century herbalist Carol Clusius is believed to be responsible for the spread of the potato through the low countries of France, Germany and Switzerland. During the early years, however, the potato was cursed as an evil food and its cultivation was resisted by all but the poorest people. The Scots refused to eat it because it was not mentioned in the Bible and others attributed dire illnesses to its consumption. Many Europeans wanted nothing to do with this evil plant, and for nearly 200 years the potato remained a botanical curiosity.

Yet not all were against it. Lord Byron, for instance, believed the potato had aphrodisiac qualities. Its botanical family, Solanaceae, includes hallucinogenic and narcotic cousins, so his prognosis may not be unfounded. By the 18th century, its irresistible expansion had led it to become the abundant food source that experts say was necessary for the expansion of Europe's industrial base.

One key to this expansion was Frenchman Antoine-Auguste Parmentier, who survived as a prisoner of war in Germany in 1757 on nothing but potatoes. When he returned to France he found his countrymen were facing famine but refused to eat the potato due to its bad reputation. Parmentier convinced King Louis XV to grant him an abandoned field near Paris to grow a crop. Parmentier had royal guards stationed at the field during the day and withdrew them at night. Local farmers, convinced that the plants in the field were something special, stole the potatoes and planted them in their own fields. From then on the potato spread and became an indispensable part of French cuisine.

Sir Walter Raleigh first introduced the potato to Ireland when he planted it on his estate. Other absentee English landlords followed suit and in time Irish peasants grew, or were allowed to grow, virtually nothing else. When the potato blight came, the population's only food source was almost wiped out and millions died or emigrated. From Ireland it spread to Scotland, Norway, Sweden and Denmark. Potatoes weren't known in the US until 1621 when they were introduced by way of England and Bermuda. The potato chip was allegedly invented in 1853, according to Rhoades. "In Saratoga Springs, New York, short-order cook George Crum, an American Indian, got revenge on a customer who had complained about his thick fried potatoes. Crum defiantly prepared a batch of super thin slices and deep-fried them. The rest is history. Today potato chips are an industry that yields about US$3 billion a year."

The Multi-Talented Spud

According to Rhoades the potato is so nutritious that a man in Scandinavia lived healthily for 300 days on only potatoes dressed with a bit of butter. It takes seven pounds of them—about 23 potatoes—to total the 2,500 calories that an adult needs daily. So eating a spud without sour cream and butter is no more fattening than eating an apple. The potato is, in fact, 99.9 percent fat free. Potatoes also serve other purposes. They are used to make vodka and aquavit, processed into a starch, paste and dye and distilled into an alcohol suitable for car fuel.

"The potato yields more nutritious food, more quickly, on less land and in harsher climates than any of the other major crops such as wheat, corn, or rice," says Rhoades. On average it matures faster than any of these staples—in a period of 90 to 120 days. Nutritionists rate the quality of potato protein higher than that of the soybean, and a single spud can supply half the daily vitamin C requirement for an adult, as discovered by sea captains who carried potatoes to prevent scurvy among their crews. The potato is so adaptable that it grows anywhere from below sea level in the Netherlands to up 13,000-feet in the high Andes mountains of Bolivia. Europe and the republics of the former Soviet Union currently grow 75 percent of the world's potato crop.

On the shores of Lake Titicaca, Justo Choque, an Aymara Indian farmer, stomps on potatoes that aren't good enough for seeds or storage. The potatoes are spread out on the ground and exposed to below freezing temperatures and then left to dry in the sun. The potatoes are soaked in bags along Lake Titicaca and freeze-dried during the chilly altiplano nights. Farmers extract the water from the potatoes by stomping on them with their bare feet. Through this process of producing freeze-dried chuño Choque and over two million Bolivian Indian farmers assure their food supply for the dry season, or through drought spells.

For hundreds of years, herds of llamas have carried chuño from the highlands to the lowlands where they barter it for coca leaves and dried meat. Llama herders continue this cross-Andean journey today.

This marvelous and often little under-stood food crop continues to play an important role in Bolivia. Perhaps one day a top quality book or CD-ROM on the potato's fascinating history can be produced. It's a product so diverse and with such a long and fascinating history that it is not difficult to imagine the creation of a world-class museum devoted entirely to this important food staple. Maybe someday the potato, which provides employment to so many Bolivians and feeds so many people, will get the attention now reserved for the coca leaf and will take its place as the true sacred crop of Bolivia.

5

CONTEMPORARY ART
AND CULTURE

BOLIVIAN LITERATURE

BY LUIS H. ANTEZANA J.
TRANSLATED BY CARYN HOFF

Prominent features of Bolivian Literature include its modernist poetry, transformed by Rubén Dario, at the end of the nine-teenth-century. In the nineteenth century, three of the most important Bolivian poets, Ricardo Jaimes Freyre, Franz Tamayo and Gregorio Reynolds, are recognized for their distinct "mod-ernist" verses. Jaimes Freyre is celebrated for the lyricism of his poetry ("Imaginary wandering dove"); Tamayo for his search of Andean roots ("Yo fui el orgullo como se es la cumbre"); and Reynolds for his exploration of man ("¿Si morir será descansar?"). Shortly before, the works of Adela Zamudio (poetry and narrative) and Nataniel Aguirre's Juan de la Rosa (1909) addi-tionally rose to prominence.

Bolivian literature developed two very important themes. First, Alcides Arguedas' novel Raza de Bronce (1919) instigated the indigenous motif, which generated multiple res-onances in Bolivia and in other Andean coun-tries. At the same time, in the 1920s, a genre developed specific to Bolivia entitled the "encholamiento costumbrista." The "encholamiento" is both a social and racial type of mestizo: a criollo of the upper class falls in love and marries a "chola" (a white-Indian mes-tiza) belonging to the lower social stratum. The lovers are almost always "criollos" and "cholas." Although there are many books encompassing this theme, the most famous are the stories La misk'isimi (meaning "sweet mouth" in Quechua) by Adolfo Costa Du Rels and Carlos Medinaceli 's novel La ch'askañawi ("Eyes of Stars"). As

the titles indicate, the beauty of the cholas resides in those places (sugar, stars). Costa Du Rels wrote his works in French; Medinaceli, on the other hand, was an excellent literary critic. If "indigenismo" examines the problematic life of the indigenous in Bolivian society, the "encholamiento costumbrista" examines evolv-ing social relationships between criollos and cholas. Both genres emphasize rural life, taking place in the country or in small villages.

Between 1932 and 1935, Bolivia was at war with Paraguay. Although it lost part of its ter-ritory (in the "Southeast Chaco"), in retrospect, many consider the war and Bolivia's subse-quent defeat as crucial for the later development of the country: the necessity to transform the country would motivate the National Revolution of 1952 (nationalization of the mines, agrarian reform, universal suffrage and education reforms). The Chaco War became a common subject in Bolivian literature, poetry, song, and narrative. Three prominent works taking place in the Chaco region include Augusto Céspedes' Sangre de mestizos (1936), Oscar Cerruto's novel Aluvión de fuego (1935) and Costa Du Rels' Laguna H-3 (1944). (Those who enjoy poetry and song, may enjoy Jenny Cárdenas' CD "Homenaje a una generación histórica," a compilation of traditional music from the Chaco region. Cerruto's Aluvión de fuego refers to the Chaco War and integrates the indigenous prob-lem with the struggle of the "encholamiento." It, additionally, gathers from another tradition of Bolivian Literature: the mining narrative.

ART AND CULTURE

The genre of "mining literature" began in the era of Spanish colonization and continues until the present day. Bolivia, as it is well known, has always been a country dependent on mining: first silver (with the hill of Potosí during the Spanish Colonization) and, then, tin (during the republic). The colonial city of Potosí inspires a great deal of short stories and novels. For example, the celebrated Historia de Potosí [(1705-1736), 1965) written by Bartolomé Arzans de Orsúa y Vela included multiple stories which have been published as much in English (The Tales of Potosí), 1975, R.G. Padden [ed.]), as Spanish (Relatos de la Villa Imperial de Potosí, 2000, L. García Pabón [ed.]). Néstor Terán's novel Manchaypuytu (meaning "Large Pot," in Quechua, 1977) transpires in colonial Potosí and details the city's traditions. The "manchaypuytu" is a tragic love song.

Mining literature focuses on the "exterior" and "interior" worlds of the miner. In the "external" world, social and political problems are explored. The "internal" world examines, above all, a mythical world describing indigenous origins. Between the Chaco War and the National Revolution of 1952, the mining narrative denounced worker exploitation and the dangerous working conditions of the cavern. This narrative form was, albeit indirectly, part of the process which led to the Nationalization of the Mines in 1953. Novels that protest the dangerous work of the miners include Fernando Ramírez Velarde's Socavones de angustia and Augusto Céspedes' Metal del diablo (1946) about the life of a famous tin mogul, Simón I. Patiño. The novel denounces the uses and abuses of power in miner exploitation. (Metal del diablo is a mining version of Citizen Kane). In the 1970s, a transition occurred from the "interior" narrative to its "external" form. René Poppe's Los compañeros del tío (1977 demonstrates this new type of narrative, where fiction alters from traditional realism. "The uncle" indicated in the title is a metaphor for an idol, with devil's characteristics, that one might find at the entrance to the miner's caverns. It is customary to offer the idol cigarettes, coca leaves, or a little alcohol before beginning work. At the end of the 1960s, the Bolivian narrative undergoes a change in perspective from classical realism (traditional) to fiction. Two books, above all, mark this transition: Oscar Cerruto's Cerco de penumbras (1959) and Marcelo Quiroga Santa Cruz' novel Los deshabitados (1960). In this period, the Bolivian narrative was influenced by Latin American innovations in literature. Subjects such as the death of Che Guevara would be treated from these new perspectives and techniques, such as Renato Prada Oropeza's Los fundadores del alba and in Julio de la Vega's Matías, el apóstol suplente.

Meanwhile, Bolivian poetry did not lose the levels reached by its modernist poets. There are various anthologies—by Juan Quirós, Yolanda Bedregal and Edward Mitre (Mitre is not just an investigator, but an excellent poet)— that indicate its development. Let us honor two poets of the twentieth century. Oscar Cerruto is noted for his poetic perfection. Two compilations of his poetic work exist: Cántico Traspasado (1975) and Poesía (1985, P. Shimose [ed.]). Jaime Saenz' "Recorrer esta distancia" (Obra poética, 1975) is his most famous poem (tr. Italia, USA). His illustrious novel Felipe Delgado (1979) reinvented the city of La Paz from the viewpoint of an "aparapita" (an Aymaran immigrant stevedore). A new type of urban literature developed in La Paz, such as Juan de Recacochea's detective novel American Visa (1994) or in poetry called "Bohemia del averno" ("El averno," or "The Hell" was a bar for delinquents, the unemployed and poets [this may be seen in the first scenes of the film "Question of Faith" by Marcos Loayza]). Recently, in the United States, a compilation of Bolivian short stories was published (The Fat Man from La Paz, 2000, Rosario Santos [ed.]). The Fat Man from La Paz a good example of contemporary narrative, but the title is misleading ("From La Paz"). I am referring to Jorge Suárez' "El Otro Gallo" which occurs in Santa Cruz, and not La Paz, the same setting as the adventures of Luis Padilla, the "Bandido de la Sierra Negra."

Usually one thinks of Bolivia as an Andean country only, but in fact, 60% of its territory is tropical (the Amazonian plains and the Southeast Chaco). In the Chaco, there is another literary tradition. Jesús Urzagasti, for example, has written about the Chaco in relation to La Paz. His novel En el país del silencio (1987, translated to English in 1994) summarizes these worlds and their ties. Urzagasti's prose is notable for it's poetic quality. Manfredo Kempf Mercado's novel Luna de locos narrates the social life of the large haciendas in the Amazonian plains. Tito Gutiérrez Diseña's novel Mariposa blanca, on the other hand, describes individual and social upheaval in the Chapare zone where coca is cultivated. Other "tropical" writers include the "classic" Raúl Otero Reiche – Santa Cruz's Casa de la Cultura takes his name— and the poet and author of, among others, "Reflexiones maquiavélicas" (1985, Poemas 1988).

Reading Bolivian literature provides one with the possibility to cross its territories and relive its history. Orson Welles has compared Bolivia to the Vienna of the Third World: its multiple political, economic and social problems are accompanied, paradoxically, with remarkable aesthetic productions.

Cochabamba, August 2002.

Yolanda Bedregal

Yolanda Bedregal, poet, novelist, storyteller and sculptress, was proclaimed "Yolanda of Bolivia" in 1948 by the intellectual youth of the country represented by the national group "Gesta Bárbara," and "Yolanda de América" by the Society of Argentine Writers.

Bedregal was born into a family of artists and intellectuals in La Paz in 1916. She studied Art Composition at the Academia de Bellas Artes, where she subsequently taught sculpture and history of art. She was also a professor of esthetics at the Greater University of San Andrés. In 1936, she moved to the United States where she became the first Bolivian woman to obtain a scholarship for studies in the Barnard College at Columbia University.

Bedregal carried out a tireless effort towards the diffusion of literature through the multiple institutions she has founded and headed, such as the National Union of Poets and Writers and the Committee of Literature for Children. She has also served as the Director of the National Council of Culture of Alcaldia in La Paz.

Yolanda Bedregal is considered one of most significant authors in all of Bolivia, and in her long literary career she has published more than sixteen books comprised of poetry, stories, novels and anthologies. Naufragio, her first book, was published in 1936. Other publications of hers include more than fifty articles on a child's approach to the history of art, as well as articles on teaching, religion, myths, folklore, and the art of the Aymara and Quechua peoples. Many of her stories and poems have been translated into various languages and included in magazines and anthologies in both the United States and Europe.

She has received various honors for her work, including: the National Prize of Poetry, National Prize of the Department of Culture, National Prize of the Novel "Erich Guttentag" for her book Under the Dark Sun, the Great Order of the Bolivian Education, the Pedro Sunday Murillo Civic Honor, the Medal of Merit, the Shield of Weapons of the City of The Peace by Distinguished Services, and the Culture of the Foundation Manuel Vicente Ballivián medal. In 1993 The National Counsel of Rights for Mexican Women presented her with the title ¨Lady of America¨. In 1995 she received the Franz Tamayo medal in the degree of Great Cross and in 1996, she was awarded the Gabriela Mistral Honor by the government of Chile. In 1997 the Congress of Bolivia awarded her the medal from the National Parliament in the degree of the Gold Flag.

After she passed away the 22 of March 1999, the Bolivian state established the Yolanda Bedregal National Poetry competition to recognize a new generation of Bolivian Poets.

COTEMPORARY BOLIVIAN VISUAL ART, WHERE IT CAME FROM

BY PATRICIA TORDOIR

Little is known internationally of what Bolivia has to offer in the contemporary visual arts. Lack of promotion is coupled with the mentality of an indigenous people that reflects a land locked country stretching from Andean peaks to rainforests - inaccessible and separated from the rest of the world. As in most countries, society has dictated the form and development of the arts, but in Bolivia geography and the lack of possibilities open to an ignored population has played an important role. Education and voting rights only became available for the majority of the people in the middle of this century, and it can be said that until then, the arts followed a socially acceptable course.

Pre-Hispanic culture has survived in the textiles and customs of the people, while ceramics have taken over the styles of the ancient clay works. During the colonial times, religious figures were used to show the indigenous how appealing the Catholic world could be. With independence came the heroes and the portraits, a form of art that lasted until the turn to the twentieth century. During the first half of this century, land and cityscapes were the most important elements in Bolivian painting, as awareness arose of the beauty of the country. José García Mesa (c.1840-1905), while living in Europe, painted Bolivian landscapes from photographic images.

In 1937, Juan Rimsa (1898-1975) arrived from Lithuania and greatly influenced the young artists of Sucre and Potosi with his German expressionism. He used heavy palettes to depict the interaction of the Indian with nature. Arturo Borda (1883-1953), with a sense of social commitment, was probably the first accepted artist to depict the indigenous of the country, and brought about a recognition of the existence of the forgotten people. Cecilio Guzmán de Rojas (1899-1950) combined his interest with the colonial period with that of the Incas, and produced many society portraits with Inca features. Rimsa left for Mexico at the about the same time as Borda and Guzman de Rojas died, and a socialist government came into power in Bolivia.

The social revolution of 1952 that attempted to give identity to the indigenous folk of the country also managed to promote corruption, factionalism, and intolerance of political opponents. With the philosophy of renewing national awareness, culture was given a boost with the initiation of annual awards and exhibitions. The "Generation of '52" was formed by a group of younger artists who commented on the situation by portraying their political opinions. Two distinct groups emerged, those of the radical left with revolutionary ideas, and those who preferred to follow the non-committing form of abstractionism, but each developing its own form of nationalism. Muralism, taking a similar form to the Mexican expressionism of the 1920's, became very popular, bringing art to public buildings by depicting the class struggle. Miguel Alandia Pantoja (1914-1975) is known for his Palace mural that was destroyed by the military government in 1965. Walter Solón Romero (1925) and Gil Imaná (1933) are probably the most notable names of this period and also founders of the Grupo Anteo, which promoted the visual arts for the people. With a military take-over, ending the reign of a revolutionary government in 1964, muralism was prohibited and Gil Imana emerged as a canvas painter depicting solitary figures (usually women) coping with the harsh life of the Andes. Together with this change of power came an end to governmental support for the arts, and many socially committed artists fled the country, taking up residence in Europe or New York.

Maria Louisa Pacheco (1918-1982) and Marina Nuñez del Prado (1910-1995) are the best known names among Bolivian contemporary artists. Maria Louisa embraced indigenism early in her career, but over the years, living in Madrid and New York, her works took on a more abstract form, often with the mountains of her homeland. Nuñez del Prado was a sculptress of great influence to the Bolivian artist, always remaining true to her deeply ingrained love for the country.

Other notable names of the Generation of '52 are Enrique Arnal, Ted Carrasco, Oscar Pantoja, Ricardo Pérez Alcalá, Fernando Montes, Alfredo La Placa, and Inés Córdova, who all developed their individual styles with influences acquired from travels, combined with inspiration from their home country. Enrique Arnal (1932) uses dramatic brush strokes to depict his themes that have ranged from workers, condors, and nudes, to mine interiors and Andean peaks. Ted Carrasco (1933) works mainly in the different stones of Bolivia, erecting monuments to

man's relationship with nature. His stylised forms often offer the female figure as an earth Goddess. Oscar Pantoja (1925) has evolved into the only true abstractionist of Bolivia, producing vast canvases of poetic tranquillity. Ricardo Pérez Alcalá (1939) is revered in Bolivia as the master of the watercolour even though many of his greatest works have been executed in oils. His paintings show a tranquil form of Bolivian life. Fernando Montes (1930) has been a resident of London, U.K. since the '60s, but finds his inspiration in the mountainous regions of Bolivia. His paintings depict life on the "Altiplano" with a grey, earthy palette. Alfredo La Placa (1929) uses his domination of oils with a personal technique to convey the luminous colours and textures of the Andean world in his unique abstract forms. Inés Córdova (1927) uses textiles or metal in collages suggesting space without sky in the mountainous regions.

The Generation of '52 responded to the search for national identity that was encouraged by the government, but slowly moved away from pure indigenism. It is interesting to note that those who returned to Bolivia did not continue painting typical scenes, while Perez Alcala (Mexico) and Montes (England) have done so. There are a few names that must be noted, but do not belong to the generation of '52, nor to the new generation that emerged after democracy returned to Bolivia. Raúl Lara (1940) shows his interest in the Bolivian folklore, combining elements of colonial themes with that of local traditions. His magic realism gives him the title of being the most Latin American of all the contemporary artists. Luis Zilveti (1941) portrays the drama of a silent, cold, but extremely expressive world with cloudy, mystic use of pale palettes. Gonzalo Ribero (1942) has progressively found his inspiration in the daily objects of Bolivian valley life, using sharp colours to emphasize the shapes.

The generation born and brought up during the revolutionary days started painting during the military years, and while the generation of '52 had produced social comments, the new generation was dedicated to protest. Roberto Valcárcel and Gastón Ugalde are the most notable names from this era, as they developed into artists beyond the need for protest, and opened the way for the latest generation that expresses itself with non-traditional forms on a very international level. Roberto Valcárcel (1951) has combined his multifaceted talent with his extensive studies abroad to become one of the most influential artists as far as the present day artist is concerned. Being equally able to portray realism as he is a capable architect, Valcárcel has taught many of the younger generation to explore and question their own works. In 1977, he created the Valcárcel Group, incorporating seven imaginary artists in one person (himself), to explore the contrasts that exist between the different media and aesthetic values in the visual arts. Gastón Ugalde (1946) uses non-traditional media to express his fascination with his country. Probably the best known of the bohemian generation, Ugalde makes use of whatever natural material available to produce outstanding installations, happenings, sculptures, and paintings. His style can be defined as questioning and experimental, the results often being quite stunning.

There are others who should be mentioned for their continued search among the new values. Francine Secretan (1948) was born and educated in Switzerland, but since settling in Bolivia in 1974 has used her distinctive talent to combine Andean ideas with modern media, producing monumental sculptures in both wood and metal. Cecilia Lampo (1952) has adapted the clean lines and contrasts learnt during her many years in Sweden and Germany to the colour fields so often found in Bolivian art. Fernando Ugalde (1949) incorporates his perfect drawings into paintings that combine the illustrative with the abstract, while Sol Mateo (1956) enhances old photographs with symbols that reflect an irony between religious themes and sexuality. Mario Sarabia (1953) has taken the traditional art of ceramics and transformed it to reflect the present.

While many of those who opened the road after the middle of the century are settled in their ways, a new generation is making an impact on the term "Bolivian contemporary art" by questioning values that seem to be outdated. Many of these present-day pioneers are women. Guiomar Mesa (1961) adapts traditional realism to depict symbols of local images. Patricia Mariaca (1961) uses texture to explore the questions of being, while Angeles Fabbri (1957) masters fields of colour to demonstrate enormous understanding of her concepts. Having settled in Bolivia in 1982, Ejti Stih (1957) has chosen the humour of daily life for her comment on society. Tatiana Fernández (1962) is able to transform whatever material into a well-balanced composition, and Erika Ewel (1970) looks towards the conceptual and abstract. With her extensive studies of ceramics, Raquel Schwartz (1963) constructs magnificent installations from hundreds of small pieces. Other than the women, there are of course, men asking the same questions. Keiko Gonzáles (1964) finds his contrasts in circles, lines, squares, and figures, and uses bold strokes with a heavy palette. Fabricio Lara (1967) works with mixed media, combining the contemporary visual elements with an ancient local culture. Leif Yourston (1963) came to Bolivia in 1989, and uses his intellectual humour in an interpretation of abstract forms in large colour fields. The technically well painted canvases of Marco Alandia (1957) are frequently described as

ART AND CULTURE

simple and unoriginal on the one hand, and brilliant on the other. Roberto Mamani Mamani (1962) gained the necessary experience to express himself in paint by watching life unfold on the streets, and has found international recognition using large colour fields to depict local ideas.

The art world is forever changing, and the development in Bolivia has produced a younger and very dynamic generation. Valeria Mueller, Adriana Bravo, Vahlia Cavalho, and Fabiola Alvarado are just a few of the names to be watched in the future.

Since 1982, Bolivia has enjoyed a democratically elected government, and the days of revolution and military dictatorships are over. As the country has turned towards a decentralised system, giving more power to regional governments, the national identity has developed into one that shows the diversity of the country. The highlands are no longer recognised as the mainstay, the valleys and lowlands being given equal importance. It has been over the last ten years that an international awareness has found its way into Bolivian art, moving steadily away from national themes. The national identity is found in the sharp use of colour, often creating vast plains of striking contrasts.

The questions being asked by the younger generation, and the awareness of a world outside the Bolivian borders, are the reasons for the new-found competitiveness in the country. What is the national identity? Does it exist, or is it something bestowed on us by a former generation? Although indigenism continues, and ethnic scenes are still being painted, the last ten years of Bolivian contemporary art reflect how communication and travel have made the world a smaller place, and Bolivia a bigger one.

MUSIC IN BOLIVIA

BY MARCELO DE URIOSTE

Music has an uninterrupted tradition of 1,700 years in Bolivia. On the frieze of the Gateway of the Sun in Tiwanaku, a stone musician plays the phututo, a trumpet made from a periwinkle. There are also kerus (ceremonial cups) and champis (bronze statuettes), which represent Tiwanaku people playing the quena (a flute which has no mouthpiece), the siku or zampoña (Pan's flute), the pinkillo (a flute with a mouthpiece), the wankaras (drums with two membranes) and other instruments like the campanillas (bells), raspadores (grating instruments) and bastones sonajeros (cane rattles). All these discoveries about the Classical Period of Tiwanaku, which began in the 3rd century, were made by archaeologist Arturo Posnasky.

The history of Bolivian music has evolved in six stages: the Prehistoric period from B.C. 20,000 to 300 A.D., the period of the Andean cultures (300-1532); the Renaissance (1532-1630); the American Mestizo Baroque, (1630-1780); the Neoclassic style (1780-1825); and National Romanticism (1825-1960).

Pre-Hispanic Music

The music of the Tiwanaku empire (Aymara) and the Inca empire (Quechua) is distinguished by several characteristics: in the first place it was predominantly pentatonic -- it employed only five notes. In some areas more archaic tonal systems were used, like the bitonal (two notes), the tritonal (three notes) and the heptatonal (seven notes).

Another characteristic that impressed D'Harcourt and D'Harcourt in La Musique des Incas et sa Survivance, is their pentamodal system. Western music has two modes: major and minor. The Andean system had five: two major, two minor and one neutral. Andean music did not know harmony. Its predominantly melodic character was based on only one voice, sometimes repeated one octave higher. Their basic rhythms were binary, with the frequent use of free syncopes and rhythms.

The Andean empires did not have any type of musical notation. The aru amunyas (the art and science of sounds) was taught at the Yachay Huasi (houses of knowledge) by the amautas (wise men). The melodies and musical techniques were traditionally transmitted by ear. There were very diverse styles, as there were 28 different cultures living in the region. Aymara music, for example, was not sung, it was instrumental, severe and vigorous. Quechua music, on the other hand, was melodic and sweet and had a predilection for singing.

Of the 27 genres of songs found by anthropologists, the most important were the jaillis (sacred agricultural and epic hymns); the taquis (dancing songs of free themes); the arawis (melancholic songs); the wawanki (dialogue songs by groups of young boys and girls); the waino (dancing songs); the kukulis (songs of love for the doves); and the wankas (elegies for the dead).

The music of the dances was even more varied. Father Díaz Gainza has classified 79 pre-Hispanic dances: 18 mythical-religious; 14 totemic; 9 historic; and 38 profane. Some of these dances can still be seen in some country festivals, although modified by nearly 500 years of cultural mixture, such as the achachilas, hanchanchus, auqui-auquis, mallkus, kusillos, choquelas, chaka chiriwanas, kullawas, arachis, chunchus, sikuris, tundiquis, mukululos, jacha sikuris and llameradas. Other famous dances like the morenada, the diablada from Oruro and the sayas come from the Viceregal period of the 17th and 18th centuries.

Viceregal Music

A UNESCO project was able to collect more than 1,800 scores of masses, oratorios, villancicos (Christmas songs), requiems, chorals, organ music, profane music and concerts, which are kept in the National Archive in Sucre. This music was composed between 1560 and 1811 in the territory that is now Bolivia. This was a golden era in the history of American music.

In this way, composers who enjoyed great fame in their lifetimes were rediscovered, like Gutiérrez Fernández Hidalgo (1553-1620), who introduced renaissance polyphonic mannerism; Francisco de Morales, the first concert guitarist; Hernán García and Juan de la Peña, who founded the first Academy of Music in 1568; J.P. Bocanegra, who in 1631 composed a Mass in Quechua, mixing the baroque system

with the Andean pentatonic; Juan de Araujo (1646-1714), the most important maestro of the Baroque Mestizo and composer of more than 600 orchestral works and chorals; Doménico Zípoli (1688-1726), an organist and composer who introduced the Italian School to Charcas; Estanislao Miguel Leyseca, a maestro from Chuquisaca who composed works for the violin in the Italian gallant style; and Manuel Mesa y Carrizo, a Neoclassic composer famous also for his masses and popular themes.

The LP recorded in 1980 by Coral Nova and the National Symphony Orchestra contains works by Bocanegra (Hanacpachap Cussicunin), Araujo (Aves, Ninfas, Selvas, Flores and Los Cofrades de la Estleya), Leyseca (Hoy a la dulce crueldad), Doménico Zípoli and other composers. This recording permits us to appreciate the splendor of Viceregal art, at the time of the greatest splendor of silver mining in Potosí.

Creole Music

National Romanticism is the predominant school of cultured Bolivian music since 1825. If musical biculturalism began early in the 17th century, it was at the time of independence that composers began to look to autochthonous sonority for the basic font of their inspiration.

The Bolivian 19th century saw musicians like Pedro Jimenez de Abril, a neoclassical maestro who was educated in Paris; Mariano Pedro Rosquellas, first violinist at the Court of Ferdinand VII (this king gave him the Stradivarius with which Rosquellas delighted Bolivians for three decades); Adolfo Ballivián, a child prodigy who in 1874 would become president of Bolivia; and Jose Salmon Ballivián, whose famous Aymara Suite and Indian Trilogy are still heard today.

In the 20th century, the refined works of José María Velasco Maidana and Humberto Viscarra Monje are outstanding. An example of this school, can be seen in LPs recorded by pianist María Antonieta García Mesa, who interprets the works of Simeón Roncal (1830-1953) and Angel Valda (1885-1950). Roncal, famous for his cuecas, is the greatest composer of creole music for piano in the country. In the record Boleros de Caballería, we can also appreciate notable examples of this trend: Terremoto de Sipe-Sipe and Despedida a Tarija by Saturnino Ríos. The works of Teofilo Vargas, Eduardo Caba, Adrián Patiño, Mauro Nuñez and Gilberto Rojas are dispersed among national recordings. They are the most relevant composers of nationalist music.

Bolivian Folk Music

Popular music is the most developed facet of Bolivian culture. Because of its variety, vigor, creativity and attachment to tradition, this art has merited a special interest. There are serious studies of Bolivian folklore music (see Bibliography), but what is most interesting is that it is a living tradition in a permanent process of creativity.

Its Hispanic-Andean mestizo forms remains relatively sound. In the Diablada from Oruro, for example, we can appreciate a Medieval religious play. In the Sikuris of Italaque, a pre-Hispanic martial orchestra.

Those interested in the music from Tarija (characterized by its poetic richness) can listen to the records of Los Montoneros de Mendez, the best group of that area. The music of the Bolivian Chaco (violin, drum and guitar) has outstanding interpreters in the Canarios del Chaco. The instrumental music from Cochabamba, of Quechua roots, has in the Canata group its best exponents. The Banda del Pagador interprets the rhythms of the Entrada of the Carnaval of Oruro. Luzmila Carpio sings the songs of the north of Potosí, as do the Ajayus.

For the music of the Altiplano there are several groups of quality: Kollawara, Los Jairas and Incallajta. A very interesting

record of this area's music is the one by the group Rumillajta. The mestizo-urban song book is represented by a vigorous group, the Khory Wairas. Other important interpreters of Bolivian folk are: Gladys Moreno, Zulma Yugar, Enriqueta Ulloa and Pepe Murillo.

A very special chapter are the records Folklore I and Folklore II recorded under the Campo seal by Ernesto Cavour, Alfredo Domínguez and "El Gringo" Fabre. These are two masterpieces of Bolivian popular music. The charango Centellas records by Ernesto Cavour and Celestino Campos are the best in relation to this stringed instrument. Alfredo Domínguez is a special case. In 1976 he was named by the European critics as one of the ten best folklore guitarists in the world. His records, especially Vida, Pasión y Muerte de Juan Cutipa and Algo Más de Alfredo Domínguez are true classics. The guitarists Ricardo Bleichner and Tito Yupanqui should also be considered in this select group.

The piano became a common instrument in Sucre and La Paz in the 19th Century. Though considered to be a salon instrument, it was not long before it was incorporated into select popular music. The Chuquisaca school is of special importance, and its primary exponent was the composer Simeón Roncal. Cuecas, bailecitos, kaluyos, huayños and yaravies have been played with elegance since the 19th century. The most important pianist today is the maestro from Chuquisaca Fidel Torrícos, author of several records.

In the 17th century, in the middle of the Viceregal era, small, string orchestras were already being formed, using bandores, vigüelas (ancient type of guitars), guitars and mandolins. Since the end of the 19th century these groups have been called estudiantinas, and incorporate the sound of the charango. A small instrument coming from the tango orchestras has been added

ART AND CULTURE

to the estudiantinas since 1930: the bandoneón, a large concertina. Unfortunately, the estudiantina is a special chamber orchestral form, now largely disappearing. The musicians are old gentlemen, especially veterans from the Chaco War who come together and form musical associations. One example is the Estudiantina Illimani. In general, all the records made by estudiantinas on the market are good.

Band music is also a specialty of the country. At the beginning of the Republic the first military bands were formed. Several of the most important Bolivian composers have cultivated this genre, among them, Antonio Montes Calderón, Adrián Patiño, Daniel Albornoz and Eduardo Caba. Thanks to them, an exalted tradition has been developed. Illustrious examples are the Andean foxtrots composed by Adrián Patiño, one of the most creative contributions to national music. There are several recordings in this genre, recorded by army bands.

Today there are some musical groups who have acquired international prestige. Theirs is a stylized modern folklore. One of these groups is Savia Andina of great instrumental professionalism. The other, Los Kjarkas, renewed the traditional melodic lines of Bolivian music. A third very special case is the Wara Group. The first three recordings by this group, Maya, Paya and Quimsa ("One," "Two" and "Three" in Aymara) stand out because of the mixing of Aymara sonority with electronic music and rock.

As has happened in other Latin American countries, a movement has developed to renew traditional songs among young composers and singers. This renovation includes the use of electronic instruments, the exploration of new poetic themes and the heterodox use of the popular tradition. Some representatives of this new trend are Manuel Monroy, Carlos Suárez and Adrián Barrenechea. A special case is

Matilde Casazola. A poet and guitar teacher, Miss Casazola is a fine composer. She recorded Matilde Casazola. In 1984, the Portales Cultural Center of Cochabamba edited an album of her scores accompanied by cassette entitled De Regreso.

Ethnographic Music of Bolivia

Recently, some very good studies and recordings have been made of ethnographic music. Outstanding in this respect are the two LPs promoted by the Portales Cultural Center of Cochabamba, based on the "Luzmila Patiño" festivals. The first includes a complete text, which explains the instruments, the genres and the regions of Bolivian ethnic music. Portales Cultural Center has the most important archive of ethnographic recordings. At the musical department of the Bolivian Institute of Cultural (IBC) there is also an important archive: one can get there an illustrative text about Altiplano music, which comes accompanied by ethnomusicological recordings.

Another interesting document about music is one by ethnomusicologist Max Peter Bauman on the Quechua songs of Cochabamba. Under the name Quechua takis: 60 Canciones del Quechua Boliviano, the Portales Cultural Center has published these scores and accompanied them with a live cassette. There is another ethnographic record, under the Campo seal, Música de los Andes Bolivianos. It contains themes recorded live by non-professional groups made up of farmers.

Bolivian Musical Instruments

There is a great variety of typically Andean instruments that have aroused the curiosity of musicians, anthropologists, ethnomusicologists and tourists. Besides the universal instruments that began to be used after the arrival of the Spaniards (guitar, mandolin, violin, harp, organ, flute) and of those that have been used since the 19th century (piano, trumpet, trombone, accordion, bandoneón), there are several instruments of pre-Colombian and colonial origin which are very interesting.

One of the most important of these is the charango. Originally, it was a copy of the Spanish vigüela, an ancient type of guitar made by local artisans. With an armadillo carapace and with llama gut as chords, they made a small guitar with five double chords. This instrument began to spread out all over the Andean region in the 17th century. Beginning in 1780, one of the third chords began to be turned one octave higher; the inventor of this variation is unknown. Beginning then, the charango became what we know today. In Chuquisaca a group of players of three and even four sizes of charangos with different voices is traditional. The most important interpreters of this instrument are Ernesto Cavour, Mauro Nuñez and Celestino Campos. The latter is the author of an excellent method of study for it: El Charango: Su Teoría y Práctica Musical.

In the Andean region, chord instruments were unknown, but the sonorous variety of its wind instruments is amply recognized. Today there are artisans who make perfectly tuned ones, with the whole chromatic scale of 12 notes included. The more widely known instruments are:

The Quena. It is a flute, usually made of reed, which is characterized by not having a mouth piece through which to blow the air. As is the case with all Andean instruments, there is a family of quenas: a small one, a mid-sized one and a large one. The typical mid-sized one is between 30-40 centimeters long. There are several methods to learn to play it; one of them, by Ernesto Cavour, is very practical since it comes with a cassette of exercises. The most important players of the quena are Gilbert Fabre, "El Gringo" (who played with Los Jairas and in the two important recordings mentioned

before of Cavour-Domínguez-Fabre) and Lucho Cavour.

The Siku. Siku is the Aymara name for the zampoña or Pan's flute (antara in Quechua). It is the most important pre-Hispanic Andean instrument. It is formed by several reed tubes of different sizes held together by knotted string. These tubes give several tones when blown into by the musician. Now sikus tuned with the entire chromatic scale are made. The old sikus were made in pairs, the iras and the arkas. Each one of them was made with different notes and necessarily had to be played by two complementary players. Although many of them had very ample sonorous scales, only the pentatonic scales were used. There is a method for learning the siku, which also belongs to Ernesto Cavour, with a cassette included. The family (or "troupe" as it is called in the Andes) of sikus is made up of the malta-siku, the likusiku, the chuli-siku and the taika-siku. These are put in order from the high tones to the low tones.

Tarkas, pinkillos and mukululos. Other very typical instruments are the tarkas (flutes of carved wood), the pinkillos (flutes with a mouth piece) and the mukululos (low, deep-sound flutes of folded wood). All of these instruments come in various sizes, and some of them are elaborated with a high aesthetic sense. When the instrument is too large to be played normally through the mouthpiece, the artisans connect a curved reed so they can be played comfortably. In this way families of gigantic transverse flutes have been created.

Erkes and phututos. The phututos were the old pre-Hispanic trumpets. Originally they were made of sea shells, wood or ceramic. Now the horn of a bull is used. The phututos give a low, deep, frightening sound. They are used by the communities to call meetings and they have been used in the great Indian rebellions as a war instrument. In Tarija, the bull's horns are

ART AND CULTURE

used to make the erkes. These are instruments identical to the phututos, but with the difference that they are tied to some long reeds (some as long as 12 feet) and they are played collectively. Usually, these instruments can only play melodies in the tritonal scale. Other erkes are made with a reed mouthpiece similar to those used on oboes. In this way they produce a more metallic sound.

Places to Hear Music

To enjoy popular Bolivian music, one should go to the peñas. These places usually present varied shows and in some instances they serve typical food and drink. In La Paz, the most important are Peña Naira, Khory Tika and Casa del Corregidor. In Sucre, go to Centro Cutural Los Masis, and in Santa Cruz, Piedra Libre.

Ethnographic music can be heard in several popular festivals. La Fiesta del Gran Poder is celebrated in La Paz in June; the Carnaval of Oruro, which is possibly the most important tourist attraction in the country, is celebrated the weekend before Ash Wednesday, usually in February. On the borders of Lake Titicaca there is another event which yearly attracts many groups of autochthonous musicians: the Festival of Compi. This takes place 62 miles (100 kms) by paved road north of La Paz. In Cochabamba one can enjoy good music at the Luzmila Patiño Festival at the Portales Palace. This takes place on March 2. On each occasion emphasis is given to the music of a different region. The Sombrero de Sao Festival is becoming more important in Santa Cruz de la Sierra, which specializes in music from the eastern lowlands.

The most attractive festival in the Department of Chuquisaca is the Carnaval of Tarabuco, which is celebrated in the town of that name 50 miles (80 kms), from the city of Sucre. The people from Tarabuco, famous for their colorful weavings, are the most elegant farmers in the country. Their dances and songs each year attract a growing number of tourists.

In Tarija there are two festivals where one can hear quality popular music: the Carnaval (usually in February) and Easter of Holy Week. On these occasions the tarijeños, people with a notable poetic and musical sense, dust their violins, guitars and erkes to express their joy.

The villancicos, folk songs of adoration of the Christ child sung by children, can be heard all over Bolivia at Christmas time.

Because of an old custom from the Viceregal era, the Bolivians like to listen to music in the plazas and promenades on Sunday and feast days. Unfortunately, this beautiful tradition is not kept with the same devotion as before. Nevertheless, when the concert begins, one has the unique occasion to listen to the numerous works composed especially for bands. When a veteran from the Chaco War is buried, or some prominent military authority dies, the funeral sounds of the boleros de caballería can be heard. These continue to be one of the most emotional genres of popular music.

Select Music: Interpreters and Composers

Bolivia boasts a select group of virtuosos of international prestige. Such is the case of violinist Jaime Laredo, who at 18 won the Queen Elizabeth of Belgium Award. Pianist Walter Ponce is also a well known maestro. A very special case is the child pianist Ana María Vera, who was the youngest concert pianist ever invited to play at the Kennedy Center, where she was accompanied by the National Symphony Orchestra of Washington, D.C. A master of classical guitar is Javier Calderón, who received a doctorate in music in the United States. Also outstanding is Agustín Fernández, a young cellist and composer of great talent. The most important composer today is Alberto Villalpando.

The passion for good music in Bolivia comes from way back. By 1568 there was a first rate music academy. In 1835 the first philharmonic Society was founded. Today the country has a National Symphony Orchestra; a Municipal Chamber Music Orchestra in La Paz; choirs like the Sociedad Coral Boliviana, the Coro Polifónico Nacional, Coral Nova, the Simón Bolívar Normalist Coral in Sucre, El Coro de los Valles directed by the prestigious maestro Franklin Anaya in Cochabamba, and Coro Santa Cecilia in Santa Cruz.

A very important contribution to contemporary music is the creation of the Orchestra of Native Instruments organized by the Prudencio Brothers. A score by Sergio Prudencio played by this orchestra was recorded recently in Havana along with a score by maestro Leo Browder.

There are good concerts regularly at the Municipal Theater of La Paz; at the Casa de la Cultura "Franz Tamayo" in La Paz; at the Casa de la Cultura "Raúl Otero Reich" in Santa Cruz; at the Portales Palace in Cochabamba and at cultural institutions such as the Goethe Institute and the Centro Boliviano Americano in La Paz.

The following are not only records; these are the beautiful columns of a sonorous door; a door that can be opened if we want to enjoy one of the artistic treasures of Creole and Indo-Hispanic America - - Bolivian Music.

Bibliography of Bolivian Music

There is an ample bibliography of Bolivian music. We shall cite only those texts which are readily available on the market.

La Historia de la Música Boliviana by Atiliano Auza, is the best general history. It is edited by Los Amigos del Libro. The Historia Musical Boliviana, by José Díaz Gainza,

continues as the best existing study of pre-Columbian music. In regard to the music of the eastern jungle people, Canción y Producción de un Pueblo Indígena, by Jurgen Riester, is the most complete compilation to date. Ethnomusicologist Marcelo Tórres has made a classic study, El Huayño en Bolivia, edited by the Bolivian Institute of Culture (IBC). Max Peter Bauman is the author of a study with scores, 60 Canciones del Quechua Boliviano, edited by the Portales Cultural Center in Cochabamba. This same institution also edited a booklet on ethnic music. Argentine musicologists Carmen García Muñoz and Angel Rodan are the authors of Un Archivo Musical Americano, the most complete study of the Viceregal music of the Audiencia de Charcas. A book that is today a bibliographical rarity is Aires Nacionales de Bolivia in four volumes, edited in 1928 by maestro Teófilo Varga. It contains the scores of the best traditional folkloric songs in the country. Finally, the methods of Ernesto Cavour for the study of the creole guitar, the quena, the siku and the charango should be mentioned.

Recommended Recordings

La Música Virreinal de Bolivia recorded by Coral Nova and the National Symphony Orchestra.

The works of Simeón Roncal and Angel Valda, interpreted by María Antonieta García Mesa.

Boleros de Caballería, recorded at Discolandia by the band of the National Army.

The two recordings of ethnographic music recorded at the Luzmila Patiño Festival, of the Lauro seal.

Música de los Andes Bolivianos recorded by Campo.

Folklore I and Folklore II, by Cavour, Fabre, Domínguez, and the records of Los Montoneros de Méndez by Discolandia.

The records of Masis and Ajayus,

Canata, Kollawara and Incallajita.

The records of Gladys Moreno and Zulma Yugar.

The singular record Vida, Pasión, y Muerte by Juan Cutipa, and Algo más of Alfredo Domínguez, Bolivia's best folk guitarist.

The records of the charanguista Ernesto Cavour and Celestino Campos.

In contemporary neo-folklore, the records of Savia Andina, the Kjarkas and Rumillajta. Also the first three records by the Wara Cultural Group, Maya, Paya and Quimsa. De Regreso, the book and cassette by Matilde Casazola, edited by the Portales Cultural Center; Matilde Casazola recorded by Heriba.

The guitar recordings of Tito Yupanqui and Guitarra by Augusto Bleichner.

The record Charangos Famosos, edited by the Lauro seal.

Several records by Estudiantinas; the piano recordings of Fidel Torricos.

A HISTORY OF BOLIVIAN CINEMA

BY PETER FRASER

"...ONLY WITH ART CAN WE FREE OURSELVES AND SURVIVE THE SUICIDAL
SELF-CONTEMPT THAT THREATENS BOLIVIA." - JORGE SANJINES

Bolivian cinema began in La Paz, in the flickering light of the Municipal theatre. That was the year 1897. In 1904 the first film was made in Bolivia, "Retrato de Personajes Historicos y de Actualidad" ("Portrait of Important Figures from the Past and the Present"). Luis Castillo and J. Goystillo were the first Bolivian filmmakers. In 1912 they shot "Vistas Locales" ("Local Sights"), appropriate for the blend of intimacy and self-dissection that would mark the national cinema.

Aymara Heart

This history is not comprehensive. It highlights main figures, films and themes so that the reader may investigate further. There has never been a major film industry in Bolivia - there is no Hollywood here - but proportional to its output, Bolivian film has achieved a high level of recognition worldwide.

By 1915 there were four theatres showing films in La Paz. Among the first documentaries, and one of the few to survive the silent era, was Professor Muller's expedition to Tiahuanaco. In 1923 an Italian entrepreneur named Pedro Sambarino came to Bolivia and started the Production Company "Bolivia Films". By 1925 he had equipped the first laboratory to process, develop and copy celluloid.

Sambarino's "Por mi Patria" ("For my homeland") was premiered the following year. A series of short clips concerning

Bolivia's customs, it was welcomed by press and public alike. His next was "Corazon Aymara" ("Aymara Heart"), based on indigenous literature and theatre, it was the country's first long film.

Sambarino was setting a trend. Although the medium itself was initially reserved for learned city-dwellers rather than for the rural majority, neglected cultures such as Aymara communities have continued to obsess Bolivian filmmakers. Amid the country's many traumas this modern medium has returned to native customs as a recurring symbol of other possibilities, an alternative Bolivia.

Censorship

The censor intervened in 1925 with a film by Jose Maria Velasco Maidana named "La Profecia del Lago" ("The Prophecy of the lake"), featuring a love affair between a Pongo (indigenous sharecropper) and the wife of his landowner. An attempt to incinerate the negatives failed.

That film teased social and racial prejudices but two films in 1927 ran into trouble due to their overt political content. They detailed the actual events of a scandalous court case in which a family was accused of murdering Ex-president General Pando in 1917. The military identified youngest son Alfredo Jauregui as the culprit and executed him despite appeals for clemency.

The two films were: "El Fusilamiento

de Jauregui" ("The execution of Jauregui") by Luis Castillo and "La Sombria Tragedia del Kenko" ("The Sombre Tragedy of Kenko") by Arturo Posnansky. The first was a short film that showed only the execution while the second reconstructed events from the killing of Pando to the execution of Jauregui so that the public might judge for themselves. The censor tried to prevent their exhibition but Castillo went to the Supreme Court and won.

Luis Castillo collaborated with the archeologist Arturo Ponsnansky in 1926 on "La Gloria de la Raza" ("The Glory of the Race") and afterwards on "El Ocaso de un Imperio" ("The Decline of an Empire"). Both sought to convey archeological theories to a wider audience and made innovative use of scale models and camera trickery.

Love and War

In 1928 Jose Maria Velasco created "Urania films". He also directed "Wara-Wara," set during the Spanish conquest. It was one of the biggest productions of the silent era and was released in 1930 with great success. It was filmed around Lake Titicaca and centered on a romance between the daughter of an Inca chief and a Spanish captain.

The film involved the most prominent intellectuals of the day. The novelist Antonio Diaz Villamil wrote it, while painter and novelist Arturo Borda and sculptress Marina Nunez del Prado acted the two main roles. Young technicians Mario Comacho and Jose Jimenez worked with Velasco. The picture required the grandest and most costly sets of the age, and because of its ambitions the film was compared to the epics being made in Hollywood.

"Hacia la Gloria" ("On Towards Glory"), from Mario Comancho and Jose Jimenez, created a stir four years later due to a plot in which a high society woman has an affair with the minister of war. Ashamed of her

baby, she abandons him in the countryside where he is raised by campesinos. He becomes a pilot and goes to war, eventually reuniting with his mother and discovering that a girl who once rejected his advances is actually his sister.

The 1932-1935 Chaco war between Bolivia and Paraguay proved an enticing theme for Bolivian filmmakers. "Infierno Verde" ("Green Inferno") by Luis Bazoberry was premiered in Barcelona to widespread indifference but today is well respected. It records the signing of the armistice and fraternization between enemy troops.

"La Campana del Chaco" ("The Chaco campaign") was put before General Kundt, commander of the Bolivian forces, who was less than pleased. The public disagreed making it the most successful production of the silent era. Kundt tried to negotiate a propaganda film with Paramount pictures but instead they made "Alas sobre el Chaco" ("Wings over the Chaco") which romanticized the conflict but at the very least reflected that Bolivia had lost the war.

Breaking the Silence

"Wait a minute! Wait a minute! You ain't heard nothing yet!" Cinema was moving towards sound. In 1927 Al Jolson uttered his immortal first words in "The Jazz Singer" changing cinema forever but for Bolivia change came slowly.

In 1932 "Hacia la Gloria" ("On Towards Glory")had used a system of phonographs behind the screen to provide its soundtrack, similar to a system developed by Warner Bros which was obsolete in America by 1931. Before that in 1930 the Municipal theatre had staged the first projection with sound, albeit at a poor standard.

Among the last silent hurrahs of the era in Bolivia was "Historia de la Decadencia Aymara" ("History of the Aymara Decline"), fittingly a reflection on indigenous culture. It took Bolivia many years to adapt to sound. "We started in the years 1958 and 1959. We made the first sound movies in Bolivia. We worked with a colleague of mine who has already passed away. His name was Augusto Roca." Jorge Ruiz (1999).

At this time Jorge Ruiz and Augusto Roca were still teenagers messing about with 8mm. Kenneth Wasson, a North American, founded "Bolivia Films" and gifted them a 16mm camera. The talented twosome formed a partnership - filmmaker and cameraman - and in 1949 collaborated with Alberto Perrin Pando on the first Bolivian film in colour. Named "Donde Nacio un Imperio" ("Where an Empire was Born"), it was filmed on Lake Titicaca. Ruiz heralds the beginning of the modern era for Bolivian cinema.

Jorge Ruiz

Jorge Ruiz directed "Vuelve Sebastiana" ("The Return of Sebastiana") in 1953. It is considered one of the most important films in Bolivian history. It depicts an altiplano people close to extinction and was the first Bolivian picture to receive an international premiere.

Ruiz has made many valuable documentaries, returning again to native peoples with "Voces de la Tierra" ("Call of the Earth"), about indigenous music, which won international prizes. In 1958 he released "La Vertiente" ("The Slope"), his first long film, which detailed the construction of a system of drinking water in Rurrenabaque.

"La Vertiente" also contained a romance between the mistress of the village and an alligator hunter in Rurrenabaque but true to his documentary instincts and the traditional strengths of Bolivian cinema Ruiz left this as a backdrop to the social realism.

"Mina Alaska" ("The Alaska Mine") in 1968 was an attempt at something more commercial. It followed the adventures of a gold prospector and is one of the few films ever in which the running time matches the time passing in the film itself.

Ruiz has continued to work and last year received the National Bolivian Award for Culture. One of his most important films of later years is his maritime-theme "El Clamor del Silencio" ("The Clamour of Silence") from 1979.

After the Revolution

In March 1953, 11 months after the 1952 revolution, the MNR government created the I.C.B (Institute of Cinematography in Bolivia). Intended to develop the national cinema, it had many well-respected members including Ruiz and Roca. Between 1953 and 1966 Bolivia produced more short films than ever before and was among the top five producers in Latin America.

Between 1956 and 1964, Jorge Ruiz managed the I. C. B. After the fall of the MNR in 1964 the new Barrientos administration offered the management to a key figure in modern Bolivian cinema who was just starting his career: Jorge Sanjines.

Sanjines had returned to Bolivia from the Chilean Film Institute in 1960. He made the short film "Revolucíon" in 1963 which has been termed "The Potemkin of Sanjines" after the Russian film by Sergei Eisenstein. It shows Bolivian history through a montage that lasts little more than ten silent minutes. Universally acclaimed, it won the garland of the Festival of Leipzig.

Sanjines was manager of the I. C. B. from 1965 to 1967. He had filmed short propaganda pieces for the MNR through the Institute and perhaps the new government expected something similar when he shot "Ukamau" in 1966. But they were outraged with the result, Sanjines resigned his position and the Institute later became Channel 7, a television station.

ART AND CULTURE

Ukamau

In 1960 Sanjines formed the "Kallasuyo" group with Oscar Soria and Ricardo Rada. Soria was a renowned scriptwriter destined to work with three generations of filmmakers. He co-wrote "Ukamau", the group's first long film and the first film in Aymara, which related the rape and murder of an Aymara woman by her mestizo (mixed-blood) landowner and her husband's subsequent revenge.

"Kollasuyo" now became the "Ukamau," group with the addition in 1968 of Antonio Eguino, another important presence, as Director of Photography.

"Yawar Malku" ("Blood of the Condor") was their next in 1969. It was selected in 1995 as one of the hundred most important films in World Cinema, partly because it alerted people to an actual sterilization program being undertaken on Campesino women without their consent by the American Peace Corp.

In the film the village chief discovers this and raises his people in violent protest. As in "Ukamau" non-professionals were used as actors. The film was almost banned by the government but demonstrations from students and the intelligentsia ensured its release and the American Peace Corp was expelled from the country.

The first "Ukamau" film in color was the 1971 "El Coraje del Pueblo" ("The Courage of the People"). It abandoned the trappings of fiction to recount the facts of the massacre of San Juan in 1967 during which dozens of miners were killed under the orders of President Barrientos. Survivors relate their traumatic experiences and act their own parts.

With the 1973 military coup and the fall of the leftist administration Sanjines emigrated and "Ukamau" split into two.

Sanjines and Eguino

In Peru Sanjines made "El Enemigo Principal" ("The Principal Enemy") about a group of Peruvian guerillas determined to liberate campesinos who judge and then shoot a landowner and foreman. The poster clearly indicated the true enemy by painting the title in the colours of the U. S. flag.

1977, Sanjines filmed "Fuera de Aqui" ("Away from Here") in Ecuador about a religious cult trying to convert campesinos.

Meanwhile in Bolivia Eguino-Soria had released "Pueblo Chico" ("Village Boy") in 1974 and "Chuquiago" (the Aymara name for La Paz) in 1977. The first concerns a young man who returns to Sucre to work in the countryside and finds that agricultural reform has failed due to corruption, hypocrisy and conservatism.

"Chuquiago" follows four individuals from different social classes in La Paz, inviting viewers to compare their stories. It became the most successful film in Bolivian history.

The Hidden Bolivia

Danielle Caillet's "Warmi" introduced a female perspective. It dealt with women's roles in Aymara / Quechua communities. Caillet had already collaborated with her husband Antonio Eguino on his previous films.

Eguino's 1984 production was named "Amargo Mar" ("Bitter Sea"), fulfilling his ambition to make a film about the 1879 War of the Pacific. His revisionist stance was quite controversial.

Having returned from abroad Sanjines directed "Las Banderas del Amanecer" ("The Flags of Dawn") which recorded the fight against military dictators and the efforts of the Bolivian people to regain democracy. Begun in 1978, it wasn't released until 1984.

Another film of the early eighties was "Mi Socio" ("My Associate") by Paolo Agazzi, which contrasted La Paz with Santa Cruz, showing a divided Bolivia beyond the indigenous peoples.

He followed this with "Los Hermanos Cartagena" ("The Cartagena Brothers") in 1985. It covers the period from the agricultural reform in 1952, until the mid-1980s,and has two brothers as its focus. It contains explicit scenes of violence that are rare in Bolivian cinema and consequently caused seat-stirring in some quarters.

The same year, Juan Miranda, a photographer who had worked with Ruiz, Eguino and others made "Tinku - El Encuentro" ("Tinku - The Encounter"), an attempt at a commercial film. The first modern film conceived and financed outside La Paz, it concerns a campesino youth who grows up to be a great pianist but who returns to confront his culture and his race.

"La Nacion Clandestina" was released in 1989, a vital later work by Jorge Sanjines, which won the "Gold shell" at a film Festival in Spain. The main character Sebastian leaves his campesino village to work in the city for the secret police but cannot fit in. He tries to return to his village but when they no longer accept him he takes extreme measures to belong again.

Lights, Camera...Action

"...Bolivia has a cinema despite the state, which has offered us pleasing words. But the words are only words." - Luis Espinal, film critic (1970).

A positive step for the preservation and publicising of Bolivian cinema was made in 1976 with the creation of the "Cinemateca Boliviana", a non-governmental initiative. At the same time the "Condor de Plata" prize was created to encourage short films.

The General law for the Cinema (law 1302) was passed in 1991 and represented a leap forward. It had four fundamental concerns: to encourage production, to educate, to preserve the cinematic heritage and to regulate the audio-visual market.

This culminated in the creation of

CONACINE (the National Council of the Cinema) which supports Bolivian film with the FFC (the Fund for the promotion of Cinema), providing loans for projects approved by the Director. FFC finance led in 1995 to an unheard-of situation: the premieres of five Bolivian films in one year. "Cuestion de Fe" ("A Question of Faith"), the first film of Marcos Laoyza, was a huge success, gaining premieres at many international festivals, and was noteworthy for its good-natured humour.

Another of those five films was "Jonas y la Ballena Rosada" ("Jonah and the Pink Whale") by up-and-coming director Juan Carlos Valdivia, controversial for its sex scenes. Jorge Sanjines also had a new picture: "Para Recibir el Canto de los Parajos" ("To Receive the Song of the Birds") about the Spanish Conquest.

Even more startling than five films in one year is the fact that in 1997 Bolivia produced a Science Fiction film named "El Triangulo del Lago" ("The Triangle of the Lake") featuring among other things a monorail bisecting a future La Paz.

With the State

In 2002 there are another five films planned for production and the new "Cinemateca" is due to be opened with three screens. Four commercial cinemas in La Paz show mainly American movies despite the popularity of films such as "Cuestion de Fe". The situation is the same accross the country.

Other problems are not unique to Bolivia such as competition from television and video and video, piracy (particularly widespread in this country). Bolivian films have no share of the lucrative video market.

A network of finance, distribution and recuperation is needed and with the FFC and the expanded "Cinemateca" we are perhaps witnessing the first steps toward such opportunity. Pedro Susz, director of

ART AND CULTURE

the Cinemateca, has said "we have the best conditions ever for Bolivian cinema at the moment."

But Bolivian filmmakers have suffered setbacks before. At time of writing the 2002 elections lie ahead and we cannot know what the policies of the new government will be. We should remember that whatever the future holds, Bolivian cinema has always survived. More than that, it has provided an essential conscience for its nation.

Luis Espinal

"For the Bolivian critic there is absolutely a before and an after Espinal" (Carlos D. Mesa). Luis Espinal arrived in Bolivia in 1968 and went on to become the country's most outspoken and influential film critic.

Espinal considered Bolivian cinema in broader political, economic and cultural contexts, which had never been done before, writing and broadcasting on the radio. He also assisted with filmmaking, for example as Director of continuity on "Chuquiago" (1977).

Educated and ordained as a Jesuit priest in his native Spain he developed a passion for cinema through private studies with the Spanish critic Juan Ripoll. In 1967 he directed "The Vital Question", a series for Spanish TV highlighting marginalized groups. The program had to continue without him because he would not be censored.

He came to this country and directed a similar series for Bolivian TV on subjects such as drugs, violence and prostitution. He wrote tirelessly on the national cinema until his death in 1980, killed by unknowns. 50 000 people gathered at his funeral and his "History of the Cinema" was published posthumously in 1982.

EXPORTING BOLIVIA NOTE BY NOTE

BY ANNA STINA LINDAHL

In a society that is getting increasingly capitalistic, the music industry is facing several dilemmas, the greatest of which is how to counter the influences of modern instruments and sounds to the cost of the tradition. Contemporary Bolivian music is today at an impasse. Outside influences are integrating themselves with the traditional melodies and in some cases over shadowing them. Still there are some musicians that are working hard to modernize the traditional and introduce it to the general public in competition with western pop music. To Bolivians, music has always been more than merely entertainment; it has been intented to lift the spirit and speak to the audience. As such there are today two types of music, that of the body and that of the soul. The former moves you to dance and the latter speak a message to the heart. Music remains an integral part of the lives of the people, but the purposes of the music vary between communities and cities. In the cities there is a growing capitalist trend and old values have been largely forgotten. Music is seen as an industry to exploit. Even street kids realize the opportunity that music brings then, and within days of new music being released over the radio, pirate copies are to be found all around the streets.

In the countryside the values of music and tradition are different, although more urban thinking is slowly integrating itself even there. Religion is one factor that has influenced musical evolution. Communities that have embraced religious syncretism between catholicism and indigenous religions still play traditional music. However, psalms and hymns sung in churches now complement the traditional music.

Music is thought to have more power than just amusing an audience; it is thought to heal and is even a form of expressing worship of nature and the deities. Music is linked to the seasons and the harvesting. From October onward the Pinkinllo is played to give seeds energy to grow toward the surface. Similarly in November and December the Moseños is played, and in February the Tarka is used to celebrate the new harvest.

Folk music groups and traditional music are seeing resurgence as it is mixed with new and modern sounds. This new music is sold in the cities because the countryside lacks the equipment and the money to be able to buy or even play newly recorded songs. Even with traditional elements returning to popular music, the sound is still predominantly western. The music industry in Bolivia is not particularly big and it is very difficult for musicians to live off their art, whereas in other countries musicians receive compensation for instruments and concerts, it is rare in Bolivia.

Bolivian music is very popular abroad, where the traditional instruments offer an

ART AND CULTURE

exotic sounds that are largely unknown in western music. The instruments imitate nature, like the panpipes the winds. With the new generation it is becoming more and more difficult to find skilled instrument artisans. It has always been passed down through generations, but recently youthsare turning away from the craft, and the old ways are beginning to be forgotten.

Bolivian music is interesting for more than just the instruments that are used. Technically the instruments are played like those of any other Latin American country, but aesthetically there is a different phonetic sound. The old Altiplano traditions are integrated into the music. Concepts such as the Aymara idea of time are felt throughout the music. The Aymaras thought not of time linearly as westerners do; they though of time as a circular space including that all that has been and all that will be.

Many people outside of Bolivian may not know the country, but recognize the music as one of sensibility and versatility. Nowadays it is possible to hear many Bolivian street musicians all throughout Europe, and though this hampers the efforts of record producing groups, it also brings the music closer to people who would not have a chance to experience it otherwise. It has even happened that popular western groups, such as Simon and Garfunkle's "El Condor pasa", have adapted traditional music, which was originally an interpretation of traditional Andean music that was in a collection registered by Alomia Robles. Los Kjarkas also had the melody of their song, "Llorando Se Fue" reinvested in the ever-popular " Lambada", but they at least received some compensation, though Bolivian culture receives little protection in terms of laws to help musicians. The longevity of the popularity of these songs attests to the integrity of Bolivian music and value of the traditional ways even in the face of modern synthesizers and dance enter-

tainment. The music of the heart still has a place in not only Bolivian society but also in the realm of the world music.

TRANSITION AND REVIVAL IN THE BOLIVIAN CERAMICS

BY RYAN TAYLOR

In the early mist-shrouded hours of the Andean morning, Bolivia's Mario Sarabia rises to enter his studio on the outskirts of La Paz, seemingly on top of the world, in a place known to locals as the Valley of the Moon. For the past 15 years, this mostly selftaught potter has managed to create beautiful pots and sculpture in a hostile environment. At altitudes reaching 12,000 feet above sea level, oxygen and vegetation needed for firing are sparse.

When Sarabia first started producing ceramics, he gathered materials around La Paz, the Altiplano and in the lower valleys. Today, he continues to explore the area, walking the earth in search of good clays to be ground, sifted, slaked and wedged in his studio. "In Bolivia, there's no such thing as a clay supply house where you can just walk in and buy all the materials prepackaged," he says. "You have to get out there with your shovel and dig it up."

Standing amidst millions of cubic tons of pale reddish clay deposits on the road to the ancient ruins of Tiwanaku (a culture thought by some to be the cradle of American civilization), Sarabia tells stories, part fact and part mystery. He describes, for example, how the Tiwanaku people must have dragged their gigantic 20 ton stones across the top of this red clay during the rainy season, because they would have moved more easily across a slick surface. "I believe in telling people stories to get them interested, and the area around Tiwanaku is fantastic," he says.

Although he uses the same clays as in the prehistoric pots found in the area, he is careful not to identify himself too closely with the Tiwanaku soul. "Tiwanaku has already been made. It wouldn't be respectful for me to be reproducing Tiwanaku ceramics instead of creating my own.

And the pieces Sarabia creates speak of his involvement in the Bolivia of today, a country with an incredible social and cultural panorama, and a natural diversity ranging from the high, snowcovered Andes mountains surrounding Lake Titicaca, to the verdant Amazon basin far below.

Inspiration for his work comes from personal experiences, such as the seven-month canoe trip he once took from Bolivia to Venezuela—from what he saw and from the stories that were told, from the remains of people buried on the banks of the river who, in time, become a part of the clay.

From his studio on the other end of the Andean–Amazon nexus, Sarabia has the opportunity to witness the daily tensions and disparities of a society in constant transition. One series, known as "Los Viejos," refers to the old beggars on the streets of La Paz. Often covered by mantles of richly textured weavings, they beg from passersby by tapping on their knees. Sarabia has seen many "fancy" people walking right by without paying any attention whatsoever. He finds it ironic that a person unwilling to help a beggar with 5 cents would pay between $200 and $300 for one of his ceramic "beggars."

He is not making a political or social statement, but merely expressing the daily reality that surrounds him in a multiethnic country characterized by extremes in poverty. "I don't understand political problems all that much," says Sarabia, "but I do see things that could be handled politically."

The series came about from a misshapened thrown bowl. "I just wanted to fold it in, and as I folded it the piece was there," he recalls.

Ten years ago, no gallery in Bolivia would show his work because at that time ceramics was considered craft and no one took it seriously. Despite the history of fine pre-Columbian pottery, 500 years of Spanish domination had left Bolivia with only utilitarian ware and almost no ceramic art tradition. But Sarabia persisted. By going back to galleries year after year, he initiated a change, and now galleries call him, requesting his work. His efforts have had a major impact on representation opportunities for his fellow ceramists as well.

Sarabia's goal is to teach people in Bolivia how to look at contemporary ceramics. "Until someone points out to you a sunset, you may not even notice it," he says. "You have to likewise mention ceramics, you have to talk about it, you have to inspire curiosity in how it was made, what it should be, what it can express.

It has taken a long time, "a lot of shows, a lot of work, a lot of stress probably. To maintain myself as a studio potter here, supporting my family and all—just staying with it—is very hard. You know I believe in what I'm doing, I believe in clay. I believe it has got a force to it."

He admits, however, that if hand-made ceramics are to be revived in Bolivia, there has to be a change. For the past 500 years people have been using lead, straight pure lead, to glaze their pots. Before the Spanish conquest, no glazes were used, only slips and minerals on burnished ware. He feels a responsibility to educate common people about what they are drinking and eating out of.

Firing at extremely high altitudes is difficult. But with the advent of electric kilns, glazed ware can be produced without the use of lead. It is now possible for Bolivian potters to jump to highfire, leadfree glazes.

Like sentinels on the road between decline and revival, Sarabia's clayworks are witnesses to dynamic cultural and social change. Yet his studio is a free, neutral space where students are encouraged to seek their own direction. "I don't expect them to follow my road. I want the student to want to do clay his or her way. It's my responsibility not to have that enthusiasm die."

Mario Sarabia's workshop is at Calle 4 in Mallasa. Tel. 2745199. Casilla: 3-12253, San Miguel, Calacoto, La Paz-Bolivia. E-mail: mario_sa@unete.com www.ceramicsarabia.com

6

THE MANY FACES OF BOLIVIA

AFRO-BOLIVIANS RECLAIM THEIR HERITAGE

BY KOREY CAPOZZA

I n the isolated lowland area of Los Yungas, a little-known chapter in Bolivian history lives on. A legacy of colonial Bolivia under the Spanish conquistadors, African-Bolivians first came as slaves who were forcibly settled in this region more than 450 years ago. In the remote region of the Bolivian tropics a unique cultural exchange produced the cultural syncretism that characterizes Afro-Bolivian communities. Today, Black Bolivians are reclaiming their cultural heritage and demanding their place in Bolivian society, in spite of their long history of oppression.

A dilapidated dirt road leads from La Paz to the subtropical lowlands marking perhaps the same route that 17,000 African slaves followed nearly half a century ago. From the Yungas town of Coroico a winding path leads through dense tropical foliage dropping several hundred feet to the Coroico River. A two-hour climb from the river along a hillside patterned with plots of coca, citrus fruits and coffee, sits the tiny Afro-Bolivian community of Tocaña where 30 families eke out an existence as small-crop farmers.

Señora Angelica Pinedo, a sturdy old woman with a face creased by hard work and time, was born in Tocaña 78 years ago and has lived there all her life. Pinedo is one of the few people left in Tocaña who recalls the history of the community. "The Spanish brought us here and made us work as slaves," she says. "But now we are our own bosses and life is much better."

African slaves were typically brought to South American coastal regions to work on sugar plantations and in other labor-intensive agro-industries. Bolivia, which has a predominantly indigenous population, is seldom considered in academic discussions of Afro-Latin history. Few historical documents remain about the course of events that brought African slaves to Bolivia, but the ones that do exist indicate that from the year 1530 on, the slaves were transported by the Spanish from Argentina and Peru to work in the mines of Potosí.

Unable to adapt to the harsh climate of the Altiplano which lies almost 4,500 meters (15,000 feet) above sea level, the Africans died rapidly. "Thousands of our African ancestors fell in Potosí for three reasons; mistreatment, the altitude and from being over-worked," says Monica Rey, president of the Afro-Bolivian Saya Cultural Movement. The Spanish soon realized that the use of African slaves in the mines would not be a profitable venture given the high mortality rate, and decided to sell the remaining Africans to plantation owners in the temperate zone of Los Yungas. Bolívar tried to abolish slavery when he created the republic of Bolivia, but his reforms were reversed by Mariscal Andres de Santa Cruz who feared the reforms would hurt the plantation economy. "It wasn't until 1953 with the

MANY FACES OF BOLIVIA

agrarian reforms of Victor Paz Estenssoro's government that we were really freed," says Rey.

Despite these agrarian reforms, Afro-Bolivians have remained among the poorest sections of Bolivian society. "Our life is very difficult," says the 78-year-old Señora Pinedo as she lifts large bags of coca leaves. Part of the problem is that Afro-Bolivians were forbidden from entering schools until 1953, and couldn't afford to send their children to study when it was actually made legal. "Most of us can't read; we were never educated," says Angelica, looking away with embarrassment.

After the abolishment of slavery, Black Bolivians formed stable communities and adopted a lifestyle very similar to that of Aymara peasants. "We can no longer talk about 'cultural purity' because a cultural syncretism is what we actually have," says Monica Rey. As was the policy in colonial North America, the Spanish separated African slaves of similar language groups in order to eliminate the possibility of a rebellion. The Spanish also feared a solidarity movement between Blacks and Indians which could potentially topple their precarious system of exploitation. Slaves and Aymara were thus deliberately socially separated and pitted against each other. Despite these efforts, the African-Bolivians were well-received by the Aymara, and a peculiar cultural symbiosis formed over the years.

"We get along well with the Blacks," says Lucy Luky, one of the few Aymara residents living in Tocaña. "They are a very happy people," she added. Señora Pinedo, dressed in a typical Aymara pleated skirt and bowler hat, laments the loss of African traditions to indigenous ones. "We have lost our African names and we are now 'Bolivian'," she says. "Bolivians are more humble and we've learned this from them.

However, situated as satellite towns around the semi-urban areas of Coroico and Chulumani, the Afro-Bolivian communities still bear the names created by their African slave ancestors. The village of "Soledad" (or Solitary), for example, was named after a king of the Afro-Bolivian people who allegedly escaped from his owner and lived in isolation until he formed a runaway slave community at the location. The story goes that under King Bonifacio Pinedo, the Black Bolivians re-created an African tribal social structure and re-invoked their cultural traditions.

Like their Aymara neighbors, the Afro Bolivians cultivate small plots of coffee, coca leaves and citrus fruits. On stone-laid platforms beneath the powerful Yungas sun, families lay out their harvests of deep red coffee beans.

Sitting next to his sun-drying crop, Jose Marín admires his view of the sprawling river valley before him. Wearing a typical Aymara woolen hat and a t-shirt that bears the name of a Canadian baseball team, José Marín's contrasting dress symbolizes the interplay of modern and traditional influences that are continually re-inventing Afro-Bolivian culture. As more and more teenagers leave for the cities, Afro-Bolivians are increasingly adopting urban Bolivian elements. For some Tocaña residents modern imports seem alien and incomprehensible. I told Marín enthusiastically that his t-shirt bore the name of my hometown. Confused, Marín scrutinized his shirt as though he had never really noticed it. "I didn't know," he said. "I can't read."

Cultural Revival

One of the few authentically Afro-Bolivian cultural traditions that remains central to Black communities is the dance of the saya. The saya that is performed in Bolivian popular festivals bears little resemblance to the original dance that was born in the Yungas and which is a cultural expression of the experience of Black Bolivians. The saya was intended to be a communal experience where Afro-Bolivian people retell the history of their people. "In the 1980's we started losing the saya because it was increasingly becoming a public spectacle," says Rey who has written her doctoral thesis on the significance of Afro-Bolivian dance. "Our ancestors, the black slaves, invented the instruments and the dance but we abandoned the saya for modern music that came to our village," says Angelica Pinedo of Tocaña.

In 1988, Rey and a group of Afro-Bolivians living in La Paz decided that something needed to be done to preserve the cultural heritage of their people. Naming themselves the Afro-Bolivian Saya Cultural Movement (MCSA), the group studied the roots of the dances and began to revive the African traditions that were being lost. According to Rey, the saya in Bolivia has been commercialized to the extent that it bears little resemblance to the traditional "African" expression.

"We decided that the dancers had to be Black if the dance was to be right," says Rey. Some dances, including the semba still bear African words that tell of the history of Bolivian slavery. "We sometimes stayed up until 2 or 3 in the morning trying to get the (dance) movements just right," says Rey. "Then we took the dances to the communities and taught them to our people."

Today, the MCSA is spearheading a social, political and cultural revolution among Afro-Bolivian communities. The recuperation of the saya was just the start for Rey and her group. "Before 1989, few people even new that we (Afro-Bolivians) existed," says Rey. "We were only known for our dance, and we were really an invisible part of Bolivian society," she says.

In 1989, the MCSA organized a "Black Bolivia" day and marched with a group of supporters on the government palace in La Paz demanding recognition as a distinct ethnic group. After this first success the MCSA began to make contacts with other African cultural groups outside the country. In 1995, the group attended a conference of "Andean African Peoples" held in Peru. Then in 1996 the group joined forces with the U.S.-based group, the Organization for the Advancement of People of African Ancestry (OAA). With its international contacts, the MCSA was able to negotiate a contract with the Inter-American Development Bank to receive funding for development projects in the Black Yungas communities. "We've learned that if we continue with our struggle we can achieve almost anything," said Rey.

MANY FACES OF BOLIVIA

BLACKS OF THE BOLIVIAN YUNGAS

BY SARAH BUSDIECKER

Beside a pile of oranges laid out on the sidewalk in the Villa Fatima neighborhood of La Paz, a cholita sits waiting to make a sale. She wears the typical bowler hat, braided hair, and multi-layered pollera skirt of any other cholita but she stands out. Amidst the varying shades of naturally brown and inevitably sun-baked skin of the Aymara Indian women seated nearby, her near ebony skin color presents an unexpected contrast.

After a month in Bolivia I had not set eyes on a single black person, until I saw that cholita. Many Bolivian and foreigners are likely to assume that the occasional black glimpsed on the streets of La Paz, Cochabamba, or Santa Cruz is from some other country, not from the overwhelmingly Indian-mestizo nation that is Bolivia. Sometimes the assumption is correct. When I saw this cholita, however, I had the distinct feeling that the assumption did not apply to her. But, my mind was filled with questions. How did this black woman become a part of the Bolivian population? Were their more black Bolivians and, if so, how many and where? Why was she wearing the clothing of an Aymara woman? I was intrigued and began to ask around, but the Bolivians with whom I spoke seemed to have very little information to share with me. I heard statements like, "there are hardly any blacks in this country", "blacks here are like any other Bolivian, just darker", and "if

there are any, you'll find them in the Yungas".

From the same neighborhood where the black cholita sells her oranges, Villa Fatima, a stream of minibuses, flotas, and camiones, make their way into and out of the Yungas region north-east of La Paz. Outside of the city, a stretch of highway passes through the cold altitude of the Cordillera Real, eventually dwindling into a narrow dirt road that winds precariously along thousand foot precipices as it heads down into the warmth and lush greenness of the subtropical Yungas. It is here that the answers to questions about Bolivia's blacks lie.

Two middle-aged black women in polleras sat in the dim front room of a house in the tiny community of Chijchipa, Nor Yungas. This was the first house I entered in the first Yungas community I visited. Upon my entrance into the house, I was met by a tide of questions almost as soon as names had been exchanged. Doña Juana, the older of the two women, led the way. "Where are you from? How is it that you speak Spanish if you are from the United States? And how can you be from the United States – you're not as tall or as white or as loud as other gringos. Tell me, how did you get hair like that? And skin like that? What do your parents look like?" Her questions were in response to my mixed-race (black and white) appearance – an appear-

MANY FACES OF BOLIVIA

ance that locally elicits the label samba or mulatta. My travel companion volunteered that I was a "gringa negra", which led to the question, "So, there are blacks in the United States?" to which I answered, "Yes, many more than here in Bolivia". With eyebrows raised, Doña Juana replied, "I thought there were only Blacks like us [dark skinned, rural, poor] in Bolivia!".

During this brief exchange, I felt these two black women were reaching across the African Diaspora, recognizing something of their own blackness in me and trying to place and understand it. The fact that they were black and I might be as well was important to them and that fact convinced me that this was a segment of the Bolivian population deserving of special attention regardless of the assertions that there are "hardly any Blacks in Bolivia" or the claims that "Blacks are just like any other Bolivian".

Time spent in the Provinces of Nor and Sud Yungas in the Department of La Paz reveals that while Blacks share much in common with other Bolivians, their difference goes beyond the color of their skin. In the Yungas, Blacks live in small rural communities in simple adobe homes just as other campesinos in the area do. Like their Aymara neighbors, they are primarily farmers who grow fruit, coffee, and, in particular, traditional-use coca. Their religious practices and beliefs demonstrate a Catholic-Andean syncretism present throughout Bolivia. Black women wear the same distinct dress and braided hair as Aymara women. While Spanish is the language of Bolivia's blacks, some elders and Blacks in integrated communities also speak or at least understand Aymara. The list of similarities goes on, but nevertheless, Bolivia's blacks do have their own unique cultural heritage which arises from their unique history, a history rooted in Africa and the trans-Atlantic slave trade.

The earliest Spaniards to arrive in the Andes in the 1530s, including the conquistador Francisco Pizarro, did so in the company of black slaves. Slaves were imported from Africa and into the area that is now Bolivia by way of Argentina and Peru with the intention that they would work in the silver mines of Potosí. The rugged cold and the high altitude of Potosí proved too much for these slaves from a distant land and, after a period laboring as silversmiths and coin minters in the Casa de la Moneda, they were moved to the Yungas region to work on plantations. In 1851, during the presidency of Isidora Belzu, slavery was finally abolished in Bolivia. It was not until the Agrarian Reform of 1952, however, that blacks were freed from indentured servitude in the haciendas of the Yungas and finally allowed to own their own land.

Abuelo Manuel, 82, of the community Tocaña, explains the presence of Blacks in Bolivia in this way, "We're not Bolivians, we're from Africa. Every Black is from Africa, my parents told me that. We were brought here from Africa by some men, brought in a box like you would bring eggs – a pair of black men and a black woman, and once here in Bolivia it was from these that the race was made". He goes on to sing, "Nosotros somos los primeros negros que llegamos en Bolivia / Ahora que vamos a hacer / Ahora que vamos a hacer / Somos ricos bolivianos".

The institution of slavery in the Andean region was not as big or as economically successful as in the Caribbean or the countries bordering the Atlantic. Blacks were few in number and so did not end up influencing the appearance and culture of the majority population as they did in countries like Haiti or Brazil and Venezuela. Perhaps for this reason, the history of Blacks has been largely ignored both inside and outside of Bolivia. It is not surprising to find, therefore, that many Bolivians, including blacks, know little about the history of this population.

Honor y gloria
Isidora Belzu bandera ganó
A los primeros negros
Ganó la bandera del Altar Mayor...
Que llegaron a Bolivia,
Que murieron trabajando
Muy explotados
Al cerro rico de Potosí.

In the 1980s, blacks formed the Movimiento Cultural Saya Afro Boliviano. Blacks began to refer to themselves as Afro-Bolivians and called attention to their presence in the Bolivian population through saya, a form of music and dance unique to Afro-Bolivians and heavily influenced by the rhythms of Africa. The above are saya lyrics, the first making reference to the black slaves brought from Africa, and the second (an introductory verse used in Nor Yungas to begin every saya), referring to emancipation. If Bolivia's history lessons have been silent on Blacks, saya has prevented the silence around Blacks from being complete. The lyrics of saya represent a means of communicating history, social concerns, and everyday sentiments over time and space within the black community and to the wider public and government. Blacks throughout the Yungas play saya and it has become the most representative element of the Afro-Bolivian population. One popular saya says:

Somos yungueñitos señores
presentes
Somos de la raza de la saya
Trayendo lindas tonadas
Para salir de Bolivia.

In many ways, the saya has come to overshadow other uniquely Afro-Bolivian cultural expressions. Other forms of afro - Bolivian music include the baile de tierra or cueca negra and the zemba. These dance forms were being forgotten until the emergence of the Movimiento Saya in the 80s, when an effort was made to recover them. At that time, the only people in the all-black community of Tocaña who remembered these dances were Abuelo Manuel and Awicha Angelia, now 80. Baile de tierra is associated with black wedding ceremonies and zemba with the Afro-Bolivian monarchy.

The monarchy is an Afro-Bolivian tradition with somewhat unclear origins. Reportedly, in the 1600s, a slave was brought to the hacienda of Mururata, Nor Yungas, and this slave was of royal kikongo Senegalese origin. In 1932, Bonifacio Pinedo, a descendant of this slave, was crowned king of the Blacks and was the object of special respect and authority. In 1992, his grandson, Julio Pinedo of Mururata, was crowned his successor. Juan Carlos, 24, of Tocaña explains, "The current Black king is a common ordinary person like anyone else. He has no real authority, his role is merely symbolic. The last king was crowned more out of an attempt not to lose the tradition than anything else".

Recognition of the Rey Negro has generally been restricted to the communities around Mururata, Nor Yungas. In Chicaloma, Sud Yungas, "el pueblo de los negros", the existence of a Black king has meant little. This is just one example of the internal diversity of the Afro-Bolivian population. Chicaloma, like many communities in Sud Yungas, has an integrated population of blacks and Aymaras who have racially and culturally mixed in ways not common in Nor Yungas. Apart from Tocaña and Chicaloma, there are concentrations of Blacks scattered throughout the Yungas in places like Chijchipa, Mururata, Kala Kala, and Colpar. No one knows for certain how many blacks are in Bolivia as they have not been counted on the national census. Estimates vary quite a bit, but the most popular is in the range of 20,000. They are certainly less than 1% of the country's total population. Rather than making them insignificant, however, this makes them especially interesting because they have managed, despite their small number and the powers that originally denied their humanity, to preserve certain cultural expressions and the blackness of their skin for over 400 years.

On a dirt road, with towering green mountains in the background, five black men stand in a row and take each other by the hand. They begin to swing their arms up and down and walk rhythmically forward, singing, "Mauchi, mauchi, candambira mauchi, candambira mauchi, candambira..." Behind them lies Tocaña's cemetery, overgrown with weeds hiding unmarked graves, and exiting the cemetery is a cluster of residents come to mourn the death of the community's oldest member, Awicha Irene, 95.

The sight is one few people have seen or even heard of. It is mauchi, the entierro negro, a burial ritual performed only by Afro-Bolivians for Afro-Bolivians. Only adult men sing mauchi and only when adults and married persons have died. The words they sing, as they make their way from the grave to the house of the deceased, are a mixture of Spanish, Aymara, and an unknown African language that the singers no longer understand. The ritual has disappeared everywhere but in Tocaña, where its words and rhythms seem echoes of a distant and unknown African past that has managed to survive, however transformed, in the lives of the blacks of the Bolivian Yungas.

THE JAPANESE SETTLERS IN THE TROPICAL LOWLANDS

BY PETER MCFARREN

Tokusho Miyagi fought the Russians and Americans in World War II and spent two and a half years as a prisoner of war in a Siberian coal mine. Today he oversees a 430-acre farm on Bolivia's tropical frontier, half a world away from his Okinawa homeland.

Miyagi is one of more than a million Japanese who settled in South America after the war and contributed to the region's development. Miyagi, now 72, lives three hours away by car from Santa Cruz in a comfortable concrete bungalow with his family. Beside the house is a garden filled with Chinese cabbage, tractor sheds and a windmill atop a water tank.

"In Okinawa, 300 families would have what I have here," he said in broken Spanish. His wife, who speaks only a few words of Spanish, served coffee. "I was a prisoner of war in Siberia, and after I returned to Okinawa, there was no work," he added.

In 1954, Miyagi, his wife and five children joined 400 other Okinawans and headed for Bolivia. They crossed the Pacific with documents issued by the U.S. Civil Administration of the Ryukyu Islands, which controlled Okinawa until 1972, when it was returned to Japan.

The former Japanese ambassador to Bolivia, Tadatsuma Yabu, recalled in an interview that "we lost a great deal of territory after the war. Japan was in a miserable state. There was no place for over one million people who lived in Taiwan, Manchuria and other regions, and who had grown accustomed to a different way of life."

Thus, one million Japanese left for South America, with loans and relocation expenses provided by the Japanese and U.S. governments. Most settled in Brazil while 80,000 made their way to Peru, 30,000 to Argentina and 10,000 to Bolivia.

"We have are still very grateful to Brazil, Peru, Bolivia and Argentina for having opened the doors to our immigrants," Ambassador Yabu said. "We have very special ties with South America."

Brazil's Japanese community, the largest outside Japan, centers around the industrial hub of Sao Paulo. Many Japanese work in agriculture, but they also have a strong presence in industry, commerce, government services and academia.

The first few hundred Japanese arrived in Bolivia as long ago as 1899 to escape harsh living conditions on the Peruvian plantations to which they had migrated. When the big postwar exodus began, the earlier immigrants helped the new arrivals get settled.

Miyagi and his family were among the pioneer settlers of the community now called Okinawa in the inhospitable eastern tropics of Bolivia. The Bolivian government gave each family 50 hectares (124 acres) of land. The United States provided tractors and other farm equipment.

Okinawa and San Juan de Yapacani, a colony 85 miles to the west, were carved out of rain forests inhabited by pumas, wild pigs, alligators, piranha fish and native tribes. In the first six months, 15 Japanese died in a mysterious epidemic. Many fled to Brazil and Peru or returned to Japan. Flooding destroyed their first rice harvests, and drought killed the cotton they planted later.

Wells had to be dug for drinking water. Santa Cruz, the nearest city, was reachable only by a two-day horseback ride because trucks could not make it over the swampy terrain.

Okinawa and Santa Cruz are now linked by a dirt road maintained by the Japanese International Cooperation Assistance program. Two modern hospitals built with Japanese government aid serve the area's 1,600 Japanese and 4,000 Bolivians.

Modern tractors bought on credit from Tokyo plow the Okinawa colony's 45,000 acres of arable land, which averages a production of 97,000 tons of rice, wheat, soya and sugar cane, and 550,000 dozen eggs. A cooperative of Japanese settlers is in charge of marketing.

Okinawa and San Juan de Yapacani have introduced rice, chicken farming and modern agriculture methods to the area, and now produce half of Bolivia's poultry and eggs. Thanks to Japanese farmers, Bolivia now exports rice.

Okinawa's social and political life centers around the Bolivian-Japanese Association. It organizes festivals and Spanish and Japanese language classes, registers births and runs the colony's two hospitals.

The association's former president, Kori Yamashiro, also arrived in Bolivia with his wife and three children. Recalling visits back to Japan in 1974 and 1982, he said; "I saw what life in Japan was really like. The people are very busy and have no time for pleasure. One has to work hard to maintain a family. . . I'm content here. At first it was hard, but now I'm used to life in Bolivia."

Sitting next to him, his wife, wearing a Japanese-style housedress, watched a Japanese musical show on a Japanese-made VCR. Against the whitewashed walls of their home is a shelf filled with Japanese books and magazines. Yamashiro maintains his faith in Shinto, the native Japanese religion of ancestor worship. His sons, like most Bolivians, are Roman Catholics.

Kiomi Nakazo, 30, arrived as a toddler in 1959 during a second wave of postwar immigration. She now works as a nurse at the Okinawa hospital, and has married a Japanese she met last year while studying in Japan.

"Japan is another world," she said. "I liked it very much. There is more comfort in Japan, but spiritually I prefer to be here."

Many children of the first postwar immigrants have moved to Bolivian cities, some have returned to study in Japan and others have taken over their parents' farms. Most consider themselves Bolivians, but still maintain ties with Japan.

THE CHIPAYAS

BY JORGE ASIN

Pushed and menaced by other cultures, determined to remain ethnically pure, and searching for food (mainly wild game), the Chipayas moved from place to place along the Bolivian altiplano and finally, early in this century, settled in the barren, frightening and yet beautiful empty space known as Chipaya. Located at some 1600 km from the town of Oruro, somewhere between the town of Huancalla and the Salar de Collpasa, Chipaya is a lovely town from which you can see a belt of snowy mountains. Unfortunately the mountains are too far away to provide protection against summer floods or to allow for better agricultural production.

Built with local materials, volcanic rock, adobe and straw, the typical Chipaya architecture spreads over the flat fields of their relatively small domains. Their houses, phutukus, are of two main construction forms and sizes: the larger one, built in a pyramidal form with a circular base, covered with the same material as the walls but with additional straw for impermability, constitutes the permanent family dwelling. A smaller cone-shaped form is found apart, amidst the empty space. This second phutuku is the night watchman's protection against freezing temperatures and is used as a protection base from which to watch their game (a blind). The beauty of this simple architecture is considerably hampered by a more recent use of a more common, parallelogram shaped house built for the ease of construction.

Similarly, the originality and brightness of their dress is being replaced by the less expensive, indifferent-looking modern fashion--mainly blue jeans and common shirts and jackets. Both cases represent a loss of cultural identity and possible adaptation to a more common standard that tends to predominate throughout the altiplano. Much of this change is in response to economics and practicality.

Chipayana, the language, is the best-preserved cultural trait. Derived from the ancient pukina tongue, this functional language of unknown origin is used only by members of this culture and their kin, the Hirohitos, and very few others. No more than two to three thousand people communicate in Chipayano. Their language provides a sense of community and culture, although versed in other altiplano languages, they use Chipayano as their first means of communication.

The soil of Chipaya is very infertile due to the altitude, freezing cold and salinity of the land. Agricultural production exists only at a minimum, and only renders quinoa as a product. Llama and sheep are the main animal products. Chipayas leave their town to work seasonally outside their own fields. The hire themselves out for sharecropping in Chile and other parts of Bolivia.

Who are these mysterious people?

There are myths about their wanderings in the altiplano. Some trace their origins to ancient times when floods forced them into hiding in caves for periods of time, while other assume that their origins are in the Polynesian Islands. The latter view is expressed in various texts, (one of them written by Felix Barrientos Ignacio in Chipaya, in 1990). Chipayas' ability to survive poverty and beauty of their culture are on a collision course with the demands of modern existence.

RELIGION IN AYMARA CULTURE

BY VINCENTE MAMANI BERNABÉ

AS AYMARAS, WE ARE A DEEPLY RELIGIOUS PEOPLE AND THE IDEA OF THE SACRED PERMEATES OUR CULTURE. WE RECOGNIZE OUR DEPENDENCE ON A SUPREME BEING, EVEN THOUGH WE CANNOT EXPLAIN IT WITH WESTERN CRITERIA AND LANGUAGE.

We Aymaras have lived on this land since time immemorial. However, no written chronicle exists: our history and religion are written on stones, in tapestries, ceramics and in our collective memory. In one way or another we still maintain the same way of life and the same religion as our ancestors.

Despite five centuries of oppression, our elders have not let themselves be influenced by Western culture, although the majority of young people are on a path towards alienation from the Aymara culture due to Western influences. This will ultimately lead to a loss of our cultural identity.

We are a people with thousands of years of history; we have created our own scientific ways of nourishing our people, our own religion, art, science, technology, organization, etc. Our life principle is solidarity, reciprocity, honesty and responsibility. We have a saying that describes our way of living: "From one cob of corn can come two; from that which I serve to myself, you too can eat".

The Aymaras are a deeply religious people and the idea of the sacred permeates our culture. We recognize our dependence on a supreme being, even though we cannot explain it with Western criteria and language.

The God of Life

The Aymaras are continually looking for God everywhere because it is this Supreme Being who gives us security in our daily lives. The God of Life manifests him/herself through the deities, such as those of the mountains, the water, the wind, the sun, the moon and the Waq'as (sacred places).

That is why we give wax'ta (offer-ings), wilancha (llama sacrifices), ch'alla (sprinkling alcohol on the ground) to the achachilas (the protecting spirits of the family and the whole community), the Pachamama (Mother Earth), Kuntur Mamani and Uywiri (protecting spirits of the home) as a sign of gratitude.

The Importance of the Mountains

The apachetas (remote mountains) area profoundly positive symbol. When the Aymara jaqui (man) goes on a long trip, he must cross the apacheta, the highest peak. As he passes his sacred place he shows great respect: he takes off his hat, kneels down and, with his face lifted to the heaven, his eyes open and his hands raised towards Tatitu Suma Awqui (Good God), he prays. Having realized this act of faith, he can go on, confident of his ability to overcome any difficulties he may encounter.

In a quotation from La Cultura Aymara, Domingo laque says, "for the Aymara the most sacred places are the high moutains, far from human problems: It is here that they have built their altars to offer worship, to communicate with their God and to ask for-giveness".

The Importance of the Community

In Aymara, the achachila means grandfather, a great-great grandfather, of a family. Ayllu marka means protector, in this case not of an individual but of the whole community. The acahachilas are the protectors of the community and are God's representatives.

Evil spirits like the anchañcho, supaya, saxra oppose the achachilas, the guardian spirits. These evil spirits are always looking for ways to bring harm to humanity.

The rites of waxt'a to the sacred hills take place for the most part in August; they are community celebrations. All rites, offerings and sacrifices are performed facing the East.

Many different rituals are celebrated. There are those within the family, in the mountains, for the planting and the harvest. There are rites to ask for rain or to ask for protection against hailstorms and frosts, and there are ceremonies for Mother-Earth.

Yatiris and the Coca Leaf

All rituals are led by Aymara yatiris, who are male or female priests. "The Yatiri is a wise person, someone who knows. He or she is the community' spiritual and moral guide. Through a method of divination that involves the reading of coca leaves, the yatari guides individuals in their personal decision making".

This green leaf related to nature, is the sacred leaf. It is used as a medicine and as a way of communicating with the God of Life. The coca leaf is now being threatened and condemned. Due to the problem of drug trafficking, it is being persecuted and eradicated. However, for the Aymaras, the coca leaf is the symbol of life, hope and faith.

Akulli, which means to share, is the name for yet another Aymara religious ceremony. Unity is called for while chewing coca. Without coca, almost nothing of importance can be realized in the community.

The Pachamama

Pachamama, or Mother Earth, occupies a very privileged place in Aymara culture, because she is the generative source of life. We carry out liturgies to Mother Earth, because there is a very close relationship between jaqi (human-ity), and the Pachamama.

"Man was created from the land, and thus man is fraternally tied to all the living beings that share the earth. The earth is our mother, and it is on the basis of this understanding that all of human society is organized, always maintaining the cosmic norms and laws. Women's and men's relationship with nature are what we call ecology, harmony and equilibrium".

According to my elders, before 1953 the land was cultivated in aynoqas (communal work), according to certain systems of reciprocity such as the ayni, the minqa or the waki. In other words, the land is part of the whole community (ayllu). After the Agrarian Reform Decree of 1953 collective property was broken up, the land was divided into individual parcels and the private individual minifundio was created. Each year there is less land and every day it is in worse condition.

We believe that in these last few years the land has not been producing as in the past because it is tired of producing year after year without resting. The use of chemical fertilizers is killing and poisoning our land and ourselves. The present condition of the land is lamentable. Many families are forced to cultivate very small plots; others have only a few rows, while others have been left with no land at all. This situation leads to conflict between brothers and has transformed us into fugitives of our maternal earth. Despite these dire consequences, large landowners still continue to usurp the native people's land. For the Aymaras, the type of land tenancy practiced by these large landowner is a social sin because we believe the land is for everyone. It is meant to .be shared and not only used for the benefit of a few.

Land is life because it produces all that we need to live. Water emanates from the land as if from the veins of a human body. There is also the natural wealth of minerals, and arid pasture also grows from it to feed the animals. Therefore, for the Aymaras, the Pachamama is sacred and since we are her children we are also sacred. No one can replace the earth, she is not meant to be exploited, or to be converted into merchandise. Our duty is to respect and care for the earth. This is what white people today are just beginning to realize and are calling ecology. Respect for the Pachamama is respect for us as she is life. Today, she is threatened with death and must be liberated for the sake of her children's liberation.

Carlo Intipampa has described the concept of the Pachamama in this way: "...the ritual of the Pachamama can in no way whatsoever be considered as a work of evil. On the contrary, it is in this very concept that the high level of religiosity rooted in the Andean people is preserved. Secondly, the Pachamama is considered to be the mother of this culture, because life itself is possible thanks to Mother Earth. She is an inexhaustible source of life".

MANY FACES OF BOLIVIA

THE CHIRIGUANOS, A PROUD RACE

BY PETER MCFARREN

The Chiriguanos, a brave and proud people who do not want to disappear, still subsist as an integral part of the great Bolivian nation, with a valuable historical past, a problematic present and a future of little hope.

The Legend of the Toad

The legend of the toad was related by Dr. Tesoro Chávez who received it from a Chiriguano grandmother from Ñaurenda, a ranch to the south of Monteagudo owned by Dr. Chávez's family.

"The Chiriguanos knew that there was going to be a great flood which would cover the whole earth. To save their race they chose a boy and a girl. They placed them in a big pumpkin. It rained and rained and everything was flooded. Almost every creature died in the floods that came. When the water evaporated, the pumpkin which contained the children came to a stop on the bank of a river. They knew what their mission was. They came out of the pumpkin and felt intense grief at what they found. The vultures were one of the few animals that survived."

"At that time all animals talked. The poor children were very cold and frightened. They heard some voices and realized that it was the vultures preparing a barbecue. The vultures had saved fire from a tree that was hit by lightening. The children were hungry, but they could not go near the meat for fear of the vultures."

"A toad which had survived the flood appeared, calmed them and promised to steal the fire for them. The toad approached the vultures' fire and got a small burning branch. A vulture noticed and put water in the toad's mouth to put out the fire. The poor, battered toad returned as fast as he could to the children and spit out what little fire was left. It was in this way that the children saved the fire, and the people again occupied the land."

Now when there is a great drought, they tie a toad between two stakes, belly side up so that Tumpa (God) will take pity on the toad and send them rain.

Living in a world made up of impenetrable forests, deserts, great rivers and streams, mountainous regions and plains of the Bolivian East, the survivors of this race form a powerful alliance with nature. The Chiriguanos from Ingre are now employed on the lands that formerly belonged to their forefathers. They live united by a tradition that is transmitted from one generation to the next. They are a proud and hard-working people. Their ancestors came in great waves from Paraguay in the 16th and 17th centuries. It was a slow migration over thousands of kilometers. Though they were looking for better lands to ensure their material existence, they were also fighting for spiritual contentment in all aspects of life.

On reaching the eastern side of what is now Bolivia, they had to face the Inca empire and the Chane, the Arawak tribe which controlled part of the area. To stop the Chiriguano invasion, the Incas built forts, among them Samaipata.

The Chiriguanos, who came from the great Chaco, subjected the Chane, who were a peaceful tribe and did not offer resistance. They enslaved the men and married the women. Then there came about a division among the Chiriguanos because of differences in tradition and regionalism. There were the Chiriguanos from Izozog who live in the southern part of Santa Cruz and in the Ava, and Chiriguanos who live in the eastern part of Chuquisaca, partly in Santa Cruz and in the north of Tarija.

With the arrival of the Spaniards, the Chiriguanos had to defend themselves against the invaders. They rose up against the power of the Spaniards, and under the command of their chieftains they began a war which lasted until the last years of the 19th century. The Spaniards resorted to every means to annihilate these people. The missionaries arrived with the soldiers, but the Chiriguanos continued their rebellion, aware that the missionaries were the harbingers of those who would come later to enslave them.

According to Pinkert in his book, The Chiriguano War, the Chiriguanos were the only native race against whom the Viceroy Toledo, in the name of the King of Spain himself, declared a war to the death, but was unable to conquer. The resistance of these people ended with the Battle of Kuruyuki, a massacre that occurred in 1892, and the death of their great chief Apiaguaqui-Tumpa in Monteagudo at the hands of the Spaniards.

Chiriguanos are a people who have nonetheless maintained a strong spirit of tribal cohesion. According to Dr. Hernando Sanabria Fernández, author of the book Apiaguaqui-Tumpa, "it can be said that they were the bravest and most warlike indige-nous group in this part of the continent, and therefore the most unwilling to submit and the most obstinate defenders of their liberty."

"Proof of this is the fact that while other native groups from the mountains and from the plains were conquered and absorbed by the white man in the short- or long-term, the Chiriguanos resisted for centuries, until the very last."

Occult Powers

The Chiriguanos live in relation to occult powers that float in nature. Health, work, travel, hunting, time itself and the well-being and order of the family depend on the harmony and potency of these powers.

Through contact with Catholic and Protestant missionaries, and the penetration of the Spanish colonists, the foreign cultural and religious values were absorbed. Only in Izozog in the south of the department of Santa Cruz have many of the Chiriguano traditions been maintained. It is there that Dr. Jurgen Riester, a German anthropologist and author of several books about the indigenous cultures of the East, has done commendable work in documentation, development and protection of the traditional values of these people.

In his book, En Busca de la Loma Santa ("In Search of the Holy Hill"), Dr. Riester writes about the influences of the Catholic settlements on the lives of the Chiriguanos.

"The objective of these Catholic settlements, and of the Catholic and Protestant missions, was the transformation of the unworthy way of life of the Indians who, in the eyes of the missionaries, ran freely in the jungle without order, religion or real work. The result was the invasion of landowners, merchants and other foreign elements that initiated the enslavement, the kidnapping and violation of the human rights, the economic exploitation, and in many cases the physical extermination of the indigenous people."

Their Situation Today

The way things are today among the Chiriguanos can be seen through the family of Alexandro Chávez, a Chiriguanos cowboy, his wife and their eight children. His reputation as a cowboy, horse tamer, guide, violinist and worker in leather reaches from the Iguenbe Valley across the Parapeti River as far Rosario del Ingre. He is famous for his loyalty, his sense of humor and his knavery. His wife, Lidia Chávez, a descendent of the great Chinica, is an expert in the preparation of buyape (corn biscuit), caguiye (corn soup), baipu, ka-a, arapasi and many other Chiriguanos dishes. She is respected for her gentility and amiability. Her initial reserve with a stranger disappears after the greeting "icavinio" and after sharing a glass of a cold corn drink.

Certain customs and traditions of her ancestors have come down from many generations, but one can see that the penetration of modern ways is changing the Chávezs' way of life.

Ceramics have been replaced by plastic, the violin by the radio, women's textiles by nylon, the horse by the tractor. Some of the sons have gone to the city, partly obeying their parents' wish that they receive a good education.

Their Values

The Franciscan priest, Father Bernardo Niño, worked many years with the Chiriguanos. In 1912 he published a book, Chiriguano Ethnography, in which he speaks of the religious values of the Chiriguanos:

"When the soul of the Chiriguano leaves the body, it does not die; all of them, without realizing it or even suspecting it, have this idea of the immortality of the soul. Related to this, there is the mourning and the feelings of loss, the burial and the things that they place on the casket when someone dies."

"The Tumpa is the principle of the goodness in every virtue, of everything that is good, Tecocavi. With this idea that they have of God, the Chiriguanos naturally conclude that God admits in his company only the good people, those who are virtuous and free of all evil."

The late Dr. Hernando Sanabria, a distinguished historian, former director of the Gabriel René-Moreno University library and author of the book about the Chiriguano, Apiaguaqui Tumpa, referred to the work of the missionaries among the Chiriguano in an interview before his death:

"The Franciscan missionaries had the Guaranís congregated in groups. But the missions were secularized, which permitted the landowners to exploit them. When the Franciscans left, they were alone. The evangelists, who where very strict, came and did not permit them to maintain their culture. They prohibited the traditional songs and dances; they considered them diabolical. The unfortunate result is that the Indians, upon losing their own culture also lost their identity, and became easy prey for the exploitation of the corregidores, landowners and also of the union leaders."

Dr. Sanabria referred also to the Indians who came to the area around the city of Santa Cruz. With the loss of their cultural values under the influence of the missions, and their need to work outside the tribal context in sugar harvests, they lost their identity and began to adopt the worst values of the predominant culture of the region.

"Apiaguaqui-Tumpa? No, I don't know who he is..." Thus answered a Guaraní youth who lives in the Valley of the Ingre, south of Monteagudo. The Chiriguanos are a sub culture of the Guaranis.

The reality of the Chiriguano people has also been affected by the educational system. In Angoa, a small village in the Valley of the Ingre, there is a Guaraní school built with the aid of the German Catholic Church and the collaboration of local residents, especially of Mr. Alberto Guzmán, owner of the Ipati Hacienda.

Although the school fulfills an important function in the area, it has an educational focus that does not consider the history, the language or the culture of the Chiriguanos. According to Dr. Sanabria, many of the Guaraní schools have teachers who do not speak the language and are not aware of the Chiriguanos' reality.

"An inferiority complex is fostered in the schools. The teachers prohibit the students to speak Guaraní. The language is condemned to disappear if something is not done, There are no educational materials, and the normal school, which was established to prepare teachers who spoke Guaraní, has not been able to fulfill its purpose."

On their part, the scientists from the Center of Anthropological Studies, in their publication, The Chiriguanos, affirm that "to give these communities economic, social and cultural reinforcements will make it possible for them to live like independent men with full rights within Latin American societies. Language constitutes a basic factor in the existence and the process of liberation of each indigenous people."

It is abundantly clear that the Christians, with the patience and the perseverance of an anchorite and risking their lives in many circumstances, little by little took possession of the whole territory. Today there is no corner where there is not a Christian family living.

In many places, the Chiriguano tribe has disappeared completely, sometimes due to the epidemics, other times due to their lost liberty. In some places there are still a few rather large groups, often subject to a boss because of the debts acquired by the people.

In the Rosario del Ingre Valley, in the southern part of Chuquisaca, there is much interest in maintaining and promoting the Chiriguano traditions. Several young professionals formed a group called Ava, which means "man" in Guaraní, with the objective of protecting the natural and human resources of the region. It is their desire to create a small museum in that area.

A festival has been organized in which both Chiriguano and Christian traditions are exhibited. Ironically, many of the people interested in promoting the traditions and the culture of the Chiriguano people are the sons of the bosses.

In Santa Cruz, a group called "Aid for the Indian Farmer of the Bolivian East" has been formed by several anthropologists. Through the work carried out by this group, the Casa de la Cultura, the Cooperativa Cruceña de Cultura and the effort of many people, something is being done to protect the Chiriguano culture.

Nevertheless, the backing of all the people is essential, Dr. Tesoro Chavez said, "it is important that the Bolivian people accept and respect the Chiriguano people as an integral part of our nation. It is the rich variety of our people which gives us our identity. It is a richness formed through the centuries, and if we do not defend it, we will be losing something of great value."

NOTE: The Chiriguanos of the Ingre Valley celebrate Carnaval, which falls either in February or March, with dances and beautiful masks. The town's main festivity is during the Fiesta del Rosario. Sucre or Camiri is the starting point to a visit to the Monteagudo region, which is located in southern Chuquisaca. Both buses or trucks serve this town. For an excellent description of the relationship between the white landowners and the Chiriguano farmers in the Monteagudo region, be sure to read the book Caciques y Patrones by American author Kevin Healy.

CHIMANES' FIGHT FOR THEIR TERRITORY

BY BOLIVIAN TIMES STAFF

IN BOLIVIA'S AMAZON BASIN, GANGS OF CHAIN SAWERS COMPETE WITH HUNTING-AND-GATHERING TRIBES FOR OLD-GROWTH MAHOGANY TREES. THE CHIMANES INDIANS WHO HAVE TRADITIONALLY USED THE MAHOGANY ON THEIR HOMELAND TO MAKE DUGOUT CANOES, NOW FACE HUNDREDS OF IMPOVERISHED LOGGERS WHO ARE ENTERING THE CHIMANE RESERVE TO EXTRACT MAHOGANY. THE RESERVE WAS CREATED TO GIVE NATIVE PEOPLE RIGHTS TO THEIR HOMELAND. BUT CHIMANES LEADERS SAY THEY ARE CONSTANTLY REMINDED THAT, TO A LARGE DEGREE, IT EXISTS ONLY ON PAPER.

Cutting through early morning mist, a logging gang makes its way up the Maniqui River, an Amazonian tributary that flows through the center of the reserve. The chain saw gang left the last dirt road behind five days ago, and they are traveling slowly in this vast wilderness because their wooden canoe is heavily loaded with supplies: alcohol, chain saws, food and gas.

Chain saw gangs in the Chimane Reserve are much like hundreds of other gangs that operate in Bolivia's expansive Amazonian basin: they saw mahogany and other valuable hardwoods that are exported to Argentina, the United States and Mexico. The chain saw gangs use minimal amounts of equipment. In fact, most gangs own only a few chain saws and an outboard motor. The gangs don't use trucks, so to get the logs out of the jungle they must saw the mahogany trees into two-hundred-pound sections and carry them on their shoulders. Trails hacked into the dense undergrowth lead from the remote logging camps to rivers, where the mahogany is lashed onto rafts and then floated to the nearest town.

When they are carrying the timbers to the river, the gangs form a line in which each logger has a section about one hun-dred paces long. The work starts when the first logger staggers toward the end of his section with a timber, where he will pass his load off to the next logger in line. That person will then carry the timber to the next worker. The relay system is slow, so at times it takes an entire day for a gang to move a batch of forty timbers half a mile. While some workers are carrying the timbers, others saw new logs into 200-pound sections--a job that takes a great deal of skill because they must repeatedly cut ten-foot-long boards free-hand with only one-quarter-inch error in their width. The whole extraction process requires next to no infra-structure; streams, rivers and trails cut by machetes are the only necessary ingredients. The simplicity of the process means that the loggers are free to cut wherever they want, as long as no one stops them.

"It's like the old Wild West in the U.S.," said Preston Pattie, a consultant with the U.S. Agency for International Development in Bolivia (USAID). "Loggers have tradition-ally gone where they wanted to [in Bolivia], taking timber wherever they pleased." Pattie said this is why the remoteness and lack of governmental control in the Chimane territo-ry have made this, and other areas like it in Bolivia, vulnerable to opportunistic busi-nesses.

MANY FACES OF BOLIVIA

The chain saw gang's outboard motor screams over the drone of the rapids near the headwaters of the Maniqui River. Here, facing the jungle-covered mountains of the southern edge of the Chimane Reserve, lives a Chimane Indian named Apo (In order to not compromise safety, "Apo's" real name is not used in this article). Apo's son has heard the motorboat, and is now waiting for it in a tree by the river. Soon the dugout canoe grinds onto the sandy shore below him, and the group of loggers jumps into the shallow water. The men wear shorts, cleated soccer shoes and ripped shirts. Because the gang must hike several miles to their logging camp, the workers carry backpacks made from feed sacks.

The men head toward a clearing filled with the sounds of chickens and parrots, where Apo squats with his wife by a cooking fire. "Apo," the gang's boss says, "we are going to log mahogany here." The muscular Chimane looks up at him, and then back down at his food. He doesn't argue--Apo knows that, for the loggers, the borders of this million-acre reserve are simply lines on a piece of paper, and that on the ground these lines are next to meaningless.

The Chimanes try to remain apart from the rest of Bolivia. In fact, the tribe remains so isolated that very few of the 5,000 Chimane even speak Spanish, according to Anthony Stocks, a Professor of Anthropology at Idaho State University. Chain saw gangs often "employ" Chimane to scout for mahogany trees, which is one of the only interactions the Chimane have with the rest of Bolivia. But the Chimane receive little in return for their work in the logging camps. A group of Chimanes will commonly spend a whole month locating 80 mahogany trees. A gang can sell the lumber from these 80 trees for US$60,000, yet the Chimanes receive less than US$500 worth of food and other goods in exchange for these trees. The Chimanes say the loggers cheat them,

and they criticize their own leaders and the Bolivian government for failing to keep the gangs out of the Chimane Reserve.

Westerners often speak of Amazonian logging as if it were one homogeneous group. But in fact, it is a highly stratified industry, and those who enter the forest to cut trees are at the very bottom. Tied to their work by a debt-peonage system, most loggers can't even leave the jungle when they want to. And while those who carry the mahogany out on their backs receive less than 70 cents an hour for this labor, the lumber companies who import the wood into the United States, Argentina and Peru make a handsome profit.

Pablo grips the blade of his five-foot-long chain saw and throws it over his shoulder. The 29-year-old chain sawer steps away from Apo's cooking fire and thinks of how much he wants to leave the forest. But, like most members of this chain saw gang, Pablo can't leave because he is heavily in debt to his boss. In fact, Pablo owes so much money to his boss that he may have to stay in the jungle for five months before he can leave the gang. Pablo hasn't always been so desperate for work. He says that several years ago his father had his own chain saw gang, but he was an alcoholic and drank away the family's income. Pablo dropped out of school when he was in his early teens so that he could learn how to drive a truck and operate a chain saw. After his dad's lumber business collapsed, Pablo drifted among logging camps in the Madidi National Park, about 75 miles northwest of the Chimane Reserve. When all the mahogany was cut in the park, Pablo joined the rest of the loggers from his town and traveled to San Borja, where he got a job logging in the Chimane Reserve.

Like most men on the chain saw gangs, Pablo started logging because the pay--between US$5 and $6 a day--makes the work one of the best jobs for a non educated laborer in the Bolivian lowlands. In the months that Pablo has spent in the remote logging camps, he has learned to live without dancing, women and the late night bars he enjoys so much in the steamy tropical towns where he would otherwise live.

At night, instead of going to a bar, Pablo hunts red howler monkeys, pacas and gray brocket deer. These nightly hunting trips are necessary because the gangs only bring white rice, noodles and salt from town. Those supplies frequently run out, so the loggers often work having only eaten plantain and the animals they have killed. Plantain is a major part of the diet in the logging camps, and all of the plantain comes from trading with the Chimane. But the Chimanes are often cheated in these deals, which only add to their anger at the foremen of chain saw gangs for refusing to fairly compensate them for the mahogany they take.

Jack Weatherford, professor of anthropology said at Macalester College, said that while indigenous peoples have land titles throughout South America, they are often not enforced. "Their rights are only as good as the willingness of the governments to enforce them," he said. "They may have rights in theory, but somehow those rights get lost between the capital cities and the rural areas." Apo would agree with Weatherford. "We don't have nothing, nothing here," he says softly. "They cut all the [mahogany] trees we had here. [These loggers] sell all the mahogany, so we don't have nothing for our canoes." Looking at the ground he adds, "the [logging] machines scare all the animals away now, if we want to go hunt, there is nothing, we can't find anything."

Lero, a Chimane who has visited towns outside of the reserve, is also painfully aware that, despite the rights the Chimane have to their land, these rights do not translate into protection from opportunistic businesses. "The loggers say, 'you Chimane have nothing, you can't do anything. You don't have chain saws, [you] are useless, and [you] don't know how to work," Lero explains. Lero says the loggers tell him he is not utilizing the forest, and so it is justifiable for outsiders to log in the Chimane homeland. Lero counters that he and other Chimane do use the forest, and that they are angry with the loggers for entering the reserve and stealing items from their homes and the trees they would keep for canoes. Both Apo and Lero agree that to preserve the last of their mahogany trees, they have to control the chain saw gangs. But they don't expect the Chimane Reserve's borders to be policed anytime soon.

Policing the reserve would likely require resources the Bolivian government doesn't have. For example, in 1997 the Bolivian Forestry Service had an operating budget of US$6.5 million, and was responsible for managing an area two-thirds the size of the U.S. National Forests. So, it is not surprising that government oversight has been virtually nonexistent, especially in light of the fact that in the United States, the U.S. Forest Service has fifty thousand employees and an annual budget of more than US$2.5 billion.

"The presence of the government in a lot of these places is limited," Pattie of USAID said as he smoked a pipe in his consulting office. "I don't see that there is any capability, or means of gaining the capability, to regulate an industry that is thrown across such a vast uncontrolled area with limited access. And with a history of powerful local people controlling in places like San Borja, the town closest to the Chimane Reserve." Certainly, Pattie's assessment casts doubt on the ability of international aid organizations to positively affect change in the region. The last organization to try to do so, Conservation International, pulled out several years ago amidst accusations from

Bolivians that they had made the situation worse in their almost ten-year involvement in the area surrounding the Chimane Indian Reserve.

Jorge Añez, the leader of the Chimane tribe, is more optimistic than Pattie. Añez believes that guarding the Maniqui River is the most efficient means of regulating the loggers because the river is the only means of transportation in the territory. The local police, Aflez said, are not going to help him do this. Instead, Afiez envisions a Chimane border patrol, for which he is looking for funding. Añez said he believes Chimane guards are necessary because, based on the widespread corruption in the Bolivian courts and law enforcement agencies, he lacks the legal resources to effectively fight the gangs. But other Chimanes, who have more contact with the loggers, wonder if a few guards can keep settlers and opportunistic outsiders from exploiting the rich resources in the million-acre wilderness.

Cursing their heavy backpacks and blisters, Pablo and his gang walk away from Apo's hut on a well-worn animal trail that leads to their logging camp. As they walk, they count the number of mahogany trees left in the area. They estimate that there are less than five. Soon their conversation shifts to what they will do once all the mahogany is removed from the Chimane Reserve. They are not sure which species of hardwood they will cut next, but they agree that whatever it is, it will be exported. One thing, however, is for sure: the gang isn't planning on leaving anytime soon.

For more information contact: Carolina Zumarán, Outreach Coordinator, **Beni Biological Station, Bolivian Academy of Sciences**, PO Box 5829, La Paz, Bolivia. Fax. 2352071. Also **Conservation International**, E-mail: CIBolivia@conservation.org or: www.conservation.org.

CROSS COUNTRY CURES OF THE KALLAWAYAS

BY ERIC LATIL

BOLIVIA'S ITINERANT FOLK HEALERS, FROM THE KALLAWAYAS CULTURE, HAVE BEEN WANDERING THE REGION FOR MORE YEARS THAN PEOPLE CAN REMEMBER, COLLECTING MEDICINAL PLANTS AND SELLING HERBS AND CURES TO PEOPLE IN REMOTE AND FAR FLUNG REGIONS. THERE ARE PLANS TO ASSIST THE KALLAWAYAS IN PRESERVING THEIR LORE BEFORE TOO MUCH OF IT IS LOST FOREVER.

Bolivia's patchwork ethno-cultural identity is altogether thrilling, problematic and complex. Even as the government searches for a united national identity, many Bolivians still follow the precepts and traditions of their own heritage.

The Quechua, Aymara and Guarani attract the most attention, but there is one indigenous group whose penchant for herbal healing and making hundred kilometers 'house calls' on foot set it apart. Living in the high valleys of Charazani, in the province of Bautista Saavedra, La Paz, they are the Kallawaya.

At one time they even had their own language, says Hilarion, a 64-year-old Kallawaya folk healer in Charazani. "We (today's Kallawaya) know a little, but we're forgetting. They use that language for speaking among themselves. It's secret, special."

Though there have been numerous studies on the culture, the Kallawayas' past and present are elusive topics. Their history, particularly their relation to the Incan Empire, is an enigma. What investigators do know is that the Kallawaya's ancient practice of traditional herbal medicine stretches back as far as anyone can remember.

French cultural promoter Erik Latil recently accompanied Kallawaya folk healers Hilarion and Alejandro and ritualist Pedro Huaqui on an excursion to study their herbal medicine practices and itinerant sales methods. Some of the goals were to walk along, gathering plants and find individuals who needed herbal medicines or a prescription.

Besides shepherding and farming, the folk healer travels cross-country to sell his organic cures. Once or twice a year, he leaves his home, wife and children to travel by truck, bus or foot to cities as far away as Santa Cruz.

He usually travels in August and September, when farming chores ease up. He may travel for up to two months, leaving domestic responsibilities to his wife.

Hilarion believes today's folk healers only "travel briefly." He says that the folk healers used to travel much farther, more often and by foot to Argentina, Chile, Peru and Colombia.

"The trips sometimes lasted months—three or four," he says. Some even walked as far as Panama, when the canal was being built, "but all of them have already died."

Hilarion took up herbal medicine because he never studied adobe construction, an alternative local profession. His parents and grand parents built with stones. Also, "we never left [this area]. We didn't know about anything but plants."

Hilarion began traveling when he was 16, with healers of various ages. "That's how I learned to heal and sell the products," he recalls.

Before the group set out to make the rounds, they entered the hills to prepare a mesa (a ritual performed to bring good luck).

They traveled by foot, first to Peru, stopping at every farm. They practiced in Rinconada, Pinamari and Yavere, sometimes spending two or three days in barren outback.

"We slept in the hills, sometimes without food," says Hilarion. "Such is the traveler's life."

They usually took along toasted beans, ground pita and sugar. They drank whatever water was available.

Afterwards, on two occasions Hilarion walked to Chile with other folk healers. On the second trip he reached the city of Arica, in 30 days, then continued on to the towns of Taca and Iquique.

Besides being a means of income, healing with plants also lets man commune with nature, the Kallawaya believe. Numerous natural elements or sacred sites, called "achachilas," play a very important role in their daily lives. They believe the sites help maintain an equilibrium between man and Pachamama (Mother Earth).

The achachilas are hills, lakes and rocks, which the Kallawaya believes, have a certain power. All sorts of rituals are performed in and around them. The Kallawaya particularly venerate those places that bring pleasant trips, health for family and livestock, rain and a flush harvest.

For them, the achachilas are like people; they have a name, personality and qualities. The Kallawaya folk healers are responsible for maintaining the power of the sacred place, "feeding it," by performing rituals there.

When a sacred spot is neglected, they believe, the power diminishes. Such is the case of the achachila, Larwachijuani, in General Gonzalez, where healers used to perform rituals before traveling to Peru. "It's been more than 50 years since a ritual has been performed here," says Hilarion, 64, from Charazani. "We keep the brazier and some clay plates (ritual utensils) here in town, but now there's nothing.

"We could repair [the place], but it wouldn't be so easy, because we could get sick. Its power would punish us. First we have to perform a little ritual, which is like getting its permission.

"It's like a person. For example, if I take your hat from you without asking for permission, you're going to get angry. If we pay it with food, we can repair the place and be at peace."

Kallawaya treatments do not only involve the use of medicinal plants. When herbs are not enough, folk healers employ spiritual rituals or read coca leaves or cards.

"My father in law can heal in another way; he's a yatiri," says Hilarion's nephew Alejandro, 30. "He's not so interested in herbs. He heals things that plants don't."

For example, Alejandro says, if a man falls in a gully or something scares him, a few months later he will 'fall ill. "Even if you take medicine or (use) plants, you won't get better," he says. "That's why you have to look for someone who's a yatiri, like my father in law."

The victim must show the yatiri how and where the accident occurred. There, the yatiri heals the victim by performing a ritual using a black rooster, a live dog or sometimes a dried llama fetus, Alejandro says. "It's as if the place had power over the person," he says.

Cultural promoter Latil's project has produced a pedagogic and introductory document on the properties of the Kallawaya's medicinal plants. Also, project participants donated a mounted collection of reports on 24 staple plants to the Kallawaya School of General Gonzalez. This July and August the project's findings will be presented in various botanical gardens in France, including one of Europe's most famous, the du Col du Lautaret.

Latil wishes to later complete a true cultural exchange by introducing Bolivia to the French management and culture of traditional medicine. Latil proposes a tour of Bolivia—under the auspices of the Association of Latin American Exchange and Cultural Solidarity (ECLAT)—to exhibit a series of medicinal plants from the Alps and the Kallawaya region.

Latil's project received financial aid from the French minister of Youth and Sports, the University of Aix en Provence, CROUS de Marseille, Les Mejeones de Valaurie, Santoline de St Remy de Provence, Solidarité Bolivie and Les Amis du Jardin Alpin du Col du Lautaret.

The project received support from the Directorate of the Bolivian Ministry of Biodiversity, Ulla Ulla National Reserve in Bautista Saavedra, the La Paz Prefecture Department of Tourism, the herbarium and botanical garden of La Paz's Cota Cota neighborhood, the French Embassy, the Alianza Francesa of La Paz, the US Peace Corps in Bolivia, the non governmental organization CISED and Linares Photography Studio in La Paz.

If you are interested in consulting a Kallawaya specialist contact Dr. Walter Alvarez Quispe at **SOBOMETRA**, Calle pasaje Gonzales 140, San Pedro, La Paz. Tels/Fax. 2313783, 2331724. Casilla 12585.

Kallawaya, Curanderos Itinerantes de los Andes: Louis Girault. *Investigación sobre prácticas medicinales y mágicas.* La Paz, 1987. Ed. Unicef, OPS, OMS, PL 480. © ORSTOM, Paris. Also available in French.

MANY FACES OF BOLIVIA

AYOREOS CLASH WITH THE 20TH CENTURY

BY MIKE CEASER

For most peoples the journey from the Stone Age to the space age has been a long one--but not for the Ayoreos. The Ayoreo indigenous people living in extreme poverty in Santa Cruz's Bolivar neighborhood have only to go back a few decades or travel a few hundred kilometers south into the Chaco scrub country to rediscover their Stone Age past. The Chaco is where the Ayoreos were living their hunting and gathering lifestyle as they had since time immemorial, until the 20th century intruded violently and irreparably.

The Ayoreos, a tiny tribe numbering about 3,000 people, had evidently had some contact with others. The Guaranis called them "Yanaiguas" (forest dwellers), and the Jesuits called them "Zamucos," but they never succeeded in evangelizing them. During the 1932-1935 Chaco War between Bolivia and Paraguay, troops occupied desert water holes, forcing the shy Ayoreos north to survive. But after the war the soldiers left the inhospitable area to the Ayoreos, who went on unnoticed with their traditional ways.

It was religion and a railroad to Puerto Suárez that permanently changed the Ayoreo's lives. When crews began work on the railroad in the 1940s, the Ayoreos, who had little concept of private property, sacked and stole from the workers' camps. Military troops protecting the railroad work retaliated in what some called an "Ayoreo hunt", killing Ayoreos, although it's unclear whether this was official policy. About the same time, missionaries, mostly from the United States, began efforts to convert the Ayoreos. But not all Ayoreos were eager for contact.

In November, 1943, a group of six American missionaries were killed by Ayoreos, generating publicity in the U.S. More missionaries came and set up missions from which they gave Ayoreo groups free food and clothing. The strategy worked and the Ayoreos, motivated also by infighting between their groups, began adopting a semi-nomadic existence in which they settled near the approximately ten Evangelical and Roman Catholic missions, but still came and went. "They were the last natives in the department (of Santa Cruz) to make contact with whites," said sociologist Antonio Rivero of Support for Campesinos and Indigenous Peoples of Eastern Bolivia (APCOB), who works with the Ayoreos on land issues. The missionaries tried teaching the Ayoreos western ways. After awhile, for example, missionaries stopped giving things away and instead required the Ayoreos to work for goods, eventually replacing this system with one in which the Ayoreos were paid and had to purchase things. U.S. Evangelical missionary, Jamie Dunne, tracked down what may have been the final group of Ayoreos to make contact with white culture, near the Paraguay border, in 1965. Dunne died in 1993, but his Bolivian wife, Eida, said that her husband spent nine years roaming the Chaco scrub in his pickup truck searching for a group of uncontacted Ayoreos to evangelize.

When Dunne met them, the Ayoreos were living a simple existence, wandering about hunting tortoises, wild boars and armadillos and gathering honey. Men wore only loincloths and women pieces of fabric wrapped around their waists. They carried children about in bags woven from plant fibers and had almost no possessions. During rainy seasons, they drank from water holes and rain puddles. In dry seasons, they squeezed roots for moisture. The Ayoreos worshipped a bird god, the Kuyavo, important for their culture because the bird's singing announced the change between the wet and dry seasons. They also had a complex mythology, passed along orally, which emphasized that many parts of the animals they hunted were taboo and inedible. For diversion, they told stories, sang and beat gourd drums and played a game resembling tag. The Ayoreos also had practices which we find cruel, but which made their severe lifestyle possible. When an older person could no longer keep up with the group, he or she would ask to be buried alive. This also was the traditional way of killing unwanted newborns.

At first, to win the Ayoreos' trust, the Dunnes traveled about with them. "It wasn't easy," she said. "The first years we were nomads. After two years, we settled in one spot, and they came and went." She said Ayoreos recognized life with the missionaries as easier. "When they saw there was help, they stopped wandering because (nomadism) isn't easy," she recalled. "You suffer from the sun, heat, bees. When there's no hunting, there's nothing to eat." The Dunnes helped the Ayoreos build houses and at first gave them free food. "Later we told them, 'We're going to teach you to work,'" Dunne said. "We gave food to those who went to work and nothing to those who didn't." Then the Dunnes began paying the Ayoreos cash for working in order to teach them to earn and buy things. The Dunnes' method--a common one used by missionaries--was used to try to "civilize" the Ayoreos. In 1985, the Dunnes moved with their group of Ayoreos to a mission nearer to Santa Cruz and then returned to their home in the small town of Camiri, where they established an orphanage in 1992. Dunne said that the couple felt they had accomplished their goal. "My husband's goal was to evangelize them, and we couldn't continue feeding them from the markets of Camiri. They had to live on their own." Today, some of those Ayoreos live in missions, others in Santa Cruz's Bolivar neighborhood.

In many outward aspects, the Ayoreos changed quickly under the missionaries' wings. They adopted western dress, stopped scarifying themselves and abandoned many other traditions. "[The missionaries] ended their games, their dances, their music," Riveros said. "The dancing, for example, [was] very erotic." Anthropologists have noted that Ayoreos did adapt quickly to a money economy, which, combined with their extreme poverty, was perhaps a forerunner to their current participation in prostitution and drug dealing. But in other ways, their nature resisted civilization. "There have been many attempts to turn them into farmers," said Rivero, "but they are by nature hunter-gatherers. They plant and harvest what they want to eat, which is a form of gathering." Riveros said that fundamental changes require more than a few decades or even generations. One anthropologist, Riveros said, has theorized that the Ayoreos continue using a "hunter's logic" in the city; that is, they still think in short term. "Their contact with whites has been very sudden and brutal," Riveros said. "Changing the customs of a culture takes generations. It's not a five-year project."

Since they made contact with whites, the Ayoreos have also suffered from western diseases, such as tuberculosis and smallpox, which afflicted other native peoples centuries ago. The Ayoreos are naive in many ways. Riveros said that when politicians visit their communities, promising assistance, the Ayoreos take them at their word and later visit their offices demanding the aid. "They're very straightforward," Riveros said.

An old Dunne video shows the Ayoreos telling stories, beating gourd drums and laughing as they climb in and out of the missionaries' truck. The Ayoreos living in Santa Cruz must laugh a lot less now. In the city, their community is beset by many social problems, including drug use, prostitution, unemployment and crime. In the Bolivar neighborhood, a group of about 110 Ayoreos has lived for thirteen years in wood shacks roofed with blue and orange plastic sheets through which the rain drips. The land is littered with trash and there are few latrines. The community drinks from a pair of water taps, which are also used for bathing. The half-built church doubles as a rudimentary school, which many children do not attend. Neque Picaneray, one of the community's leaders, said the Ayoreos moved to Santa Cruz because in the countryside there was little medical attention or work. In Santa Cruz, the men work irregularly, clearing land with machetes, and the women weave handbags for sale. Picaneray said conflicts with non-Ayoreo neighbors are one of the community's principal difficulties. "Sometimes they don't take us into account as citizens. They don't listen to us. They don't want to approach the Ayoreos to find solutions. They want to create more problems."

The Ayoreos' neighbors said it was the Ayoreos who caused the problems. Patricia Gonzalez, part-owner of a restaurant around the corner from the Ayoreos, said that most nights, groups of Ayoreo men gathered to drink across the street. She pointed toward the Ayoreo community. "At night on the corner there are five or six (Ayoreos) who rob old people and neighbors," she said. "The adults work, but the youth don't." Gonzalez said the neighbors were organizing to try and expel the Ayoreos. Manuel Dosapey is the Ayoreos' development representative to the Santa Cruz Ethnic Peoples Coordinator (CPESC), which includes representatives from four indigenous peoples. He said that CPESC was working on obtaining land titles for Ayoreo communities in the countryside.

Dosapey said Ayoreos first came to Santa Cruz to work, but that many were not paid and so could not pay the fare home to their missions. They settled around the old train station, where some women engaged in prostitution. In 1985, with help from city officials, many Ayoreos moved to the Bolivar neighborhood where they live now. Smaller groups live in other neighborhoods. Dosapey said they now have legal title to the land, since they have been there more than ten years.

Dosapey acknowledged that the Ayoreos are responsible for some of the conflicts with neighbors. They have committed crimes, such as robbing people who passed by their community. Women and children beg on downtown sidewalks. Some Ayoreos also took over The Campesino's House (La Casa del Campesino), a lodging place in Santa Cruz intended to be used by rural residents visiting town to shop or see sick relatives. Instead, some Ayoreos lived in the house and sold drugs nearby. Those residents were evicted late last year and Dosapey said that, since then, Ayoreo leaders have been cooperating with authorities. "We've supported the police by searching (for criminals) among our own people," he said. "We're going to clean up . . . so that they don't speak badly of the Ayoreos."

Dosapey defended the practice of begging. "We spoke to a missionary. He told us, 'We also beg for alms and the government begs from other nations. Not only the Ayoreos beg.'" Dosapey said a group of young people had studied mechanics, nursing and teaching, but that the people's general educational level was still very low. Few can read or write and none have attended university. "Other indigenous people are much more advanced," he said.

Being from the Department of Santa Cruz has garnered the Ayoreos more sympathy than Santa Cruz's other beggars, like the Potosinos who come, especially around Christmas. Maria Julia Gutiérrez is the president of the Women's Civic Committee of Santa Cruz, which helps Ayoreo women market their weaving. She said the Ayoreos are taking positive actions, such as sending children to a home to study and expelling some members. "According to a leader, they've sent the prostitutes and the drug addicts back to their lands," she said. "They're moving forward."

Adult Ayoreos remember their old lifestyle--at the missions and as hunter-gatherers--as healthier. Hortensia Etore is the Bolivar community's leader. Her family moved from a mission to Santa Cruz to be closer to the hospitals. She said the Ayoreos beg for medical care from doctors who know them and sometimes treat them for free. Although in the countryside there was no medical care, Etore said, "The life there was good, because the young men didn't drink. It was a healthier life." In recent decades, most of the missions have reduced their activities or shut down completely, leaving many Ayoreos feeling betrayed. "When there were gringo missions, we lived well, but not anymore," said Bolivar resident Marta Chiqueno. "The gringos threw us away like trash."

Many Ayoreos continue living near the missions, continuing a semi-nomadic existence. Dosapey's father, Chakaidi, who estimates his age at seventy, lives near a mission but visited Santa Cruz recently for a medical checkup. He said the Ayoreos' traditional dietary taboos protected them in bush country, but that present-day habits have weakened the people. "When the grandparents lived in the forest, everyone was very strong," Chakaidi said through Zamuco, an interpreter in the Ayoreo language. "Now the youth are weak, because before their grandparents had many taboos. They didn't eat many things. If today's young people return to the countryside, they won't have the strength the people once had, because they eat too much butter." But others said that change would be difficult. "You get used to the city," said one young man.

Missionary Dunne recognized the problems the Ayoreos have suffered in the city. Years ago, she visited an Ayoreo girl who worked with several others in a brothel near the train station. "She was a girl who was already a Christian, who left the countryside," Dunne recalled. "She was crying. She was already sick from tuberculosis. Another woman asked us, 'Why don't you take her away? She's useless.' But the Ayoreos have a tradition that once a girl falls into prostitution no man will marry her. So we couldn't take her." Dunne is hoping to bring a group of Ayoreo children to live and attend school in her children's home, but she said she did not feel responsible for the Ayoreos' situation. "I tell them, 'Why don't you return to the country? The door's open.'" Dunne did say, however, that two years ago a group of Ayoreos asked her to take them to the Chaco to resume their old lives, but that they returned. "There were only three men (in that group) who knew how to hunt, to live in the country," she said. "I think they have a love for the place where they were born. But, once the children knew how to track animals, knew the calls of the birds. Not anymore. It's not the same for them anymore. It will never be the same." There may still be, however, at least one group of Ayoreos still living as hunters and gatherers. National park rangers in the Chaco have found what appear to be abandoned Ayoreo campsites.

For better or for worse, sociologist Riveros said, contact with white culture was inevitable for the Ayoreos, and that outsiders' presence in their territory continued to increase. "Sooner or later it had to happen," he said, "but the circumstances weren't very fortunate." While Picaneray considers the old ways healthier, he does not believe the young people could adjust to a hunter-gatherer lifestyle. Still, he said, the community is attempting to obtain titles to land in the countryside. "We're thinking about returning the youth to the countryside."

For more information contact:
Tour companies in Santa Cruz that offer tours of the mission circuit to see missions where the Ayoreos have lived. The Bañados de Izozog, close to San Jose de Chiquitos, may have some 300,000 hectares set aside for the Ayoreos. A true wilderness, it is accessed only in 4WD private vehicle.

MIKE THE MENNONITE

BY MIKE CEASER

The Mennonite minister looked at me severely. From pants to top hat, he wore all black clothing. "I'm a reporter from La Paz," I told him in Spanish. "Can I ask you a few questions about your colony?"

I had bicycled down 20 kms of sandy road to find Santa Rita, one of the more conservative of the Mennonite colonies that populate the plains east of the city of Santa Cruz. The Mennonites are a conservative Anabaptist sect similar to the Hutterites and Amish, who originated in 16th-century Switzerland and have carried their farming lifestyle and Low German dialect across three continents and many nations.

Mennonite Origins

The Mennonite colonies in East Bolivia are the culmination of a people's odyssey across five centuries, eleven nations and three continents and their determination to preserve their lifestyle and values despite persecutions and a changing world.

The Mennonites sprang from the Protestant movement in southern Switzerland around 1520 and share roots with the Amish. There, the first Mennonites, known as Anabaptists because they rejected infant baptism, preached love for one's enemies, the separation of church and state and strict obedience to Jesus Christ's teachings.

In Switzerland, the Anabaptists suffered persecutions and even murders. They fled to Holland, where a leader, Menno Simons, gave them their name, and then to Poland. Authorities welcomed the Mennonites because of their reputation as able, hard-working farmers. But the persecutions continued, as did the Mennonites' determination to maintain their values. In 1789 they left Poland for Russia to avoid serving in the army. Russian Czarina Catherine the Great gave the Mennonites land in the Ukraine and promises of religious freedom and the right to operate their own schools.

The Mennonites' penchant for having large families gave them a constant need for wider territories. Also, the Mennonites' maintenance of their Low German dialect and rejection of military service continued to attract friction and persecution. In 1700, the Mennonites remaining in Germany and Switzerland left for North America. In 1874 large-scale emigration began to Canada from Russia, where Mennonites had experienced persecution and mass killings. The emigration accelerated after the 1917 Russian Revolution brought Communists to power. Bolivian Mennonites say that some of their ancestors were forced to sneak across the Russian border disguised as cattle.

The Mennonites arrived in Canada with government promises of religious liberty, exclusion from military service and the right to run their own schools. But, according to Mennonite literature, the Canadian Government renounced its promise of educational freedom and in 1920 the more conservative members began leaving for Latin America.

About 6,000 Mennonites went to Mexico and 2,000 to Paraguay, where they settled in the Gran Chaco region. Smaller numbers went to Belize and Argentina. In the decades since, many of those colonists have partially assimilated into the dominant cultures and the Mennonites' large families have driven their search for new lands. In 1957 the first Mennonites arrived in Bolivia, invited by then President Victor Paz Estenssoro, who wanted farmers for Bolivia's lightly populated eastern plains. (The area has also been populated by Japanese, Russian Orthodox and Sikh Indian immigrants). They have continued arriving since, searching for new lands or seeking a place to maintain their traditional lifestyle.

Rejecting the Worldly

Like other Mennonite colonies, the one I visited had no plaza or other common buildings besides its church and schoolhouses. It consisted of neat, plain homes, each surrounded by a farm. The lifestyles of the colonial Mennonites vary widely. More liberal colonies own cars and modern farm equipment, and have electric lines running to their homes. More conservative ones reject such modern conveniences. The Santa Rita colony, populated by mostly Mennonite immigrants from Mexico, was one of the most conservative. There were no electric power lines. And black horse-drawn buggies, reminiscent of another century, rolled along the sand roads.

I asked the minister, who, in contrast to his severe vestment, turned out to be quite cheerful, on what biblical command the Mennonites based their ascetic lifestyle. "God likes low people," he explained in his limited Spanish, which I interpreted to mean humble. "[They shouldn't] have radios, televisions and everything else."

Even though the minister had been born in Canada and grown up in Mexico before coming to Bolivia "in search of more land," his Spanish was very limited and his English non-existent. Like other Mennonite colonists, he spoke the Low German dialect of the first Mennonites in South Germany and Switzerland 450 years ago. I tried explaining to him that I was a reporter, even showing him my business card and a copy of the newspaper. But he didn't understand. Instead, he was interested in the photo on the paper's cover of houses being bulldozed on the outskirts of the city of La Paz.

He pointed to a spot of bare earth in the background. "Does anybody farm that?" he asked, extremely interested.

A Model Farm

I left the minister to find one of the colony leaders, whose farm was a few kilometers away. Cornelius Rompel's farm was a set of neatly-constructed buildings, workshops and animal pens. Even the concrete pig sty was more solid than many homes I have seen. He showed me the tractor, whose huge bare iron wheels use metal blades to bite into the earth. Conservative colonists prohibit rubber wheels on self-propelled vehicles. Rompel explained it as a mixture of custom and religion, but added another reason. "Also because many young men see (rubber) wheels as a way to visit town," he said. "Prohibited."

But some young men do go to town and Mennonites are known among colony neighbors for drinking, even though the religion prohibits it. One evening I spoke with a young Bolivian man who had worked on Mennonite farms. "They drink and they fight," a farmer in the nearby Bolivian town had told me. "The want to play pool, but they're afraid the ministers will find out."

Keeping the Colony Closed

Santa Rita children attend school from age 6 to 13. There, children learn basic reading, writing, and mathematics, all in their Low German dialect. The Bible, read in High German, is another fundamental part of their studies. In the other colony I visited ,schooling was similar, except that girls studied two fewer years than boys. "For us, the school is a platform for the church," Rompel explained. "One who studies too much wants to be an engineer. He no longer wants to be a farmer."

Large Mennonite families, some with as many as 18 children, fill the colony's schools. The tradition of having big families was one of the motors that drove their pilgrimages to new lands over the centuries. "It's as God commands," Rompel said. "There's no (birth) control." And how do families feed so many mouths? "God is great. He helps."

I asked Rompel about the other Mennonite restrictions, such as not voting, driving cars or decorating their churches, which are plain wood buildings filled with hardwood benches. He said those things were either "prohibited," because Mennonites weren't supposed to involve themselves in worldly things, or "unnecessary."

Some Mennonites who come to Bolivia from Paraguay or Mexico, where many colonies have liberalized, must adapt to these new restrictions. "In Mexico, the first ones were like us; they didn't have cars," Rompel explained. "Now they have cars."

After we talked, Rompel invited me in for lunch, a great favor since I had seen no place to buy food in the colony. The home's inside was almost as plain as the exterior. The bottom halves of the walls were painted light blue and the upper halves white, with no other decorations. We sat down on a hard, unpainted, wood bench without a back under a window covered with a plain, white curtain. The kitchen's furniture was completely utilitarian, a wood stove, a gas lantern hanging from the ceiling, and a gas refrigerator in the corner.

While we talked, Rompel's wife and daughters, dressed in flowered, green dresses and bonnets, washed dishes and painted the walls. Mennonites follow strict dress codes. The men wear long pants and, for the more conservative, blue overalls. Rompel's wife and daughters worked silently, only occasionally speaking softly to each other and barely glancing at me with serious expressions. While Mennonite men learn Spanish doing business with Bolivians and employing Bolivian farm workers, women have little contact with the outside world and speak only Low German. As a result, while Mennonite men occasionally marry Bolivian women, the opposite never occurs. When a mixed marriage does occur, the colony expels the couple.

The evening before, while riding along a rural road, I had spoken with such a Mennonite man who was returning home, drunk, in his plain buggy. He had married a Bolivian and left his colony, but said he was still friendly with some colony members. "The old folks don't like mixed marriages," he said.

Neither do the colony residents accept new members. Their genetic isolation across three continents and five centuries shows in their light skin and generally blond hair.

While I ate, Rompel showed me snapshots of one of the colony's few social interchanges with Bolivian communities. Several colonies had cooperated to send relief supplies to Aiquile quake victims. The camera that took the pictures belonged to someone else, Rompel pointed out.

After lunch Rompel took me on a tour of his farm buildings. We walked past his workshop, where his sons were building farm implements. The family makes whatever it can, including buggies and cultivators, using modern presses and drills. Although Santa Rita colonists reject power lines, electric generators are accepted. He also showed me large fuel tanks. Rompel works in several kinds of business, including selling cheese and ham to Bolivians and fuels to other Mennonites.

In addition to their need for more land, the Mennonites also came to Bolivia seeking isolation, and Rompel said they had found it. "[The government] does not come here," he said. "We work in silence. There are no problems here."

After leaving Santa Rita's trim homes and neat farms, I pedaled through the poor, neighboring Bolivian town. Here the homes were unkempt and skinny animals wandered about looking for scraps among garbage piles. But there was also the sound of children yelling and playing, young people shot pool and a group of men drank beers while they watched football.

Dissatisfaction

Not all Mennonites are as comfortable as Rompel with the sect's restrictions. The day before, I had visited a more liberal colony and met a family that had a large, modern farm. Electric power lines ran to the homes, most of which had televisions and radios. Families owned automobiles, which even women drove. Even here the women did not speak Spanish, though.

I sat on the grass and spoke with the men and their Bolivian farmhands. The father, who frequently went to the cities to do business, recounted how he had cleared timberland when he arrived from Paraguay about 30 years before.

The family had prospered and now also rented and farmed land independently. Although this colony was more liberal than others, children had few years of school, the sons told me. They learned "a little bit of

mathematics, a little reading and a little writing," one son said, adding, "There should be more school."

Despite the religious strictures, these young men told me they sometimes wear shorts and one said his sister wore pants in cold weather. "He doesn't pay attention to the ministers," a brother said of another. In another nearby colony that was even more liberal, young men played soccer, the brothers told me.

Neighboring Bolivians generally speak admiringly of the Mennonites' work ethic, even if they are a little intimidated by the "hard" religion. The Mennonites provide farm jobs and sell cheese, eggs and milk. Neighbors see them when they drive their cars or buggies into town to buy supplies or stroll around.

An Economic Force in Santa Cruz

In Santa Cruz, the Mennonite colonists have generated their own economy. The bonneted women and overalled men shopping for supplies are a common sight in one section of the city market, where Mennonites wait in a taxi office under a Low German sign reading "Good Service for Mennonites." The Mennonites also have their own bus terminal and recently established the Menno Credit Union to enable families to buy new land and equipment.

Today the Mennonite Central Committee estimates there are 33,000 Mennonites living in about 40 Bolivian colonies, where have become a major force in Bolivian agricultural exports. After overcoming the challenges of a virgin land, the colonists have prospered and today are a major part of the region's agricultural industry.

"If we Mennonites hadn't come here, Santa Cruz wouldn't have grown so much," a minister told me.

Leonidas Saucedo, assistant and advisor to the president of the National Mennonite Church, an evangelical sect whose members live conventionally, said the colonists do not base their lifestyle on a specific biblical phrase. "Strictly speaking, there's no biblical command," he said. "But the idea is not to contaminate oneself with worldly things."

The prohibition against mixed marriages does follow a biblical principle against wedding a person of another faith, he said. But he said that across the centuries, many of the religious bases for the lifestyle had faded. "There's a mixture in which one can no longer tell whether it's religion or custom," he said. The closed colonies have resulted in several reports of marriages between relatives, he said.

Although Saucedo said the Mennonite colonists in Bolivia are the sect's most conservative members, he felt there was a variation among them. Some had TVs, radios and cars, "things that would scandalize the others," and one colony even taught Spanish in its schools. "To speak of the colonies is to speak of diversity," he said.

Opening Up

In Santa Cruz, the Mennonite Central Committee, a non-governmental organization, operates a center providing German and English books for colonists. "We work to get the Mennonites to open up a little more to society," Saucedo said. "As long as they don't open up, they become more bitter."

Saucedo sees the colonies evolving, just as the Mennonites have across the centuries. "How much longer will the young people accept the religious strictures and how will the liberal colonies affect the others?" he asked. Little by little, Saucedo sees a division occurring, in which the conservatives migrate east, away from urban influences.

Despite their self-imposed challenges, Saucedo observed, the colonists had flourished agriculturally as "people who make the land produce, where it once didn't." In Paraguay's Prado, he said, they turned a "desert" into a "green paradise."

Saucedo predicted that eastern Bolivia is big and empty enough that the colonists will not need to move to another nation soon. In those great expanses they will be able to preserve their lifestyle and traditions for some time yet, he said. "It's another way of life, neither better nor worse than ours," he said.

Meanwhile Rompel, of Santa Rita, does expect the Mennonites' earthly wanderings to continue, but he is unsure of the next destination. "Where? I don't know where, but we'll have to, because the land fills up," he said. "We have no land. Our land is in heaven. God only lends us the earth. We're visiting here, awaiting the other life."

CHÉ IN BOLIVIA:
A FRESH LOOK AT AN OLD STORY

BY MIKE CEASER

Ché and Fidel: allies or enemies? Tania: Ché spy, mistress, or double agent? A new English-language edition of the diary of Ché Guevara shows the evolution of thinking about the characters involved in the drama that ended 37 years ago with the legendary revolutionary's death in the heart of Bolivia. The new edition, published by Cooper Square Press, contains more than Ché's11-month diary. It also includes the captured diaries of three of the other guerrillas, as well as many photos taken by the guerrillas themselves and a pair of introductions: one written by Ché biographer Daniel James for the diary's 1968 edition, and another written by Ché researcher and writer Henry Butterfield Ryan for this latest printing. Both introductions offer enlightening analyses of the Cuban/Argentinean revolutionary's circumstances and the reasons why his attempt to foment a Latin America-wide revolution from Bolivia failed so miserably. Ché Guevara was Fidel Castro's most famous ally during the years of the Cuban Revolution. He then occupied high Cuban government posts and wrote a famous book about guerrilla warfare before returning to fomenting revolution himself.

Ché first tried and failed to start a revolution in the Congo before travelling secretly to Bolivia. Ché believed that Bolivia's central location would make it possible to ignite a continent-wide revolution.

Ché also believed that Bolivia's political and social conditions -- the nation is perennially poor and unstable, and was then governed by dictator-turned-democrat René Barrientos -- made it promising revolutionary territory. Ché's effort failed utterly and miserably. He received no campesino support, was isolated or rejected by urban collaborators, and suffered hunger, thirst and disease during his losing struggle against the Bolivian military. The new diary edition features two introductions, one written for the 1968 edition by Ché biographer Daniel James, and the other written last year by Henry Butterfield Ryan, author of the book "The fall of Ché Guevara." Both provide interesting insights into Ché's cause and a perspective on how interpretations of Ché's experience have changed over the years.

Ché and Fidel: feuders or friends? One central controversy has always revolved around Ché's relationship with Castro. Some argue that Castro wanted to rid himself of an incendiary figure, and so he left Ché to fail without support in the Bolivian jungle Others say that Castro gave Ché's adventure all the support he could, and that there was no way that Castro could have rescued his ally from the center of a continent where he was surrounded by hostile forces. In this debate, James comes down on the side of those believing in the feud theory, whereas Ryan argues that Castro did all that he could. Belief in a Ché-Fidel feud has declined in the past decades, according to Ryan. Another interesting point of contention is whether Tania, the Argentine/East German woman who did Ché's advance work in La Paz and later died with the guerrillas, was actually a double agent also working for the East Germans. James says that she was, based on the declarations of an East German intelligence agent. Ryan, in his book, argues that she wasn't. This is a point which Ché buffs likely will continue debating while they have breath. James and Ryan also bring out the pathos and military failings of Ché's band. As James points out, the little group of warriors seems to wander through the hills without much overall strategy. Ché also disregarded huge opportunities to strike psychological blows, if not strategic ones. Why, for example, asks James, did he not sabotage petroleum pipelines in the region? Why didn't he repeat the bold stroke of his lightning occupation of the town of Samaipata, an act that made international headlines and gave the impression that the Bolivian military was losing the battle when in fact the reverse was true?

As James points out, although Ché had written a famous book on guerrilla warfare, he did not follow many of his own precepts. for example his advance knowledge of the region he selected was faulty. His men studied the native language of Quechua even though the area's dominant tongue is Guarani. Another example of this is when an unexpected clash with soldiers forced Ché to begin fighting before he had finished his preparation, his diary barely mentions the disastrous implications of this event. Perhaps, as James suggests, Ché expected the Bolivian military to be a pushover. And in fact, the Bolivian soldiers did prove to be quite incompetent, and yet Ché still lost. In his diary's monthly summaries of his efforts, Ché repeatedly hits two themes: the lack of campesino recruit-

ment, and casualty totals, which, until the end, favored the guerrillas. The lack of campesino support was a huge contrast with Ché's experience during the Cuban revolution, when people flocked to support the fight against a hated dictatorship. In Bolivia, conversely, many rural people were fond of the charismatic President Barrientos, and most campesinos supported the military against the strange-looking foreign guerrilla fighters.

Ché's casualty totals seem particularly futile, as Ché, with his band of never more than 60 men, could not hope to win on the casualty front even by killing 100 enemy soldiers for each loss of his own. In fact, even in the absence of a hostile army, Ché might have lost the war to sickness and accidents. The diary is a sad account of a group of supremely dedicated men suffering and failing at a hopeless task. James does, however, suggest another way Ché might have won: if the U.S. had poured in troops to defeat the guerrillas, causing a continent-wide reaction and producing the "hundred Vietnams" Ché dreamed of. However, the U.S. was wise enough to limit its involvement to advisors and CIA agents, and the nationalistic reaction did not occur. The guerrillas also nearly succeeded in destabilizing Barrientos' government sufficiently to make it fall. At one point, Ché even regrets not having 100 additional fighters. However, there is little likelihood that a communist one, particularly considering Ché's break with the Bolivian communist parties, would have replaced a Barrientos regime.

Story of the Diary's Publishing

Ryan, for his part, gives a fascinating account of the intrigue, suspicion and international rivalries that surrounded the publishing of Ché's diary. He also describes the changes in perspective on Ché that have occurred since James wrote his introduction. And Ryan also points to another eternal question: why did Ché want his presence in Bolivia kept secret, since that information would undoubtedly have attracted more fighters and international support? Perhaps Fidel knows, but he is not talking. The new edition contains diaries of three other members of Ché's band.

While none of these diaries are as complete as Ché's, they do offer insights into the guerrillas' nature there was a lot of interfighting between the band members, for example and Ché's own personality. At one point, for example, diarist Pombo, a Cuban who survived the guerrilla struggle, records that Ché threatened thieves with death. Of the three other diaries, Pombo's is the most interesting because of his reflections on the guerrillas' wider strategy, which included plans for an urban uprising and a continent-wide revolt, his humor, and his insights on the other personalities, not to mention his appraisals of campesinos' daughters. Pombo also points to several of Ché's basic errors. For example, he mentions that the guerrillas could use the petroleum pipeline traversing the area to make an international impact, something, which Ché never attempted. Pombo also points out a fundamental difference between the campesinos' circumstances in Cuba and Bolivia, where a 1953 land distribution had given campesinos small pieces of property. "We must not forget how little the fight for land means, because (Bolivian campesinos) have thousands of hectares of idle lands," Pombo wrote. Finally, Pombo wrote that it was necessary to have a parallel revolution in a coastal nation, concluding that "if this doesn't happen, this revolution will be smothered."

A Hurried Translation

One slightly bothersome aspect of the diary edition is the translation that includes occasional "Spanglishisms" in grammar and capitalizations. According to Ryan, this is because the translation was done in a hurry when the publishers were racing to be the first on the market. While the errors were certainly understandable then, in the decades since, it certainly seems that somebody could have cleaned up the English. Another flaw of the book is the lack of an index, which would be a very useful tool for historical researchers. Imperfections aside, the Ché's Bolivian diary makes for compelling and fascinating, if not sad, reading which anybody interested in Bolivian history can benefit from. As James points out, by dying young and heroically in Bolivia, Ché left a much stronger legacy than he would have by living to an old age as a mediocre bureaucrat.

The Complete Bolivian Diaries of Ché Guevara and other Captured Documents, edited by Daniel James (Cooper Square Press, 2000) is available through Amazon.com

Michael Blendinger, Nature Tours offers interesting tours of the area.
Tel/Fax. 9446186
www.discoveringbolivia.com
E-mail: mblendinger@cotas.com.bo

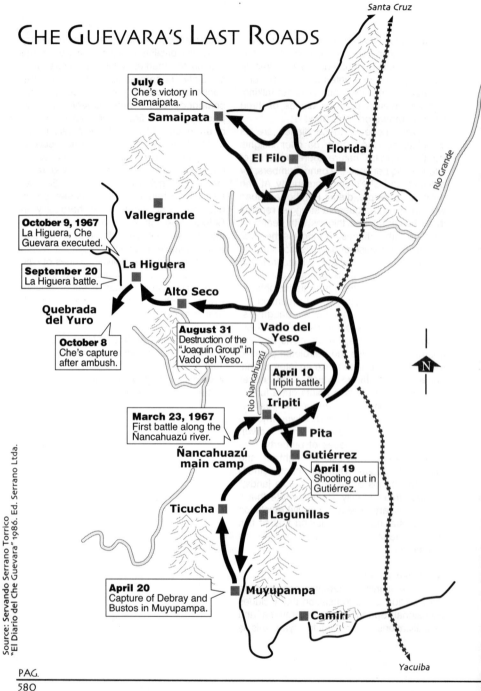

CHE GUEVARA'S LAST ROADS

July 6
Che's victory in Samaipata.

Samaipata

Santa Cruz

Florida

El Filo

Rio Grande

Vallegrande

October 9, 1967
La Higuera, Che Guevara executed.

September 20
La Higuera battle.

La Higuera

Alto Seco

Quebrada del Yuro

August 31
Destruction of the "Joaquín Group" in Vado del Yeso.

Vado del Yeso

October 8
Che's capture after ambush.

April 10
Iripiti battle.

Rio Ñancahuazú

Iripiti

March 23, 1967
First battle along the Ñancahuazú river.

Pita

Ñancahuazú main camp

Gutiérrez

April 19
Shooting out in Gutiérrez.

Ticucha

Lagunillas

April 20
Capture of Debray and Bustos in Muyupampa.

Muyupampa

Camiri

Yacuiba

N

Source: Servando Serrano Torrico "El Diario del Che Guevara" 1986. Ed. Serrano Ltda.

DEATH IN THE ANDES:
BUTCH CASSIDY & THE SUNDANCE KID

BY ANNE MEADOWS AND DANIEL BUCK

At the end of the movie *Butch Cassidy and the Sundance Kid*, Paul Newman and Robert Redford reload their six-shooters and exchange a final round of wisecracks, then dash valiantly into a plaza rimmed with Bolivian soldiers. The movie, a box-office smash in 1969 and a late-night-television chestnut today, closes with the wounded outlaws facing almost certain doom. The frame freezes before the anti-heroes fall, however, leaving open the barest possibility of their survival.

The movie is based on a true story. The outlaw known as Butch Cassidy, born Robert LeRoy Parker on 13 April 1866, was the eldest of thirteen children in a Mormon family in Utah. His admiration for a young cowboy named Mike Cassidy and a stint as a butcher inspired his *nom de crime*. A stretch in a Wyoming prison for the theft of a five-dollar horse impelled him toward a life on the run.

The Sundance Kid, born Harry Alonzo Longabaugh in the spring of 1867, was the youngest of five children in a Baptist family in Pennsylvania. After heading west at the age of fifteen, he ranched with relatives in Colorado, then knocked around the U.S. and Canadian Rockies working as a drover and bronco-buster. He earned his nickname by serving eighteen months in jail at Sundance, Wyoming for stealing a horse.

Sundance's companion in the movie was Etta Place. His companion in real life was an enigma. Although she has been described as a prostitute, a teacher, or both, no one knows her true origin or fate. Even her name is a mystery. The Pinkerton Detective Agency called her Etta on its WANTED posters, but she called herself Ethel, which may or may not have been her real name. Her true last name is unknown. Place was an alias borrowed from Sundance's mother's maiden name.

Butch and Sundance belonged to a loose-knit gang that included men like Elzy Lay, Matt Warner, Harvey "Kid Curry" Logan, Ben "Tall Texan" Kilpatrick and Will Carver. Dubbed the Hole-in-the-Wall Gang, the Robbers Roost Gang and the Wild Bunch, the band held up trains, banks and mine payrolls in the Rocky Mountain West and made off with a total of some $200,000 (the equivalent of perhaps $3 million today) between 1889 and the early 1900s.

With rewards on their heads and Pinkerton agents on their tails, Butch and Sundance fled to South America with Ethel in 1901. The movie takes them directly from New York City to Bolivia, but their initial destination was actually Argentina. After steaming into Buenos Aires on the British ship *Herminius* in March and taking the train to Patagonia in June, they settled in the Chubut Territory, a frontier zone in southern Argentina sparsely populated by immigrants, pioneers and Indians. Although most of the immigrants were Welsh or Chilean, several North Americans had journeyed to the same corner of the world looking for open ranges. The bandits' nearest neighbor, for example, was John Commodore Perry, who had been the first sheriff of Crockett County, Texas. Butch and Sundance also traded and socialized with a Texan named Jarred Jones, who lived two days' ride north, near Bariloche.

Calling themselves James "Santiago" Ryan and Mr. and Mrs. Harry "Enrique" Place, the Wild Bunch exiles peacefully homesteaded a ranch in the Cholila Valley, raising sheep, cattle and horses. All three got on well with their neighbors, and if anyone came to know about Butch and Sundance's shady past, it never interfered with their friendship. They were so highly regarded that when the territorial governor, Julio Lezana, visited the valley in early 1904, he spent the night in their home, a well-kept four-room log cabin on the east bank of the Río Blanco. During the welcoming festivities, Sundance played sambas on his guitar, and the governor danced with Ethel.

Meanwhile, in March 1903, the Pinkertons had sent agent Frank Dimaio to Buenos Aires, after receiving a tip that Butch and Sundance were living in Argentina. Dimaio traced their whereabouts, then cabled his superiors, saying that the rainy season prevented him from making the journey to Cholila. He returned empty-handed to New York, and the Pinkertons had to content themselves with supplying the Buenos Aires police with Spanish translations of the bandits' WANTED posters.

On 14 February 1905, two English-speaking bandits held up the Banco de Tarapacá y Argentino in Río Gallegos, seven hundred miles south of Cholila, near the Strait of Magellan. Escaping with a sum that would be worth at least $100,000 today, the pair vanished north across the bleak Patagonian steppes. Although the descrip-

tions of the culprits didn't fit Butch and Sundance and their neighbors said they were in Cholila at the time of the holdup, they became the prime suspects because of their backgrounds.

Responding to a directive from the Buenos Aires police chief, Governor Lezana issued an order to detain Butch and Sundance for questioning. Before the order could be executed, however, Edward Humphreys – a Welsh-Argentine sheriff who was friendly with Butch and enamored of Ethel – tipped them off. In early May, the trio hustled north to Bariloche and took the steamer *Cóndor* across Lake Nahuel Huapi to Chile.

Almost nothing is known about what the bandits did in Chile, but they apparently spent time in Antofagasta, the center of the nitrate trade on the northern coastal desert. The Pinkertons learned from a postal informant that Frank D. Aller, the U.S. vice-consul in Antofagasta, had bailed Sundance (alias Frank Boyd) out of a scrape with the Chilean government in 1905.

Late that year, the outlaws returned to Argentina on business: on 19 December, Butch, Sundance, Ethel and an unidentified confederate heisted 12,000 pesos (worth about $80,000 today) from the Banco de la Nación in Villa Mercedes, a livestock center four hundred miles west of Buenos Aires. With several posses chasing them, they slogged west over rain-swollen pampas and the Andes to Chile.

A few months later, Sundance briefly visited Cholila to sell some sheep and mares he and Butch had left with their friend Daniel Gibbon, a Welsh rancher. By then, Ethel was in San Francisco, having returned to the United States for good, and Butch was in Antofagasta, en route to Bolivia.

In 1906, Butch (alias James "Santiago" Maxwell) found work at the Concordia Tin Mine, 16,000 feet up in the Santa Vela Cruz range of the central

Bolivian Andes. Sometime after selling the livestock in Cholila, Sundance (alias H.A. "Enrique" Brown) hired on with contractor Roy Letson, who was driving mules from northern Argentina to a railroad-construction camp near La Paz. Sundance worked a while breaking mules at the camp, then joined Butch at Concordia, where their duties included tending mules and guarding payrolls.

Assistant manager Percy Seibert, who had first met the pair at a Christmas party at the Grand Hotel Guibert in La Paz, knew that they were outlaws. Nonetheless, he "never had the slightest trouble getting along with" either of them. He found Sundance somewhat taciturn but grew quite fond of Butch. After Seibert became the manager at Concordia, they were his regular guests for Sunday dinner. To avoid unpleasant surprises, Butch always took the seat with a view of the valley and the trail to Seibert's house.

Having been forced to give up his quiet life in Argentina, Butch still wanted to settle down as a respectable rancher. In late 1907, he and Sundance made an excursion to Santa Cruz, a frontier town in Bolivia's tropical eastern savannah, and Butch wrote to friends at Concordia, saying that he had "found just the place [he had] been looking for 20 years." Now forty-one, he was burdened with regret. "Oh god," he lamented, "if I could call back 20 years . . . I would be happy." He marveled at the affordability of good land with plenty of water and grazing, and made a prediction: "If I don't fall down, I will be living here before long."

The bandits quit their jobs in 1908, after an inebriated Sundance bragged publicly about their criminal exploits. Although there is no proof of their having been anything other than model employees during their tenure at Concordia, Seibert later credited them with several holdups in Bolivia. He said, for example, that they had robbed a railroad-construction payroll at Eucaliptus, south of La Paz, in 1908. The payroll was actually robbed twice that year. According to newspaper accounts, the perpetrators of the first holdup, which occurred in April, were "three Yankees who had been employed as contract-workers." The newspapers provided no details about the second robbery, which took place in August, after Butch and Sundance had left Concordia.

Later that month, they turned up in Tupiza, a mining center in southern Bolivia. Intent on robbing a local bank, perhaps to finance their retirement in Santa Cruz, the outlaws needed a place to lie low while making their plans. They found a perfect hideout at the camp of British engineer A.G. Francis, who was supervising the transportation of a gold dredge on the Río San Juan del Oro. Now calling themselves James "Santiago" Lowe and Frank Smith, Butch and Sundance appeared at Francis's camp at Verdugo, fifteen miles south of Tupiza, and asked to rest their mules for a spell. Their legendary charm soon won Francis over, and they wound up bunking with him for several weeks.

While Sundance stayed with Francis, Butch made frequent forays into Tupiza, casing the bank and formulating his plans. Meanwhile, a detachment of soldiers from the Abaroa Regiment, the Bolivian army's celebrated cavalry unit, came to the region on maneuvers. With the Abaroa officers ensconced in a hotel on the same plaza as the bank, Butch turned his attention to the Aramayo, Francke y Compañía, which had mines in the area. Although the operational headquarters were at Quechisla, a three-day journey to the northwest, the Aramayo family lived in Tupiza, and the money for the payrolls came through the Tupiza office. In conversations with an unidentified Aramayo employee, Butch learned that manager Carlos Peró would soon be taking an unguarded 80,000 peso payroll (worth $500,000 today) to Quechisla.

In late October, Butch rode into Francis's new headquarters at Tomahuaico, a few miles south of Verdugo, on the west bank of the Río San Juan del Oro. After exchanging pleasantries with Francis, he took Sundance aside and briefed him about their new target. Shortly thereafter, the pair decamped to Tupiza and checked into the Hotel Terminus.

Early on the morning of November 3, Carlos Peró picked up a packet of money wrapped in homespun cloth from the office behind the Aramayo family's Italianate mansion, Chajrahuasi. He then set off for Quechisla with his young son Mariano, a peon and several mules, trailed discreetly by Butch and Sundance. Peró and his companions spent the night at the Aramayo hacienda in Salo, then resumed their journey at dawn. The outlaws were now ahead of them, watching through binoculars as the group made its way up Huaca Huañusca (Dead Cow Hill), the peon and the boy on mules, and Peró on foot in the rear.

At 9:30 a.m., Peró's party rounded a curve on the far side of the cactus-studded hill and found the trail blocked by Butch and Sundance, who wielded brand-new small-caliber Mauser carbines with thick barrels. Dressed in dark-red corduroy suits, with bandannas masking their faces and their hat brims turned down so that only their eyes were visible, the bandits had Colt revolvers in their holsters and Browning pocket pistols tucked into their cartridge belts, which bulged with rifle ammunition.

Sundance kept his distance and said nothing. Butch politely ordered Mariano Peró and the peon to dismount and asked Carlos Peró to hand over the payroll. Unable to offer any resistance, Peró replied that they could take whatever they wanted. Butch began to search their saddlebags but could not find the money, so he told Peró to open their luggage. Speaking in English, Butch explained that he was not interested in the money or personal articles of Peró or his companions but only in the 80,000 pesos they were carrying for the Aramayo company. When Peró replied that they had only 15,000 pesos (worth $90,000 today), the larger payroll having been scheduled for the following week, Butch was stunned into silence. He then took not only the packet of money but also a fine, dark-brown mule that belonged to the company.

After the bandits departed, Peró's party continued north toward the village of Guadalupe. At noon, they encountered a muleteer named Andrés Gutiérrez. Peró scribbled a note in pencil and gave it to Gutiérrez to deliver to the Aramayo hacienda in Salo. Another messenger took the note from Salo to Chajrahuasi, and the alarm went out via telegraph to local authorities in surrounding communities, as well as to Argentine and Chilean officials in all the nearby border towns. Military patrols and armed miners (whose pay had been stolen) were soon combing the ravines, watching the roads, guarding the train stations and looking for strangers in villages throughout southern Bolivia.

Peró spent the night in the mining camp at Cotani, a day's journey shy of Quechisla. In a letter detailing the morning's events to his superiors, he surmised that the brigands had "undoubtedly planned their retreat carefully; otherwise, they would not have left us with our animals, or they would have killed us in order to avoid leaving witnesses or to gain time."

In the meantime, Butch and Sundance had made their way south, through rough, uninhabited terrain. They skirted Tupiza under cover of darkness and arrived at Tomahuaico after midnight. Butch was sick and went to bed at once, but Sundance stayed up late, telling Francis about the holdup.

The outlaw also spoke of having "made several attempts to settle down to a law-abiding life, but [said that] these attempts had always been frustrated by emissaries of the police and detective agencies getting on his track, and thus forcing him to return to the road." Nonetheless, he averred, "he had never hurt or killed a man except in self-defense and had never stolen from the poor, but only from rich corporations well able to support his 'requisitions.'"

Although Francis disapproved of his visitors' misdeeds, he had found them "very pleasant and amusing companions" and did not intend to betray them to the authorities.

The next morning, a friend hastened to Tomahuaico to warn the bandits that a military patrol from Tupiza was headed in their direction. Butch and Sundance packed their belongings and saddled their mules. To Francis's horror, they insisted that he accompany them. Expecting them to flee south to Argentina, he was surprised when they said they were going to "Uyuni and the north." (Their destination may have been Oruro, which had several thousand foreign residents, among whom the outlaws would have been inconspicuous. In any case, the Hotel Americano in Oruro was Sundance's last known address.)

Fearing that he would be caught in the crossfire if the soldiers overtook them, Francis nervously led the bandits south and west along the Río San Juan del Oro, then north through a narrow, twisting ravine to the village of Estarca. Francis arranged for them to spend the night in a room at the home of Narcisa de Burgos. Early the next morning, Butch and Sundance thanked Francis for his help and let him go, with instructions to tell any soldiers he encountered that he had seen the bandits making for the Argentine border.

They paused for directions in Cucho, ten miles north of Estarca, then followed the long, rugged trail to San Vicente, a mining village in a barren, dun-colored bowl 14,500 feet up in the Cordillera Occidental. At sundown on November 6, 1908, they rode into town on a black mule and the dark-brown Aramayo mule, and stopped at the home of Bonifacio Casasola. Cleto Bellot, the corregidor (chief administrative officer), approached and asked what they wanted. An inn, they responded. Bellot said that there wasn't one but that Casasola could put them up in a spare room and sell them fodder for their mules.

After tending to their animals, Butch and Sundance joined Bellot in their room, which opened onto Casasola's walled patio. They asked Bellot about the road to Santa Catalina, an Argentine town just south of the border, and the road to Uyuni, about seventy-five miles north of San Vicente. They then asked where they could get some sardines and beer, which Bellot sent Casasola to buy with money provided by Sundance.

When Bellot took his leave, he went straight to the home of Manuel Barran, where a four-man posse from Uyuni was staying. The posse, made up of Captain Justo P. Concha and two soldiers from the Abaroa Regiment and Inspector Timoteo Rios from the Uyuni police department, had ridden in that afternoon and had told Bellot to be on the lookout for two Yankees with an Aramayo mule. Although Captain Concha was unavailable when Bellot reported the arrival of the suspects, Inspector Rios and the two soldiers loaded their rifles at once.

Accompanied by Bellot, they went to Casasola's home and entered the patio. As they approached the bandits' room, Butch appeared in the doorway and fired his Colt, wounding the leading soldier, Victor Torres, in the neck. Torres responded with a rifle shot and retreated to a nearby house, where he died within moments. The other soldier and Rios also fired at Butch, then scurried out with Bellot.

After a quick trip to Barran's house for

more ammunition, the soldier and Rios positioned themselves at the entrance to the patio and began firing at the bandits. Captain Concha then appeared and asked Bellot to round up some men to watch the roof and the back of the adobe house, so that the bandits couldn't make a hole and escape. As Bellot rushed to comply, he heard "three screams of desperation" issue from the bandits' room. By the time the San Vicenteños were posted, the firing had ceased and all was quiet.

The guards remained at their stations throughout the bitterly cold, windy night. Finally, at dawn, Captain Concha ordered Bonifacio Casasola to enter the room. When he reported that both Yankees were dead, the captain and the surviving soldier went inside. They found Butch's body stretched out on the floor, one bullet wound in the temple and another in the arm, and Sundance's corpse sitting on a bench behind the door, hugging a large ceramic jar; he had been shot once in the forehead and several times in the arm. According to one report, the bullet removed from Sundance's forehead had come from Butch's Colt. From the positions of the bodies and the locations of the fatal wounds, the witnesses apparently concluded that Butch had put his partner out of his misery, then turned the gun on himself.

The outlaws were buried in the local cemetery that afternoon. The Aramayo payroll was found intact in their saddlebags. Once their possessions had been inventoried and placed in a leather trunk, Captain Concha absconded to Uyuni with the lot, leaving the Aramayo company to battle for months in court to recover its money and its mule.

Two weeks after the shootout, the bandits' bodies were disinterred, and Peró identified them as the pair who had held him up. Tupiza officials conducted an inquest of the robbery and shootout, interviewing Peró, Bellot and several other area residents, but were unable to ascertain the dead outlaws' names.

In July 1909, Frank D. Aller, Sundance's benefactor in Antofagasta, wrote the American legation in La Paz for "confirmation and a certificate of death" for two Americans – one known as Frank Boyd or H.A. Brown and the other as Maxwell – who were reportedly "killed at San Vicente near Tupiza by natives and police and buried as '*desconoci - dos.*'" Aller said that he needed a death certificate to settle Boyd's estate in Chile. The legation forwarded the request to the Bolivian foreign ministry, stating that the Americans had "held up several of the Bolivian Railway Company's pay trains, as also the stage coaches of several mines, and . . . were killed in a fight with soldiers that were detached to capture them as outlaws."

In late 1910, after considerable procrastination, the Bolivian government finally responded with a summary of the Tupiza inquest report and "death certificates for the two men, whose names [were] unknown."

In May 1913, a Missouri carpenter named Francis M. Lowe was arrested in La Paz on suspicion of being George Parker (which the Pinkertons' WANTED posters mistakenly listed as Butch's real name). With the aid of the American legation, Lowe established that his was a case of mistaken identity. In filing a report on the matter, an official at the legation advised that "certain Englishmen and others here assert that a man known as George Parker (whom the La Paz police were seeking) had been killed in one of the provinces two or three years ago while resisting" arrest.

Shortly before Lowe was detained, William A. Pinkerton had heard about the San Vicente shootout, but had dismissed "the whole story as a fake." The agency never officially called off the search for Butch and Sundance. Indeed, in 1921, Mr. Pinkerton told an agent that "the last we heard of [the Sundance Kid] . . . he was in jail in Peru for an attempted bank robbery. Butch Cassidy had been with him but got away and is supposed to have returned to the Argentine." Needless to say, the Pinkertons never caught up with the pair.

Authors' Bio:

Daniel Buck and Anne Meadows are contributing editors of *True West* and *South American Explorer*. They have made numerous trips to Argentina, Bolivia and Chile during the past two decades to research the story of Butch and Sundance's fate. Meadows is the author of *Digging Up Butch and Sundance* (Bison Books, 1996).

For more informations see: http://our-world.compuserve.com/homepages/danne/

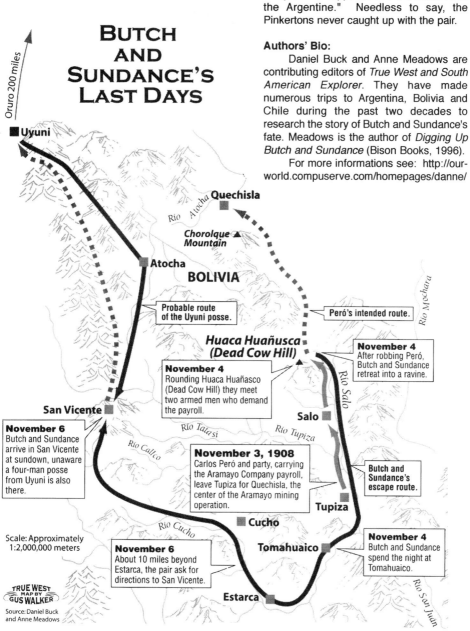

BUTCH AND SUNDANCE'S LAST DAYS

Oruro 200 miles

Uyuni

Quechisla

Rio Atocha

Chorolque ▲ Mountain

Atocha

BOLIVIA

Rio Mochara

Probable route of the Uyuni posse.

Peró's intended route.

Huaca Huañusca (Dead Cow Hill)

November 4
After robbing Peró, Butch and Sundance retreat into a ravine.

November 4
Rounding Huaca Huañasco (Dead Cow Hill) they meet two armed men who demand the payroll.

Rio Salo

San Vicente

Salo

November 6
Butch and Sundance arrive in San Vicente at sundown, unaware a four-man posse from Uyuni is also there.

Rio Tatasi

Rio Tupiza

Rio Callco

November 3, 1908
Carlos Peró and party, carrying the Aramayo Company payroll, leave Tupiza for Quechisla, the center of the Aramayo mining operation.

Butch and Sundance's escape route.

Tupiza

Cucho

Rio Cucho

Scale: Approximately 1:2,000,000 meters

November 6
About 10 miles beyond Estarca, the pair ask for directions to San Vicente.

Tomahuaico

November 4
Butch and Sundance spend the night at Tomahuaico.

TRUE WEST
MAP BY
GUS WALKER

Source: Daniel Buck and Anne Meadows

Estarca

Rio San Juan

CHAPTER SEVEN

7

EXPLORING
BOLIVIA'S ENVIRONMENT

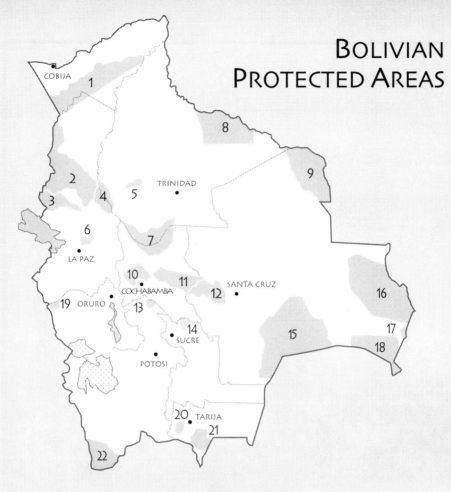

BOLIVIAN PROTECTED AREAS

1   Vida Silvestre Amazonica Manuripi National Reserve
2   Madidi National Park and Integrated Management Area
3   Ulla Ulla National Fauna Reserve
4   Pilon Lajas Indigenous Territory and National Park
5   Beni Biosphere Biological Station and Reserve
6   Cotapata National Park and Rural Integrated Management Area
7   Isiboro Sécure Indigenous Territory and National Park
8   Itenéz Forestry Reserve
9   Noel Kempff Mercado National Park
10 Tunari National Park
11 Carrasco National Park
12 Amboró National Park
13 Toro Toro National Park
14 El Palmar Integrated Management Area
15 Kaa-Iya of the Gran Chaco National Park and Integrated Management Area
16 San Matias Integrated Management Area
17 Otuquis National Park and Integrated Management Area, Rio Pimiento Zone
18 Otuquis National Park and Integrated Management Area
19 Sajama National Park and Integrated Management Area
20 Cordillera of Sama Biological Reserve
21 Tariquía National Flora and Fauna Reserve
22 Eduardo Avaroa National Reserve of Andean Fauna

BOLIVIA'S ENVIRONMENT

CARBON CREDITS FOR CLEAN AIR

BY MIKE CEASER

In the Amazon basin of eastern Bolivia, an experiment is underway whose success or failure could affect the very livability of this planet. Scientists believe that the carbon dioxide produced from burning hydrocarbons in factories, planes and cars is changing the composition of the Earth's atmosphere. As carbon dioxide levels increase, the atmosphere traps more of the sun's energy, warming the planet and potentially causing dire changes, such as increases in the sea level and expansion of deserts.

Tropical forest plants are one of the world's primary consumers of carbon dioxide, but fires, oil and gas development and agricultural expansion are destroying the forests. Under an agreement signed in 1996 between the managers of Noel Kempff Mercado National Park, located in the Department of Santa Cruz, and several U.S. companies, the companies are financially contributing to the park's conservation in return for credits for the carbon gases the park consumes. They could later use these credits on an anticipated carbon credit market. "We met with companies interested in mitigating their emissions and they've put up money to protect the forests," said Alain Muñoz, communication chief of Fundación Amigos de la Naturaleza (FAN), which manages the park.

The three companies, which have jointly contributed US$7 million, are electricity generator American Electric Power and petroleum companies Pacific Corp. and British Petroleum's U.S. division. The environmental organization, The Nature Conservancy, also contributed US$2 million. The money will go towards purchasing park equipment, paying park rangers and subsidizing scientific research and the sustainable development programs of local communities. In thirty years, the park will consume an estimated thirty million tons of carbon. The companies involved will receive carbon credits for half and the nation of Bolivia for the other half.

In 1990, world energy industries produced 21.7 million tons of carbon and Latin America's industries 1.1 million tons of that. Muñoz expects that within five years industrialized governments will force companies to take responsibility for their carbon emissions, a policy that some countries are already backing. "When that moment arrives, these companies will tell their governments, 'I have a number of tons of carbon credits already,'" he said. "The companies deserve the credit, because [if not for their money] in thirty years the agricultural advancement will eliminate the park."

For companies, it's much cheaper to obtain carbon credits this way than by actually reducing their own pollution. "Bolivia could be able to sell its carbon credits to industrialized nations," Mufioz said. When the agreement was signed, the park was also expanded from 706 to 1.5 million hectares and the new portion contains most of the carbon-consuming forest.

The carbon agreement is not unique. Muñoz said that similar deals exist in Costa Rica and Belize. Mufioz added that there is potential for similar deals concerning other privately managed Bolivian parks or the reforestation process in Bolivia.

For more information contact:
Parque Nacional Noel Kempff Mercado, Calle Bumberque 1100, PB Colegio de Bioquímica y Farmacia, Tel. 3556800, Fax. 3547383.
E-mail: gpena@farm_bo.org
Fundación Amigos de la Naturaleza, Casilla 2241, Santa Cruz. Tels. 3535426, 3524921, Fax. 3524921.
www.botanik.uni-bonn.de/system/fan.htm

LOST AND FOUND

BY STEVE HENDRIX

Sixteen years ago, a young Israeli named Yossi Ghinsberg flipped his handmade raft on Bolivia's Tuichi River, a tributary of the Amazon, and found himself lost in the jungle for three agonizing weeks. A lot of people are very glad he did. Tico Tudela a once impoverished Bolivian hunter who now wears a thick gold watch and drives a Land Cruiser--is glad Yossi Ghinsberg got lost. A new merchant class of hoteliers and restaurateurs in the dusty town of Rurrenabaque in the Department of Beni are glad. The five hundred people of San José a tiny rain forest village that recently secured a US$1.25 million grant and opened a world-class ecotourism lodge are glad. And finally, thousands of adventure travelers that have embarked on some truly eye-popping tours of Bolivia's Amazon basin are glad Yossi Ghinsberg got lost. I'm a member of that later group.

If it weren't for Yossi Ghinsberg's near-death misadventure in 1982, I wouldn't be sitting where I am now in the bow of a thirty-foot dugout canoe, chugging upstream along the most spectacular river corridor I've ever seen. Before Ghinsberg, this remote corner of northwest Bolivia was all but unknown to travelers. But now here we are, where the Amazon lowlands ripple into the first valleys of the Andes, flanked by riverbanks that alternate between stark red cliffs and impenetrable walls of jungle. We see absurdly colored parrots on the cliffs, clinging to the sheer red walls as they pick at nutrients in the clay. My sense of privilege at being here is growing. This is a distinguished place. It's also a dangerous place. There are six paying tourists aboard, if US$50-a-head for four well fed, expertly guided days in utterly unsullied rain forest can be considered even paying.

We're in the care of two Bolivian guides, one in the stern with his hand on the tiller of the ragged outboard, the other in the bow rhythmically stabbing a pole in the current to gauge the ever-shifting depth. Every twenty minutes or so, the bowman sings out in Spanish, the captain cuts the engine, and we all leap over the sides to shove the boat over the shallows, water racing around our straining knees. One slip on the rocky bottom could drive a person under, and the risk of being roller-pinned by the massive hull is real. Of course none of us would be here at all if this river hadn't once handled Yossi Ghinsberg so roughly.

The story of how the mishaps of a young Israeli adventurer sparked a tourism industry in this back corner of the Bolivian wilderness is a case study in survival, enterprise and the lengths travelers will go to see nature at its most unspoiled. And it all started, as sagas so often do, with someone's bright idea to go looking for gold. "Bolivia was just one stop for me," Ghinsberg told me in Rurrenabaque a few years ago. "It didn't work out that way." Ghinsberg was several months into his grand tour of South America when he reached Bolivia in 1982, fresh from his stint in the Israeli Navy. One day in La Paz, Ghinsberg and two fellow vagabond travelers fell in with an Austrian expatriate named Karl, who held himself out as a gold miner, expert jaguar hunter and all around master of the forbidding Bolivian jungle. The mysterious Karl offered, for a healthy fee, to guide the three gringos to a remote indigenous village and some sure-fire gold sites along the Tuichi River. Ghinsberg--a thoroughgoing adventurer--accepted at once. A few days later, with a couple of bootleg rifles and a few bags of rice, the four of them were in a bush plane plunging down the slope of the Andes to the lush green floor of the upper Amazon basin. But after weeks of arduous trekking through the jungle, the three began to doubt Karl's woodcraft as well as his veracity. His promised indigenous village--and the rich gold site it supposedly guarded--never materialized. Eventually, tired and discouraged, they backtracked to their starting outpost and commissioned some locals to build them a balsa-log raft.

The plan this time: to float down the swift Tuichi in comfort to the airfield of Rurrenabaque. The river, however, was no kinder than the forest. From the first mile, it was obvious they weren't prepared to cope with much beyond placid flat water, and after two days of prolonged panic--with the worst white water fast approaching--their group split apart. Two of them, Karl the guide and Marcus, a young Swiss, refused to continue. They divided the provisions and began walking back upriver. Marcus turned and waved good-bye as they disappeared into the thick foliage. What happened to them after that remains a mystery. Neither was seen again.

Yossi and Kevin, an American, returned to the raft and launched it back into the current. Things went wrong immediate-ly. The river contracted; the banks rose from the flat beaches to sheer walls; the speed and force of the water quadrupled. They suddenly found themselves hurtling toward a roaring hydraulic hell that could only be the infamous and unrunnable San Pedro Canyon. The raft rammed into a rock and was pinned by the relentless current. Kevin jumped out and made it to the shore, but only in time to watch the raft slowly shift free and plunge down a waterfall and into the canyon proper, with Yossi clinging helpless-ly to the logs. He didn't last long on the back of that bucking raft, but he didn't drown. An eternity of minutes and infinity of miles later, Ghinsberg found himself stranded on a nar-row gravel beach, battered, breathless, and utterly alone.

Over the course of the next twenty days, there must have been times when he would have preferred never to have sur-faced at all from the black grip of the Tuichi. It's hard to do justice to what Ghinsberg endured over those three weeks as he wan-dered about the deep jungle in search of some kind of trail, some kind of food, and some kind of help. Here's but a meager cat-alog of the trials the rain forest had ready for him: The days the search planes passed overhead, deaf and blind to his frantic calls beneath the forest canopy; the day he sank to his chest in quicksand, and the next day, when he did it again; the night he urinated on himself out of exhaustion, only to wake up and find a swarm of termites devouring his salty clothes and huge patches of skin; the night he woke up with a jaguar breathing on his face; the day the red, skin-rotting fungus on his wet feet finally made walking not just agonizing but impossible. Finally, there was the day when the drone in his head wasn't a hallucination and it wasn't another ferocious insect--it was a boat, guided by a burly river man named Tico Tudela. Leaning over the bow, calling Yossi's name, was his friend, Kevin. He was

BOLIVIA'S ENVIRONMENT

rescued. Tico and Kevin carried the emaciated castaway down river to Rurrenabaque. And that, effectively, is the happy ending to Ghinsberg's tale of survival in the rain forest.

But it's only the beginning of the story for Tico, his town, the river, and the tiny, remote village of San José. A few years after returning to Israel, Ghinsberg wrote a thrilling book about his adventure called Back from Tuichi. Among the keenest readers, were young Israeli travelers, who swapped the book around at youth hostels from Cuzco, Peru to Sao Paulo, Brazil. Inevitably, one hot day in 1985, a group of seven Israeli backpackers climbed off a dusty bus in Rurrenabaque and asked where to find Tico. "They came to ask me if Yossi's story was true," says Tico, an amiable bear of a man with a neat black beard and a jaguar's tooth around his neck. At the time, he was still scratching out a living on the river, hunting and trading. "They asked me to take them up the Tuichi, to show them everything." Tico shrugs and smiles. "So I started a business." Word of Tico's jungle tours buzzed like a swarm of mosquitoes along the travelers' telegraph, and suddenly a new destination was added to the backpacker circuit. Bolivia: A Lonely Planet Travel Survival Kit gave Tico's tours rave reviews, and before long signs in Hebrew, German and English were popping up in Rurrenabaque shops and cafes.

By the time Ann and I arrived in Rurrenabaque during a summer in Bolivia, Tico's Agencia Fluvial had grown from a two-canoe operation to one of the largest employers in town, behind only the big timber and oil operations. Tico also owns a hotel, catering largely to the hundreds of tourists a month he takes to his camps on the Tuichi and in the nearby wetlands called the pampas. He still wears the jaguar tooth, but now his clothes are a bit newer than the Rurrenabaque average, and he's a bit more harried than his old compadres on the river. Tico's hard work shows. The trip up the Tuichi is an unforgettable voyage. Our home for three nights is a cluster of log, sleeping platforms high on a riverside bluff. Our dining room is a screened hut the size of a one-car garage. Days are spent walking the jungle trails, swimming the river, and following the ever-pointing fingers of our astonishingly knowledgeable local guides. We see spider monkeys, black monkeys, toucans, parrots, white owls, crocodiles, trees that bleed, trees that ooze poison, trees that give water and--my chilling favorite--thumb-size ants with Doberman jaws and a bite that can paralyze an adult for a day. On our final morning, we build a balsa raft of our own and float tranquilly back down the river.

All in all, the Ghinsberg effect shows no sign of fading as more operators offer tours up and down these waters. It's part of a general tourism boom in Bolivia. Tucked between Peru and Brazil, Bolivia has long offered one stop adventure travel to hardcore mountaineers and jungle expeditionists drawn by the country's rugged beauty, Andes-to-Amazon variety and cultural richness (Bolivia boasts South America's only majority indigenous population). But now a fragile economic renaissance and a stretch of political stability have opened the door to more mainstream travelers, and tourism is increasing by as much as twenty percent a year. But sadly, neither that boom nor much else in the way of economic development has ever quite reached all the way upriver to San José, the Tacana-Quechua village that Yossi searched for in vain during his time in the jungle. With young people fleeing to La Paz, some visionaries in San José decided they needed to create a tourism boom of their own. And who better to ask than the original Tuichi tourist, their friend Yossi Ghinsberg. Ghinsberg came through for San José in two key ways: he put them in touch with the Inter-American Development Bank, which ponied up a US$1.25 million grant to build a state-of-the-art, solar powered ecolodge in the middle of the jungle and to train the local people how to manage it. Secondly, he put San José in touch with Conservation International, a Washington environmental group that has pioneered much of the ecotourism field, and that was instrumental in getting 4.5 million acres around San José declared as Madidi National Park. With access to a powerhouse team of resort designers, ecologists, and community development experts, what San José came up with may be unique in the world, a spectacular, community-run ecolodge called Chalalán.

I visited Chalalán as a work in progress while on assignment for International Wildlife magazine. It was impossible not to be dazzled by the spooky beauty of its setting: a misty jungle lake ringed by low hills. Now construction is complete on a compound of stylish cabanas, lodges and trail networks, all several stars above the other rugged camps available on the river. Tour companies in Texas, Canada and Colorado have already booked the first groups of tourists to Chalalán. Visitors after a short flight from La Paz to Rurrenabaque--will begin their trip to the jungle with a simple boat trip along the unpredictable Tuichi River. Just as Yossi Ghinsberg did.

For more information contact:
Parque Nacional A.N.M.I. Madidi, Av. Busch, Rurrenabaque. Tel. 8922540. E-mail: info@madidi.com www.Madidi.com
Conservation International, Tel. 8922419, Fax. 8922309. E-mail:chalalan_eco@yahoo.com ci-bolivia@conservation.org

RIVER OF THE FORGOTTEN

BY CYNTHIA THOMPSON

On March 5, 1997, Hugo Saavedra Cortez, a small, wiry, seventy-year-old man, who I'd met on the Beni River twenty years ago, and I were ready to travel 1000 kilometers down the river from Rurrenabaque to Riberalta on a callapo (balsa log raft) measuring 3 by 2.5 meters. The callapo was loaded and friends who'd gathered to see us off were saying goodbye when the Port Captain arrived to stop us from leaving. He said the Navy Commandant wanted to see me immediately. The Navy had heard on Radio Fides news that morning that I was traveling to Riberalta on a "rustic" balsa raft to gather material for a book about life along the rivers in the Beni. Their concerns were numerous: it was too dangerous to navigate the river during this year's unusually heavy flood; we had no safety equipment, and they had no way to rescue us if we had difficulties; it was dangerous to travel by raft-- especially a foreign woman accompanied only by an old man. A group of foreigners had be assaulted and robbed on the river last year. One was shot and seriously injured. Their embassy took issue with the Navy over the incident and much bad press ensued. They even mentioned that Peruvian terrorists might enter Bolivia through the jungle and cause trouble in the region. I understood the Navy's position, but was set on making the trip. I had made the trip twenty years ago in a dugout canoe and

knew what I would be dealing with. I trusted Hugo's judgment and river expertise, and was certain we could make it to Riberalta safely. I also thought it important for my writing that I see the effects of the floods on the river communities. I found two life jackets to fulfill the Navy's requirement, made several calls to the American Embassy to ask for their support, spoke to the Navy command in La Paz, signed a notarized statement that the Navy warned me of the dangers and was not responsible for my actions, and forty-eight hours later, was given an official written permission, a zarpe, to sail.

The morning of March 7, 1997, we had loaded the callapo and were preparing to leave again. Friends, well-wishers, and the press gathered for the second time to see me off when the Navy arrived on the shore to apologetically ask me to return the zarpe because they had received urgent orders to stop me from sailing--this time due to a phone call from someone at my embassy who had expressed concern about my trip. Frustrated, I spent another day making phone calls to La Paz, pleading my case and refusing to accept the proposed compromise of either traveling by motorboat or departing in April when the floodwaters receded. By the end of the day, I was given permission again. On Saturday, March 8, we finally departed. The Navy was present, but only to document with photos that we were wearing life jackets as we set off. The sky was overcast but the river calm, and it felt almost anticlimactic after all the warnings and struggle to depart. Later in the day, battling a raging storm, I thought of those warnings in a new light. That night we camped on a wide, recently flooded beach. It was the last time we would see a beach on our trip. The river was so high for the rest of the journey that all the beaches were under water and the river often flooded over the banks and back into the forest.

I had terrible dreams that night, a kaleidoscope of all the warnings I had received before departing. At three in the morning, I woke up and left my tent to check on the raft. It was still there. The river was flowing with great force. The edge of the beach was breaking off and crashing into the river. Hugo had told me to wake him if during the night I heard an increase in these landslides nearby. The mosquitoes had disappeared and I stood for some time listening to the river and the sound of night in the jungle. Clouds moved in to cover the sky but the Southern Cross was still visible. I saw a shooting star, wished for a safe trip, and returned to my tent. Some people suggested that traveling by raft would be slow and boring. It was never boring, nor with the river so flooded, was it slow. The strong current and flooding caused by the powerful storms we passed through, forced us to be constantly active and vigilant. I was always learning. Each day was different. Each evening at sunset, brilliant color spread across the humid sky like paint dropped into water. The haunting call of the howler monkeys, something of a chant and a roar combined, moved through the forest accompanying us for many days on our journey.

Hugo knew every bend of the river, where it had recently forged a new course, where it had run twenty years ago. He named every village and knew every hut. He spoke with the Esse Ejas, the river nomads, and exchanged words in Tacana

with the few old timers who still remembered the language. His stamina and strength amazed me. He told me about the legends and spirit world of the Beni and taught me to recognize the Mapajo tree, one of the most majestic in the jungle, whose tall, thick trunk is said to be where the duende, a forest spirit, seeks shelter.

We slept in the jungle and reached the badly flooded village of San Marcos on the third day of our trip. The river had recently receded leaving debris, piles of sticks, logs, and thick mud all through the village. Lakes still covered the main paths in the village. All the grass had been washed away. One man had stepped on a stingray as he waded through the muddy water outside his home. Electric eels were also a danger. It rained steadily and I wondered how the people could stand the endless days of mud, rain, and flooding. Children ran through the village barefoot, splashing through large puddles of contaminated water. The adults looked worn and worried. I felt we had arrived in a disaster area but there was no rescue team in sight. "The worst is yet to come," a villager told me. "As the water recedes, health problems increase, and it is the children who will suffer the most. Many will die from diarrhea and disease." A delegation from the village had traveled to Rurrenabaque seeking emergency help and asking for a place to relocate their village. Their crops had drowned or rotted and food was scarce. Hugo offered food to the children who gathered around to watch us eat. He threw scraps to the skeletal-looking dogs. We stayed, camped in the mud, for two days because the heavy rain wouldn't let up. As we left, the river was rising again.

The village of Carmen sat up on a bank of high ground. The children there, as in many places on the river, came up to touch my skin and hair. They marveled at the freckles on my arms, thinking they were insect bites. They ran about naked in the rain and played precarious games, swinging each other out over the fast moving river. I noticed that children on the river rarely cried, even when sick, hungry, injured, wet or cold, as if they learned early on to stoically endure these hardships. We stopped in the village of Moliendo-Monterey, which had also been seriously flooded. The hut where Hugo's friends lived stood only five feet from the edge of the river, which flowed just inches below the ground level. The bank continued to erode while we were there.

Juana, whose home we stayed in, was thirty and had seven children. She talked to me about the complications women in the region suffered during pregnancy and childbirth. One woman's baby died just before birth and rotted in her womb. She became deathly ill and finally the villagers worked to extract the dead child using a fishhook. The woman never fully recuperated. Death during childbirth and infant mortality were common. Juana was ill, physically worn, and didn't want to have any more children. I asked her if using birth control was an option. She said yes, condoms were used and accepted, but the commerciantes--merchants who traveled the river with goods to sell--came down river infrequently and rarely brought them. Repeatedly, the things I witnessed and stories I was told, impressed upon me how precarious life was along the river. One day Juana told me, "There is so much danger, illness, and disease in our lives, that we survive here by the grace of God alone." So it seemed, for there was no one else to help them.

From Puerto Cavinas to Riberalta, the river had fewer difficult passes. It was less meandering and easier to navigate. River traffic increased notably. Motorboats of varying sizes plied the river and some, quite large, came to pick up the Brazil nut harvest and the workers returning to Riberalta as the season ended. The villages on this stretch of the Beni were suffering epidemics of malaria. In Puerto Cavinas, the nurse at the small medical post had arrived four days earlier from La Paz with her two-year-old daughter. She worried her daughter would come down with malaria. The child was covered with infected insect bites. Eighty percent of the people in Cavinas had malaria, she told me, and her supply of medicine was not enough to treat the epidemic. Every village from Candelaria to Riberalta had the same problem. Years ago, these villages and the centers back in the forest where the Brazil nut gatherers live during harvest, had been fumigated with DDT and other pesticides donated by foreign governments. It was decided that these pesticides were dangerous and the fumigation stopped. Since then, malaria has been on the rise. A new pesticide, supposedly tested to be safe, is available, but lack of funds and political disputes have held up its distribution.

The only medical assistance on the river is provided by ADRA, a non-profit organization run by Seventh Day Adventists, who send a boat from Riberalta to Puerto Cavinas every forty-five days. It stops briefly in each village and offers cheap medical consultations and medicine at cost price. They accept chickens, rice, bananas, and so on for payment because most people have no money. The service is limited though and one person said of ADRA, "If you can't pay, you die, and many of us don't have the goods to trade for medical help." Still, they are better off than the people on the river south of Puerto Cavinas who have no medical assistance at all. The people on the river use medicinal plants to cure everything from malaria to broken bones and hemorrhages, but if that doesn't work, for most there is no alternative.

Hugo and I traveled the Beni River for twenty-six days. The river was too filled with sediment to fish, the forest too flooded to hunt. I didn't bathe for the first six days because the water was so muddy it would have been pointless. Further down river, we searched for clear water streams that had not been flooded by the Beni or used collected rainwater to bathe in and wash our clothes. The most difficult part of the travel was dealing with such basic needs as bathing or going to the bathroom. I came to think of the most rustic outhouse as a great luxury. I was often uncomfortable, hot, wet, dirty, and insect bitten. Yet I loved being on the river. The people I met, and the insight I gained into their lives, made it all worthwhile.

The whole way down the river, people told me they felt isolated from the rest of Bolivia, abandoned and forgotten. One man, echoing the voices of many, said: "No one comes here to talk to us, to learn what we need, to see how we live. Every five years the politicians come to buy our votes, offering us sacks of rice and making empty promises. Then they disappear until the next election. Aid that is meant for us never makes it here. The Beni is the future of Bolivia, but those running this country turn a blind eye to us. They can't see further than the major cities. Maybe you can carry this message from us and write that we are the forgotten people."

ETHNOECOTOURISM IN THE BOLIVIAN AMAZON

BY JAMIE GRANT

The candle flame seems to ebb and flow with the conversation. It's the only light, flickering on the group of faces lit out of shadows around the table. All around, dark night is pressing in hard. The talk slows, falters and we sit for a time in silence listening to animal calls in the jungle outside. The group starts up again, describing the creatures they see in the forest, imitating their voices: the puma, jaguar and yellow-breasted macaw; the anteater with its high pitched whistle and long leathery tongue for dipping into ants' nests; the mountain pig (Chanco del Tropo) that marches in packs of up to one hundred through the undergrowth and can be heard from miles away, cracking nuts with its teeth. The group pauses to talk amongst themselves in their own language--Mosetén or Chimán--before the conversation switches from the forest to their ethnoecotourism project, and into Spanish. There is much to discuss: accounting, environmental management, the next three months work plan and where to take the tourists. The community of Asunción is gearing up for the new millennium.

Their project, named Mapajo after the oldest and grandest tree in the region, is in its early stages. The tourist cabins are yet to be finished and the communities' first visitors aren't expected until the middle of next year. But when they come, the plan is to offer tourists much more than a standard jungle tour of crocodiles, macaws, and biting insects. "When the tourists come, we are going to show them our culture, our customs and our traditions; and then the forest, the vegetation, the Mapajo tree, medicinal plants and the animals," said Jose Caimani, one of the project's prime movers in the community.

The Mapajo Project draws in six small villages scattered upriver from the Quiquibey, a tributary of the Beni River in the heart of the Pilon Lajas Reserve and indigenous territory in the Bolivian Amazon. As all of these Chimani and Musaten peoples, some 300 in total, are joint owners of the indigenous territory, it has been decided that they are all to have an equal stake in the project's ownership and development, running and benefits. "We have consulted with all the upriver communities like San Luis and San Bernardo, and we hope that they all participate," said Caimani.

Although seemingly cut off from the rest of the world, these communities are no strangers to the world of ecotourism, despite not having had much say in tourism until now. Tourist agencies from the nearest town, Rurrenabaque, have been running boatloads of tourists up the river for years, often dropping them off for a while in the villages to wander around (uninvited) to take photos before heading off again. The project plans to give these communities greater control over the development of tourism in the area and to help ensure that they see some of the benefits. Despite being set up with funds from outside, the project is being conceived, planned, and put into practice by the people of the Quiquibey. Marco Langevin and David Campfens of the Canadian organization, Cuso, have helped find US$40,000, mainly from British and French corporations and the Programa de Apoyo a los Pueblos Indigenas (PRAIA) for the first year's capital investment. This mainly covers large expenses such as computers, construction material and a motor for transporting the tourists, as well as carpentry to help build and furnish the cabins. The real investment, however, is from the communities. They are currently putting up the cabins themselves, using local materials such as timber and ferns, or Chuchillo, from the forest. "It's very cooperative, because there are no salaries for us," said Jose Caimani. "We are making sacrifices because it's our project." The two Canadians are helping manage the project's setup by providing support with administration and accounting, new worlds for these communities. But the communities already handle the money and decide how it's to be spent, and by the middle of next year will be ready to do it entirely on their own. "By mid-2000, we will hand everything over and only maintain some long-distance support," said Langevin.

Rather than lining a few people's pockets, profits made from tourism are to benefit the communities as a whole. The money made is to be put back into smaller projects to improve living conditions for the six villages of the Quiquibey. Many of these villages still don't have potable water, provisions for basic health care, or even the means to educate their children. "We want to improve the water, put in latrines, and have a little better food for the children," commented José Caimani. "In all these areas we are lacking, because the government doesn't do very much here." In health care, there has already been an important

advance. Project Mapajo's budget includes funding to set up a medicine bank in each community to compliment the use of traditional medicine from local curative plants. At the women's organization, the Centro Feminino in Asunción, medicines are to be prescribed on a barter system. Two doctors are now making regular visits from Rurrenabaque to help provide the stock and give advice on its use.

Of course the project is not without its risks. It is well known that a rapid transition from subsistence to a market economy, let alone with a big influx of tourists, can often have a devastating impact on indigenous peoples. Marco Langevin recognizes that such a sudden change can cause "alcoholism and a loss of traditional values," particularly amongst the young. His hope is that such a change will be gradual, and more sustainable than other activities in the cash economy such as logging. "They are trying to get out of a bad economic situation; you can't expect them to stay trapped in poverty," said Langevin. The communities themselves are just as aware of the dangers, and are determined not to let the project disrupt their rhythm of life. They have chosen to build the tourist cabins a short walk outside of the village of Asunción, and no more than eight tourists will be allowed to stay at one time. "We're not going to allow it to damage or change our customs. We're going to continue hunting, marrying, and speaking Mosetén or Chimán," said Jose Caimani. The project may even act to reinforce traditions and customs in danger of being lost with the older generations. As tourists who visit are to be shown traditional practices such as basket and textile weaving and the use of medicinal plants, knowledge of the forest's resources and their application is finding fresh impetus. "We are remembering and practicing anew," commented one of the women from Asunción, Regina Gualvo. The people of Quiquibey are starting much more than an ethnoecotourism project. They are embarking on a long road of cautious--and hopefully sustainable--development on their own terms. Their vision is that the project will nurture them just as the Mapajo tree, with its huge branches, lends support to the trees that surround it. "We are happy and we hope that the project that is planned will become a reality," said Gualvo.

For more information contact:
Reserva De La Bioesfera y Territorio Indígena Pilon Lajas, Tel. 8922246, Fax. 8922445 in Rurrenabaque. In La Paz, Calle Republica Dominicana 2109.
Travel companies based in Rurrenabaque.
Agencia Fluvial, located in the Hotel Tuichi. Tel. 8922372.
Eco-Tours, located in the Hotel Berlin. Tel. 8922450.
Transamazonas. Tel.3350411, Fax: 3360923.

REINVESTING IN COMMUNITIES

BY MIKE CEASER

Tourism enriches the tour operators in the big cities, but may bring trash and distorted values to communities near the tourist sites. Such is the case of the salt lakes in southwest Bolivia, which despite their international fame are surrounded by some of Bolivia's worst poverty. Few of the tourists who flock to the Tiawanaku ruins ever visit the town of Tiawanaku itself. Apart from selling cheap clay figures, the campesinos living there have not shared in the income generated by tourism to this archaeological site. But an exception to the rule is taking place on the Mamoré River near Trinidad, where Fremen Travel and Tourism of La Paz is working with local communities to help them capture part of the tourist income and use it wisely.

The project began in 1994 when Fremen met with communities along the Mamoré River, which its tourist boats had encountered for a decade, and drew up an "Ethnoecotourism Plan" based on three principles: community development, environmental conservation and profitability. The project was to be jointly managed by Fremen and the three small communities, consisting of about forty families from the Yuracaré and Moxeño indigenous groups. "They not only participate, but have a fifty percent decision-making power," said Fremen Manager of Receptive Tourism, Michele Livet. "The only problem we have is that everything is done with a certain slowness. The rural people have another concept of these things." Under the agreement, the communities receive a set fee for each tourist who enters or takes a tour. They also sell the tourists clay and other artwork. Part of the income goes to a common fund, which the community decides how to use at the year's end. Fremen also assisted with a loan to buy an oven for making clay works. The community paid back the loan through their income, according to Livet. "We don't do anything at a loss," Livet said. "We're not an NGO." The communities also set rules for visitor's behavior, such as whether or not they will allow smoking. Now the communities intend to use part of their earnings to build a viewing tower, which tourists would pay to climb.

Another way in which Fremen's role is different from an NGO's, Livet explained, is that the company is committed to working in the area for the long haul, rather than just a short span of, say, five years. Fremen has also helped in other ways, such as when the local school was in danger of being shut because it didn't have the minimum of twenty students. Fremen, community members, and tourism officials all wrote letters to education authorities and saved the school. Fremen has also paid biologists to study the area's ecology.

Livet hopes that instead of warping indigenous peoples' culture, as it often does, tourism will actually help the indigenous people recover cultural values such as traditional foods and art, which they have been losing. "What we want is for them to realize on their own that it's in their interest to return to those customs," he said.

The cultural interchange is not unidirectional. When tourists visit the community's school, they tell the students where they are from, sing a song, and tell about their nations' customs. In return, the community tells the tourists about their customs and how they live in the jungle. Then a community member and a biologist take groups of tourists on jungle walks, in which they explain about both the jungle's biology and the way natives use the plants. While the indigenous people contribute knowledge of their traditions and environment, Fremen contributes business and tourism experience. "We know our tourists," Livet said. Ultimately, says Livet, Fremen would like to hand over all the guiding duty to the indigenous peoples. "What we are trying to do is transform ourselves someday from a tour operator to nearly just transporters. We arrive and drop the tourists off at the community's doors and they manage from there."

For more information contact:
Fremen Tours, La Paz, Avenida Mariscal Santa Cruz, Galeria Handal Center Of. 13. Tels. 2407995, 2408200.
E-mail: vtfremen@caoba.entelnet.bo
Calle Tumusla 245, Cochabamba,
Tel. 4259392. Fax. 4117790.
E-mail:fremencb@pino.cbb.entelnet.bo
Avenida Cipriano Barace 332, Trinidad,
Tel. 4622276, Fax. 4652251.
E-mail: fremen@sauce.ben.entelnet.bo
Calle Beni 79, Santa Cruz,
Tel. 3338535. Fax. 3360265.
E-mail: fremen@cotas.com.bo
www.andes-amazonia.com

FIFTEEN YEARS OF BIODIVERSITY BREAKTHROUGHS

BY TOM WILKINSON

The Biodiversity Leadership Awards are given to individuals who have made an exceptional contribution to conservation. Dr. Timothy Killeen, a botanist and conservation biologist who has dedicated the last fifteen years of his life to studying Bolivia's lowland tropical ecosystems, received one of the year's five awards, bestowed by the U.S.-based Bay Foundation and Josephine Bay Paul and C. Michael Paul Foundation. Killeen first visited Bolivia in 1980, one month after the start of the bloodiest and most corrupt dictatorship the country has ever experienced. Nevertheless, captivated by Bolivia's natural beauty and the generosity of its people, he returned in 1984 to conduct his Ph.D. research on the taxonomy and ecology of the grasses of the eastern lowlands. Today, he leads a multifaceted, multidisciplinary research program with collaborative projects that range from botanical exploration to studying how climate change will affect biodiversity. His research program has been specifically designed to strengthen Bolivia's internal research capacity to study both its physical and human dimensions. Killeen applies his research to conservation problems and then works to ensure that the information derived from that research is incorporated into the decision making process of environmental organizations. He believes that one of the most important things he has done in Bolivia is publish a guide to the country's trees. As part of a preexisting USAID research contract, he was obligated to write a guide of the region's trees to promote the sustainable management of timber resources. But Killeen decided to increase the scope of the work to include the trees from the entire country and did it with the active participation of almost every single botanist in Bolivia. The resulting book, Guia de Arboles de Bolivia, was written by thirty -nine young people and co edited by Killeen, with the collaboration of Stephan Beck and Emilia Gracia of the National Herbarium of Bolivia. It was completed in the relatively short span of eighteen months and has been recognized, not just as a magnificent contribution to the country's knowledge of Bolivian flora, but as an example of the importance of collaboration in conservation research. That project's most important legacy has been its impact on the botanical research community within Bolivia, which has become a well organized, dynamic force for the advancement of science and is a key component of Bolivia's greater conservation community.

In 1993, Killeen moved to Santa Cruz to pursue his longtime goal of studying the biodiversity of Noel Kempff National Park. This protected area is situated on the extreme southern limit of the Amazon jungle and is one of the most biologically diverse areas in South America. Killeen recruited a team of students from across the country.

For the next four years, they collected thousands of plant specimens and established a network of biodiversity monitoring plots in the park's different habitats. The plots are being used in an ongoing research program designed to improve understanding of the patterns of biodiversity and the functional processes responsible f or maintaining biodiversity. In his quest to better understand habitat diversity, Killeen began using satellite imagery to map the different plant formations in Noel Kempff. This effort grew out of a collaborative relationship with NASA's Goddard Space Flight Center. Using remote-sensing data to study natural habitats and natural disturbance phenomena, they produced a vegetation map widely considered to be the best example of a digital classification of a tropical area produced to date. Killeen is now using remote-sensing technology to identify areas within the park that may have experienced a change in the position of the savanna-forest border in recent geological time. Once identified, these areas are being examined through ground-based studies that will reveal the direction of change (e.g. forest encroachment on savanna, or savanna expansion into forest).

In a related project, Killeen is collaborating with scientist Francis Mayle, who is studying pollen profiles in lakebed sediments within the park. Preliminary data shows that Amazonian forest vegetation has only recently arrived in the area. One interpretation of this information is that as the Earth has warmed since the end of the Pleistocene Age, the Amazon has become a more humid ecosystem, causing it to expand southward. This trend towards forest expansion, in areas free from human intervention, may increase in the future, since most models of climate warming predict increasing rainfall for tropical and subtropical regions. This information has led to a change in the management of Noel

Kempff National Park. Most of the endemic species within the park are restricted to the savanna ecosystem, and their survival depends on the maintenance of grassland habitat. Previous to these studies, park administrators had an anti-fire philosophy. Now, they understand that it is a natural part of the savanna ecosystem and the long-term survival of many endangered species is dependent upon a judicious use of fire as a management tool. Noel Kempff National Park was the focus of another important climate change initiation when it was recently expanded to 1.5 million hectares via a carbon offset agreement between the Fundación Amigos de la Naturaleza (FAN), The Nature Conservancy, and a consortium of North American energy companies in 1996. The US$9 million agreement was initiated under the auspices of the Initiative for Joint Implementation of the UN Convention on Climate Change and is the largest carbon offset agreement reached to date, both in terms of its total value, as well as in the amount of forest protected.

Fielding a team of ten biologists and twenty workers, Killeen has created a network of six hundred biomass estimation plots in under six months. These plots will be resampled in the years 1999, 2001 and at subsequent five-year intervals for thirty years in order to monitor the amount of biomass being sequestered by the carbon offset agreement. Killeen's success in coupling remote-sensing data with field studies prompted NASA to invite him to a workshop dedicated to promoting the use of remote-sensing technologies by conservation biologists. During that workshop, he proposed that a remote-sensing data center be established in Bolivia to provide easy access to satellite imagery for biologists and conservationists. His proposal was accepted and the Noel Kempff Museum in Santa Cruz is distributing satellite imagery from NASA's historical archive. The data center initiative has only existed for four months, but has already distributed imagery to administrators and researchers working in the Beni Biological Station, the Kaa-Iya Gran Chaco National Park, Noel Kempff National Park, Amboró National Park, and the Pilón Lajas Biosphere Reserve.

For more information contact:

Parque Nacional Noel Kempff Mercado, Calle Bumberque 1100, PB Colegio de Bioquímica y Farmacia, Santa Cruz. Tel. 3547383, Fax. 3556800. E-mail: gpena@farm_bo.org

Parque Nacional A.N.M.I. Kaa-Iya Gran Chaco, Av. Irala 452, Santa Cruz. Tels. 3365337, 3370508, 1942293. E-mail: kaaiya@roble.scz.entelnet.bo E-mail: tluisfer@yahoo.com

Parque Nacional A.N.M.I. Amboró, Calle Los Limos 300, Barrio Fleig, Santa Cruz. Tel. 3453040, Fax. 3452865. E-mail: amboro@latinmail.com

Reserva De la Biosfera y Territorio Indígena Pilon Lajas, Tel. 8922246, Fax. 8922445, Rurrenabaque. In La Paz, Calle Republica Dominicana 2109.

Estacion Biológica Del Beni, Tel. 8952124, Fax. 8952004-5, San Borja. In La Paz, Av. 16 de Julio 1732, Academia Nacional de Ciencias de Bolivia, Tel. 2350612.

THE SALAR AND BEYOND

BY ADAM TOWNSEND

EDUARDO AVAROA NATIONAL RESERVE OF ANDEAN FAUNA.

It was minus 26 degrees Celsius the first night we slept in the altiplano's far southwest. The radiator of our 4WD froze completely solid, apparently oblivious to the anti-freeze in the coolant. Down below the park bunkhouse, flamingo corpses were spread about the ice and borax of Laguna Colorada. Our host and driver, Louis Fiery of Ecological Expeditions, and helpful Park Avaroa wardens debated and applied various cures to the car as the temperature began its rapid morning climb. The southwest area that includes the Salar de Uyuni and the National Park Eduardo Avaroa features some of the worlds most beautiful and bizarre landscapes. Its altitude, climate, geography, fauna and flora combine to create an awesome effect. It is empty and desolate, yet has multi-colored lakes which brim with bird life. It is freezing at night, yet the harsh sun sends temperatures soaring in the day. Its dawns are incredible; its sunsets unique. It is desert, but snow lies beside the roads, and ice covers lakes beside warm hot springs.

Our trip took us past geysers 4,850 meters high, Laguna Verde, Laguna Colorada, the five consecutive lakes, hot springs, across rivers, through small frontier settlements, among the fields of quinoa and across the vast salt pan, the Salar de Uyuni. We slept two nights in the comfortable bunkhouse at Laguna Colorada that is run by the National Park administration and one night at the Hotel Playa Blanca, built entirely of salt. The authorities in charge of protecting the park and of regulating tourism in the area are stretched to the limits. Incursions by Chilean tour operators, garbage strewn about, harassed wildlife and ever widening roads are the challenges they face. At the same time, many government employees and tour operators who serve the area would like to see the infrastructure improved, to attract better paying tourists and to preserve the region.

To many people, Bolivia and the altiplano (high plain) are synonymous. Making up only 10 percent of the country's land area, the altiplano remains the most densely populated zone. The altiplano stretches down the western border of the country from north to south and ranges in east-west breadth from 100 to 200 km. The far southwest corner of the altiplano is Bolivia's harshest climatic region. The few communities that survive do so only through a constant battle with the isolation, the infertile and salty soil, the low precipitation and the freezing nights and chilling winds. Temperatures as low as-35 degrees Celsius have been recorded. The altitude of the southwest altiplano ranges from 3,560 m in the salt basin of Uyuni to 5,000 m a further 250 km south, at the border with Chile. The peaks are much higher, many of them reaching 6,000 m and permanently capped with snow.

BOLIVIA'S ENVIRONMENT

Lakes of various color and size are spread about, most drawing their water from underground and lending it to the occasional watercourse that keeps pockets of land fertile. The lakes featured in Eduardo Avaroa National Park include Laguna Colorada (Red Lake), the five lagunas one after the other, the stunning Laguna Verde (Green Lake) that touches Laguna Blanca (White Lake), and more remote Laguna Celeste (Heavenly Lake). Not far behind Laguna Celeste, and crossing a 5,900 m pass, the service road to the Uturuncu sulfur mine may be the highest road in the world. Laguna Verde lies at around 5,000 m, below the watchful eye of the Licancabur Volcano reaching to 6,000 m and marked with the visible remains of Inca trails that lead to its summit. Licancabur marks the southwestern border of Bolivia, and standing on its west flank the view over the land dropping away into the salt basin of San Pedro de Atacama far below is absolutely unbelievable. From the east side of the volcano's summit, the curved lines of the Laguna Blanca and Verde mold into a landscape that is reflected, sometimes flawlessly, on the colored surfaces of the two lakes.

The flagship of the bird life in the area is the famous flamingo. The three types of flamingos are, like the human inhabitants of the park, on the very edge of subsistence, and the weak and the young often die in the cold nights. The sun, a flightless bird smaller than the ostrich is present, too, but rare, as the park's human inhabitants value the bird's eggs for their apparent medicinal value. The park holds a number of viscachas (a sort of rabbit), the Andino Fox, the Andino Cat, and of course the llama and vicuña. The vicuña were killed off in large numbers on account of their resistance to domestication and the value of their coats. At the only place breeding vicuña for their fur, the animals must still be tranquilized in order to shear them. They are protected in the park and their numbers are thought to be growing. Certainly they are often visible.

Despite its origin as sediment, the soil throughout the area was long ago rendered relatively infertile by the low precipitation and the high concentration of salt and other minerals. The vegetation consists mainly of a type of low, tufty yellow grass and yareta. The yareta is a type of moss growing green and slowly across the rocks. Director of the park, Jaime Peñaranda, says that one of the aims of the creation of the park was to protect yareta. Quinoa is the only crop grown by the inhabitants of the area in any quantity. The people consume, trade, and sell quinoa. They use its husks as fuel and much of their labor organization and ceremony is arranged around its cycles. The Inca civilization introduced the crop to the area, arranging for private ownership of plots of land with a system of shared labor. There was an owner for each piece of land- albeit with limited rights of alienability, but all residents would work the land, rotating from plot to plot as arranged. Antonio, a quinoa farmer from the settlement of Colcha "K," said the year had been very dry and the crop would suffer because of it. "The people are all leaving the villages here anyway," he added. "They go to work in Chile, Santa Cruz and the south, and they are not coming back."

There is no doubt that Bolivia's southwest is an established stop on the tourist trail. In 1998, more than ten thousand tourists passed through Uyuni, many coming to see the Salar and the southwest. In 1999, with the northern summer yet to begin, Uyuni had already seen half of last year's total. The Park Director, Jaime Peñaranda, believes equal numbers of tourists depart from the Chilean town of San Pedro, (just across from the border) as do from Uyuni. The Chilean-based companies claim to operate legally in Bolivia under a vague Bolivia-Chile Tourism pact, but the fact is that they are bringing tourists across the border without passing through immigration, a patently illegal situation--the tourism pact notwithstanding. Regulating and managing the flows, especially the ingressions from Chile, is proving very challenging in the face of limited resources and central government help. "They have cut our salaries to US$21 a month," said a park warden in Laguna Colorada, "And what is more, they haven't paid us for two months." "Most of our funding comes from the World Bank," said Mr. Peñaranda. "But the current problems with funding are due to the national government canceling the environment fund."

The park administration plans to levy a new charge of US$10 per visitor from early July 1999. Louis Fiery, Director of Ecological Expeditions La Paz, agrees with the idea of introducing a charge but has two worries. "We have to make sure the money is used to upgrade the facilities in the park to attract better paying tourists and protect the environment." He is also worried the Chilean companies will avoid the charge. Mr. Peñaranda says there are plans to build a camp at the border above Laguna Blanca to collect the charge and regulate the flow of tourists from Chile. But with even basic funds in question, nobody seems to know where funds for infrastructure will come from.

With an abundance of operators (twenty-two companies in Uyuni alone), the careless nature of some of the companies is beginning to impact the park. Drivers taking their vehicles off the trails in search of a smoother ride have widened the poorly defined trails. Tins and other garbage lie alongside the road in places and when we stopped at one lake, a group of tourists threw rocks at flamingos to get pictures of them flying. "I am normally an animal lover, but I really want a good photograph," said one Israeli tourist.

On the popular Isla de Pescadores, located on the world's largest salt basin (Salar de Uyuni), toilet paper, garbage, broken cacti and numerous trails are threatening to divert from the island's natural attractions. As tourism continues to grow, the park staff will find it harder just to do their basic job and protect the wildlife, vegetation and geology of the park without increased infrastructure spending. At this stage, with wages of US$21 a month proving too much, the park administration needs funding urgently. Many of the tour companies are demanding the improvement of standards of accommodation and food hygiene, and upgraded infrastructure to attract tourists who won't throw rocks at flamingos and bottles out of cars.

For more information contact:
Reserva Nacional Fauna Andina Eduardo Avaroa, Tel. 6932225, Uyuni. E-mail: orocha@latinwide.com
TROPICO, Asociación Boliviana para la conservación. La Paz, Tel. 2435005. Calle Campos corner with 6 de Agosto, Ed. El Ciprés, Of. 5A Casilla 11250. E-mail: tropico@acelerate.com www.tropico.org

Tropico has also published a good guide book on the park.

PANTANAL JOURNEY

BY MICHAEL LEVITIN

BOLIVIA STRUGGLES TO PRESERVE WILDLIFE AND INDIGENOUS COMMUNITIES IN THE WORLD'S LARGEST FRESHWATER SWAMP.

In the lush marsh and channels that weave across Bolivia's far east, the river boat stirs through dense copper-colored waters beneath the blaze of an afternoon sun. Small green parrots shriek across the sky and, as twilight approaches, a mother capybara leads her young through grass along the shore. Troops of howler monkeys crowd onto the limbs of tall trees. And the black eyes and double-barreled snouts of caiman wait motionless on the water's surface. A day's journey from the dusty Bolivian port town of Quijarro on the border with Brazil, our crew of 18, on a trip financed by the World Wildlife Fund, is exploring the waterways of the Pantanal, one of nature's wildest and most remote places—one we hope stays that way.

The world's largest freshwater swamp and the best place to view wildlife in South America, the Pantanal is facing a series of environmental threats that are challenging the economic and human resources of Bolivia, the continent's poorest nation. Illegal trafficking in animal species—the world's third-largest contraband industry after drugs and weapons—has caused considerable damage to the biodiversity of the area, which is shared by Brazil (75 percent), Bolivia (20 percent) and Paraguay (5 percent).

In this unique ecological zone, home to anaconda, tapir, macaw, piranha, giant anteater and the highest density of jaguars

on the continent, some species have edged toward extinction in recent years. The giant blue parrot, which measures three feet from beak to tail and had been decimated by black market hunters, received protection last year under the International Convention on Trafficking in Endangered Species.

The fate of other species in the Pantanal, like the river otter, hunted for its costly pelt, and the borochi—a large fox-like animal sought for its medicinally valuable bones—are still uncertain. And the decline of the gama, a horned savanna deer, has biologists baffled and alarmed. "Gama used to show up in groups of five and six," says Marcel Caballero, a Bolivian wildlife biologist. "Now they are rarely seen more than one at a time. They might be too sensitive to the presence of humans. Once these animals are scared, they stop reproducing, just like in the zoo."

In the 1860s, Bolivia's senile and dictatorial President Mariano Melgarejo cut a deal with Brazil: In exchange for "a magnificent horse," he laid his hand on the map and, covering a swath of territory in Bolivia's far east, declared it the property of Brazil. The site of gold discovery and colonization in the early 18th century, the Pantanal was mostly left alone well into the 20th century, when unrestricted cattle grazing and an extensive road network started to eat away the wild region, particularly on the Brazilian side. By 1998, more than 23 million head of cattle roamed the swamp. Less developed than Brazil—which preserves just 10 percent of its Pantanal as the Matogrossense National Park—Bolivia still has reason to be concerned about its side of the swamp, which at 11,600 square miles is approximately the size of Holland.

Now that Brazil has cracked down on illegal hunting, fishing, logging and mining in the Pantanal—punishable by up to four years in prison—some Bolivians are worried about an increase in poachers crossing the border to continue their assault on species and resources. Since 1990, Bolivia has had a general ban on hunting and trade in wildlife, though the law has been poorly enforced.

In addition, runoff from chemical fertilizers and pesticides for soybean and other cash crops grown on nearby ranches endangers the region's ecological health. Controlled burns by farmers expanding cattle-grazing areas often rage out of control, devastating large areas of plant and animal-rich grassland. And mercury still used for gold mining in the swamp's interior has killed scores of fish of which the Pantanal contains some 260 species.

On a more organized scale of human meddling, Shell, Enron and Bolivian hydrocarbon company Transredes have run a gas pipeline directly through the San Matias Protected Area and the Chiquitano Forest, the largest dry tropical forest in the world. The project's long-term environmental costs are anticipated to be $20 million, for which a "conservation fund"—managed by the gas companies themselves—has been created.

On this journey up the Paraguay River and its tributaries, our crew is a mix of indigenous leaders, park officials, naval officers and a cook who fries up the dozens of piranha we fish out and eat nightly. I am the only non-Bolivian aboard the two-deck military boat, and the events of our journey are varied: Several times a day, we speed off in a johnboat to see rare clusters of the giant pictoria plant, or pull up on land and walk knee-deep through marsh and mud to isolated ranches where we talk with farmers in Portanol—a mix of Portuguese and Spanish—about their living and working conditions.

The excursion's goal is to explore and confirm national boundaries within the swamp, and to meet with indigenous communities living there, explaining to them the status of the San Matias Protected Area. Created in 1997, San Matias is the most recent of Bolivia's 20 protected areas, which comprise nearly one-sixth of national territory. An estimated 6,000 people—half under the age of 15—live among the 17 indigenous communities in the region, growing yucca and rice, raising chickens and pigs, and gathering fruit that falls from the trees. For some the native language and culture is Guarani, while others are Chiquitano, and although they outfit themselves in basic western apparel of T-shirts and shorts, their lifestyle of agri-culture, fishing and animal husbandry appears largely unchanged by the decades. The Bolivian government employs just eight workers—a director, a protection chief and six park guards—to supervise its portion of the Pantanal. Though the staff of San Matias receives financial and technical help from the World Wildlife Fund, its members admit that present resources are inadequate to oversee the area's preservation. Lacking in personnel, aircraft, vehicles and communication with the interior, park guards say they rely more on the cooperation of indigenous communities than on government funds to protect their wilderness. "The people here are easy to speak to about conservation," says park director Jorge Landivar. "They are conscious that they can use nature responsibly."

But seated on wood benches in a dirt

yard of Puerto Gonzalo, an indigenous community some 24 hours by boat from the Brazilian city of Corumba, site of the nearest hospi-tal, we see the people whom progress has left behind. The town has neither a doctor nor medical goods, and its one-room schoolhouse has sat empty since the last teacher left years ago.

A poor farmer and his family offer us cups of water. The man has a pink pigmentation on his hands, neck and lips and the rest of him is a leathery brown. He says his only vices are mate and cigarettes, and he's missing four top front teeth. With canvas shoes torn at the seams and his callused toes protruding from them, he talks about how little water there is in the laguna at this time of year.

There is an awkward, uncertain silence at the meeting, where men sit on one side of a semi-circle, women with fidgeting children sit on the other, and our assemblage of park guards, a cameraman and a foreign journalist make modest attempts at dialogue from the middle. Their grievances are real, their living conditions hard and poor, and it is impossible to promise them that any of this will change. Another man says, "We hope you come again, that you don't just go and forget about us."

The Bolivian government and the World Wildlife Fund hope to attract "eco-tourists" to the area, which could allow Puerto Gonzalo and other remote indigenous communities to continue their farming lifestyle while helping enforce preservation in the region. Bolivia generated $179 million in tourism in 1999, and the government estimates that its current mark of 500,000 visitors a year will reach a million by 2004, providing 150,000 new jobs. Riding the surge in tourism into the Pantanal might be the compromise the swamp's communities make to retain their old ways of life.

The lure of cash through ecotourism

as well as a drop in the price for cattle has already prompted many Brazilian farmers to convert their ranches into fazenda-lodges, accommodations that serve visitors on excursions into the swamp's interior. In the Pantanal's rugged and mountainous tropical landscape, both high-and low-end tourism are on the rise. River trips in the region have even been popularized by writers such as John Grisham, who structured his novel The Testament around an adventure that takes lace in the Pantanal.

But Bolivia faces the task of developing an ecotourism strategy from scratch, one that competes with Brazil while having a minimal impact on the environment. According to Ascensio Ares, vice president of a local indigenous association, the Bolivian communities must adopt a higher standard of living before they can host tourists in their backyard. "If we don't strengthen this type of development," he says, "the problems in the area will only continue.

Its history mired in poverty and corruption, Bolivia is still struggling to develop a basic infrastructure of roads and indus-try, the lack of which has helped keep vast portions of its jungle intact, more so than its tropical neighbors. But to succeed with ecotourism, some fundamental progress will be necessary. "You can't have tourism if there is no road," explains Hernan Banegas, an architect from Puerto Suarez, a town that borders the Pantanal and is reachable only via the ancient railway line known as the "death train," which rattles 400 miles east from Santa Cruz.

A successful transition to ecotourism in Bolivia already has one clear example: Rurrenabaque. Located outside what is now Madidi National Park in the northern La Paz region, this small jungle town whose economy used to revolve around the timber trade —particularly the illegal sale of mahogany— now relies solely on ecotourism.

Still reeling from the shock of privatization enacted by neoliberal leadership in the mid-'80s and continued by ineffectual administrations through the '90s, Bolivia continues to underfund its environment, while many of the country's top officials guard close ties to major logging, mining and energy interests. Maybe less often mentioned in poor nations like Bolivia is the latent public consciousness of the need to pre-serve its wild, unspoiled places. "In the past no one spoke of conservation, of ecology," Banegas says. "They cut trees, they killed animals—thousands upon thousands of alligators just to sell the skin and eat the tail. By necessity and ignorance we exploited nature. Only 10 years ago, we didn't know the word medioambiente (environment). Now they tell us our Pantanal is the biggest lung of the planet."

It might be the indigenous communities themselves who have the most to do with guarding the region's long-term health. According to Landivar, generations have kept the vast swampland in its relatively unaltered form and the native people still living there understand their responsibility to live within it in that same way. "If the Bolivian Pantanal is less damaged by man, it's because the region's inhabitants took only what they needed for centuries," he says. "There is no other place like it in the world."

El Pantanal Hotel Resort,
Tels. 9782020, 800104111, Fax. 9782092,
E-mail:informaciones@elpantanalhotel.com
Close to the Brazilian border El Pantanal
is a five stars hotel. Single, $53;
Double, $67; Suite junior, $109;
Suite Pantanal, $116.

Michael Blendinger, Nature Tours
offers interesting tours of the area.
Tel/Fax. 9446186
www.discoveringbolivia.com
E-mail: mblendinger@cotas.com.bo

IS BOLIVIAN TOURISM A DANGEROUS GAME?

BY ERIK LOZA

In Bolivia, government officials and average citizens alike are looking to tourism as an alternative form of development to lift the country out of Third World status. This national industry is increasing every year and is "the only non-destructive form [of development] for forests and other fragile ecosystems," according to the Vice President of Green Cross International-Bolivia (GCIB) Andrés Szwagrzak. "For the majority of La Paz citizens," he says, "and for many foreigners, above all tourists from the Nordic countries, there is a paradigm that makes one afraid of the Bolivian tropics- the green hell'—where 'the savage beasts' and 'tremendous tropical diseases' rule." The risk of contracting tropical diseases is undeniable and the insects that carry them are in no short supply. The fleas that ride around on rats still transmit the plague in some sectors and ticks can transmit rickets, though instances are rare. These, however, are the small time carriers.

The greatest culprit of spreading disease worldwide is the blood-sucking mosquito anopheles, which has 60 different varieties throughout the continents. Twenty of these are the most deadly, however, because of their high incidence rate and ready adaptation to poisons. Six species in particular plague Bolivia and three of them can be found in the Department of La Paz. Anopheles, the most dangerous, and darlingi, found mostly in the north of La Paz, is responsible for 90 percent of reported cases of illnesses, according to Director of Diseases Transmitted by Vectors Benjamin Alcón in La Paz. These two species of mosquitoes can carry a variety of diseases, from leishmaniasis (also known as espundia or white leprosy) to yellow fever, dengue, elephantiasis, filariasis and even AIDS.

The greatest killer, and leading impediment to tourism, however, which reportedly struck about 50,000 Bolivians last year, is malaria. Malaria comes in a dozen varieties. Bolivia's endemic ones isn't devastating as those in the Caribbean and Africa and Bolivia's varieties of malaria are few. But the future is still dim. With increasing human traffic impulsed by the construction of transcontinental highways, "we can soon expect the appearance of all classes of malaria," say Szwagrzak, "along with more high-risk rural zones." Already in central Pando, inhabitants have migrated from numerous locales within the provinces of Madre de Dios and Manuripi. At the beginning of 1994, citizens of Santa Rosa, the capital of Abuna Province, also left their homes and evacuated the area's military headquarters.

"Analyzing a profile of tourists' interests," says Szwagrzak, "we see that the majority of people that visit the tropics wish to see the Amazon jungle and the maximum variety of biodiversity possible." Because of accessible roads and available transportation, many tourists' agencies direct travelers to Rurrenabaque, "the pearl of the Orient." What they may not know is that the cities of Reyes, San Buenaventura and Rurrenabaque comprise a malaria-infested triangle, "a virtual hell" in reference to the disease, according to Szwagrzak. Alcón says the main high-risk areas are in the Departments of La Paz, Pando and northern Beni. Reports say that almost 80 percent of malaria cases originate in La Paz, which has three high-risk locales: Palos Blancos, a tropical plains area, the mountainous zones of the Yungas (Coroico to Chulumani) and the Inquisivila Province, in the sector of Cajuata. In certain areas, the malaria factor has already impacted tourism. In Irupana (Department of La Paz) the foreign sponsors of a tourism complex withheld financing because of the zone's "high malaria risk."

Since the 1950's, the number of registered malaria cases has been mounting exponentially. "Despite the efforts of the Ministry of Health, National Service of Malaria and enormous expenditures to control the proliferation of the carriers of the sickness," says Szwagrzak, "no considerable effect has resulted." The medical world is struggling with a sure vaccination and repellents are costly and "little effective." Even the chemicals cloroquine and malerex, among others, are more dangerous to people's health than to the mosquitoes," according to Szwagrzak. "Moreover," he adds, "as history shows, the varieties of malarias will quickly produce defenses against any cures." People's fear of these contaminated zones, of digesting food and drink with chemical traces and of exposure to the bites of pesky, yet potentially deadly, insects will surely impede tourism's growth, unless a solution is found.

GCIB is attempting to develop an environmentally safe solution to the mosquito dilemma. Until that joyous day arrives, how-

ever, travelers need to take precautions. "If someone enters a high-risk area for a very short time, the chance of receiving a disease is almost less than probable," says Alcón, but if visitors plan on staying for a while, they should be aware. Light but long-sleeve shirts and long pants are recommended and travelers should always cover their feet and, whenever possible, their hands. Both are preferred delicacies for mosquitoes. In some areas, mosquitoes will even enter the house if it isn't well fumigated. In this case, very fine, impregnable mosquito nets serve well, especially against the minuscule mosquito that transmits espundia. As always, a good repellent also helps. Finally, people should stay away from humid areas and groups of animals, because female mosquitoes are always looking for blood, human or non. Even with these precautions, "we don't guarantee [immunity]," says Alcón. "It's practically a lottery," but with one out of every 4,000 mosquitoes infected in high-risk areas, according to the latest figures, the chance of contracting a disease is .025 percent.

REACHING FOR THE CRYSTAL-CLEAR SUMMIT

BY SERGIO GÓMEZ

Climbing a mountain that surpasses 6,000 m in height is not a snap; it requires good physical conditioning, a routed course, and some equipment. We drove off towards Huayna Potosi that weekend as a quartet: a Spaniard, a Swiss and two Bolivians loaded with all the necessary equipment. The excursion began early in the morning. We left La Paz and headed for one of the most fascinating and accessible mountains of the Bolivian Andes, both for its geographic location (approximately 40 km from La Paz), as well as the low level of technical knowledge necessary for its summiting. We chose a route that would normally guide us to the Zongo Valley, one that, for the climber's comfort, passes by the base camp located on the Zongo Terrace-- at 4,600 m above sea level, our first pit stop and the next point of departure for the ascent.

As we began our ascent, majestic Huayna Potosi stood up, challenging us with its imposing height of 6,099 meters. The two days of climbing that awaited us would require great physical and mental endurance. We strapped on our equipment and began to climb. After an hour and a half of foothill trekking, we arrived at the glacier's base (5,100 m) where we equipped ourselves with crampons for the scaling. At the end of two hours, we reached the first day's goal: the Zongo camp at 5,500 m. We set up camp--pitching tents, preparing our

indispensable mate de coca to better acclimate our bodies to the altitude, preparing supper--all this done in a hurry considering that in a few minutes the summit would slowly drop its shadow over us, bringing with it a considerable drop in temperature (-2 degrees Celsius).

The hour programmed to begin the next day's assault on the summit (3 a.m.) obliged us to hit our sleeping bags early. During the night many routine incidents happened due to the altitude: headaches, diarrhea and, during the short moments of sleep, continuous respiratory crises. A difficult time awaited us after getting up for breakfast: the wind blew strongly, impetuously breaking against the tent and plunging us into a fearful state. After having breakfast, we gathered the necessary equipment, prepared the safety cord and now, without much weight in our backpacks, undertook the climb's last stretch. Following the usual route, being careful to keep to the path due to the surrounding crevices, we ascended with the city of El Alto's lights to our left. The dawn spectacle required an obligatory break to look upon the sun's fascinating ascent; an intense, awesome red dot on the horizon. In a few minutes, we were climbing the last obstacle before the peak, a 45-50 degree wall of snow that towered approximately 200 meters above our heads. We reached the top at 8:30 a.m. few moments are as memorable as this--hugs, congratulations, and a tear. A wine bottle forgotten in the snow by some other group then made me reflect on the care that the mountain is receiving. Along the way, food remains, cans, plastic bags, and gas bottles lay strewn about. The descent was different, like an all-out rush: a rush to pack up camp, to follow the schedule, to arrive comfortably at the base camp, and later, to return to La Paz.

Through this short story, I would like to plant a seed of awareness and curiosity for Bolivia's mountains, valleys, prairies, deserts, and forests so that more organization and planning for ecotourism projects can be developed. I propose, unpretentiously, solutions such as putting three garbage cans at Huayna Potosi; one at the base camp, one at the beginning of the glacier, and another at the high camp area. And we shouldn't limit ourselves to this mountain, but rather concern ourselves with all the areas that are visited, year after year, by growing groups of tourists.

TIWANAKU, THE GATE OF THE SUN

TIWANAKU, SUNKEN TEMPLE TOWARDS THE KALASASAYA TEMPLE

TIWANAKU, THE PONCE MONOLITH

SAMAIPATA, SANTA CRUZ DEPT.

SAMAIPATA, SANTA CRUZ DEPT.

Samaipata, Santa Cruz dept.

Oruro carnaval

ISLAND OF THE SUN

AYMARA PACUCHIS DANCERS, TITICACA LAKE

WACA WACA DANCERS, TITICACA LAKE

SAN IGNACIOS DE MOXOS, MACHETEROS DANCERS, BENI DEPT.

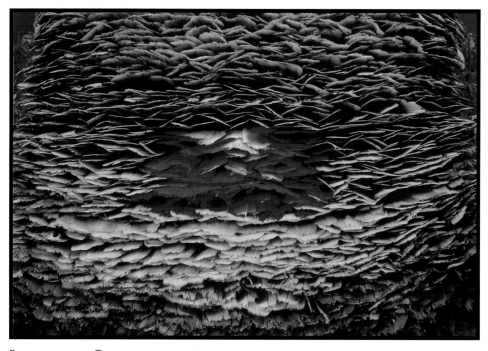

FEATHER ART FROM TIWANAKU

Bolivian andean textile

Lagunillas, La Paz dept.

AYMARA COMMUNAL MEAL ON THE ALTIPLANO   LA PAZ

QUINUA FIELD, TITICACA LAKE

Yatiri, andean kallawaya healer in Curva, La Paz dept.

Titicaca lake

CERAMIST MARIO SARABIA

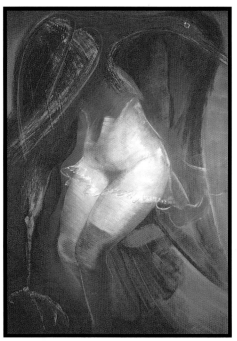

PAINTING OF GUSTAVO LARA

PAINTING OF GIL IMANA

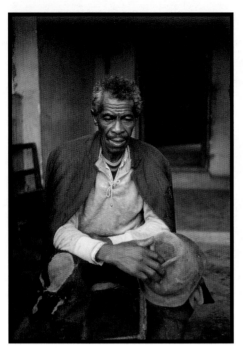

AFRO BOLIVIAN OF THE YUNGAS, LA PAZ DEPT.

A VILLAGE OF CHIPAYAS, ORURO DEPT.

JAPANESES SETTLERS IN OKINAWA, SANTA CRUZ DEPT.

KALLAWAYA IN CURVA, LA PAZ DEPT.

AYMARA GIRL, ALTIPLANO

QUECHUA GIRLS IN VILACAYMA, COCHABAMBA DEPT.

CHIRIGUANO WOMAN IN IPATY, SUCRE DEPT.

FAMILY IN BENI DEPT.

WOMAN HARVESTING BRAZIL NUTS, PANDO DEPT.

COWBOY, SAN JUAN DEL BENI

THE FREMEN RIVER BOAT ON THE MAMORE RIVER

Amboró Nat. Park, Santa Cruz dept.

Llamas at the foot of the Andes, Yungas

Uyuni salt flats, Potosí dept.

Huayna Potosi, La Paz dept.

Milluni lake, La Paz dept.

Cordillera Real

8

HELPFUL SPANISH,
AYMARA, QUECHUA
WORDS AND PHRASES

HELPFUL SPANISH, AYMARA, QUECHUA WORDS AND PHRASES

TRANSLATED INTO AYMARA BY FREDY YAPU GUTIERREZ
TRANSLATED INTO QUECHUA BY PRIMITIVO NINA

	SPANISH	AYMARA	QUECHUA
Basic conversation and courtesies			
Hello	Hola	Kamisaki	Imaynalla
Good morning	Buenos días	Aski willjtakipan	Allin p'unchay/qansina
Good afternoon	Buenas tardes	Jayp'u urukipan	Allin p'unchay/qansina
Good evening	Buenas tardes	Aski Jayp'ukipan	Allinp'unchay/qansina
Good night	Buenas noches	Aski arumakipan	Qansina
Goodbye	Chau	Waliki-jikisiñkama	Askamalla
See you later	Nos vemos	Qhipurkama	Tinkunakama
Thank you	Gracias	Juspara	Pachi
Please	Por favor	Amp suma	Ma, ama jina kay
Yes	Sí	Jisa	Arì
No	No	Janiwa	Mana
How are you?	¿Cómo estás?	Kamisaki	Imaynalla
I am fine/not good	Estoy bien/mal	waliki-jan waliki	Allillan/mana waliq
My name is . . .	Mi nombre es	Sutijaxa	...Sutiyqa
	Me llamo . . .		
What is your name?	¿Cuál es tu nombre?,	Kunas sutimaxa?	Imataq sutiyi?
	¿Cómo se llama?		
Where are you from?	¿De dónde es?	Kawkhankiritasa?	Maymantá kanki?
I am from . . .	Yo soy de . . .	Nayaxa...	...Manta kani
Pleased to meet you	Mucho gusto	Ancha waliki	Kusikuni, imaynalla
I don't understand	No entiendo	Janiw yatkti	Mana unanchanichu
Please speak slower	Más despacio,	K'achhatak amp suma	Pisipisimanta ma/
	por favor		allillamanta
Go away!	¡Vayase!	Saram!	Ripuya
Excuse me	Permiso/Perdón	Pampachita	Qhispichiway
Soliciting Information			
Where is...?	¿Dónde está ...?	Kawkhankisa?	Maypitaq ...kasha
... the bathroom	el baño	Yaq'añuta	Jispiarikuna wasi
... the bus station	la terminal de buses	Autu suyaña	Karru sayana/tirminal
... the airport	el aeropuerto	Awyun suyaña	Pista
... the police station	la estación de policía	Policiya chaxwa	Pulisiya wasi
		askichayir uta	

English	Spanish	Aymara	Quechua
... the supermarket	el supermercado	qhatu utaxa	Qhatu
... the post office	el correo	Chaski uta	Chaskiwasi
... the bank	el banco	Qullqi uta	Qulqiwasi
... the park	el parque	Anatawja	Puqllanawasi/parki
... the stadium	el estadio	Peq'uta anatañaja	Kancha
... the museum	el museo	Nayra yanak imaña uta	Wawa puqllanawasi
... the movie theater	el cine	sini	Sini
... the tourist office	la oficina de turismo	Turism uta	Turismuwasi
... the theatre	el teatro	Tiyatru	Aranwa
... the restaurant	el restaurante	Manq'añ uta	Mikhunawasi
... the telephone office	centro de llamadas	parlañ uta	Waqyanawasi
... the exchange house	la casa de cambio	Qullqi turkaña utaxa	Qulqi chinpunawasi
... the pharmacy	la farmacia	Qulla aljañ uta	Janpiwasi
... the hospital	el hospital	Qullaña uta	Janpinawasi
What is the exchange rate?	¿Cuál es la tasa de cámbio?	Qullqi turkawix qawqhankaskisa	
How much does it cost?	¿Cuánto cuesta?	Qhaw qhas chamipaxa?	Mayklapitaq
That's fine	Está bien	Walikiwa	Allin kashan
That's too much	Es demasiado	Anchawa	Ancha
What's your best price?	¿Cuál es su precio mejor?	Kawkirisa suma chamipaxa?	Mayqintaq aswan waliq
How do you say ...	¿Cómo se dice ...?	Kamsañasa?	Imaytá nikun?
Why?	¿Por qué?	Kunata?	imarayku?
Who?	¿Quién?	Qhitisa?	Pí?
What time is it?	¿Qué hora es?	Kuna pachaxisa?	Maypiña inti?
It is ...			
... 1:00	Es la una	Mapach jayp'u?	Uq tardiyay
... 3:30	Son las tres y media	Kimsapach chikan	Kinsa kuskanniyunqña
... 8:15	Son las ocho y cuarto	Kinsa Kuskanniyuq Kimsaqallq	Pusaq pagarimuy Chunka phisqayuq minutu
... 10:45	Son las once menos cuarto	Chkalwa uruxiwa	Chunka uqniyuqpaq chunka phisqayuq
When does the leave/arrive?	¿A qué hora sale/llega el autobús?	Kuna pachas autux purini/mistuxa?	Ima uratá pluta luqsin/chayamun?
in the morning	por la mañana	Alwawa	Paqarinta
in the afternoon/evening	por la tarde	Jayp'uruwa	Chawpi p'inchaymata japayman, tardinta
at night	por la noche	Arumjaruwa	Ch'isinta

Numbers

English	Spanish	Aymara	Quechua
one	un, uno/una	Maya	Uq
two	dos	Paya	Iskay
three	tres	Kimsa	Kinsa
four	cuatro	Pusi	Tawa

SPANISH, AYMARA, QUECHUA

English	Spanish	Aymara	Quechua
five	cinco	Phiska	Phisqa
six	seis	Suxta	Suqta
seven	siete	Paqallqu	Qanchis
eight	ocho	Kimsaqallqu	Pusaq
nine	nueve	Llatunka	Isqun
ten	diez	Tunka	Chunka
eleven	once	Tunka mayani	Chunka uqniyuq
twelve	doce	Tunka payani	Chunka iskayniyuq
thirteen	trece	Tunka kimsani	Chunka kinsayuq
fourteen	catorce	Tunka pusini	Chunka tawayuq
fifteen	quince	Tunka phisqani	Chunka phisqayuq
sixteen	dieciséis	Tunka suxtani	Chunka suqtayuq
seventeen	diecisiete	Tunka paqallquni	Chunka qanchisniyuq
eighteen	dieciocho	Tunka kimsaqallquni	Chunka pusaqniyuq
nineteen	diecinueve	Tunka llatunkani	Chunka isqunniyuq
twenty	veinte	Patunka	Iskay chunka
twenty one	veintiuno	Patunk mayani	Iskay chunka uqniyuq
twenty two	veintidós	Patunk payani	Iskay chunka iskayniyuq
thirty	treinta	Kimsa tunka	Kinsa chunka
thirty one	treinta y uno	Kimsa mayani	Kinsa chunka uqniyuq
thirty two	treinta y dos	Kimsa tunk payani	Kinsa chunka iskayniyuq
forty	cuarenta	Pusitunka	Tawa chunka
fifty	cincuenta	Phiskatunka	Phisqa chunka
sixty	sesenta	Suxtatunka	Suqta chunka
seventy	setenta	Paqallqtunka	Qanchis chunka
eighty	ochenta	Kimsaqallqtunka	Pusaq chunka
ninety	noventa	Llatunk tunka	Isqun chunka
one hundred	cien	Pataka	Pachaq
one thousand	mil	Waranqa	Waranqa

Directions

English	Spanish	Aymara	Quechua
How do I get to ...?	¿Cómo llego a ...?	Kunjams...purirista?	Imaynatá...chayayman
to the left	a la izquierda	Ch'iqaxam	Lluq'iman
to the right	a la derecha	Kupixam	Pañaman
straight ahead	recto	Chiqapa	Chiqanta
block	cuadra	Ma jacha mansaná uraqi	Uq muyurinaman chayasi
street	calle	Jaqi sarnaqhaña thaki	Puriy ñan
hill	colina	Quntu	Pata, ch'utu
mountain	montaña	Qullu	Urqu
up/above	arriba	Alaxa	Pata/janaq
down/below	abajo	Aynacha	Ura
near	cerca	Jak'a	Sispa

far	lejos	Jaya	Karu
next to	al lado de	Thiya	Kayman kutirispa
behind	atrás de	Qhipaxa	qhipa manta
in front of	adelante de	Nayrjaru	Ñawpaqinpi

Days of the Week

Sunday	domingo	Wanturu	Intichaw
Monday	lunes	Q'illuru	Kinachau
Tuesday	martes	Ch'uxñuru	Atichaw
Wednesday	miércoles	Laqpuru	Quyllurchaw
Thursday	jueves	Larmuru	Illapachaw
Friday	viernes	Kulluru	Ch'askaxhaw
Saturday	sábado	Chapuru	K'uychichaw

Months of the Year

January	enero	Chinula	Musuq intiraymi killa
February	febrero	Qhulliwi	Kamaq killa
March	marzo	Achuqa	Pacha puquy killa
April	abril	Llamayu	Jatun puquy killa
May	mayo	Q'asiwi	Jawkay kuski killa
June	junio	T'aqaya	Kuski aymuray killa
July	julio	Phawawi	Jawkay kuski killa
August	agosto	Thalari	Situwalki killa
September	septiembre	Awtila	Chaqraypuy killa
October	octubre	Satawi	Qhuya raymi killa
November	noviembre	Lapaka	Aya marq'ay killa
December	diciembre	Kutili	Raymi killa

Other useful words and phrases ...

food	comida	Manqa	Mikhuna
drink	bebida	Umaña	Uqyana
beer	cerveza	Machjayir uma	Simi sirwisa
napkins	servilletas	Pichasiña	Pichakuna
purified water	agua purificada	Q'uma uma	Ch'uya yaku
fork	tenedor	Tinitura	Tinidor/tinki
knife	cuchillo	Tumi	Kuchuna
spoon	cuchara	Jisk'a wislla	Wislla
toilet paper	papel higiénico	Picharasiñ laphi	Pichakuna papila
room	cuarto	Ikiñ uta	Wasi
pillow	almohada	Ch'ijma	Kawsira
bed	cama	Ikiña	Puñunawasi
blanket	frasada	Pirsara	Phullu/qhatakuna
towels	toallas	Picharasina	Ukhu ch'akichikuna
doctor	medico	Qulliri	Jampiq/yachaq
stomach	estómago	Puraka	Wisa
head	cabeza	P'iqi	Uma

pain	dolor	Usu	Nanay
fever	fiebre	Phuthut usu	Chirichiri
altitude sickness	soroche	Suruxchi	Suruqchi/chhuchunkiya
blood	sangre	Wila	Yawar
pills	pastillas	Umampiqulla umaña	Misk'i
without meat/sugar	sin carne/azúcar	Jan aychani/	Mana aychayuq,
		Jan asukarani	mana misk'Ichanayuq
I am a vegetarian	Yo soy vegetariano	Nayax ch'uxña	Nuqa mana
		achunak manq'aniritwa	aycha mikhuq kani

MAPS INDEX

BLACK & WHITE MAP SYMBOLS

Road	——	Campsite	△	Mine	✗
Trail	·············	Soccer Field	▣	Jesuit mission	🏠
Railroad	••••••••	Ruins	∴	Church	✝
International Border	— - - -	Cemetery	✝✝✝ ✝✝✝	Hotel Restaurant	🏠
River	～～～	Mountain	∧∧∧	Forest	🌲
Town, Capital	○ ◉	Bridge	≍	Lake	🗺
		Horse Riding	🐎		

MAP OF BOLIVIA

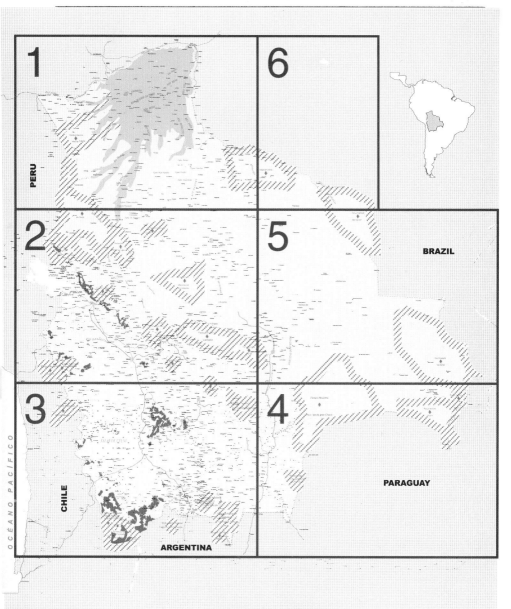

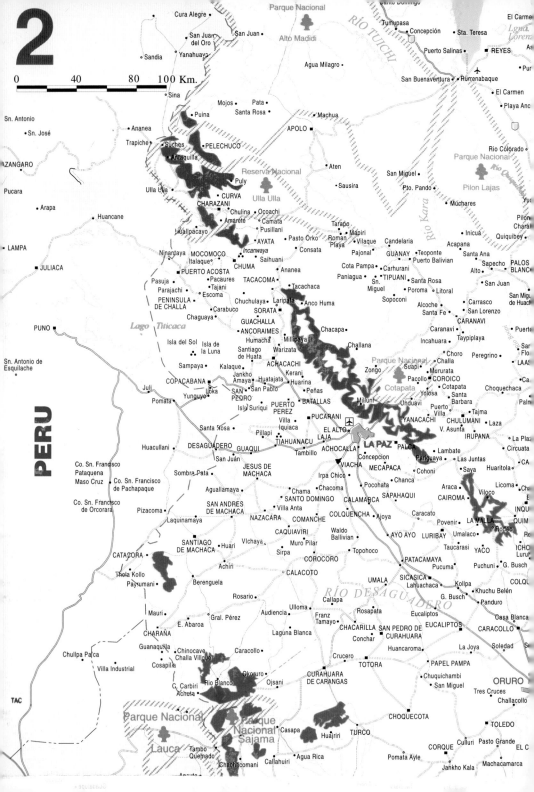

Igba. Bravo

SANTA ROSA Sn. Miguel Camba Muerto Galilea La Esperanza San Pablo La Cruz
Macho El Carmen Boliv
Vibosi Cachal El Encanto La Reforma San Pedro Nuevo
Florida Vallegrande Nazareth Verdum Sn. Bernardo
Reserva Nacional San Jose Viejo SAN JAVIER Sn. Lorenzo
del Beni Guadalajara La Capital Fortaleza
esperanza El Tesoro Loma Suarez TRINIDAD San Jose
Progreso Villa Dorita Pto. Almacen Macedonia V. Banzer
SAN BORJA La Escala SAN IGNACIO DE MOXOS Sochojere Miraflores
Carlos La Laguna Chirigua Victroria San Lorenzo Peroto San Rafael Nacupina
Napoles La Selva SAN ANDRES Sn. Bartolo
San Miguel El Villar San Rafael La Loma San Pablo
de Apere El Mangal San El Cecero LORETO
San Lorenzo Francisco San Antonio Espiritu
Pitai de Lora Camiaco Sn. Rafael Palmarito
San Francisco Girasol Berlin Bella Vista La Caracha
San Lorenzo Limoquije Canta La Piedra Las Abras Caimanes Adent
Parque Nacional Primavera Psto. Nueva Esperanza La Laguna
Isiboro Secure La Boca Embocada
Santa Elena (Area Indigena) RIO MAMORE Tres Cruces La Chita
Pto. Borracho
Guadalquivir
Sn. Silvestre
Rio Santa Elena Palacio
Rio Cotacajes Pto. de Las Flores
bel Pto. Patino Sasama Santa Maria Pto. Ibibobo
Cotacajes San Francisco IBARE Puerto
San Agustin Reteramazana Villa Barrientos Todos Santos Mamore
Rosay Valle Porvenir Miraflores PUERTO VILLARROEL
Icari VILLA TUNARI Palmeras
DEPENDENCIA Pucarani Tablas San José Central CHIMORE La Enconada
Machaca Chichiri Palca Busch Mariposas Ivirgarsama
MOROCHATA Tunari Coran Mendoza Valle Ivirsa Puerto Grether Villa Sucre
Charapaya QUILLACOLLO Locotal Parque Nacional Rio Ichilo
Coriri SIPESIPE COCHABAMBA COLOMI Carrasco San Isidro San Carl
Leque Incarracay Suticollo Calliri Palca Chuluchuncani Yapacani BUENA VISTA
TAPACARI Ramada SACABA Ucuchi TIRAQUE "A" Monte Puncu
Huayllamarca Itapaya SAN BENITO PUNATA VACAS Incallajta San Mateo Parque Nacional
Challa SANTIBANEZ CLIZA VILLA RIVERO Chuchu Palca Amboro
Ventilla ORCOMA TARATA POCONA Epizana POJO Guarayos
Changolla CAPINOTA TOKO Pallicha Duraznillos San Juan
TACOPAYA SICAYA ANZALDO La Aguada TOTORA Manzanal del Potrero PAMPA
Challa Uma ARQUE Khaallusta Marcavi Villa MIZQUE COMARAPA GRANDE
Corpani Pararani Viscarra Chujllas Oconi San Isidro
Ituras BOLIVAR Iturata Siquimira Tintin SAINA Mataral SAMAIPATA
Jarenkho Yaricoya Acasio Julo Grande Vicho Vicho OMEREQUE San Lu
Negro Pabellon Jaruma SACACA Huaylloma AIQUILE Pena Ele Ele PULQUINA Angostura
HACAMARCA Tarwa Chapi TORO TORO Colorada Perereta San Juan de
JUN Katari Khaua CARIPUYO TOROTORO El TRIGAL el Rosario
OOPO Nequita Colloma SAN PEDRO PASORAPA Lagunillas Muyurina Quirusillas
Sicoya DE BUENA VISTA Viru Viru San Juan de
LLALLAGUA Irupata Moscari Maizal La Ladera
ANTEQUERA UNCIA Senajo San Marcos Quiroga Acevedo VALLEGRANDE Tierras Postrer Valle
Calacala Tacarani Chayala POROMA Nuevas
Guadalupe

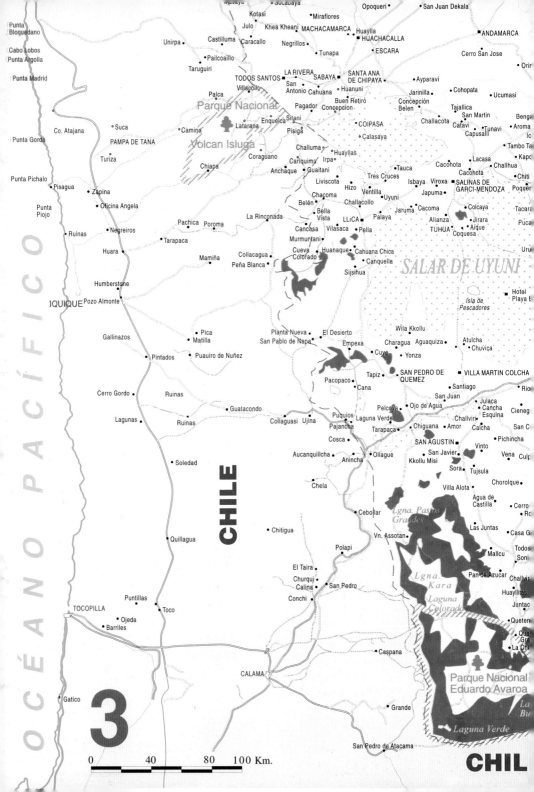

ARGENTINA

SUCRE
POTOSÍ
TARIJA

Parque Nacional Cordillera de Sama
Parque Nacional Turiquia
Parque Nacional Baritu
Monumento Natural Lago de los Pozuelos
La Rinconada
Reserva Forestal Rio Grande Masciuri
Área Protegida El Palmar

COLQUECHACA · Guadalupe · Pitantora · La Palca · Buena Vista · Pirayhiri
POCOATA · Rosario · Wila Lahua · Huari Pampa · Pasopaya · Rodeo · MOJOCOYA · PUCARA · Loma Larga
Penas · Ventilla · Macha · OCURI · RAVELO · Huañufaya · Chuqui Chuqui · Masicure
Huancacato · Ayoma · Pacollo · Tomuyo · Huata · PRESTO · Nuevo Mundo
STGO. DE HUARI · Maragua · Aeropuerto · Mojotoro · Villa Serrano · P. Grand
LLAPATA · Santiago de Huari · Thola Palca · Ayo Ayo · Potolo · Rodeo · YOTALA · TARABUCO · ZUDAÑEZ · VILLA SERRANO · Urriolagoitia · Torrecilla
JARIO JILLACAS · Urmiri · Lagunillas · TINGUIPAYA · TACOBAMBA · YAMPARAEZ · Faldilli · VILLA TOMINA · Tarabuquilla · PADILLA · El Palmar
Mendoza · Vichajlupe · Cahuayo · Uli · Calavi · Colla Camani · Nancahuaz
Sevaruyo · Sorasora · Chullpa Khasa · Concepción · Potobamba · Puente Mendez · Pocopoco · ICLA · VILLA ALCALA · Yuqui
Taraja · Salinas de Yocalla · YOCALLA · Machacamarca · Millares · Troja Pampa · Sorama · El Rosal · La Per
Calacala · Chusekhani · Santa Lucia · Torapoaya · Don Diego · BETANZOS · Oron Kkota · San Pedro · Lagunillas · Puente Azero · Ticucha
Coroma · Carhuayco · Vila Khollu · Paco Grande · CHAQUI · Coipasi · Esquiri · Rupasca · Sumalla · Tarca Pampa · EL VILLAR · LAGUNILLAS · Aratical
Anaraya · Catavi · Yura · POTOSÍ · Duraznos · Juana A. de Padilla · MONTEAGUDO
Chaucantaca · Opoco · Killpani · Viluyo · Vinto · PORCO · Condoriri · Talaco · PUNA · Miculpaya · Turuchipa · Sunchu Waykho · VILLA ORIAS · VILLA VACA GUZMAN
Quilla Quilla · Chaquilla · La Lava · Uruchiri · Mariscal Braun · Las Casas
Quehua · Ventilla · Apacheta · Cuchagua · Llajtavi · Kollpa · Palca Chanca · Vilacaya · Tarvita Alta · Fernandez
Cala Cala · Calazaya · Palca · CAIZA D. · Tambillo · Queque Huisi · AZURDUY · Hapendi
Chita · TOMAVE · Ticatica · Tatuca · Tauru · Ketuche · Tuctapari · Otavi · SAN LUCAS · Antonio Lopez · Sauceritos · Meson · Muri · Yumao
Chacala · Tholapampa · Olleria · Chana · VITICHI · Ayuma · Puca Tambo · Ajchilla · Algodonal · Sauci Mayu · Vallecito · Las Abr
Haricocha · Huanchaca · Totora · Vilaque · Jahuisla · Padcoyo · Malliri · Chinimayu · SAN PABLO DE HUACARETA · Bororigua
Pulacayo · UYUNI · Ubina · Toro Palca · Calcha · Quehuaca Grande · Jacahuito · Supas · Bombona · La Hoyada · Puca Mayu · Añimbo · Boicobo
Quisma Karillas · Arislaca · Khara Khara · Chati · Ara · Estumilla · Tacaquira · Santa Elena · Pucara · Huajlaya · El Fuerte · HUACAY
Pucara · Mina Tazna · Tocla · Pulaxi · Rancho · CAMARGO · Nacamiri
Corregidores · Cerdas · Rio Blanco · Vichacla · La Carreta · Rio Chico · Palca Grande · INCAHUASI · Puca Pampa · La Redonda · Timboycito
Sulche · Quechisla · SANTIAGO DE COTAGAITA · Quemada · Higuera · CULPINA · La Loma · El Palmar · Tartagalito · Ivoca
Siete Suyos · ATOCHA · Vintro Esquina · Jailla · Kollpa · Salitre · Cienega · La Cueva · Rio Nuevo
Gran Chocaya · Laitapi · VILLA ABECIA · Arenal · Casa Alta
Porko · Horno Pampa · Guadalupe · Cornaca · Higuerayoj · Pampa Grande · Tomatirenda · Caruruti
Uyuni · Agua Blanca · Ramadas · Almona · Portillo · Parchu · San Lorencito · Cañon Verde · Timboy
Cocani · Tatasi · Yana Rumi · Mochara · EL PUENTE · Las Carreras · Tomayapo · Canasmoro · Huayco
San Vicente · Sorocaya Chico · Oploca · Santa Rosa · SAN LORENZO · SELLA CERCADO · Narvaez · Chimeo · Palos Blancos
Huayllas · Chilco · Impora · Taraya · Carrizal · Huarmechi · TARIJA · Tambo · Entre Rios · Suararo
Pululos · Cerrillos · Chifloca · TUPIZA · Mal Paso · Curqui · Iscayachi · Los Naranjos
Ramadillas · Viluyo · Khuchu · Palquiza · Tocloca · Reynecilla · Belén · Tablitas · URIONDO · La Cueva · Saladillo
SAN PABLO DE LIPEZ · Santo Domingo · Tapaxa · Quiriza · San Francisco · Noquera · Parque Nacional Cordillera de Sama · Salinas · CARAPARI
Esmoraca · Huaripaca · Chapi Waykho · Checona · Yuruma · Asloca · Churquis · Campo Pajoso
Mojinete · Estarca · Mojo · Tojo · YUNCHARA · Chiquiaca · YACUIBA
Puda Khasa · Guadalupe · Sarcari · Casira · Chagua · Sajnasti · San Marcos · Quebradillas · PADCAYA · San Jose de Pocitos
SAN ANTONIO DE ESMORUCO · Orkho Quillacas · Berque · Cuartos · Sococha · La Merced · Parque Nacional Turiquia · EL CERRITO
Oratorio · Quebrada Grande · Arenales · Salitre · Rota · Mecoya · La Capilla de Bermejo · Cambari · Madrejones
LA QUIACA · Yavi · Santa Victoria · Vaden · FILO CONCHAS
Puma Huasi · La Rinconada · Limal · Parque Nacional Baritu · TARTAGA
Carahuasi · Cangrejos · Candado Grande · BERMEJO
Rinconada · Abra Pampa · Iruya · Chanar · Talita · Fortin Campero (Puesto Militar)
Antiguya · Cochinoca · Tres Cruces · Turbe · SAN RAMON

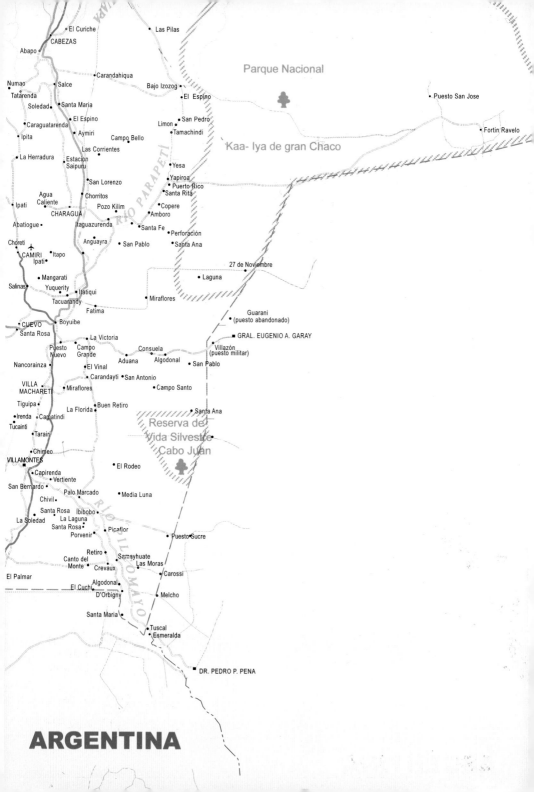

Bella Vista • •Santa Ana de Chiquitos
Todos Santos•
Venticuatro• •Ascención del puquio
•El Carmen
El Cairo • •
Campo
en Medio •
San Silvestre • •Est.Yacuses
Triunfo • •
Cupesi• San Roque
Rosario •

Sa.
Puerto Nuevo• Francisco
El Alba• •San Antonio
Salmo XXIII •Tuyuyu
•Pimenteira

Parque Nacional
Otuquis

Puerto Suárez
Tacuaral •San Miguicho
•El Carmen
•San Pedrito

CORUMBA
Quijarro

•Formiguento

Parque Nacional

Otuquis

Tacuaral•
San Juan•
Mutun

Puquio

•Porto de Manga
Manoa •

El Encanto •
Quebracho•
•Guapango
•Esperanza
•Retoño
•Camelia
Cabana Rica• •Pénjamo
•Santa Elena

BRAZIL

PARAGUAY

Cruz Del Sur
Valdemar• •Isla Santa Fe
•Puerto Busch
•Puerto Pacheco
Bahia Negra•

4

0   40   80   100 Km.

5

0   40   80   100 Km.

▪ MATTO GROSSO

BRAZIL

• Las Petas   SAN MATIAS ▪
✈

• Candelaria

▪ San Juan

La Gaiba •

Area Protegida
🌳
San Matias

•
Santo Corazon

Rincón del
Tigre •

ROBORE
• Santigo de Chiquitos

MAP SYMBOLS

6

————— **Paved Roads**
————— **Main Roads**
————— **Dirt Roads**
············· **Other Roads**
———————— **Tracks**
— — — **International Borders**

Department Capitals

▪ **Towns**
• **Villages**
Lakes
Salt Flats
Rivers

🌲 ///////. **National Parks & Reserves**
Mountains
✈ **International Airports**
✈ **Airports**
∴ **Archaeological Ruins**

SCALE APROX. 1:2.430.555

0   40   80   100 Km.

GUAPORÉ
San Antonio
Versalles •
• Porvenir
• Pedras Negras

Reserva Forestal
🌲
Itenez
• Chocolata   Versalles
Mategua •
Camargo •

• San Juan

BRAZIL

Laranjeira

RÍO ITENEZ O GUAPORÉ

Remanso •
Piso Firme •
RÍO PARAGUAY
• Puerto Leyton

• Puerto Saucedo

THE QUIPUS CULTURAL FOUNDATION

The Quipus Cultural Foundation is a non-profit organization (NGO) founded in 1985 by a group of prominent Bolivians concerned with the preservation and promotion of Bolivia's rich tradition and culture. Our mission is one of education: We seek to inform both the Bolivian people and visitors of this country about the traditions and histories that have created today's diverse and multi-ethnic culture.

Quipus continues to contribute to the educational development of Bolivia through a variety of programs, projects, and productions, including The Laikakota Cultural Complex in La Paz which houses the Kusillo Children's Museum of Science and Play and the Tanga Tanga Children's Museum in Sucre. Future plans for the La Paz site include a Museum of Bolivian Arts and Cultures as well as a planetarium and digital theatre complex. Quipus is also implementing a National Craft Development Program and a Computer for Schools program

To date, The Quipus Cultural Foundation has overseen the editing and publishing of over ten books of photography and history including *La Fe Vida: las Misiones Jesuitas en Bolivia, Vilacayma: un Pueblo Quechua , Masks of the Bolivian Andes, Guia Cultural y Turistica de Bolivia, Robert Gerstmann- Photographs of Bolivia 1928, Alcides Dorbigny and Expresiones de Fe: Templos en Bolivia.* The organization also produces popular postcards and prints from Quipus president Peter McFarren as well as tourism maps of the country, all manufactured here in Bolivia. This is the fourth edition of the internationally popular An Insider's Guide to Bolivia.

For more information on how to get involved with the Quipus Cultural Foundation please visit our website at *www.quipusbolivia.org* For matters concerning An Insider's Guide to Bolivia, you may contact us via email at *insidersguide@quipusbolivia.org.* Or contact our office directly at Casilla 1696, Pasaje Jáuregui 2248, La Paz, Bolivia. Tel. 591.2.2444311 Fax. 591.2.2442848.

Look for these Quipus publications coming soon: *The EcoTourism Guide to Bolivia, Textiles en los Andes Bolivianos* as well as *Lake Titicaca,* a book of photos by Peter McFarren.

CALLE SAGARNAGA ° 225
LA PAZ · BOLIVIA

Maximun comfort, total luxury.

HOTEL EUROPA
★ ★ ★ ★ ★

A touch of european elegance in the business district of La Paz. The beautiful garden lobby of "Hotel Europa" transports travellers from the noisy city streets to a calm serene environment, perfect for the fatigued traveller. This incomparable sensation continues into the hotel's elegant and spacious rooms, restaurants, recreation areas, and conference rooms.

For this reason and many more, "Hotel Europa" is the finest, most comfortable and elegant hotel in La Paz. We invite you to get to know the "Hotel Europa", a pleasant surprise.

ACCOMODATIONS

- Ample work space with swivel chair
- Desk with Internet & fax connections
- Universal outlets
- Goose down pillows & comforters
- Electronic safe
- Telephone with direct national & international dialing
- Television with swivel base
- Cable TV
- Fridge Bar
- Radio clock
- Magnetic locks for better security
- Individually-controlled heating
- Finn Club - (health club)
- Meeting and Conference Center

RESTAURANTS

- Eurocafé - Bistro
- Le Gourmet - Sophisticated cuisine
- El Solar - Grill and Fondues
- Le Balcon Bar - Sushi Bar
- Café Bar Meeting Place

SERVICES INCLUDED

- Buffet breakfast
- Internet access
- Use of the Business Center
- Use of indoor pool, sauna & gym at the Finn Club
- Cellular telephone (you pay only for calls made)
- Oxygen
- Local paper
- Shoe shine
- 24 hour security

HOTEL EUROPA
★ ★ ★ ★ ★

Simply unique

Calle Tiahuanacu No. 64 • Teléfono: 591-2-2315656 • Fax: 591-2-2113930 • Toll Free Nacional: 80010-5656
www.hoteleuropa.com.bo • E-mail: reservas@hoteleuropa.com.bo - ventas@hoteleuropa.com.bo
Casilla: 1800 • La Paz - Bolivia

Because we really
connect the Country

Línea aérea

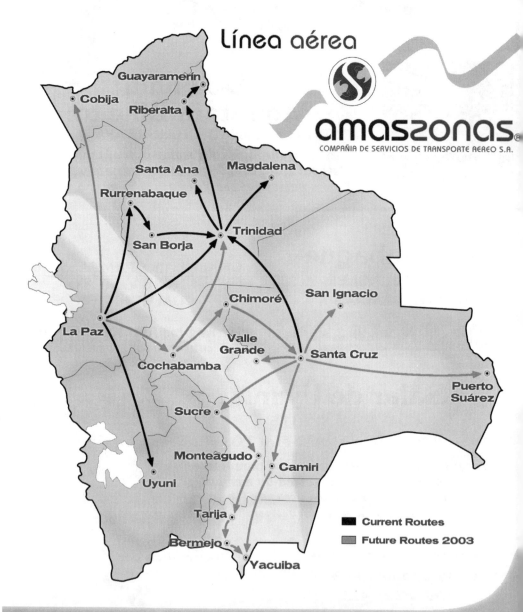

amaszonas®

COMPAÑIA DE SERVICIOS DE TRANSPORTE AEREO S.A.

■ Current Routes
■ Future Routes 2003

La Paz: Tel.: (591) 2 -2220848 • Trinidad: (591) 3-4622426 • Santa Cruz: (591) 3-3578983 • Rurrenabaque: (591) 3-8922
San Borja: (591) 3-8953185 • Riberalta: (591) 3-8523933 • Guayaramerín: (591) 3-8553731 • Magdalena.
e-mail: reserva1@entelnet.bo

Domestic
Routes

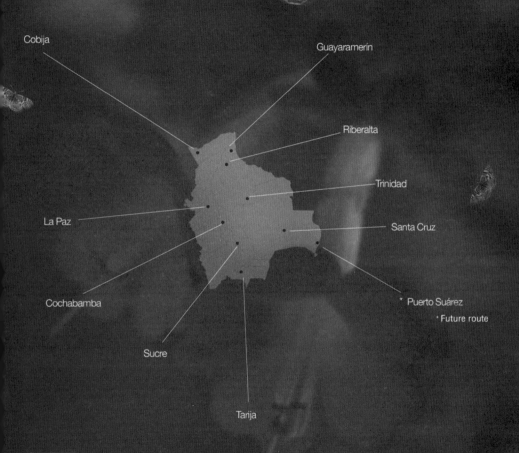

Cobija

Guayaramerín

Riberalta

Trinidad

La Paz

Santa Cruz

Cochabamba

* Puerto Suárez

* Future route

Sucre

Tarija

LAB takes you all over Bolivia... 9 magnificent destinations in only one country. Unforgettable!

Ask about the LABPASS program

LLOYD AEREO BOLIVIANO